In Search of the Common Good

Utopian Experiments Past and Future

Charles J. Erasmus

THE FREE PRESS
A Division of Macmillan, Inc.
NEW YORK

Collier Macmillan Publishers
LONDON

Dedicated with Love to
Helen O'Brien Erasmus

The Free Press
A Division of Macmillan, Inc.
866 Third Avenue, New York, N. Y. 10022

Collier Macmillan Canada, Inc.

First Free Press Paperback Edition 1985

Printed in the United States of America

printing number

1 2 3 4 5 6 7 8 9 10

Library of Congress Cataloging in Publication Data

Erasmus, Charles J.
  In search of the common good.

  Originally published: New York : Free Press, c1977.
With new pref.
  Bibliography: p.
  Includes index.
  1. Utopias—History. 2. Utopias. I. Title.
[HX806.E65 1985]   335'.02   82-25877
ISBN 0-02-909640-5 (pbk.)
ISBN 0-02-909630-8

Contents

Preface to the Paperback Edition

BACK IN THE late 1960s and early 1970s when university students were emulating the Red Guards of the Chinese Cultural Revolution, Maoism was being hailed as the political philosophy of the future, a noble pattern for the First and Third Worlds as well as the Second. Such ethical and political concerns, especially on the part of college students, were proof that a New Moral Man was emerging in America, a composite of communist or socialist ideals and anarchistic life styles. At last the world was seeing market economy in its true colors, a playground for corrupt, profit-seeking misanthropes and mafia-like corporations. Capitalism would soon be dead.

This book grew out of lectures designed to present evidence for a contrary view. To make labels less emotional, millennialism took the place of communism, and Rousseau's ideas on progress and inequality served me well as a substitute for Marx's. A strategy good for lectures, however, may not be the best one for a book. Students remained in their seats instead of running for the exists and finally got the point. But readers who complained about the book's anti-capitalist bias surely exited too soon.

Much has happened since the book's publication to enhance its credibility. Mao has been dead only seven years, and already China is a different country. Ten years ago I was telling students they would live to see such changes while not expecting to myself. It has been the rate of change in the last decade, not the direction, which has surprised me. Now I look for changes equally dramatic within the Soviet Union during my lifetime.

Maoism is no longer the inspiration and guiding model of development for the Third World. It has been replaced even in China by the experience and methods of such countries as Japan and South Korea. Increasing involvement in market economy by the Chinese masses will produce an explosion of development dwarfing even Japan's. By then if not before, Russia will be forced by her historic dread of mongol hordes to release her own great human potential at the expense of tired old utopian doctrines.

The kibbutz movement, too, has changed with suprising speed, though again in the direction expected. By solving its profitability problem through industrialization, it has propelled itself rapidly along the same path taken by nineteenth-century Amana. Most kibbutzim have virtually become shitufim just as shitufim members predicted they would only fifteen years ago.

Market economy continues to spread everywhere with similar consequences. Growing self-determination by the masses ("habit rationality" in the book) is one. Concern by government for faster "trickle-down" is another. Ideological change is a third. Some neo-marxists, for example, are even breaking with the master over dispensability of the market. Industrialization was created not by entrepreneurs and capitalists but by the masses. As ordinary people throughout Europe during the Middle Ages sought and obtained more and more of the material things that made life comfortable ("consumer choice" in the book), they created the market that made industrialization possible. Thus market economy was truly a democratic development. We need only separate it from capitalism—all evils such as exploitation and monopoly—to finally purify it. And Karl Marx becomes but the shade of Adam Smith.

The great utopian social experiments of the twentieth century have taught us lessons after all. Comprehensive planning at the top perpetuates patrimonial despotism; it does not liberate the creative energy of the masses. Decentralization has become the key word everywhere. We are even finding it deep inside those of our large corporations that show true "excellence."

The nations of the world are on converging tracks. While details of this convergence are not predictable, the gross outline is already with us. Does it matter whether we call it welfare capitalism or market socialism? It does to those who read sinister differences into the words. Precisely because of personal preference, not in spite of it, we can each claim to work for *the* common good when in fact we can only work for *a* common good that defies agreement. Since good intentions continually adapt to experience, adaptive "muddling-through" becomes the only game around when everyone gets a fair chance to play. And since no compromise will ever satisfy everyone, the common good will always be an issue, an issue keeping us forever imperfect as we forever seek perfection.

Charles J. Erasmus

University of California at Santa Barbara
September, 1984

Acknowledgments

So MANY PEOPLE whose lives have touched mine over the past 30 years have contributed to this book in one way or another that to thank them all would fill as many pages as the book. First, let me thank the hundreds of students at the University of California at Santa Barbara who provided an invaluable critical audience as I worked out the structure of this book in lectures and seminars between 1969 and 1975. In particular I wish to mention those doctoral students who went on to seek the truth for themselves: Waldemar Smith, who studied the capitalist invasion of rural Guatemala and its effect on older forms of status seeking; James Eder, who studied the origins of inequality among Philippine settlers in a developing frontier; Alison Bland Sánchez, who at Ravenna, Italy, studied the oldest collective farming movement in the world; Peter Westerlind, who studied recent changes in the Israeli kibbutzim; Jill Cordover Byron-Cooper, who did the same for the Israeli shitufim; Josette Murphy, who made a comparative analysis of government-sponsored agricultural production cooperatives in rural France; Diane Bray Heiken, who devoted several summers to a study of recent changes among the Hutterites; George and Sharon Gmelch, who studied the persistence of poverty culture among the Irish Tinkers; Mary O'Connor, who is reexamining cultural and ethnic persistence among the Mayos of Sonora, Mexico; and Sheldon Rosen, who is preparing to compare worker participation in the management of kibbutzim and shitufim factories. The stimulation one receives from students such as these can never be repaid nor fully acknowledged. Their books and theses are in various stages of preparation.

Special thanks go to my very special friend and colleague, Tom Harding, who has so generously exchanged ideas, criticisms, and references with me for 15 years. Sincere thanks go also to Don Symons, Don Brown, and Mat Mines, whose careful reading of my manuscript spared me numerous embarrassments.

I am also grateful to Clifton Wharton and the Agricultural Development Council, of which he was then vice president, for the grant which made possible extensive travel in Africa, Israel, and Western Europe during 1968—a trip that resulted in a drastic revision of my professional objectives. During that odyssey many people went far beyond the call of professional duty or international goodwill to assist me in my quest for information. Space permits me to thank only a few of them here. By country they are: Ghana—Nana Ababio and Sarkodee Addo; Uganda—M. Assedri and Jason Male; Tanzania—Griffiths Cunningham and Bernardo Kilonzo; Israel—Joseph Shepher, Shlomo Kenan, Kurt Ohrenstein, Moshe Wolff, Phil Feingold, and Benjamin Eliassow; England—A. J. S. Cox and Margaret Digby; Norway—Jon Arnstad and Lars Bull-Berg; Sweden—Nils Bengtsson and Goran Nilsson; France—Raymond Bras and Jacqueline Peroche; Spain—Miguel Bueno and Joaquín Ruiz-Gómez; and Italy—Magnani Valdo and Decimo Triossi.

Chapter One

Introduction

FORTY YEARS AGO, in the middle of a worldwide economic depression, the eminent British archaeologist V. Gordon Childe tried to cheer up mankind with a book entitled *Man Makes Himself*.[1] The previous century, he pointed out, had accepted progress as fact, for the climate of growing prosperity had generated boundless enthusiasm. Since then, however, World War I and the Great Depression had so undermined this earlier optimism as to call into question the very idea of progress. Taking a long-range view—nothing less than mankind's entire planetary existence—Childe set out to show that there had been continual progress through the lows as well as the highs of man's history. Although creative, culture-bearing man was the progenitor of his own progress, its engine was a long series of technological accomplishments clearly demonstrated in the material record of prehistory. As for his judgment of progress, Childe sought a neutral criterion that could be measured "impersonally" and "scientifically." Correlating human population expansion with technological growth, he "objectively" demonstrated progress through species success, the numerical increase of humankind.

What a difference there is between the pessimism of Childe's day and the pessimism of ours! Childe's measures of progress are at the very roots of contemporary pessimism, antiprogress, and antimaterialism. In the view of many, technological and population growth have been so diabolically successful that they threaten the very existence of our species. Besides looting and polluting our environment, technology eventually exploits and even alienates its creator. And in sheer growth of numbers the human population threatens to reach and surpass the carrying capacity of the planet. All such processes, moreover, proceed at an exponential rate that may overwhelm man before he can take corrective action. The riddle of the lily pond succinctly captures the major thrust of the Meadows' influential book, *The Limits to Growth*.[2] A water lily on a certain pond doubles in size each day and unchecked will cover the water in 30 days, thereby choking off all other life in the pond. The early growth of the lily plant is deceptively slow, so the pond owner decides not to worry about

1

cutting it back until half the pond is covered. On what day will he clear it? On the 29th—only 24 hours before disaster.

The pessimistic forecasts of some scholars today read almost like dystopian science fiction. Economist Robert Heilbroner sees convulsive change forced on us by future demographic and environmental limits.[3] Nuclear weapons become widely disseminated among nations, and world food shortages precipitate nuclear blackmail and "wars of redistribution." Threatening to wipe out New York or San Francisco, starving nations force us to share with them our food and other goods. Even within nation-states, conditions of scarcity bring about Hobbesian struggles for equitable distribution, forcing both capitalist and socialist governments toward totalitarian extremes.

Roberto Vacca, an Italian systems analyst, depicts a future "dark age" initiated not by starvation or scarcity but by the breakdown of great technological systems through sheer overcomplication and instability. As the most technologically advanced nation, the United States is the first to experience catastrophe.[4]

Not everyone is so pessimistic. The University of Sussex's social and technological forecasting team, which published *Models of Doom,* a critique of *The Limits to Growth,* is highly suspicious of "doom writing." [5] The authors of *Models* consider contemporary system dynamics a social movement similar to the Technocracy movement of the 1930's and accuse the limits-to-growth school at the Massachusetts Institute of Technology of messianic adherence to the new movement. They believe that the MIT group greatly underestimates the possibilities of continuing technical progress, and they feel that political and social limits to growth deserve more attention than the purely physical limits stressed by MIT.

The Sussex group agrees that the world faces population, pollution, and energy problems far too serious for complacency. But it accuses the system-dynamics forecasters of overlooking the human animal's essential role in this drama. Men can act to change their fate and are capable of upsetting all the doomsday predictions.

George Land, in his book *Grow or Die,* takes the position that man will continue to modify his environment in ways that challenge, and select out for, higher forms of technology and social organization.[6] Those who want to stop growth, in his opinion, fail to see it as a multilinear process in which some lines die out as others multiply and transform. Therefore those who oppose growth are nothing but unwitting symptoms of current developmental changes in which lower, outmoded lines of growth are being replaced by higher levels of organization. A total state of equilibrium that arrested all lines of growth would result in extinction, not survival. Growth and life are inseparable. At no time in the history of life has any "life system" successfully returned to a past or balanced state. On the contrary, disequilibrium has always been an integral part of life and environmental systems.

Although economist E. F. Schumacher is sympathetic with many antigrowth positions, he has made a telling point about deterministic systems isolated in laboratories or on drawing boards.[7] These systems yield only what he calls "exploratory calculations"—not true forecasts or predictions. The latter deal with the uncertainties of the real world and can never be more than probability statements. But exploratory calculations, conditional to the artificial parameters of a deterministic system, can achieve mathematical certainty while remaining completely inapplicable to the real world. Were it not for human creativity and choice, man's social behavior would be as predictable and as amenable to the same methods of study as the subject matter of the natural sciences.

The recent drop in the U.S. fertility rate to a level below that necessary for population replacement was not predicted by most demographers. While environmentalists are pleased by this unexpected turn of events, many progrowth economists are outlining a new form of doomsday—a 21st-century world with too few young workers to support all the old people living on social security. Others say it is too early to make such "pessimistic" judgments since large families could once more become popular. Man is certainly an unpredictable animal—as unpredictable as he is adaptive. It is this very quality of unpredictability, therefore, that holds high promise of problem-solving capability in the social world as well as in the material or technological realm.

Whether they be progrowth or antigrowth, pessimists seem to share a distrust of human nature; nothing so unpredictable could be anything but capricious. Since the animal's reasoning powers are undoubtedly contaminated by primitive emotions, two favorite views of the future involve breakdown into a disorganized form of anarchy on the one hand, and on the other, the achievement of organization and plan through totalitarian government. In some views the first leads to the second. In any case, a world of increasing scarcities propels man into a kind of Hobbesian choice: either to slip back into a "war" of all against all or to accept a strong "Leviathan" state—at best a "friendly fascism" —ruled firmly by an elite of Guardians or Planners dedicated to the collective good. Were the great philosopher Thomas Hobbes alive today, says Richard Peters, he would recommend that one nation be given overwhelming superiority in nuclear arms and allowed to maintain international peace according to its own dictates.[8]

Political scientist William Ophuls has written a provocative essay on the Hobbesian problem by comparing Thomas Hobbes with Garrett Hardin, an eminent contemporary biologist and vigorous champion of population control.[9] Ophuls is concerned with a specific essay by Hardin, "The Tragedy of the Commons," which has attracted widespread attention. In it Hardin takes the position that the human population problem has no technical solution; it requires a political solution. In his metaphor of the commons, all members of a community of herdsmen have equal access to a common pasture; but as each herdsman endeavors to expand his herd, none concerns himself with the preservation of the commons. Unless the community acts to regulate the size of herds, all families in the community must eventually face ruin. Such regulation cannot be left up to individual conscience; it requires "mutual coercion mutually agreed upon."

As Ophuls points out, Hardin's tragedy of the commons illustrates the central concern of all political theory in Western civilization: how to get men to rise above self-interest and act in the best interests of the collectivity. Nor is this concern peculiar to the West. Maoist ideology has always emphasized "fighting self" and working for the common good.

The tragedy of the commons also raises the question central to this book—a question that has pursued me most of my professional life: How and why do men provision collective good? As students of social behavior improve their answers to this question they can better judge whether men like Ophuls and Hardin are correct in endorsing a Hobbesian solution—in believing that a spaceship earth with finite resources needs a strong captain to enforce and protect the public interest.

Almost 30 years ago I spent 12 months in a small, poverty-stricken Mexican-Indian village where families lived very independently of one another despite the leisure time available to make collective community improvements. Almost all traditional forms of mutual aid and community service had disappeared. Villagers even hired one another when they needed help. The community possessed pasture and thorn-forest commons, their *comunidad indígena,* but the land was eroding badly from overgrazing by sheep and cattle, and the forests were being denuded by woodcutters. The villagers blamed Mexican outsiders for all their troubles—for illegally chopping wood and for keeping cattle on the commons without permission. They wanted to do something about it, but they said they had no power. They were poor, and the rich governed. Thus, those so inclined increased their livestock or cut more wood for sale—to get what they could before the outsiders got it all. The only time the village gave nearly unanimous support to a public good was during a fiesta to honor the village saints. Although reasons for participation varied, everyone was able to derive some satisfaction from the event. All felt equal, and the affair was under their control.

In the early 1950's, while working as an applied anthropologist for U.S. technical-assistance programs in South America, I first came up against the problems of provisioning public good in development situations. How could technical personnel get the natives to adopt and operate a new irrigation project, a community-development program, improved public-health practices, or badly needed soil-conservation techniques? "Why won't the people cooperate?" I was often asked. In most cases I soon discovered the question really meant, "Why don't the people do what we want them to do?" I learned to distrust the word "cooperation." For some people—particularly bureaucrats with a strong sense of mission—the word had a devotional significance that was almost religious; for others—particularly farmers who had at one time or another been organized into "cooperatives" by government personnel—it was a pejorative term. Moreover, the word "cooperative" includes so many forms of organization in different parts of the world as to be almost meaningless. Some cooperatives make payments to capital shares just like joint stock companies; others reward members only for work, and some presumably work only for a good to be enjoyed by all. The range of behaviors customarily associated with "cooperation" is so broad that the word is almost a synonym for social behavior. I avoid it as much as possible in this book.

The same people who failed to give their full support to programs designed for their collective good often maintained traditional customs of mutual aid among themselves. But almost everywhere in western South America mutual-aid customs were breaking down and disappearing, and I tried to find out why.

Some 20 years ago I was privileged to study the amazing economic development of northwestern Mexico, specifically the area of southern Sonora and northern Sinaloa. Here the Mexican government built great power and irrigation dams for the public good and divided over half the cultivable land into small farms for the landless. Then it turned the region over to the invisible hand of the market, and the world of Adam Smith was recapitulated. Thousands of people, frenetically working for their own private interests, were developing a new frontier for the collective benefit of an entire nation. I was so impressed by this experiment, especially in comparison to the people-manipulation programs of technical assistance, that it took me many years to see it in a more balanced perspective.

In 1963–64 I went to Bolivia and Venezuela to study land-reform programs and while there had an opportunity to compare their collective-farming experiments with those I had previously seen in Mexico. The peasants co-opted by these experiments seldom liked them; failure was the consistent pattern everywhere. The complaint of collective and excollective farmers was always the same. Those who worked hard resented "supporting" those who leaned on their hoes. Work levels generally fell to the level of the poorest worker, and high labor costs led to insolvency. Again people failed to provision a collective good, and again I tried to find out why.

During 1968 I traveled to Africa, Israel, and western Europe to observe more cases of "cooperation" in agriculture. The projects I saw in Israel and Spain were unusually successful, although for entirely different reasons. Since then I have combined my own experiences with information on 19th-century communes and the great social experiments of Russia and China. All the data in this book bear on the central question: How and why do people provision collective good? And when they do not, what goes wrong; what is lacking?

Successful communes like those of Israel and some of the 19th-century American experiments were all deliberately formed. They were "intentional" communities and to some extent "planned." Collective farms are also intentional associations, but they are almost always organized by government and planned by government; and unless a Hobbesian sovereign maintains them by force, they soon collapse. But judging from the successful communes, there are clearly times when collective good can be provisioned so enthusiastically and unanimously by an entire community that Rousseau's nebulous concept of general will seems credible after all. In such cases plan, regulation, predictability, and consensus seem to coincide—at least for a while.

For those who are not yet ready to close the door on man's future and who feel out of step with a time in history when prophecies of doom are the vogue, are there any grounds for optimism? Is man verging on extinction, or has he scarcely begun to achieve his full potential? Can he adapt to the limits of his spaceship earth without sacrificing freedom and individuality and without terminating all hope for some kind of progress? Can the planning animal learn to plan more comprehensively than in the past with wider participation by a public better able to appraise the social and environmental contingencies of both collective and private good? Can man be both a comprehensive planner and an individualist? Can he learn to control his technology and economy and still retain a free, cosmopolitan society without Hobbesian overlords?

No one in his right mind would promise final answers to such questions. I can only offer the evidence for optimism as I see it and let each reader come to his own conclusion. In presenting my evidence I shall concentrate on social incentives. Throughout most of this book behavioral terms such as "reinforcement" or "reward" can be substituted for "incentive" if the reader so desires. I prefer the term "incentive," however, because of the teleological side to human action that is absent in the reinforcement or rewarding of animal behavior. Social groups can deliberately and consciously establish contingencies of reinforcement which their members just as deliberately and consciously can pursue or circumvent. The special interest of this book is in those incentives related to the support of collective or public good.

I shall use as a basic reference point that well-known distinction among capitalist, socialist, and communist incentives based on capital, work, and need. For purely literary convenience I shall label these macrocategories "Capitalist Man," "Socialist Man," and "Millennial Man." In all three types, individuals are expected to work up to their ability; but only one type, Socialist Man, is rewarded strictly according to work. Capitalist Man is rewarded for capital as well as work, and Millennial Man receives only according to "need." Socialist Man owns all productive property collectively and equally but distributes benefits unequally according to effort and skill.

Most Americans, to take a Capitalist Man example, are employees rather than employers or entrepreneurs. They are rewarded according to effort and skill as Russians and Chinese are, except that pay differentials are much greater under capitalism than under socialism. American workers who save part of their salaries in bank accounts can receive interest payments on capital in addition to their salaries, and the same applies to Russians and Chinese. But unlike Russians and Chinese, many Americans own capital far in excess of small bank deposits. Capitalist Man owns most of his productive property privately and unequally and benefits from it unequally according to ownership shares that have no necessary relationship to their owner's effort or skill.

Millennial Man, like Socialist Man, shares equally in the ownership of productive property and like him receives no payments on capital, for the most part. Unlike Socialist Man, however, he is rewarded not according to effort and skill but according to the size of his family and the standard of living deemed reasonable by the society in which he lives.

Millennial Man fits the Marxian dream of a millennial communist world in which the state has withered away and everyone works for the sheer pleasure of supporting the collective good. It was the ideal of early Bolshevism and of radical Maoism. But Millennial Man has never been successfully established at the leviathan level; so far as the real world is concerned, he crops up very sporadically at best and only in small, social-movement or religious-movement communities—a major reason why I call him "millennial." Another reason is that "Communist Man," the logical alternative to "Millennial Man," would have pejorative connotations for many readers.

All three types refer to material incentives only. They include the wages and wage goods (personal or consumer property) of Capitalist and Socialist Man and the productive property of Capitalist Man. Millennial Man, it should be noted, has no individual incentives at all if we take a purely materialist position. Ideally his individual incentives are primarily internal, one might even say "spiritual." However, in real-world, Millennial Man societies such as those compared in subsequent chapters, strong individual incentives are definitely present; but they are social, not material. In fact, we shall see that social incentives are present in all three types of societies and that to a large degree the so-called material incentives are simply a vehicle for social incentives peculiar to a certain kind of society.

Chapter 2, "Altruism, Progress, and Utopia," provides introductory background primarily on the nature of the human animal. It has two major purposes: (1) to view man's development as a planning social animal over the course of his brief existence on this planet; and (2) to introduce concepts and assumptions basic to the arguments of succeeding chapters.

I divide man's history as a planning social animal into three stages. In the first and by far the longest stage, man's innate capacities for planning and living in social groups are formed. He becomes a "reciprocal altruist" during this stage rather than the "pure" or nonreciprocal type of altruist exemplified by social insects. In the second, very brief, stage, beginning roughly with the industrial-scientific revolution, man adopts ideas of progress and purposive development. The third stage, if it exists at all, is just beginning; it may turn out to be nothing more than a utopian anticipation. In short it is a hypothetical stage in which man achieves planning dominion over his technology, economy, and social order. Presumably progress will be controlled and in many areas selectively arrested.

Chapter 3 examines certain "Primitive Man" incentives to demonstrate the fundamental importance of social reinforcement within relatively small groups. We shall find that while Primitive Man is not Capitalist Man, Socialist Man, or Millennial Man he provides common roots and common denominators for all three. I shall focus particularly on mutual-aid practices of precapitalist farmers and the conscription of community labor for public-work projects. My purpose is to provide models of mutual-aid practices that were not only prevalent in precapitalist societies but that best illustrate the conditions under which social incentives support collective good in relatively small, egalitarian groups. These "conditions of social predictability," as I shall call them, are essential to the analysis of incentives in the egalitarian utopias of subsequent chapters.

Because this book is concerned primarily with social incentives, it is essential that one chapter be devoted exclusively to material or property incentives for background and comparison. Chapter 4 compares the property incentives of Socialist Man and Capitalist Man and examines the differences between personal and productive property incentives. We see how closely material and social incentives are tied together and how questionable it is to regard productive property as a universal individual incentive. Its effectiveness seems limited to very special circumstances. Pursuit of personal property, on the other hand, becomes and remains an impelling materialistic game at the very heart of Schumpeter's "civilization of capitalism." [10] In this context I introduce Huizinga's concept "Homo Ludens," or Man the Play Animal.[11] This personal-property side of the capitalist game comes to dominate the industrial era as it replaces the diverse, colorful games of the preindustrial. We see why this game spreads everywhere and why, despite the crass materialism many intellectuals ascribe to it, it has not been without positive consequences for the masses who play it.

Chapters 5 and 6 concentrate on the incentives of Millennial Man. Although real-world examples of Millennial Man communities sufficiently "successful" to have lasted 30 years or more are few and relatively insignificant compared to total world-population figures, our cases from modern Israel and 19th-century America represent priceless social experiments whose importance far outweighs their size and numbers. We examine carefully the social-incentive conditions of these communities, including those of social "predictability," "commitment," and "visibility." And we analyze a process of incentive changes that tends to destroy or transform these societies in strikingly similar fashion nearly everywhere.

As I have said, man seems to be moving toward more comprehensive social planning, including a greater concern with such new subjects as "futurology." The coming generation will probably be inundated with all sorts of utopian schemes for a new world dominated by a concern for the collective good. In Chapter 7 we gain practice in evaluating the incentive structures of utopian models by contrasting five Millennial Man utopias with the results of our real-world comparisons. My choices of fictional models are five of the most widely read utopias of all time. We shall find that utopians who design "chessboard" state communes can be relatively insensitive to the severe social-incentive problems inherent in the very scale of such large group games. The players of their games, as we shall see, would undoubtedly become the objects rather than the subjects of the rules of play. The contents of this chapter, therefore, are crucial to the distinction between the utopian behaviorism of B. F. Skinner and the philosophy of humanistic behaviorism that permeates this book.

Chapter 8 returns us to the real world with a comparison of two Socialist Man leviathans, Russia and China. Implications of the preceding chapter are confirmed. Despite egalitarian, nonmaterial, Millennial Man goals, the utopian state can effect only Socialist Man rewards, and even these remain highly materialistic. Relegated largely to object playing on their totalitarian "chessboards," the masses find few ways to increase their participation as subject-players except through the pursuit of personal property. In this context we consider for the first time the conditions of "legal predictability" that prevail in large, complex societies. These we shall compare with the "social-predictability" conditions prevailing in the small, relatively egalitarian groups that were our chief concern up to this point.

Some utopians blame the very size and nature of state society for the failure of Millennial Man incentives. They would eliminate the state and replace it with a grass-roots democracy rooted in communities that are united, through some kind of associations such as worker alliances, into regional confederations. Other utopians believe that Capitalist Man or Socialist Man incentives would work in more egalitarian and humanitarian fashion under stateless or limited-state conditions. For this reason Chapter 9 is devoted to utopian anarchism and a comparison of anarcho-capitalism, anarcho-socialism and anarcho-communism. Unfortunately, we are again limited mainly to fictive models, which I analyze in the light of the real-world data covered in preceding chapters.

We shall see that anarcho-communism is probably more unworkable than any other scheme for provisioning collective good discussed in this book. The case of anarcho-capitalism is not so clear; some versions seem as romantic as anarcho-communism and others but slightly modified versions of the capitalism we all know. Chapter 9 zeros in, therefore, on a version of anarcho-socialism much discussed at present in the capitalist as well as the socialist world—worker participation in management. Because of the limited, ambiguous nature of the available real-world data, I include in this chapter the results of personal observations on farm collectives managed by their members.

The pursuit of collective good described in Chapters 2 through 9 covers a sequence of social situations, from small to large, simple to complex, egalitarian to asymmetrical. After a brief examination of precapitalistic models we see how the civilization of capitalism alters the total situation and how dissident groups reject the capitalist alternative, for a while at least, by intensively playing a Millennial Man game in small, distinctive communities, eventually seduced by "progress." Next we observe how entire states try to defy the civilization of capitalism but in doing so sacrifice their Millennial Man ideals to Socialist Man compromises including monolithic, "patrimonial" bureaucracies. Finally we turn to the utopian dream of civilization without bureaucracy, of a society with the material advantages of large size and industrial complexity that preserves all the alleged advantages of life in small, egalitarian groups.

This sequence proved convenient not only to my inquiry into the provisioning of collective good but to my correlative search for answers to some of the disturbing questions of the late 1960's. Could mankind stop "progress" even if most men wanted to do so? Is progress necessarily "materialistic"? Is all materialism necessarily bad? How much equality is desirable? How much is possible? Is the best road to human fulfillment to the left of our capitalist road? If so, how far left?

I have made an honest attempt to let the data in Chapters 2 through 9 speak for themselves. Only in the final chapter do I indulge my personal feelings. But while the writing of this book undoubtedly nudged me to the right, it has not made me a spokesman for capitalism, even in the final chapter. I invite the reader, however, after finishing this book, to ask where on the face of the earth any great society has ever come closer to "utopia" than the one—despite its many faults—in which we are privileged to live. And if the pudding tastes good, perhaps we should all take a closer look at the recipe.

The one personal commitment that does permeate this book I would call, for lack of any better name, "humanistic behaviorism." Although I avoid the jargon of behaviorism as much as possible, the emphasis throughout is on "contingencies of reinforcement" within specific social environments. And that is precisely why I find the "Homo-ludens" view of man a necessary and healthy balance, for it emphasizes the important problem of participation. We must never allow contingencies of reinforcement to be designed for us by "specialists." We must all be active players on the field of moral judgment, for here is precisely where equality deserves its most vigorous defense. It is for this reason that I return repeatedly in this book to Jean-Jacques Rousseau.

Scholars differ widely in their interpretations of Rousseau, and while those who espouse the interpretations adopted here are perfectly respectable, they are vigorously opposed by others who are equally respectable. My choice is therefore a matter of preference rather than credence, convenience rather than veneration. No one can know with certainty what lies within the head of another man, much less one dead two hundred years. History, however, is a useful stage on which to dramatize contemporary issues. And the reminder that greater minds than ours were already puzzling over similar problems long before we were born contributes to a healthy atmosphere of humility. Any author, moreover, who presents his own predilections under a well-known historical label can modestly reduce his usage of the first-person pronoun.

Chapter Two

Altruism, Progress, and Utopia

MAN'S HISTORY as a planning animal I shall divide into three broad, heuristic stages of adaptation: the multiecological, the supraecological, and the mono-ecological. During the first stage, which begins with the earliest tool-using hominids and ends approximately with the onset of the scientific-industrial revolution, man evolves biologically in response to planning opportunities while adapting culturally to an expanding range of physical environments. Possessed of only a rudimentary technology throughout most of this period, he makes cultural adaptations that vary with habitat. These adaptations are "determined" only in the passive sense of specific environmental limitations, but in that passive sense we can call this a period of "geographic" or environmental "determinism."

With industrialization man acquires some dominion over ecological differences as he learns to "carry his environment with him," so to speak, and to flatten out many salient geographic "determinants." He now becomes technologically "determined"—although in the same passive sense—as those aspects of culture most closely affected by technology drift toward global homogeneity.

The third stage has scarcely begun. In fact, its existence to date is largely at the metaphysical level of anticipation. In this stage the spaceship earth becomes a single, finite, ecological niche, and man's physical environment again becomes the preeminent determinant of his adaptation. As it does, technology becomes increasingly the instrument of public, rather than private, good; and man becomes the master, rather than the slave, of his technology.

Although the captions for my three stages are ecological, this chapter is not a discussion of ecological determinants. Incentives are the central concern of this book, and this chapter provides essential background for their discussion. I am taking ecological and technological "determinants" for granted and am concentrating here on man's perception of himself as a social animal capable of initiating and sustaining collective good. I am concerned primarily with "human

11

nature" and how it relates to ideas of altruism, progress, and a utopian future.

The first section, on "multiecological man," is about primitive man and leads into Chapter 3. In this section we look at the relationship between the new and the old evolution and the effects of tool use and group size on man's planning capacity and, through "reciprocal altruism," on the quality of his entire "moral ecology."

The second section, on "supraecological man," is concerned with the progressive ideas of scientific-industrial man and how they began. We shall also introduce in this context the early antiprogress notions of Jean-Jacques Rousseau. Of particular concern will be the views of early Capitalist Man that have so dominated the progressive ethos of Western civilization throughout the period. Concepts basic to future chapters are introduced and illustrated through the materials of this section. The most important of these are: "new moral man," "reasonable need," and the "zero-sum view of inequality." This section is also background to Chapter 4, on property incentives.

The final section, on "monoecological man," introduces us to the differences between progress and utopia, to the hypothetical problem of adjusting progress to a spaceship earth, and to the possibility of a stationary-state utopia. It also introduces two important Rousseauean conditions for maximal support of collective good—the equality and high visibility of society's members.

Multiecological Man

We may never know precisely what adaptive steps led to the planning animal, but we do know that they took place much more slowly than the cultural changes that followed. Once the "old evolution" reached a critical threshold in the hominid line, what George Gaylord Simpson has called the "new evolution" took off at an exponential rate.[1]

To help visualize the magnitude of this transition from old to new evolution, imagine a 20-foot blackboard at the head of a large lecture hall, and imagine a line drawn across that blackboard to represent the curve of technological development beginning at the far left, where the first hominid toolmakers are labeled conservatively "two million years ago." Our line goes half way across the board to "one million years ago" before we reach the approximate appearance of Homo erectus, a creature of the same genus as ourselves but of a different species. We come to our own species at the 250,000-year mark with only two and a half feet of blackboard remaining. During all this time there has been relatively little change or development in tool traditions. They remain primitive with little specialization of function, and our blackboard line remains flat with as yet no perceptible upward curve.

Only when we get to modern man, about 30,000 years ago—on our blackboard only three and one-half inches from the right-hand edge—do we find the first spectacular diversification in the variety and elaboration of stone tools and other artifacts. One inch from the edge, "8,000 years ago," man begins to farm in the Old World; and by the time of Christ almost nothing remains of our 20-foot board. The Middle Ages, the Renaissance, the rediscovery of the New World, and the industrial revolution cannot be represented, for all that part of our cultural-development curve during which most of the exponential growth took place would have to fit into a space less than the width of a chalk line. The most intensive period of development, that of the last 120 years, would be represented by only one one-hundredth of an inch.

For most of our development curve the archaeological record reveals little change. This is the period when the history of life overlaps and dominates the history of culture, when the old evolution of adaptive radiation or natural selection was preparing the new evolution of adaptive rationality. Man did not blossom into a modern tool manipulator any more suddenly than he blossomed into a modern man. The first tool-using man-apes had a long way to go. In the early stages it can fairly be said that tools played as great a part in making man as he played in making them. Once our ancestors began to make tools any genetic variation toward greater planning and tool-making capacities would have afforded enormous adaptive advantages. But genetic change—the old evolution —was a tediously slow process compared to the new evolution once the adaptively rational animal had reached that developmental threshold from where cultural change could proceed on its own without being tied to further genetic changes.

This crucial point may have come with the physical changes, either vocal or neural, that made modern language possible. The simple kinds of tool traditions that dominate most of the technological curve could have been passed on without language as we know it. But the specialization and elaboration of stone tools that began some 30 to 50 thousand years ago would certainly have required language, and the animal that developed it would surely have been living in social groups for many thousands of years. It is at this point in man's history that "human nature" (all the limitations and potentialities of his phylogenic development) was set for better or for worse. Many pessimists today believe it was set for worse, and such assumptions have important consequences for "predictions" about the future.

Why worry about human nature? What good is a constant when what we really want to understand are differences and changes? How can a constant explain differences? A constant does not have to explain differences all by itself to be a necessary part of a complete explanation of those differences. In other words, it can be a necessary part of all, most, or many explanations of culture without being a sufficient part of any of them. In that event it may be uninteresting in the sense that it is nondiscriminatory and can be taken for granted. To say, for example, that men are motivated by hunger and sex drives may be a necessary part of any complete explanation of human dietary and sexual customs; but the more we become involved in accounting for group differences in such customs, the more trivial and uninteresting this "necessary" (and constant) part of the explanation becomes.

Sometimes scholars use human-nature constants as sufficient explanation for broad categories of behavior. It is especially in cases such as these that their assumptions about human nature can have powerful consequences for their prognostications. A case in point would be the contemporary emphasis on animal aggression stemming from the work of Konrad Lorenz and popularized by Robert Ardrey. Among other things war, crime, and private-property incentives are attributed to a biologically adaptive pattern of aggression that in effect is instinctive. Erich Fromm believes that such views find a ready audience not on the merit of the evidence presented but because they help people who feel frightened and powerless to accept their feelings of impotence and to abrogate any sense of responsibility. He believes that man developed a healthy, defensive aggression that helped him survive in the primitive state, which Fromm labels "benign aggression" to distinguish it from the "malignant aggression" that is cultural, not phylogenic.[2]

Even B. F. Skinner accepts the notion of an innate human aggressiveness that was once biologically adaptive but is now potentially "lethal."[3] Is it possible that this behavioral psychologist par excellence, who spurns all "mentalistic" explanations of behavior, has finally slipped into mentalism himself? Any reasonable man who wants to explain human behavior must accept some general motivational constant to put the animal in motion, but Skinner is not really interested in explaining behavior through nonobservable agents inside the head. He is concerned only with the various (and therefore interesting) contingencies of reinforcement that may direct this constant (and therefore uninteresting) energy source into channels deemed socially healthy or even "lethal."

In the same vein I accept here a self-interest on the part of mankind that can be channeled in various directions by different cultural contingencies. As we have said in connection with early toolmaking, any brain changes enhancing future-oriented decisions would have tremendous adaptive advantages. But an animal phylogenically rewarded by such contingencies of selection would be led to invest increasing amounts of labor in tool manufacture. And these investments of time would be justified by the animal's anticipation of future occasions when the tools would make a food-procurement effort more rewarding than it would have been without them. Greater ability to visualize future situations reflects an expansion of the memory function—a projection of past into future. But the more future oriented the animal becomes—the more it plans for future contingencies and the more it projects itself into future situations— the stronger becomes its self-awareness or ego consciousness. Future gratifications of the self become increasingly a matter of present concern.

The importance of memory for identity and future orientation has been dramatically demonstrated through the study of brain damage. As Howard Gardner explains in *The Shattered Mind*, each person normally constructs a "metaphor of self" in an ongoing process linking new experiences to those of the past.[4] The process by which each individual continuously adds to and revises his metaphor of self depends upon a "comprehensive" memory function unique to the human animal. When a malady such as Korsakoff's disease impairs this uniquely human dimension of memory with its "abstracting," "verbal-symbolic" capabilities, the individual can no longer encode the new information necessary to revise the mental metaphor. Identity and self-awareness are frozen at an earlier point in life history, and the individual becomes immune to the normal reinforcement processes that make it possible to relate accurately to the present environment or to plan rational future acts. The patient's ability to separate "individual-as-subject" from "individual-as-object" suffers permanent impairment as does "autonomy" of self.

The adaptive evolution of man's memory function and ego awareness took place in a social context that included reciprocities of food and sex. Such reciprocities made future satisfactions and ego awareness relative to, and contingent upon, the satisfactions and ego awareness of other members of the group. When, for example, asymmetrical reciprocities of food occur over any length of time, the memory of them can affect the distribution of future reciprocities. Ego awareness of future gratifications is open to invidious comparison with other persons' gratifications. Permanent asymmetries can intensify such comparisons and lead to interpersonal behavior of the kind we now consider indicative of status differences. Concern for future satisfactions would become much the same as concern for future status.

Here we see the genesis of what Immanuel Kant, in 1784, called "the unsocial sociability of men." [5] They are drawn into association with one another for their mutual advantage, yet each individual strives to direct everything "according to his own mind." In this regard men are quite unlike the social insects although both are labeled "social" animals. Thomas Hobbes was quite aware of this difference in 1651 when he used it to support the argument of his *Leviathan* that men need the coercive power of a sovereign to keep them sociable.[6] Among social insects "common good" and private good are the same, according to Hobbes, because agreement among them is "natural." Today we call it "genetic," the result of "phylogenic reinforcement" or "contingencies of selection" (the old evolution). Men, on the other hand, says Hobbes, by competing continually for "honor" and power, breed among themselves the "envy and hatred" that necessitates the "artificial" agreement of legal contract—what today we assign to the cultural realm of "ontogenic reinforcements" (the new evolution).

The societies of men and social insects are analogous, not homologous, yet ironically the terms of analogy used in descriptions of insect societies make the two sound much the same.[7] Although the insect social unit is really one big family, it is called a "colony"; the mother is "queen," and the various specialists known as "castes" are individually characterized as "workers," "soldiers," "nurses," "millers," and the like. "Slave raids" are carried out by ants that steal grubs from the nests of other species and raise them as their own workers.

"Totalitarianism" is practiced by insects that kill off certain specialized workers after their seasonal mission has been accomplished but before they become a useless drain on the colony's food reserves. Zoologists who use these terms do so for the sake of vivid, economical writing and are perfectly conscious of their literal inaccuracy. But such terms tend to minimize and hide the important difference between what I call the "genetic ecology" of insect society and what philosopher A. R. Louch has aptly called the "moral ecology" of human behavior.[8]

Louch illustrates his meaning with the former Bushman practice of leaving the aged to die of exposure in the South African desert. White colonials used to cite the practice to demonstrate the animal nature of the African native, a "moral judgment" quite different, says Louch, from the "moral assessment" of that same behavior by a social scientist. The latter takes into account the entire moral ecology: the harsh environmental circumstances weighed by the band in its decision, the grief of younger relatives and friends at the parting, and the resignation of the aged to a fate they deem necessary for the good of their loved ones. For Louch this approach also illustrates "moral explanation," the closest the student of human behavior can come to "scientific" explanation.

When groups such as the Bushmen and Eskimo abandon their aged or incapacitated in this manner, we label this willingness of the condemned individual to sacrifice himself for the group by the word "altruism"—a self-detrimental act performed for the benefit of others. Zoologists metaphorically employ the same word for analogous behavior among social insects. Cases that might be labeled "totalitarianism" by some observers can just as easily be labeled "altruism." Suppose, for example, that when honeybee workers push the drones from the nests at the end of summer, we emphasize the acquiescence of the drones rather than the aggressiveness of the workers. The metaphor can now be rewritten to portray the drones allowing themselves to be exposed to cold, hunger, and eventual death as altruistic self-sacrifice for the good of the colony. And when harvester ants kill off their "millers" once they have done their job of cracking open the colony's seed grains, we could metaphorically emphasize the fact that the millers offer no protest. They do not organize to demand their right to distributive justice. They altruistically bow to their fate and to the good of the greater number.

Both of the "moral explanations" applied to these insect cases—totalitarianism and altruism—are absurd. There is no moral ecology among honeybees and harvester ants—only genetic ecology. Even some zoologists object to the word "altruism" for nonhuman behavior and would prefer a neutral term such as "social donorism." But as Edward Wilson says, altruism instantly conveys the basic idea in a package familiar to everyone.[9]

Given, then, that the altruism of social insects is so different from the altruism of men as to have no "moral explanation," how do we explain it? We explain it along lines first set out by Charles Darwin, who found the social insects particularly difficult to accommodate to his view of natural selection.[10] How could sterile worker castes evolve, for example, if they had no offspring? He resolved the difficulty by postulating group selection at the level of the colony-family. The fertile members of the group carried the genes for sterile, "altruistic" members. The readiness of social bees and wasps to "sacrifice" their lives for the good of the colony originated in the effectiveness of this behavior and the fact that the altruism of the victims was perpetuated in the genes of their surviving kin.

When human societies are metaphorically likened to those of social insects, the intent is usually derogatory; during the Great Leap Forward, for example, communist China was frequently compared to an "ant hill." In this vein it has often been pointed out that precisely on those occasions when men are caught up in a mass movement and are at the peak of group commitment and enthusiasm they most resemble social insects. If it could be said that at such times man comes closest to true sociability, then Eric Hoffer's convincing indictment of the "true believer" can be seen as an impassioned plea in favor of the unsociable half of Kant's famous equation. Like social wasps men are also capable of extravagant altruistic sacrifice of lives. But there is no group selection in the genetic sense for true believers. Those who survive do not carry on the genes of true believerhood for those who died. Members of mass movements are not close kin like the residents of an ant hill; they are the products of that peculiar attribute of man—the moral ecology. How could such an anomalous form of altruism arise?

Robert Trivers has endeavored to answer precisely this question.[11] Since he is not primarily interested in the group- or "kin-selected" form of altruism typical of social insects, he focuses on altruistic behavior occurring between organisms distantly related—sometimes so distant as to be members of different species. For example, in the cleaning symbiosis between two species of ocean fish, the wrasse and the grouper, the former cleans ectoparasites from the mouth and gill chamber of the latter. The wrasse "altruistically" rids his grouper host of a pest, and the grouper "altruistically" avoids eating his cleaners and may even chase away their predators. But for this kind of altruism to arise among distantly related participants, there must be adaptive benefits for both. The host is healthier while the cleaner is better fed and less likely to be eaten. Both are better able to survive and are more likely to pass their "altruistic" genes to their descendants. To distinguish this kind of altruism from the kin-selected, social-insect variety, Trivers calls it "reciprocal altruism."

In kin-selected altruism (which I call "nonreciprocal altruism") the altruistic behavior does not have to benefit the organism performing the behavior because his close kin benefit, and they pass on the altruistic genes for him. In reciprocal altruism the organism performing the behavior cannot, or does not, pass on altruistic genetic changes through close kin; therefore, the organism must itself be favored by contingencies of natural selection, in other words, by phylogenic reinforcement.

Trivers lists four principal biological conditions that favor development of reciprocal altruism. First, a relatively long-lived species will have more opportunities to encounter and respond to altruistic situations. Second, if the organisms have a low dispersal rate, they will have more occasion to encounter the same set of neighbors with whom to exchange favors. Third, when a small set of individuals group together for mutual dependence, the chances for reciprocal interaction are increased. Fourth, groups in which dominance hierarchies are minimal (chimpanzees as compared to baboons) will offer more opportunities for altruistic symmetries. Most of these conditions, Trivers feels, apply to higher primates, and he suggests that during the Pleistocene epoch reciprocal altruism began to evolve in a hominid species which met these conditions.

However, these same circumstances—small bands of closely related individuals—also favor kin-selected altruism. In my opinion, reciprocal altruism would have been favored over kin selection in the human line by the correlative development and expansion of tool use. Take, for example, care of the young. As hominid infants were born in more foetal condition than other primate infants, allowing greater brain-case growth (probably after tool using increased phylogenic reinforcements for brain development), they would be less able to cling to their mother's fur as do, for example, infant baboons. The more foetal the infant, the more of an armful it literally becomes. Unlike the baboon mother, who goes right on foraging with her brand new infant clinging to her back, the hominid mother would be increasingly disadvantaged. This problem might have been solved by kin-selected, nonreciprocal altruism in the form of cooperative breeding behavior.[12] Band interest in new infants, which extends among some primates even to grooming the mother, might have developed into group feeding of both mother and infant. Although a much lower order example, the adult members of African wild-dog packs instinctively regurgitate food in the presence of pups.

Such phylogenic altruism was not the main route taken, however, because another route proved more adaptive for a tool-using animal with a rapidly developing brain. The father of the infant was by now investing labor in tools for future use, and he could readily use the same adaptive rationality to invest labor in social relationships and exchanges. He could help support the mother in return for future economic and sexual benefits, and the infant could become his social security policy for old age. In a tool-using animal reciprocal altruism could more quickly become cultural and part of a new process of ontogenic, rather than phylogenic, reinforcement.

In the early stages, however, there would still be considerable phylogenic reinforcement; and much of it, as Trivers points out, could have favored brain development even as much as did tool use.[13] At this point Trivers introduces the concept "cheating," by which he means "failure to reciprocate," implying moral assessment rather than moral judgment, a concept that closely parallels the "free rider" of economists. Selection would work against the "gross" cheater who did not reciprocate at all by favoring discrimination against that individual. "Subtle" cheating, however, in which an individual gives enough to maintain benefits to himself but consistently gives less than is received, would be adaptive and selectively reinforced. But it sets up dynamic tensions in the reciprocal process. As brain changes make some individuals more successful at subtle cheating, they also make other individuals more successful at detecting cheaters.[14] Thus, the original human dialectic may have been an adaptive phylogenic process which accelerated selection for a complex brain capable of moral assessment and moral explanation. Gradually ontogenic dialectic replaced phylogenic dialectic, and the new evolution was on its way.

Selective pressures would also have reinforced any emotions that helped regulate this new kind of reciprocal altruism, such emotions as friendship, hatred, guilt, sympathy, gratitude and what Trivers calls "moralist aggression and indignation."[15] These would help motivate altruism and would help provide a basis for encouraging reciprocity and discouraging cheating. Such a development would also accelerate the shift to ontogenic, rather than phylogenic, reinforcements of reciprocal altruism; and reinforcements could themselves become part of the cognitive animal's planning repertoire. Generosity and friendly behavior can be planned either to induce their return or to disarm a mark before cheating him, and moralistic aggression could be used against cheaters to provoke guilt and reparative behavior or could be used by cheaters to divert suspicion and detection. The very complexity of the reciprocal possibilities would exert selective pressure for more complex psychological and cognitive powers.[16]

At this point I wish to make clear that I am deliberately avoiding either a man-is-basically-good or a man-is-basically-evil position. I agree with geneticist Theodosius Dobzhansky that the most important consequence of natural selection for man was "plasticity of behavior" and "genetically established educability."[17] Only further research can clear up current debates over the degree to which "egotism" and "altruism" are phylogenically fixed in man and how their selection might have taken place. It is my belief, and a basic assumption here, that in man any such phylogenic behavior patterns will prove rudimentary and attenuated compared to their ontogenic counterparts. The reciprocal altruism that concerns us in this book is the product of man's plasticity and educability and is a dynamic part of his moral ecology rather than his genetic ecology.

Nonreciprocal altruism or kin-selected altruism comes closest to the idealistic connotation the word normally evokes. In the idealistic sense an altruist devotes himself to the welfare of others without seeking any return. But this kind of behavior, which occurs metaphorically among social insects, is an attribute of kin selection and is therefore a part of a genetic ecology where no idealism exists. Ironically, the ideal form is the cognitive invention of an animal that developed altruism through reciprocity; through giving services to receive services; through balancing public interest against self-interest. Thus, as in Kant's dialectical phrase, man's sociability has its built-in unsociability. But this form of sociability and altruism is much more flexible than the nonreciprocal form resulting from kin selection. An insect society is a response to selective pressures over thousands of years, whereas a human society can respond drastically to selective pressures in a single generation. Although the source of much of our trouble, this very circumstance may justify some hope for the future.

Here we must tread carefully, however, for utopian futures have often inspired the "idealistic" nonreciprocal form of altruism so normal among social insects—self-sacrifice including even self-destruction for the collective good. Honeybee workers leave their entrails and their lives along with the barbed sting they embed in the enemy of their colony. How like them were the Japanese kamikaze pilots of World War II or the thousands of Germans who sacrificed themselves for the glory of the Third Reich. Observers like our own proletarian philosopher, Eric Hoffer, do not view such forms of human altruism as utopian. Quite the contrary they tend to see them as social pathologies.

Hoffer, however, does not remove self-interest entirely from pathological forms of altruism.[18] He emphasizes the dramaturgical character of the mass movement, the make-believe nature of a mass performance in which each actor sees his own death as a heroic theatrical gesture before an audience of contemporaries. At the same time Hoffer sees a "passion for self-renunciation" in the mass movement quite unlike the practical organization's direct appeal to self-interest through self-advancement. The pathological extremes of human altruism seem to him like a reversion to the primitive small society in which each individual is a highly visible member of a group to which public allegiance is almost inseparable from identity of self.

To compare the primitive small society to a contemporary mass movement involving millions of people is more insightful than it might appear at first glance. Modern man fully evolved physically some thirty thousand years ago while living in small hunting-gathering bands. But the very adaptability and flexibility of man's reciprocal altruism with all its emotional and cognitive attributes may have left the door open to pathological excess once he began living in large urban societies. Detection and correction of cheating behavior evolved in small—not large—hominid groups.

Judging from those that survived to modern times, hunting-gathering bands averaged about 25 persons. So common is this band size that Michael Jochim refers to it as the "magic number." [19] In an ethnohistorical analysis of the Pai Indians of the Southwestern United States, John Martin found that Pai bands averaged 25 to 28 persons, a local group built around approximately 4 mature males who comprised an optimal hunting party for this environment.[20] Returns for effort were good without overtaxing local resources. Since a majority of the members in any primitive band were women, children and subadults, the mature males made up a small, face-to-face, decision-making core in each. Even hunting-gathering bands as large as 50 would have had a decision-making core of less than 10 individuals.

Group experiments by social psychologists have shown that affection and trust among members decrease as group size increases, and as they do, the coordination of members' activities requires stronger leadership. According to Paul Hare, the average individual in a group situation cannot accurately keep track of the separate views and social activities of more than six or seven persons.[21] Beyond that number the individual tends to classify fellow members in subgroups and begins to treat other subgroups than one's own in stereotypic fashion. A leader is then likely to arise who coordinates, in hub-and-spoke fashion, the subgroup leaders.

In his now classic paper "The Magical Number Seven, Plus or Minus Two," George A. Miller argues that man has a limited "channel capacity" for making absolute judgments of visual, auditory or tactile stimuli that averages around 6.5 categories of distinguishable alternatives.[22] Man increased his total channel capacity, however, by perceiving and judging along more than one sensory dimension at a time. Miller believes there were adaptive advantages in being responsive to a wide range of stimuli in the environment, in other words to knowing a little about a lot of things rather than a lot about a relatively few things. Man learned, moreover, to increase the span of absolute judgment by developing and applying memory function and his verbal ability to "recode" experience. Even the span of immediate memory, as shown by test situations, is limited to approximately seven items. But the amount and quality of information that can be contained in the immediate memory span can be increased by the construction of information "chunks." By forming groups of information items into few enough chunks, man could recall many more of them, a process accomplished by translating into a verbal code. Language thus served man as an enormously useful tool for culture building by providing a mnemonic and taxonomic device to compensate for limitations of absolute judgment, limitations which at one point were an adaptive advantage by demanding responsiveness to a wide range of stimuli.

The fact that Hare's group-size limitations for keeping track of other people also distribute themselves around the "magical" number seven as well as the fact that members of groups above this number tend to "chunk" one another in subgroups would indicate that man's limits of channel capacity and memory span apply to the social, as well as physical, environment. Hare devised a formula to show the exponential increase in potential social relationships with increasing group size and concluded that when circumstances demand finely coordinated social relationships groups will tend to be small.[23] Effective leaders, however, by reducing large-group psychological complexities to a series of dyadic relationships between themselves and each member can actually become an alternative to size reduction.

Returning to modern man's original social group, the hunting-gathering band, we see that so far as the decision-making core is concerned, "the magical number seven plus or minus two" approximates the range of band size. With strong male dominance the band would readily chunk into household subgroups represented by the mature males. Totally wrong in his picture of "natural" man, Hobbes was by no means wrong in assuming that urban man needed to live by formal contract and effective authority structures. He was right for the wrong reasons. In those original social groupings in which man physically evolved, he could live by mutual trust rather than by formal contract and strong authority. Members of a seven-man decision-making core can inspectionally evaluate each other's behavior and correct "cheating" without laws and police.

By committing themselves to a charismatic leader under mass-movement conditions, large numbers of people can so drastically— perhaps pathologically— simplify the psychological complexities of social interaction as to achieve a quality of small-group unity. But neither the Hobbesian anarchy of "natural man" nor the total mass movement is characteristic of the day-to-day behavior of human societies. Man has adapted remarkably well to life under urban conditions, unbelievably well for a small-group, hunting-gathering animal. Recoding and chunking capabilities have given man an amazing flexibility.

So flexible has the human animal proven itself that thinkers like the late Abraham Maslow, the great Brandeis psychologist, have seriously entertained the notion of a new "authentic person" or "self-actualizing" man capable of transcending cultural and social provincialism to become more and more species-oriented and less and less bound to a local group.[24] And when one considers the primitive condition, this view of an expanding moral ecology may not be just idle romanticism.

In a rare study of primitive morality carried out among the Gahuku-Gama of highland New Guinea, K. E. Read depicts a moral order that fits closely to patterns of subgroup chunking and reciprocal altruism.[25] The Gahuku-Gama have a strictly tribal morality, not one that is universalistic and species oriented. They could not understand Read's friendship with certain European neighbors based only on mutual regard. To explain the phenomenon to themselves, they chunked Read and his friends together as "age mates" or "clansmen." They themselves were not free to choose associations on idiosyncratic grounds but categorized their fellows according to a system of rights and obligations. Moral obligation among these people was "distributive" in that it varied with the particular relationship and especially with the distance of each. There was no common morality for all situations. Nor did the Gahuku-Gama concern themselves with the morality of actions that did not directly involve them. They had no interest in abstract notions of right and wrong. Their moral statements clearly took the pattern of reciprocal altruism: "help others so they will help you," and "give food to those who visit you so they will think well of you."

The cultural behavior and moral ecology of man in the first stage of development varied from place to place with the adaptation to a multitude of environmental niches around the planet. But this book is not primarily concerned with the cultural relativism of that stage. More pertinent are certain aspects of life related to reciprocal altruism that were broadly similar everywhere such as food sharing among hunters, mutual-aid practices among primitive farmers, and the earliest forms of public support of a collective good through labor taxation. The latter two subjects occupy us in considerable detail in Chapter 3.

Opinion differs as to whether man's moral ecology has grown or progressed since the multiecological stage of adaptation. Some feel it has only diversified more. Others not only feel it has progressed since the band and the primitive state, they even preserve a late 18th-century brand of optimism. Maybe those contemporary thinkers who would solve the world's problems by decentralizing all society into small local groups are simply arcadian utopians after all. Perhaps those analysts are right who, like Herbert Kaufman, view the primitive or peasant village as more tyrannical and stifling than the city or who, like Michel Crozier, see our moral ecology as expanding or progressing away from the "rule of morality" of the closed, traditional, religious society to the "rule of negotiation" of the open, enlightened, cosmopolitan society.[26] But we are getting ahead of our story. It is time now to turn to our second heuristic stage in man's development.

Supraecological Man

The second, and by far the shorter, of our first two stages—the width of a chalk line in our previous blackboard metaphor—begins a little before the industrial revolution. It begins with the idea of progress, when men first became conscious of the upward curve of material development. French historian Jean Bodin as far back as 1565 attacked the notion of an ancient "golden age," followed by degeneration.[27] He gave the ancients their due, but labeled their time one of "iron," compared to his own day. Mankind could not possibly have degenerated since the days of the Greeks and Romans as medieval history taught, for the "discoveries" of men of his own time far outranked those of the ancients. Of the magnet and the compass they knew nothing, yet this discovery had opened the whole world to commerce and colonization and to the union of all men into a kind of world society. In addition, men of his day had made great advances in geography, the technology of warfare, and the weaving industry. The art of printing alone surpassed all the inventions of the past.

In 1688 Bernard de Fontenelle carried Bodin's contrast of ancient and modern times a step further and suggested the inevitable advance of science and knowledge into an indefinite future.[28] He warns, moreover, that nothing retards natural progress more than too much admiration of "the ancients." By the early 18th century, says Crane Brinton, the achievements of scientists from Copernicus through Newton had advanced the notion of scientific progress generally among intellectuals, and by the middle of that century material progress was becoming evident even in the everyday world of the layman.[29] Roads were improving, coaches were getting places faster, and even indoor plumbing was becoming fashionable. By the end of the 18th century an old man could look back over his life and reminisce about the poorer living standards, inefficient tools, and greater hardships of his youth.

Peter Gay records the observations of Dr. David Ramsay, an American physician prominent in his day, who on the first of January, 1801, wrote proudly of all the progress made in medicine during the preceding century.[30] He invited his oldest readers to think back 40 or 50 years and recall the great number of women who died in childbirth and the countless children born with deformities. Only 4 or 5 children per family reached adulthood then compared to the 7 or 8 who now survived. And where, he asks, does one see children anymore with the pock marks that blemish the faces of their grandmothers? Progress had become so inspectional by 1800, concludes Gay, that it was visible even on people's faces. No wonder that by the end of the 18th century men had grown so optimistic about what they could accomplish through the powers of reason that they believed mankind could also build a happier, more ethical world! And as material improvements spread to everyone and not merely a privileged few, it would become a more just world as well. When the 18th century opened, writes Sidney Pollard, the idea of progress was generally restricted to science and technology; but before it had closed, progress had been applied to wealth, society, the arts, and even human nature.[31]

Recently, historian E. R. Dodds has argued convincingly that a genuine belief in progress existed among the Greeks for a brief period during the fifth century B.C.[32] While this negates an oft repeated assumption that the idea of progress was completely foreign to the ancient world, Dodds' evidence becomes the exception that demonstrates the rule. For the idea of progress lasted only a brief period at a time when Greek civilization was experiencing an advance so broad and apparent to all that it managed to create its own expectation. But once the actual experience of advancement ended, says Dodds, so did the expectation of further progress.

During the 18th and 19th centuries the empirical evidences of progress became so convincing that by the middle of the 19th century it had been awarded a volition and inevitability all its own—a kind of law of indefinite cumulative change. As Carl Becker wrote in 1934, the doctrine of progress of the 18th-century philosophes embodied a faith in man's conscious, rational ability to create an earthly utopia.[33] With the influence of Darwin, Marx, and others, progress by the second half of the 19th century had become a deterministic force external to man. But the form in which the 18th-century philosophes formulated the modern idea of progress, Becker argued, was simply a modification of the Christian doctrine of redemption.[34] The Heavenly City of God was brought down to earth and made a tangible possibility in this world through the perfectibility of man and his environment. In the process, "posterity" took the place of God and was invoked reverentially in a Biblical idiom documented by Becker with quotations from the period.

This concern with posterity, which was to become so important a part of the ideology of progress, had actually begun much earlier and in a much more secular form among 15th- and 16th-century craftsmen. To them Edgar Zilsel credits the earliest beginnings of the notion of scientific progress.[35] As the economic competition of early capitalism began to undermine the power of the guilds, innovative artisans turned into incipient capitalist manufacturers. At a time when people who worked with their hands were still disdained, these ambitious men sought avenues to justify their achievements in the eyes of society. Where could they turn? Science as we know it today did not exist; the classical science of the period was closer to what we would label philosophy. And the humanists of Renaissance times were masters of a literary style devoted to the display of classical erudition.

In case after case, Zilsel documents the fact that 15th- and 16th-century artisans were breaking free of the guild tradition of secrecy to publish manuals of craft technique and treatises on technical improvements and new discoveries. Lacking the scholarly erudition and polish of the humanists and defying guild secrecy, they apologized for their presumptuousness and lack of learning and justified publication in the name of posterity and the public good. In their modest treatises they eschewed any desire for private fame and emphasized their desire to serve the public benefit by leaving behind a record on which other craftsmen could build. They argued for gradual progress in the arts and sciences through the sharing of knowledge and the painstaking perfection of inventions. Men should not be maligned, they contended, for searching out and publishing the secrets of their crafts. Rather, blame should go to those who keep new knowledge to themselves; for had all men so behaved since earliest times, mankind would differ little from animals. How little difference there is in the spirit of these pre-Baconian treatises and that of Bertrand Russell's credo four hundred years later that "our supreme duty to posterity" is to further, not diminish, the achievements we bequeath to the next generation.[36]

Some of the treatises antedated Francis Bacon by a hundred years or more. Thus, the ideology of modern science and the concept of scientific progress were already long in existence before Bacon formalized and popularized them in the early 17th century. Zilsel concludes that the concept of science we normally think of as "Baconian" was really an essential and unavoidable correlate of incipient capitalism and capitalistic technology with roots as far back as the 15th century.

Science, capitalism, and belief in progress have been close companions during most of the supraecological stage. Recently, philosopher Henryk Skolimowski has criticized the strong ideological connection between the "scientific world view" and the "illusions of progress" of Western intellectual heritage.[37] He considers it an improvident marriage that has resulted in the exploitation of our planetary ecological system at the expense of the many for the benefit of a small elite. This is not too different from the Marxian view of the relationship between capitalism and progress.

As political scientist Henry Pachter points out, the *Communist Manifesto* contains the most enthusiastic tribute ever written to the role of the capitalist bourgeoisie in carrying progress to the four corners of the earth.[38] But for Marx and Engels progress was dialectically both good and evil. The progress of capitalism creates tremendous productive forces to liberate man from superstition and want and to replace backwardness with scientific and technical knowledge. As it accomplishes this material objective, however, it also achieves that climax in the history of social evil when human oppression must finally be replaced by political and social equality.

As for the connection between capitalism and science, Joseph Schumpeter summed it up well when he made them two indispensable concomitants of "the civilization of capitalism." [39] Capitalism, by establishing the monetary unit as the unit of account, introduced rational cost-profit calculations into human affairs. Mathematics and science ("mathematico-experimental science") grew out of practical problems of commercial arithmetic, architecture, and craftsmanship as part of the "rise of capitalism." Together science and capitalism became the instrument and force for the "rationalization" of human behavior such that all the products of science and its application are simultaneously the product of the capitalist process.

But for those critics of modern society who, like Skolimowski, stress the relationship between progress and the technical or industrial-scientific order, the modernizing socialist world can be just as guilty of short-sighted materialism as the capitalist world. And anyone who has read *Andromeda,* the Russian, government-approved, science-fiction novel by Ivan Efremov, cannot help being impressed by the inordinate concern for posterity in this progressive, communist world of the future. [40]

Bernard Kiernan has forcefully argued that the ideology of progress has so gripped the developing or "emergent" world in its desire for rapid modernization that communism or socialism has an historically determined part to play in the process. [41] Since the First (industrialized) World has already set the course for development, a totalitarian elite dedicated to the material improvement of its masses and to the welfare of posterity can now plan and carry out an accelerated version of the capitalist experience. By creating a kind of war economy through the politics of crisis, a committed, ideological elite can marshal the human capital of a nation to advance together in an egalitarian movement that effects the savings necessary for industrialization and progress. China, Kiernan feels, has become the outstanding model for this Second (socialist) World approach to the development problems of the Third (emergent) World.

Throughout the socialist world and those emerging nations taking the socialist route to progress, the need has repeatedly been stressed for a new kind of man, a "new moral man" also called a new "socialist man" or "communist man" or even in the case of Cuba a "new Cuban man." This new moral man according to some ideological statements puts the collective or public good ahead of self-interest in almost nonreciprocal fashion. Such a view of man is quite the reverse of the laissez-faire capitalist view that the public good is a consequence or product of conflicting self-interests rewarded under perfect (nonmonopolized) conditions of market competition. This capitalist view fits the model of reciprocal altruism. Yet there are those who feel that a new moral man such as that endorsed by the socialist world will be essential to any kind of planned, harmonious society on our future, spaceship earth.

Many people tend to forget that capitalism once had its new moral man too—Calvinist Man, if I may call him that. Benjamin Nelson, in his engaging little book on *The Idea of Usury*, introduces a three-stage scheme of man's relation to fellow man during the early development of Western civilization and illustrates it with historical changes in the interpretation of usury.[42] The first stage, the "tribal brotherhood," is illustrated by Old Testament, Hebraic law. Deuteronomy 23: 19–20 proscribes loaning anything "upon usuary" (on interest) to a brother but permits such behavior toward a "stranger"—someone outside the brotherhood. Medieval Christianity, according to Nelson, tried to apply Deuteronomy to all of Christendom by opposing usury throughout the Western world, an unsuccessful attempt to create a "universal brotherhood." With the Reformation, and especially Calvinism, objections to interest charges broke down and were replaced by the utilitarian liberalism of the "universal otherhood." Calvin argued that the political union of the Jews was different from "our union" and that usury was not unlawful unless it disrupted brotherly relations. So he invoked everyone to employ the golden rule—to not do to *others* what one would not want done to himself—in deciding what interest was just or unjust. The decision was left to each man's conscience in anticipation of God's full and final judgment.

As Christopher Hill has pointed out, Calvin also insisted that each man always put the public good ahead of his own private gain; and in that same spirit the puritan preachers of the 16th and 17th centuries assured their congregations that industrious productive work by the pure in heart could not help but benefit the common good.[43] Specialists, in producing for the marketplace, simultaneously benefited all others while benefiting themselves. Since God had made the marketplace, men could be both rich and holy as long as in their hearts they sought riches for God and their fellow men and not just for themselves.

The new moral man of capitalism is by no means dead; Abraham Maslow's self-actualizing man is in many ways a modern, secularized version of the Calvinist form.[44] The self-actualizing man, who strives to attain the maximum self-fulfillment of his own idiosyncratic potential, is also capable of rising above the distinction between selfishness and unselfishness. He derives as much pleasure from the pleasure and self-actualization of *others* as from his own. This self-fulfilling involvement in the otherhood is a kind of nonreciprocal altruism that makes Maslow's form of the capitalist new moral man almost indistinguishable from the socialist form. And while Calvin's mid-16th-century version was too early for a clear statement of the idea of progress, it is strong in Maslow's. The self-actualizing man will never rest on his laurels but will always strive to enhance his blessings, an eternal process of human improvement reaching "into the future forever."

Although the idealistic form of Capitalist Man tends toward nonreciprocal altruism, the puritan form above had reciprocal overtones that led straight to Adam Smith. Along the way, however, these reciprocal attributes were exposed to the satirical social criticism of Bernard Mandeville. In his *The Fable of the Bees: Or Private Vices, Publick Benefits*, the final complete edition of which was published in 1724, Mandeville links the prosperity and opulence (public benefits) of a growing, "stirring," "trading" country with the avarice, prodigality and pride (private vices or sins) of its citizens.[45] In such a nation the demand for consumer goods will keep enough ahead of supply to insure full employment and steady growth of national wealth. A truly virtuous country, on the other hand, would have to be small, spartan, frugal, and poor. To live in such an honest, virtuous land the average Englishman, says Mandeville, would have to give up most of the comforts and enjoyments he now considers necessary. Since men are obviously unwilling to make such a sacrifice, why should they go about bemoaning the vice that insures their continued prosperity?

In Mandeville's scheme a people's prosperity is generated by their selfishness particularly in the form of pride—the insatiable pursuit of public honor. "Pride," "sloth," "sensuality," "fickleness," "avarice," "envy," and "ambition" are the great motivators of men. These are, moreover, the very attributes which make men "sociable creatures," and support their "trades and employments"; yet, he says, these are precisely what men lump together as the "evil" of this world. A prosperous society, he concludes, will decay as soon as evil ceases.

When Adam Smith published *The Wealth of Nations* over half a century later (1776), he had obviously been influenced by Mandeville. Self-interest was the prime mover of economic and social progress in Smith's scheme, too; for as he noted in his oft quoted phrase about the butcher, brewer and baker, we do not count on their "benevolence" to provide us with our dinner but on "their regard to their own self-interest." [46] But for Mandeville to equate self-interest with vice was for Smith a play on words—a "sophistry." If public benefits such as "elegant arts," "improvements of human life," in "dress, furniture or equipage," and outstanding "architecture" are invariably classified as the sensuous indulgence of "ostentation" and the latter in turn classified as vice, then indeed everything readily becomes evil.[47]

Smith is not nearly so sanguine as Mandeville about self-interest. For him the drive within each individual to improve his lot is "so powerful a principle" that it alone can carry a society to "wealth and prosperity" particularly when it operates through "frugality" and "industriousness." [48] Part of man's self-interest drive is his "propensity" to "exchange" which leads him to a division of labor that in turn creates "general opulence." [49] Thus, a steady improvement results which no one ever "foresees" or "intends." Smith's progress is not the result of a master plan but the consequence of competitive, self-seeking behavior guided only by the "invisible hand" of the market. In this model of society the individual works for his own private interest and usually has no intention of promoting the public interest nor any awareness of when he does. Nor is this bad in Smith's view, for the man who concentrates on his own interests often benefits society more than the man who puts society's interests first.[50]

In Louch's terms it might be fair to say that Adam Smith was making an honest attempt to arrive at a moral assessment of his society while Mandeville in the spirit of satire was passing a moral judgment upon it. But both men certainly viewed "altruism" in the reciprocal sense. The public or collective good had to follow from some private reinforcement. But not only was the link between public and private benefits not premeditated, its existence when exposed was sometimes a shocking surprise.

In 1784, only a short time after Smith's famous work, Immanuel Kant praised the "unsocial sociability" of man, that "great tendency to individualize" which impels him to strive for honor, power, and rank and creates the "mutual antagonisms" peculiar to human society.[51] He praises this "selfish propensity" in man because without his "envious jealousy and vanity" and his "insatiable desire of possession" and "power" he would have been content with the life of an "Arcadian shepherd" and all his "talents would have forever remained hidden." Mankind can achieve fulfillment only in a society which guarantees the greatest liberty for this antagonism as long as a just civil government insures its mutuality so that the freedom of some members does not limit the freedom of other members.

Writing earlier than either Adam Smith or Immanuel Kant, Jean-Jacques Rousseau in his *Discourse on the Origin and Foundations of Inequality among Men* (1755) finds little to his taste in the same world admired by Smith and Kant. He sees no virtue in selfish competition and mutual antagonisms. Like Mandeville he is aware of the vices of his time, but unlike him he is not inclined to justify them with any so-called public benefits.

Rousseau follows partially in the path of Montesquieu, who in the *Spirit of the Laws* (1748) reversed Hobbes's sequence of a natural "state of war" followed by civil society. "Is it not obvious," asked Montesquieu, that the conditions of human conflict arise with society rather than precede it? [52] For Rousseau the conflict of the natural state was continued and exacerbated by the civil society of Hobbes, Smith, and Kant.

Men in society compete for social status—honor and riches—and in doing so become "enemies." Man's increasing avariciousness "stifles" natural compassion for others and propels him into a perpetual "state of war" against them. "Progress" and "knowledge" "deprave" men by creating the conflicts of interest that foster mutual "hatred." Thus, civilization brings "honor without virtue" and "reason without wisdom." Man's reason actually undermines the humane sentiments, for the rational man of civilized, urban society, says Rousseau in an example that seems even more relevant to our day than to his, will not even get out of bed when he hears his fellow man being murdered outside his window. Instead he puts his hands over his ears and fights back every inclination to identify with the victim.[53]

In another passage that seems very modern in its social criticism, Rousseau alludes to what we today call the "rat race." The average member of society, he says, is always pushing and tormenting himself by undertaking more and more arduous occupations. He works himself to death getting ready to live. And much of this frenetic activity is performed to acquire unnecessary new "commodities" which "degenerate" into "needs" that no one is really "happy to possess" but everyone is "unhappy to lose." Not only could men do without these new goods, they "soften body and mind." While the rich, for example, end up with foods "overly refined," the poor end up without enough to eat. Like his own domesticated animals, man becomes dependent upon conditions that lead to his degeneration.[54]

So early and yet so modern is Rousseau in most of his condemnations of progress that he can fairly be called "the father of antiprogress." And since his condemnations occur in the context of a discourse on the origins of inequality, his measure of antiprogress becomes inequality itself. The state, he says, was sold to men on the grounds that it could "protect the weak from oppression," and so they "all ran to meet their chains." For in effect it ended up putting "new fetters" on the poor and giving new strength to the rich. By institutionalizing inequality of property rights, it magnified and perpetuated social inequalities, "authorized" the status of rich and poor, and converted "legitimate power into arbitrary power." [55]

A correlate of this emphasis on expanding inequalities was that the very circumstances that constituted the progress of some men caused the degradation and impoverishment of others. Not only is the prosperity of one man achieved through a corresponding loss to others, all men have "a hidden desire to profit at the expense of others" as part of their consuming ambition to succeed. Thus, each successful man obtains his profits through other men's misfortunes. What is worse, the unnecessary luxuries of the rich man are prized by him less for their intrinsic merit than for the enjoyment of seeing others deprived of them. The rich, says Rousseau, would cease to be happy if those they deprived ceased to be miserable; luxury, therefore, demeans everyone.[56]

Here Rousseau illustrates for us two important ideas that I refer to repeatedly throughout this book. The first of these is the concept of *reasonable need*. As we see in subsequent chapters, utopians frequently design a society in which the growth of needs is contained at a level deemed reasonable by the utopian, a purely relative notion. Rousseau obviously feels that even the society of his day has gone too far in the creation of unnecessary consumer goods, and we see below how much in this respect he resembles not only Plato and Thomas More but even Mao Tse-tung.

The second important concept Rousseau illustrates for us is the zero-sum view of inequality. The term "zero sum" comes from game strategy and refers to a closed-system game situation in which the winning player wins at the expense of the losing player or players. Take, for example, a poker game with four players all of whom start off with $10 apiece. At the close of their evening's entertainment, player A has $40 and Players B, C, and D have none. Player A has won $30 at the expense of Players B, C, and D who have each lost $10. The sum of the winnings (+$30) and the losses (−$30) equals zero.

When I use the term "positive-sum view," I refer to the opposite situation— a view of the world in which everyone is considered to be winning though not necessarily winning in equal amounts. This view assumes an open system in which new wealth is created for all without depriving anyone. It is essentially the view of progress that characterizes our second period of human history—the supraecological stage. It is also the view that best characterizes Adam Smith. Driven by self-interest but led by civil society to engage increasingly in a division and capitalization of labor that greatly magnified its productivity, men were able to augment wealth and opulence to the enjoyment—though not equal enjoyment—of all. Savages, Smith said, worked as hard as civilized men but were "miserably poor." Among civilized men, however, many did not work at all; yet everyone was "abundantly supplied" such that even the lowest and poorest workmen had more of the "necessaries and conveniences of life" than the wealthiest savage.[57] Here, indeed, was a progress over time that held great benefits for all even though the category "poorest workmen" indicated that these benefits or winnings were by no means evenly distributed.

Immanuel Kant, as we have seen, joined Smith in making the unsociable part of man's nature—his vanity and desire for power—the underlying energy of progress; but the channel was civil society itself. Comparing men in society to trees in a forest, he says as each endeavors to take all the available air and sunlight they force one another to seek the air and sun above; thus all of them "grow beautiful and straight." [58] The zero-sum competition for scarce resources has positive-sum results by virtue of a civil society that allows the greatest freedom for the "antagonism of its members" while limiting each individual's liberty so that it may "coexist with the liberty of others."

As Italian philosopher Lucio Colletti has pointed out, Rousseau was backward in his economics and never grasped the dynamic, positive-sum economic view developing in his day.[59] He adhered to an earlier, static, zero-sum economic view. One might say he was a double anachronism; by being behind the times at precisely the right moment, he emerged for posterity as a man well ahead of his time. His out-of-date position became a foundation for Marxian views that Marxists have not properly acknowledged; for Rousseau's position implied that the positive-sum game of progress was a long-term mirage and what really mattered was its zero-sum consequences for the present. His position provided the basis for modern embourgeoisement doctrine: a worker may be misled by the absolute, long-term, positive-sum benefits (his income compared to his father's) to overlook the fact that relatively (compared to the present top) he may be worse off than his father and grandfather were in their generations.

But Rousseau published his social critique a generation before the "dynamic" views of Smith and Kant and in many ways was transitional between them and earlier writers such as Hobbes, Locke, and Mandeville. The earlier writers had not been as fully influenced by ideas of progress as had Smith and Kant. In Hobbes's system, the civil state or leviathan was far better than the state of nature in which man led a life that was "solitary, poor, nasty, brutish, and short." [60] But Hobbes does not emphasize progression. Man's competitive struggle for power in the natural state is a zero-sum contention made more vicious by the very fact that men by nature are fairly equal to one another.

Being fairly equal they tend to have equal aspirations and thus inevitably become enemies in a "state of war" the moment two or more covet something they cannot share. The leviathan brings security to men by constituting a common, coercive power, an "artificial man" to protect property. Hobbes is stressing peace and security in 1651 rather than the dynamic positive-sum economics stressed by Adam Smith 125 years later.

John Locke in 1689 comes much closer to Smith's positive-sum view of things; all the ingredients are there in his "Second Treatise" on civil government, but he never clearly combines them into one dynamic system. Like Hobbes he emphasizes security, especially the protection of property; but he does imply that progressive long-term public benefits accrue from this security. Unlike Hobbes, however, he does not adopt a zero-sum view of the state of nature. For a long time, he says, the world had plenty of "natural provisions" and "few spenders"; each man could take what he needed without quarreling with anyone else. But in a comparison of savages and civilized peoples so close to Smith's as to have probably been the latter's inspiration, Locke says even a great chief among the Indians of America "feeds, lodges, and is clad worse than a day-laborer in England." This was to illustrate that people living in a bountiful environment without "improving it by labor" would not have "one-hundredth part of the conveniences we enjoy." Human labor accounted for most of the value of civilized man's products—about ninety-nine percent of it by his rough estimate. But this labor theory of value was of more help to Karl Marx than to Adam Smith. Locke's labor component lacks the dynamic, exponential quality Smith gave it through the process of specialization. Instead, he recognized that men differed in degrees of industry—the amount and quality of labor they expended, which resulted in unequal "possessions." [61]

Locke also emphasized the importance for civil society of money, which was to be another indispensable ingredient of Smith's system as catalyst for the division of labor. For Locke it was crucial to the explanation of unequal possession.[62] Before money most goods were perishable, so to avoid spoilage no one produced or accumulated more than he could use. But money made it possible for the industrious to greatly extend their supply of permanent possessions. Thus, a "disproportionate and unequal possession of the earth" came about in the natural state through "the consent of men" even before civil governments and their laws were created to regulate property ownership. With unequal ownership of durable goods, quarreling among men began, and men were compelled to unite in "commonwealths" for "the preservation of their property."

Adam Smith not only followed Locke's reasoning on the association between private property and civil government, he even specified the point at which the latter becomes necessary, when the members of a society are able to accumulate property worth three or more days of labor.[63] And in wealthy societies great inequality is inevitable. For every rich man there will be at least five hundred indignant, envious, poor men ready to strip him of the accumulation of a lifetime of hard work.

It was precisely this kind of thinking that Rousseau was to convert into his conspiracy-of-the-rich theory for the origin of civil society with all the built-in inequality he abhorred. Both Locke and Smith, however, seem to imply that unequal possession goes with unequal effort and thereby constitutes an incentive for the labor so important to the difference between civilized and savage living standards.

Mandeville went much further with property incentives than did Locke.[64] Employing a more elaborate version of the same Lockean example, he says that if one traced the most prosperous nations back to their origins he would find that the richest men during those "remote beginnings" had none of the "comforts of life" that now even the most "humble wretches" deemed a necessity. While civilization had certainly brought with it a higher standard of living for all, it had not, however, distributed its largesse in equal amounts to all, and it was Mandeville's opinion that inequality of benefits was essential to motivate "working people." Any working man, he says, who can provide himself with the essentials of life by working only four days a week will never be persuaded to work five. Laborers are so dominated by a "proclivity to idleness" that they can be "obliged" to work only "by immediate necessity." So within Mandeville's positive-sum game of advancing civilization there is also at any one point in time a zero-sum game between capitalists and laborers that allows the former a large discretionary income and the latter none at all, a difference essential to the motivations of each and to the long-term, positive-sum results that benefit both.

Adam Smith was not nearly so pessimistic about motivating the laboring masses. He argues against the view that most working men labor only to survive and therefore work less when goods are cheaper or wages higher.[65] They want more goods and conveniences and are willing to work for them. Moreover it is in those countries which are progressing fastest that wages are highest. England, he says, is a richer land than North America, but North America is progressing faster and pays higher wages. Where progress is taking place at a quicker pace, labor is in greater demand. In a stationary society such as China where there is little or no progress, many people compete for a limited number of jobs, and the poverty of the lowest classes is far greater there than in Europe. Smith consistently emphasizes the positive-sum characteristics of capitalist progress even for the working masses.

These early writers of the second stage of development illustrate in simple fashion the capitalistic world view that accompanied industrial development. The dominant view of this period as influenced by scientific industrial capitalism greatly extended planning at the level of private interest but emphasized the *consequential* rather than *purposive* nature of public interest. In other words it endorsed a reciprocal altruism very close to the adaptive model of biology by putting the emphasis on individual—not group—reinforcement.

But as human groups became larger with increasing commercialization and industrialization, the face-to-face conditions under which "cheating" was originally controlled were replaced by the laws of the leviathan state. Men like

Mandeville, Rousseau, and Marx were disturbed by such phenomena as vice, selfishness, abuse of power—all words to describe the "cheating" behavior of reciprocal altruism magnified under large-group conditions. The complaints of men like Rousseau also illustrate an aspect of the human condition unique to the adaptive biological model. Man is the only animal with a moral ecology making moral judgments, moral assessments and moral explanations. The "cheating" and cheating-control behavior we neutrally and dispassionately observe in other species is the very substance of human moral ecology. This is the point the Jean-Jacques Rousseaus of this world keep trying to drive home.

Monoecological Man

Ironically the same concern for posterity that was so important and hallowed a justification for early notions of progress is now the rallying cry of those advocating the end of progress. For many observers the positive-sum game of industrial expansion that was supposed to benefit posterity as well as the living has become a zero-sum game benefiting the living at the expense of posterity. According to economist Kenneth Boulding the open-system view of positive-sum capitalist economics is all wrong.[66] It either assumed unlimited resources or simply did not take limits into account. Boulding calls our second stage of capitalist progressivism the period of "cowboy economics," a reckless period when the pistol-packing entrepreneurs of capitalist exploitation shot up our environment while maximizing their short-term, private benefits. Consumption during this period was regarded as a great, collective good—the end point of a "flow" process emphasizing a "throughput" that began with raw-material extraction. The cowboy economy, says Boulding, must be replaced with a closed or "spaceman" economy which views the planet realistically as a spaceship with limited "reservoirs" both for resource extraction and pollution deposits. To get away from the notion ingrained in modern economics that unrestrained production and consumption are good, rather than bad, we must start giving posterity a "voice" and a "vote." To emphasize the "relevancy" of posterity consciousness, he threatens any society that abandons its positive links to posterity with immediate disintegration, a threat based on undisclosed "historical evidence."

In similar vein economist E. F. Shumacher argues that man has treated "nonrenewable" resources such as fossil fuels not as irreplaceable capital assets but as unlimited income.[67] The open-system, positive-sum economy is a mirage based on bad bookkeeping that has failed to record in the debit column the true costs of our material development. Moreover, Schumacher emphasizes a zero-sum contest over resources between the rich and poor nations of the world. Despite the fact that the populations of poor countries are growing much faster than the populations of rich countries, the latter continue to do most of the exploitive damage to the planet because of their insatiable needs and high levels of consumption.

In many ways Schumacher is a modern version of Rousseau. He advocates a reduction of needs to some reasonable level, and he believes the continued pursuit of universal prosperity via greed and envy can only destroy the intelligence and happiness of man. He would also like to decentralize modern society into the kind of small, autonomous groups in which people are "comprehensible" to one another. We can carry on close, brotherly relationships, he says, with only a limited number of people at any one time.

In discussing Rousseau above, I do not mention the small, egalitarian, ideal society of his *Social Contract* because its proper place for discussion is here in the monoecological "stage" with more utopian schemes. This stage is not so much a real time period as an expression of concern about the future. It may be a utopian or dystopian anticipation that never comes to pass; at best it is what Schumacher calls "exploratory calculation." At this point it is appropriate to say a few words about the nature of utopia, particularly how it differs from the idea of progress and from what I shall call "eutopia."

In the first place, the notion of utopia is much older than the concept of progress. A. L. Morton traces it back to primitive folklore.[68] But we do not have to go that far back to differentiate it from progress. A medieval utopian concept first recorded for the 13th century, but which reaches much further back into antiquity, is the vision of the village wonderland known as Cockaigne.[69] Here all earthly desires are fulfilled in paradise fashion—in plenty and without effort. Roasted meat is always at hand, beer and wine flow in natural streams, houses are of gingerbread, and a fountain of youth makes everyone young again.

When we get to the utopias of written history, they tend to become much more than fantasies of paradise. They portray a better world, the virtues of which stand in sharp contrast to the vices of this one. In effect, they become a vehicle of social criticism. The word itself comes from Thomas More's book *Utopia* (1516), a title he constructed from Greek roots signifying "no place." Because "utopia" and "eutopia" (good place) are pronounced the same, More was able to imply the existence of a good place—an improvement on early 16th-century England—that was really no place. I adhere to this distinction in subsequent chapters. "Utopia" refers to fictional good societies, while "eutopia" refers to those community experiments in the good life that have had a real time and place. "Dystopia," bad place, has become a label for pessimistic fictional views of the future such as George Orwell's *1984* or Anthony Burgess's *A Clockwork Orange*, and I shall use it here only in that sense. Some persons have regarded the Soviet Union, for example, as a real-world dystopia; but no matter how we judge the outcome, this was a eutopian experiment in its intent.

Early visions of utopia were static, and Thomas More's book certainly fits this pattern. The perfect society, once organized, needs no improvement. And More's island paradise was no Cockaigne; everyone was well provided with the essentials of life, but there were no frills. Nor did Utopian needs expand; quite the contrary, they remained austerely "reasonable."

The first progressive utopia was Etienne Cabet's *Icaria* (1840), which adopted labor-saving machinery and gradually but steadily raised its citizens' material standard of living. Since its social order was perfect, however, no further social changes were needed or desired.

Efremov's *Andromeda* (1960), mentioned above, also depicts a social order which has achieved the permanence of perfection—the world communist society of the future. Material living standards have leveled off at optimum need-satisfaction, so no further changes in consumer goods are necessary here either. Yet the world is a more progressive society than ever before, for everyone has become a trained scientist contributing to human knowledge for both personal intellectual satisfaction and that of posterity. Thus, *Andromeda* depicts a utopian view of the future in which the world has socially and industrially achieved a steady-state condition but in which progress marches on in an exaggerated version of its original, 17th-century form—a continuing expansion of science and knowledge into the indefinite future.

It is not surprising that *Andromeda's* picture of the future is close to Friederick Engels's millennial view depicted in the closing passages of his *Socialism: Utopian and Scientific* (1892). When the competitive anarchy of capitalistic production comes to an end, man's social and economic environment—instead of controlling humanity as it has in the past—will at last come under man's dominion. Contrasting the laws of nature with the laws of man in a form similar to Montesquieu's 18th-century distinction, Engels declares that laws of social action will no longer count among the laws of nature but will now become man-made and man-controlled, thus opening up a whole new dimension of human freedom.[70]

According to some writers, the 19th-century view of progress as influenced by Marx and Darwin took on a developmental determinism.[71] In the 18th century, progress was the product of reason; in the 19th it was the manifestation of inexorable historical laws. But as Henry Pachter has recently argued, Marx and Engels, by the time of the *Communist Manifesto*, had abandoned the historicist position for one of social action.[72] They considered the capitalist bourgeoisie an unwitting carrier or agent of progress, much as did Adam Smith, but in their scheme this unplanned state of change was to be replaced after the proletarian revolution by a planning or "decisionist" society.

Coordinated worldwide planning at a monoecological or spaceship-earth stage does not, however, obviate historicist explanation. If a future monoecological stage may be viewed as the result of population pressures and resource scarcities, then man's final planned environment, planned social action, or planned social law—however one cares to label it—will ultimately be determined by the limitations of the spaceship. In other words, *if* these ultimate pressures occur, man will be forced to make the most optimal compromise possible between the predictability of natural law and the predictability of man-made law. In that event a planning stage will be the product of the same "non-predictive determinism"—to use an apt phrase of George Gaylord Simpson—that has characterized all evolution, both old and new.[73]

Among those who believe that some such ultimate planning stage will adaptively evolve, opinions differ as to whether it will be a world worth living in. The views of Marx, Engels, and other socialists are often euphoric and even millennial in tone. But many thinkers outside the socialist camp have shared their enthusiasm. John Stuart Mill, writing at mid-19th century, believed wealth could increase only within certain limits at which point the progressive state would change into a stationary one, a change he thought would be for the better.[74] He hated to think of humans forever "trampling and elbowing" one another in the struggle "to get on" and preferred to think of his own progressive era as a temporary and disagreeable, albeit necessary, stage. Eventually the world will achieve an egalitarian affluence, and the "coarse stimuli" of economic competition will give way to "improving the Art of Living."

Writing in 1930, economist John Maynard Keynes also predicted that the "strenuous purposeful money-makers" would carry everyone along with them to an era of "economic abundance" after which people could turn to cultivating the "art of life." [75] But he believed the time of abundance was at least another hundred years off, and meanwhile vice, avarice and usury would be in command until they had led us all "out of the tunnel of economic necessity."

Keynes and Mill both follow in the footsteps of Mandeville and Adam Smith. Ugly competition labeled "coarse stimuli" or outright "avarice" still performs an enormous public benefit by reducing and eventually eliminating "economic necessity" or poverty. But to the Mandeville and Adam Smith schemes Mill and Keynes have added a utopian finale in which the amoral, or downright immoral, rat race gradually evolves into an intellectual's paradise.

Joseph Schumpeter, writing not long (1942) after Keynes, did not believe a stationary state very likely since he found it difficult to conceive of human needs ever reaching "satiety." [76] But if they ever did, the ensuing stationary state would make the creative entrepreneur obsolete, and capitalism would be replaced by a very "sober" bureaucratic socialism. Schumpeter's exploratory calculations on the demise of capitalism follow a different route from the previous model of satiation through rising affluence. His causal reasoning is much more subtle. The scientific rationalism so integrally a part of the civilization of capitalism breeds a critical frame of mind that eventually undermines the moral authority of the capitalist order. He says the bourgeoisie eventually discover to their amazement that the rationalist attitude they have sponsored and fostered shifts its attacks from "kings and popes" to private property and all other sacred bourgeois values. By its very nature the civilization of capitalism is built to self-destruct. Again, planning becomes the consequence of unplanned, nonpredictive determinism. But Schumpeter's determinism focuses on adaptive rationality rather than upon ennui or limitations of the physical environment. It differs from Marxism mainly in that the agent of change is the educated intellectual rather than the working proletariat.

Schumpeter's educated intellectual, however, is no different ethically from a bourgeois capitalist. If there were ever a stationary state, he says, business would no longer provide an outlet for egotism, and the best brains would soon be attracted into other adventures. Human self-interest and the desire for prestige go so much deeper than capitalism that society will never be able to rely entirely on a "purely altruistic" (nonreciprocal) commitment to the public good. The new society will have to harness somehow the energy of self-interest in its own behalf by finding some other way of allocating prestige than through private property. If it impressed one's fellows enough to win their deference and respect, says Schumpeter, the privilege of sticking a penny stamp on one's trouser could do as much to motivate the wearer as an income of a million dollars a year does now.[77]

Geneticist Gunther Stent has still another deterministic model for the end of progress.[78] In his case the reversing mechanism is not satiety or rationality but security. The motivational source of progress is a will to power created by necessity, the characteristic of "Faustian Man." But once progress has proceeded far enough to guarantee security for everyone, the social ethos changes and with it the parental discipline that previously fostered a strong power incentive in children. Faustian Man will then be replaced by a "Polynesian Man" who can face the prospect of universal leisure without terror. Or possibly he will be replaced by Dennis Gabor's "Mozartian Man," who finds creative inspiration in leisure rather than in conflict and competition.

Stent, however, believes the creativity of the future is doomed at best to a kind of involutional pedanticism as the scientific disciplines all reach their intrinsic limits. Just as geography reached its disciplinary boundaries once it had described the features of the earth, so genetics, chemistry, and biology are all doomed to reach theirs in the near future. Scientific work will then become redundant, trivial and Parkinsonian.[79]

One biologist's picture of the future, however, may not necessarily appeal to another. Nobel prize-winner Peter Medawar, for example, believes we are mere beginners at the game of progress.[80] Improvement lies ahead, and he chides pessimists who submit to discouragement because they see no quick and easy solutions to all our problems. "To deride the hope of progress," he concludes, "is the ultimate fatuity, the last word in poverty of spirit and meanness of mind."

Utopian and dystopian models of the monoecological future are games of exploratory calculation. But scholars who advocate giving "votes" to posterity in support of programs for spaceship economics or behavioral engineering act as if they *know* what is best for posterity. To know, they must be able to do more than make exploratory calculations; they must be able to make high-probability predictions. And since, as we have seen, they cannot do that except through the enforcement of a plan the rest of us have consented to, we are right back where we started—the leviathan state. But now we have a super-leviathan that not only protects the public interest in the present, it plans and protects it for posterity as well. And how does even a superleviathan know what is best for posterity? How does one collect votes from the unborn?

Perhaps the venal, pistol-packing, cowboy stage of progress was a necessary evil just as men like Mill and Keynes have thought. Perhaps the careless, exploitive use of nonrenewable capital was intrinsic to a primitive industrial stage that had to precede the technological and scientific sophistication necessary for new breakthroughs in the harnessing of energy. Perhaps Adam Smith was right: the individual who follows self-interest for today and the immediate future is wiser than the one who deliberately works for the collective good of a future which can be only improbably anticipated; for our precise drawing-board models, as noted earlier, may have no approximation to reality whatsoever. Perhaps the old commonsense adage that a bird in hand is worth two in the bush is still *good* sense.

Our self-educated, proletarian philosopher Eric Hoffer has warned us in several books about the frustrated intellectuals who would have us all reach for those two birds in the bush. Mass movements feed on "vivid visualization of a glorious future," and he bids us all beware the leader who promises the millennium.[81] Maybe cowboyism is still more pragmatic than spacemanship.

A planning, or super, leviathan will need planners, and who will they be? Man, said Immanuel Kant, is an animal who needs a master; yet there is none to serve as master save yet another man made from the same "crooked material." [82]

According to Rousseau the perfect "lawgiver" would have to be a god; no mere mortal would be up to the job. Thus, in his *Social Contract* (1762), the father of antiprogress does not rely on guardians or planners.[83] To keep sovereignty in the hands of the people, he allows no legislators to represent them; the people make their own laws in town-meeting assemblies where they enact their legislation by a "general will." As mentioned above, scholars have differed widely in their perception of Rousseau's meaning; for some the general will is totalitarian while for others it is a manifestation of perfect liberty.

The passage that so many find bothersome is the one in which Rousseau equates ultimate freedom with conformity to the general will. If anyone refuses to obey the general will, he must be "constrained to do so by the whole body" which, says Rousseau, means that "he shall be forced to be free." [84] For Crane Brinton this statement turns Rousseau, the great individualist, into a prophet of modern collectivism.[85]

At the opposite extreme Ellen Wood has recently argued that Rousseau's general will is really a principle of procedure.[86] On each problem that arises, Rousseau's citizen does not consult personal interest or those of any particular group but considers what the consequences will be for the public good. The general will is not a "collective consciousness," says Wood, but rather an individual consciousness capable of compassion and of universalizing itself. It is a union within each individual of the public and private good. Peter Gay takes much the same position when he says that the general will comes into being as men concentrate on their "common interests." [87]

In one case Rousseau is damned for constructing a collectivist leviathan, and in the other he is praised for creating a new moral man who seems to be guided by pure (nonreciprocal) altruism. Actually, we can readily bring these two extreme positions together by making Rousseau's citizen the member of a mass movement, a "true believer" in Eric Hoffer's sense. The true believer, as we saw earlier, merges individuality with the group identity. The very conformity to group behavior becomes a denial of self and of any interests apart from those of the group. Such a person may come very close in his behavior to the nonreciprocal altruism of a social insect.

Conceivably the pressures of a monoecological stage might create a mass movement in which private good, collective good, and a concern for the interests of posterity would be all conjoined. Were scarcities to become so great as to seriously and permanently affect our daily lives, public and private interests might coalesce in each individual. Catastrophes like those predicted by doom writers would thus bring together present and future, short and long term, and private good and collective good.

Rousseau, however, was not describing a mass movement. He was trying to design a society in which the power concentrated by the leviathan in the hands of a few could be distributed more equitably among its citizens. In the Hobbesian model individuals were too distracted by their private interests to achieve a harmony of wills; so the sovereign became the guardian of the collective interest; the "mortal god" had to transcend private interest for the public good. By agreement among themselves, individuals voluntarily established this sovereignty to reduce their plurality of wills to one will. This single will or "mortal god" then had the power to compel individuals to conform to the covenants of the commonwealth. In so doing, all were set free from the insecurities and conflicts of the state of nature so they could "nourish themselves" through their "own industry." [88] Hobbes's man like Rousseau's was also "forced to be free." The consistent difference between the two is that the "force" comes from the "whole body" of Rousseau's society rather than from a monarch or legislature as in Hobbes's. Rousseau wants to spread equally among the population the power he finds so unequally distributed in the world he knows. Only when power is equitably distributed will private and public interest become the same.

One way he fights inequality is to remove all luxuries, for these corrupt the rich "by possession" and the poor "by covetousness." [89] Change is not emphasized, for Rousseau, as we have said, probably never understood positive-sum development. But zero-sum conditions are eliminated as much as possible. Equality is not absolute in his good society; but he felt that to maintain equality of power equality of wealth should be "considerable." Moreover, since all participate directly through town-meeting-type assemblies in the making of their laws, the society must be small, one in which members are well known to one another. It is only in large societies where all citizens are mutual strangers that "talents" go "hidden, virtues ignored," and "vices unpunished." [90]

There is an arcadian quality to this highly personal, ideal society in which everyone is visible to everyone else. Rousseau is calling for those conditions of high visibility under which the counter-cheating behavior of reciprocal altruism was originally applied. If peasants seated under an oak tree can expertly conduct the affairs of a happy country, he asks, why do sophisicated nations make themselves "wretched" with all their intrigue and "mystery"? [91]

It hardly seems likely that the whole world will revert to life in village communities, although as we see in the chapters below, various forms of socialist and capitalist decentralization have been advocated. Not long ago *The Ecologist* published a special edition, "Blueprint for Survival," in which life in small communities was recommended to reduce individualism, excessive consumption, and the harmful impact of population on the environment.[92] Rather than bring modern complex society down to the high-visibility level of primitive and traditional villages, it seems more probable that we shall look for ways to carry the high visibility of the small society up to the level of large, spatially mobile, human populations. How else can we reconcile high-visibility conditions with another Rousseauean dream, that of a "common brotherhood" among men?

In his "Essay on the Origin of Languages," Rousseau pointed out that primitive men "had the concept of a father, a son, a brother, but not that of a man." [93] Beyond the local group everyone was both stranger and enemy. Here Rousseau's view of the primitive moral ecology is strikingly similar to Read's observations on the Gahuku-Gama discussed earlier. He goes on to say that tender emotions of love and compassion were experienced among the local group in this narrow, familiar sense, but all felt only hatred for "their species."

"Social feeling," says Rousseau, develops with "enlightenment" and "knowledge"; it is activated by "imagination," which in turn depends on the "comparsion of ideas." [94] Here Rousseau is firmly in the 18th-century Enlightenment tradition. Through reason and knowledge man can expand the horizons of his sociability. It was also Immanuel Kant's hope that this would prove to be "the highest purpose of nature" and would culminate in a "universal cosmopolitical institution." [95]

But how does one reconcile the idea of the small, high-visibility society with that of a world state experiencing common brotherhood? Schumacher believes it can be done by somehow creating an "articulated structure" of many "small-scale units" whatever this may mean. He would also reduce or eliminate that high degree of modern spatial mobility Alvin Toffler eulogized under the label "transience" in his book, *Future Shock*. Modern rapid transportation and communications facilities, according to Schumacher, tend to destroy freedom by increasing insecurity.[96] But without them can men still expand the horizons of their experience through the comparison of ideas? Martin Buber's solution in his *Paths in Utopia* was similar to Schumacher's.[97] He felt a true "organic commonwealth" would be a "community of communities" much like a giant federation of kibbutzim. But as we see, even in Israel only a small percentage of the population chooses to live in this kind of community.

Summary

Development of the one and only planning animal, man, has been depicted in three stages. In the first, phylogenic and ontogenic adaptations work together to produce an unusual intellect. An inevitable concomitant of that intellect, however, is a self-awareness that accounts for the animal's "unsociability" as well as its "sociability." This unique animal can not only be sociable—can support a collective good—for reasons of self-advantage, it can also cheat and free ride for those same reasons. The most intelligent product of evolution is, therefore, its only morally concerned product. Since all of this animal's actions take place in a moral ecology, all studies of them by specialists become moral assessments. In addition to its own experience, the individual animal can weigh moral assessments by specialists before reaching its own moral judgments. All moral judgments, however, are made in the context of reciprocal altruism.

"Reciprocal altruism" is preferred to terms such as "reciprocity" or "exchange" for literary emphasis. The very concept of pure altruism is a unique product of our moral ecology. In practice, pure—nonreciprocal—altruism works only in genetic ecologies like those of social insects. Reciprocal altruism is the marvelous evolutionary concomitant of an intelligent animal with a moral ecology. To emphasize the point that reciprocal altruism is the most developed form of altruism as well as the only one we have, it is the preferred term throughout this book.

Man's unique intelligence leads to cumulative developments of knowledge and technology that eventually become self-evident. This new level of self-awareness, corresponding roughly with the beginnings of modern science and the industrial revolution, initiates the second stage. Man begins to realize that short-run planning over the ages has had progressive, long-run consequences for the collective good that were not foreseen, much less planned. Science, capitalism, and the idea of progress unfold together in the positive-sum view of a long-run collective good inspired by the short-run pursuit of individual self-interests. One negative view of the process, represented in this book by Rousseau, sees too much inequality in the short run; long-run progress cannot justify short-run cheating. True progress must serve not only posterity but the masses who live and die in the short run.

The third stage is hypothetical. Pressure on world resources—now viewed as finite—provokes criticism of previous ideas of progress and long-run collective good. Comprehensive planning is advocated as well as an end to progress based on the unintended consequences of the pursuit of self-interest. Some look forward to a static state in which everyone works for the good of all. Would such a state require an ant-hill altruism irreconcilable with that of an intelligent, moral animal? Would the moral judgments of the masses determine its design? Could a utopia of small, semiautonomous communities combine reciprocal altruism and the fruits of our progress to date? Or would the utopian static state reflect only the moral assessments of planning specialists? By what means would their assessments prevail? These are questions to which subsequent chapters are addressed.

Chapter Three

Mutual Aid: Preindustrial Forms

A MISTAKEN NOTION persists among some students of primitive life that Rousseau extolled and romanticized this period in man's history. Actually the father of antiprogress was a great optimist about the future; the progress he opposed was a lopsided materialist version that neglected man's moral ecology. Rousseau believed society could be redesigned to engender a new moral man; but this new man lay ahead of, not behind, us.

The savage, according to Rousseau, was ignorant due to self-sufficiency. Without any progress in education there was none in intellect or reason. Savages thought little about the future and had "neither foresight nor curiosity." Their "generations multiplied uselessly," each one "always starting from the same point" so that "man remained ever a child." Since in this natural state man was "neither good nor evil," Rousseau considered Hobbes wrong in picturing man as naturally bad. Rousseau saw in the primitive's great capacity for compassion and pity the foundations for a better man. Unfortunately, the self-seeking, materialistic progress of civilization was developing the worst in man's character. Rousseau wanted a progress that would make man more moral, as well as more rational; reason by itself could be downright immoral.[1]

For all practical purposes, Rousseau's natural state did not differ much from Hobbes's. In Hobbes's version there was always "war of every one against every one"; but he did not mean "actual fighting"—only "the known disposition thereto." [2] Similarly primitive men, said Rousseau, might attack one another when they met, "but they rarely met. A state of war prevailed universally, and the entire earth was at peace." [3] Both authors were using the state of nature as a model for contrast. Rousseau is clearer than Hobbes on this point, for he states categorically that he is not attempting to write history or discover actual origins.[4] Even the savage populations of his own day are of little help in constructing a model of the natural state since they had diverged from the original condition just as had civilized peoples. Instead he is undertaking "hypothetical" reasoning, he says, like "our physicists" do to aid in clarifying the "nature of things."

According to Durkheim, Rousseau was using the state of nature as a methodological device to isolate man's inherent psychological structure from all social attributes.[5] He was dramatizing a transition from the "de facto order," in which man thought only of himself, to the "de jure order" of the civil state, in which he can and must achieve a higher morality by reconciling individual will and general will.

Selective Incentives and Collective Good[6]

Let me illustrate Rousseau's problems of immoral reason, individual versus general will, and transition from de facto order to de jure order, with some examples of collective good. Suppose four farmers living some distance from a highway recognize the advantage of collectively building and maintaining a feeder road to connect their four adjacent properties to the highway. But one man's farm is many times larger than the tiny farms of the other three. The material advantages of this road are so much greater for the man with the big farm, who will make much more use and profit from it, that he may decide to provision this collective good unilaterally and simply invite the other three to contribute any work or funds they care, or can afford, to provide. In this case there can be no cheating behavior on the part of the three minor contributors to the collective good since they are under no obligation to support it. Altruism in this case appears nonreciprocal only because an asymmetry of wealth has, in effect, converted a public good into one man's private good.

Now let us suppose that the four farmers all have farms of equal size, all stand to benefit equally from the feeder road, and all are equally anxious to obtain this collective good. Let us also suppose that the location of the farm properties is such that once the road is constructed all four men cannot help but have equal and unobstructed access to it regardless of whether each does his share to construct and maintain it. One of the four, Farmer Jones, believes that the other three want the road badly enough that they will build it even if he does not contribute his share of work and capital. He therefore decides that by not participating he can save time and money and still get the benefit of the road. The other three farmers may regard Jones's decision as cheating behavior and may decide to employ counter-cheating behavior against him.

By definition there is no way the three men can make the collective good in this case into an incentive that is "selective" for Jones; for once the road is built, he will be able to use it and profit from it as much as they. Every year at harvest time, however, the four men are accustomed to pooling their labor and equipment to help each other get in their grain crops before the rains can damage them. Jones is told by the other three farmers that they will no longer help him at harvest time. They threaten him, in short, with such a severe loss in labor and equipment that he feels a strong negative, selective, material incentive to support the collective good. Moreover, they warn Jones that no one else in the community will help him after hearing of his cheating ways; his social standing in the community will be irreparably damaged. To the negative material incentive they have now added a negative social incentive, and both are selective since both apply specifically to Jones.

In this case the costs of not provisioning the collective good are so great that Jones considers it much cheaper to do his share. In fact, if he willingly and cheerfully does even more than his share, the other three men not only remain his friends, they are likely to treat him more generously than usual the next time he asks for their help at harvesting. His reputation also rises in the community. Clearly there are positive material and social incentives highly selective for Jones if he enthusiastically participates in provisioning the collective good. In fact Jones never threatens to cheat at all, for the entire strategy we have reviewed here goes through his head the minute he even thinks of cheating. Jones is a rational man, and in this case it is clearly rational to provision the collective good.

Now let us go to the lowland province of Portuguesa in western Venezuela where the federal government is opening up virgin lands for settlers from the overcrowded highlands. A new farming community of some four hundred settler families needs an all-weather secondary road to link it with the nearest highway. The government promises to loan the community bulldozers and road-grading machinery if the families will donate the labor. The settlers have all been given farm plots of equal size, they stand to benefit equally from the road, and all are expected to participate equally in its construction. As in the previous case, however, once the road is built, there is no convenient way of making this collective good selective in itself as everyone will have equal, unobstructed access to it.

In this community, the equivalent of Farmer Jones is Settler Fulano, who also considers the consequences of cheating. He reasons that his labor and financial support of the project would be such a small proportion of the total that it would probably not be missed if he failed to provide it. Instead of being one-fourth of the total support as was Jones's, his is only one-fourth of one percent of the total. Even if someone notices that Fulano is not doing his share, what harm can come of it? The settlers are all from different parts of the highlands and do not know one another. They have no ties to each other and do not even have social standings among themselves to go up or down. Obviously there are no selective incentives—material, social, negative or positive—in this situation to induce Fulano's support. If he cheats, no counter-cheating behavior will oppose him. Fulano is a rational man, so he cheats; he does not support the collective good.

Fulano's community illustrates the civilized world Rousseau found so immoral. Visibility is low in this community, and selective incentives to support the collective good are weak. Like the rational man in Rousseau's example, who hears his neighbor being murdered outside his bedroom window and simply pulls the pillow over his head, Fulano acts rationally but immorally. He has entered a moral ecology where material progress may be taking place but where the worst attributes of "natural man" find stimulation through that very same reasoning process that creates his material progress.

In Jones's community, however, visibility is high and so is participation. Each man sees the advantage of the collective good; each individual will is in full conformity with the general will, and virtue is served. This situation comes much closer to the Rousseauean ideal in which reason and morality go hand in hand. Whether Rousseau would have admired Jones's reasoning as I describe it is another question and one I do not try to answer.

As we shall see, the Farmer Jones situation has much in common with primitive forms of mutual aid and represents the past better than the future. It is for this reason that Rousseau's utopian hopes for the future often seem arcadian today. But Rousseau was writing before the industrial revolution was really under way. At that time Jones and Fulano situations could well have seemed more like contemporary alternatives than stages in a contemporary transition.

The Jones and Fulano examples also illustrate the wisdom of the Locke and Montesquieu critiques of Hobbes. Locke did not believe the state of nature was one of war. It was a time when men lived together by reason alone, without a "common superior." [7] And Montesquieu, as we have seen, was of the opinion that the state of war began when men entered into civil society, not when they lived in a state of nature. [8]

As noted in the previous chapter, Hobbes was right for the wrong reasons. Through expanding commercial relationships, the brotherhood becomes an otherhood; strangers become quasibrothers, and the high visibility of the small community is replaced by the low visibility of large communities with spatially mobile populations. Reason grows stronger as experience and choice expand, but the moral ecology grows weaker as visibility falls. The war of each against all fills the vacuum left by a weakened moral ecology, and the leviathan or de jure order becomes necessary to strengthen and restore the moral ecology.

In Fulano's community, as more and more individuals adopt his line of reasoning, support for road construction decreases. Fewer and fewer settlers show up for work, and those who do say, "Why should I do all the work while those lazy malingerers stay home?" So they stay home, too, and work comes to a standstill. Is there no solution to the problem? The solution is very simple; the leviathan steps in and taxes each settler a share of the road-building costs and employs a contractor to build the road.

The way in which cheating behavior is corrected in the Jones and Fulano examples illustrates a distinction referred to throughout this book between what I call "social predictability" and "legal predictability." The conditions of social predictability are those which social psychologists, who study small groups, label conditions of small-group trust. Legal predictability covers the formal legal sanctions by which large societies order their internal relations to effect collective good.

The Farmer Jones case fits the conditions of social predictability. The four farmers in this case had been neighbors all their lives and had worked together and exchanged services for many years. They had developed means of controlling each other's outcomes; and their behavior toward one another not only affected their mutual exchanges, it affected behaviors toward them by other "third" persons external to these relationships.

In the Fulano case none of these conditions of social predictability existed. Members of the community were truly strangers to one another, and predictability in this case had to be established by the laws of the state. Taxes must be paid, and if they are not, the offender is fined or put in jail. Selective incentives under legal predictability tend to be much more negative than under social predictability. Their punitive character makes them predominantly material in form though such punishments may also involve a loss of social esteem.

Social predictability may still exist alongside legal predictability in the civil state; but in the primitive societies that preceded civil government, social predictability prevailed. Beyond their small groups many primitive peoples endured a situation very similar to the Hobbesian state of war. But within the smallest face-to-face communities, "reason" ruled relationships without any authoritarian superior much as Locke supposed. Anthropologist Napoleon Chagnon's recent study of the South American Yanomamo provides a dramatic illustration of this reconciliation of views.[9] A Yanomamo headman leads by example and persuasion rather than by force, and he produces more food than anyone else in order to give it away at feasts. Other men help him at his gardening, and all men as hunters share their game with other members of the village. Ideally each gives away most of the game he kills. Despite reciprocal altruism, however, villages fission once they reach 100 to 150 persons in size at which point internal disputes finally tax the persuasive leadership to its limits. On the other hand, groups never drop below 40 persons in size because they would be too vulnerable to attack from other groups. Thus, reciprocal altruism works optimally in groups up to 100 members above which the forces of cheating and counter-cheating become too disruptive. And except for protective, women-exchanging alliances with a few other groups, each group is essentially at war with all others.

Robert Trivers, in his discussion of the development of reciprocal altruism, correctly notes that aggression within hunter-gatherer bands is often provoked by real or imagined inequalities in food sharing.[10] I do not focus on hunter-gatherers in the sections below, but rather on examples of mutual-aid practices typical of primitive and peasant farmers. I choose these because of first-hand familiarity with them. They illustrate: (1) how reciprocal altruism works through selective incentives at the primitive level; (2) what happens when the conditions of social predictability are replaced by conditions of legal predictability; and (3) in what sense the roots of Capitalist, Socialist and Millennial Man were already present in Primitive Man.

Exchange Labor

Widespread among primitive and peasant farmers is the practice of exchanging labor days. A man needs help at planting, weeding, harvesting, or some other farm chore and asks one or more neighbors to assist him. In return he is obligated to provide each of them with the same number of work days upon request. So strict in most cases is his obligation to reciprocate that if he is unable to go on the day requested (for reasons of ill health or pressing personal business), he must send a substitute in his place. The labor is then owed to the substitute, who can be repaid at a more convenient time. These exchanges are customarily made among neighbors, who are predominantly relatives and close friends, and the groups are invariably small. Estimates of their size, which I collected in Africa and South America, averaged 4.5 while estimates from 23 library sources averaged 6. These averages are probably high, for informants who talk of groups of 4 to 6 men will often add, "Usually just 2 men work together."

What collective good if any is involved in this preindustrial form of cooperation? The harvest of each farm belongs to the man who occupies the land, so the immediate outcome and purpose of the joint effort is strictly an individual or private benefit in each case. The collective good in labor exchange is very elementary; it consists of the mutual aid itself—the availability of a labor pool to help meet peak work loads on subsistence farms.

A subsistence farm large enough to maintain a family may at certain periods of the cropping cycle require more labor than the family can provide on its own. Weeds may come up faster than the family can remove them, or a crop threatened by rain may have to be harvested faster than the family can do it alone. By anticipating such needs in advance, however, friends may arrange to help one another before planting even begins. But how can neighbors farming under the same conditions have time to help each other? When Farmer A needs Farmer B to help him weed or harvest, why is it that Farmer B does not simultaneously need the help of Farmer A?

The reason is very simple. Neighbors seldom have exactly the same planting schedules. Peak labor loads do not hit all neighboring farms simultaneously. In the tropics, for example, there is not only wide latitude in planting schedules, but even crops may vary. In mountainous areas, neighboring farms may lie at different altitudes allowing different planting and harvesting dates. Farmers exchanging labor near a Norwegian lake explained to me that the lake had such a determining effect on local climatic variation that they picked exchange partners according to their distance from it. In countries or areas where irrigation is practiced, rotation of irrigation periods can also result in different cropping schedules. Exchange labor partners in some parts of precommunist China deliberately staggered their planting dates, and in Haiti 50 years ago they even diversified their crops to avoid conflicts in working schedules.[11]

Some people are still inclined to think of primitive and peasant peoples as being "naturally" somewhat socialistic or communistic. But to judge from this prevalent, worldwide form of mutual aid, preindustrial man—in one special sense at least—was closer to Capitalist Man than to either his socialist or millennial counterparts. While the arrangements obviously involved at least short-term (seasonal) planning and therefore some appreciation of the collective benefit of a labor pool, the major collective good in this case was a consequence rather than a primary objective of the cooperation. I refer to the enhancement of community survival that this practice affords, a collective good which is a by-product of an incentive that is material and highly selective. The direct and immediate benefit of each joint effort is the family harvest, a product that is both material and private; no incentive could be more selective. In a simple, subsistence-farming setting the short-term and long-term benefits of this practice coalesce, and community survival becomes a correlate of family survival. As Adam Smith might have put it, primitive farmers enjoy a collective good in this case because they are effectively pursuing their own self interests, not because they are pursuing a collective good per se.

Granted there is a strong material incentive to participate in exchange labor, what social incentives apply here? Let us suppose that Farmer A decides to cheat Farmer B by working less industriously on B's farm than B works on his. What counter-cheating behavior can B bring to bear? The answer to this question illustrates the social predictability of the small, traditional community. But before describing the exchange-labor patterns involved, I must first provide additional background on conditions of social predictability.

On the basis of experimental studies of two-person game situations, psychologist Morton Deutsch has identified certain conditions that facilitate mutual assistance or cooperation because they encourage trust.[12] By this he means that under these conditions any person endeavoring to cooperate with another is more likely to act with confidence in committing himself to a trustful choice. However, because it connotes a psychological state, the word "trust" has a mentalistic quality I prefer to avoid. Since confidence in such a choice implies that interactions between two people have achieved a predictable pattern, I prefer to substitute "predictability" for "trust" and place the emphasis on behavioral contingencies rather than a mental state.

The strongest form of mutual trust or predictability occurs, according to Deutsch, among close relatives or between husband and wife.[13] In such relationships exchange is so all-encompassing and involves so many long-term, as well as short-term, reciprocities and benefits that it would be impossible to do mental bookkeeping and absurd to balance particular exchanges. Farmers exchanging labor with a close relative might not always care whether this particular exchange was balanced or not. It is worth noting that labor exchanges among brothers or between father and son are common.

Social predictability occurs, however, without such all-encompassing exchanges. Deutsch is able to develop it between strangers in two-person game situations when the following four conditions are satisfied: [14]

1. *Knowledge of the other person.* Knowing a person's background or past behavioral patterns makes his future behavior more predictable. With such knowledge one can better judge the advisability of committing oneself to a cooperative arrangement with him.

2. *A system of procedures.* If two people have an opportunity to communicate and work out arrangements for cooperation, mutual responsibilities can be defined as well as means for handling violations of the rules.

3. *Mutual control of outcomes.* If two persons can influence each other's outcomes, behavior deviating from those procedures acceptable to both can more easily be corrected.

4. *Third-person controls.* If behavior deviating from the accepted procedures not only adversely affects a person's exchange relationships with another but as a consequence adversely affects relations with additional persons, these third-person contingencies will help correct the behavior.

Each of these four conditions of predictability is met in the case of traditional labor exchange. The first, knowledge of the other person, is particularly appropriate to the exchange labor relationship. Partners choose each other specifically because they are known and predictable to one another. Farmers have often told me that for an exchange to be successful an individual must pick exchange partners who know how to work; they must have the same work habits as their partner. To the question how one knows this in advance, the typical reply is, "We are all neighbors, are we not?" All have lived in the same community most of their lives, and friendships are of long standing.

The second condition, a system of procedures, is a part of community knowledge and custom in the case of labor exchange. Procedures are traditional, ready-made, readily remembered and readily adopted. People have confidence in them because they go back as far as anyone can remember.

While the first two conditions help to prevent cheating, the third and fourth conditions—mutual control of outcomes and third-person controls—help to correct it. Mutual control of outcomes is a condition peculiar to exchange labor because exchange labor is basically dyadic in its organization. When, for example, Villagers W, X, and Y help Z weed his fields on a certain day, they may have exchange relationships with Z alone. A few days later when W asks Z to return the day's work, the work party on W's field may be comprised of villagers W, Z, L, and P. And later when Z helps Y, Villagers L, Q, and S are present. In such cases the reciprocal work parties consist mainly of dyadic exchanges and have no permanent memberships. If one member of a dyad begins to lower the quality of his contribution, however, the other member can make new exchange arrangements before the asymmetries grow too unfair. Thus each member of a dyad can affect the other's outcomes, for each knows the quality of a partner's performance will be the measure of its return.

Since any given work group is usually comprised of more than one dyadic exchange, "third persons" to each dyad are present who can also evaluate the quality of each partner's effort. It is to each villager's advantage to look well before these third persons since they belong to the same labor pool from which he seeks exchanges. The farmer who cannot find exchange labor partners is in an unenviable position.

Now we can return to our original exchange-labor question: How does Farmer B keep Farmer A from cheating? By making A and B lifetime residents of a small, traditional community, we greatly reduce the probability that A will ever deliberately cheat Farmer B or vice versa. Their decision to exchange labor was based on a record of mutual reciprocities free of any serious cheating behavior over an extended period of time. Thorough familiarity with the tradition of exchange labor also reduces the likelihood of cheating between Farmers A and B because each knows exactly what is expected and exactly how to meet those expectations.

But even under the best of circumstances, problems can arise. So again we come back to our original question: What if Farmer A decides to give less work than he gets? What corrective steps does Farmer B take? For one thing he can reciprocate by lowering effort to the same degree on his return workday, or for another he can threaten to break off the exchange. Finally, if A does not improve, B can carry out his threat and enter into an exchange-labor agreement with someone else. Moreover, B, in explaining to others why he no longer exchanges labor with A, helps to lower A's credibility with the rest of the community. Other "third persons" present during the work party can confirm B's judgment and further lower A's credibility. The ethnographic literature is full of anecdotes about what happens to individuals who fail to keep faith with exchange-labor commitments.

In the Solomon Islands, anthropologist Ian Hogbin knew a man compelled to live in a leaky, disreputable shack simply because no one would help him rebuild his house after it collapsed.[15] Since he had always been remiss in helping others, everyone was now enjoying the opportunity to repay him in kind. Hogbin notes also that two or three individuals in the same village had very small gardens because no one in the community would help them; they had never been willing to help anyone else. In Borneo, a Siang Dyak, who for any reason found an exchange-labor relationship unsatisfactory, would simply decline to exchange with that person again and would make arrangements with a different family the following year.[16] At Ch'u Hsien, in precommunist China, an individual who attempted to take advantage of his fellows in exchange labor was pointed to as one "who did not want face" and was soon unable to get anyone's help.[17] In Ireland an individual who failed to return a labor obligation was publicly condemned by the entire community including his own kin.[18] In early pioneering days in the Mississippi valley, public sentiment is said to have been a stronger guarantee than law in maintaining reciprocity.[19] Among the Tarahumara, of northern Mexico, taking part in labor parties was one of the duties of every individual and a refusal to do so was considered an offense against the entire community.[20]

Although exchange labor in western South America is usually a temporary and informal network of dyadic agreements, there is a distinct tendency for the same small groups of people who know each other intimately to exchange repeatedly. Sometimes a group forms for the length of time it takes to complete a round of reciprocities. Less frequently the same group may help each other throughout a complete farming cycle, and occasionally the joint ownership or pooling of equipment may give such a group considerable permanence. Among the Araucanian Indians of southern central Chile, for example, the membership in some equipment pools had been in operation for several years at the time of my visit in 1952.

Such groups are usually very small, less than eight members, and what little leadership is required is persuasive, not authoritarian. Yet in such groups the leadership is sufficient to replace the dyadic quality of the common exchange form. The leader tends to represent the entire group in relations with individual members; and when one tries to cheat, it is the leader, who in the group's name, activates counter-cheating measures against the malingerer through reprimand and threat of expulsion. In short, the group leader becomes a surrogate of what we might call the "general other" or "third person at large." It can be said that in a sense Hobbes's "leviathan," alias "mortal god," alias "artificial man" has its roots as far back as the persuasive leader of the small face-to-face group.[21] As we see below, in reference to corvée labor, the leader who represents an entire community in dealings with any one member has become a powerful third-person surrogate. The exchange relation has shifted from one between two equal farmers to an "exchange" between ego and the representative of third-person-at-large.

Let us take the case of an exchange-labor group I encountered in 1963 at a land-reform settlement in Venezuela. The group called itself the "Mondragón Cooperative" and had been formed to obtain farm credit from the federal Agriculture and Livestock Bank. The members wanted credit to clear additional land for cultivation and to purchase farm machinery. The members' farms were near one another but not contiguous. Together, however, members went successively from plot to plot during each stage of the farming cycle. Even harvesting was done jointly though crops were not pooled; each man owned and marketed the produce of his own plot. Only machinery, labor, and credit were collective.

Mutual control of outcomes in the dyadic sense of simple labor exchange had disappeared in this formal organization although members had modeled their "production union" on *mano vuelta,* the traditional Venezuelan labor exchange they all knew so well. The major collective good was still the same, a labor pool of benefit to all members. But now each member of the work party was literally exchanging with all the rest. If we still wanted to speak of "dyadic" exchange, it would now consist of an exchange between Ego and Group. Ego works for Group on several succesive days, and then Group works a day for Ego. But if for some reason Ego is not satisfied with Group's work, Ego does not complain to the members individually, but informs elected Leader of Group who acts as surrogate. And if members of Group are displeased with Ego's work, they pressure him to conform through Leader.

The leader of this Venezuelan production cooperative was a strong personality. He had organized it, he was an efficient work boss, and he was the principal reason to date for the group's success. The group, however, had begun with 12 members and was down to 8 when I visited it. Four had been expelled, and one more was being forced out that year. The leader was especially vigilant in apprehending and expelling shirkers and malingerers. He was confident, however, that the remaining 7 members were made of the stuff he needed for a viable cooperative. "You have to get up early to be a good farmer," he told me. "We want just the hard workers." Here is Hobbes's "mortal god" in microcosm.

This case of exchange labor is not typical of the general primitive or peasant pattern. Actually it is in part a product of civil government, for the labor pool is no longer the only collective good. To it have been added machinery and credit, two major instruments of government inducement used for changing rural habits in developing nations. The microcosmic leviathan is linked directly to the macrocosmic leviathan. It is in organized forms like this that labor exchange often survives after the informal traditional variety has disappeared.

Most of my observations on reciprocal farm labor were made in South America a quarter of a century ago, although for stylistic convenience I use the present tense. But even then the traditional patterns were rapidly disappearing; and in most of the places where I was still able to observe and record them in the early 1950's, they have since disappeared. Exchange labor was practiced by subsistence-farming equals who had little or no cash. With commercialization of agriculture, the increase of monetary exchange, and the growing inequality of farm operations, the traditional form of exchange labor ceased to be convenient.

For example, along the Cayapas River of coastal Ecuador in 1952 commercial banana production had only recently become a booming enterprise among peasant growers. Those peasant entrepreneurs who were industriously extending their plantations into the jungle ran into exchange-labor difficulties right away. As several of these individuals described the situation to me, they soon owed so many labor days to their exchange-labor partners that they had trouble making repayment in person. And as their plantations became larger, these required more day-to-day management on their part. To ease the situation, the entrepreneurs began hiring day laborers to stand in for them when called upon to repay labor obligations, but their exchange-labor partners immediately protested against this practice. In return for the hard work the partners were giving the entrepreneurs, they were getting back indolent, careless work over which they had no control. The day laborers were not even their own employees. Reluctantly, the entrepreneurs abandoned labor exchange and put the hired laborers to work on their own plantations directly under their supervision. "Then the day laborers knew they would not get paid if their work was badly done," I was told.

It may seem incredible that these farmer-entrepreneurs would not have begun hiring labor the minute they increased the scale of their operations. But traditional patterns are habit patterns, and the route by which they change sometimes seems circuitous and naive. There is another reason as well in this case. Everywhere in the world that I have asked the question, even where exchange labor was dying out, farmers have been unanimous in their judgment that exchange labor is preferable to hired labor. As one Colombian farmer put it, "When two friends exchange days of work, each works for the other as he would work for himself. A hired laborer never works *con toda voluntad* [with complete free will and devotion]."

Yet the convenience of monetary payment is so great that even close friends begin to employ one another once cash becomes prevalent. Bergantín is a land-reform settlement in northeastern Venezuela near the city of Barcelona. When I visited it in 1963, it had become a prosperous community of cassava-bread bakers. On the small parcels of land distributed by the reform, each Bergantín family was growing manioc and processing it into the manioc flour from which each made its cassava bread. The city of Barcelona had proven to be an enthusiastic market for this native delicacy, and Bergantín had proven just as enthusiastic in meeting the demand.

Manioc is a marvelous tropical tuber which ripens quickly and then stores itself; some varieties last up to two years in the ground after ripening. Bergantín families had learned to stagger their plantings so they had a continuous supply of manioc and thereby a steady cash income as self-employed farmer-bakers. At certain critical stages in the manufacturing process, however, each family required outside help, and for this they customarily relied on certain other families with whom in precassava days they had exchanged farm labor. The same patterns of labor reciprocity were still there, but now families paid one another after each day's work. This was easier, they said, than trying to remember who owed whom and how much. Moreover it automatically solved the problem of balancing reciprocities between families who needed unequal amounts of help. "All labor debts are automatically canceled with each payment," they explained, "and now we do not quarrel as much." This was a discovery that gave them considerable satisfaction even in the telling.

But once hired labor replaces exchange labor, an important qualitative change takes place. In the small, traditional community a man who cheated on his labor-exchange obligations was a target for the disapproval of his entire social world. The selective incentive to conform was negative and social but came from the whole social body in the Rousseauean sense. When wage payment becomes the rule, adjudication of disputes becomes a problem for local civil authorities; legal predictability replaces social predictability.

Festive Labor

The festive form of reciprocal labor (common in frontier America as "work bee" and "barn raising") proved even more vulnerable to the change from subsistence to commercial farming than the exchange form. While exchange labor might hang on for a while among poor peasants with little cash or among more enterprising peasants combining labor exchanges with machinery pools, I found that festive labor was always the first to disappear and tended to go abruptly. Moreover, once it was gone, hardly anyone had a good word to say for it.

Although both festive and exchange labor are forms of reciprocal labor, the obligation to reciprocate is usually less binding or contractual in the festive form. Peasants in South America frequently referred to this obligation in the festive form as a "moral obligation" or an "act of devotion." If a person is sick or otherwise indisposed, a replacement does not have to be sent. Only close friends and kin have a deep sense of obligation to attend each other's festive work parties.

Labor reciprocity is weaker in this form for the simple reason that the festivities provided by the host constitute an immediate repayment for the labor contributed by the guests. By contrast the hosts of exchange-labor groups provide common, everyday fare when even this has not been dispensed with by a mutual agreement among participants to provide their own. But a true festive work party usually includes an alcoholic beverage and plenty of meat, the two most indispensable ingredients of any festive occasion. Sheer abundance of food and liquor is another attribute of a good festive work party.

People would never work at exchange labor just to eat; all participants have work of their own sufficiently demanding to require a labor repayment. The host in either form of labor is known in South America as the *dueño del trabajo*, "owner of the work," but while participants in exchange labor are always work owners, festive labor parties are often attended by individuals who are not. For example, young men without lands of their own may come neither to represent nor replace a work owner, but simply to enjoy the festivities. For this reason festive-labor groups are purely temporary, and participants vary with the occasion.

The distinction between festive and exchange labor is not an analytic convenience of the observer; people who practice these two forms of labor reciprocity are the ones who make the distinction. In South America festive labor is known by such names as *convite*, *minga*, and *mingaco*, all implying festivities. Among the many labels for exchange labor are *vuelta mano*, *día trocado*, *cambio de tiempo,* and *torna peón,* all referring to an exchange of hands, days, time, or workers. Similar distinctions are made in Africa, China, Borneo, and elsewhere throughout the world.

Another important difference between exchange and festive labor is the size of the work party. Festive work groups are usually much larger than exchange groups. Farmers' estimates in Africa and South America averaged 31 participants for festive labor (compared with 4.5 for exchange) and library sources averaged an estimate of 54 (compared with 6 for exchange). While exchange-labor arrangements are usually made for peak labor loads in the agricultural cycle that are calendrical and predictable, festive work parties are used in emergencies. Because of illness or attention to other pressing duties, a farmer may get behind in some farm chore such as weeding and to avoid crop damage may need a large number of helpers immediately, more than convenient to repay with labor. The festivities obviate this heavy labor debt.

The collective good in this case is the same as for exchange labor. It is the availability of a labor pool to meet extrafamilial labor needs on subsistence farms and thereby contributes to community survival. Again, the material good directly and immediately involved is the individual crop, the benefits of which constitute a selective incentive only for the family to which it belongs.

In a closed traditional community the conditions of social predictability make for strong selective incentives. Members of the community are well known to one another and are bound together by many social ties. The procedures of festive labor are traditional and common knowledge. But unlike exchange labor, festive labor involves no direct mutual control of outcomes. In exchange labor Farmer A works hard and well for Farmer B so that B will work hard and well for him; each man's crop is the selective material incentive under mutual control. This is not true of the festive form since a strict obligation to reciprocate labor is usually absent. Control in festive labor depends on third-party sanctions, and the third party in this case is the community at large. A host who has a poor reputation as a festive provider will not get many helpers, and the man with a poor reputation as a festive worker will not get many invitations.

Actions of both host and guest must be highly visible if the third-person-at-large is to detect and counter cheating behavior on the part of either one. In this regard the conditions of festive labor are a degree more complex than those of exchange labor. In the latter case the work group is relatively small and each contribution relatively large. If A invites B, C, and D to help him weed, B's contribution to the joint effort is one-fourth of the total and affects one-fourth of A's crop. In such a small face-to-face group the visibility of each contribution is very high. As peasants assured me in all the countries of western South America, it is seldom possible for any participant to reduce effort without prompt detection and resentment by the rest.

Because work groups tend to be much larger in the case of festive labor, various techniques are employed to raise worker visibility and to enhance the community's ability to apply selective social incentives. At Haitian *combites* (festive work parties) workers in the old days were under the direction of a *chef d'esquade*, who began the work, set the pace, encouraged the efforts of good workers, and drove away the lazy ones.[22] Sometimes the chef divided the work force into two groups that competed to be first in finishing their assigned tasks, a common procedure in West and East African work parties and among the Araucanian Indians of southern central Chile.[23] At plowing parties Araucanians would often divide a field among several ox teams that competed to finish first, and in the southern United States a century ago festive groups of corn shuckers raced each other to the middle of the pile.[24]

Near Sonsón, Colombia, workers often joked with latecomers by accusing them of attending only for food. Araucanians would shout at late arrivals "Now the sun will come up!" The Chamí of Colombia and the Otavalos of Ecuador made fun of slow workers left behind by the rest of the clearing line. In both cases the best workers were placed at the ends to set the pace for those in the middle. At land clearing along the Cayapas River of Ecuador, each man took a section, and those who finished first, the "best" workers, helped the rest. To need such help could be cause for teasing and derision. In all such cases workers served both as participants and as an audience of community peers. Slackers were targets for jokes and ridicule, visibility of individual effort was high, and third-person approbation or condemnation was immediate and selective.[25]

The visibility of the host or festive "work owner," is inevitably high. No matter how few or how many guests join the work party there is only one host, whose generosity or stinginess cannot escape detection. Where festive labor had strong community support, the host was highly motivated to display distributive generosity. What is today the Caldas (Colombia) coffee belt around Pereira, Cartago, and Armenia had just the right conditions for festive labor near the turn of the century. In 1952, elderly farmers could still recall the circumstances clearly.

In those days there was little commercial cropping. Land was abundant and markets far away. It was a period of colonization and of slash-and-burn farming, and corn was so abundant it was fed to pigs. But few men drove pigs to market because for most the nearest market was so far away they had to walk the fat off the pigs just to get there. So corn was converted into pork and chicha (corn beer), and everyone ate well and entertained one another at festive work parties. Festive labor was almost as calendrical as exchange labor.

Some men were known to be better hosts than others. These were friendly, gracious individuals who lavishly entertained their workers with chicha, meat, music, and dancing. Since their work parties were better attended, these men were able to crop more extensively and produce larger harvests. And since under these conditions the harvest surplus could render no commercial profit, it was "recycled" into the festive system which produced it and which reaffirmed the reputation of the host as a generous and affectionate neighbor. In short, some men used festive labor to become prestige entrepreneurs in the redistributive fashion of primitive economics. The prestige entrepreneur in this game gets far more work from his guests than he gives in return, because the community has allocated to him, through personal respect and affection, the right to entertain them with the product of their own labor. Such behavior was not peculiar to turn-of-the-century Caldas colonists nor to South America. It has been reported for west,[26] east,[27] and south [28] Africa, the Sudan,[29] the South Pacific [30] and Southeastern Asia.[31] Chiefs or "wealthy" men sponsored festive work parties to reaffirm their status through the generosity made possible by those same work parties.

Just as we found elements of Capitalist Man in exchange labor so we find elements of Millennial Man in the festive form. The atmosphere of the ideal festive-labor situation is one in which the host is more concerned for his guests than for himself and the guests are more concerned with helping their host than in the table spread before them. Such concerns may not be the real motivations, but the behavioral etiquette of the situation demands that they appear to be. In other words, the altruism of a festive work party ideally conducted should appear to be nonreciprocal rather than reciprocal. The host distributes more food and drink than is ever returned, and the guests provide more labor than could ever be repaid.

Everyone, moreover, receives according to "need." The generous host distributes a surplus of wealth in the form of comestibles which he and his household could not possibly consume by themselves and ends up with no more than he can use. What is not needed has been equitably distributed among the guests, who must have "needed" this supplement to their usual fare or they would not have attended. Moreover, everyone has worked in a spirit of "devotion" which insures that everyone's effort has been commensurate with his ability.

But "nonreciprocal" altruism as well as "needs" apply in this case only to material incentives. As in all real-world, Millennial Man situations, reciprocal altruism is still present though now largely in social form. In a spirit of friendly rivalry the workers are organized to compete for selective social incentives while the host competes with other hosts for the status of generous big man and for the privilege of co-opting the community labor necessary to make his status possible. Strongly selective social incentives work at both ends of the spectrum.

In all such comparisons and contracts the biggest problem is the concept of "need," which is always relative and highly elastic. The very fact that people work beyond the bare subsistence level to provide a surplus for social enjoyment introduces a dynamic element that is held in check only by the limited availability of goods. Take the cap off the primitive bottle and out pops the genie of Capitalist Man. He was in there all the time. The social entrepreneur rapidly converts into capitalist entrepreneur.

The big man who has captured festive labor by virtue of his reputation for generosity gains no permanent advantage over his guests so long as their labor is converted into locally consumed food crops. But when he diverts that labor to commercial crops, particularly noncomestible ones, he gains a permanent advantage over his guests. Anthropologist Nadel pointed this out many years ago as he watched Nuba chiefs switch from food crops to cotton in the Sudan.[32] Since the cash crop brought a return of permanent value that could multiply a chief's working capital in the most modern sense, the old prestige entrepreneur was transformed into a modern capitalist overnight on the impetus of festive labor.

Once the host begins to combine capitalist entrepreneurship with social entrepreneurship, the worker-guests quite understandably begin to take a zero-sum view of festive labor. In 1968, farmers in Ghana voiced to me the same complaint against festive labor that I had heard in Venezuela in 1963 and ten years before that in Colombia, Ecuador, Peru, and Chile: "Why should I work for nothing to help someone else get rich?" Workers were no longer content to work for food and beer; they wanted money to buy wrist watches, bicycles and transistor radios.

Even in the role of host, farmers begin to take a zero-sum view of festive labor. To the host it seems that guests come only to eat and carouse and do as little work as possible. But because they are "guests," the "host" should not discipline or control them. Consequently, festive work is said to be more costly than hired labor. Even worse, the work is often bad enough to lower crop yields. Once both host and guests of a festive work party take a zero-sum view of the proceeding, they each tend to behave in ways that verify each other's moral judgment. Hosts become less generous and more calculating in the distribution of food and beer, and guests become more demanding and less industrious.

During 1952 and 1953, almost everywhere I went in western South America, I found festive labor either gone or in the process of disappearing. In either case the transition was usually recent enough to be fresh in people's minds and still an issue that provoked strong opinions, mostly negative. In few areas had it been gone long enough to be recalled with nostalgia. But even in those cases my elderly informants assured me that while festive labor was right for its day it could not work once people started producing for market. Everywhere the reasons given were the same, and they all add up to another illustration of Schumpeter's spreading "civilization of capitalism."

As farmers grew more market-conscious, they began to intensify and specialize their production. Money and the cost calculations it involved began to pervade their lives. Men began to figure the cost of festive labor in monetary terms and compare it with the cost of hired labor. In some parts of South America in 1952 and 1953, farmers voluntarily itemized the costs of both forms of labor for identical jobs to "convince" me of the "uneconomical" nature of festive labor. These were places where the practice had disappeared very recently, and farmers were still in an argumentative frame of mind. Independently in Colombia, Ecuador, Peru, and Chile, they showed me figures demonstrating that the cost of festive labor ran approximately two to three times that of hired labor. In all cases they had become conscious of the discrepancy after specializing in a cash crop and reducing food-crop production.

In becoming more dependent on the market for their own food, they automatically became more dependent on it for festive-labor supplies. And once they had to buy food and drink for a work party, they had a pecuniary basis for an exact quantitative comparison with wage labor.

The same process has been documented for other parts of the world. About the time I was collecting my data in western South America, other observers were recording this process for Brazil, Mexico, and Haiti.[33] The same two-to-one discrepancy in costs was recorded at Marbial, Haiti, in 1950 by Alfred Metraux.[34]

In Africa and Asia the major shift against festive labor may have taken place earlier, prior to World War II, when the same concern for expenses was recorded by observers in west, east, and south Africa, and in Korea.[35] George Homans documents the change for England during the 13th century.[36] Manor records for this period admitted that the lord's expenses for the food and drink dispensed to villagers on the day of a bene (festive work party) exceeded the value of the work done. And when the pros and cons of a prospective apple-paring bee were being discussed by late 19th-century New Englanders Hildy and Aunt Jerusha in *Danvis Folks,* Aunt Jerusha pointed out that bees were "turrible wasteful an' mussin' an' gen'ally cost more'n they come tu." [37]

Cost analysis by itself was not sufficient to turn people from festive labor; the civilization of capitalism is more inclusive than that. Antioquian farmers a hard day's ride by mule from Sonsón, Colombia, knew that wage labor was cheaper than festive. To supplement their food-crop income, they had been growing coffee for market several years by the time I talked with them in 1952. But despite their market and monetary sophistication they were still enthusiastic supporters of festive labor. They explained it to me this way: "In Sonsón there are movies and pool halls and cantinas. But we are a long way from Sonsón. Here we entertain each other with our festive work parties."

A year later I encountered the same attitude in remote highland communities around Cuzco, Peru. At one village I helped a group of men add up the expenses of their festive work parties using local market values of the ingredients. When the results showed festive labor cost over twice as much as hired labor, they were greatly amused. They had not known this, they confided. To my question whether they would now hire their labor instead of sponsoring work parties, they laughed. No, they said, they enjoyed their festive labor; and besides, they had lots of food but very little money.

These Antioquian and Peruvian communities were still too isolated to feel the full impact of the civilization of capitalism. It was quite the opposite situation on the Cayapas River of Ecuador where all the peasants had turned to banana production by 1952. There, men proudly showed me their new wrist watches though none had set them properly and some could not even tell time. As a great variety of manufactured goods became available everywhere, prestige entrepreneurs turned to demonstrating their success through the ownership of durable goods rather than through the redistribution of perishable foodstuffs.

What has come to be called the process of "privatization" was initiated everywhere by the spread of capitalist civilization. As families privately concentrated on the acquisition of consumer goods, they lost interest in the community-bound game of festive labor.

As in the case of traditional exchange labor there was no strong third-person surrogate, no leviathan, to support festive labor and to back it up with legal predictability once the conditions of social predictability broke down. People still knew each other well in most of these communities, and they knew the procedures of festive labor; but when community interest in the custom was gone, there was no third-person authority left to apply negative selective sanctions against cheating guests and cheating hosts. No one cared any more.

The argument of many South American farmers that festive labor never had been careful or reliable is to some extent correct. It was often associated with slash-and-burn farming, and as one Venezuelan farmer expressed it, "What did it matter if mistakes were made during clearing? Once we set fire to the brush, we erased them all." An abundance of land with extensive, rather than intensive, cropping fitted well with festive labor. Productivity under these conditions was low per unit of land area but high per man-day of labor. As population densities and cash cropping increased, however, farming became much more intensive and demanding. Productivity per unit of land grew more important; and as it did, work had to be more exact. As one Caldas coffee grower summed it up, "Women, children, and drunks were all right for weeding swidden [slash-and-burn corn plots]; but hoeing around coffee trees, they were a disaster!"

Monetary calculation, rational-scientific techniques, the "business spirit," and the capitalist style of life—all ingredients of Schumpeter's capitalist civilization—were too much for the primitive status game of festive labor.[38] This type of collective good had no place in the new civilization.

Corvée Labor

The collective good provisioned by our third and final example of primitive cooperation is of the same substance as the feeder road in the introductory example. In fact, roads have always been one of the most important collective goods provided by corvée. In some parts of rural Spain even today, farm roads are maintained by this primitive form of labor tax. Every household in the village must provide one adult male for road work when the mayor sets the date, usually during slack periods in the agricultural cycle.

The so-called ancient or primitive civilizations were based largely on corvée. During those times of the year when farm chores were least demanding, manpower was organized for various construction projects including roads, public buildings and irrigation or drainage projects. Ancient Mesopotamia and the preconquest Inca empire are two outstanding examples of primitive civilizations based on corvée development. All citizens as taxpayers shared the burdens of community service, and all shared—though not always equally—in the benefits of the public works it produced.

The collective good in this case is not a labor pool to supplement family labor on private plots as in exchange and festive labor. The plan and purpose of the two forms of reciprocal farm labor, as we have seen, was a private good—the success of each family's crops. The plan and purpose of corvée, ideally, at least, is the provisioning of material public goods not individually selective in their benefits. A more complex form of reciprocity is involved.

In our discussion of exchange labor we see that Ego could be viewed as exchanging with Group in cases in which individuals had formed permanent, formal, exchange organizations. But in these cases each member is receiving a direct private or selective benefit on his own farm plot whereas corvée tends to produce public goods that benefit all members of the community nonselectively. This does not mean, however, that corvée is a form of nonreciprocal altruism. The relationship between Ego and Community (General Other or Third-Person-At-Large) is still an exchange; and when a local chief or government official acts as surrogate of General Other, the "exchange" may formally take place between Ego and Chief. Ego donates labor to General Other, and General Other provides Ego with a good that is not Ego's exclusively—it is used by General Other as well—but which would not be available for Ego's or anyone else's use without this exchange arrangement.

General Other, however, is now a community or primitive state, not just a small group of exchange laborers. The exchange relationship between Ego and General Other has become much more asymmetrical, and this fact has two important sequiturs. First, Ego is much less visible to General Other; it is harder for General Other to monitor Ego to make sure he is keeping his share of the bargain. Second, Ego has become much smaller and weaker vis-à-vis this enlarged General Other, less able to resist General Other's enforcement of the obligations of the bargain. In the development of corvée the second condition has tended to correct the first with the result that the selective incentives employed by General Other for maintaining Ego's commitment to the exchange become increasingly negative or punitive in nature. The General Other becomes the genesis of Hobbes's leviathan long before civil government as he conceived it.

When speculating on how the corvée pattern began, one is well advised to ponder the fact that much if not most of the corvée labor of some primitive states was devoted to food production. In ancient Mesopotamia the citizens of each temple community took turns working on the fields of the temple god, and in each community of the Inca empire citizens did likewise on fields belonging to the state and to the church. The grain produced by this labor tax supported the bureaucracies of church and state, provisioned the annual cycle of public festivities, and even fed the taxpayers themselves when recruited for corvée construction projects that took them away from home.

Here we have a possible link between corvée in its most advanced "primitive" form and the festive-labor prestige entrepreneur who redistributes the product of neighbors' help in the form of public entertainment. The festive-labor big man institutionalized as "chief" can begin supporting festive work parties for the construction of permanent public goods as well as seasonal festivities. In this sense festive labor did receive Third Person support and did survive. But it survived in a different form, that of the corvée, which had evolved long before festive labor was seriously threatened.

In 1968 I had a chance to visit various villages in Ghana and to talk with elders there about changes in corvée over the years. They still remembered how it was organized and conducted in the old days to make the participation highly visible. Corvée work parties—called "communal labor"—were convened by the chief for such tasks as clearing weeds from the village outskirts, clearing footpaths between villages, cleaning wells and stream beds, constructing bridges, and maintaining the chief's house and the palaver grounds. During work, group competitions were organized much the same as for festive labor, and in the old days workers and watchers attended the event in a festive mood. Men and women too old to work brought contributions of palm wine for the rest and remained as an audience to the proceedings, loudly ridiculing slow workers. Cooperation was insured in extreme cases of malingering by such negative social incentives as community ostracism or public ridicule by the women. A headman would rebuke and shame a lazy individual by assigning him piecework, a separate area to finish by himself under the critical eye of the old women. He would also congratulate good workers and point them out to the shirkers: "Look what they can do." The rest would laugh.

On the positive side there was high social esteem for community service. A common Ghanaian proverb states that "a good name is better than riches." Elaborating on this proverb, an informant said, "Some people are very rich but have no place in the community. But if a town has got something from a man—funds, advice or personal effort—he is honored in the community; he has a good name."

These kinds of social incentives are much like those used to maintain optimal performance in the case of festive labor. We see the same procedures, typical of the traditional community, for insuring high visibility of individual effort. The conditions of predictability can thereby be successfully reinforced in communities of considerable size though still sufficiently closed that everyone can know everyone else. But third-person control of outcomes has now been reified in the person and office of the chief, who instigates the work parties and is personally concerned with their success. The authority of his office added considerable weight to the usual social incentives. He was an adjudicator of disputes as well as a dispenser of favors, and those who did not heed his call to communal labor could hardly expect him to be an impartial judge when they later brought a case before him. In more recent times, he would fine people who did not attend work parties, usually in palm wine but sometimes in cash. At Yamfo, if a man refused to pay his fine, a strong young man was selected to fight him. "After one blow he was ready to pay."

During colonial times the district commissioners used the corvée tradition to supplement wage labor in effecting local improvements. By the 1920's communities were building pit latrines, schools, bridges, culverts, and roads. Even missionaries organized their congregations to construct schools and churches. After independence official Community Development agencies continued these practices, and most Ghanaian farmers I talked with were of the opinion that federal enforcement of "communal" (corvée) labor reached its peak during the postindependence Nkrumah period, 1957–1964. In 1968 fines were still the most commonly mentioned sanction at all communities I visited, and persons unable to pay sometimes spent a week or two in jail.

At a council meeting I attended in a village near Kumasi, one young man vigorously denied that communal labor was a truly "cooperative" enterprise. For him cooperation implied an exchange agreement as in *nnoboa,* the traditional custom of exchange labor. "In nnoboa one does not feel reluctant to work; in communal labor people do, and they are punished." Cooperation, he thought, should not involve force. The young man did not know it, but he had discovered Hobbes's leviathan. Unlike Hobbes, however, he preferred the natural state in which power, as he saw it, was more equitably distributed. One wonders what he would have thought of Rousseau, who also favored equality but simultaneously idealized the corvée.

Rousseau championed *les corvées* near the conclusion of his *Social Contract* during a vigorous attack on representative sovereignty.[39] For a people to be truly sovereign, he said, they must personally attend all assemblies and ratify all laws; they must never pay others to legislate for them. The business of the state must be their principal concern, which it ceases to be the moment they begin serving it with their "purses" instead of their "persons." Once they do that, the state will be enslaved by its armies and swindled by its representatives. At this point in his argument Rousseau pledged his citizens to the ultimate commitment; to be really free they must not buy exemption from any service to the state. Even taxes should be paid with service—the corvée rather than with money.

Rousseau's principal concern was the equitable distribution of power and the avoidance of zero-sum exploitation. In this context corvée labor becomes part of total participation in government by a citizenry that values freedom above all else. As we saw earlier, Rousseau was apparently a bit too early to understand the positive-sum economics of Adam Smith with its recognition of the importance of specialization. A society in which everyone pays taxes with labor is an unspecialized society; and that is why corvée was the major capital-formation technique of primitive or ancient civilizations.

In advocating corvée, Rousseau was consistent with his earlier opposition to materialistic progress and exploitive inequality. But he was not altogether consistent with his hope for a new man who would think of the general good before his own. It is hard to conceive of any sustained growth of the human "intellect," such as he approved, without specialization of labor. In Rousseau's day people were buying their way out of corvée obligations just as they were to do in West Africa two centuries later. An examination of this contemporary process makes the arcadian implications of Rousseau's position more evident than they were in his day.

My visit to Ghana in 1968 to observe Community Development corvée projects was motivated by a desire to compare these West African experiments with similar projects previously observed in Latin America. In 1964, for example, I attended the inauguration of a school and health clinic at a Venezuelan land-reform community near the city of Maracay. Speeches by Community Development officials and the governor of the state strongly praised the cooperative spirit of this "progressive" community, which had constructed these public buildings with its own (corvée) labor. But this community was even more progressive and enterprising than the officials realized. Located on the outskirts of a major metropolis, the villagers were industriously raising poultry, swine, and vegetables for the urban market. Others had taken permanent jobs in town to which they commuted daily on bicycles. "We are too busy to play carpenter and stone mason," they told me.

Nearly all the households paid a day's wages in lieu of personal service each time it came their turn for corvée. Accepting these payments as wages, two household heads, a carpenter and a stone mason, built the school and health clinic with the help of a few hired laborers. In effect, the villagers circumvented the labor tax organized by officials and contracted the construction through a monetary tax used to pay specialists.

The situation in Ghana was no different. Yamfo, an Ashanti cocoa-farming community of about 4,500 inhabitants, is a prosperous community, for farm sizes average higher here than for most of the country. The town is progressive in every sense and has paved its main street and built 4 schools, a town market, a slaughter house, a clinic, a post office, a community center, and a potable water system. When the people of Yamfo began their town improvement projects, they had used traditional communal labor; but they soon gave it up. Most men were too busy managing their farms, and some also had service businesses or other employments. They still convened in festive spirit for the traditional clearing or weeding jobs around town, but modern construction projects were another matter. These required skills most villagers did not have, so they decided to tax their own cocoa production and contract the labor. "We are cocoa farmers, not artisans."

Community size and the commercialization of farming had had much to do with this transformation in the provisioning of collective good. In small isolated communities the old ways were still effective for jobs like cleaning wells or building schools of traditional mud-and-wattle construction. Large communities in areas of extensive cash cropping began long ago to allow some members to hire replacements to do their share of corvée work. Eventually as a standard monetary payment became acceptable, many people found it more convenient to pay their taxes in money than in labor. Busy farmers and merchants preferred to manage their cocoa plantations and businesses and pay "artisans to do the work of artisans," as the men at Yamfo expressed it.

Corvée labor was no longer a community "event" in which everyone personally participated. The festive, competitive atmosphere and the high visibility it had maintained were lost. While absenteeism remained visible and easy to punish, malingering on the job was another matter, and the quality and quantity of corvée labor declined. As it did, authorities found it fairer and more efficient to demand equal payment from everyone in monetary form and pay contractors to construct the public goods. Contractors could control their laborers through wages and threat of dismissal. This is precisely the way in which the primitive labor tax evolved into a modern monetary tax in many parts of the world. As economist Mancur Olson has emphasized, no modern state can support itself through voluntary contributions; taxes are necessary, and they are compulsory by definition.[40]

Corvée labor has proved just as unacceptable to the civilization of capitalism as has exchange and festive labor. Although community-development programs in many Third World countries have tried to effect development by this means, it goes against the grain. People busily pursuing diversified employments no longer have a common "slack" season during which they can enthusiastically join together in public-work projects. And once some members of the community start paying others to work in their place, the atmosphere of friendly rivalry and festive camaraderie is destroyed. A monetary payment for all becomes the convenient and unavoidable solution.

The socialist or Second World countries are another matter, for corvée has been used by all of them. If we can fairly say that exchange labor embodied elements of Capitalist Man and festive labor elements of Millennial Man, then we are certainly justified in finding Socialist Man foreshadowed in the primitive corvée. Russia and China have both made extensive use of its principles. In Stalin's day each collective farm in Russia contributed a prescribed number of laborers annually for the construction and maintenance of local roads, bridges, and public buildings.[41] These public-work brigades were in addition to the forced-labor camps of political prisoners so vividly portrayed in Solzhenitsyn's *The Gulag Archipelago*.[42] Employed in construction, mining, lumbering, brick making, cement manufacture, and transport, these forced laborers totaled about seven million on the eve of World War II. According to Swianiewicz they made up about eight percent of the total Russian labor force at that time.[43]

In China during the Great Leap Forward of the late 1950's, collective farms reorganized as giant communes provided enormous quantities of corvée labor for construction projects. In addition, the People's Liberation Army has always served in part as a corvée construction army participating in such public works as land reclamation and water conservation. In 1959 alone, it contributed 40 million man-days of corvée labor.[44]

In Castro's Cuba, campaigns to mobilize voluntary (unpaid) workers during the late 1960's and early 1970's attracted worldwide attention. This modern-state experiment in applying corvée labor went far beyond the traditional community boundaries of high visibility and social predictability. By the mid 1960's, the supply of wage goods had decreased to a point where monetary incentives were becoming ineffective and with them the elaborate wage system modeled on the Russian *trudoden*.[45] As Castro himself was to remark, monetary incentives are not much good when there is nothing for people to buy.[46] At first the few available consumer goods including refrigerators, motorcycles, and houses were awarded as prizes to the winners of "socialist emulation" competitions in industry and agriculture. But so few workers received prizes that little enthusiasm was generated.[47]

Influenced by Maoist ideology, Che Guevara began to push the concept of a Cuban New Man, who was to be the opposite of Capitalist Man. This New Man would put the collective good first and realize personal well being through the collectivity. Capitalistic self-centeredness would be replaced by unselfish dedication to the New Society.[48] One major way of internalizing this collectivist sentiment, Guevara believed, was through participation in voluntary, unpaid labor (corvée).[49] Another way was through participation in mass movements, rallies and campaigns. Guevara had noted that commitment to the Cuban cause had been greatest among workers during the Bay of Pigs emergency; therefore the state should perpetuate a sense of imminent danger. Combining a state-of-emergency psychology with collective action programs would break down individualism and indifference and replace it with strong personal involvement.[50]

Relegating material incentives (money and wage-goods) to second place, the New Man program emphasized "moral incentives," or what we here have called "social incentives." These included a great number of ingenious attempts, in the Russian and Chinese socialist tradition, to raise the visibility of worker participation. Good workers received public praise by leaders, certificates of socialist accomplishment, plaques, banners, pennants, praise on factory bulletin boards and in factory bulletins, and election to the Communist Party.[51] Bad or lazy workers were criticized by the other members of their work group and shamed publicly by prominently displayed posters describing all their faults.[52] Although sympathetic with this attempt to apply social or moral incentives on a national scale, Robert Bernardo concludes that the Cuban GNP was probably lower in 1970 than it was in 1959.[53]

Corvée labor in agriculture frequently resulted in crop damage and waste due to lack of experience on the part of workers and their poor motivation. Though called "volunteer" labor, it was invariably induced by a variety of social pressures.[54] Social-emulation programs remained formally bureaucratic and never involved workers in the planning of goals and work norms.[55] The rewards themselves were debased through "prize inflation"; too many title prizes were distributed by too many organizations and authorities.[56] Yet in his "We Have Failed" speech of July, 1970, Castro blamed a growing manpower shortage for Cuba's inability to realize the dreams of the socialist revolution.[57]

Simply as a result of population growth, however, the total work force by 1971 was probably greater than in 1957 in spite of the fact that over half a million persons had been allowed to emigrate since the revolution. Moreover, "emancipation" of women had added huge numbers of former housewives and domestics to the productive work force. Sectors of the population organized for corvée labor in agriculture included: employees working weekends, vacations and after hours; unemployed women organized through the Federation of Cuban Women; high school and university students working after school, on weekends and during school vacations; political prisoners; and recruits serving their three years of compulsory military service.[58] Carmelo Mesa-Lago estimates that in 1967 this corvée or "unpaid labor" accounted for 8 to 11 percent of the total Cuban work force.[59]

Yet in spite of all these procedures for increasing the total volume of Cuban labor, economic productivity decreased. Malingering and absenteeism became endemic as Cuban workers discovered they could subsist on 15 to 20 days of work per month. They had little desire to do more than that, for there was nothing on which to spend discretionary income, and few wanted to work just for pennants and hero medals.[60]

In two speeches late in 1970, Castro equated the laziness of many Cuban workers with theft. The lazy person steals from the dedicated worker, he said, by disorganizing production and leaving the hardest part of each job for others. Here we have our first example of the socialist zero-sum game—the loafer or malingerer increases his leisure at the expense of his fellows. Labeling such malingerers "the new exploiters," Castro warned that a "rational and just" society has the right to take "coercive" measures against them.[61]

Early in 1971 a new law against loafing was passed. People could be interned in "rehabilitation institutions" doing productive labor for as long as 2 years if they were absent from work for 15 days without a legitimate excuse or if they received more than two reprimands from their work council. Moreover, the name of a person guilty of the crime of loafing could be turned in to police by any loyal individual or organization.[62] It was this growing trend toward administrative centralism of a semimilitary character that finally led to the disillusionment and disaffection of two staunch old friends of the Cuban revolution, European Marxists René Dumont and K. S. Karol.[63]

The Cuban experiment demonstrates on a national scale the tremendous difficulties inherent in any attempt to achieve high visibility and conditions of social predictability in large populations. According to what Mesa-Lago has labeled the "Sino-Guevarist line," unpaid "voluntary" labor was an essential means of "raising" the "consciousness" of the masses to the unselfish, fully socialized New Man level. Through voluntary contributions of work to national development, the masses would achieve a greater sense of solidarity and a stronger devotion to state and community.[64] Though such notions may be inspired and even briefly sustained by social-movement conditions, the trend over time is for those in power to rely less on personal charisma and humanistic inducements to effect work output and more on punitive sanctions. Legal predictability dominates, but it becomes the legal predictability of a strong, centralized leviathan. It has little in common with the quality of legal predictability envisioned by Rousseau in his town-meeting type of popular government, his view of corvée as voluntary social service, and his egalitarian, self-reliant version of the new moral man.

The Cuban case also points up the convenience of material incentives for large populations and the difficulty of replacing them with social incentives alone. During the first half of the 1970's, Cuba has abandoned Sino-Guevarism and returned to the modern Soviet line. Material incentives are once again being emphasized, and the use of corvée labor has been drastically reduced.[65]

Compared to the corvée or labor tax, monetary taxation requires much less disruption of the daily life of its citizens and much less personal manipulation by the state. Tax Foundation Incorporated of New York City has calculated that the average American wage earner works 13 hours and 10 minutes during each 40-hour week just to pay taxes.[66] This amounts to approximately a third of his time on the job. Suppose that instead of paying income and sales taxes, the average American paid taxes by corvée. Imagine the disruption of the week entailed in joining, for example, road-repair crews, one and three-quarter workdays per week to say nothing of the unpleasantness of meeting state-prescribed work norms at unfamiliar tasks. The quality of compulsion in a monetary taxation system is far different from that of a labor-taxation system. If the latter seems totalitarian, it is not because taxation per se is totalitarian but because the form in which those taxes are paid requires pervasive supervision under constant threat of strong, punitive sanctions.

Monetary taxation, by allowing the individual to choose the way taxable income is earned, gives him greater control over his time and labor than in corvée. There is more freedom, in other words, to pick one's own game instead of being a pawn in someone else's. Even the kind of work done by corvée, however, can be a game for some people as long as it is voluntary.

Take the case of an old man by the name of George McPherson, who decided to clean up his neighborhood in downtown San Francisco. He wanted to do some "good" for others before he died, but his neighbors and the police decided otherwise. He was taken to the police station and warned to stop. So George McPherson moved to Guerneville, a town of 2,200 people in northern California, and began sweeping the streets, a voluntary, unpaid service he proceeded to perform day after day and year after year with no other income than his small Social Security pension. At first the townspeople simply wrote the old man off as an eccentric. He seemed harmless enough so they did not interfere. But with time his single-minded dedication to their collective good was impossible to disregard. Eventually everyone in town came to know George McPherson and never went by without a greeting and kind word. Passing police cars always honked their horns in friendly salute. Housewives brought him freshly baked pies, and mechanics repaired his truck for nothing whenever it broke down.

When his house trailer accidentally caught fire and burned, the townspeople took up a collection and bought him a new one.[67]

A bored and lonely old man wanted some game to fill his time—one not beyond his talents yet one that could bring him attention and appreciation. In a voluntary public service that gave him high visibility, he made an overture of selfless altruism that could not be ignored. An entire town reciprocated in full measure, at first mainly with positive social rewards and eventually with material ones as well.

George McPherson was wise or lucky enough to pick a small town in which he had high visibility, the same condition under which corvée workers performed their competitive group games in traditional African villages, as we have seen. A more modern form of public service performed in many ways like a competitive game was that of the volunteer fire departments that abounded about a century ago even in our largest cities. In fact, Albert Brisbane used New York volunteer fire departments to illustrate the utopian ideas of Charles Fourier in his book *Social Destiny of Man*, published in 1840.[68]

Fourier wanted to construct utopian communities (phalanxes) organized into "emulative groups" whose activities would be highly visible to one another and to the entire community. Each phalanx was to be divided into series, and each series was to consist of at least five groups. Each group, in turn, was to contain at least seven people. These agricultural, industrial, and public service units would turn the drudgery of work into a spontaneous and enthusiastic game through "corporative emulation." Progressive, healthy rivalry of group versus group, series versus series, and phalanx versus phalanx would turn work into fun, resulting in excellent "products" while accelerating overall cultural and social "progress." The sum of these competitive forces, stimulated and coordinated through "serial organization" was called "compound emulation," one of the utopian roots of modern "socialist emulation."

Fourier's scheme even included social incentives much like the "moral incentives" of modern socialist states. Members of a series renowned for its excellent products were identifiable through special badges, much like the "insignia" of Edward Bellamy's *Looking Backward* (discussed in Chapter 7). Moreover, outstanding individuals within series were privileged to add special badges and medals of honor.

Brisbane compared the fire departments "in our large cities" with Fourier's series and the fire companies with his groups. The basic unit of competitive "energy" was the attempt of each individual to excel all the others in his company. But individual competitiveness was spared the disrupting influence of envy due to the strong "corporative feeling" involved in the rivalry between companies and departments. First man to reach the engine was given the privilege of holding the water "pipe" and of guiding the stream on the fire in full view of his fellow firemen and all the onlookers who regularly gathered at early 19th-century fires to enjoy the show. But when water had to be relayed long distances from one engine to another, members of each fire company had to work together to pump the water to the next engine as fast as it was pumped to them. An overflow before the audience of onlookers would have been a great disgrace. New York companies that had never suffered an overflow were particularly anxious not to damage their reputations.

Santiago, Chile, is the largest city in the world still depending on volunteer firemen. Judging from insurance rates and safety records, Santiago's fire department is better than the professional departments of most other Latin American cities. The 20 fire companies distributed throughout Santiago are comprised of some 40 active members each. These are small, tightly knit fraternities that Chileans themselves label *hermandades* or "brotherhoods." To become a member is a great honor, for it is not easy. There is a long apprenticeship period after which the candidate's company votes on his application through a secret ballot in which at least 75 percent of the members must be in his favor. Some of the companies, such as the English-speaking 14th, are ethnically distinct and homogeneous. The station houses are exclusive clubhouses with their own bars and dining concessions. Companies design their own parade uniforms and dress helmets and paint their fire trucks and equipment in distinctive company colors. In all of this they get considerable public attention and are highly competitive. Although all officers are elected annually by majority vote, there is a strict hierarchy of authority within each company, and members who break rules are dealt with severely. To be voted out of one's company is a great dishonor.[69]

Both George McPherson and these volunteer fire departments provide examples of public service for the collective good at jobs much like that done by corvée labor. But the examples are quite different from corvée in their voluntary and spontaneous quality. In these cases individuals are game playing as the subjects, not the objects, of play. In so doing, they are giving time and effort out of personal choice. Man is a playful animal, but it makes a big difference whether he plays his own game or is the object of play in someone else's. It is on this note that we begin the next chapter.

Summary

Focusing on egalitarian, preindustrial examples of mutual aid and the provisioning of collective good, we have seen that primitive man was not a capitalist, socialist, or communist although the roots of all three incentive systems can be found in his behavior.

Incentives to provision a collective good were highly selective for the individual in the social context of small, intimate groups whose members could reciprocally reward or punish one another—the conditions of social predictability. Moving from primary groups to entire communities, we saw that deliberate mechanisms grew up among preindustrial peoples, often in the form of competitive games, to maintain high social visibility in the face of growing numbers. As group size increases, however, exchange between individual and group becomes more asymmetrical and the conditions of social predictability ever weaker.

In primitive groups and communities, reciprocal altruism prevailed as participants controlled each other's cheating through direct application of social punishments and rewards. The egalitarian cases favored in this chapter illustrated social predictability under conditions of maximum membership involvement. But even under the most egalitarian circumstances, some individuals, as we saw, received more social rewards than others.

As societies grew larger, more spatially mobile and more commercial, material rewards proved more convenient than the more directly social forms of the past. And as people engaged in a wider variety of productive and leisure activities, provisioning of the collective good fell to specialists supported by monetary taxation. Wherever large, complex societies endeavor to maintain labor taxation and direct social incentives, the intrusion of state or community into people's lives tends to become comprehensive and oppressive. The combination of positive material and negative legal incentives allows a reciprocally altruistic animal living in large social units to provision collective good with minimal supervision. Exceptions include unusual cases of voluntary commitment by members of some kind of group "game" enjoying high visibility within the larger society.

Chapter Four

Property Incentives:
Origins of Capitalist Man

PRIMITIVE FARMERS, as mentioned in Chapter 3, often organized their festive and corvée work parties into competitive games. By doing so, they not only raised the visibility of their performance before a critical audience, they also made possible a piecework division of tasks among competing individuals and groups. Both these characteristics of their competitive game playing made it possible for the community to apply social incentives. The dramatic and "heroic" nature of fire fighting gave this activity high visibility, too, even in relatively large populations. In all these cases of voluntary participation in competitively organized work, the emphasis of Chapter 3 was on ascertaining the social conditions under which successful provisioning of the collective good was most likely to occur. There is another dimension of this game playing, however, which is more relevant to the subject matter of this chapter. The example of exchange labor helps make clear what that other dimension is.

An important consequence of exchange labor for the collective good, as we saw, was the availability of labor to supplement that of the family in emergencies. Applied to certain urgent tasks, this supplementary labor supply enhances the survival of the entire community. But exchange labor is applied to many jobs that one has plenty of time to do by oneself. If Farmer A can clear a given plot of land in six days, why should he ask Farmer B to help him clear it in three? For as soon as they finish, Farmer A works another three days helping Farmer B. Both work six days either way. Why exchange?

The point is that while each man *can* clear his plot in six days all by himself, he frequently does not. He goes out to his farm early in the morning, but as the sun rises in the sky he begins to notice the heat, and the amount of clearing he has done seems insignificant compared to all he has left to do. He takes a rest. When he resumes clearing, he notices the sun is even hotter than before; he feels thirsty and hungry. After working a while longer, he returns home for an early lunch. He naps after lunch and on waking finds the afternoon already well advanced. Although he has worked less than half a day and in a very dilatory fashion, he decides it will be better to start fresh tomorrow.

When two men work together, however, neither wants to be the first to rest. Each tries to outdo the other, and neither will admit to feeling tired or hungry. They stop only briefly to eat, and they work long past their normal quitting time. Thus, while each man accomplishes competitively no more than he *could* have accomplished alone, he actually accomplishes two or three times as much. This is how peasants have explained it to me in South America, and it is the way New Guinea natives explained it to Ian Hogbin.[1] As one of Hogbin's informants graphically expressed it, clearing land all by oneself is like trying to empty the ocean with a canoe bailer. Turning work into a competitive game can make it go faster and more enjoyably.

What has all this to do with the subject of property incentives? The answer to that question is to a large degree the subject matter of this chapter. By looking at man as Homo ludens (Man the Player), we shall see that the social or "moral" incentives that dominated the reciprocal altruism of the traditional, closed community are continuous—not discontinuous—with the material, property, or so-called "acquisitive" incentives that dominate the supraecological stage. For some people these material incentives become so salient that the word "altruism" no longer seems in any way appropriate as a label for human behavior. A Homo ludens perspective helps us gain a sense of detachment. Hopefully, it can help us expand our moral assessments of the present while reserving moral judgment.

Why should we even concern ourselves with material incentives in a book devoted mainly to an investigation of social incentives? To weigh the plausibility of a monoecological stage in which social incentives regain predominance, we must certainly devote at least one chapter to the material incentives of the civilization of capitalism. In fact, the subject matter of this chapter provides essential background for the social and cultural comparisons that follow.

The first two sections of this chapter introduce terms important here and for the remainder of the book. These include Homo ludens, material incentives, property incentives, and the differences between productive and personal property. The bulk of the chapter is a discussion of the latter two forms of material incentive both for primitive society and for the civilization of capitalism.

Material Incentives

Socialist writers tend to catalogue all incentives under two major headings: material and moral. In practice, moral incentives usually turn out to be social incentives, so I use these terms synonymously. Such a decision cannot, of course, please those idealists who believe man capable of internalizing such inclusive concern for collective good as to make possible a golden age of nonreciprocal altruism. For such persons "moral incentive" implies an altruism that is nonreciprocal whereas "social incentive" as used here is consistent with the selective nature of reciprocity. The viability of the idealistic meaning is a problem I prefer to postpone until the final chapter.

In practice, "material incentive" is largely coterminous with "property incentive," so I also use these terms synonymously. One can imagine a negative incentive such as incarceration whose punitive consequences are material as well as social, yet we would hardly call it a "property" incentive except where it leads to loss of property through loss of freedom. In this chapter, however, we are concerned mainly with positive material incentives of Capitalist Man progress, and in that sense "material" and "property" become much the same.

I shall also follow the practice of socialist writers in subdividing the property category into productive property and personal property. The latter in capitalist vocabulary is called consumer goods, wage goods, and consumption property. I use these terms interchangeably. Acquisition of personal property is an acknowledged work incentive in socialist as well as capitalist countries although some socialist countries would prefer to reduce existing inequalities in this form of reward. The major area of dispute between the capitalist and socialist worlds concerns private ownership of productive property, particularly distributions of rewards "to each according to his capital"—what socialists regard as "unearned income."

In his "Critique of the Gotha Program" (1875) Karl Marx indicated that the Millennial Man reward, "to each according to his needs," would only be possible in a "higher phase" of communism when all bourgeois influences on the personality had been outgrown.[2] Until then the individual worker had a right to a reward proportional to his product. Labor, to serve as an accurate measure of a man's productivity, would have to be defined in terms of "duration" and "intensity," which may vary with individual abilities. These natural differences in individual productive capacity confer a "right of inequality"; they confer the "bourgeois" right to share in the joint product according to one's work— "an unequal right for unequal labor."

In their *Communist Manifesto* (1848) Marx and Engels make clear to what kind of reward "right of inequality" pertains.[3] It does not pertain to "bourgeois" property, which must be abolished. Bourgeois property is productive property enabling capitalist exploitation of the worker, a zero-sum antagonism in which the former grows ever richer at the expense of the latter. Inequality of worker rewards pertains to "hard won," "self-earned," "personal property."

Marx's distinction between productive and personal property and his recognition of the right of the worker to earn in proportion to the product of his work have allowed the Marxian socialist states to legitimize private ownership of personal property as a selective incentive to increase production for the collective good. In practice, personal property has come to include anything in the category of consumer or wage goods that is not put to any kind of income-producing use. It should provide creature comforts but cannot constitute a productive investment. For example, over one-third of the urban dwelling space in Russia and over 90 percent of both rural and urban housing in China is privately owned. In both countries, however, home ownership is a prominent field for abuse of personal property privileges. Individuals who buy and resell homes become "profiteers" manipulating personal property to produce "unearned" income.[4]

In their outlook on productive property, including their zero-sum view of Capitalist Man, the Marxian socialist states follow in the path of such notable utopians as More, Cabet, and Bellamy, as we see in Chapter 7. They diverge from them in their treatment of personal property, for they permit those unequal accumulations of personal property that for More, Plato, and others led to competitive, ostentatious and avaricious behavior. In the real world, however, legal distinctions between comfort and ostentation are harder to make than those between consumption and profiteering. A Russian citizen with 11 new overcoats in his possession is likely to be convicted of "speculation," not of conspicuous consumption. Nor is the Soviet official who owns a vacation cottage in addition to his house in town accused of being ostentatious. But if he regularly rents the cottage, it is open to confiscation for producing unearned income.

Only China, of all the socialist countries, has shared the utopian concern for ostentatious accumulation of personal property, and even there it is confined largely to Maoist ideology. "Comrades," wrote Mao, must "remain modest" and "preserve the style of plain living and hard struggle."[5] According to John Hazard, observers in the Soviet Union and elsewhere attribute such statements to a Maoist tendency to treat necessity as a virtue until production catches up to the rest of the socialist world.[6]

Inheritance practices in socialist countries confirm the selective-incentive power attributed to personal property, for citizens are not prevented from transmitting accumulated wealth to the heirs of their choice. Since hereditary wealth can consist only of personal property, it cannot produce unearned income or lend itself to the exploitation of others. If, for example, a family inherits a second house (not a summer cottage), it must choose one and sell the other; it cannot keep one as a source of rent. Especially in the Soviet Union and Eastern Europe, where wage differentials can be considerable, the incentive effect of such differences is regarded as significantly enhanced by the right to leave personal property accumulations to one's heirs.[7]

American socialists differ widely in the importance they attach to property incentives. Leo Huberman and Paul Sweezy, for example, come very close to the utopian pole, whereas Michael Harrington and Norman Thomas veer so far in the other direction that they often seem more American than socialist.

In his "The ABC of Socialism," Huberman clearly states the zero-sum position on productive property: neither worker nor capitalist can succeed except at the expense of the other. Productive property must be taken out of private hands in order to expand private ownership in the legitimate area of "use" and "enjoyment"—the area of personal property or consumer goods.[8] Both Sweezy and Huberman, however, are highly critical of the Soviet Union's expansion of the consumer-good sector. When "private incentives" are fostered in the form of houses, appliances, automobiles, and so on, a new socialist man is not created. Instead, socialism reverts to the same selfish, greedy, ostentatious "old man" it is attempting to replace. They feel these material incentives should be de-emphasized, preferably through a cultural revolution similar to that effected in China, one involving a "repoliticization" toward socialist objectives. Sweezy and Huberman prefer a form of reasonable need expansion in which everyone would go up together, and items such as apartment houses, cars, and laundries would be used collectively.[9] They come very close to the progressive, Millennial Man states of Cabet or Bellamy, and their basic moral objection to property incentives goes back to Plato and More.

Harrington and Thomas are considerably more flexible on the subject of property incentives than are Huberman and Sweezy. Although Harrington would like to extend collective ownership of productive property as far as possible while conceding that greater "inefficiency" will result, he wants a slow transition through taxation rather than through outright expropriation. He even respects the theory that men work harder if they can leave capital to their heirs, and he favors a Saint Simonian type of inheritance tax that is relatively light on the transfer from first to second generation and heavy on the transfer from second to third generation.[10]

Norman Thomas, in one of his last articles, wanted to extend collective ownership but not to the extent of eliminating individual initiative and the mechanisms of price and profit. He would have liked to see social ownership extended to natural resources such as coal, iron, oil, and forests and to public utilities and the steel industry. But he felt there was such a deep and universal human desire to own land that he was willing to allow its private ownership for "use" and "occupancy." He advocated a tax on the inflation of land values, as does Harrington, and "very heavy" inheritance taxes.[11]

Homo Ludens

For many people, the moral issues surrounding property and property incentives are fighting issues and altogether a serious business indeed. By viewing those emotionally involved in such concerns as "players"—no matter how serious their commitment to the game—we are better able to preserve our own detachment. But what do we mean by Homo ludens or Man the Player, and how does this notion apply here?

Homo Ludens (1944) was the title Johan Huizinga, a distinguished Dutch historian whose specialty was the Middle Ages, chose for his pioneering work on the relationship between play and culture. During his studies of the Middle Ages, Huizinga became convinced that culture had originated as a form of play. He was emphatic in insisting that culture did not arise *out of* play but rather that the two evolved as one.[12]

Play for Huizinga was essentially an "antithetical" phenomenon that included all kinds of contests. Among primitives, these typically took the form of competitions in gift giving and even reached such extremes as the potlatch ceremony at which goods were competitively destroyed. The Middle Ages, however, were permeated by a spirit of play to a degree unequaled by any other period. There were, for example, the medieval tournaments or "sham fights," the chivalry of knighthood, and even the disputatious scholasticism of the medieval university.[13]

As culture continues to develop, play gradually recedes into the background, according to Huizinga. Although it is still there and is capable of breaking free at any moment "in full force" as a mass movement, it is swallowed up by utilitarianism as we approach "our own times." Work becomes the ideal, play turns into business, science becomes applied, and even warfare loses all of its former quality as "a noble game." [14]

Huizinga admitted that it was harder to be objective about the present than the past, and it is on this point that he has been most severely criticized.[15] Up close, play can look like very serious business. What seems like "work" to us today may seem more like a game to historians of the future. And were we able to go back and live in a primitive village or a medieval town, we might find their "games" more like work and less like play than they seem to us from our present vantage point. As Jacques Ehrmann has pointed out, if play is part of the civilizing process, then civilization today should be full of more games than ever, and he believes that it is.[16] The seriousness of a game cannot disqualify it as play, for even Huizinga noted that when players totally abandoned themselves to a game it can become "profoundly serious."

Ehrmann believes play is as much a part of culture as it always was. To link it only to leisure and luxury in the present rather than to work is ethnocentric. Where Huizinga went wrong, in his opinion, was in failing to distinguish between subjects and objects of play. In his romantic view of the Middle Ages he focused on participants largely as the subjects of action. When Huizinga looked at his contemporary world, however, he saw people being manipulated by others. A world full of employees everywhere at the beck and call of their employers had become a world of work, not play. But since Huizinga did not make these distinctions, he may not have been fully aware of them. He had a one-dimensional view that even led him to overlook or slight the object players of earlier periods, including those of the Middle Ages.[17]

As for the question when does play become too serious to be play, Erving Goffman long ago provided a handy sidestep.[18] In his dramaturgical view of game playing, a "sincere" performer is one so completely caught up in his routine as to be thoroughly and seriously committed. The "cynical" performer, on the other hand, is one who preserves enough detachment to be an audience to his own acts. The latter can more deliberately manipulate his performance to affect his outcomes. The whole question changes from one of seriousness to one of awareness.

Looking at it this way, we can see that both subject and object players may be either sincere or cynical. Some individuals can "play" others with sincere involvement or with cynical detachment, and in both cases the ends may be either "noble" or "selfish."

The view that play and culture developed together may not be just metaphor. One distinguished anthropologist, Alfred Kroeber, took the possibility very seriously about the same time Huizinga did.[19] Since mammals in general are playful creatures, especially their young, it occurred to Kroeber that play was related to higher intelligence and to the learning process itself. Extending his speculations further, one could say that as the animal that depends most on learning throughout life, man is understandably the most play oriented. And if ontogenic cheating-versus-counter-cheating adaptations did contribute to the phylogenic evolution of his brain, then man is indeed a creature of play in whom culture developed together with social gamesmanship.

The subsequent two sections of this chapter show how changes in the quantity and substance of material incentives have created only recently in man's history a new kind of game playing—the civilization of capitalism. Under primitive conditions material goods were limited; productive property was largely in the form of land held under group tenure, and personal property was limited in amount and variety by the low degree of specialization. Game playing was largely of the social-entrepreneur type described in the previous chapter in connection with festive labor. Wealth accumulations tended to be in the form of perishable foodstuffs given away in return for social esteem.

Specialization and the use of money rapidly increased the amount and variety of both producer and consumer goods, and conspicuous giving readily converted to conspicuous getting. Men still pursued social esteem but now through the acquisition, rather than the redistribution, of property. Privately owned material goods became conductors and symbols of prestige free of the small-group conditions of social predictability. Status seekers could now obtain social rewards in material form free of the social restrictions of the traditional community. New kinds of cheating became possible which had to be countered with new kinds of formal, institutionalized negative incentives. The legal predictability of the state had to supplement, and increasingly take precedence over, the social predictability of the traditional community.

We see next how productive property made it possible for the social entrepreneur to become a capitalist entrepreneur and in what sense productive property has limits as a material incentive. The final section of this chapter shows why personal-property incentives have become the most pervasive and influential aspect of the civilization of capitalism. While the pursuit of productive property is a game limited always to a small elite, the pursuit of personal property is a game that intrigues and captures the masses. The latter seem to play this game as subject players, but in doing so they make possible concentrations of productive property. And in the view of some, these concentrations make it easier for a few privileged individuals to "play" the masses as objects.

Productive Property

Thomas Hobbes, John Locke, and Adam Smith all viewed the rise of the civil state as essential to the protection of property. "Where there is no commonwealth," wrote Hobbes in his *Leviathan* (1651), "there is no propriety; all men having right to all things." [20] Some 40 years later Locke, in a similar vein, claimed property was so insecure in the state of nature that men found it necessary to join together deliberately in political societies or commonwealths in order to preserve it. [21] As we noted in Chapter 2, neither Hobbes nor Locke attached any clear statement of progress to this transformation although the implication is strong a century later (1776) in Adam Smith's *Wealth of Nations*. [22] For Smith, too, the establishment of civil government was a precondition of property, but property in an obviously entrepreneurial and productive sense. Rousseau (1755), as we noted previously, saw only injustice and inequality in this situation. [23] It was the rich who wanted to protect their property and who conspired to do so through the creation of civil government—"the most deliberate project that ever entered the human mind." On the pretext that government would "protect the weak from oppression," the rich cleverly turned their "adversaries" into "defenders" as men "ran to meet their chains." A hundred years later (1848) Marx and Engels were to urge the workers of the world to throw off these same chains and unite together against the owners of productive property. [24]

Smith, Rousseau, and Marx illustrate three basic positions with regard to productive property incentives. In the first case the acquisition and extension of productive property in the right hands leads to progressive benefits for all. In the second case the accumulation of productive property is purely exploitive and unjust. And in the third case it is both of these; but once the positive-sum forces have created an abundance of wealth, the time comes to divide it equitably among all. Let us go back for a moment to that "state of nature" which 17th- and 18th-century philosophers mentioned so frequently but on which they had so little concrete data.

John Locke's views on the origins of property in his *Of Civil Government* (1689) seems insightful even today. [25] There were still some very primitive rural communities in the England of his day; and perhaps his model of pre-state society ("state of nature") was better than others of his period simply because he stuck closer to the real world of experience. Locke emphasized the relation between labor and ownership. Each man, he said, begins with the property of "his own person" which he extends to objects of nature by "mixing" them with his labor. Just as his own person is exclusively his own property, so he comes to exclude from "the common right of other men" those natural goods on which he expends his personal labor.

Locke was right; labor was certainly the most important determinant of possession among primitive peoples. [26] The labor investment of the producer established ownership of the property in question. A family's tools, housing, clothes, food, and utensils were products of its labor and constituted its belongings. Community survival, however, placed a high premium on sharing. When crop failure afflicted some members of the community, they received food supplies from more fortunate kin. Thus the fortunes of all were much the same in the end. While such practices were a kind of insurance for the primitive community, for the individual household they created a disincentive to produce much above immediate need. A family that produced more food than it could consume must expect to share it with others. Similarly, if it manufactured more tools or utensils than it could put to immediate use, excess items were likely to be borrowed. Deliberate "overproduction" was limited to festive occasions when food and goods were shared with guests, or for exchange in an atmosphere of reciprocal generosity. But "overproduction" in such cases refers to consumption of personal property rather than tools of production.

The major item of productive property among primitive farmers was land, but its ownership was of such a quality that it has often been referred to as "communal land tenure." The word "communal," however, has pejorative connotations for some people, and casual reference to communal ownership of land as "primitive communism" has repeatedly resulted in confusion between collective ownership and collective production. For example, no less an authority on Marx than Alfred Meyer claims that Marx, Engels, and the 19th-century anthropologist Lewis H. Morgan viewed primitive production as communal.[27] But a careful reading of all three shows they were talking about land tenure, not production. All distinguished between land as a "communal" property and land as a private "possession" for individual or family use. Production, as they correctly realized, was private and not collective.[28]

Both Marx and Engels, however, wrote of communal production in reference to household units or "family communities," and both mention the "Slav" family or *zadruga* as an example. The zadruga, as we now know, was simply an extended family of about ten members. One reason they lived and worked together was to reduce the per-capita effect of household taxes, and once this artificial advantage was removed, the institution rapidly disappeared.[29] In his *Pre-Capitalist Economic Formations* (1857), Marx wrote of a "secondary" (household production was "primary") form of communal production resulting from conquest.[30] Peru was his example, but Engels later noted that "tillage" there, too, was "individual." [31] Undoubtedly Marx had in mind what we now know to have been a labor tax on state (Inca) lands and which was no more "communal" or collective in the sense of crops collectively produced and divided than the labor performed by medieval European serfs on their lord's demesne.

In part to avoid such confusions, modern anthropology substituted the phrase "corporate land tenure" for the older "communal land tenure." Recently, however, some authorities have challenged the accuracy of the word "corporate" because it implies a degree of organization and associational perpetuity that may not be appropriate in many primitive and peasant circumstances.[32] I therefore will use the phrase "group land tenure."

The distinctive feature of group land tenure is that members of the community have inheritable use rights to land within the jurisdiction of the community but no right to alienate such land from the community. The "community" in this case can apply to a kin group, village, region, state, or to all of these in a hierarchy of overlapping rights. Primitive farmers generally practiced group land tenure; the Russian mir is a famous example lasting until recent times; the individual (noncollective) form of the Mexican *ejido* is a modern land reform example; and the Israeli *moshav ovdim* is a modern settlement form.

Basing his suppositions on the disposition of land "commons" in the England of his day, John Locke again came up with a fairly modern view of prestate property rights, this time with respect to land tenure.[33] He recognized the fact that individual possession was nonnegotiable under group tenure and that such practices were most common when land was plentiful. Each family cultivated what it needed, and there was still plenty left over. Before money came into use and before farmers began producing for market, there was no incentive to possess more land than each family needed to sustain itself. However, each farmer petitioned the "consent of all his fellow commoners" before he appropriated any part for his own use. And "fellow commoners" were specifically the members of a local county or parish, not "all mankind." In any case, the land to which each family had possession rights was land on which it expended its own labor.

Three characteristics of group land tenure emphasized by Gerard Clauson come very close to Locke's view of prestate tenure.[34] First, land is not a negotiable commodity except within the group itself—family, lineage, or tribe as the case may be. Even in instances of internal negotiability participants usually distinguish between the land and the work ("improvements") invested in the land. As informants on an Indian *comunidad* (reservation) in Sonora, Mexico, explained to me many years ago, "No one can sell his farmland here because here no one owns farmland; the comunidad—all of us—owns the land. But one who has cleared land and fenced it and worked it for many years has improved it. He can sell these improvements (*mejoras*); but when he does, it is the labor that is sold, not the land."

Second, a family's rights to any part of the land held by the group depends on use. If it ceases to cultivate a parcel of farmland, it loses its use rights to it. In the same Sonoran comunidad, one old man attempted to reclaim a parcel of farmland he had abandoned more than 20 years earlier when he had left the area. A council of elders determined that all evidences of the old man's labor had completely disappeared by the time the present owners had recleared the parcel. The present owners were not liable to him. On the contrary, if he wanted to repossess the land, he would have to reimburse them for all the labor they had invested in it over the past ten years. "It would be cheaper for you to clear a new parcel," the council told him.

Third, if a family dies out or leaves the area permanently, its rights are inherited by the group at large. In the previous case, the new owners of the farm parcel had requested permission of the community council to reuse the land before they had cleared it. At that time the community decided the land had been abandoned by the previous user and was available to any comunidad family in need.

Where group land tenure prevailed among primitive farmers, it would be difficult to speak of productive property incentives in the same sense as among farmers with private tenure. Division of land within the group makes it possible for each family to claim a product directly proportional to its effort. The harvest is the material incentive, not the land per se. Locke seems to appreciate this difference in explaining that group tenure changes to private ownership as a result of population pressure and the general use of money.[35] Once land becomes scarce, society has to regulate its distribution; but were it not for money and the buying and selling of land, there would still be far more than enough for everyone. If some men now acquire more land than they can labor personally, acquisition of land has become an incentive in its own right.

Rousseau follows this same distinction in explaining the origins of inequality.[36] In the first place farming helped make inequalities possible by necessitating a division of the land. Why, he asked, would any sane person work hard to produce a crop if he could not with reasonable certainty expect to reap it? Like Locke, Rousseau implicitly accepts the necessity of a selective material incentive. And though it is only the primitive cultivator's labor that allows the right to the product, the planter must insure that right by retaining possession of the soil until harvest. Thus, by becoming continuous from harvest to harvest and year to year, possession gradually turns into ownership. But this process alone does not turn a product incentive into a property incentive. Acquisition of land becomes an incentive only after population pressure creates scarcity and some cultivators begin to extend their holdings at the expense of other cultivators. Taking a zero-sum view of Locke's conclusion, Rousseau aims his negative moral judgment of inequality at the property incentive of land ownership.

Roughly a hundred years later, in the middle of the 19th century, John Stuart Mill stressed another important reason for the prolongation of possession that both Locke and Rousseau had neglected despite their focus on the relation of labor and ownership.[37] Not only must a cultivator keep possession of land long enough to harvest what is planted, possession must be retained long enough to get full benefit of all the labor invested in such improvements as buildings, fences, terraces, irrigation canals, and drainage ditches. The user of a piece of land is not going to make improvements on it, says Mill, if these are destined to benefit someone else.

Not only will the possessor of a piece of land not improve it if there is no guarantee of tenure; he may not even properly maintain it. This the Plymouth Colony discovered to its dismay in 1624.[38] After collectively clearing its group-held lands, the colony divided them into equal plots, which it distributed among the individual families for independent cultivation. To make sure no family would be permanently disadvantaged by the assignment of an inferior parcel, all plots were annually redistributed by lot. But as members found themselves receiving plots not as well tended as those they had worked hard on the year before, everyone grew more lax, and carelessness began to lower the efficiency of the entire colony.

Even when the 19th-century Russian mir periodically redistributed its lands, every effort was made by this group-land-tenure body to return the same plots to those families which had been most diligent in manuring them. Redistributions, moreover, were far more frequent in the fertile southern provinces of Russia than in the north, where manure was indispensable. And in those villages that had both manured and unmanured mir lands, it was only the latter that were redistributed with any regularity.[39]

In any event, at the hypothetical stage depicted by Rousseau, each household is an independent production and consumption unit working to meet subsistence needs. As long as each family survives, each receives according to need; and as long as each is self-sufficient, it receives according to work. The primitive farmer in this paradigm is both Millennial and Socialist Man. Is he also a Capitalist Man? Does he receive according to capital? In John Stuart Mill's sense he certainly does. The primitive farmer who has invested several years of laborious work in terraces and canals that increase his farm's productivity has capitalized the farm, and his current rewards are in part a return on that capital. But in this hypothetical primitive case the farmer's capital is simply an accumulation of his own labor. He is indeed a synthesis of all three "men"— Capitalist, Socialist, and Millennial. All three coalesce when unspecialized, subsistence-farming labor determines capital, need and product.

Can we say that at this stage the Rousseauean primitive has a productive property incentive? The improvements he has made on his farm certainly constitute an elementary form of fixed capital and one that guarantees him continued possession of his share of community-held land. To the extent the cultivator takes pride in leaving his handiwork to an heir, he can be said to have a productive property incentive, for his labor investment cannot be separated from the land. But at this Rousseauean stage when Capitalist and Socialist Man are one, there is no zero-sum antagonism. Each household economy is separate, land is abundant, and no family enjoys a return on its capital at the expense of any other family.

Rousseau's model of prestate society, however, is very misleading in its picture of pure equality. As we saw in the festive-labor model in Chapter 3, even the simplest primitive community could have a persuasive leader or big man to whom other members of the community were willing to make gifts of labor repaid with festive generosity. There is no productive property incentive in such cases although the big man is able to "possess" and crop a larger share of the group land than his fellows by virtue of their assistance. Except for the festivities, social incentives dominate the reciprocities involved.

The ingredients of the festivities constitute an important material incentive for the community, but it would be hard to classify them as property which is either productive or personal, although in a sense they are both. They are a form of capital produced by the big man to "pay" for festive labor, but they are a capital that has no permanence. Food spoils without use, so this extra production is purely for redistribution. The festive ingredients might also be considered the personal property of the big man except that neither he nor the community produces them for his private enjoyment. The purpose is collective, rather than private or personal, consumption.

This situation is by no means strictly egalitarian. Though his talents be persuasive rather than coercive, this big man has the "power" to induce others to work for him. Even at a time when labor was practically coterminous with both productive and personal property, there was no Rousseauean equality. According to Rousseau's scheme, the zero-sum antagonisms of inequality arose in two ways.[40] They arose, as already noted, when population pressure on the land produced competition for a resource in scarce supply. But they also arose when the exchange of goods led to specialization, for then the strong gained an advantage over the weak and the clever over the ingenuous. As our example illustrates, however, exchange is intrinsically a part of human social behavior and existed long before it was intensified by money economy. And in those times, too, some people were ingenuous and others clever.

John Stuart Mill steered a middle course between zero-sum and positive-sum inequalities.[41] He would probably have viewed the difference between the primitive big man and his festive-labor constituency as one of positive-sum inequality, an inequality resulting in collective benefits for all. This is why Mill's position could be so much like Rousseau's in some ways while being so different in others.

Mill made a crucial distinction between "moveable" property and land. One can acquire considerable moveable property without preventing another from acquiring the same kind of property. Each can buy the machinery and tools needed to carry on business. This is a positive-sum situation. But whoever occupies land is preventing someone else from occupying it. Thus, if the occupier is not making productive use of land and is not improving it, the community is deprived of its full benefit. Obviously Mill is not thinking of an abundant land situation but of one in which land has become scarce and each farmer must do more than support a family; each must also produce food for the growing urban market. Therefore, as a valuable production factor in limited supply, "landed property" should not provide a sinecure for lazy proprietors. He questions the justice of allowing any land not destined for cultivation to be privately owned. Where such ownership occurs, the possessor should hold the land purely "by suffrance of the community." [42]

At this point Mill comes close to Rousseau's conviction that the possession of large tracts of land by one individual was "possible only by punishable usurpation." Rousseau believed "usurpation" could be changed into "true right" of possession by subordinating the individual's rights to those of the community.[43] In short, Rousseau proposed a return to group land tenure.

The difference between Mill and Rousseau, however, is significant. While Rousseau identified equality with the collective good, Mill identified progress, improvement and efficiency with it. He implied that a landowner not serving the general welfare through efficient cultivation and improvement of the land should be replaced by one who would. Implicit in Mill's position is the inevitability of inequality and the implication that those most capable should be given the means and incentives to make the best possible use of scarce resources for the good of society. Mill in the end is true to the proprogress view of the supraecological stage of capitalism.

A recent and very strong reaffirmation of the importance of productive-property incentives for the civilization of capitalism has been provided by Douglass North and Robert Thomas in *The Rise of the Western World*.[44] Covering the economic history of Europe from 900 to 1700, North and Thomas argue that such factors as technological innovation, economies of scale, and capital accumulation are the manifestations rather than the causes of modern economic growth. As they see it, the industrial revolution was a result of important changes in the structure of incentives that began taking place in Europe long before the second half of the 18th century. By establishing more effective productive property rights, these changes encouraged the specialization and innovation that made the industrial revolution possible.

In effect North and Thomas are reaffirming the importance given to private property rights by Hobbes, Locke, and Adam Smith and to the crucial role of the nation-state in protecting those rights. Effecting economic growth required the special effort and ingenuity of only a very small proportion of the population, but these individuals needed the proper selective incentives. To get them to work for the long-term benefit of society, the "private rate of return," say North and Thomas, had to come close to the "social rate of return." [45] In other words the collective benefits had to include sufficient private benefits to justify the costs of undertaking activities leading to growth.

Let us return for a moment to the feeder-road examples used to illustrate selective incentives in Chapter 2. In the case of the four farmers, three of whom had very small holdings and the fourth a very large farm, the asymmetry of benefits from the proposed road was such that the social rate of return from the road was almost the same as the private rate of return for the fourth farmer. The road was so nearly a private good anyway that the owner of the large farm was sure of realizing benefits commensurate with his investment. But in the example of the four hundred settlers with equal land holdings, let us suppose that settler Fulano has the capital, know-how and desire to build the secondary road all by himself. His benefit from the road building, however, would be only one-fourth of one percent of the normal use of the road. In other words his private rate of return would be only one-fourth of one percent of the social rate. Since this rate of return would hardly justify his costs, Fulano would, as the situation dictated, either play "free rider" and wait for others to build a road he could then use at no expense to himself or play taxpayer and pay his share of the costs of a road constructed by government contract. A third possibility, however, illustrates the North-Thomas paradigm of bringing the private rate of return into closer parity with the social rate of return. Fulano tells the government he is willing and able to build the road at his own expense if the government will authorize his right to charge all the other settlers a toll rate for its use. By sharing part of his neighbor's benefits through toll charges, Fulano is now able to realize a private rate of return closer to the social rate (closer to the net effect of the road on the entire settlement). Since the potential benefits to Fulano from this arrangement far exceed his costs, he builds the road.

The role of the state is crucial in this example, for it guarantees Fulano's productive-property rights to the road for a period long enough to handsomely reimburse him for his effort. The state must also apply punitive sanctions to enforce the collection of charges. Actually the transaction costs to Fulano and the government for collective tolls would today probably exceed those for collecting a single road tax and contracting Fulano to build it. But privately owned and constructed toll roads and transport canals were common in the late 18th and early 19th centuries.

With the expansion of the market economy during the Middle Ages, there was increasing need for private-property protection, especially in long-distance trade. Political organization capable of controlling large areas could give coercive support to the commercial law that had been developing outside feudal courts as an integral part of mercantile custom. Money economy made this possible since governments could now employ standing armies instead of depending on an exchange of labor services. At that point governments could protect property rights much more efficiently than voluntary groups, and the latter in turn became more willing to trade taxes for government enforcement of those rights.[46]

For unique historical reasons England led most of Europe in two important legal developments that North and Thomas regard as having been crucial for productive property incentives. First was the fundamental change in land law during the 13th century which gave freeholders almost fee-simple ownership rights to their land.[47] From this point on the gradual breakdown of "commons" and feudal land tenure arrangements enhanced the incentives for proprietors to improve and capitalize their farms. Second was the Statute of Monopolies of 1624 which included a patent system that encouraged invention and innovation.[48] Before that time an innovator had had to keep improvements secret to enjoy a selective benefit from them. But the development of patent laws stimulated the innovator to experiment in the face of high research costs because they insured a private rate of return closer to parity with the social rate of return. The recognition and enforcement of productive property rights in knowledge and innovation put England and Holland at the vanguard of industrial development.

By emphasizing the productive-property incentives afforded by the legal predictability of the nation-state, North and Thomas close the gap between John Locke and Joseph Schumpeter. For Schumpeter the agent of the civilization of capitalism was the entrepreneur, an individual who could recognize and exploit technological innovations that revolutionized production.[49] This was a person, said Schumpeter, who could proceed with confidence beyond the range of the familiar. Only a tiny percentage of the population had the aptitudes required; but as the civilization of capitalism begins to self-destruct, these special aptitudes no longer serve a purpose. The entrepreneur was a doer more than an inventor. Today, however, innovation is performed by teams of specialists, and the economic process becomes more and more automatized and impersonal. The person who might once have been a great entrepreneur is rationalized and specialized into just another member of the office team. As for those factory buildings and other tangibles which the old entrepreneur watched grow with a sense of creative accomplishment, the capitalistic process substitutes shares of stock. Factories end up in the hands of employed managers while absentee owners hold the pieces of paper.

The strength of productive-property incentives during the early entrepreneurial phase of industrialization actually made it possible for England to lead the industrial revolution while lagging behind in development of the joint-stock company. As David Landes has pointed out, England, by being first, was able to build its enterprises "from the ground up" and did not need the greater initial financing the joint-stock company could provide.[50] It remained for those countries industrializing later to put it to use more readily, yet England was more responsive to the opportunities of the industrial revolution than any other country in the world.

Josiah Wedgwood, whose 18th-century plant at Etruria, England, introduced the factory system to the pottery industry, is an early example of industrial entrepreneurship.[51] He took great pride in his success and in the expansion and development of his plant, and he died a wealthy man. It would be inaccurate, however, to describe his income as "unearned" or the expansion of his capital as a zero-sum process. During the expansion of his business the population of Etruria trebled, workers' income doubled, and their housing and life style improved dramatically. Wedgwood organized his workers in specialized production stages, limited the scope of each worker's task to increase skills, and introduced new standards of punctuality, safety, attendance, cleanliness, and discipline. He worked long hours, controlling every detail during the early years including product design, construction of kilns, supervision and disciplining of workers, and inspection of their products. He performed all his own clerical chores late at night after the plant had closed or early in the morning before it opened. He helped revolutionize an entire industry while building his capital and increasing his workers' income.

Industrial capitalism opened up a new era of geometrically progressive technological change—a positive-sum game of moveable property that soon dwarfed the zero-sum characteristics of agrarian capitalism. In the early stages of industrialism, owner-managers like Wedgwood undoubtedly felt pride of ownership in their enterprises. In contemporary Mexico I have seen prosperous small farmers shining brand new tractors parked alongside their mud-and-wattle houses. And in New Guinea, Ben Finney found that Gorokan entrepreneurs had a veritable "passion" for investing in highly visible forms of productive property such as big trucks, stores, and plantations.[52] Native big men were getting financial backing from their local constituencies to invest in conspicuous productive property in which the entire local group took pride. And successful big men later returned the favor by helping fellow tribesmen in their business enterprises.

Even in our own society proprietors of small businesses such as restaurants, stores, and machine shops may take considerable pride in their new buildings or equipment. In such cases there is display value in this ownership similar to that for personal property. Both provide the owner with status satisfactions that overlap on the area of social or "nonmaterial" incentives. Included here would be the sense of power that often accompanies ownership of productive property. Wedgwood, for example, was very autocratic and enjoyed disciplining his workers; they became his human clay as he attempted even to mould their personal habits. Like many primitive industrialists of his time he was an extremely paternalistic employer and fully believed he was helping to correct an improvident and immoral society. However we may assess his motives or judge his results, the Wedgwood type of early entrepreneur was not only a subject player in the sense of manipulating productive property, he was also a manipulator of others. To some degree his subject playing converted others into object players.

That phase in the development of capitalism when ownership and control of important industrial enterprises were in the hands of one man was relatively brief. As we have seen, such productive property today is held by large corporations owned by stockholders who have little or nothing to do with management. Since stockholders have no visible share of the productive property in which they invest, productive property incentive is essentially no different from that of contemporary Russians or Chinese who invest savings in the socialist, state-owned bank.[53] The Russians or Chinese are, in a sense, buying shares in their government, which owns all productive property. The interest on shares may be less than the dividends paid by most United States corporations, but they do not have to worry about a fall in their market value. And U.S. shareholders with modest investments are probably, like the thrifty Russians or Chinese, building a retirement supplement. In most cases they are planning to spend the money at some future date on consumption goods; investments in productive property actually stem from personal-property incentives.

In the classified advertisement section of the daily newspaper one frequently sees apartment houses listed for sale with the caption "Pride-of-Ownership Units." Many small investors, particularly in the real-estate field, still take pride in acquiring visible, tangible pieces of productive property. But many investors are contemptuous of appeals to "pride of ownership," and if a profitable slum property is for sale at the right price, they buy it. In either case, however, the investors are expanding "unearned income" to raise their living standards or to bless their old age.

The enterprise manager who owns little or none of the productive property controlled is motivated to operate the enterprise profitably to keep his job and to earn bonuses and salary increments. This is as true in Russia and China as in the United States except that rewards to top management in the socialist countries are much smaller relative to the minimum wage (25 to 1 in the USSR) than in the United States (over 100 to 1).[54] In all these countries the successful manager enjoys a higher-than-average standard of living. Today in most industrial countries the productive-property incentive translates into a "power" incentive or a deferred form of personal-property incentive.

So far as power is concerned, anti-Soviet Marxists sometimes refer to state ownership of productive property as "state capitalism." The bureaucratic elite which controls the state's property does not own that property, but the power and privilege they obtain through its control turns them into the equivalent of a capitalist bourgeoisie. More dispassionate comparisons of capitalist and socialist stratification systems point out a major difference between the two. Since state ownership precludes the inheritance of productive property, the socialist class structure does not include ownership classes; achievement weighs heavily in determining the membership of the occupational and political elites. Nevertheless both societies have elites, and both are characterized by inequality of power, income, status, and control of wealth. For our purposes, however, the essential question raised by this comparison is to what extent, if any, private ownership of productive property is a necessary or viable incentive in advanced industrial society.

According to some students of capitalism, property incentives in Russia and the United States are converging as a result of the growth of corporate capitalism. In the United States today, as Berle and Means have shown, very little individually owned wealth is productive property in the sense of owner-used and owner-managed tools of production.[55] Most productive property consists of the corporation stocks of "passive" owners who neither control nor manage the enterprises concerned. So concentrated have these industrial enterprises become that a mere six or seven hundred of them now account for 70 percent of all commercial operations (other than agricultural) in the United States. Some of these corporations have millions of stockholders, "owners" who do not manage.

Almost half of all individually owned wealth in the United States is personal property of which by far the largest share, as in China and Russia, consists of family homes. As for productive property, Peter Drucker claims that pension-fund ownership of stocks is rapidly moving the United States toward a socialism that is far closer to the Marxian ideal than is the "state capitalism" of the socialist world.[56] By making labor both the "source of all value" and the full beneficiary of production, the private pension funds, says Drucker, "socialize" the economy without "nationalizing" it and will gradually lead us to genuine "decentralized market socialism." If Russia in turn continues to develop "market socialism" through decentralization of managerial planning and decision making, the differences between the two systems might become more nominal than real.

Before turning to the category of personal property, one final aspect of productive property merits brief consideration: the mechanized family farm. The U.S. farmer feeds more people per worker-year of labor than any other farmer in the world, yet American farming has remained predominantly a family operation. Is the high productivity of American family farming evidence for the strength of a productive-property ownership incentive? The answer to this question is probably to be found in the fact that the American farmer is not much different from any farmer since the beginning of agriculture. On a national scale or on a community scale, family farming is basically a piecework system that allows the individual to appraise the reward in relation to one's skill and effort. Ownership of the land or even of equipment is not the crucial factor. Family farming is also the predominant form in Israel where it is entrepreneurial, competitive, and competent; yet the land is owned and leased by government.

As long as there is a climate of confidence in land-tenure arrangements, farmers will invest in permanent improvements whether or not they have negotiable title to the land. This is true in Israel where settlers find their government landlord helpful rather than exploitive and unpredictable. Even Venezuelan farmers in 1964, shortly after a major land-reform movement, were making heavy investments in farm improvements because the government had established a predictable policy of generously reimbursing owners of expropriated lands. Bolivia, on the other hand, had redistributed land to thousands of peasants; but in 1964, ten years after the land reform, few farmers anywhere were making permanent improvements. Owners of expropriated lands had not been reimbursed, and confidence had been destroyed by an unpredictable, revolutionary climate.[57]

Even private ownership of farm machinery is not essential to productive efficiency. It is true that most socialist countries which have collectivized their agriculture have had severe problems at some time or other with the care and maintenance of livestock and equipment. They have all had to learn that responsibility for equipment must be individually assigned; for when many persons share in the ownership and maintenance of a piece of machinery, no one takes care of it. Successful machinery cooperatives in Western European countries place one member of the cooperative or a permanent employee in charge of each machine. Bonuses are often paid to those individuals who keep their equipment in best repair with lowest maintenance costs. Under these conditions farm machinery is often used more efficiently than where it is privately owned and operated.[58]

It is true, however, that in Western Europe as in the rest of the capitalist world, most farmers do not join machinery cooperatives and many of them overmechanize as a consequence. And there is no doubt that one of the main reasons for overmechanization, besides the convenience of having one's own equipment and being able to use it independently of other people's needs, is pride of ownership and the display value of the equipment. One way in which an entrepreneur can announce financial success without wasting resources on ostentatious luxuries and consumer goods is to invest in productive property that is highly visible to all his friends.

It has been said that in 1850 approximately 80 percent of the working population of the United States was self-employed while only 20 percent consisted of employees. A hundred years later the proportions were reversed: 80 percent employees and only 20 percent self-employed. During the early phases of the industrial revolution and the mechanization of agriculture, there were probably very strong incentives among self-employed producers to acquire and own productive property for pride of ownership as well as for convenience and profit. Even today in many small, owner-operated service businesses these same incentives still apply. So much does the success of such enterprises often depend upon these incentives, that critics of socialism wonder if the productive property of the service sector could ever be nationalized without drastically lowering the "efficiency" of all services. In the opinion of Michael Harrington, socialism would be well worth this sacrifice.[59] But if actions speak louder than words, people living under socialism do not agree with him. According to Hedrick Smith, the "creeping capitalism" of Russia's "thriving counter-economy" is a direct response to such inefficiency, and throughout eastern Europe the predominant trend is toward more private entrepreneurship in the service sector, particularly restaurants, bakeries, repair shops, and the professions.[60]

Personal Property

Many years ago, while studying economic development in northwest Mexico, I made the acquaintance of an old Indian who had never heard of Jean-Jacques Rousseau but who had strong Rousseauean convictions concerning the vain pursuit of possessions. Living alone on a small farm by the Mayo River, Don Braulio was in his middle sixties and had only recently left his wife and home in the San Fernando Valley to return to a less demanding way of life in his native Sonora. Some 40 years earlier he had migrated to southern California from this very farm, a young Mayo Indian with little education. He had prospered in Los Angeles, married a Mexican-American girl, and raised a family. But as he grew older, he became disenchanted with "civilization." "In the United States," Don Braulio explained, "a man spends all his time working to make the payments on his house and his furniture and his car. And whenever his friends and neighbors get something new, he has to go out and get it too. Every time I got one damn thing paid off, I started paying on another. I got fed up with the whole rat race."

When his mother died a year before, he returned to occupy the family farm. Except, however, for his little garden of subsistence crops, he was only half-heartedly attempting to work the land; and the old family adobe was in a state of disrepair bordering on ruin. None of this bothered Don Braulio as he stretched out in his hammock to philosophize. It saddened him that Sonora was becoming like California. Everyone was accumulating new consumer goods bought on credit just to keep up with the Fulanos. "There's no escape; the rat race is spreading everywhere."

Don Braulio reminisced about a visit to the farm made early that summer by his three grown sons and their wives and children. His sons had liked Mexico, but his Mexican-American daughters-in-law had not. "They missed their washing machines and their electric stoves and their refrigerators. They hated having to carry their water from a well. Finally the children got sick, and they all went home. Can you imagine! *My* grandchildren sick on Mexican water!"

But even Don Braulio had gone soft after 40 years of civilization. On my next visit, a few months later, I found his house abandoned. He had fallen ill during the winter months and, according to his neighbors, had gone back to his wife in California. "He said the medical care was better there, so he wired his sons to come and get him." When things got rough, even Don Braulio felt the pull of civilization. As Rousseau noted two hundred years earlier, in the state of civilization people have created many new "commodities unknown to their fathers" which have become a "yoke" both for them and their descendants. These commodities "soften body and mind," said Rousseau, and eventually "degenerate" into "needs" that people can no longer do without even though they are made no happier by possessing them.[61]

Individuals like Don Braulio who reject even part of the progress equation are numerically unimportant in those areas of the Third World that are rapidly changing. Few are given his unique opportunity to straddle two eras, the industrial and the preindustrial, in a single lifetime. Even when they are, they seldom draw his critical conclusion. Most people eagerly join the competitive-consumption marathon and never question it. What is the nature of this powerful, personal-property incentive that not even the socialist countries have been able to escape? They try to contain consumerism, yet they find they have to reward according to work and that wages are the most convenient way of doing so. But wages have little incentive value, as even Fidel Castro discovered, without wage goods on which to spend them. How did all this come about? What was the situation before the civilization of capitalism? What was the role of personal property among primitive peoples of the multiecological era? What happened to make personal property so important in the second stage?

In a recent book on the ecology of development, Richard Wilkinson makes a distinction between what he calls the "leisure preference" of preindustrial societies and the "work" or "consumer preference" of industrial societies.[62] This distinction is very reminiscent of Huizinga's contrast between the play behavior of primitive and medieval people and the serious business of contemporary life. Wilkinson's notion of leisure preference, however, coincides with a phenomenon economists call "inverse elasticity of supply." J. H. Boeke called attention to this phenomenon long ago in contrasting the industrial and preindustrial sectors of "dual" or colonial societies.[63] When the price of coconuts goes up, the commercial farmer produces and sells as many as possible to increase profits. But in the preindustrial (also called "peasant," "primitive," or "precapitalistic") sector the grower brings fewer coconuts to market. The individual's very limited needs are easily saturated; and once the grower has purchased the few items regularly bought at the store such as kerosene, salt, matches, cloth and thread, there is no further need for cash and therefore no need to sell any more coconuts. Conversely, if the price of coconuts goes down, the precapitalistic peasant brings in more than usual and drives the price down even further. No matter what the market value of the product the individual seeks just that cash necessary to buy the few trade goods he is accustomed to consuming.

The same phenomenon applies to wage laborers. If, says Boeke, the manager of a colonial plantation tries to be nice to workers by raising their wages, the risk run is severe absenteeism. In the precapitalistic sector of the dual society, workers do not seek discretionary income increases to buy more wage goods; they convert income increases into increased leisure. Pamphlets on urban labor problems printed in England during the early half of the 18th century testify to the precapitalistic leisure preferences of London workers just prior to the industrial revolution. According to one such tract published in 1739, laborers are said to work only as much as they find necessary "to live and support their weekly debauches." A laborer who earns enough for two days' work to keep drunk the rest of the week will surely spend the other five days in a "tipling-house." Only by reducing wages, suggests the pamphlet, can employers make the working class industrious and virtuous.[64]

Wilkinson dates the big change from leisure preference to consumer preference in Western civilization during the latter half of the 18th century as the industrial revolution got under way.[65] The difference between Adam Smith's views on worker motivation in 1776 and those of Bernard Mandeville in 1724 illustrate this change. Smith contradicted the inverse-elasticity-of-supply arguments of his day and ascribed them to the bias of employers who preferred the greater docility displayed by workers during periods of high prices and scarce jobs.[66] Mandeville on the other hand portrayed man as a "slothful" creature who exerts himself only when forced by necessity to do so.[67] Put men in a mild climate with more land at their disposal than they can till, and they will be easygoing, virtuous, poor, and ignorant. But take the same society and increase the population to the point where land is scarce and some individuals are forced to specialize in trades and manufactures while all become increasingly invidious of each other's possessions, and there you will create an opulent, industrious society with flourishing businesses, arts and sciences.

There is a definite neo-Mandevillian quality to Wilkinson's ecological view of development, for he too believes necessity, principally in the form of population pressure, is the prime mover of development. He uses this model to explain the dramatic economic development of North America under conditions of abundant land and scarce labor, and he uses it also to explain the great change under capitalism to a work-preference society in which people willingly work overtime to increase income and consumption. His explanations are ingenious but less than convincing. A major problem of his entire thesis is the very nature of his leisure-work classification. And in this regard, Wilkinson is probably less to blame than the anthropologists from whom he gets notions about work and leisure.

In anthropology of late there has been a tongue-in-cheek tendency to romanticize primitive life in a way Rousseau has long been accused of doing but never really did. As we saw earlier, Rousseau developed a natural-man "type" or "model" to contrast with the civilized life of which he was so critical. He was not writing about "real" primitives as some anthropologists do today when characterizing them, for example, as the "original affluent society." [68] According-ing to this contemporary view, which is deliberately exaggerated I believe, primitive groups achieved a stable population plateau in their adaptation to a particular ecological niche, did not exhaust or threaten their resource base, and, given their limited needs, succeeded in leading a leisurely existence under conditions of material plenty.

In such portraits of primitive life, the time people devoted to ritual, dancing, head-hunting, competitive feasting, and so on, is counted as leisure activity or as a form of play. Yet all the manpower devoted in our society to the manufacture, sale, and maintenance of such things as Cadillacs and luxury housing is classified as work. The protestant ethic, alias work ethic, has somehow managed to make our status-seeking game playing look like serious business compared to the exotic, prestige-seeking frivolities of primitive people. What is surprising is that some contemporary anthropologists have been as susceptible to this conceptual distortion as was Huizinga. They find it hard to see in civilized man the same Homo ludens they describe for their "leisure-preferring, affluent," primitive societies. But for the society in question, counting coup, potlatching, competitive yam-growing, women stealing, camel raiding, competitive pig feasting, or trance-dancing may be very serious business indeed; and it is serious business that often goes far beyond the least-effort requirements of the particular ecological circumstances.

This does not mean that for much of man's behavior a least-effort interpretation is invalid. Ester Boserup, for example, has shown convincingly that primitive slash-and-burn agriculture is highly productive per unit of labor while low per unit of land.[69] As long as there is plenty of land, swidden farmers would be irrational indeed to adopt intensive cropping patterns that increased yields per unit of land but reduced them per unit of labor. In this case "progress" to more modern forms of cultivation is forced on people by population growth that increases the demand for land and food. The change from the two-field to the three-field system in medieval Europe was a very slow transition for the same "rational" reasons. The three-field system was much more productive per unit of land area than the two-field system; but since the two-field system produced more per unit of human effort, people did not make the switch until it was forced on them by population growth. North and Thomas, however, are careful to note that this change did not constitute any real progress in efficiency as measured by labor productivity.[70]

We come back to the point made by John Stuart Mill that the relation of people to land is far different in degree from their relation to "moveable" goods. Because of his people–land ecological perspective, however, Wilkinson has taken Boserup's slash-and-burn farming model as the basis for his entire history of civilization. But when it comes to "moveable" goods, the principle of least effort can work to increase the productivity of human labor.

Seldom has humanity been content to sit back and watch the clouds roll by. The same people who apply the principle of least effort to their food-procuring activities may expend unlimited energy in the pursuit of other rewards both material and social. During the multiecological stage innumerable status-seeking games were developed that varied with the ecological circumstances. The Plains Indians counted coup and stole ponies, the Northwest Coast Indians sponsored competitive potlatches, and the Ifugao peoples of the Philippines accumulated wealth and took heads in order to qualify some day as sponsors of kadangyang feasts. The preconquest Maya Indians of Yucatán practiced a form of slash-and-burn agriculture that was highly productive in terms of labor costs. Agriculture could not have taken much of their time, but they left behind impressive ruins as testimony to the fact that they found other things to do with it. Yucatán's rocky limestone peninsula provided the Mayas with an abundantly available building material. Rocks and mortar were readily extracted from every farmer's field. The Mayas, in effect, found themselves living on top of a natural erector set, and they got caught up in playing with it.[71]

One of the most important changes in the shift from the multiecological to the supraecological phase was the homogenization of game playing effected by the civilization of capitalism. Primitive game playing varied in its details with differing ecological restraints or opportunities. But the civilization of capitalism, in effect, converted these various games into an international, real-world version of "Monopoly." With the spread of money, what Schumpeter called "rational cost–profit calculation" automatically established universal scoring procedures for a game everyone could readily learn despite differences of language and culture.[72] As Schumpeter noted, precapitalist man was "no less 'grabbing' than capitalist man," by which he meant no less self-interested. But the self-interest of precapitalist man led him in multiecological directions, and the spread of money and markets converged these to a single track, the civilization of capitalism.

Primitive peoples owned little in the way of material objects or goods, and even that little was usually manufactured by each family for its own use. A member of a hunting band might have been "wealthier" than all his fellows on a day when his luck was good, but such wealth was temporary and perishable. There was no money or durable trade goods into which the hunter could convert a temporary surplus, so he exchanged it for good will by giving it away. On a day when he was "poor" and another member of the band was "rich," his generosity on previous occasions would be remembered, and he would become the beneficiary of someone else's largesse.

There was no incentive, however, to produce beyond one's needs simply to supply others, and a hunter who gave up working with the intention of living off the others would soon be an outcast from the group. The incentive to share food surpluses with others was based on the expectation of reciprocity and the greater security it provided the band. But let us suppose, for the sake of an example, that one member of the band was much more talented as a hunter than the rest. If he produced up to his ability, he might consistently surpass his own needs and in the long run give away much more food than he got back. Was this talented hunter a Millennial Man, in producing according to his ability and receiving according to his need, who helped to support the entire community? Is this simple savage the epitome of that nonreciprocal altruism idolized by utopians?

Primitive bands did have talented hunters who consistently caught more game than their fellows and who distributed more than they got back. In return they received the group's respect and approbation including labels of respect such as "big man." A big man distributed surplus food for nonmaterial or social rewards that fully met the conditions of reciprocal altruism. And with agriculture, particularly of the primitive slash-and-burn variety, he could move from the simple distributive behavior of a skillful hunter to the redistributive behavior of a social entrepreneur able to enlist the labor of his fellows for his own and the common good. In Chapter 3 we saw how this could initially have been accomplished through some form of festive work party; but with greater centralization of third-party control, it readily transforms into the corvée or labor tax.

Ancient civilizations using corvée accomplished great engineering feats of irrigation and produced impressive amounts of grain, but they did not effect any lasting rise in the real incomes of their masses. Their populations always bred up to each increase in food production. The few consumer goods not produced within the peasant household itself were largely luxury items enjoyed by a privileged elite comprising less than two percent of the population. The production of personal property and the division of labor it requires were limited by the extent of the market, in this case a market of privilege comprised of a tiny elite. The full-time specialists who produced luxury goods for this class were supported by state food supplies produced by corvée.

Some emulative consumption of luxury goods undoubtedly took place within the nobility, or elite class; but because status was predominantly ascriptive, it was not on a scale that would justify calling it competitive consumption. Among the peasant masses traditional forms of festive or ceremonial consumption prevailed with little or no emulation by them of the sumptuary privileges of the elite. In fact, the luxury goods of the nobility were symbols of ascribed rank that reinforced class distinctions including attitudes of awe and deference among the masses. Feudalism in precapitalist Europe was simply a more decentralized form of the same market of privilege. Specialization was confined mainly to the internal economy of the manor, and similarly corvée labor was limited to manorial tasks and to the cropping of the lord's demesne.

The spread of commerce facilitated by money economy broke open these redistributive economies and prepared the way for an industrial market. The specialist was no longer dependent upon a market of privilege nor dependent on exchange with unskilled labor. A village or tribal blacksmith who made hoes only until all the planting chores on his subsistence farm had been done for him by his clientele was inclined to halt hoe production before satisfying demand. But once he could take a money payment and defer his real reward to suit his own convenience, he had an incentive to continue hoe production beyond the labor requirements of his subsistence plot. In fact, he could drop all pretenses of being a farmer and buy his food from those who used to exchange their labor for his.

Similarly, the lord of the manor could now control labor directly through wages instead of indirectly through perquisites and social reciprocities. Even the former serf was soon free to specialize in the most lucrative commercial crops while buying staples in the marketplace. And the public works formerly constructed by corvée could now be done by specialized contractors paid from tax monies.

A recurring theme among both utopian and socialist writers is the eventual elimination of all forms of money. Even American socialist Michael Harrington has recently advocated that society start moving toward its abolition.[73] Yet there can be no doubt that money was one of society's greatest inventions. By reducing transaction costs of exchange it greatly enhanced freedom of choice in day-to-day living. The great drawback for some observers is that money simultaneously commits people to an irreversible process of specialization involving increasingly complex and impersonal economic relationships.

While much of this specialization process was in response to new opportunities, some of it was undoubtedly the product of necessity. As North and Thomas have emphasized, the growth of the European population during the Middle Ages created the opportunity for an expanding market economy.[74] But both opportunity and necessity worked together in this development. As population increases in local areas led to diminishing returns to labor, part of the labor force found it advantageous to establish new frontier settlements in outlying wilderness areas. But since the older areas still had a denser population than those more recently populated, different land–labor ratios were created. These in combination with local differences in resource endowments encouraged variation in types of production and regional exchange. As a result, the Middle Ages became a period of dynamic, market-economy expansion initiating a process that was to continue with increasing vigor into the early modern period.

Economic historians have been giving increasing attention to the demand side of economic growth, the expansion of consumer needs among the Western European masses during the two to three centuries that immediately preceded the industrial revolution. As L. A. Clarkson has shown, English agriculture was already highly commercialized by the period 1550–1750 compared with modern underdeveloped countries in Africa and Asia.[75] Urban growth was enlarging the wage-earning class, which depended on the market for its food requirements. The population of London increased from 50,000 in 1500 to almost 700,000 in 1750. Although no other English towns approached London in absolute size, many grew at an even faster rate during the same period. As early as the 16th century at least half the population of the towns was comprised of wage earners as was between a fourth and a third of the rural population. In all cases these laborers bought their food; they did not grow it. Farmers grew accustomed to producing commercial food crops, livestock, dairy products, poultry, wool, hides, and such industrial crops as flax and hemp all for the internal market demand. As incomes of farmers went up, they increased their purchases of manufactured goods and thereby helped to stimulate the enterprises employing the workers who bought their farm produce.

Meanwhile the town and country wage earners were not only increasing and diversifying their consumption of farm products—especially meat and dairy produce—they were consuming a wider variety of manufactured goods as well. In the long run, the latter proved a strong incentive to economic development since demand for manufactured goods is much more elastic than consumption limited by the capacity of the human stomach. Diversification of products was especially marked in the textile industry. New woolen cloth was produced that was lighter and cheaper and could appeal to fashion changes even among the poorer classes. Thus, says Clarkson, while no important changes took place in methods of production or scale of operations in English manufacturing during the three centuries preceding the industrial revolution, volume and diversification increased dramatically.[76] The appetite for consumer goods, or personal property, had definitely been whetted.

In his meticulous research into the economy and living standards of Worcester, England, during the 16th century, Alan Dyer found that the real wealth of the population increased very little if at all during that period, for incomes barely kept pace with the increasing price of food.[77] Yet living standards improved appreciably through the consumption of new consumer goods such as furniture, utensils, linens, curtains, and glass. Dyer's explanation of this seeming contradiction is that early in the century families kept money in cash or invested it in loans or real estate; but as the century progressed, they tended to spend more on house furnishings. He found clear evidence of growing status consciousness and competitive consumption. Many families were beginning to advertise their financial standing through the appearance of their homes. And since there were no social barriers to prevent a rise from the middle to the upper social class, there was enough mobility to encourage its pretension by any who might try.

For the 17th century Eric Kerridge notes even greater changes in British consumption habits.[78] Fresh meat, cheese, butter, and wheat bread became available in greater quantities even on the table of the poorest farm workers. Clothing improved as it became cheaper and everyone grew more style conscious. Some people complained that they could no longer tell master from servant. And as brick houses became more common, chimneys replaced the former smoke holes. Even homes of the lowest classes now had glass windows, floors of brick instead of trampled earth, and roof tiles in place of the traditional thatch. With these construction improvements, house rats began to disappear and with them the recurring plague.

For the early part of the 18th century, still prior to the takeoff of the English industrial revolution, none other than our old friend Bernard Mandeville paints a vivid picture of emulative consumption.[79] He describes the well-dressed, lower-class woman who joins Easter and other holiday celebrations at which large crowds cloak her in their anonymity. There for a few short hours she can rise above her station and even pretend to herself that she is worthy of the courtesy and esteem shown her by those persons of higher status whom she may chance to meet.

Mandeville obviously does not like to be fooled by lower-class ladies disguised in garments common to their "betters." He would prefer that everyone's station in life be conveniently apparent. While he does not approve of the leveling effect of these new consumer habits, he is describing what was to be precisely one of the major positive-sum results of the rising living standards made possible by industrial production. Rousseau also overlooked the leveling effect inherent in this desire for "luxury;" for in the mass pursuit of personal property the father of antiprogress saw only vanity and exploitation.

The lady disguised in clothes above her station is careful, Mandeville notes, to give no clues to her address or employment. By Mandeville's time, urbanization in England had reached a point that new clothes might indeed make the man or woman in them. The small community, in which everyone knew everyone else, would never have been so easily fooled. Here again we see the effect of Toffler's transience or spatial mobility that so impersonalizes and equalizes the social relationships of modern society. Mandeville's lower-class lady is simply a precursor of the contemporary shipping clerk who after working hours drives about town in a Cadillac or Porsche. The incentive to acquire a personal-property disguise is the same in both cases despite their separation in time of two and a half centuries.

After dealing with his lower-class lady of the Easter crowds, Mandeville amuses himself with the competitive, social-climbing aspects of the same phenomenon.[80] The wife of the poorest laborer in the parish starves herself to buy the second-hand clothing of a shoemaker's or barber's wife so she can feel "more genteel." And the shoemaker and his wife try to dress like the family of a prosperous shopkeeper. Meanwhile the shopkeeper begins to dress and live like a merchant, while the latter's wife, in her desperate attempt to keep her distance from such inferiors, copies the styles of the "women of quality." This so thoroughly alarms the ladies at court that they diligently set about to devise the new styles that will put them once again ahead of those impudent city women.

For Mandeville, as we have seen, the "push" factors of population pressure and land scarcity are the prime movers of development, but once these conditions are ripe, the "pull" effect of emulative consumption takes over, and the vice of vanity becomes the source of public benefit. "This emulation and continual striving to outdo one another," says Mandeville, "sets the poor to work, adds spurs to industry, and encourages the skillful artificer to search after further improvements." [81]

British sociologist David Lockwood has recently described some of the contemporary consequences of these same "pull" factors after two hundred years in operation.[82] He roughly divides the British working class into two kinds of industrial communities: "traditional" and "privatized." Traditional workers are found in older forms of industry such as mining, docking and shipbuilding and live in small towns or working-class enclaves where their horizons do not extend much beyond the boundaries of their communities. Workmates are often neighbors and kin, and usually spend their leisure time together. Because the communities tend to be socially isolated and endogamous with low rates of spatial and social mobility, they also tend to be cohesive and to demand financial and personal support of traditional consumption patterns emphasizing "present-oriented conviviality." All know their place and no one gains status in the group by trying to be different or by spending on pretentious consumer goods.

Privatized workers, on the other hand, are spatially mobile and work in large, mass-production factories in big cities. They move around so much and are so socially isolated from one another in separate family units that they become literally strangers to one another. They seek status through conspicuous or "competitive" consumption and attach a high degree of importance to their standard of living and their ability to acquire material possessions.[83]

Again the crucial common denominator in these cases is the spatial mobility of Toffler's "transience." [84] But while Toffler carries the process to its logical extremes in his view of the future, transience has a history that parallels the industrial revolution. As families are torn from the small community and thrown into association with the anonymous other, personal property becomes increasingly important as an indicator of social position. Even before the industrial revolution, urbanization in England had resulted in considerable spatial mobility.[85] Rural families were migrating to London and other towns in large numbers after 1650, and many were even moving from one rural area to another. In the latter event, families tended to move from land-poor areas to those with more employment opportunities, especially those with rural industries. Rapid expansion of framework knitting in the east Midlands, for example, attracted many migrants. Some rural areas experienced a complete turnover in their populations within a single decade. As one effect of this transience, the English, by the time of the industrial revolution, were living predominantly in nuclear family units composed of parents and their unmarried children. Whether the nuclear-family pattern developed entirely as a result of spatial mobility is not yet clear, but it was a development highly propitious for privatized family life and its competitive consumption.

Had it not been for the privatization of English workers, the factory system would have had an even harder time overcoming their leisure preference than it did. As David Landes has shown, the preindustrial putting-out system was an indispensable stage leading to industrial capitalism.[86] It increased specialization, stimulated the demand for durable goods by reducing their market price, increased the population of towns, and absorbed the countryside into the capitalistic economy. But the system had reached its limits by the 18th century. Beyond a certain point, the work force preferred leisure to an increase in wages— the proverbial inverse elasticity of supply. Consequently during those periods when a manufacturer had the greatest opportunities to maximize profits, the available labor decreased. The owner also found it extremely difficult to prevent embezzlement of raw materials by workers who clandestinely processed them into products sold illegally for their own profit.

By organizing workers into coordinated units under the direct supervision of management, the factory system brought a degree of discipline and self-correction to the production process that was impossible under the old system. Laborers, however, were extremely reluctant to leave their cottages and small shops to enter the new mills, and, according to Landes, it took several generations for the factory system to create an efficient and punctual work force. But the new system made such unprecedented gains in productivity that reduced prices led to increased demand. Undoubtedly the factory system did more to solve the problem of worker motivation through its own expansion than through any disciplinary measures per se. By making available a greater variety of inexpensive goods that privatized workers could competitively consume, it became possible for work preference to increase gradually at the expense of leisure preference. In other words, it created conditions for a new kind of prestige-seeking game that eventually replaced the older traditional forms.

As Boeke pointed out with regard to the traditional sector of the "dual" society, community opinion is a strong determinant of standards and values.[87] If a Madurese farmer, for example, considers a bull ten times more valuable than a cow, it is not because the bull is that much more useful in a Capitalist Man sense. On the contrary, the bull's value is determined by the prestige it brings its owner at the local bull races; its value is determined by idiosyncratic conditions typical of multiecological man. In a relatively undisturbed traditional community, Capitalist Man values may intrude only very slowly on the older ones. And as anthropologist Clifford Geertz has shown with regard to Java, the dual society was deliberately preserved in Indonesia by Dutch colonial policy.[88] Afraid that opening up Indonesia as an extensive market for industrial goods would only bring it under increasing British or Japanese influence, the Dutch kept "the natives native" while getting them to produce for world markets through corvée labor on Dutch plantations. Tradition was not disrupted by transience, and villagers were not introduced to competitive consumption.

In the Guatemalan highlands a situation accidentally similar to that of Dutch Indonesia was studied some twenty years ago by anthropologist Manning Nash.[89] A textile factory had existed in the Indian community of Cantel since 1876, but it had changed traditional lifeways very little. The eight hundred workers employed by the factory came from those families with the least land. Land scarcity had "pushed" them into factory employment of a traditional-worker kind without transience or privatization of consumption. Factory raw materials were shipped into the community and textile products shipped out with no effect on local marketing or retailing.

Comparing Canteleño factory workers with Canteleño farmers, Nash found the level of living of the two groups much the same although wage goods such as bicycles, wrist watches, and radios were more common among the former. Factory workers also consumed more high-priced food and on festive occasions were more expensively dressed. But if factory workers were showing a greater ability than farmers to acquire new private-property incentives, they were nevertheless just as inclined to retain traditional social rewards. Not only did they participate just as much as farmers in the annual religious fiestas, but due to their higher incomes they actually contributed more than the farmers to their financial support.[90]

While this Guatemalan factory had made possible some new personal-property incentives, in the main it had adapted to the traditional prestige system more than it had changed it. The history of the factory was a history of concessions to worker convenience as management attempted to reduce personnel turnover. A system of four-hour shifts was instituted so Canteleños could cultivate their small plots or perform domestic duties. Workers who became fiesta functionaries were given leaves of absence, and during Easter week the factory shut down completely. Protected by high government tariffs, the factory adapted to its tradition-oriented labor force without sacrificing its competitive position; it had none. It never researched its markets and changed products only when retailers complained of overloaded inventories. It did no cost accounting of its production or plant efficiency and kept no record of absenteeism. While Nash was there, a government commission spent six weeks going over the factory's books, but it left completely unable to figure out how the company set its prices.[91] Obviously this was not the competitive kind of industrialization that characterized early 19th-century England. Instead of subtitling his book "The Industrialization of a Guatemalan Community," Nash could just as accurately have labeled it "The Deindustrialization of a Factory by a Guatemalan Community."

When I visited Cantel in 1970, I found the factory extensively modernized.

Nearly all the equipment had been replaced since Nash's time; the work force had been cut 25 percent, and Canteleños were now eager to secure factory employment. Significant changes had also taken place in community consumption patterns, but the factory had had little or nothing to do with these changes.

A "Catholic Action" attack on the native *cofradía* or fiesta system by the local clergy had produced an effect quite the opposite of that intended. Instead of increasing Catholic devotion, it had gained many new adherents for the local Protestant movement, and a new "Protestant" life style was spreading throughout the community. Families were giving up such vices as liquor and Catholic religious festivals to save for improvements in family living and investments in family enterprises. Everyone was giving more attention to their children's education and to the purchase of a wider range of consumer goods. The traditional system of fiesta sponsorship with its "conspicuous-giving" expenses had been replaced with a formal contribution system (*hermandad*) involving radical reductions in expenses.

A major catalyst in the change was the new paved highway passing Cantel on its way from Quezaltenango to the Pacific coast. Regular bus service provided ready access to the city, where many families were sending their children for further education. There, too, Canteleños could observe and emulate the rising affluence of enterprising Indian families, many of whom now owned important shops along the main thoroughfare.

A few hours' drive to the north of Cantel, the highland Indian town of San Pedro Sacatepéquez has recently undergone more drastic changes than Cantel and without the presence of any large factory. According to Waldemar Smith, who studied the area for two years, economic development in San Pedro enjoyed a broader base than in Cantel through the active participation of many small entrepreneurs.[92] The highway system again was a crucial factor in opening the town to new marketing opportunities. Many San Pedranos became truckers, starting out with small second-hand vehicles and ending up with several large trucks and their own warehouses. The international market for handicraft textiles stimulated expansion of the weaving, tailoring and knitting industries and a putting-out system reminiscent of preindustrial England.

San Pedro entrepreneurs showed a strong tendency to forego purchases of personal property while investing in the productive property essential to the growth of their enterprises. According to Smith, a clear preference for "conspicuous investment" preceded conspicuous consumption. While building a business, the entrepreneur took considerable pride in the visibility of productive property, and Smith's informants speculated that in a country as rich as the United States every citizen surely had at least one big truck. Once San Pedro entrepreneurs had their businesses on a firm footing, however, they would begin to improve their houses, buy new furniture and wear more stylish clothes.[93]

As San Pedro interests turned more and more to conspicuous investment in productive property and conspicuous consumption of personal property, the traditional pattern of fiesta consumption changed radically. Some fiestas were abandoned completely, and others were changed to the brotherhood (herman-dad), dues-paying form of financial support modeled on the modern Guatemala City pattern. Occurring first in San Pedro proper, the changes soon spread to the surrounding villages and hamlets as well.[94]

The San Pedro example illustrates at the municipal level a process of development that took place on a regional scale in northwest Mexico during the late 1950's. Don Braulio was right when he complained that Sonora was joining the rat race of conspicuous consumption. For those who have had the opportunity to watch northwestern Mexico develop over the past 30 years as I have, the transformation has been almost unbelievable.[95] Desert villages have turned into modern towns and cities, and a network of paved roads covers an area that when I first saw it after World War II had none at all. Cars and trucks still forded the major rivers when the water was low and boarded hand-drawn auto ferries when it was high. Not long after World War II the Mexican government began damming the rivers that cut across the Sonoran desert between the Sierras and the Gulf of California and began building vast irrigation, road, and public-power networks. Hundreds of thousands of acres of thorn forest were gradually converted into rich agricultural land cultivated by ejidatarios (land-reform beneficiaries) and small private farmers.

These developments increased incomes and business opportunities dramatically over a wide area and attracted immigrants from many parts of Mexico. Conspicuous consumption was not entirely new to most of these people, but prosperity increased it by making the game available to an expanding number of players who gravitated in greatest numbers to the towns where the game was most intense. As the towns grew in size and impersonality so did the importance of the symbols of affluence. These communities became a meeting ground for individuals who no longer knew each other's family background. Social mobility became a strong ideal and families jockeyed for position in the status hierarchy. And as manufactured goods became cheaper and more abundant, even the rural areas began to purchase them and to sacrifice their traditional patterns of social and ritual consumption.

Townspeople distinguished three social classes which they labeled "first," "second," and "third." The third class was made up largely of manual laborers or owners of very small farms. In the second class were owners of moderate size farms, owners of small stores and repair businesses, and office workers. Professional people, owners of large farms, owners of big stores, and so on, made up the first class. Wealth, education, and success in business or farming determined the family's social position and the social clubs it was allowed to join. Club membership was the most visible criterion for locating people in the class system, and a family's life style, the symbol of its business success, was the key to club membership. Competitive consumption had become a major game in the towns and a game played particularly hard by second-class families and the socially mobile.

Major activities of the clubs were the dances and social events at which courtship could take place under well-chaperoned conditions. Families became more club conscious as their daughters approached marriageable age and grew increasingly concerned with their social image. At this point in the family life cycle the greatest effort was made to fix up the house and provide it with new furnishings. The rising affluence and productivity of the region created an atmosphere of such financial optimism that consumer credit became as readily available as investment capital. A credit chain developed that enabled the entrepreneur not only to invest in the expansion of his enterprise but to extend credit to his clientele. Even Indians and mestizos in the rural villages could buy bicycles and radios with small down payments and save for consumption after the fact. As David Landes has noted for the growth of domestic consumption in 18th-century Britain, mobility is ambiguous in its effects with respect to consumption rates.[96] While some people are frugally saving for the climb ahead, others are ostentatiously consuming to announce their arrival. In Sonora, probably more than in San Pedro, the booming economy and expansion of credit made it possible for the socially mobile to announce their arrival while still in the act of climbing.

Recently, Frank Parkin has criticized what he calls the "status-seeking thesis" of such writers as Vance Packard and C. Wright Mills.[97] He does not believe that status in a modern stratification system is achieved through the ostentatious display of personal property. "Reputational status" among class peers may be affected by such behavior but not the "system of ranked positions" which makes up a "national prestige structure." In other words, competitive consumption may become a very serious game within a middle class or a working class without actually affecting the boundaries between them. Competitive consumption is not aimed at those boundaries, for people do not normally try to emulate the life style of social strata above them; they compete with the flesh-and-blood inhabitants, the Joneses and Fulanos, of their immediate world. Parkin, moreover, follows Lockwood in stressing the utility of consumer goods and feels that the status-seeking argument emphasizes their symbolic function to such a degree that their usefulness is almost totally forgotten.

Parkin has made a valuable point. The socialist and capitalist countries both have elites which enjoy a different life style from the masses. But it is not their personal property that determines their status; their status determines their personal property. Both elites occupy their superior position by virtue of control over productive property. The reason personal-property incentives are not very helpful in understanding stratification systems, however, is the very reason that makes them so important for understanding economic growth. The competitive and utilitarian consumption that takes place among peers or near peers stimulates the demand side of the market and presumably the productivity of the workers.

Psychological experiments have shown that individuals are more likely to dislike competitors who narrowly defeat them than competitors who surpass them by a wide margin.[98] Ego tends to view the person who beats him by a wide margin as someone too different for meaningful comparison. But the person who narrowly wins threatens one's self-esteem and can readily become the recipient of strong dislike. These research results support the view that keeping up with the Joneses is a form of competitive emulation much more likely to occur among peers than between persons of differing social strata.

In Sonora, for example, when neighbors complimented a family on its new refrigerator and quickly added, "But we are getting a bigger one," they were all persons of the same peer group. This behavior on the part of friends and neighbors living in a growing new suburb of Obregón or Navojoa would fit Parkin's category of "reputational" status seeking. The behavior of the women in Mandeville's chain of emulation also fits this category. The wife of the laborer emulated the dress of the barber's wife—not that of the ladies at court. The first was surely closer to her means while sufficient to put her above her peers; she had no dream of surpassing the merchant's wife.

When an Indian in a Sonoran village, however, buys a new wrist watch and expensive clothes to impress the city people with whom he does occasional business, he is engaging in a type of reputational status seeking quite different from that which was traditionally pursued in the village. In the old days he would have sponsored religious festivities and thereby spent his savings on ceremonial consumption to raise reputational status within the community. Now the successful Indian entrepreneur cares more about his reputation within the wider regional context; and as he does, highly visible personal-property items such as watch, clothes, and pickup truck become more instrumental to his goals than ceremonial or social consumption. Both personal and productive property become an increasingly effective material instrument for reputational status seeking as an individual shifts reference group from a traditional context of high social visibility and high interpersonal familiarity to one involving the interpersonal relations of transience with their greater anonymity, lower social visibility and lack of personal familiarity.

Those scholars are right, however, who warn us not to forget the utilitarian aspects of personal property while focusing on the reputational status seeking of competitive consumption. One of the greatest motivational engines of the civilization of capitalism has been the double reinforcement effect of personal property. A Sonoran household acquiring its first refrigerator in 1958 would now consume more fresh meat and dairy products and could enjoy cold drinks at the peak of the desert summer. The fact that it was temporarily the envy of other households who had not yet saved enough for the down payment was also a strong source of pride and satisfaction. This powerful combination of incentives has proven strong enough everywhere to overwhelm easily the misgivings of a few Don Braulios.

It would be just as wrong, however, to overlook the social-incentive aspects of personal property by blindly emphasizing utility. To overlook reputational status seeking in the acquisition of utilitarian personal property would result in underestimating one of the most important tendencies of the civilization of capitalism: the tendency for social incentives to take a more material and private form. The diversified status-seeking behavior of primitive man was more directly social than that of Capitalist Man. But when we stress the material incentives of the civilization of capitalism, we often forget that utilitarian satisfactions are only one part of the package. Nor is it easy to determine the relative weight of these two satisfactions in any particular case. Given that in a society in which automobiles are owned privately by nearly all families, these artifacts can be said to have a certain universal utility. But when a small car can perform most of the utility functions of one of the larger models so wasteful of energy, raw materials, and atmosphere, is the demand for the latter dictated more by the utilitarian side of Capitalist Man materialism or the status-seeking side? In modern Capitalist Man society is it ever possible to speak of a material incentive per se? If this question is not always in mind when distinguishing between material and social incentives, the arbitrary nature of the distinction is too easily forgotten.

As we have seen, transience, or the spatial movement of peoples, enhances the social-incentive value of property. But it must also be remembered that as the civilization of capitalism matures and the number of employees increases in proportion to the number of self-employed, the social-incentive strength of productive property loses out to the social-incentive strength of personal property. As noted above, in the first half of the 19th century 80 percent or more of the working population of the United States was self-employed, mostly as farmers or small businessmen who were in a position to derive prestige from the display of productive property. As late as 1875, when Charles Nordhoff published his description of 19th-century communes, he considered the chief danger of the trade-union movement its acceptance of "hireling" status as permanent.[99] For American workers ever to give up the hope of achieving independence through the acquisition of productive property would be one of the greatest disasters that could strike our nation. Yet by mid-20th century the condition of a century earlier had reversed itself, and 80 percent of the working population of the United States had become employees. What 19th-century Americans had viewed as a possible future calamity became everyday reality for Americans of the 20th century.

Sonoran development in the 1950's was also characterized by a high percentage of self-employed families again in farming and small business. And again these families took great pride in the visibility of productive property such as retail stores, pop-bottling plants, movie theaters, transport trucks, farm machinery, warehouses, and so on. While it was true that a family's class position depended on its social-club affiliations, which in turn depended on the life style it presented to the community, it was also true that each family's life style, its consumption and accumulation of personal property, depended on its wealth in productive property. There were farmers, for example, in all three social classes, but only wealthy farmers with large holdings were normally found in the first class. Similarly, there were retail merchants in the first and second classes, but the first class included only the largest and most important.

Parkin's qualifications with regard to competitive consumption certainly hold true for Sonora. First, there was a strong utilitarian bent to this consumption, even the domestic variety. The convenience of indoor plumbing, refrigerators, and gas stoves, for example, was obvious to everyone. Second, the emulative behavior involved did not of itself determine social-class categories. In fact, this behavior if anything tended to blur class lines by extending the symbols of affluence and success and by strengthening the regional conviction that most families could progress with thrift and hard work and eventually become part of an amorphous, comfortable Mexican middle class.

Fifteen years ago the Sonoran case inspired me with considerable optimism about the future of developing countries. I wrote a book which in retrospect seems very Mandevillian.[100] The status-seeking pursuit of property for conspicuous display was described in the satirical terms of Thorstein Veblen. But like Mandeville, I saw this "vice" as working for the long-term public benefit, and I hoped that other countries could follow Mexico's example in developing first those areas which offered the greatest potential response by small entrepreneurs to social-overhead capital investments such as power dams, irrigation systems, and roads. And like John Maynard Keynes, who voted to let the hell of materialistic competitiveness go on long enough to lead the world "out of the tunnel of economic necessity into the daylight of abundance," I voted to encourage it everywhere for the same reason.[101]

Unfortunately, northwest Mexico was an unusual case which for two reasons had little applicability to other underdeveloped areas even in Mexico itself. First, it was an area with vast quantities of underutilized land that needed only roads and irrigation to make it highly productive. Add to this the new, high-yielding wheat varieties developed for this area, and the salutary effects on income and productivity are staggering. Few places in the world provide an opportunity to apply multidirectional technological inputs to such good effect.

Second, competitive consumption in Sonora was stimulating the enthusiastic participation of a different kind of incipient "middle sector" than in most of the Third World. The Sonoran middle was more like early 19th-century English and Anglo-American middles. In most of the Third World, however, the term "middle class" applies to a life style for which contemporary United States and Western Europe act as models. But it seldom applies to a true middle sector; families that Americans and Europeans regard as "middle class" are really privileged elites in their countries. Moreover, they are predominantly employees, not farmers and small businessmen.

Since the middle of the last century when most of the working population was self-employed, the United States, as we have said, changed into a nation of employees. Conspicuous consumption has far less opportunity or reason to include productive property than it did a hundred years ago or than it still

does today in southern Sonora. When the elites of Third World countries emulate the modern American middle class, they are emulating the behavior of
affluent employees, not ambitious entrepreneurs juggling their budgets between
"climbing" and "arriving."

Let us examine the case of incipient, social-class formation in Jos, a small
city of Nigeria, described by Leonard Plotnicov.[102] At the time of his study an
elite had formed in this community comprised of those families with the most
wealth, who held the most prestigeful occupations, who were the most European in their speech and life style, and who belonged to a particular local social
club that admitted only this elite. What is interesting about this case and most
different from the Sonora example is the fact that the members of the Jos elite
were predominantly bureaucrats. In addition, the elite included some independent
professional people and a few wealthy entrepreneurs. Many of the bureaucrat
families had lived abroad, and these formed the core of the elite. Of the local
business entrepreneurs only the most wealthy were allowed into the private club
mainly to enhance its economic viability. "Wealth" within this elite as a whole
referred primarily to personal property and life style rather than to productive
property. Jos exemplifies the diffusion of the contemporary employee life style
of the affluent Western World to a Third World setting.

Stanislav Andreski, in separate books on· Africa and Latin America, attacks
what he calls the "parasitism" of the administrative bureaucracies that make
up the bulk of the "middle classes" or elites in the Third World "kleptocracies." [103] Although in Latin America these so-called middle classes often include many active business entrepreneurs and farmers, they are comprised
mostly of public-administration bureaucrats who contribute little to productivity while milking their countries for their own competitive-consumption
purposes. In Africa there are even fewer productive members within these
elites than in South America; bureaucrats illegally accumulate small fortunes
worth many times over the salaries they are paid while struggling traders live
miserably by comparison. Frequently educated in Europe and America, the
members of these elites mimic the middle-class life styles they have seen abroad
and return home to consume in ways "lavish" and "ruinous" for their own
countries.

Here in the context of modern Third World underdevelopment we come
back to the zero-sum view of personal property held by Jean-Jacques Rousseau
and, as we shall see, by utopian Thomas More. As described by Andreski, competitive, ostentatious consumption is pursued by a privileged bureaucratic elite
at the expense of the masses. This kind of conspicuous consumption is more
like that of the ancient agrarian state than the positive-sum variety of our English, San Pedro, and Sonoran examples.

Many in the middle-class Third World elite fit also into Andre Gunder
Frank's category of "lumpenbourgeoisie." [104] By pushing the production and
exportation of raw materials rather than the expansion of internal markets, the
lumpenbourgeoisie foster "lumpendevelopment." The latter is very similar to

the dual-economy development mentioned above concerning Indonesia. In this kind of development most of a Third World country's natural and human resources are exploited for the benefit of foreign and indigenous corporations. These employ a managerial bureaucracy of native lumpenbourgeoisie whose vested interests insure the perpetuation of lumpendevelopment policies. Even when local industries are supported, the durable goods they produce seldom reach the masses, but are consumed predominantly by the elite "middle classes," the lumpenbourgeoisie. For Frank, the only solution is armed rebellion by the masses followed by the building of a socialist state.

For a socialist solution to the problems of Third World modernization, Bernard Kiernan believes China offers the most provocative model.[105] As Kiernan sees it, there is a "configuration of circumstances" in the emergent world that makes rapid modernization necessary and inevitable. Yet because of these very circumstances the emergent world cannot copy Western or United States development. In place of a class of lumpenbourgeoisie dedicated to the zero-sum game of luxury consumption, the Chinese way offers a core of tireless revolutionaries dedicated to the positive-sum welfare of the collectivity. Without the gross inequities of productive and personal property inspired by the capitalist route, all members of the socialist state advance together. Now we are back in part to Plato's guardians and in part to Etienne Cabet's progressive view of utopia.

Wheelwright and McFarlane, two sympathetic observers of the "Chinese road" to socialist development during the Cultural Revolution, likened Chinese Marxism to a religious movement of massive revivalist proportions.[106] They believed Mao directed an unprecedented experiment in the creation of a new moral order, but they were not sure how long his religious crusade could last. Would the "iceberg theory" critics prove right, they wondered. Was the moral ideology espoused only by a small percentage at the top of the social hierarchy who were completely unrepresentative of the Chinese masses? Was the other 97 percent of the population biding its time, waiting for some relaxation of ideology in order to indulge self-interest in a frantic pursuit of consumer goods? Maoism was endeavoring to restrain the population from the pursuit of "unreasonable" needs and was sponsoring regional autonomy and rural industrialization to keep people in their traditional villages and less subject to transience and privatization.

Is Maoism a modern version of an age-old utopian dream finally vindicated by the Chinese socialist experiment? Can property incentives be eliminated from the world of the future? How we answer such questions must depend to some degree on how we perceive the socialist catch-up game as being played. Is Chinese socialism truly a team game? Can such large masses of people participate in collective development as subject players, or are they only manipulated object players? Is it possible to "play" people on such a massive scale, or must we assume that the masses themselves are caught up in this collective pursuit of the collective good? Before coming back to these questions in Chapter 8, we examine smaller, less complicated team experiments in playing the game of eutopia.

And after seeing how the members of successful eutopian communities operate as subject players of the Millennial Man game, we look critically at utopian designs of this game for larger, state societies. This experience should better prepare us for the next step, our assessment of the eutopian socialist states in Chapter 8.

Summary

Increasing use of money, regional differentiation of production, and spatial mobility favored the growth and dissemination of a whole new game for Man the Player. The varied forms of social entrepreneurship that characterized the multiecological era were superseded by a game that employed and expanded material incentives everywhere. Using a quantitative language, universally intelligible, the new game disseminated easily. An era of rapid material progress ensued, one that engaged the masses to an unprecedented degree. Knowledge, technology, and human comforts expanded dramatically.

For the masses competitive consumption was a powerful inducement to switch from the older games, grouped by some authorities under the label "leisure preference," to the new so-called "work preference." The transition remained relatively slow until the quantity of inexpensive goods, expanding with the factory system, opened up the game. Acquisition of personal property not only brought new creature comforts, it also brought competitive status rewards. And in conjunction with increasing social anonymity among the players, competitive consumption had leveling tendencies that further amplified the competition. So many people began to mimic those just above them on the scale that everyone had to struggle—some even had to improvise—to keep ahead.

During the early phase of capitalist development, when a high proportion of family heads were self-employed, productive property tended to involve the same combination of utility and status rewards as personal property. In developed capitalism it persists mainly among the small, family businesses in the service and agricultural sectors. To the extent that its productive-property incentives diminish, the First World converges toward the Second. And as the Second World expands the incentive power of personal property among employees, and even productive property incentives in the service sector, the Second World converges toward the First. In Third World "kleptocracies," cheating, in combination with enormous social inequalities, may prevent the masses from full involvement in the capitalistic game. In such cases, a Millennial Man social movement that enjoins the masses—even if for only a few years—in a fight-self game of progress-with-equality may effect essential improvements.

Chapter Five

Nineteenth-Century Communes: Millennial Man in Eutopia (I)

THE PROPERTY INCENTIVES of primitive man were very rudimentary, as we have seen. They were attenuated by group land tenure, simple technologies, and the relative inelasticity of the major consumption good, food. The roots of productive- and personal-property incentives were present; but social incentives dominated, and when material goods became the instrument of social incentives, they tended to do so through conspicuous giving or social consumption rather than through conspicuous ownership or private consumption.

The attenuation of property incentives in the multiecological era was not due to any conscious policy; we must look elsewhere for deliberate "natural" experiments in the elimination of property incentives. Moreover, we must examine such experiments in interaction with the civilization of capitalism if we are to gauge their lesson for the monoecological era ahead. Though many persons have written of imaginary utopias that have outlawed such incentives, the number of real-world Millennial Man experiments which have successfully done so have been few indeed. For this reason the handful for which we have anything approaching reliable data have an importance far out of proportion to their numbers.

Our interest here is restricted primarily to the communal, Millennial Man eutopias in which all productive property was held in common and all personal property distributed according to needs defined equitably and minimally for the entire society. Such community experiments enable us to see how individuals can operate as subject players in an intensive, team-played game of eutopia. Furthermore, we are interested only in those eutopias which lasted long enough that we can fairly credit them with finding successful alternatives to property incentives. Of the 8 eutopian movements considered here and in Chapter 6, none lasted less than 35 years while 3 lasted a hundred or more. The Shakers became a communal movement about 1800 and were still a thousand strong at the beginning of this century. The Rappites adopted communism in 1805 and did not dissolve until 1905. The Zoarites were communists from 1819 until their demise in 1898, a life of about 80 years. The True Inspirationists of Amana, Iowa, had been communists approximately 90 years when they became a corporation in 1932. The famous Oneida community, however, had been a commune only 37 years when, in 1881, it also made the switch from commune to corporation. Although the Hutterites first took up communism in Europe in 1528, their North American communes are only a hundred years old; but of all the 19th-century communes they are the only ones that are still strong and prosperous today. Except for 12 Shaker ladies who live in the 2 surviving communities at Canterbury, New Hampshire, and Sabbathday Lake, Maine, the Shaker movement today is virtually over.

In Chapter 6 we examine 2 more contemporary commune movements, both of them Israeli. Of these, the kibbutz is the older and better known. The average age of the 225 kibbutzim in existence is almost 30 years, but the oldest kibbutz is over 65. The moshav-shitufim communes are much younger than the kibbutzim and far fewer in number, but the oldest is now 40 years old and therefore well above our 35-year minimum.

The total population of our communal farming communities past and present is infinitesimal in comparison with world population figures. Maximal estimates for all 19th-century and Israeli communes at their population peaks would total about 200,000, about half of whom are living in Israeli communes today. If we eliminate the 19th-century communes that lasted less than 10 years, the total would not reach 140,000 souls of whom the living communists (Hutterite and Israeli) would comprise about 90 percent. Communal farming communities that have lasted more than one generation have indeed been rare.

Despite the relative insignificance of their numbers, these successful commune movements have profoundly influenced human thinking. Even before the middle of the 19th century Friedrick Engels was using the Shakers, Rappites, and Zoarites as empirical evidence that communism could be economically successful.[1] The people in these communities did not fight for individual possession of their common property, nor did they avoid hard and unpleasant manual labor, the two major practical arguments against theoretical communism in Engels's day. Not only had communist society been proven practical by these experiments, said Engels, but in direct competition with capitalism, communism had clearly outperformed it.

Even allowing for some exaggeration on Engels's part, how was such a thing possible? Had man at last achieved a state of nonreciprocal altruism? As we see, successful communes all make powerful use of social incentives, and in this regard are like traditional communities. They maintain high visibility of membership and employ rewards and punishments that are strongly selective.

But our communes are much more deliberate and self-conscious in these procedures than traditional communities. The successful commune is an intentional community which begins as a social movement with a high degree of membership commitment. Subject playing of the team game is intense during this high-commitment phase, and the organization that develops during it determines how well the community will endure once the original social-movement stimuli have disappeared.

Martin Buber, as we note in Chapter 2, looks to some sort of federation of communal communities like the kibbutzim as the answer to world problems. Although he does not mention Rousseau, the virtues of the communal community, as he sees it, seem close to Rousseau's requisites for a "true democracy." [2] According to Rousseau, however, true democracy could never be more than an ideal, for he doubted if any real-world society could meet his requirements. He did not live to see the 19th-century communes, but they came remarkably close to meeting them.

Rousseau's first requirement for a true democracy is small size. The "state" would have to be small enough for everyone to assemble readily and frequently together in a town-meeting type of legislative body and small enough for everyone to know everyone else quite intimately. Here he is stipulating what we earlier termed conditions of social predictability, and as we see below, the successful communes achieved these conditions remarkably well.

Second, the culture of true democracies would have to be relatively simple and unsophisticated. This requirement is to spare them the disruption of unnecessary forensics and complex economic problems. The only one of our 19th-century eutopias that does not clearly fit this requirement is Oneida, and it had the briefest lifespan of all.

Third, for equality to prevail both in rights and authority, it would be necessary for a true democracy to have "a large measure" of social and economic equality. Note that Rousseau does not insist on absolute equality, for he never considers the capacity for absolute equality except in that hypothetical state of nature in which everyone is completely self-sufficient. Here again our 19th-century eutopias fit the requirements. All maintained highly egalitarian living standards, yet there were perceptible status differences in all of them.

Finally, Rousseau insists that in such a democracy citizens must live without luxury. Here he follows in the footsteps of Plato and Thomas More by insisting on an austere level of reasonable need, for luxury "corrupts both the rich and the poor." All of our 19th-century eutopias fulfill this requirement; in fact their insistence on a simple, egalitarian level of reasonable need is one of their most salient characteristics prior to change or decline.

If these eutopias could be considered Rousseauean it would only be in the sense that they embody features the father of antiprogress considered desirable, not in the sense that he considered them feasible. The very rarity of our successful communes supports Rousseau's judgment that any such combination of characteristics is surely improbable. It is all the more important, then, that we endeavor to determine the circumstances which favored them as well as those leading to their demise or alteration.

First, however, it is necessary to make clear what is implied by a communal farming eutopia and how it differs from collective or corporate farming. Second, for historical background the characteristics of that famous, widespread commune of the Middle Ages, the monastery, are briefly reviewed. Third, a brief historical profile of our six eutopias is an indispensable prerequisite to their analytic comparison. Fourth, conditions of social predictability will be compared among the six eutopias. Fifth, a similar comparison is made of membership commitment, for it is unusually strong commitment that gives these eutopias their intentional and organizational quality and distinguishes them most from traditional communities. Finally, we examine the reasons why five of these successful 19th-century communes eventually failed and why one of them has survived.

Communal, Collective, and Corporate Farming

With the exception of Oneida our eutopias are, or were, primarily farming communities. All but the Hutterites, however, developed some industries as they matured, a trend true of the Israeli communes as well. All members of a commune work according to their ability, and all products or profits are shared by the members according to need. So far as incentives are concerned, these eutopias are truly Millennial Man societies. Material or property incentives are minimal.

The land worked by communal farmers is held in group tenure although it may be leased (Israeli communes) as well as owned (19th-century communes). Production is carried out collectively on the land without subdividing it into individual or household plots. All other productive property in the form of livestock, machinery, and so on, is collectively owned although responsibility for the care and maintenance of animals and equipment is individually delegated.

Much of what noncommunists—even socialists—normally think of as personal property is collectively owned by communal farmers. While the kibbutz, in its early years, even tried to eliminate private possession of clothing, the clothing of all communal farmers is among their few personal effects. Even furniture is collectively owned, at least nominally, before societies begin to change or break down. Housing is often in the form of dormitories, as among the Shakers and Oneida Perfectionists, or in the form of apartments as among the Hutterites and kibbutzim, although separate family domiciles are also common (that is, shitufim, Zoarites, and Amana Inspirationists). In the case of individual family dwellings, however, the units are standardized so that no family occupies a better home than any other. And no family can alter its house without community permission, since the building and its furnishings are community property. Communal farmers, moreover, are strictly limited in their consumption habits by community-determined levels of need. No one is free to purchase consumer goods indiscriminately; members are allowed only those items approved by the entire community, and these are usually allotted in equal amounts to all families or individuals.

Collective farmers practice group land tenure also except where collectives are formed by associations of individuals pooling their private holdings. In such cases the collective may rent the land from the members. Production on the group-held (owned or leased) land or the pooled individual plots is carried out collectively. Collective farmers, however, are not rewarded according to need as are communal farmers, but are rewarded according to work. In this sense they conform to Socialist Man incentives not those of Millennial Man. In other words, harvests or profits are divided among members in proportion to their labor contributions. While an association of collective farmers jointly owns its productive equipment just as do communal farmers, it does not collectivize its consumption. Members are free to spend their share of the collective income as they are able or see fit. Nor does the collective necessarily attempt to establish consumption norms or levels. (We examine socialist and Third World collective farming experiments in Chapter 9.)

In corporate farming the reward system is that of Capitalist Man. Income is distributed among the members according to work and capital. In cases where the members perform some or most of the farm labor themselves, they may distribute part of the income in shares proportionate to work just like collective farmers, or they may pay themselves a salary according to work like capitalist farmers. Usually, however, a corporate farming association hires much of its labor and may reach the point where it hires all of it. In that case the members become collective owners or stockholders, and they divide income entirely according to capital.

A division of income according to capital is like that of a joint stock company. The value of each farmer's contribution of land and equipment to the corporate pool constitutes his percentage of the total capital, his "stock" as it were; and this stock determines his share of the annual net income. Unequal shares result when members of a corporate farming association pool individually-owned lands of unequal size and value. When lands of a corporate farm are held by its members under group-land-tenure arrangements, members usually have equal rights to the land or "capital." In that case members share equally in the net income provided all work is done by hired laborers. This situation can occur in the case of land-reform collectives, for by definition a collective farm automatically becomes corporate when the members hire others to do the work and then divide income in equal parts among themselves after paying wages.

Almost without exception, collective farms are instigated by government action whereas communal and corporate farms are the product of voluntary, spontaneous association. As we see in Chapters 8 and 9, membership in the collective farms of the Socialist World is obligatory while in Third World or First World experiments it is voluntary. But in the latter instances government plans the collective organizations and provides members with such inducements as free land, cheap credit and subsidized farm machinery. However, governments that try to form communes—even socialist governments—fail, as the Russian and Chinese examples show. In Israel, government has collaborated well with kibbutzim and shitufim, but neither type of community was originally designed or initiated by government any more than any of the 19th-century communes were.

Corporate farms are primarily a voluntary and spontaneous type of organization also. Recently, however, England and Spain have provided inducements such as inexpensive credit and farm machinery to coax small farmers into pooling their resources in corporate form. And some Third World collective farming experiments have evolved into corporate farms although not by government plan or intent.

In the Second (socialist) World when entire communities are collectivized, a collective farm may be coterminous with a village. But Third World collective farms are usually associations rather than residential communities. Communes, on the other hand, are very definitely residential; in fact, community life is essential to that very practice which gives the commune its unique character, collective consumption.

As we see below, it is the community life of the farm commune that makes possible the conditions of social predictability without which the commune would be unable to apply selectively its indispensable social incentives. During the most vigorous period of its life, a residential communal farm becomes the entire social world of its members. In contemporary sociological jargon, membership group and reference group become one and the same. But while this can be true of a traditional community as well, there is an intensity to commune membership that stems from its messianic or social-movement intentionality. The farming commune is an organization, and the commitment of its membership takes dimensions common to all organizations.

Authorities on organization James March and Herbert Simon have made five useful generalizations about individual commitment to a group.[3] According to them the strength of that commitment will vary directly with: (1) the number of individual needs satisfied within the group; (2) the frequency of interaction among its members; (3) the extent to which goals are shared among them; and (4) the prestige of the group or organization in the larger society. Conversely, the strength of individual commitment will vary inversely with: (5) the amount of competition among members.

Commitment is higher in a farming commune than in a traditional community or a collective farming association because collective consumption is such a vital part of its social-movement character. Collective consumption greatly intensifies all five dimensions of commitment. Because of it, nearly all goods in a commune are part of the collective good, and all are used to meet membership needs. No group could attempt to meet the needs of its members so completely without itself becoming a commune. One must remember, however, that as a social movement the farm commune also determines the limits or "reasonableness" of its members' needs and thereby maximizes its ability to satisfy them completely.

Again, because of collective consumption, commune members are seldom out of each others' sight. Collective production keeps them working together, but because of collective consumption they also eat together, prepare food together, pray together, plan together, relax together, and share the same amusements. Some observers abhor the lack of individual privacy, so pervasive and constant is the high frequency of interaction.

By meeting the same needs for all members and by requiring continual adherence to the limits of reasonableness it defines, collective consumption automatically reinforces the unanimity of group goals and simultaneously makes everyone's devotion to them continually visible to everyone else. Any member who appears lax in this devotion is readily suspect and a target of negative social sanctions.

Farming communes usually arise under conditions of persecution that can have an effect similar to group prestige. Persecution raises the group visibility within the larger society and makes it harder for members to withdraw. And as all alternatives are cut off, dependence on the commune is intensified. Later in its life, however, a successful commune often achieves a position of prestige in "the world" and is visited by famous and important "outsiders." In fact, visitors may increase to the point where permanent hotel facilities become one of the commune's more lucrative enterprises. But here again collective consumption is usually what makes the group most conspicuous and thereby a target either for persecution or respectful curiosity. Moreover, in the early social-movement phase of a commune the practice of collective consumption is likely to be an act of political protest against inequalities of wealth in the larger society—or at least it may be so perceived by the larger society; this in itself can invite persecution or harassment.

Finally, collective consumption in the commune stresses egalitarianism with distribution according to need. Leveling is deliberately practiced and competition deliberately discouraged. Probably no other human organization has ever been so successful in minimizing competitive consumption within its membership.

Background: The Monastery

Many years ago Karl Kautsky argued that collective consumption rather than collective production was the primary instrument of primitive Christian communism.[4] Primitive Christianity was an urban phenomenon and did not seriously invade the countryside until the development of the monastic movement in Egypt and the Middle East during the fourth century. Even in ancient times collective production was made difficult by conditions of city life. Only in a rural environment did the movement come to include collective production.

The communism of early Christian congregations centered primarily around common meals. Common ownership of productive property would have been highly inconvenient for the urban artisans of the period while among free workers, slaves, peddlers, porters, and shopkeepers there was little on which to base collective production. Except for small groups the sharing of a common residence was equally difficult.[5]

Early Christians were predominantly lower class and in the urban environment were witnesses to the rise of a new kind of wealthy man, the merchant, who effectively increased ownership of durable goods through investment in land, buildings, ships, and even luxury goods. No longer a redistributive big man, this primeval capitalist truly seemed to increase wealth at the expense of his neighbors.[6]

Hatred of the rich by early Christians is especially evident in the Gospel of Saint Luke, which assigns the rich man to hell simply because he is rich and in which Jesus proclaims that a camel will pass through the eye of a needle before a rich man will make it into heaven. And the famous passage from The Acts of the Apostles (2: 44–45), "all that believed were together, and had all things common; and sold their possessions and goods, and parted them to all men, as every man had need," emphasizes renunciation of wealth or property and return to a redistributive economy. It illustrates again the primary concern of early Christianity with collective consumption, not collective production.[7]

As the urban congregations grew, the common meals became a symbolic ritual for many of the participants. To enhance the charity side of common meal taking, wealthy persons were admitted to the congregations in increasing numbers. But wealthy members had better food at home; so their participation in congregational activities met spiritual and social, rather than physical, needs. And as the economics of Christian charity became more complex with the increasing size and heterogeneity of the congregations, the administration became more formal and bureaucratic. The financial administrator or overseer (*episkopos*) became a full-time city bishop employed by the congregation.[8]

By early in the fourth century Christianity had been recognized by the state. It had a clerical bureaucracy and had become the religion of rich and poor alike. Primitive Christian communism now moved into the countryside in the form of a monastic movement outside the official church, which at first opposed it. Renouncing wealth or property, the movement renewed the early messianic revolt against the urban form of nonredistributive wealth. Since Christianity in the fourth century was still an urban phenomenon, the monks who invaded the pagan countryside were mainly from the cities.[9]

Many of the first monks were hermits or "anchorites," but quite early in the movement they started assembling in communities where they became "cenobites." Beginning with the cenobite communities organized by Pachomius in Egypt early in the fourth century, the monastic movement spread throughout the Middle East as well as to Italy and the islands of the Mediterranean by the century's end. The cenobite monasteries were often organized on the basis of trades although work was apparently individualistic rather than collective. As in the early urban congregations, the communism of the first monasteries was primarily in the form of collective consumption, a pattern probably true of the pre-Christian Essenes as well. But the rural environment and the tendency in many cases to achieve self-sufficiency encouraged the growth of collective production.[10]

After Benedict's influence early in the sixth century, European monasticism became much more formal than the Eastern variety. Work was sytematically organized in true collective fashion with each monk producing directly for the monastery although each was allowed to specialize according to his talents and aptitudes. And each did his share of all disagreeable and domestic duties such as cooking, washing dishes, and cleaning rooms no matter what his social background. Former nobles worked in the kitchens alongside former serfs. Monasticism now had a strong pre-Protestant work ethic with a positive emphasis on manual labor. It had become a true farming commune practicing collective production as well as collective consumption.[11]

The European monastic commune illustrates all the factors of social predictability and commitment so important in the 19th-century and Israeli communes. Each monastery had a candidacy period for novices. No one became a permanent member until the rest knew him well enough to feel sure he would work hard for the collectivity and not be a disruptive influence.[12]

Third-person controls probably included many positive social incentives for the hard-working, dedicated brother, but history records mainly negative incentives. Careless treatment of community property, laziness or malingering at work, lack of religious devotion, and "murmuring" against the rules of the order and the abbot were sufficient reason for negative sanctions. An errant brother was given two admonitions in private, first by another brother and then by the abbot. If these secret warnings failed to correct the behavior, the brother was given a public rebuke. He might, for example, be put in the "pillory of the lazy" on public display before the entire brotherhood to his embarrassment and shame.[13]

If none of this worked, the errant monk would be excommunicated. In its mildest form excommunication simply meant taking one's meals alone. In its severest form it meant total separation from the rest of the brethren during meals, prayer, and work. The errant brother was still expected to work as hard and long as everyone else, but he was assigned his own fixed task apart from the rest much like the treatment mentioned earlier for a lazy worker at a West African corvée work party. At all times the brethren avoided the excommunicated member as if he had the plague. Since the monastery was virtually the entire world for each of its members, during his excommunication a brother lived in a world that had turned its back on him. And to add to his shame, an excommunicated monk was forced to humiliate himself in other ways such as groveling face down in the dust at the door of the oratory as his fellows filed in or out. If the culprit still persisted in his errant ways, corporal punishment was administered; and if this too failed, he was expelled, the final and complete form of excommunication.[14]

As in the case of later successful farming communes the combination of collective production and collective consumption helped maintain a high degree of commitment among the brethren. This was particularly true in the case of the young monastery where the frugal austerities of daily life were acts of messianic devotion to the major principle of primitive Christian communism, renunciation of wealth and property. The limited needs of the monks were met entirely by the self-sufficient collective community. Working together, praying together, consuming together, the monks were a closed community maintaining a high degree of internal interaction and allowing little contact with the external world. Benedict, moreover, recognized the dangers of clique formation. He warned that little coteries of monks who regularly worked or dined together could become a group within a group, a faction that could too readily challenge the authority of the abbot.[15]

Given high frequency of interaction evenly distributed within the membership and given eternal vigilance against "murmurings" of subgroup dissension, the goals of the group must certainly have achieved a high degree of singlemindedness. As for the prestige of the monastery in the larger society, this undoubtedly varied from time to time and place to place, but in general its status was high throughout most of the Middle Ages.

Finally, internal competition was minimized by one of the primary tenets of the monastic community, the monk's total self-surrender through the renunciation of self and individual will. As some scholars have pointed out, the formal Benedictine commune ended up destroying the very individuality which had orginally given rise to monasticism during its earliest anchorite phase.[16]

But the individuality the monastery destroyed or sought to destroy kept reasserting itself throughout monastic history. The life cycle of a typical monastery began with a period of highly efficient collective production. A small group of dedicated monks needed little capital to clear new lands in some nearby frontier forest; and by living frugally as one collective household, they kept costs of production low. Then as their numbers grew, they could begin to take advantage of the differences in member aptitudes and achieve further economies of scale through internal specialization. Moreover, with group land tenure and collective ownership of all productive and personal property the community patrimony had an immortality that could not be lost or divided by inheritance. Inevitably the monastery became wealthy, and as it did, the members' earlier devotion to austerity and hard work began to relax. By now a village or town had grown up around the monastery with serfs and hired laborers available to perform work once done by the monks themselves. Even the dirty jobs of kitchen work and cleaning could be assigned to servants. And as the monastic commune gradually turned into a monastic corporation, the brother-stockholders began to individualize their consumption.[17]

In its pristine, messianic phase the monastic commune allowed no personal property. No monk could receive any gift from outside without permission of the abbot. Gifts were turned over to the abbot for distribution to all or for collective use. A monk could call nothing his own—not even his pen and writing paper. He did not even have room or space of his own; everyone slept in dormitories without screens and with the abbot in their midst.[18]

When a monastery reached the affluent stage, however, monks tended to have their own separate cells or rooms for privacy, sleeping, and the storing of personal possessions. These possessions inevitably grew in number and variety as permissiveness increased. In the most flagrant cases brothers even took mistresses and had personal servants. Occasionally younger monks would rebel against these evidences of corruption and would band together in a small messianic group to clear lands or drain swamps for a new monastery, thereby starting the whole cycle over again.[19]

The history of European monasticism after Benedict is a history of reform movements each trying to reassert the original Benedictine rules of austerity and organization. The last large-scale reform movement was that of the Cistercian or "white" monks which spread over Western Europe during the 12th and 13th centuries. This monastic order followed the same life cycle as its predecessors. It began as a reform movement stressing poverty, seclusion from the world and a strict, literal interpretation of the Rule of St. Benedict. It went further than its predecessors in renouncing the usual "feudal" sources of income such as mills, serfs, rents, and tithes. It resolved to accept land only for its own habitation and to work it with the manual labor of its own membership. But in coming upon the scene so late, the Cistercians found it difficult to keep apart from the rest of society. Even the initial endowments on which their monasteries were established frequently involved financial obligations to their benefactors. Unable to separate themselves economically from the world while slowly amassing wealth through their combination of Easternlike asceticism and hard work, they eventually strayed from the Rule like all the rest.[20]

As the monastic movement entered its final period of decline, it was replaced by the Dominican and Franciscan brotherhoods—movements which prohibited their members from even so much as setting foot inside a monastery. The friars devoted themselves to public service in the "world" and became the first Christian social workers in the slums of the growing cities.[21]

Even by the time of the Cistercians most of Europe's frontiers were gone. By the 14th century the population of Europe had reached its peak for the Middle Ages, and there was little frontier land left where rebellious young monks could readily start up new farming communes out of sheer fervor and hard work.[22] And as we saw in Chapter 4, the internal markets of Europe were greatly expanding during these centuries and with them the number and variety of durable goods available for private consumption. In early Christian times, as Karl Kautsky pointed out, there was little opportunity for what he called the "individualization of wants," the phenomenon of privatization. There was not the variety of consumer goods to tempt the devout from their life of austerity. Actually, Kautsky in this context was trying to explain the early demise of the 19th-century communes of the United States in contrast with the long history of medieval monasticism. But his insight applies equally well to late monastic times.[23]

Commune Profiles[24]

All six of our successful 19th-century communes began as Christian congregations and later adopted collective consumption and collective production in emulation of early Christian communism. While still congregations, there was a tendency, especially among those groups being harassed or persecuted, to share wealth and property. But the five congregations composed largely of peasants or farmers shifted easily into collective production. The shift proved particularly appropriate for the German separationist movements emigrating to the United States; they were homogeneous cohesive groups culturally and linguistically distinct from their new fellow citizens and were facing the tribulations of frontier-settlement conditions.

In all cases, however, when the groups formally organized as Christian communists, they adopted collective production simultaneously with collective consumption. It is only with the breakdown and change of these movements that the primacy of collective consumption asserts itself. As privatization of consumption undermines the social incentive structure, collective production either totally collapses or changes into corporate production. (This process of breakdown or transformation is reviewed below.) Here we briefly sketch the histories of our six commune examples.

The Shaker movement began late in the 18th century under the leadership of Ann Lees, known affectionately to her followers as Mother Ann. Convinced—after her four children died in infancy—that cohabitation was the source of all evil, Mother Ann became the leader of a celibacy-advocating sect of dissident Quakers in Manchester, England, in 1773. Moving to America the next year with a few followers, she arrived at a time when New England was still experiencing repercussions and recurrences of the Great Awakening religious revivals that had begun in 1734. Joseph Meachum, a lay preacher who led a 1779 revival in New Lebanon, later joined the new sect and became Ann's "first born son" in America. By 1784, two years after Mother Ann's death, the Shakers had become an American religious movement with Meachum at its head. Without his organizing genius and leadership ability over the next ten years, the sect might not have lasted until the 19th century, much less the 20th.

Under Meachum the Shaker movement shifted away from the proselytizing emphasis it had had under Mother Ann to one of communal life and separation from the world. By 1800 the sect had become a new American form of monasticism with 11 member "colonies" each divided into several "families" or communes. A commune consisted on the average of about 50 adults with men and women occupying separate dormitories. During the early years most of the children in the communes were those born to adult members before joining the order while later they were mainly orphans or apprentices adopted from the "world."

The beginning of the 19th century saw another period of religious activity, the Great Revival, which concentrated in the states of Kentucky, Ohio, and Indiana. The strange body movements and trancelike states that afflicted worshipers at these camp meetings resembled Shaker religious behavior, a fact which led the latter to send missionaries into Kentucky. The communal sect spread westward with the revival movements adding another 7 communities to those already established in New England and New York. About 1830 it totaled some 19 communities divided into 72 communes. Total population of the sect at its peak reached between 5,000 and 6,000 souls.

The Shakers began their gradual decline in the 1830's and by 1874, the year Charles Nordhoff made his census, membership had fallen to 2,415, roughly half the total at its peak. In 1891 there were still 1,728 members living in the 15 surviving communities. By 1950 only 4 communes with a handful of members remained, and by 1974 only 2 with a total of 12 members, all elderly women. Although the Shaker communal movement has endured 175 years, it was declining for 120 of them, the last three-fourths of its life. In addition to farming, their primary occupation, Shaker communes also manufactured various handicraft products including brooms, spinning wheels, plows, and baskets.

The second 19th-century group with which we are concerned arrived in the United States from Germany in 1804. Their leader, George Rapp, was a peasant preacher and a separatist from the Lutheran Church. Father Rapp's small society, at its largest only some 800 souls, has been known by a variety of names, Rappites, Rappists, Economites, and Harmonists. Like the Shakers, the Rappites began as a religious group and later adopted communism (1805). They too adopted celibacy (1807), and beginning about 1827 membership gradually declined in much the same fashion as the Shakers'. Unlike the Shakers, however, they began as a homogeneous ethnic group, most from the same place, Wurttemburg.

The group settled first at Harmony, Pennsylvania, 25 miles northwest of Pittsburgh. Deciding the land was not as fertile as they wished, the members sold all 9,000 acres with buildings and improvements for $100,000 (only half of which they collected) and in 1815 established New Harmony on 20,000 acres of land along the Wabash River in Indiana. Another 10 years later (1825), bothered by the malarial climate and difficulties with their neighbors, the Rappites again sold out, this time for $125,000. Moving back near their first home, they established the community of Economy, 16 miles down the Ohio River from Pittsburgh. The Indiana properties were purchased by Robert Owen, who established there his famous eutopian socialist community of New Harmony that was to last less than 3 years.

In Indiana the Rappites had developed a prosperous textile industry, which they now expanded at the expense of their agricultural enterprises. Only 3,000 acres of farmland were purchased at Economy mainly to meet their own food requirements. Dissension in 1832 led to the withdrawal of 200 members, about a third of the total membership. By 1862, 15 years after Father Rapp's death, there were less than 200 members left. When William Hinds visited Economy in 1876, most of the remaining 100 members were over 60 years of age. As in the case of the Shakers, celibacy obviously involved recruitment disadvantages, and after 100 years the society was liquidated (1905) and over a million dollars divided between its last 2 members.

German separatists from the same town of Wurttemburg established the Zoar (Ohio) community in 1817. Their leader, Joseph Bimeler (originally Baumeler), was also a preacher of peasant origins, and they too formed a communistic organization (1819) after establishing themselves in their new community. Celibacy was also practiced by this group; but in 1828 Bimeler decided to marry, and the rest soon followed his example. The Zoar society never totaled more than 500 souls, a third of whom died in a cholera epidemic about 1834. The community numbered 254 adults and children at the time of Hinds's visit in 1876 and 222 in 1898 when it dissolved.

On their 7,200 acres of land the Zoarites grew grains and fruit and raised both cattle and sheep. In addition they owned and operated a saw mill, two flour mills, and a woolen factory. Hinds estimated their worth in 1876 at three-quarters of a million dollars although at the time of breakup Randall appraised it at a third of a million. The commune had lasted 80 years.

A third German religious sect that emigrated to the United States and established a communal society after its arrival called itself The Community of True Inspiration. A major difference between this group and the previous ones was that it merely advocated celibacy; it never practiced it. From 1843 to 1846 the original 800 immigrants established their first American community, Ebenezer, on 5,000 acres of land about 6 miles from Buffalo, New York. They were later joined by other German immigrants, mainly from Ohio, and within 10 years totaled some 1,200 souls.

In 1854, the members agreed to communal ownership of all their property and initiated plans to move away from the contaminating influence of nearby Buffalo. A fertile but isolated 25,000-acre tract of land was purchased on the Iowa River 20 miles from Iowa City. Gradually the old Ebenezer estate was divided up and profitably disposed of while the new community of Amana was built and populated. By the time the transfer was completed in 1864, 6 villages had been constructed (Amana, West Amana, South Amana, High Amana, East Amana, and Middle Amana) and a seventh, the nearby village of Homestead on the Mississippi and Missouri Railroad, had been purchased outright.

The Amana community prospered even more than Ebenezer had, and shortly after the turn of the century numbered some 1,800 souls. Agriculture was the principal Amana enterprise in the early days, but its woolen and other industries increased so much in importance that by the early 1900's much of the farmland was being rented. In 1932 the society changed from a communal organization to a joint-stock company, and ownership was amicably divided among the remaining 1,400 Inspirationists.

The religious leader and organizational genius of the Amana society during its early days was Christian Metz. He was head of the sect in Germany before it emigrated, and he directed both moves. So well did he perform his job that the society endured as a commune almost 90 years. Moreover, in numbers it was stronger when it changed form than when it began.

The 37-year duration of Oneida (1844–1881) makes it the most short-lived of our 6 communes. Like the Shakers, the Oneida Perfectionists were comprised predominantly of English-speaking recruits from the native-born American population; they were not an immigrant group nor were they ethnically homogeneous in the same sense as the German communities. Moreover, they came from all walks of life. Many were farmers; occupations of the rest included bookkeeping, architecture, manufacturing, printing, shoemaking, clerking, and teaching. There was even a lawyer and a doctor. Instead of requiring or idealizing celibacy like the previous communes, Oneida practiced "complex marriage," in effect group marriage.

John Humphrey Noyes, founder of Oneida, attended Yale Divinity School and, at the young age of 22 in 1833 developed his own religious philosophy, a rejection of currently accepted notions of sin and eternal damnation. "Perfectionists" could be free of both. He began to collect a following in Putney, Vermont, where in 1840 he formed the Putney Association, at first a purely religious organization. In 1844, however, the association (28 adults and 9 children) adopted communism and established itself as a community on 500 acres of land. Two years later complex marriage was initiated, and by 1847 the incensed townspeople of Putney were charging Noyes with adultery. At this time a small group of Noyes Perfectionists was starting a communal settlement on Oneida Creek in Madison County, New York. Noyes transferred his Putney following there and in 1848 formed the Oneida Association with 87 adults and children. Over the next few years some 200 more persons joined the community.

Farming did not prove sufficiently profitable to sustain the community, and during its first ten years Oneida consumed almost half of the initial $100,000 capital contributed by its members. Very early, however, it began to expand its business ventures, and by the mid-1850's its manufacture of animal traps was doing well. Ten years later, in 1865, Oneida was a prosperous industrial center worth $185,000 and by the end of the next decade was worth more than $500,000.

In his later years Noyes began to withdraw into himself, and in 1877 he turned the management of the community over to a committee headed by his son, Theodore. Internal dissensions began, and one faction made an issue of

Noyes's practice of initiating the young girls into the sexual life of the community. The fact that most of them were indoctrinated shortly after the onset of menstruation made Noyes eligible for charges of statutory rape. In 1879 Noyes fled to Canada, and within two years the Oneida Community became a joint-stock company, Oneida Community, Limited.

In 1874, the very year that Charles Nordhoff was visiting all remaining communal societies in the United States, collecting the data for his famous book, *Communistic Societies of the United States,* the Hutterites were in the process of moving from Russia to the Dakota Territory. In that year, as Nordhoff discovered, there were still 7 established communal movements in the United States comprising together some 72 separate communities, all of which later dissolved or converted into joint-stock companies. But the Hutterites, who numbered less than 800 when they established their first 3 colonies between 1874 and 1877, had by 1974 grown to a population of 21,521 persons occupying 229 colonies in the United States and Canada. In size they are not only much larger than any of the other communal movements that existed in North America, they now surpass the total population of all those which preceded them. While they are only one-fifth the size of the total Israeli kibbutzim population, the latter have recruited their memberships from many lands; and the Hutterites, who rarely take converts, have increased their membership through a phenomenal birth rate and the effective indoctrination of their young.

Like the Mennonites and Amish, the Hutterites stem directly from the Anabaptist movement of the Reformation. By the early 16th century the breakdown of feudalism had left many landless persons, including artisans and craftsmen, ready to join these nonconformist groups some of which, like the Hutterites, believed in communal living. The Hutterites began as a strict group of Swiss Brethren opposed to war, taxes, and fighting. When asked to leave Nikolsburg, Moravia, in 1528 because they did not attend regular worship services, they were invited to nearby Austerlitz, where the liberal barons considered them ideal tenants for their estates. On the way they adopted communism and in Austerlitz set up their first common household, or Bruderhof. There they were joined by an Anabaptist leader from the Tyrol, Jakob Hutter, who adopted their communism, became their leader, and so effectively organized the new movement before being martyred in 1536 that the group took his name.

The Hutterites have endured over four hundred years of alternating periods of peace and persecution. Although they always had a reputation as good farmers and craftsmen and were in demand by landed nobility, they were repeatedly the object of persecution by church and state. Driven out of Moravia in 1547, they fled to Hungary, but there, too, the sympathetic lords were finally forced to expel them. After the Peace of Augsburg, between 1555 and 1593, the Hutterites enjoyed a "golden age" in Moravia where they established 85 Bruderhofs and grew to a membership of fifteen thousand. But when war broke out between Turkey and Austria in 1593, the Hutterites were raided by both armies, and by the end of the Thirty Years War, which followed, those Hutterites who had not been killed or carried off into captivity had been driven from Moravia to Slovakia where they began to abandon communal living in the late 17th century. By the 18th they were ripe for the Jesuit campaign to reconvert them to the Catholic faith, and after much harassment most of them joined the Church.

A few finally found refuge in Russia in 1770 as a result of Catherine the Great's liberal policies toward German immigrants who had advanced farming methods. But there, only a short time after they revived communal living, a change in the Russian attitude toward them led to their decision to emigrate to the United States. The earlier military exemptions granted by Catherine were rescinded by the universal military training act of 1872. At this time the United States and Canada were looking for good farmers; their plains and prairies were as yet only sparsely inhabited. President Grant personally assured the Hutterites that in time of war freedom of conscience would be respected.

In the United States, with some early financial help from the Rappites and the Amana Society, the Hutterites prospered until World War I when their German background and their refusal to bear arms made them the target of the patriotism of the time. The sadistic treatment of four Hutterite boys, first at Fort Lewis and then at Alcatraz and Leavenworth, which finally led to the death of two, is remembered by all Hutterites. The majority emigrated to Canada in the first few years after the war.

The Hutterites are communal farmers who live in small colonies, Bruderhofs, of about a hundred persons and, unlike many previous communal societies in North America, do not operate industries. They are excellent modern farmers, however, and are usually ahead of their neighbors in adopting the latest agricultural techniques. Like our other 19th-century American communalist societies they have found no conflict between their ideology and technological improvements in agriculture.

Social Predictability

Group Size and Leadership

As we saw in Chapter 2, conditions of social predictability (knowledge of other, system of procedures, and third-person control) make possible the provisioning of collective good in groups of considerable size when high visibility of individual contributions prevails. Visibility was a characteristic of most traditional communities, and most had means of intensifying that visibility for important events such as group labor. But typical traditional communities did not maintain visibility levels with the deliberateness of the monastic communities or our six 19th-century communes.

In size, our communes fall well within the range of traditional communities. A few of the largest kibbutzim have populations between 1,500 and

2,000, but many West African communities larger than this were able to provision collective good through social incentives, particularly before their farming became highly commercialized. Successful commune movements, however, have invariably been divided into communities averaging less than five hundred inhabitants.

At the peak of their development the Shakers numbered more than 5,000 persons, but they were distributed among 18 communities further divided into "families" or communes, the common-property, collective-production units. Using Nordhoff's reconstructed figures of the maximum membership of 52 "families" at 14 communities, we get an average membership of approximately 80 persons per commune and 300 per settlement. No community ever got much above 600 souls and few communes much above 100. During their florescence the communities still had many children. However, by 1874 when Nordhoff visited all 14 settlements, the Shaker population had dropped by half. Settlements averaged only 150 people, and communes only 45.[25]

The Amana Society peaked at 1,800 inhabitants, but it was divided into 7 villages none of which had more than 500.[26] Together the 2 Oneida communities (Wallingford and Oneida) never totaled much above 300 inhabitants[27] while Harmony and Zoar, as we have seen, peaked at about 800 and 500 respectively.[28] During most of their life spans they consisted of fewer than 500.

Hutterites intentionally keep their communes small, with the result that the number of decision-making adults in each one is usually well below 20. When the population of a Hutterite colony reaches 130 to 150, half of the group moves on to newly acquired lands to form a new Bruderhof, a process called "branching out." The ideal size of a new colony is between 50 and 75, but Hutterite fertility is so high that the average colony is ready to divide again within 15 years. Hutterite married women average approximately eleven live births during their reproductive years; and children under 15 account for 50.6 percent of the total population, a remarkably youthful and prolific one since infant mortality rates are low.[29]

The average Hutterite colony or community has approximately 100 inhabitants with slightly more women than men. About half the members are over 15 years of age, and of these roughly half are married. With an average of some 12 married couples per community, the management of colony affairs is in the hands of a small group of 12 or 14 men. This follows for two reasons. First, women do not formally participate in colony decisions because of their "inferior" status. Second, young men do not have voting privileges and are not eligible for the more responsible work assignments until they have been baptized, usually just a short time before their marriage. The number of controlling males in a new colony of only 50 members would therefore be about 6, and in a mature colony of maximum desirable size (150) about 18. These are small, face-to-face management groups, and Hutterites deliberately keep them this way. They realize cliques and factions develop in a colony that gets too large and that these can weaken or destroy the familial atmosphere. Branching may even take place prematurely when a colony splits into two opposing factions. At worst the interpersonal relations in a large colony become more formal, and much of the intimacy Hutterites prefer is lost.[30]

According to the small-group experiments mentioned in Chapter 2, group consensus decreases as group size increases, calling for ever more skillful leadership to redress the balance. Even the Hutterites acknowledge a leadership problem. If factionalism and quarreling disrupt a colony, inadequate leadership is considered a principal cause. But branching and the face-to-face quality of life in a small, egalitarian community with small-group management reduces much of the leadership problem. The fact that Hutterites recognize leadership inadequacies in larger colonies is part of their reason for keeping them small and face to face.[31] This remarkable small-group adaptation recapitulates in a deliberate, "rational" form the same kind of splitting that took place among primitive peoples and still does among such groups as the Yanomamo mentioned above. It is an adaptation that accounts in large measure for the Hutterites' phenomenal expansion over the past 95 years without the charisma of a John Noyes, Christian Metz, George Rapp, or Joseph Bimeler.

Of all the societies in our sample the one whose creation probably depended most on the personal characteristics of its leader was the Oneida Community. John Humphrey Noyes was often labeled a despot by his contemporaries, but to his followers he was a divine despot. The community openly admitted that his personal government was a "theocracy," but concluded that if it was "despotism, it was a glorious one. . . . Christ was just as much of a despot as this." During the formative years of the society, however, many people withdrew, for Noyes's dominant personality attracted only those who could readily accept his doctrines and give him complete obedience. Only after he relinquished tight control during his declining years did a faction finally arise to oppose him.[32]

Despite George Rapp's patriarchal hold over a congregation that even called him "Father," in 1832 a third of his followers were disaffected and led off by the notorious "Count" Leon. This counterfeit nobleman had enough charisma of his own to challenge Rapp's leadership on issues of celibacy and patriarchal government. As a result, Economy's industrial enterprises lost many of their best workers and began their slow decline.[33]

The severe factionalism that terminated Zoar did not occur until long after Bimeler's death. The schism in this case was due to a revolt of the younger members. In many ways Amana was the strongest of all 19th-century eutopian communities with the exception of the Hutterite settlements. Without slowly fading away like the celibate Shakers or dividing into warring factions, the Inspirationists successfully indoctrinated enough of their young to maintain their numbers; and when eventually faced with financial disaster—a full two-thirds of a century after the death of Christian Metz and almost a century after coming to America—they amicably and democratically modified their organization.

Knowledge and Procedures

Comparisons of 19th-century communes reveal several interesting tendencies among those which were most durable or "successful." They were much more often religious than secular, much more likely to have been organized for a long period before establishing communities and practicing communism, and usually were ethnically homogeneous. These characteristics are interrelated, for religious communes were more likely to arise from religious associations that had developed over a considerable period of time. Such religious associations, moreover, were likely to develop in rural areas of ethnic homogeneity.

All six of our communes began as religious congregations before adopting communism. Shaker groups formed among neighbors in small towns and villages, and their earliest communes developed among associations that had been in existence more than ten years. Both Rapp and Bimeler had been preaching to their Wurttemburg congregations for over ten years before they led them to the United States, and the Separatist organizations to which they belonged had an even longer history. Christian Metz's pietist group of Inspirationists belonged to a religious sect that began in 1714. He too was a leader and organizer of his following for more than ten years before the move to America. Oneida Perfectionism was also a religious congregation several years before adopting communism.[34] Not only did organizations precede communal living in these cases, there was plenty of time for the leadership to have a selective effect on the permanent membership.

Except for the Hutterites, who almost never take new members from outside but prefer to raise and indoctrinate their own, most groups relied on probationary or candidacy periods for selecting new members. Amana carefully recruited new members only from Germany and kept them on probationary status until everyone including the candidates were sure that permanent membership was desirable. Zoar sometimes admitted hired laborers after a one-year probationary period.[35]

The Shakers generously opened their doors to nearly all comers, but most were unable to accommodate to their strict ways and would leave before their first year was up. Oneida was very careful in its selection of members since Noyes considered the process crucial to commune success. Applicants sometimes had to study Perfectionist beliefs for years before being accepted. Even so, many left after a trial period of a year or less.[36]

In spite of the intentional quality of most successful communal farming societies, much of their internal structure was spontaneous and adaptive in a way very like that of tradition-patterned groups. The Shakers, for example, developed an elaborate behavioral code over the years, their Millennial Laws, which were never printed nor widely distributed. Sections of these statutes were read and reread at meetings although never made available in their entirety for "common perusal." [37] All the 19th-century societies had some constitution, by-laws, or articles of incorporation to give them legal status for owning land and carrying on their commercial affairs. These regulations had to do with their status as part societies within the larger nation. When written down, the mutual responsibilities and procedures of these societies were largely a crystallization of custom. Like all custom they helped make internal relationships predictable.

Controls

Observers of all the more durable communal societies invariably reported that members who did not do their fair share of the work felt too uncomfortable to remain long in the group. Such a person felt out of place. According to Nordhoff even the so-called "winter Shakers" worked hard.[38] These were "shiftless fellows" who would take refuge in Shaker communes at the beginning of winter, professing at that time a desire to join the society. But they would gradually succumb to the orderly atmosphere of the Shaker community and end up working as hard as anyone else until spring when they would again take to the road.

The example set by a eutopian community would undoubtedly have a strong influence on the behavior of new members as well as a selective effect on candidates. But while the familial atmosphere of the 19th-century communes embodied many positive reinforcements, the negative incentives stand out most clearly and are remarkably like those of the Benedictine monastery.

Among the Rappites a member was admonished first by the head of his "family," who later was backed by the rest of the community. A fellow "brother" is the first to speak to an erring Hutterite, and if this has no effect, the preacher will speak to the individual. If this does no good, the "sinner" may be requested to appear before the colony council and finally before the entire Sunday morning religious meeting. Among the Shakers it was a moral obligation on the part of all to reveal a brother's or sister's transgressions to the elders for proper censure; one who did not shared the guilt. Public rebuke before the entire congregation was a powerful deterrent at Amana as well as among the Shakers and Hutterites.[39]

Among most of the groups some form of excommunication came next. The Hutterites still practice a form of ostracism called "den Frieden nehmen," taking away the individual's peace of mind, a practice that goes back to the 16th century. The offender is not allowed to talk to other members, including his own wife, and may be assigned a special room in which to sleep apart. Although expected to perform regular duties, the individual must eat meals alone after the rest are through, and at church services must sit in the back some distance from the others. Similarly, at Zoar a difficult member was deprived of the right to attend meetings and participate in social functions, and at Amana an errant member was excluded from church services and all other community activities until having made a proper confession. An offending Shaker stood at the rear of the congregation until confession earned full reinstatement. Depending on the severity of the offense an Amana member could be prohibited from attending weekly prayer meetings for a week to one year. In such cases the

Amana member, like the errant Shaker, could be reinstated only after publicly confessing before the village congregation. To shame a member before the community in this fashion was among Amana's Twenty-Four Rules for True Godliness. Some errants considered the experience so embarrassing that they preferred to abandon the colony and make their way in the "world." [40]

Oneida employed a system of social control it called "mutual criticism." Members criticized one another and then publicly confessed their failings. As the society increased in size, criticism was carried out in committees of ten members each. Even children as young as four years of age were taught to hold their own mutual-criticism sessions. Anyone defiant in the face of such criticism was ostracized until finally submitting to the community's judgment. Subsequent approval and reinstatement by the society is said to have brought the offender a great sense of relief. [41]

The Rappites in their early years had a similar custom. Father Rapp divided his community into six groups: old men, old women, young men, young women, boys, and girls. Each group met once a week in "mutual improvement" sessions to correct each other's "deportment." At Amana members were subjected to an annual spiritual examination, unterredung, at which they confessed their faults to one another under the scrutiny of the First Brethren, the elders. [42]

Expulsion was the final recourse of all communities for extreme cases, but as a formal act it was seldom necessary. Members usually left of their own accord. Sometimes, as was true at Oneida, a member might be asked to leave; but it was rarely necessary to put the matter to community vote.

Since all of our 19th-century communes were religious societies, they were able to add supernatural reinforcement to their social sanctions. Amana's spiritual leaders, Christian Metz and Barbara Heinemann, were "instruments," werkzeuge, for divine revelation. In a trance state at church meetings, the werkzeuge, either Metz or Heinemann, would reveal God's will or judgment. More than one errant member rebuked in this fashion fell to his knees promising in tears to sin no more. Even expulsion of members could take place through such "testimony of the Lord." And when Metz wanted to legally institute communal property arrangements within the Society in 1854, he met so much resistance from the more affluent members that it took a special revelation from the Lord to change their minds. Speaking through His medium, Metz, God pronounced a curse on all who would obstruct His communal sharing. The reluctant members quickly got in line. [43]

An unusual grading system at Amana included both positive and negative social incentives. Each village population had three distinct congregations, and promotion or demotion within this ranking system had a powerful and continuous influence on members' behavior. The first grade, or Versammlung, contained all the oldest and most pious members, who held Sunday morning service in a special room within the main church. Everyone hoped someday to become a member of this, the most prestigious congregation. The second Versammlung was for the middle-aged members, who held their Sunday service in another special but smaller room. The third Versammlung included all the young married members and children above the age of seven. A member's status within each Versammlung was indicated by position in the room, and advancement was accomplished by being moved further toward the back. Seating position and grade were not determined, however, by age alone although it was generally believed that older members were more pious. For misdemeanors and sins a member could be moved forward in the church group or downward in Versammlung. These Sunday seating positions became such an important social index that any demotion was looked upon as a severe punishment.[44]

Commitment

Prestige and Persecution

Although John Humphrey Noyes had difficulties with his neighbors at Putney, it could not be said that Oneida was a persecuted society. Oneida, however, generated a great deal of curiosity in its day, and members were conscious of the fact that they were part of an unusual social experiment of great interest to the larger society. According to William Hinds, who visited Oneida in 1876, the community attracted as many as 1,500 visitors in a single day. They came from every state in the Union and all the countries of Europe.[45]

The two separatist groups, the Rappites and Zoarites, were not so much persecuted in Germany as harassed by government and clergy. In the United States both sects gained a reputation as hard-working farmers; the Rappites became famous as industrialists as well. Intellectuals always had a high degree of interest in the two groups and many visited and wrote about them. So well known did they become that both groups eventually maintained profitable hotels.[46]

The Amana Inspirationists had an 18th-century history of persecution and like the other German groups found their religious freedom severely restricted in Europe during the early 19th century. They, too, moved to the United States in search of greater freedom. During most of the 19th century their Iowa location was much more isolated than Economy, for example, which was only a few miles from Pittsburgh. But by the early 20th century, Amana had its hotel too, and Old Amana village alone was receiving some 1,200 visitors annually.[47]

The Hutterites have a long history of European persecution going back to the early Reformation, and most observers agree that it has contributed to the success or longevity of their society. According to John Hostetler, Hutterites themselves are aware of the integrative and cohesive consequences of hostile acts against the society and acknowledge the fact that as relations with the outside world become more amicable internal factionalism increases. For this reason Hutterites deliberately keep the memory of the world's past injustices against them a living and vivid part of their cultural heritage.[48]

The Shakers were the only one of our 19th-century groups to be persecuted in America. During Mother Ann's proselytizing missions into New England, she and her followers were often met with hostile mobs. And because of the movement's English leadership during its early years, which coincided with the Revolutionary War, it was considered by some to be a subversive and disloyal organization. In the early 1800's malicious rumors about the Shakers led to mob attacks on Shaker congregations and to the destruction of Shaker property. In time, however, the Shakers earned much respect for their industry and the quality of their manufactures and became, as we have seen, world famous for their demonstration that communism was economically feasible. By the second half of the 19th century the Shakers were well aware of their world renown and were taking pride and interest in the broader socialistic implications of their way of life.[49]

Goals

According to Nordhoff, some people believed the cementing force of fanatical religious conviction was indispensable to commune longevity while others felt that members of a successful commune could hold widely divergent beliefs. He disagreed with both positions. Members of a successful commune needed to be "of one mind upon some question which to them shall appear so important as to take the place of a religion, if it is not essentially religious." Given the religious nature of most of the communities he observed in 1874, Nordhoff was, in effect, anticipating the kibbutz. Moreover, he believed this unity of conviction and purpose derived from circumstances and conditions within the larger social environment that the commune members deemed unbearable: "Communism is a mutiny against society." [50] Nordhoff came close to a modern view of social movements.

A social movement that has crystallized into some form of organized community life will have a much more highly visible unity of purpose and belief than the business firms that normally concern students of modern organizations. Most of the communities compared here clearly have social-movement origins; a fact related to the persecution and harassment in their early histories. The 19th-century German groups and the Hutterites stem from reformation movements and later splinter movements. As for the Shakers, Mother Ann began to shape her sect in Manchester, England, at the very time and place the industrial revolution was born. And she transplanted it to the American colonies at a time when a rash of religious revivals was still widely recurring. Here too the stable small community was being disrupted by the beginnings of industrialization and transience.

Oneida's commitments to perfectionism and complex marriage gave it a distinctiveness that helped select a homogeneous membership. But the distinctiveness in this case was probably more closely linked to the charisma of one man than to a rejection of society.

Another quality of 19th-century communes that intrigued Nordhoff was their highly utilitarian bent. There were no decorative frills or intellectual extras to their way of life. This led him to believe that communism could succeed only among people dedicated to hard work and contented with manual labor. He doubted that it could be successful among intellectuals.[51] Here he was close to another important attribute of many social movements, particularly of the kind he was dealing with. Long-term goals are put ahead of more immediate satisfactions, future objectives before present consumer choices. This emphasis on long-term goals can lead to a utilitarian treatment of the present, but that it can influence "intellectuals" as well as peasants the kibbutz movement has shown. Communal living is itself a way of restricting immediate satisfactions, and in all our religious groups it was an instrument to millennial goals and a preparation for the afterlife rather than a goal in itself. In all these cases it was linked to the communism of primitive Christianity, and in all it was an organizational or economic expedient adopted by a group already existing for primarily religious rather than political purposes.

Needs

All our communes endeavored to achieve self-sufficiency in food, at least early in their history. The first 19th-century communes tried to be self-sufficient in all consumption goods, but this was before the era of mass-production industries. Communes made their own clothes, shoes, furniture, and so on, and produced their own meat, vegetables, and grains; some even operated community dairies, wineries, breweries, and bakeries.

There was no unemployment. If for some reason there was a depression in a commune's manufacturing enterprises, members could give their full attention to farming and still survive, as the Rappites discovered quite early.[52] Moreover, peak labor loads usually came at different times in the various enterprises, and members at less urgent assignments could lend a hand at those of higher priority.

Members were and are provided with medical and dental care, and when necessary with nursing care. Anyone physically incapacitated by accident or illness does not have to worry about the consequences of such misfortune for one's family. Orphans and widows are automatically cared for as are the aged and retired. Recreation is provided and even reading materials in some cases.

To Nordhoff, life in the 19th-century communes seemed one of order, system and security—an "eternal Sabbath" free of the world's usual "hurly-burly." He confessed to being puzzled by the fact that people living in the United States could be content with so little and concluded it was due to the comforting certainty that they would be cared for in their old age or in case of "helplessness."[53] According to John Bennett, Hutterites jokingly refer to their society as one big "retirement scheme," and freely admit that this is one of the principal reasons for their low defection rate. As one young Hutterite said to Bennett, "Where else can you get a good deal like this for a lifetime?"[54]

Frequency of Interaction

The very nature of communal life insures the high frequency of interaction between each individual and the other members of the group. So frequent is the interaction that most observers are struck by the extreme lack of privacy. Nordhoff considered this a general characteristic of the 19th-century communities, each of which was like a "great family."[55] Among the Hutterites privacy has not been condoned since the 16th-century; apartment doors are not locked, and members visit one another without knocking.[56]

The common dining hall occurred (or occurs) among the strongest American communes, the Shakers, Hutterites and Amana Inspirationists. Oneida had it as well. Other community services such as bakeries and laundries frequently occur in communes, even those in which members live in family or small household units. In the latter case, as at Amana, Economy and Zoar, they increased the frequency of interaction outside the family. Since all production is collective, community members work together at many tasks although all have had a tendency to specialize according to skills. By working collectively at jobs no one likes to do, Hutterites dispose of them quickly without unfairly burdening a few. Oneida formed work "bees" for much the same reason, to make a job that would be monotonous for only one or two persons into a pleasurable group activity. Sometimes members would get together as early as five in the morning to gather broom corn, pare apples, or make bags "by storm."[57] Among the Hutterites entire colonies frequently exchange work parties for harvesting, haying, and construction.[58]

Some of the religious communes had an extraordinary number of weekly meetings. Shakers knelt together in prayer when they got up in the morning, held "grace" periods of 10 to 15 minutes before every meal, knelt in prayer at the dining table before eating, and worshiped in the meeting room every evening. In addition, some evenings were dedicated to singing and others to business meetings.[59] Even by the early 20th century, when attendance was already declining, Amana had 11 weekly services exclusive of those on special holidays. They held prayer meetings every evening in neighborhood groups, a meeting by orders, Versammlungen, on Wednesday and Sunday mornings, and general meetings on Saturday mornings and Sunday afternoons.[60] At Oneida, every day was supposedly sacred although no established prayer times or formal services were set for any day, not even Sunday. Every evening at 8 o'clock, however, Noyes met with his followers to instruct them in self-improvement and to criticize evidence of anything less than complete, spiritual dedication.[61]

The family competes with any group for the commitment of its members as modern students of organization all know. But Karl Kautsky clearly perceived the importance of this conflict half a century ago when he pointed out ways in which the early Christian congregation attempted to minimize the influence of the family.[62] In the Gospels of Saint Mark (3: 31) and Saint Luke (4: 59ff, 14: 26) the brotherly relations within Jesus' following, the Christian congregation, are strongly emphasized to the neglect, abandonment and even hatred of nuclear family ties—ties to father, mother, wife, children, brothers, and sisters. Even in pre-Christian times some Essene groups had adopted celibacy and others a kind of group marriage with cohabitation only to perpetuate the society. Christian monasticism, as it developed, took the celibate route. To Kautsky, the significance of all this was not the conflict between the family and collective production but between the family and collective consumption. He correctly recognized that family consumption has an individualizing or privatizing effect that can be more dangerous to the integrity of the commune than any other single factor.

Oneida's battle with the natural family took the route of complex (group) marriage with a special dormitory for children. The commune itself was looked upon as one big family. No couples were to show "exclusive love" for one another; and if a man and woman began to have a disproportionate number of sexual encounters, they were corrected at "mutual criticism" sessions. Similarly no parent was supposed to show "exclusive love" for a child. Children were "communized" by making them "the property of the whole Community." After infancy they were raised together in the Children's House; and to expand "pa- and ma-hood," mothers sometimes exchanged children or temporarily adopted children not their own.[63]

Other groups weakened or eliminated the family ties through celibacy. Shaker "families" were actually the movement's basic communal units. Each colony averaged about 3 families of 30 to 90 members who carried on their own industrial and farming activities, had their own store and office, and shared the same dining hall and sleeping quarters, the latter divided into separate dormitories for men and women. A membership of about 50 was considered the ideal size for a "family"; if much larger it became impersonal, and if much smaller it lost all the advantages of both group effort and a workable division of labor.[64]

"Families" among the celibate Rappites were much smaller than Shaker "families," and the village, not the "families," was the commune. Each family was a household that prepared its own meals and had its own garden and chickens. These celibate households ranged in size from two to eight members; modally they had about five or six. The sexes were distributed fairly evenly among them, but the "brothers" and "sisters" in each were not necessarily related. Zoar was celibate at first, but gave up the practice after a cholera epidemic severely decimated their numbers. They then tried raising children communally, a system much like the contemporary kibbutz, but after one generation gave this up too.[65]

Nuclear-family living units were maintained at Amana although many collective services such as dairies, bakeries, kitchens, and dining halls were provided by the village commune. The oldest communists, the Hutterites, have kept the nuclear family intact although families eat in communal dining halls and occupy apartments within communal "long houses." Moreover, the factionalism that sometimes leads to premature splitting of a colony is usually due to friction between families. In addition to restricting and invading its privacy as previously mentioned, Hutterites attack the family indirectly by limiting husband-wife and parent-child relationships. Childrearing, according to Hostetler, is the responsibility of the colony rather than the private concern of the child's natural parents. And the division between male and female subcultures so emphasized by Hutterite society strengthens the wife's loyalty to her sex at the expense of her relationship to her husband.[66]

Competition

That unique feature of communal eutopias, collective consumption, greatly simplifies the problem of competition. Consumption within the community is controlled through egalitarian distribution of supplies. Each member receives according to need, not according to capital; thus, any differences in capital must be erased. Members on joining sign over all their property, an irreversible investment since they usually sign away the right to reclaim it should they ever change their minds. The Rappites went so far as to burn, in 1818, their records of the original contributions to the common property. This was done so those who had contributed the most could not feel superior to the poorest members.[67]

Distribution of consumer goods in the communal society tends to be uniform and austere. In the 19th-century communes all families received the same quantity and quality of goods from the community stores. Clothing fabrics were uniform in color and quality and among the Shakers, Rappites, Zoarites, and Amanites were tailored in the same style. This is still true of the Hutterites. No jewelry or adornment of dress was allowed. The Shakers reasoned that differences in wearing apparel would create jealousies and "wants would bear the sway over needs." Constant changes would be necessary, and a great deal of money would be improvidently spent to maintain equality.[68] The Shakers in their early days seem to have had a clear appreciation of the consequences of Mandeville's "private vices."

Housing and furnishings were always plain and the amount of furnishings sparse. Where family housing was provided, the dwellings were made as much alike as possible to avoid differences in comfort. At Oneida, rooms used by the entire community were tastefully and attractively furnished, whereas in members' private rooms decorations were not allowed.[69]

Differences in material goods are much easier for communes to avoid than are differences in status and rank. As Nordhoff noticed in his travels among the 19th-century communes, "Brains seem to come easily to the top." [70] Ability, particularly managerial ability, is always in limited supply, and communal societies like any others must make the best allocation of their resources. But in letting their most capable people come to the top, the egalitarian commune must be careful that no symbolization of this status undermines group equality. Among the Shakers, for example, a "trustee" (business manager) who became too impressed with his own importance was transferred to another commune if of outstanding ability. But if those talents were not too highly regarded, the individual was simply demoted to common membership.[71]

Here we encounter another parallel to St. Benedict's monastic rules. Any monk with a special skill was admonished to practice his craft with utmost "humility." If ever such a craftsman became proud of his work or the profits it brought the monastery, he was assigned to ordinary labor until humble once again.[72]

Hutterites do not overtly regard an office as an honor or defer to office holders, because to do so would counter their strong dedication to fighting self and renouncing individual will. Men do not compete for positions and no overt praise is awarded the talented administrator. Anyone who gives the appearance of being personally ambitious will soon be admonished or called before a colony meeting.[73]

Occasionally differences in rank clearly asserted themselves in the communes dependent on strong leadership. Although Father Rapp is said to have shared the same style of life as all his followers, he occupied the largest and most impressive house. Here he entertained friends and guests of the community. Joseph Bimeler not only had the largest house at Zoar, it was far from plainly furnished. He enjoyed "exclusive luxuries" for which he was severely criticized by some dissatisfied members who withdrew. At Oneida, John Humphrey Noyes and other "central" members enjoyed many special privileges of rank. They were able to travel to Europe and within the United States. Noyes, in fact, went to the Great Exhibition of London in 1851 even though Oneida was having severe financial difficulties at the time. The central members also had more choice in the selection of sexual partners; and to them, and Noyes especially, fell the task of initiating the virgins.[74]

Among our six groups the Shakers, Amana Inspirationists, and Hutterites seem to have been most successful in avoiding any obvious differences in life style enjoyed by a privileged leader or small group. But all three had a hierarchical organization with a definite chain of command from "head to foot" as the Shakers put it. According to Edward Deming Andrews, the government of the Shaker Believers resembled the oligarchic Puritan state.[75]

At the head of each Shaker "family" or commune were four elders, two men and two women (eldresses). The elders of the head or "Church" commune in each colony comprised the ministry of that colony, and the central ministry (the elders of the Church commune at New Lebanon) held supreme authority over the entire United Society. The central ministry appointed, advised, instructed, judged and when necessary removed the secondary ministries. These ministries did the same for the "family" elders under their jurisdiction and for the deacons and trustees in each family.[76]

Deacons and trustees were "temporal" heads. The former were in charge of labor branches, that is, farm deacon, garden deaconess, and so on; and the trustees or "office deacons" were in charge of all transactions with the world. They purchased what the society did not produce itself, sold society manufactures, signed legal documents and so on.[77]

The Shakers believed in a "government by revelation" which meant that those revealed to be less capable and perfect were to submit to those revealed to be more capable and perfect. Appointments were based on merit; those believers who worked hardest for the society and were most esteemed by their fellows were the most likely to be promoted. Nothing but the honor of serving the rest of the members, however, was supposedly gained by such a promotion, for all had to perform manual labor and share the same living conditions as their fellows.[78]

The Amana Society was ruled by a board of trustees also known as the Great Council of the Brethren. The council consisted of 13 trustees elected annually by popular vote from all the elders of the Society. Actually they were reelected annually since rotation of offices was not an Amana practice. Only if an office holder became too overbearing and too concerned with his own personal ambition was he likely to be voted out. Men were supposed to accept an office as a sacred responsibility, not for personal honor or glory. Each of the seven Amana villages had at least one elder on the Great Council, who in his own village was known as the Resident Trustee.[79]

The Bruderrath, made up of 7 to 19 elders, was the governing board of each village. These elders were men of great piety and spirituality, not necessarily the oldest men in the community. Vacancies were filled by appointments made by the Great Council from a list presented by the Resident Trustee. The Brudderrath appointed the foremen of the various branches of village industry, and assigned all members to their tasks. The Head Elder of the Bruderrath was its spiritual head; he outranked its temporal head, the Resident Trustee.[80]

Outsiders often criticized Amana as an "aristocracy of elders." As among the Shakers, however, lines of authority were clear; and they effectively subdivided the larger society into smaller, face-to-face, semiautonomous communes. Consumption was egalitarian; power and authority were not. But the first so balanced the second that competition between the individual and the group was minimal. Moreover, authority ultimately originated with the supernatural, which justified it and tempered it with humility.

Hutterite authority is also divinely ordained, and operates at the colony or commune level through a council of 5 to 7 baptized males. All the important offices of the commune are occupied by these men, first preacher, second preacher, householder, and field manager. All are elected by the baptized males of the colony, who usually total only 5 to 18 men because of the small average size of each community. The head preacher is both spiritual and temporal head of the commune while the householder is specifically responsible for its economic success.[81]

A divinely ordained system of authority is buttressed with an effective indoctrination system, also divinely sanctioned. According to Hostetler and Huntington, a primary Hutterite goal is the "self-surrender" of the individual by breaking his will primarily at the kindergarten age (3 to 5 years) and reinforcing this surrender throughout his lifetime. "God worketh only in surrendered men." Children at the kindergarten age (preschool or nursery school age in Gentile society) are considered "willfull and useless," and Hutterites firmly believe in the need to break their "stubborn wills."[82] This attitude goes back to the very beginning of Hutterite history in the 16th century and is clearly an accommodation of the monastic renunciation of self and of individual will to a Reformation society trying to combine primitive Christian communism with preservation of nuclear family units.

So effective is this divinely ordained breaking of the will that public-school teachers find it very difficult to motivate Hutterite children competitively. If one child in a Hutterite class is praised, the rest sit in "embarrassed silence." The lack of "competitive spirit" and "aggression" noted by classroom teachers also shows up on personality tests given to Hutterite adults.[83]

Little is known of the Amana Society's indoctrination of its young during its most vigorous years, but the Amana Kinder-Stimme (children's guide) contained "orders and regulations" clearly in the same spirit as the Hutterite's monastic renunciation of self. Children were admonished not to seek honors or elevate themselves above others. They were to do cheerfully whatever served best "to break [their] will" or bring about their "humiliation." Never were they to envy another or think themselves better than anyone else.[84] Apparently this severe application of Benedictine self-surrender in the indoctrination of Amana and Hutterite children proved an effective substitute for celibacy or group marriage. As self-contained, ongoing societies these were unquestionably the most successful of all the 19th-century experiments.

The Other Eutopias

Our six communal movements were not typical of the vast majority of 19th-century eutopian experiments. All told, in the United States during the 19th century there were literally hundreds of eutopian communities, most of which were secular and most of which expired in less than five years. A brief summary of these communities is in order before analyzing decline and change in our six religious communes.

Contrasting 19th-century and contemporary communes, Margaret Mead once called the former dedicated, self-denying, and highly disciplined and the latter individualistic, parasitic, and irresponsible.[85] Obviously Mead was taking the religious movements discussed here as representative of 19th-century communitarianism. Actually the most typical 19th-century eutopian experiments have far more in common with contemporary experiments than they ever had with the six communes reviewed above. Most of the 19th-century experiments as well as the contemporary so-called "communes" are not even true communes in the full collective-production, collective-consumption sense employed here.

Longevity comparisons between the religious and secular eutopian communities of the 19th century show how important it is to consider the two types separately. Almost a third of the secular experiments failed during their first year compared with 8 percent of the religious. The 10-year level is even more significant; approximately 5 of every 6 secular communities expired in less than 10 years while three-fourths of the religious endured more than 10. And while hardly any of the secular societies lasted 25 years, almost two-thirds of the sectarians passed the quarter-century mark.[86] As a rule conditions of social predictability and individual commitment were not conducive to success in the secular eutopias.

The Owenite communities of the 1820's and the Fourierist communities of the 1840's were the most noteworthy of the secular communitarian movements, and of these, New Harmony, the first of the Owenite communities, is probably the most famous. In fact, far more has been written about Robert Owen's failure at New Harmony than about Father George Rapp's prior success there. Owen, a self-made English industrialist and philanthropist, bought all of the Rappites' Indiana property for $125,000 in 1825. There he planned to establish a scientific, rational community that would combine all the economic and social virtues of the religious communes without their religious fanaticism and unnatural sex taboos. But in two years the community had dissolved and with it most of Owen's fortune.[87]

Although the one thousand Owenites at New Harmony exceeded the number of Rappites before them, they neither put the factories into operation, nor ever even got farming underway. Without any plan for the selection of members the community ended up with no skilled craftsmen and only 35 farmers. There were members from every state in the Union and nearly every country of northern Europe. They shared little or nothing in religion, background, habits, opinions, or interests. According to one contemporary, never before had a small community of one thousand population consisted of one thousand strangers all oblivious to each other's feelings.[88]

Freeloaders greatly outnumbered workers and little was accomplished. When the community could not even grow food to sustain itself, Owen urged members to cultivate private, household gardens. Owen did not have the kind of charisma to command a community venture of this sort and did not stay on the premises long enough to use what he had. He left his sons in charge of the day-to-day operations, and when funds eventually gave out, the experiment ended. Living off Owen's largesse, the members developed neither social incentives to provision the collective good nor any strong commitment to the group. Most finally decided they could do better for themselves working individually on the outside. Without previous experience working together, they had convened from all walks of life and all points of the compass, and they dispersed by the same route.[89]

The Owenite movement inspired the formation of some 19 communities, none of which lasted more than 4 years. Few succeeded during their brief life to grow enough food to feed themselves, much less a surplus for market. Some developed crafts, but only to meet community needs. Always there was the problem of unequal contributions of effort. At all the communities industrious members complained of working to support the lazy members and malingerers. In an attempt to rectify this situation at New Harmony, work inspectors were appointed to judge the quality and quantity of everyone's labor contributions. But the craftsmen objected to any plan of equal rewards for equal work because their labor was worth $2 a day on the open market while that of a farmhand was worth only $.25.[90] At Yellow Springs a band of musicians refused to help with the harvest because music, not agriculture, was their group's profession, and a public lecturer refused to do anything but give lectures.[91]

Twenty years later, in the mid-1840's, the Fourierist movement resulted in over 30 eutopian communities most of which lasted only 1 or 2 years. Inequality of effort, heterogeneous memberships with no common ground of understanding, mutual distrust, poor management, and lack of leadership were, again, common causes of early disruption.[92] The major complaint at the Sylvania Association was that many members took advantage of the rest by doing less than their share of work and consuming more than their share of provisions. And according to a disillusioned member of the Trumball Phalanx, by advertising for its members in the newspapers, the society had attracted "mixed characters from various parts of the country," too many of whom joined "with the idea that they could live in idleness." An ex-member of the Wisconsin Phalanx claimed the community was undone by a small core of shrewd men who never expected the experiment to work but used it "to accumulate property individually by any and every means called fair in competitive society." [93]

A former participant in the Moorhouse Union experiment blamed its failure on the lack of common goals. The membership, he claimed, included philosophers, bankrupt merchants, philanthropists, and former officers of the Texas army. It was "a motley group of ill-assorted materials as inexperienced as it was heterogeneous." Everyone had different ideas, "There was no unanimity of purpose." Similarly, the demise of the North American Phalanx was ascribed by one observer to the lack of any guiding common principles although the members themselves had been a "decent sort" in his opinion.[94]

The Owenite and Fourierist communities certainly constituted social movements, and were social movements based on dissatisfaction with contemporary capitalism. Shortly after it formed in 1843, the Sylvania Phalanx, for example, published a statement accusing modern urban society of becoming "vice-engendering" and "ruinous" and of living in "isolated households" that resulted in "wasteful complication." Moreover, industries produced "destructive competition and anarchy" leading to unemployment and hunger. Children everywhere were growing up "in ignorance and vice." [95] But while dissatisfaction with society can stir up social movements, these do not necessarily produce long-range goals and long-term commitments among their followers. There has to be some process of membership selection and a way of making members predictable to one another. By beginning as religious congregations, the sectarian movements solved both these problems. But the collective consumption of primitive Christian communism was the crucial binding cement absent from most secular eutopias despite all their high ideals and plans for sharing.

Neither the Owenite and Fourierist communities nor most of the other 19th-century eutopias were true communal farming societies as defined here. Not only did they fail to produce collectively, they did not consume collectively in the sense of distributing according to need. Fourierist communities were, in fact, joint-stock companies in which payments were made to capital. Working members of a Fourierist Phalanx (community) did not have to be stockholders, and the stockholders did not have to be resident working members. Slightly less than half of all profits were to go to labor, a third to capital, and a fourth were to be distributed according to skill. Supposedly no jealousy would arise from such a division since all members could look forward to becoming stockholders with the passage of time.[96]

In practice, the distinction between capital and labor led to jealousies and dissatisfactions that disrupted the experiments. At the Wisconsin Phalanx most members thought the share of income going to capital "too large and disproportionate." Dividends at North American Phalanx, however, paid so little that the stockholders finally "dissolved the concern" without any compensation to the "honest, resident, working members" who had invested several years of hard labor in the enterprise. And at La Grange Phalanx, one member who owned nearly half the stock insisted on managing everything himself and did it so autocratically the society broke up.[97]

Not even at New Harmony was there ever community of property, for Owen did not wish to risk his entire investment. Most Owenite communities were financed by a single person or a small group of owners, and disagreement between these members and those who agitated for total equality of membership and property was inevitable. Owen favored community of property and equal distribution of benefits, but he did not advocate confiscation. Members who had no capital to invest in a community would contribute extra labor over the years of a value equal to the investments of the wealthier members. In other cases members were to pay off the capital investments of the proprietor-members with interest just as they would pay off a mortgage. Complete communism was never attained at any Owenite community nor was equal distribution ever practiced at any of them. Labor credits were awarded on the basis of production or work time.[98]

The Fourierist and Owenite communities were more like corporate farming communities than communal ones. Differences in wealth with payments to capital provided a ready basis for disagreement and internal competition. Moreover, they put an emphasis on immediate rewards that the communal form did not. For in the sectarian eutopias communal living was less an end in itself than a means to millennial, other-worldly goals. Although the Owenite movement has been described as a "secularized version of millennial sectarianism," this label fits Owenite theory much better than Owenite practice.[99] There was never the commitment to common goals among the Owenites and Fourierists that there was among the sectarian communists.

Few of the great number of contemporary rural communes would qualify as communal farming societies in the strictest sense. In his tour of rural communes throughout the United States, Robert Houriet did not find any that had achieved economic self-sufficiency.[100] Affluent "hippy patrons" frequently subsidized communities, and other external sources of support included federal food stamps, unemployment assistance, aid to dependent children, money from home, tourist handouts, and sometimes even the quarterly dividend checks received by members who had investments and inheritances. Sometimes members held outside jobs and made monthly contributions for food, utilities, and so on. Judson Jerome and Benjamin Zablocki agree in their observations that the average rural commune strives to raise as much food for subsistence as possible and gets whatever cash is needed from odd jobs, often day labor on neighboring farms.[101] Some try to set up cottage industries or some other nonfarming enterprise to obtain a cash income. Contributions of new members may be a further source of income, according to Houriet, and an important one where the turnover rate in membership is high.[102] Although incomes are sometimes pooled, Jerome believes a dual system is much more typical. Each member keeps part of his income for himself to buy personal items and turns over the rest for the group budget.[103]

Rosabeth Kanter reports that property remains essentially private among contemporary commune members even though they readily share it.[104] Using phonographs as an example, Jerome says that while everyone shares and uses them all remain quite conscious of who their actual owners are. Ownership, he says, tends to be dual in a vague sort of way.[105] New Buffalo had become "a commune of hoarders" by the time of Houriet's stay. Members had to get their eggs "right out from under the chickens," and mothers who wanted milk for their children had to go straight to the cow's udder despite a commune regulation that milk was only for children. Degree of hoarding, believes Houriet, is a measure of "communal decline." [106] Zablocki says much the same thing. At first members pool their money and may even share "one another sexually." Then jealousies arise. Some members think of the commune as a permanent home while others live only for the present. Work slows down, and the more permanent residents become increasingly resentful of the transients they view as parasites and loafers.[107]

"The less committed," says Zablocki, "gradually drive out the more committed." He gives an example of a commune in a region of severe winters whose serious members saw the need to make adequate cold-weather preparations but could get no cooperation from the summer, fair-weather members. The former eventually left to start their own community elsewhere.[108] Other observers have noted the great difficulty with which commune members cooperate to accomplish any major undertaking. A common cause of disruption is disagreement over household chores and work assignments. None of the communes would survive any length of time were it not for the willingness of members to reduce radically their consumer "necessities." If together they find it impossible to work effectively, then together they can tighten their belts.[109]

The earlier observers agreed that membership turnover in the communes was high. The groups had a brief life on the average; new ones were continually being born as old ones died, with some of the same people moving from one to another.[110] The more durable communities Kanter classified as "growth and learning centers" to distinguish them from the less durable "anarchistic" variety.[111] She placed their number at roughly one hundred (both rural and urban) at a time when Zablocki believed there were about one thousand rural and two thousand urban communes in the United States.[112] These growth-and-learning centers, according to Kanter, employed many of the practices of the 19th-century religious communes. They created an atmosphere of intimacy— an extended family feeling. Yet they often had charismatic leaders, strict entrance requirements, candidacy periods, and fixed daily routines. Mutual criticism and evening meetings were common, and encounter-group techniques frequently added a modern touch. But these communes were not truly collective in their production any more than the rest.

More recently Judson Jerome has called earlier commune statistics into question.[113] He believes there are at least 30,000 rural communes in the United States today. Most of them are small, ranging in size from 6 to 20 adults plus a few children. The modal size is probably about 8 to 12 adults. Of these, some 4 or 5 make up a permanent core group who shoulder most of the responsibilities. One or more of these core members buys the farm and holds the mortgage. Outside the core group, membership commitment varies from exploratory visiting to a kind of provisional membership. The farm itself is usually a marginal, run-down property of 30 to 100 acres.

As the contemporary commune movement grows older, it is possible that a small-group rural variety may be emerging in which membership will be more stable. Small groups building around an even smaller core over a period of years could indeed effect a selection of members that would meet conditions of social predictability. Since, according to Jerome, most of these communes seldom use radios or television sets and depend largely on internal socializing for amusement, intragroup relations become increasingly important to the individual and with them the good will and good opinion of his fellows. Yet even Jerome, a strong advocate of the new culture, believes that the number of economically successful communes is infinitesimally small and that despite "cultural cohesiveness" they so rarely make effective economic units that he is unwilling to predict a future of economic self-sufficiency for the movement. The contemporary commune, as he sees it, is a domestic unit like a family rather than an economic unit. The collective emphasis is on consumption rather than production.[114]

If a more mature commune movement has developed since the late 1960's, it is one that has definite similarities with primitive Christian communism despite its predominantly secular nature. It is primarily urban, and its collectivism is limited mainly to consumption. In the rural ambience, as Kautsky noted for early Christianity, collectivism extends into production though not too successfully. The overriding tendency is again toward pooling of individual incomes rather than true collective production. Jerome considers the commune movement a "new anarchism," but in some ways it seems an anarchism very reminiscent of the anchorite phase of early monasticism. Jerome even quotes the passage from Saint Luke in which Jesus tells his followers they must hate father, mother, wife, children, brothers, and sisters. The new culture calls for a shift of loyalties as the new "transcendent purpose" makes "private materialistic concerns" irrelevant.[115]

As Nordhoff said, communism is a mutiny against society, and certainly the new culture is as much that as was early Christianity.[116] It is a social movement with a strong Rousseauean antagonism to capitalist civilization's emphasis on material rewards and unnecessary goods. It is a movement opposed, as Jerome says, to competitiveness, acquisitiveness, and aggression. It involves what Jerome aptly calls a "revolution of alternative rewards." Instead of increasing the needs and consumer goods of society, the new culture calls for a reassessment of needs. Contemporary communards take pride and enjoyment in shopping for old clothes in Goodwill stores as they show their contempt for the middle-class values of the old culture. They seek substitutes or alternatives for the acquisition of mass-produced goods in an ambience of gregariousness and brotherly love. Though most contemporary communards live far below the poverty level, they must not be confused with the "real poor," says Jerome. Most of them come from the white middle class, but this is not the only reason for not grouping them with the "real" poor; they actually achieve a state of classlessness by deliberately rejecting the old culture's symbols of respectability. To the extent they turn their backs on the material incentives of modern society and the competitive consumption of reputational status seeking, they become members of a contemporary Millennial Man movement immune to symbols of social class.[117]

Allied with this classlessness is one very significant difference, pointed out by Jerome, between the contemporary communal movement and that of the preceding century: 19th-century communes had little to do with one another, whereas modern communards are highly mobile spatially. As they move about the country from one commune to another, communards increase the strains of membership turnover in individual communes but add to the unity of the total movement.[118] This is an important observation. Until now we have found the growth of material incentives closely associated with the growth of transience. Personal property became the instrument of reputational status among transient peers. But now we have a counter movement whose growing membership constitutes its own reference peer group, one that combines transience with the rejection of material symbols of reputational status.

But in its own form of self-surrender, which the new movement calls "I-death" or the "death of ego," it again resembles the successful 19th-century communes. That "store of ego" which each of us builds up within himself, says Jerome, "must be cracked." But rather than a suppression of individuality, this ego "cracking" calls for an open, nonhypocritical person free from the "posturing, arguing, putdowns, gamesmanship, and neurotic sarcasm" of the old society, a person who can achieve a strong commitment to group intimacy through a shedding of personal notions of privacy. In rejecting the old culture's concern of toilet and bedroom privacy and its opposition to public nudity, the new culture has made bodily exposure central to its pursuit of deliberate intimacy. Jerome tells of one commune, for example, whose bathroom was separated from the kitchen only by a glass door.[119]

One important difference between contemporary communes and our successful 19th-century cases, however, concerns the attitude toward progress in the sphere of productive property. The new culture rejects material progress and the expansion of needs in the production, as well as the consumption, sense. Our 19th-century cases, however, did not reject progress so out of hand. While they saw no need for all those pretentious baubles of civilization which appealed to the vanity of the flesh, they readily adopted any mechanical improvements that could save them labor. The emphasis in the new culture is to revive older preindustrial skills that give personal satisfaction or make pleasant, group labor possible. Efficiency purely for the sake of saving effort is not only irrelevant, it is something to be avoided. This difference may be crucial to the future of the contemporary movement, for the acceptance of progress in the area of productive property proved to be the major undoing of all of our successful communes except the Hutterites.

Decline and Extinction

Most contemporary, so-called "communes" pursue a least-effort or leisure-preference policy based on restriction of consumer wants. By maintaining a relatively low level of reasonable need, they can reduce effort and increase leisure. Our 19th-century "true" communes also maintained low levels of reasonable need in the area of personal or consumer goods yet combined this in their early years with a strong work ethic. They did not limit consumer wants for the specific purpose of increasing leisure or reducing effort; but as they grew older, they all drifted toward leisure preference. The initiating agent in this gradual drift was not the low level of reasonable need, however; it was acceptance of technological progress in the area of collectively owned productive property. Need elasticity permitted in the production sphere eventually undermined their collectivism. So far the Hutterites have been an exception to this process but one, as we shall see, that provides a special demonstration of the rules underlying it.

For a society set on maintaining a low level of reasonable need, sectarian opposition to materialistic contamination from the "world"—the larger society of which it is a part—can be a big advantage. One way to maintain that distance is to avoid credit relationships with the outside world, and the best way to avoid credit relationships is to keep all transactions on a cash basis. Since this is what most of them did, they found it unnecessary to keep anything more than the most rudimentary accounts. As Nordhoff traveled from group to group, he was continually amazed at the difficulties of obtaining even "simple statistics." [120] Communities were perfectly willing to provide whatever they had, but in most cases records were too poor to yield more than "approximate figures." Only at Oneida could he get precise information, but Oneida, he felt, was really a manufacturing corporation. By the time of his visit, as we see below, that is precisely what Oneida had become.

But even Oneida, despite the sophistication of accounts, made a deliberate attempt to pay cash for everything it purchased. Members reasoned that so long as the society owed no one it could survive any national economic crisis simply by shutting down its factories, wearing patched clothing, and living on "mush and applesauce" until times got better. This plan assumed at least some agricultural production on which to fall back; and since most of the communes were primarily agricultural they could readily reduce their manufacturing and concentrate on subsistence farming during temporary recessions as the Rappites discovered during their Indiana years.[121]

Ideally, these societies could have preserved maximal distance from the "world" by sticking to subsistence farming supplemented by labor-intensive manufacturing of just those tools, clothing items, and household furnishings used by their own memberships. This was the policy of most Hutterite colonies until recently, and they have certainly been the most successful in longevity and expansion of numbers. It was the conviction of Shaker elder Frederick Evans that the biggest mistake the Shakers ever made was to switch from subsistence to commercial production.[122] As he explained it to Nordhoff in 1874, once the Shakers began to specialize in selling certain items to the world, they discovered there were other things they could buy from the world more cheaply than they could produce them in their own workshops. They found, for example, that they could buy far more clothing materials than their own weavers could produce by taking those same weavers and putting them to work producing something for which the Shakers could obtain a relatively high price in the marketplace. In other words, as their looms became antiquated and labor-intensive relative to the world's textile industry, the society was better off channeling its labor into those enterprises in which it was technologically more competitive.

As Evans saw, this trap allowed no escape once the communal society lost its self-sufficiency through commercial specialization. But his negative view of the consequences was not shared by Oneida founder John Humphrey Noyes who, four years before Nordhoff's visit to Oneida, criticized the Fourierist eutopian experiments for being too land hungry and subsistence conscious.[123] In his opinion they should have gone into manufacturing "as soon as possible." What Noyes did not know, however, when he confidently published these words was that his own manufacturing eutopia was to fail as a commune within the next ten years. And as we see in Chapter 6, the industrialization of the kibbutz is producing changes in that movement strikingly similar to those which preceded the demise of the 19th-century communes.

The trap Evans perceived as undermining communal life was none other than the engine of Adam Smith's scheme of positive-sum progress. As he put it in *The Wealth of Nations,* no prudent head of family should ever "make at home what it will cost him more to make than to buy." [124] The tailor should purchase shoes from the shoemaker and the shoemaker should employ the tailor to make clothes. All should concentrate their labor in a way to give "some advantage over their neighbors." And what is good for the family is good for the kingdom. "If a foreign country can supply us with a commodity cheaper than we ourselves can make it, better buy it of them with some part of the purchase of our own industry employed in a way in which we have some advantage."

As self-sufficient communities most of our 19th-century communes acquired extensive farmlands and a full complement of their own specialists: blacksmiths, tinsmiths, wagonmakers, tilemakers, potters, cabinetmakers, shoemakers, tailors, bakers, and so on. They were communities of capable people with the know-how to farm, construct their own buildings, and perform essential arts and crafts. They were fascinated by the technologies of their time and eagerly adopted any and all labor-saving mechanical improvements that were useful to them. Most of the communities even added inventions of their own although the two Yankee communes, Shakers and Oneida, were probably the most inventive.

Among Shaker inventions were the brimstone match, a needle with an eye in the middle for sewing brooms, the four-wheel dumpcart, the one-horse buggy, a washing machine, the circular saw, a revolving harrow, the screw propeller, a turbine water wheel, a threshing machine, cut nails, a pea sheller, the common clothes pin, a revolving oven, and flat brooms. After developing a new herb-pressing machine, Elisha Myrick of the Harvard colony wrote in his diary, "every improvement relieving human toil or facilitating labor [gives] time and opportunity for moral, mechanical, scientific and intellectual improvement and the cultivation of the finer and higher qualities of the human mind." As Father Meacham had said long before, "We have a right to improve the inventions of man, so far as is useful and necessary, but not to vain glory or anything superfluous." [125]

Oneida was always on the lookout for ways to improve the efficiency of its operations, and the inventions of its members included a washing machine, a string-bean slicer and new accounting methods. They introduced steam heating quite early to reduce the labor of stoking stoves, and they initiated a variety of manufactures such as wheel spokes, mop handles, plows, bags, scuffle hoes, and steel traps. [126]

The Rappites, especially during their Indiana period, kept in the vanguard of new industrial methods and labor-saving devices and were among the first in the western part of the country to use steam power. They employed it to run their textile looms, to thresh and clean grain, and to operate their community laundry.[127] Early in their career the Zoarites built grist and woolen mills and even an iron furnace, which at first produced implements, such as their plows and large heating stoves, mainly for the community.[128] Amana manufactures began like those at Zoar, and by the beginning of the 20th century Amana owned only the "latest and most improved machinery" in its woolen mills, some of it "imported directly from Germany." Moreover, according to Shambaugh, Amana members invented numerous "clever devices" to increase the efficiency of their machinery. But since they made these improvements to "facilitate" work rather than for "pecuniary gain," they, like all the other inventive communards, allowed outsiders to copy and patent their inventions. Amana also made a deliberate practice of "promptly testing" any new labor-saving improvement it heard about.[129]

All of this interest in labor-saving improvements quickly led the communes to specialize like Adam Smith's "kingdoms" in those industries that gave them "some advantage." Oneida was always quick to eliminate unprofitable ventures and concentrate on those that gave the best return. Once the Rappites condescended to gin their neighbor's cotton as well as their own, it was not long until they also found themselves weaving far more cotton than they could either produce or consume themselves. Meanwhile, the heating stoves and plows produced by the Zoarites at their iron foundry became so popular in rural Ohio during the early 19th century that their manufacture grew into a highly profitable industry. And at Amana, members found the demand for their woolens growing steadily with their reputation for high quality. Concentrating on its woolen mills, Amana was soon weaving far more wool than the community's three thousand sheep could produce.[130]

Amana, like many of the other societies, gave increasingly less attention to agriculture as it expanded its manufactures. It came to depend more and more on the profits of its woolen mills to purchase the necessities no longer produced in the community. What did it give up? Despite a strong desire to be self-sufficient in agricultural and dairy products, by the end of the 19th century a year never passed that the society did not have to buy food supplies from outside to meet the needs of members and livestock. It had found that it was more economical to rent out its farm lands and enlarge its mills. And by the beginning of the 20th century, it had given up many community crafts. Ready-made clothes were cheaper than those made by Amana tailors, and it was deemed better to buy factory-made furniture than "to take the time of a good workman." [131]

When a self-sufficient community abandons some of its activities to concentrate on those it finds more remunerative, values other than economic independence have gained precedence. The relative "cheapness" of outside goods reflects a new way of evaluating community labor. The "world's" standards are now being applied. Why? All these communities had a limited labor supply, and second, they did not want to overwork. Sparing their members unnecessary toil and drudgery was one of their goals, and it was easy to follow the principle of least effort when even the group's ideology supported it. Amana members, according to Shambaugh, wanted only a modest surplus, although enough to see them through bad as well as good years. To accomplish this, however, they found it unnecessary to work "exhaustively"; it was sufficient to work steadily at some comfortable industry. And the Amana mills were not turn-of-the-century sweat shops. Shambaugh found them "unusual" despite the noisy machinery. They were "light and airy," and every worker had a cushioned chair or stool for "between times." Flowers decorated the looms, and many tables with "well equipped cupboards" were distributed throughout the factory where the workers would eat their lunch and take their midmorning and midafternoon coffee breaks.[132]

With a limited labor force Amana was faced with the choice of hiring outside labor to staff its expanding mills or put its own people to work in the mills while employing outside labor to farm its land. Factory labor was much more expensive to hire than that necessary to perform the unskilled or semiskilled farm chores from which the community released its own members. Moreover, unskilled heavy farm work was the less desirable choice for the members. But after employing increasing numbers of outsiders to do agricultural work, the society then found it more profitable to rent much of its cultivated land and concentrate its efforts in industry rather than supervise extensive farming done by hired help. Even so, by 1908 Amana was employing about two hundred farm hands to work under society foremen and superintendents.[133]

Amana was discovering that the labor-saving process involves the capitalization of human labor through the addition of machinery, a process hard to stop once begun. But with machinery added, the same unit of labor will produce more goods in the same amount of time or the same amount of goods in less time. The wants of the communists were very limited; they were not seeking more goods or greater wealth. Consequently they limited the expansion of the mills and allowed the demand for their woolens to far outrun the supply. Despite curtailment of the expansion process, Amana became highly specialized in its exchange relationships with the larger society, and such relationships entail mutual dependencies.

Amana was large enough, and its woolens enterprise successful enough, by the turn of the century that it could effectively compete with other enterprises. Some of the other groups were not so fortunate. To effect increasing economies of scale, production units must become larger; and as they do, they employ more labor. At some point a community's labor supply is exhausted, and it must employ labor from outside. Use of outside labor means contamination from the world, which all the communal societies opposed. But in each community where it occurred, the extensive use of outside labor signaled a major transformation of its economic structure. The commune was becoming a corporation; its members were becoming co-owners and co-managers of productive property worked by hired labor.

The labor problems of the Shakers and Rappites were further complicated by the effect of celibacy, a dwindling membership. The Rappites were never energetic recruiters, and the Shakers had little success adopting orphans. Only one of every ten children the Shakers raised remained to become a member. More and more their few recruits tended to be older people seeking a secure haven at an age when the "opportunity costs" of celibacy had become minimal. The more the memberships of the two societies aged, the harder it became for them to perform heavy physical labor and the more necessary it became to depend on hired laborers to work the land. Moreover, with a diminishing membership they were unable to accomplish economies of scale except by working in close association with hired workers, which they were unwilling to do.[134]

The Rappites eventually closed down all their factories at Economy and depended on income from investments outside. Their holdings included oil wells, a coal mine, and various railroad stocks. By 1890 Economy had only 44 members, of whom about half had been recently recruited to add new "vitality." But the hired hands working the Economy farms greatly outnumbered the members, and by now were even ridiculing their employers for their old-fashioned dress. The remaining members lived on like retired pensioners while poor management and bad investments depleted their capital until the final division in 1905.[135] Among the Shakers, when a colony grew too small to function properly, the members were transferred to another colony and the property sold, a slow process that today has ended in only two colonies and 12 old ladies. The dwindling membership has been living off land rents and property liquidations for almost a century.[136]

Although Zoar did not practice celibacy in its later years, it never fully recovered from the disastrous cholera epidemic that carried off a third of its members in 1832. It began hiring outside labor at that time and continued to do so until its demise in 1898. In 1877, at the time of William Hinds's visit, the total population of Zoar was only 254 and that of its labor force (including the families of its workers) was 171. When Hinds inquired about the effect of the employee population on the membership, the reply was, "Very injurious. They tempt our young people into bad habits." After the Civil War so many of Zoar's young people began defecting that by the 1890's the aging residents had become almost completely dependent on hired labor for most of the farm work. Even at the time of Hinds's visit, much of their land was being rented.[137]

The Zoar population was too small to effect economies of scale in its industries and too inflexible to grow through the hiring of labor and the improvement of its products. With time its once popular heating stoves appeared "grotesque" beside the lighter, more efficient stoves of its competitors. Gradually all Zoar's factories and shops closed down as outside products became "cheaper" than its own. By the time the society expired, it had lost almost all its industries and crafts. It was still making its members' clothes and shoes, but the cloth and leather were now obtained more "cheaply" from outside.[138]

Oneida chose to develop its economy almost entirely in the direction of manufacturing and with interesting consequences. According to the *Oneida*

Circular of October 1, 1863, the community had depended entirely on its own labor until 1861, when it hired outsiders to dig drainage ditches on the farm. After that, dependence on hired labor grew rapidly. The society was employing 27 hired workers in its various departments by 1865; 49 by 1866; 154 by 1867; and some 200 by 1869. This was the period of rapid expansion at Oneida's trap factory; the society had decided to expand its enterprises by using wage labor.[139]

Oneida later expressed some guilt over this decision in its February 20, 1871, edition of the *Circular*. There it admitted the community had come to rely heavily on "hired help" for jobs demanding the most manual labor, but it went on to explain that this situation was not due to any "lilly-fingered" avoidance of hard work by the members. The society found it expedient—more profitable— to employ its own workers in the "more remunerative employments" such as department "superintendents" and to employ outsiders in the less remunerative. But as commune members turn into corporate owners and managers, they quickly develop typical management attitudes toward their hired laborers. In another edition of the *Circular*, the society noted how much it hated to drive and push its hired laborers as employers are accustomed to do in the "vicious hireling system of the world." As a result their "hirelings" had "selfishly" taken advantage of the society's "lenity" and were causing a "great leak in the profits of [their] manufactures." Independently inventing its own brand of Taylorism, Oneida instituted piecework rates to avoid "slavery"![140]

This situation convinced Nordhoff upon his visit in 1874 that Oneida was no longer "a commune in the common sense of the word."[141] Members worked "steadily" but nearly always in a supervisory capacity and "not very hard." All "drudgery they nowadays put upon their hired people." They had even taken to employing outsiders in the service branches, in the laundry, kitchen, furnace room, shoemaker's shop, and tailor's shop. Nordhoff concluded that "Oneida is in reality . . . a large and prosperous manufacturing corporation, with a great number of partners all actively engaged in the work." His words were prophetic, for only six years later Oneida was to become in name what he had already declared it to be in fact.

Amana in a sense tried to have its cake and eat it too; it endeavored to expand its manufacture of woolens while retaining as much self-sufficiency as possible in its agriculture and crafts. It moved its own labor into the mills and employed labor from outside in the farm sector. About 1905 Amana employed some 200 farm laborers while only 18 of the 125 workers in the woolen mills were hired from outside. These hired outsiders performed only the heaviest and most unskilled chores. The same division of labor became true in other branches as well. Members objected more and more to heavy and unpleasant work. Instead of cleaning stables and outdoor toilets on a rotation basis as had been the custom, they hired tramps for such purposes and built a bunkhouse for them. Like Oneida, Amana even began to employ hired labor in its service branches, particularly the communal kitchens. Community women no longer enjoyed working in them. Older women were excused; and younger women, when it was their turn to work complained of physical ailments.[142]

For those societies able to carry "labor saving" farthest, their labor-saving "devices" eventually came to include people as well as machinery. Faced with a limited labor supply, members took the best jobs for themselves (the brotherhood) and hired outsiders (the otherhood) to perform the least desirable. The more a communistic part-society integrates its economy with that of a larger capitalist society, the more like the capitalistic otherhood it will become. It is not surprising that both Oneida and Amana were eventually to prosper as joint-stock corporations. By the time the change took place, it was purely nominal.

With commercialization the goals of a communal society inevitably become more immediate and short term. Shaker traders soon developed a reputation for great shrewdness, and Emerson remarked that "they always sent the devil to market." [143] But otherhood is hard to restrict to the marketplace; the devil can come back to haunt the brotherhood. Concerns of an immediate and practical nature can easily eclipse millennial goals, and opportunities for individualistic and competitive behavior can readily disrupt the social order.

Father Meachum, as we saw, was not against those improvements that would leave more time for intellectual and spiritual growth, but he was against superfluous baubles that appealed to fleshly "vainglory." By 1840, however, the Shakers had been so corrupted by such vainglorious baubles as "veils," "silver pencils" and "useless journals" that a revivalistic movement took place called "Mother Ann's Work." Shaker "revelations" during this period advocated a return to the earlier simple life of plain speech, plain dress, and plain furnishings. One elder argued for complete separation from the world including the abandonment of industries and a return to an agricultural economy.[144] Two generations later, Shaker Evans, as we saw above, was to wish aloud to Nordhoff that the society had taken that advice. "Only the simple labors and manners of a farming people can hold a community together." [145]

Even the Rappites' first move, to Indiana, was motivated in part by a desire to extend markets. On the Wabash they were linked to an inland waterway, and agencies to handle their products were soon established in a number of river towns. When they moved back to Pennsylvania, even the name of their new community, Economy, reflected the changing emphasis from agriculture to manufacturing.[146] It is not surprising that many members were now attracted to a new leader advocating higher living standards and less work.

In 1875, long after Oneida had committed itself to manufacturing and the hiring of labor, Noyes warned his fellow members of the dangers involved; the business could easily corrupt them. Employing a distinction between subject and object resembling that of contemporary existentialism, he said that money making as an external objective could easily subvert them from the subjective pursuit of education and personal development. Yet only a year later, in 1876, replacement of the *Oneida Circular* by the *American Socialist* marked a significant secular change at Oneida. Perfectionism had been replaced by socialism, but the latter did not provide the divine justification for Noyes's theocracy that Perfectionism had. Four years later his theocracy had ended and with it Oneida communism.[147]

With growing commercialism, short-term individualistic considerations increasingly overshadow the more long-term ideological goals of the original social movement. And as this crucial dimension of individual commitment weakens so do all the other commitment factors, especially frequency of interaction. Hinds noted a weakening of purpose and interaction at Zoar during his stay in 1876.[148] In his opinion the young people were losing their dedication to the community. There were few meetings and no mutual-criticism practices; attendance at Sunday services was poor. "There was no meeting, I was informed, in which all take part—where all hearts flow together in unity and devotion. Is it any wonder that the young people . . . lose their attraction for Community life?" By the time of Randall's visit in 1898, "All services had been abandoned . . . and as one member remarked, religious sentiment was passing away as a prelude to the departure of communism." [149]

The same dwindling participation and loss of dedication transpired at Amana. In the days when exclusion from church was a drastic punishment, attendance at all religious services was mandatory; but by 1905 Amana elders were content if young people were loyal enough to attend with "reasonable" regularity. Even the common dining halls were eventually given up at Amana. Members began to take food home to eat in family groups, and finally the communal kitchens merely prepared meals, which the family reheated on its own kerosine stove before serving. The old dining halls were used to feed hired laborers.[150]

As goods produced outside Amana became "cheaper" than its own craft products, the village stores grew increasingly important. All members of the colony received an annual allowance or credit to make their necessary purchases, an allowance that varied among the membership according to Trustee perceptions of "justice and equity." The allowance system always caused some degree of invidious comparison, but as long as the community sanctions were strong, competitiveness was kept within bounds. Shambaugh records a late 19th-century occurrence that illustrates the strength of moral persuasion at that time: [151]

> Some years ago a talented Brother appealed to one of the First Brethren for a larger sum of maintenance on the ground that the service rendered by him was of unusual value to the Community and that his position required a larger personal expenditure than that of the average Brother. The reply of the First Brother is an admirable illustration of the spirit of the Community. He sat by an open window overlooking a meadow where Eduard, a half-witted shepherd, was tending his flock of sheep. "Dost thou see Eduard yonder in the meadow?" asked the First Brother. "Yes, Brother." "Doth he not perform the task allotted to him faithfully and to the utmost extent of his ability?" "Yes, Brother." "Go

thou then, my dear Brother, and do likewise. Be thankful that the Almighty God hath endowed thee with greater gifts, for therein thou hast already received a fuller allowance. Go render unto the Community thy best service and offer up a prayer to the Heavenly Father for His special kindness and gracious gifts to thee."

According to Mrs. Barbara Schneider Yambura, who grew up in Amana during the years before it changed to a joint-stock company, many of the members by her time were "unacquainted with the old time Inspirationists" and "felt no allegiance to the ideals of Christian Metz." [152] As the original, long-term goals of the society weakened and as frequency of interaction among the members diminished, increasing privatization of needs was an inevitable sequitur. And as interests became more familial and individualistic, they became more short-term and materialistic. Individual needs began to multiply well beyond the point where the society could still be the major source of their satisfaction.

Members wanted to buy things not provided by the society and became increasingly resentful of the meagre allowance doled out by the elders. Mail-order catalogues had invaded the community, and they offered many temptations. The paved highway and the automobile now brought tens of thousands of visitors each year in place of the annual twelve hundred at the turn of the century. Members began buying radios, cameras, and bicycles in considerable numbers. Even a few pianos and automobiles appeared. The old costume was abandoned as women adopted bright colors, jewelry, and silk stockings. As one man told Shambaugh about the time of the change, "We cease to have communism the minute one member of the group gets a dime more than another." [153]

To make their individual purchases, members were earning money on their own, and some even opened private bank accounts in Iowa City. Yambura tells how her brother took a paper route to earn money and buy his first bicycle and how she subcontracted part of the job to get spending money for herself. Some members even used Amana property in their schemes of private enterprise.[154]

The drift within the communes toward privatization with its individualization and expansion of needs was bound to result in greater internal competition and friction. Barbara Yambura's story about her mother's determination to have a new bathtub with indoor plumbing in defiance of the elders vividly illustrates the disintegrative effects of new consumer wants and new private means of supplying them. After being scolded by the elders for her extravagance, she cried with shame and embarrassment. But the more she privately reflected on the matter, the more her initial remorse gave way to belligerent indignation. After all, she had saved part of her family-allowance credits for years while the very elders who accused her of extravagance had used up theirs each year and then begged for and gotten more. And she was paying much of the cost herself, anyway, with money earned from the sale of her privately grown vegetables and her embroidered tablecloths. Ever since her husband died, moreover, she had been giving the family's annual wine allotment to one of the elders who had scolded her; she would threaten to take it back! She got her way.[155]

The same individualistic, competitive tendencies showed up at Zoar and Economy before the end. At Zoar, women began washing clothes for visitors, and boys caught and sold fish and took odd jobs for private spending money. Bicycles quickly became a major consumer item. Families had always been allowed to raise their own chickens; but they were restricted to a certain number per family, and feed was rationed accordingly. But with the increase of private-enterprise schemes, families began to sell eggs to outsiders and disregarded the community restriction on the number of fowl.[156]

Even outright "cheating" against the collectivity took place in this context. At Economy, for example, an investigation into poultry raising about 1890 disclosed that one household had developed a large enterprise by circumventing the feed ration. It was feeding its chickens bread from the community bakery because bread was a necessity of life the society had never thought to ration.[157] The profits of this household's private enterprise were being earned entirely at the expense of the collectivity.

With the gradual breakdown of all dimensions of commitment, the societies lost any resemblance to social movements and became more and more like secular corporations. But the viability of a corporation depends on conditions of legal predictability, and the viability of these communes had been based on conditions of social predictability. With commitment undermined, social predictability soon went the same route. Societies not already decimated by the long-range consequences of celibacy were left with two major alternatives: they could disband, or they could reorganize under the conditions of legal predictability. Zoar disbanded; Oneida and Amana reorganized.

The breakdown of social predictability first becomes apparent with the increase of "cheating" or "free rider" behavior. Each member seeks to lower contributions to the collectivity while maintaining demands upon it. Individual bitterness within the society increasingly takes the socialist form of the zero-sum view; the greater leisure (malingering) of one member is viewed as a theft committed at the expense of the other members, for they must increase their work contributions to compensate for his decrease in effort. In Chapter 3 we saw how Fidel Castro verbalized this same view in reference to Cuban malingerers and absentee workers.

Zoar was the only case in which an outside observer actually documented members' opinions of collective production and consumption immediately prior to the dissolution or reorganization of a successful, 19th-century commune. In this regard, the results of Randall's 1898 interviews are priceless. Randall found the "inequality of the exertion put forth and of the labor performed" was one of the most common complaints and was "often expressed in no undisguised terms." The blacksmith said, "Think how much I would have now had I worked and saved for myself—some in the Society have done hardly any work." In the old shoemaker's opinion it was "not according to nature for one to work

for others. It is better that each be by himself and know what he has got."
Others were bitter that they worked every day until dark while some "got off
with easy jobs." The dairy foreman was looking forward to being on his own
and told Randall that the "communistic system gave the lazy too much lee-
way." He toiled "while others slept." [158]

One individual of particular interest to Randall was Levi Bimeler, school-
master at Zoar and grandson of Joseph Bimeler. Educated outside the Society,
he became a leading agitator for the division of Zoar property. In 1895 and
1896 he published a small paper, *Nugitna*, which he sold only to members but
which openly opposed what we might today call the communist "establishment"
at Zoar. Young Bimeler accused the society of having lost its original religious
devotion in the absence of which equality was no longer being maintained.
Some families were taking advantage of other families as "individual interest
gained supremacy over the general interest." Bimeler concluded:

> Theorists may dream of a golden time when Communism shall pervade this
> whole earth, but let them go to a Communistic Society and fill the place of a
> common laborer and they will awake to the fact that Purgatory is a blessing
> compared with their position. Communism is a curse to any and all communi-
> ties where it is established. It deadens all push, energy and ambition. It puts a
> premium on idleness and unfits a person for the battle with the world. . . . There
> is no equality of rank and fortune in Communistic Societies nor any other in-
> telligent community.[159]

Inequality of effort became a big problem at Amana, too, before the change
although there was never such an open rebellion of the young as at Zoar. Amana
was much larger, and its joint enterprises much more successful. It could
compete in the marketplace; its problem became one of maintaining the work
output of its membership. The society was going into debt paying human labor
savers to do the members' work for them while production steadily decreased.
In addition, collective consumption had become extravagant.[160]

The old controls of social predictability were no longer effective. As individuals pursued private goals in defiance of the elders, their defiance became
more and more open. The attitude at first, says Yambura, was to take "any
liberty you might wish, provided the elders did not find out about it." Finally,
no one cared what the elders thought. Few men, moreover, wanted to serve as
elders anymore. No one wanted the authority, and to reprimand other members
was too embarrassing. Unlike Barbara Heinemann and Christian Metz, the new
elders no longer named actual wrongdoers to shame them publicly during community services; they preferred instead to reprimand the entire community in
general terms. To have pointed an accusing finger at specific persons and to
have described specific cases would have embarrassed the new elders as much as
their victims. Members consequently found it easier to ignore the old restrictions. Expulsions became a thing of the past. No one had the heart to turn a
fellow member out into the cold competitive world away from friends and
kin.[161]

The free-rider effect in the form of the "hampering" brothers and sisters became far too common as a consequence of this weakening of third-person controls. After the society reorganized as a joint-stock company, some 200 outside employees were dismissed at an annual saving of $60,000, and yet there were still not enough jobs for all the members. According to Shambaugh: [162]

> Men who had been "too sick" to do an honest day's work in twenty years were loud in their demands for something to do. Jobs at the disposal of the new management were respectfully asked for by the same individuals who had rejected them as "unreasonable" under the gentle discipline of the old Brotherhood; and here and there an over-weight brother regained his youthful figure. . . . Women who formerly dropped out of the kitchen and garden routine on the slightest pretext (but sent their baskets to the kitchen-house at meal time with great regularity) learned for the first time what it means to prepare three meals a day for a family and to cultivate a vegetable garden if the family were to eat. Deduction in wages for time out resulted in a marked improvement in the general health of men who had formed the habit of being "too sick" to report for work in the field or factory when the apple trees in their own yards needed spraying or the currants were ready to pick—and perhaps to sell.

The communal kitchens were eliminated after the change, and the bakeries and dairies and so on were put on a business basis. The former members, now stockholders, had to earn wages and buy their food. The savings in consumption were enormous. Within 6 weeks the milk consumption in one village dropped to 27 gallons a day from its former average of 175 gallons. Consumption of bread and meat fell to half the previous level.[163] A similar abandonment of thrift in collective consumption had been one of the major problems at Zoar as well.

The Hutterite Adaptation

As we have seen, the same year the original Hutterite colonies moved from Russia to the United States, Nordhoff counted 7 major communal movements in the United States embracing a total of 72 communities.[164] All of these have since disappeared or converted into joint-stock companies. Yet, today, Hutterites live in over 225 colonies, an expansion that has taken place with minimal membership recruitment from the outside—only 50 persons over the past 100 years.[165] What accounts for the unique success of this amazing experiment?

The Hutterites have not been totally immune to commune failure or to membership defection. Lee Emerson Deets, the first social scientist to make a serious study of the Hutterites, was impressed by evidences of colony breakdown as early as 1929 when the Hutterites were only a fifth their present size. He described many of the same symptoms of disintegration noted for our other movements in the preceding section.[166]

Deets found young men in some colonies improvidently "loafing" and thereby provoking others to curtail their own efforts resentfully lest they work too hard themselves. On the side, members were clandestinely operating private enterprises such as trapping and handicrafts, and a few had even been caught stealing and selling colony property. To control these deviations, colonies were giving members larger personal allowances and permitting a limited amount of "capitalistic" enterprise, but they were finding that needs simply continued to grow since there is "no end to what a person wants." [167]

Subsequent studies of the Hutterites have resulted in similar observations, even as recently as the 1970's. Colonies allowing family heads to earn their own money for private consumption have suffered "serious consequences" in the form of growing inequality and the invidious comparisons accompanying it.[168]

In our previous commune examples an important initiating cause of breakdown was endorsement of progress through labor-saving mechanization. While the Hutterites have not eschewed labor-saving machinery, they have so channeled it as to contain the progressive consequences that undermined our 19th-century eutopias. More by accident than intent, Hutterite mechanization has kept within a Shaker Evans agricultural framework instead of following a John Humphrey Noyes industrial expansion. Hutterites were not opposed to industrialization per se, for they had developed extensive craft industries early in their history. But by the time they arrived in the United States, the industrialization process with which Economy, Amana, and Oneida had grown up a generation or two earlier had now become highly competitive. The Hutterites took the more secure and profitable route for their purposes and developed eventually into modern, mechanized farmers.[169]

Hutterites resemble the Shakers, Rappites, and Amana Inspirationists in their capacity to invent new tools, to make adaptations in the machinery they buy, and to be "early adopters" of improved techniques. But by restricting mechanization to farming, they did not create an expanding need for hired labor. In fact, mechanization and the practice of exchanging labor between colonies have enabled them to avoid the use of hired labor with all its disastrous consequences for community integrity. Hutterites have reaped the same benefits from mechanized agriculture as the rest of Canada where the labor requirements of farming dropped over 50 percent between 1950 and 1970 while farm productivity was increasing more than 300 percent.[170]

When mechanization of farm operations is accompanied by a high degree of product specialization to increase profits, colonies can lose much of their self-sufficiency while making themselves increasingly vulnerable to market fluctuation. There is a correlative tendency in such cases to grow dependent on goods produced more cheaply by the "world" than by their own labor. In such cases "progress" tends to run a parallel course with the 19th-century cases. But according to John Hostetler, the predominant trend has been to retain a high degree of product diversification even at the expense of "efficiency." To operate a broad range of enterprises with a small profit margin is considered better strategy than pursuing a highly specialized economy with a large profit margin. The former results in a more even work load during the year, a greater number of responsible positions for the adult males, and greater colony self-sufficiency and independence.[171]

Hutterite colonies, in other words, have been exposed to the same insidious danger of creeping affluence that plagued medieval monasticism as well as the successful 19th-century eutopias. Economic success too often breeds "moral" decay as the expansion of short-term material needs undermines long-term collective goals. The branching adaptation, more than any other single factor, has contained the corrupting influences of economic success. Though not intentionally an adaptive reversion to primitive band fission, branching has become the chief support of membership commitment.

As a social movement ages, long-term goals find it harder to compete with short-term needs, particularly as the consumption of personal property grows more competitive between individuals and families. But through their technique of branching the Hutterites have struck on a goal that is neither immediate nor indefinitely long term. Colonies divide every 15 years, approximately, and during that period the community must save the necessary capital. This provides the Hutterites with a very tangible, realizable objective to implement the more indefinite, ideological goals of their faith. And it is an objective that directly competes with the growth of individual and family needs. It helps to contain these at a "reasonable" level, one of relative austerity under the circumstances. "Wealthy" colonies that grow so "content" with their "luxuries" as to delay branching are soon disrupted by internal fighting. They become dramatic illustrations to all other colonies of the dangers of affluence not only for the colony that fails to branch on schedule but for Hutterianism itself.[172]

Not only does this intermediate goal of branching help to resolve need–goal conflicts by keeping needs more "reasonable," it helps to maintain high frequency of interaction while minimizing disruptive competition. Branching perpetuates the same kind of pioneering, creative game of continually building anew that undoubtedly vitalized the spread of medieval monasticism, though the latter was less deliberate or scheduled. Everyone must work much harder in a new Hutterite colony than in an established one, but the new colony offers its members more opportunities to fill responsible status positions. Instead of competition between individuals for scarce positions, the competitive emphasis shifts constructively from individuals to groups. Enterprises within a colony as well as entire colonies can compete in productivity. This in turn constructively directs the individual's competitive focus toward maximum work effort in each of his membership groups. One cannot let one's fellows down, thus the group game is continually reinvigorated.

All of this unquestionably helps to maintain the boundaries between the Hutterites and the "world." Community fission results in a population expansion that threatens many of the Hutterites' neighbors. Meanwhile, dedication to the fulfillment of branching encourages a single-mindedness of purpose that reinforces Hutterite segregationist behavior. Close friendships with outsiders are discouraged, an isolationism often resented by the world. Hostile acts, such as vandalism or restrictive legislation, are understandable consequences. These in turn help the elders keep alive the Hutterite view of themselves as persecuted. Thus, by strengthening all factors of commitment, branching—for as long as it is feasible—helps make the Hutterite way of life a self-perpetuating system. But an expanding system requires an infinitely open environment. The final test of Hutterite adaptability will come when branching reaches its limits.

According to Diane Bray Heiken who has been studying Hutterite defection and community breakdown during the past four summers, failure to branch usually creates severe problems for a colony. Such a colony is more likely to experience internal factionalism and high defection rates. Heiken's data indicate that while community breakdown is still relatively rare, defection and private consumption are not only far more prevalent than previously reported, they are on the increase.[173]

Summary

To test the feasibility of Communist Man (Millennial Man) incentives for the hypothetical monoecological era, we have examined real-world, 19th-century examples including the still flourishing Hutterite colonies. Like earlier forms of Christian communism these communities were religious social movements stressing collective consumption. Membership commitment far exceeded anything we would normally expect in modern organizations when measured according to the same criteria. In part, Communist Man incentives clearly depend on fortuitous social-movement conditions strong enough to produce a degree of membership commitment never equaled under normal circumstances.

This high degree of commitment must be accompanied, moreover, by the conditions of social predictability. Most of the communities were small, close to the average size of traditional, peasant villages. The smallest communities, those of the Hutterites, approach the size of primitive bands. The largest successful movements developed internal organizations which intentionally kept social visibility high. These organizations were able to maintain the conditions of social predictability, as in the case of Amana, even after commitment began to weaken.

Given all these unusual conditions, Communist Man (Millennial Man) incentives work; material rewards are distributed according to need. But while such groups are extremely egalitarian as far as property incentives are concerned, they are certainly not without selective incentives. They employ selective incentives of the same social quality as those employed in traditional communities. They are simply more deliberate and better organized. Those intentional communities that failed to effect conditions of social predictability and the selective social incentives those conditions make possible were doomed to early failure. In order to work, Communist Man incentives obviously require conditions of reciprocal altruism. Despite strong egalitarian ideals, the social incentives of successful Communist Man communities are never equal. They are unequally applied to get effective leadership and to curtail free riding.

Accepting notions of progress and labor-saving devices leads such communities toward commercial interdependence with the outside world. The needs and goals of the communards inevitably expand and diversify; and as they do, they undermine collective consumption and eventually collective production. Pursuit of self-interest replaces the original fight-self ethic. Members who pursue personal-property incentives are no longer controlled by the previous social incentives. To avoid complete dissolution, groups with successful enterprises may continue in corporate form as the communards transform themselves into juristic-person stockholders.

Although Hutterites display similar tendencies toward breakdown, their communard adaptation to frontier circumstances has made them unusually resistant. They have kept their colonies close to primitive-band size through an intentional and sophisticated form of band fission. The latter gives them an "intermediate" near-future goal to reinforce conditions of predictability and commitment.

Chapter Six

Israeli Communes: Millennial Man in Eutopia (II)

THE COMMUNES Charles Nordhoff labeled "a mutiny against society" [1] we might call today extreme cases of "counter-culture"—a kind of group game played against, or apart from, the external world by a cohesive team of members. In sheer durability the Hutterites have proven themselves most successful at this game because they developed a way to continually revitalize it. Our other 19th-century eutopias became so deeply involved in the game playing of capitalist civilization that it eventually undermined their team game.

While the Hutterites meet the conditions of Rousseauean democracy, they would hardly be an acceptable model for that more sophisticated Rousseauean civil state in which people presumably continue their intellectual and moral progress. Such a civil state would have to be much larger than a Hutterite colony, and while Rousseau felt a confederacy of small, face-to-face communities might be the solution, he confessed to complete ignorance on how to make such a system work. [2]

Suppose we found communal game players who were patriotic and nationalistic rather than simply countercultural in their proclivities? Patriotism was Rousseau's example of a "virtue" powerful enough to weld together individual interest, subgroup interest, and the "general will" or collective good of the entire civil state. [3] Could patriotic communard game players be the basis for a new kind of progressive, self-governing state? Martin Buber not only believed so, he indicated the very communities that would show the world how it could be done, the Israeli kibbutzim. [4] As he viewed the situation in 1949, capitalist civilization was impoverishing human society more each day by individualizing and atomizing it and thereby robbing it of the collaboration and association so vital to social health. Some form of socialism must replace the morally bankrupt capitalist order, but the centralist version of Bolshevik socialism was not the one. This version produces a state which so thoroughly "devours" society that in the end the cure becomes worse than the disease. Buber called for a renewal of the "utopian" ideal of decentralized socialism, a federation of fully cooperative communities that could combine into a genuine "organic commonwealth"— a "community of communities." The two "poles of socialism" between which all of us must choose he labeled "Moscow" and "Jerusalem." Thus, the fully cooperative Israeli commune becomes the most promising road to a utopian socialist future, the Jerusalem road.

The patriotic or nationalistic character of the Israeli kibbutz is what most distinguishes it from our North American eutopias. The kibbutz movement is only part of the larger Zionist movement, Jewish nationalism dedicated to the creation and protection of the Israeli state. The kibbutzim distinguished themselves as pioneer communities in the Jewish resettlement and "reconquest" of Palestine, and kibbutzniks still regard themselves as superpatriots. Many boasted to me in 1968 that kibbutz participation in the Six Day War was far out of proportion to the number of kibbutzniks. Although the latter represent a mere 3 percent of the Jewish population of Israel, those in the armed forces sustained 25 percent of the casualties. As one man explained it, "That's what we're here for; that's what it's all about."

In total population, some 90,000 persons, the kibbutz movement is still the largest commune movement the world has ever seen, about three times as large as the total Hutterite population. Its impressive size and its relative openness are not so surprising, however, when it is viewed as a nationalistic movement. Unlike the 19th-century examples, the kibbutz movement has received generous financial and technical assistance from the Jewish Agency and more recently from the Israeli state.[5] Since the latter owns 90 percent of the land, kibbutzim do not have to buy their farms as do Hutterites, for example. They rent cheaply from the state on 49-year readily renewable leases. And the population turnover rate far exceeds that of our 19th-century communes.[6] According to a kibbutz federation estimate, the number of ex-kibbutzniks living in Israel is three times as large as the number still living in the commune settlements. During the 1950's, for example, the defection rate was nearly 10 percent per year, although the total kibbutz population was simultaneously increasing by about 25 percent of its present size. While regretting the loss of converts, kibbutzniks embellish this statistic too with patriotic pride; it demonstrates their invaluable historical role in indoctrinating and acclimatizing new Israeli citizens.

Despite the relative success of this commune movement, few who are most knowledgeable about it, including educated kibbutzniks, consider it a utopian model for the rest of the world. In this chapter we see just how unreal is the hope for a Jerusalem road to socialism. We see below that the kibbutz is already contending with all the symptoms of breakdown or transformation that beset our 19th-century eutopias. And since the modified form of kibbutz known as the moshav shitufi shows many of these same symptoms to a more advanced degree, much of the chapter is devoted to comparing the two forms. We shall also see that while patriotism or nationalism can work for a eutopian community at one stage in its development it can work against it at another stage.

Kibbutz and Shitufi

The population of Israeli communes is predominantly European and Western in origin, a fact which has greatly affected the growth of these communities relative to the rest of Israel. Table 6.1 tells the story for the kibbutz.[7] The greatest period of growth took place prior to and just after statehood in 1948. The kibbutz population by 1948 was nearly 8 percent of the total Jewish population of Israel. This was at a time when European Jews made up 80 percent of that population. By 1960 the great postwar influx of Eastern, or Oriental, Jews from North Africa and the Near and Middle East had reduced the European share of the population to less than 40 percent. Since Eastern Jews preferred private farming on moshavim ovdim settlements to a collective way of life, the source of supply for the relatively more sophisticated Zionist communards began drying up soon after statehood. As it did, kibbutz expansion tended to level off in absolute numbers and to fall rapidly relative to national growth.

The earliest kibbutzim are now more than 65 years old, and the average age of all 225 is over 30 years. The oldest have not yet caught up with Amana, Zoar, and the Rappites while the average age is still less than the lifespan of Oneida.

In the early years many Zionist leaders were less than enthusiastic about the idea of communist settlements. But as the Jewish population came under increasing Arab attack, defense considerations were given priority. The communal kibbutz with its closely knit social organization and strong ideology was cheaper to establish and far better able to survive under unsettled political conditions than the more individualistic moshavim ovdim.[8]

Youth from Eastern Europe and Germany, many of them illegal immigrants,

TABLE 6.1.   *Kibbutz Population 1931–1968*

Year	Number of kibbutzim	Percentage of Jewish population	Total inhabitants
1931	24	2.5	4,000
1936	43	4.0	16,000
1947	140	7.0	47,000
1948	150	7.9	54,000
1949	211	6.5	64,000
1968	225	3.0	90,000

occupied temporary camps in the towns and villages where they supported themselves as laborers while waiting to receive land. The difficulties with the Arabs and British as well as Hitler's rise to power in Germany added even greater impetus to Zionist ideology, and the immigrants who entered the kibbutzim and remained there tended to be those most commited to it. The kibbutz became an indispensable instrument of Jewish nationalism and the defense of the Jewish community. It stored illegally acquired arms, helped organize the Jewish Defensive Force and the Palmah commando troops, and aided in illegal immigration.[9]

With establishment of the Israeli state, restrictions on immigration and colonization were removed, and preparatory kibbutz groups in Israel were quickly settled while those abroad were free to immigrate immediately. Shortly after statehood the kibbutzim outnumbered the moshavim, but within 10 years the moshav population was 50 percent larger than that of the kibbutz.[10] Moreover, defections from the kibbutzim increased greatly after independence while the kibbutz-affiliated youth movements at home and abroad found far fewer recruits than before.

The great influx of Eastern Jews following statehood created a surplus of labor outside the kibbutz just as it was beginning to experience an internal shortage. Ideological resistance within the kibbutz movement to employing this needy outside labor provoked public criticism both in Israel and among Jews abroad. In January of 1950, the kibbutz antihiring policy was denounced by David Ben-Gurion, then prime minister. Kibbutzim soon began to relent under this pressure, but most remained convinced that the hiring of labor was in direct contradiction to the spirit of the kibbutz and a direct threat to kibbutz morale.[11]

The nationalistic orientation of the kibbutz movement, which had contributed so much to its genesis and expansion, was now making claims upon it. Even the mixed agriculture of early settlement days, when self-sufficiency was important, was giving way to intensive specialization to increase profitability. And as kibbutz industrialization expanded for the same reason, the hiring of labor became harder to avoid. By 1970 when well over half the workers employed in kibbutz industries were hired outsiders, some kibbutzim were already deriving as much as 90 percent of their income from industrial pursuits.[12] Today more than 50 percent of all kibbutz income is industrial; and since its rising living standards are so much a function of this income, the kibbutz, like most of the successful 19th-century eutopias, has become dependent on "labor saving" through the hiring of nonmembers.

The shitufi has had a much different history from the kibbutz, for it began much later as a modified form.[13] The founders of the earliest shitufim between 1936 and 1938 wanted to produce collectively and share communally like kibbutzniks but without the kibbutz mechanisms for fighting the nuclear family. The moshav shitufi is often said to lie halfway between the kibbutz and the "private" moshav (moshav ovdim) because shitufim members produce collectively as do members of kibbutzim while they live and consume privately in their own family residences as do the inhabitants of the moshavim. If this were absolutely true, we would have to classify the shitufi as a collective rather than a communal-farming society. But while production is collective, the individual's contribution is not rewarded on the basis of labor time, and the individual is not free to consume whatever he pleases. As in the kibbutz, the shitufi distributes to its members according to need, and they are expected to work according to their abilities. Shitufi members, unlike kibbutzniks, however, live and consume in family units. There is no communal kitchen, and children are not reared away from their parents in special dormitories. Nevertheless, in most shitufim the family must hold its consumption within limits set by the group unlike the ordinary moshav where each family is at liberty to buy whatever it can afford. In other words, most shitufim attempt to equalize consumption, as in the kibbutzim, while allowing more range for family variation. Compared with our 19th-century eutopias, we could say that the shitufim resemble Zoar while the kibbutzim are more like Oneida.

Members of the kibbutz movement often refer to the shitufi as the "kolkhoz form" of Israeli cooperative, a designation which many shitufi members resent. The latter recognize that the shitufi is not a collective like the kolkhoz, and some even point to the absence of a private farming sector within the shitufi as additional evidence of the difference between the two. Since they do not consider the kolkhoz to be a "voluntary" cooperative like the shitufi, they regard the private family plot as an official "concession" to kolkhoz families to keep them mollified. The shitufi, on the other hand, allows members to have some fruit trees around the house and even a few vegetables as long as this produce is consumed only by the family. The fact that it cannot be sold is a restriction imposed upon the shitufim by the members themselves, not by some outside authority. And they impose this restriction on themselves to insure that all give full attention and effort to cooperative production.

Writing in 1955, Melford Spiro thought it possible that many kibbutzim would eventually transform into shitufim.[14] Yet only ten years later American economist Kanovsky felt the shitufi was already in "decline." [15] While neither view is altogether correct, neither is completely wrong.

The first shitufi, Kefar Hittim, was founded in 1936 followed by Moledet in 1937 and Shavei Zion in 1938. Except for Bert Hillel, which changed to a private moshav after one year, these three settlements constituted the shitufim "movement" from 1936 until the end of World War II. During most of the period when European Zionist organizations were forming youth groups to found and populate kibbutzim, the shitufi was not even an existing alternative. All three settlements occurred late, were largely independent of one another, and did not attempt to form a movement or publicize their cause. Because the kibbutz federations considered them an aberrant and threatening alternative, the shitufim were forced to join the moshav movement, which had little sympathy for them either at first.

Five of the shitufim in existence during my visit in 1968 were formed between World War II and 1950, all of them by soldiers of the Jewish Brigade (World War II) and the Israel Defense Army (War of Independence). Two others formed during this period have since changed to private moshavim, Kefar Monash in 1958 and Ramot Naphtali in 1962. The decade from 1951 to 1961 saw the founding of 14 more shitufim, 12 of which were originally kibbutzim. All shitufim are composed predominantly of European, American, or South African Jews; as in the case of the kibbutzim there are no shitufim comprised of Eastern Jews.

The shitufim began a little too late to become a strong competitor of kibbutzim and private moshavim, and they did not develop a movement or federation of their own. The settlements have tended to be "spontaneous" and independent of one another. It was not until the second shitufi convention held in 1950 that even certain basic principles of organization were agreed upon and not until 1962 that an intermovement committee was established to deal with matters concerning all communal moshavs. Several shitufim members told me they had lived in kibbutzim several years before becoming aware of the existence of shitufim. This lack of information has been a serious inhibiting factor in their growth, for the bulk of their membership up to 1968 was comprised of former kibbutz inhabitants. The turnover in the shitufim formed by army groups has been high, and replacement has been largely by kibbutz defectors.

At the time of my visit in 1968, there were 22 shitufim with a total population of about 4,500 persons. Included in these figures is Bet Herut, a settlement listed on some official records as a shitufi although many people in the movement refuse to include it. They do not regard it as a legitimate shitufi because it allows members to engage in private production. Since 1968, 18 new shitufim settlements have been established, most of them in occupied territories such as the Golan, the West Bank, and the Sinai. Including Bet Herut, there are now 40 shitufim with a total population of about 8,000. According to Jill Cordover Byron-Cooper, who at the time of this writing was in Israel studying the shitufim, the memberships of these new settlements consist primarily of highly ideological young Israelis from urban areas.[16] They have also benefited from the wave of Western Jewish immigrants that followed the Six Day War. At least one of the recently formed shitufim, Neve Ilan, is almost completely "industrial" and may become a prototype for future settlements.

In general the shitufi is identical to the kibbutz in its pattern of production. It maximizes economies of scale by mechanizing its operations as much as possible. In older settlements like Kefar Hittim as well as some of the later ones like Timorim a great deal of attention is given to planning, cost accounting, and improvement of production records. Field crops are emphasized although most settlements also have other interests such as oranges, avocados, chickens, turkeys, and dairy cattle. A few have begun to grow flowers for the European market, and some are planting vegetables for which mechanical pickers have been developed; pruning machines have recently been adopted for orchards. In addition most shitufim have small industries: Timorim and Kefar

Daniel produce metal furniture; Regba kitchen cabinets; Moledet prefabricated metal sheds; Kefar Hittim has a textile plant; Nir Gallim a foundry; Bet Herut a silkscreen printing plant; and Shoresh a tourist resort.

Social Predictability

Most kibbutzim and shitufim qualify as face-to-face communities in the same sense as our 19th-century eutopias. Averaging less than 500 souls in size with strong commitment characteristics, they are capable of achieving high visibility and effective social incentives. Although the largest kibbutzim reach almost 2,000 in population, they average about 400 persons in size. Of these 400, approximately 225 are members and candidates, 125 are children of members, and the remaining 50 consist of visiting children and youth and the elderly parents of members.[17] Shitufim tend to be much smaller than kibbutzim, populations averaging only 200 each. The 9 shitufim I visited in 1968 ranged in size from 70 to 400 persons and averaged 250 persons and 55 families.

In the early days kibbutzim were very small. Before World War I some had only 5 to 10 members, mostly unmarried with few if any dependents. In 1922 they averaged only 18, a figure that had increased to 67 by 1930. Today, in most official quarters it is felt that a kibbutz should have at least 80 to 100 families (at least 200 members); because of the relatively fixed service and administrative costs of kibbutzim, per-capita overhead expenses become oppressively high in the smaller communes. Such considerations reflect, again, the pressures toward settlement profitability. Many early kibbutzim began as small contract-labor groups, which as late as the 1920's derived much of their income from outside employment. It was during the 1920's that they successfully developed mixed farming to protect against market slumps and to employ members more evenly throughout the year.[18]

This kind of beginning shows how kibbutzim were able to achieve conditions of mutual compatibility and homogeneity without the selective leadership so crucial in most of our 19th-century cases. For example, the Labor Battalion of the 1920's, from which some kibbutzim stem, was originally divided in cells of ten members formed on the basis of mutual friendship and common background. The Hashomer Hatzair pioneers were organized in Poland before World War I as part of the Jewish Boy Scout movement. After the war the movement became ardently Zionist and established European centers to teach Jewish youth how to organize and live in Palestinian communes. Hashomer Hatzair members often had to wait long periods in Palestine before being settled and during the waiting period formed communal groups that hired themselves out for agricultural and construction work. Other Zionist youth organizations experimented with kibbutzim in Europe as preparation for kibbutz life in Palestine. Most of the youth pioneers (halutzim) came from Eastern Europe, but a few came from Western countries as well. They were organized in small groups, usually from the same country. On arrival in Palestine they were often located in established kibbutzim for additional training and preparation before starting kibbutzim of their own. Settler nuclei in kibbutzim have typically been very cohesive as a result of long preliminary periods of training and working together.[19]

The older and more stable moshavim shitufim also began as relatively homogeneous groups. Shavei Zion was formed by Germans most of whom came from the same town in Germany. Moledet was founded by a group of students who left Germany shortly after the Nazis came to power. Located together in Moshav Nahalal for settlement training, they organized the group that later became the founding nucleus of Moledet. Kefar Hittim was formed by Bulgarians originally scattered among several kibbutzim and among office jobs in town. In 1936 they organized a Bulgarian association in Haifa that became their settlement nucleus.

Later shitufim were not as homogeneous or tightly knit as these three. Most underwent a rapid turnover of membership, but with a candidacy period of one year and careful membership selection they produced reasonably successful groups that gradually drifted toward ethnic homogeneity. For example, the majority of Regba members are German; Bet Herut is two-thirds American; Kefar Daniel and Timorim are predominantly "Anglo Saxon"; and Nir Gallim and Shoresh are mainly Hungarian.

Kibbutzim and shitufim tend to follow the Benedictine pattern of selective negative incentives just as our 19th-century eutopias did. In both, a member's fellow workers will be first to criticize him, then the head of the work branch, then the farm management committee, and finally the general assembly. The mere threat of the final stage is usually enough to bring the person in line. At shitufi Timorim, for example, the farm manager and branch managers know what a worker should accomplish in eight hours at any job, and if one individual consistently fails to measure up, "We want to know why. We call him to a meeting of the Work Committee and let him know that if he doesn't do better his case will be discussed at the next general meeting. He improves then; nobody wants to be discussed by the whole assembly. But we do it if we have to. In a community like ours if one person fails to pull his weight, it costs all of us." Again, we encounter a vivid illustration of the Socialist Man and Millennial Man zero-sum view; no one expands his leisure relative to his fellows' except at their expense.

All writers on the kibbutz stress the importance of public opinion and informal sanctions in controlling members. Given the strong work ideology of the kibbutz, the individual who is reluctant to do his share makes himself a target for criticism whereas the person who works hard and well wins group approval and respect. This system of control has maintained a high level of output from most members. One reason it has, according to anthropologist Melford Spiro, is because the status of each member depends so much upon his labor efficiency.[20] Shirking is "spotted immediately" and jeopardizes "the respect of one's fellows."

According to Murray Weingarten, a founding member of an American kibbutz, some members do "goldbrick." [21] They work halfheartedly, are "sick" as much as possible, and in short become parasitic on the other members. But so negative is the reaction of the community that only a very insensitive person can maintain such behavior for very long.

As explained to me in several kibbutzim, there are lazy people everywhere; the problem is to keep them to a minimum. This is done first by requiring all would-be members to pass a trial candidacy period of one to two years after which membership is granted on approval by a two-thirds majority of the general assembly. During this period candidates are carefully screened although in most cases those who are undesirable become aware of the fact themselves and withdraw before the end of the period. Second, there are very overt ways of making a person feel unwanted, including outright ostracism, a kibbutz version of "excommunication." Perhaps the most common is to pass the offender from one work branch to another. One new member at a certain kibbutz had received this treatment but "had still not gotten the idea." So at a general meeting when opportunities for specialized training were being discussed, this young man asked if he could take a certain course in Tel Aviv. Another member turned to him and said with some astonishment, "What! With your attitude you expect us to send you to school?" The shirker left the kibbutz for good the next day.

The point is that an Israeli commune, particularly a small one, can find some way to make even insensitive recalcitrants too uncomfortable to remain. At one kibbutz I was told the story of a member who had been passed from one branch to another before being permanently assigned to do women's work in the kitchen. Even this did not seem to disturb him, but one day on an emergency work assignment in the kibbutz banana grove his dilatory tactics so enraged one of his co-workers that the latter threatened him with a machete. Usually kibbutzniks abhor violent behavior and loss of temper, but by now public opinion was so universally opposed to the shirker that the entire kibbutz sided with the aggressor. For several days the incident was the favorite topic of conversation at work and in the dining hall, and within two weeks the unwanted member had packed up his family and returned to Johannesburg.

The importance of social-predictability factors in the case of Israeli communes is well illustrated by two moshavim shitufim that had failed before my 1968 stay in Israel. They had already converted to private moshavs (moshavim ovdim), and I visited both to talk with families that had been founding members of the original settlements. These two former communes, Ramot Naphtali and Kefar Monash, had begun with about 40 families each, in 1946 and 1947. Of the original founding families less than half a dozen were left at either moshav by 1958 although both in that year had larger settlement populations than they had started with. The turnover rate had been extremely high in both over the years. Unlike successful kibbutzim and shitufim, neither settlement had started with a strong membership nucleus that had learned to work together before forming communes, and neither ever became a close-knit group.

In both cases most of the original members had been in the Jewish Brigade of the British Army during World War II but had not been in the same units. Not knowing each other well before forming the settlements, they remained "strangers" to one another. "We hadn't lived together before—never pulled together as a team; and a bunch of ex-soldiers don't necessarily make a team. That's why starting with a nucleus like the kibbutzim do is so important. If people are going to fall out, they should do it before starting a settlement." New members entered to replace the old, but insufficient care was taken in their selection. "There were no idealists like you need in a collective community. We were just a bunch of individuals, not an integrated society."

Not surprisingly, labor was so inefficient that profits remained poor and living standards low. Many members felt they were being "held back" by the others and would never be able to realize their full potential. Several who left subsequently became high government officials or successful businessmen in Tel Aviv. "People couldn't get together on the work. Some worked hard and some didn't."

According to one informant who had lived in a kibbutz prior to the shitufi, "There's a certain percentage of loafers in any collective, but if it gets too high you're in for trouble." At Kefar Monash, which had had a printing plant as well as a farm, the printers refused to help at farm chores during periods of peak labor load; they argued that the work would "coarsen" their hands. Others got medical excuses to avoid hard labor in the fields. "But after we became a private moshav, you should have seen how hard those sickly people worked all day long out in the hot sun."

This person's observations parallel those previously recorded for Amana after that society shifted to private production. The consequences for profitability are also strikingly similar. At Ramot Naphtali, for example, the apple orchards paid an annual income of two thousand Israeli pounds per family while production was collective. After dividing the orchard into equal parcels, the income went up to ten thousand each. "There was no increase in production," I was told. "The difference was due to a decrease in the cost of labor and the amount of waste."

In most respects Ramot Naphtali and Kefar Monash resemble the Owenite and Fourierist communes of the 19th century more than the successful religious ones. Lack of homogeneity was crucial in all such cases. The original members at Naphtali and Monash were of many different nationalities; and as they dropped out and others entered, the situation did not improve. No particular criteria were used for selecting new members, and some of the immigrants who joined were not even sure they wanted to farm or live in a rural settlement. "Each family started to do its own thing off the farm, not just sacrifice for the country. Gradually people went into other work." Under these conditions the communities never developed any of the controls of social exchange, and inequalities in the provisioning of the collective good finally led to reorganization. "Now if I work more, I get more." Group commitment never really developed at either settlement.

What is most surprising is that although neither Ramot Naphtali nor Kefar Monash was any better qualified by conditions of social predictability or commitment to be more successful than their Owenite and Fourierist equivalents more than 100 years earlier, these Israeli "failures" actually endured as communes 15 years and 12 years respectively. If we generously set the average life span of the 19th-century failures at 3 years, the Israeli failures were some 500 percent more "successful." This comparison provides a rough index of the degree to which financial and technical assistance to Israeli communes have affected their longevity. Obviously, this assistance has played an extraordinary role in the "success" of Israeli communes in addition to those circumstances contributing to membership commitment.

Commitment

Probably no movement has ever benefited more from the combined effect of persecution and prestige than that of the kibbutz.[22] Persecution of Jews in the diaspora was a fundamental cause of the Zionist and kibbutz movements. The anti-Jewish pogroms and riots in Russia, Poland, Rumania, and Germany between 1881 and the Second World War led to the five aliya, the waves of emigrants from Eastern Europe to Palestine which provided most of the kibbutz manpower. They also sparked the movements that trained and prepared youth for kibbutz life before leaving Europe. The period of most rapid growth in the number of kibbutzim (after 1927) coincided with the increase in Arab attacks, for many of the new settlements were deliberately located in the most dangerous parts of Palestine. Precisely because of the European persecutions and the severe hardships of settlement life in the new land, the kibbutz movement achieved renown throughout the diaspora. And with the achievement of the Zionist dream, Israeli statehood, the kibbutzim reached the peak of their prestige both in Israel and abroad. No other sector of Israeli society was considered more instrumental in the realization of the Zionist dream than the kibbutz population. Today many kibbutzim operate hotels for the thousands of visitors who come each year to see these famous communes for themselves. And each summer thousands of students arrive from the United States and Europe to spend several weeks working hard in kibbutzim fields for only their room and board.

The shitufi has never had the external visibility of the kibbutz. Though the early settlements were a product of the same Zionist response to anti-Semitism that motivated the kibbutzim, they occurred too late to play a significant role in the birth of Israel. Even today many people both inside and outside of Israel have never heard of the shitufi though they may have a fairly accurate picture of the kibbutz. Foreign students do not come to live and work in shitufi settlements during the summer, nor do members feel they are part of a world-famous, or locally famous, movement. There is little doubt that this difference in social reinforcement is partially responsible for a faster rate of change in the shitufim.

The kibbutz movement, as we have seen, was always a highly nationalistic movement dedicated to the Zionist goal of creating and perpetuating the Israeli state. While shitufim members are similarly dedicated to Zionist goals, they tend to consider themselves less "ideological" and more "practical" than many kibbutzniks.

Members of both movements, however, appreciate the security afforded by a collective life that provides reasonably for all their needs. As one kibbutznik explained it to me, "I may not make any money, but I have more security here than I could get in any other society in the world. If I'm killed or disabled tomorrow, my family will be taken care of. I never have to worry." Over $50,000 had been spent by another kibbutz for the treatment of one member victimized by polio, a sum that did not include the cost of building wheelchair ramps into all the buildings. At various shitufim I visited, members frequently compared themselves with private farmers in ovdim settlements. Yes, it was true that some private farmers were far wealthier than shitufi members, but shitufi members never had to face all by themselves those unpredictable disasters that can befall anyone. A private farmer just as industrious and intelligent as the most prosperous neighbor could be wiped out by an incapacitating illness or heavy medical expense, but "In a shitufi, no one has to bear the consequences of a personal misfortune all by himself."

Though not so true of many kibbutzim today, a generation ago the frequency of interaction among members was extraordinarily high. Members had little time to themselves day or night.[23] After working together all day long, they joined in some group activity nearly every evening. And in the common dining hall members were supposed to "mix," to sit with different persons at every meal. As one kibbutz philosopher explained it to me, the communal dining hall is "much more than a place to eat food. It establishes community feeling at a quasireligious level. To eliminate it from kibbutz life would end the kibbutz as kibbutz." From its inception, however, the whole point of the shitufi-type commune was to increase privacy, particularly of the nuclear family. The shitufim eliminated the common dining hall, brought children home again to sleep and eat with their parents, and replaced such collective services as community laundries with conventional "homemaking."

In their desire to maintain equality and reduce individualistic competition, the earliest shitufim were little different from kibbutzim. New members turned over all their wealth to the community as well as any property or money received subsequently such as a legacy or a German restitution payment. Similarly, any salary received by a member for work off the settlement as a teacher, government official or whatever was also turned over to the commune, which returned to that individual a "reasonable" living allowance (if living away from the settlement was necessary).

In Israeli communes as in their 19th-century counterparts, brains, as Nordhoff put it, "come easily to the top." [24] Kibbutzim and shitufim also have to make the best possible use of a limited resource. Despite strong egalitarianism, the most responsible managerial positions are usually rotated within a small elite of able and qualified members. Some persons occupy one of these central posts continuously while others are rotated from one to another. While such people obviously enjoy higher status and greater authority than most, the community is careful not to "symbolize" their status or allow them to form a special interest group or superior social stratum.[25]

In most cases the communities have been able to provide their more able individuals with social rewards for managerial and leadership functions without showing them special deference or allowing them material advantages. Such leadership is not seen as undermining the equality of the group as long as it provides the office holder with no economic advantages and his children with no inherited privileges. In fact, the kibbutz has its own "built-in" egalitarian reminders for its managerial elite and for those kibbutz members who achieve important positions outside. Stories of cabinet ministers and members of parliament made to wait table when home at their kibbutz on weekends were told to me several times during my stay in Israel. Such stories are as important as the events themselves in keeping the kibbutz egalitarian.

Although shitufi members laugh at such stories and consider them symptomatic of the kibbutz's impractical overemphasis on ideology, both kibbutzim and shitufim will quickly vote a competent member out of a managerial position—even one held many years—if the person begins to act authoritarian and possessive. At one shitufi I visited, the farm manager had recently been voted into another job because "we felt he was becoming too assertive. He was beginning to think he was indispensable." Thus, members of both types of commune believe that filling top jobs with those best qualified to fill them and keeping the same people in those jobs for long periods does not lead to "class" differences nor does it compromise the community's egalitarian ethic.

Change and Transformation

In Chapter 5 we traced the breakdown or transformation of 19th-century eutopias through a process that began with weakening commitment and led to the undermining of those selective social incentives supporting the collective good. By accepting progress in the form of labor-saving inventions and machinery, our 19th-century eutopias became dependent on hired labor and externally produced consumer goods. The curtailment of short-term materialistic needs became increasingly "unreasonable," a "privatization" tendency that increased individual competitiveness at the expense of high-frequency interaction. The Hutterites were the only exception; they restricted labor-saving machinery primarily to farming while their branching adaptation provided a pressing "intermediate" goal to help keep needs "reasonable."

The Hutterites, in short, have managed to keep their social distance from the world by effectively pursuing a game of their own. The rest were so gradually corrupted by the world's game that by the time they could perceive the consequences they were both unable and unwilling to counter them. Israeli communes, however, never tried to separate themselves from the world; as part of a "patriotic," nationalistic, social movement, they were always very much within it.

Until that common goal of the kibbutz and Zionist movements, Israeli statehood, was achieved, Israeli communes could dedicate themselves wholeheartedly to a long-term, future goal that made the restriction of short-term, materialistic needs eminently reasonable. But once statehood was achieved, the materialist present with all its mundane, immediate concerns began to take precedence. As participants in a nationalistic movement, moreover, the Israeli communes were committed to attending the needs of the new state. The latter constituted not only an outside world on which the communes had become dependent for financial assistance but an outside world that could now make demands upon them. The two most urgent demands of this outside world were that the communes try to employ those new Israeli citizens who wanted to work but did not want to become communards and that they pay back their debts. The economic function of the communes suddenly became more important than their political function.

It now seems to some Israeli communards that the very movement which created the kibbutzim and shitufim is propelling them toward transformation over which they have no control. Although far more sophisticated than their 19th-century counterparts in appraising the ultimate consequences of current trends, Israeli commune members feel just as unable to control the outside world and even less able to shut themselves off from it. Many see themselves drifting toward a corporate structure similar to that which Amana and Oneida finally adopted.

The case of Ramot Naphtali, the shitufi that failed as a commune and converted to a private moshav, is instructive from the standpoint of corporate structure. Due to the nature of its operations, Ramot Naphtali could divide into separate family plots only one part of its holdings, its irrigated apple orchards. It was not physically possible to divide the extensive fish ponds, and the dry-farming acreage devoted to wheat could not be profitably exploited in small, uneconomical parcels. The settlement continued, therefore, to manage its field crops and fish ponds collectively; it even continued to weed, cultivate, and spray the apple orchards across the new "ownership" boundaries. Apple harvesting is one of the few operations families carry out separately in this nominally "private" moshav which its members now refer to as "the company." The only difference from an "ordinary" company, they say, is that all members have equal shares. Profits from the corporate sector are divided equally among all shareholders, and all who work on the corporate sector are paid according to the hours worked although wages of field managers are now higher than those of the other members. Almost a third of the family heads have permanent jobs off the moshav and leave the farmwork to the other two-thirds and to the hired laborers employed seasonally from outside the settlement. Those who live on the settlement but work away still receive their share of profits after all expenses have been paid including the wages of the working members. This results in a clear distinction between labor and capital. New members, moreover, must now "buy in" by paying their share of capital improvement and equipment.

Not only did some members of Ramot Naphtali believe they were an advanced form of settlement toward which many shitufi settlements were heading, many people still active in the shitufi movement agreed with them. Of the nine shitufim I visited, six showed "corporate" (joint-stock company) tendencies. At Bet Herut new members were required to buy a share of the enterprise and pay for their house and turkey run. Some were being helped with loans. Comparing their settlement to a kibbutz, members told me that there was not as much idealism or "feeling of mission" at Bet Herut: "Here it's a business."

New members at Kefar Daniel had not been asked to buy shares *yet,* I was told. "But we've been talking about it. We all have a big investment in the place now." At Nir Gallim new members had to pay an entrance fee of ten thousand Israeli pounds, which was returned if they left. Some of the young family heads at Talme Yafe would have preferred to form a "farm corporation" of a few families, but they could not get any land. "It all belongs to Israel. So the shitufi is the next best thing." They believed many shitufim would eventually become like Ramot Naphtali or Bet Herut—members would "buy in," and those settlement enterprises jointly administered would employ hired labor in corporate fashion.

At Shoresh, members had held several meetings to discuss the division of settlement assets into family shares. They too thought the shitufim would become "companies" or "corporations" with time; for a big problem, they felt, was the incentive structure. Members needed to be "linked closer to income." A plan recently discussed involved a separate division of profits among the workers of each production branch. "We are people who have left the kibbutz. We are the bad people who want more responsibility and work and are not as willing to share with the community."

Just as some Ramot Naphtali members felt that shitufim in general were moving in their direction, so did many shitufim members believe that the kibbutzim were moving in theirs. They did not believe that the change would be a nominal one; the settlements would continue to call themselves kibbutzim, but they would become just as family-oriented and corporation-minded as shitufim settlements. This seemed to be a threatening notion to many kibbutzniks to judge from the strongly negative reaction it evoked among some of those I questioned about it. Yet when one considers the drift toward privatization in the kibbutz as well as the correlative processes of industrialization and the hiring of outside labor, one cannot help be reminded of Amana and Oneida just before their conversion from communes to joint-stock corporations. As noted in Chapter 5, Charles Nordhoff, in 1874, found Oneidans working largely in a managerial capacity superintending the hired labor of their "manufacturing corporation." [26] Were Nordhoff alive today he might consider most Israeli communes to be examples of the same kind of transition. Below is an attempt to appraise the extent to which this transformation has already taken place.

As we have seen, the long-term goal of the early kibbutz movement and its equivalent of 19th-century millennialism, was the formation of the Jewish state. When the state of Israel became a fact in 1948 the Millennium had arrived, and attention turned to more immediate, short-term problems and satisfactions. With its pioneering, colonizing, immigrant-absorbing, and military functions taken over by the state, the kibbutz had to shift its attention from military survival and agricultural self-sufficiency to producing for the rapidly growing urban population. Its existence could no longer be justified on colonization and defense grounds alone or on its historic role in the formation of Israel. It had to become economically successful and pay its debts; that meant increasing both its productivity and its profitability. The first proved easier than the second.[27]

Despite a period of extremely rapid growth during the first three years following statehood, the ḳibbutzim were faced with an acute manpower shortage. They had to mechanize and employ the latest scientific methods if they were to increase their agricultural productivity. This led toward greater specialization in agriculture and away from the former emphasis on mixed farming. Many kibbutzim reduced the number of their production branches to concentrate on those most profitable given local climatic and soil conditions and national and international markets.[28]

Like their successful North American counterparts, the Israeli communes were highly receptive to technological innovations and labor-saving devices. During his study of kibbutz industries, Seymour Melman was impressed by the great number of production-process innovations of a technical nature developed on the spot by the members themselves.[29] In their agricultural enterprises the kibbutzim mechanized early; and by 1954, when they accounted for 20 percent of the Jewish rural population, they owned 50 percent of all the agricultural machinery. Dairy yields and poultry production in some kibbutzim and shitufim are as high as on the best farms in the United States, a fact always brought to the visitor's attention.[30]

In overall productivity and mechanization the kibbutzim have achieved a par with Western Europe although they are still behind the United States.[31] This is a remarkable achievement for people who came to Palestine with little or no knowledge of farming, a fact I was reminded of at every commune where I talked with older members: "We weren't farmers originally. We came from the middle class, and our parents were merchants and professional people. But we had to build a new country, and you can't do that without agriculture. So we worked, and we read, and we learned. We had no traditional notions to overcome, so we took a scientific approach. We got the latest books and the best technical advice."

Accounting procedures of Israeli communes are more like those of Oneida than those of the other American experiments. Settlements often use cost-accounting techniques to improve the productivity of their enterprises, and they plan the allocation of resources, especially their labor, for each day of the month a year in advance. And in planning production, the settlement works closely with Israeli advisers who research European markets. Here again we see the close integration of commune and state.

A government study in the mid 1960's, for example, revealed that the winter market for flowers in Western Europe could absorb twice the current Israeli production. Kibbutz and shitufi settlements were offered the opportunity to initiate hothouse production of flowers with government financial and technical assistance. Of the initial costs, 30 percent were paid by the participating settlements, 50 percent by government loans, and 20 percent by government grants. Other crops, such as sugar beets, which the government feels are indispensable for national self-sufficiency in time of war, are highly subsidized. The government works closely with the settlements in establishing production goals and initiating experiments and technological changes to increase yields.

Again like their 19th-century counterparts, the Israeli communes also started up small industries. By 1970 there were some 180 kibbutz-owned factories employing about 7,000 workers.[32] While these workers constituted only 5.4 percent of Israel's industrial work force, they accounted for 7 percent of the country's industrial output.[33] Most of the plants were small; over half employed less than 25 workers and less than a third employed more than 50.[34] Farming is often a precarious business in arid areas with insufficient water, and the factories made many kibbutzim less dependent on their environment.[35] Factors affecting production could be better controlled than in agriculture, and this helped settlements stabilize work schedules and incomes.[36] They could also capitalize their labor supply more effectively and thereby greatly increase productivity per worker. Kibbutz factories, moreover, have had a competitive advantage over private industries for several reasons. They pay little rent for their land, little or nothing in the way of income taxes, and, in about a third of the factories, no wages at all. Yet they have received special advisory, marketing, and financial services from their federations that would have cost their private competitors dearly.[37]

With the mechanization of agriculture and the growth of industries, productivity was increasing at the rate of 8 percent per annum in the kibbutzim by the late 1960's although their population was increasing only 3 percent. As Amana and Oneida discovered long before, continued growth in productivity— no matter how labor saving the means—eventually requires additional inputs of labor; and when the commune's supply is exhausted, it must obtain these additional inputs from outside. If it does, it will tend to import unskilled labor first to hold down costs, and commune members will tend to concentrate more and more in supervisory and managerial positions. This process runs directly counter to kibbutz ideology, which has always opposed distinctions between managers and workers as "exploitation."

Despite the deliberate attempt of many settlements to hire foremen as well as skilled laborers from outside, the trend is for kibbutz members to become the managers and experts. At several settlements, moreover, I was told that some members were beginning to openly prefer less arduous tasks and to advocate hiring outside labor for the more menial. This was said to be having an alarming effect on the children, who were learning to distinguish between jobs suitable for members and those fit only for hired help.

Shitufi members often deride these ideological concerns of the kibbutzim As one man put it, "They have an ideological problem we don't have." At Timorim, for example, the policy was to employ as many nonmembers as possible. Members considered it their "patriotic duty" to help provide employment for new citizens who preferred the nearby urban areas to life in moshav settlements. As long as the shitufi paid the wage scales set by the Israeli labor federation, members believed they were rendering their country a service. They accused kibbutzim of eliminating jobs on principle rather than for sound business reasons, a practice which often led kibbutzim to overinvest in machinery. At Timorim, on the other hand, members calculated costs carefully; and "if the scale of production of a certain item like tomatoes is not large enough to make a new combine cheaper than wage labor, we stick with wage labor. But a kibbutz would choose the machine."

This shitufi was proud of the fact that it maintained more worker families than member families. Although none of the other shitufim I visited was able to make such a boast, the ratio of workers to members was high at all except Moledet and Kefar Hittim. These two oldest shitufim were like kibbutzim in resisting the practice of hiring labor.

With a need for more labor in the face of ideological resistance to employing it, why did the kibbutzim not recruit new members to meet the need? As we have seen, the source of recruits dried up after statehood. The Zionist youth movements that had been the principal source of kibbutz manpower before World War II were subsequently banned in all East European countries. As for concentration-camp survivors or iron-curtain escapees, few were attracted to the confining, communal life of the kibbutz. Although Zionist youth movements exist in the Western countries, only those in Latin America have provided the kibbutzim with reliable immigrants (of Polish and Russian descent) and these in modest numbers. Settler nuclei from the English-speaking countries have always proved relatively weak and unstable. Less than 4 percent of the kibbutz population is "Anglo Saxon." [38]

Another source of manpower had been young people born in Palestine who were attracted to the heroic pioneering mission of the kibbutz. By 1968 the youth movement in Israel was attracting few recruits. Leadership in the movement lost its charisma when it grew career oriented and bureaucratic. Now young people join for the social functions but resign at an early age—75 percent by age 16 and 90 percent by age 18. In the old days youth-movement members who joined a kibbutz were made to feel guilty if they later defected.

This is no longer true; there are too many prestigious alternatives including successful business careers.[39]

Zionism has lost much of its meaning for the children and grandchildren of the original pioneers. The young people born in Israel have never experienced anti-Semitic persecutions nor lived in a European ghetto under the threat of massacres. Now they learn about such things in their history courses.[40] And during the lifetime of many of them the public acclaim accorded the kibbutz has diminished considerably.

It is the Arab hostilities which have provided the best substitute for ghetto persecution. They have helped to renew Zionist ideology and to enhance the status of kibbutzniks through their exemplary patriotism in wartime. Kibbutz defection rates generally go down during periods of strife particularly in kibbutzim occupying strategic border locations. No one wants to abandon comrades under fire. According to one of Michael Gorkin's kibbutz informants, this is "one of those ironic, but fortunate, effects" of the war.[41] Like Hutterites, some kibbutzniks favor a wordly hell if it helps maintain their earthbound version of utopia.

There has always been some tendency toward internal dissension within Israeli communes when outside pressures are relaxed. During the struggle between political parties shortly after the goal of statehood had been realized, the kibbutz movement passed through what some now consider its darkest hour. Many kibbutzim split in two, thousands of members abandoned one kibbutz to join another, and in some cases even families were torn apart.[42]

One shitufi informant explained the situation to me this way: "Sociologists have come to Israel to see how we are managing to create one society out of people from so many different places and backgrounds. We aren't; the Arabs are doing it for us. In Holland I was always a 'damn Jew'; but when I arrived here I became a 'damn Dutchman.' "

Although hostilities may have helped to check defection rates, they have not created any new waves of recruits like those before World War I. The only comparable phenomenon has been the wave of volunteer labor, the young students from the West (mainly the United States) who come to Israel for varying periods to live and work in a kibbutz for room and board. Because the shitufim are not well known and because they lack the communal dining halls the kibbutz has found so convenient (as Amana discovered too) for feeding hired laborers, they have not benefited from this windfall. And a windfall it is for many kibbutzim. As one man put it, "If it costs us a dollar a day to feed and house a volunteer and we get approximately 10 dollars worth of work, that's a 9-dollar donation. And if we average about 50 kids for about 3 months a year during the season when work is heaviest . . . well, you figure it out; it comes to a nice little gift from Uncle Sam." (About $40,000.)

Yet in many kibbutzim the presence of volunteers is resented. They are believed to have a corrupting effect on the kibbutz, particularly through their influence on children. Some kibbutzim keep volunteer labor separate from kibbutz members even during working hours and may prohibit their children from associating with them at any time. Older members may refuse to eat any longer in the dining commons because of the loud, objectionable behavior of the volunteers.[43] One is reminded of the answer the Zoarites gave William Hinds during his visit in 1876 when he inquired about the effects of using outside laborers: "Very injurious. They tempt our young people into bad habits." [44]

In all fairness to the kibbutzim, they would prefer to admit their hired and volunteer laborers as members; but none of the former and few of the latter want to live permanently in a kibbutz. The solution heard over and over again in talking with kibbutzniks on their settlements or in federation headquarters is "rationalization of production." They still hope that through greater mechanization and efficiency they can maintain or increase productivity without relying on hired labor.

The kibbutz, of course, has had to continue hiring workers; but to resolve the conflict between two ideological commitments, one to the state and the other to self-employment, kibbutzim have turned to the development of industries under the jurisdiction of regional councils. These regional organizations of neighboring settlements with common ecological problems provide co-ownership of enterprises among several kibbutzim (and often nonkibbutz settlements as well). They help provide jobs without bringing the bulk of kibbutz members into continual direct contact with employees.[45]

A new danger, however, has already presented itself. Some of the most talented and enterprising members of the kibbutzim participating in these cooperative industries end up managers of hired workers. These individuals, some believe, are already becoming a managerial and technological elite more concerned with efficiency and profits than with collective principles.[46] Such premonitions are similar to those voiced a hundred years ago by John Humphrey Noyes as Oneida members turned into profit-motivated enterprisers and the supervisors of hired laborers.[47]

More serious than the problem of hired labor, in the view of some observers, has been the vacuum in kibbutz ideology which statehood created but did nothing to refill.[48] Consequently, as Israeli society has moved toward a renewed interest in education and commerce, the kibbutzim have followed suit. The very values against which many of the early settlements rebelled are gradually being reclaimed.[49]

When a communal community accepts the notion of progress not only in labor-saving technology but in creature comforts, the problem of administering the rule "to each according to his needs" becomes more complicated. The concept of need acquires a quality of elasticity that it does not have when members are all equal in poverty. Kibbutzim are no longer poverty stricken; many have large, cheerful dining halls, luxurious swimming pools, espresso bars, and new apartment buildings. As living standards go up in the kibbutz, so do everyone's needs. But not all of the new items of consumption can be used collectively as easily as swimming pools and dining halls. Today many kibbutzim are following the example of the shitufim and are giving their members regular allowances to purchase personal supplies.[50] When I asked the member of a kibbutz near Nazareth if members' allowances had been increasing over the years, the worker smiled broadly and said, "Yes, and our needs too!" Then growing sober, the kibbutznik added, "We're expanding consumption because we're doing better, but it won't corrupt us."

Needs may grow, but only by consensus. Corruption of kibbutz ideology is avoided if the community continues to satisfy all needs by limiting them to what it can afford to supply to all members equally and to those which a majority of members agrees are common needs. If members are allowed to satisfy different needs individually, competitive inequalities and jealousies are likely to arise.

During a visit to an Artzi kibbutz, I noticed that only one apartment in the settlement had an air-conditioning unit, and I inquired why its occupants should be so specially privileged. It was explained to me that an elderly woman with a respiratory ailment lived there, and the unit had been medically prescribed. "Some day we shall all have air conditioners," I was told. "Our ideology is one of equality—not of poverty. We are going up, but we are going up together."

Even kibbutzim of the Artzi federation, which belongs to the revolutionary Marxist party, Mapam, have adopted the notion of progress as long as everyone progresses equally. These kibbutzim have been most strict in holding the line against individual differences in consumption and against the intrusion of consumption goods deemed dangerous to kibbutz life, such as television sets. They have fought the longest and hardest, too, against the adoption of family refrigerators, kitchenettes, and individual differences in furnishings. But to hold their membership, they, like all the rest, have had to yield to a more progressive approach to living standards. They are the most adamant, however, on the question of equality. Whereas some liberal kibbutzim allowed members who were awarded German reparation payments to keep all or a portion of the money for personal expenses including new furniture or vacations in Europe, Artzi members were required to turn theirs over to their kibbutz for collective benefits such as swimming pools and dining halls.[51]

Consumption standards have steadily risen in the kibbutzim although even the most liberal settlements have not been able to keep pace with the rise in urban living standards. Many kibbutzim by 1968 were furnishing members with radios, bicycles, refrigerators (for keeping snacks and cold drinks), and desert coolers. Most settlements had a television in their clubhouse or recreation center, and many believed the day when each apartment would have its own set was not far off. The major objection was that "television destroys social ties." Time has proved them right on both counts; today kibbutzniks cut evening business meetings to watch their favorite television shows.

As members of a liberal kibbutz explained it to me, "In the early pioneering period we valued the spartan life and viewed all private consumption as the personification of the devil." In those days if one person had more than another it was deeply resented and created considerable jealousy. Now that the kibbutzim have grown more affluent, individual differences do not attract the same attention so long as they are not too extreme. However, if a family is allowed to keep some windfall such as an inheritance or a German restitution payment, it creates difficulties. "Suppose another family has more money than you, and they buy their children new bicycles. What do you do when your kids come to you and want bicycles too? Or suppose a friend of yours buys a new tape recorder and lots of tapes and invites you over to listen but you can't ever reciprocate. It's a matter of jealousy; people in a kibbutz are like people everywhere else." Yet sometimes when a family receives a gift from outside, the members decide to let them keep it. "Then the kibbutz has to hump to get the same thing for everybody else." This process has been a major factor in the rising living standards of the kibbutz.

The kibbutz, however, prides itself on having a different style of life from the world outside. For this reason, I was frequently told, it does not have to copy all the consumption habits of the urban middle classes. When, for example, I asked the members of one settlement how they felt their standard of living compared with that of the moshav ovdim and private farmers, they replied that the answer would depend on what was meant by "standard." "Many moshav members have their own automobiles. If owning a car is what you want, then you might be able to argue their living standards are higher than ours. But if you value things like a good education, a convenient library and the opportunity to travel, then our living standards are the best." This kibbutz had a library of fifty thousand volumes and had recently instituted a new program to send seven or eight married couples each year on a trip to Europe. Moreover, moshav ovdim farmers, they said, worked ten hours a day whereas only eight are customary in the kibbutz. "We get machines to work for us. Having the leisure to read and hold discussions is important too."

Artzi-federation kibbutzim have been opposed to family and personal allowances; they have even resisted personal clothing budgets. Their argument is that some members would use the budget wisely while others would make inadequate purchases. The result would be inequality.[52] Moreover, once a budget system is introduced for clothing, it is easily extended to other purchases as well. Members then begin to weigh consumption choices in terms of money rather than in terms of their intrinsic value. When this happens, members have reverted to a capitalistic method of evaluation and have taken the first step toward remuneration according to work rather than need.

Many kibbutzim in the more liberal (less leftist) federations have adopted a system of individual allowances for supplying personal needs: cigarettes, toothpaste, razor blades, stationery, and so on.[53] Scrip or "inside money" is used as in the shitufim. It has been found that this procedure eliminates a great amount of waste. Several kibbutzim tell almost the same "soap story." After adopting the allowance system, members discovered that soap consumption had dropped almost 75 percent. "We wondered if people had suddenly stopped bathing and why. But it wasn't that at all. When your soap is costing you something else, you don't leave it sitting in a pool of water." A close parallel to the kibbutz soap story is the shitufi electricity story. Shitufim that had originally provided each family dwelling with all the electricity it wanted effected enormous savings in their energy bills after installing private meters and deducting the cost of each family's consumption from its monthly allowance. Israeli experience in achieving economies of communal consumption through the allowance system parallels the transformation at Amana after each household was put in charge of its own economy.

The trend toward more inclusive allowance systems is proceeding just as the Artzi officials feared it would. Some kibbutzim have instituted additional individual allowances for clothing as well as family allowances for furniture. If the kibbutz is strict, it will not allow members to give any part of their allowance to another member of their family. Gradually, however, the specific allowance system breaks down, and all are combined in one budget. "Now," as I was told, "if I want cigarettes instead of furniture, it's my business."

Family budgets in such cases are still based on the number and ages of family members with so much calculated for candy, toiletries, clothes, furniture, and so on. But in the most liberal settlements, a family can allocate these funds as it sees fit. And just as in a shitufi, the family can exchange its scrip for Israeli currency and buy what it wants in town. Under the combined budget system, saving potentials are enhanced, and some families economize their spending so they can purchase large items. At one kibbutz I visited, three families had recently purchased their own television sets, and a general meeting had been scheduled to decide whether they would be allowed to keep them. "They'll get to keep them," I was assured. "In five years we'll all have them." That prediction was right; today nearly every family in the settlement has its own set.

The allowance system not only shifts more responsibility to the family, it allows each to express more individuality in dress and furnishings.[54] It also encourages family members to focus more attention on short-term, materialistic goals that emphasize family choice and family togetherness. As in the shitufim, greater competitiveness and inequality result. Even families with the same budgets are not equal in their abilities to manage them. The most thrifty and astute can increase the amount and quality of their consumer goods conspicuously above that of other members. Either such inequalities and the jealousies they may provoke are allowed, or the more ambitious must restrain their wants until the kibbutz can help the slower families catch up. In either case these kibbutzim are becoming increasingly like shitufim whether they admit it or not.

Another source of increasing inequality and internal competitiveness is the trend toward greater specialization. In the early days, physical labor was valued for its own sake and each member was supposedly able to exchange jobs with any other. Not even the traditional sex division of labor was observed. Today, however, rotation of workers among the various production branches of the kibbutz is no longer practiced. Service jobs, such as waiting tables and washing dishes at the communal dining hall, are still rotated, but jobs in agriculture and industry are not. Individuals are encouraged to specialize as soon as possible; and once skilled at a certain task or assignment, they are seldom changed. Members are sent to special training courses and periodically attend meetings with specialists in the same field from other kibbutzim where they discuss the latest information and share the benefit of their own successes and failures. At kibbutzim I visited, I was told that the prestige of blue-collar work was not as strong as it was in the fifties and that education and specialized training were more highly valued than a decade before.

An elite of production managers and technical experts has grown up in what was originally a classless setting. The control which the kibbutz general assembly once exercised over this managerial elite has become less effective; for as specialization leads to more technical problems and decisions, the average member becomes less competent to participate in those decisions. And the more these elite members are exported into federation and government service as a special class of professional functionaries, the less integrated they become with other members of their home settlements and the more likely they are to stimulate jealousy and feelings of relative deprivation among them.[55]

Some kibbutzniks I talked with justified government and federation service on the ground that it provided more ambitious and restless members, who might otherwise leave the kibbutz altogether, with a greater opportunity for individual development and self-expression. A similar argument was made at Oneida when it began to industrialize. Since differences in position did not result in differences in wealth, they could do no harm. Fortunately, the *Oneida Circular* explained, the expansion of community enterprises was smothering its young people with new opportunities.[56]

In large part these new opportunities at Oneida were due to enterprise expansions based on hired labor and consisted of supervisory positions over that labor. This suggests a further parallel with the kibbutz in regard to the latter's cooperative regional enterprises; for the managerial elite of the kibbutz also comes to occupy supervisory, executive and technical positions in businesses employing wage laborers.[57]

This gradual process of individualization has repercussions in the whole area of membership interaction. People withdraw more from community situations to give time to friendship and family relations. There are now literally hundreds of members in some general assemblies, and discussions are often too technical for the majority. In the old days when jobs were rotated and techniques were not so specialized, members understood the problems of all the different branches. And all were eager to see the various enterprises get on their feet economically. Now, the fish-pond workers do not understand the problems in the dairy division and vice versa. The majority of members no longer have an overview. They are bored by meetings and prefer to leave decisions to the elected officers. Attendance at meetings has declined drastically in many settlements, and in some the younger members are openly critical of what they consider pointless garrulousness on the part of older ones.[58]

As individuals withdraw from group activities, they tend to devote more time to their families and a small circle of intimate friends. And as they do, they come to resent community intrusions on their privacy.[59] Work schedules and holidays are arranged so family members can have more time together.[60] Members prefer to form small informal social groups or cliques composed of close friends who feel at ease with one another: "You can't be friends with everyone." [61] Even in the dining halls, members no longer "mix" as was once customary during the noon meal. Dining-hall cliques have formed at many settlements as members continue to meet daily with the same small group of friends. At many kibbutzim, families now eat their evening meal in their apartments. Food is picked up at the communal kitchen and taken home; there, as became habitual at Amana just before its demise as a commune, it is reheated in the kitchenette. This is just one more indication of a general trend toward greater emphasis on the family.

To maintain membership, the kibbutzim can no longer count on the external recruitment of immigrants. They have had to give more attention and emphasis to natural replacement through family procreation. The kibbutz population profile has changed radically since prestatehood days when settlements consisted largely of young adults and children were scarce. Today the distribution of ages in the kibbutz is the same as in the general Israeli population.[62] The change has resulted in what Talmon called a "centrifugal" emphasis on the family. With more children than ever before, more time has had to be shifted to their care and education.[63] Members began giving precedence to family relations at the expense of ideological or community relations. Children in some kibbutzim now live with their parents just as they do in shitufim. Private apartments often have their own kitchens, bathrooms, and washing facilities, and women's work hours have been reduced to allow them more time for household chores.[64]

Since many kibbutz families have now been established for two generations, kinship ties have grown up within and among kibbutzim and between kibbutz members and relatives in the towns and cities. Celebrations such as weddings, for example, which were once an exclusively kibbutz affair, are now followed by private, more personal parties of close friends and relatives. Relatives in the same community visit one another frequently and tend to sit together in the dining halls.[65]

None of these trends in the kibbutz is the least surprising to a shitufi member. After all, in claiming that the shitufi is what the kibbutz is destined to become, one in effect predicts them. Shitufim founded before 1968 are populated predominantly with exkibbutzniks who were too impatient to wait for these changes to take place gradually. As we have seen, they did away with communal kitchens, dining halls, and children's dormitories precisely to reemphasize family living. They began as a "privatized" version of the kibbutz, and they realize that their goals are distinct. They see themselves as more "practical" than kibbutzniks and more oriented toward business success and the enjoyment of family life.

The shitufi provides each of its families with a rent-free house it cannot modify in any way without community consent. Household furnishings and clothing, however, are the personal property of the family and are purchased from its allowance, the size of which depends on the number and ages of its members. The allowance is frequently paid in "inside money" which must be used at the settlement store, but members often prefer to make their purchases at urban department stores where the settlement maintains a charge account. Sometimes, if a family wishes to make a purchase on its own, the settlement exchanges Israeli currency for the family's "inside money."

Most shitufim allow much more freedom in the purchase of consumer goods than do the kibbutzim. At Kefar Daniel, for example, I was told, "If a family decides to fill its house with TV sets, washing machines, and air conditioners, that's its business." At Moledet, one of the oldest and most conservative shitufim, none of these things was allowed in 1968: "We have to guard against too high a standard of living." It was feared that if some families were unable to save enough to buy a TV set, for example, inequality and jealousy would result. But at Kefar Hittim four families had television sets because "the women managed their household budgets better than the rest and were able to save for them."

At Regba, in 1968, the only television was in the recreation center, but each household was to have its own very soon. The settlement was waiting until all but ten families had saved enough to buy their own; then it would provide financing for the remaining ten. Shoresh families had added rooms to their houses in this way. At first they had planned to let each family arrange for its own improvement loan, but when some were unable to obtain loans, "there were hard feelings." So the shitufi decided to wait and get financing for everyone. "You can't have the big differences in a small community that you get in a town," I was told. "It's more like a big family here; and in a family if you give something to one child, the rest want it too."

This requirement of "going up together," still typical of kibbutzim, has been relaxed in the shitufim. By 1968 many had given it up entirely in the sphere of household furnishings, as noted above. Bet Herut had no limits at all; almost half its members owned cars as did four families at Shoresh, two at Nir Gallim, and one at Kefar Daniel. Cars are so expensive to maintain in Israel that members who did not have them were said not to be jealous of those who did. The other five shitufim I visited, however, did not allow them. At Regba and Timorím members were permitted to drive settlement cars on weekends and holidays.

At several shitufim I was told, as the kibbutzniks had also told me, that jealousies over differences in consumption were not nearly as acute as they had been in the early days when the standard of living was much lower. With greater affluence, people were no longer concerned with minor differences. The people of Bet Herut considered themselves members of "the Israeli middle class" and regarded the standard of living of all their members as "high." They had depended on their own personal financing to develop their enterprises, and the settlement had never been in debt or in shaky financial condition. They believed their relative affluence to be the reason why they had never found it necessary to insist on equality of consumption to avoid internal jealousies. Some members even had investments outside the settlement.

The case of Bet Herut is unusual. Although this settlement is officially listed as a shitufi by the Tnuat Ha Moshavim federation, other shitufim claim it is not one for the simple reason that it allows private enterprise. Each family has a half acre of ground on which it raises turkeys sold by the settlement, a private operation that supplements the family's monthly allowance. The turkey runs were started to provide "more room for individual initiative" but have resulted in what one settlement official regarded as a "definite conflict of interest" between the private and the collective sectors. To reduce this conflict, Bet Herut was increasing its use of hired labor within the "collective" sector, a practice which was actually making that sector more corporate.

Bet Herut is not the only shitufi, however, to allow members to earn or inherit private incomes. Shoresh, unlike other shitufim, paid wives an hourly rate when they worked for the shitufi and allowed them to keep any wages earned off the settlement, both sources of income constituting a supplement to the family allowance. Two wives working in Jerusalem had been able to buy cars with this extra income. And at Kefar Daniel members who inherit money are free to save or spend it as they wish.

Israeli communes, it was noted above, have generally been more successful in their productivity than their profitability. Undoubtedly the two biggest questions in regard to profitability concern the rise of living standards and the quantity and quality of individual effort. In his study of kibbutz profitability, Kanovsky indicated a number of tangential factors.[66] The location of many communes, for example, was determined by defense considerations rather than soil and rainfall characteristics. Large numbers of kibbutz members were employed on federation staffs despite the manpower shortage in production branches. Financially weak settlements were being kept alive at all costs to avoid the stigma of failure; as a result, financial and technical aid diverted from profitable to unprofitable settlements was lowering the profitability of all. The most enterprising and skilled members were often the ones enticed away by employment opportunities in the towns and cities while the security minded remained. Ideological resistance to the use of hired labor, by forcing many kibbutzim to be excessively capital intensive, was raising their interest costs. It was also preventing many settlements from fully developing their most profitable enterprises.

The problem most difficult to analyze, however, is the effect of consumption on profitability because of the former's communal nature. It is not always clear when labor is a cost of production and when it is a form of consumption. In many cases the institutionalization of service branches such as communal laundries seems to consume more labor than when those same activities are performed on a family basis. This can raise labor costs in the income-producing branches if it leads to the employment there of additional outside labor. And although kibbutz members are not paid wages, they have been demanding a higher and more comfortable standard of living. Living standards in the larger society have been advancing rapidly, and the kibbutz part-society has had to bring its own more closely in line to avoid internal dissatisfactions and increasing defections. But increments in living standards and leisure based on norms determined by the federations rather than on the current profitability of the individual kibbutz inevitably raise labor costs and reduce profitability even further.

Dan Leon and others have objected to Kanovsky's criteria for judging profitability.[67] According to Leon, "money income" is not the only measure of economic efficiency; time spent at cultural activities, leisure and education are also a kind of profit. But this is just the point. The second kind of profit may conform to the part-society's values, but Kanovsky's values are those of the larger society. It is precisely the integration of the two, to which the kibbutz has already committed itself, that determines the whole question of profitability.

Leon, in fact, contradicts himself when he shows how standards in the kibbutz can be improved without additional cash expenditures simply by transferring workers to service branches at the expense of production branches. For, as he himself admits, if such transfers cause "the ratio of 'income-earning' to 'non-income earning' working-days to fall below a certain level, the advantages of the kibbutz system and its chances of profitability would be frittered away." [68]

Several conditions push this ratio close to the critical level. About half the labor of the kibbutz is occupied in services—kitchen, laundry, store, nursing, education, clothing repair, shoe repair, carpentry, mechanical, plumbing, electrical maintenance, and so on. Over a third of the female work force is concentrated in the education and nursery branches. The smaller the kibbutz the higher the proportion of workers required for maintaining these services, particularly those allocated for education.[69] Moreover, the percentage of kibbutz membership "recruitable" by its federation varies between 5 and 7 percent, while even more members may be at work in government posts.[70] According to some estimates 10 percent of kibbutz members are "shabbat" members, individuals who live and work outside the kibbutz and come home for visits only on the Sabbath.[71] Of the 730 days per year that each kibbutz couple has available for work, Viteles estimates that on the average 196 to 202 days are non-work days, Sabbath, holidays, sick leaves, and so on. Of the remaining 528 to 534 days, 265 to 287 are taken up by service and administrative chores, leaving only some 245 to 269 days spent in income-earning work.[72]

One consequence of this conflict between consumption-producing and income-producing labor is the pressure to increase the size of kibbutzim in order to lower the consumption–income labor ratio. But as average kibbutz size increases, there are other consequences in turn. Membership visibility decreases, and third-person control weakens. Inequality of effort has a negative effect on membership productivity, and labor costs go up.

The kibbutzim themselves have become increasingly concerned with backsliding and goldbricking, and many are growing more particular in their selection of new members. Like some shitufim they are looking for people with special training and skills, not people who want a temporary haven while down on their luck.[73] The largest kibbutzim can afford to be more particular because they are usually the ones that employ the most hired labor, much of it for unskilled jobs. Yet the kibbutzim that hire the most outside labor have the highest defection rates and the lowest productivity of labor within their membership.[74]

A man who had been a member of two kibbutzim at different periods of his life, one of the smallest and later one of the largest and most industrialized, was of the opinion that "there is much more pressure on the backslider in the small kibbutz." In the larger one people are less visible to one another and "there get to be a lot of soft jobs. These should be just for the older people, but often younger men get into them and find themselves a sinecure. After that happens, everyone gets more tolerant of backsliding." When I recounted this man's observation to officials at one of the federation headquarters, they agreed that shirking was becoming more common as the old work ideology grew weaker. But there was no need to be concerned. The ideology was still strong enough to keep most members working hard, especially in the smaller settlements. And in the larger ones "increasing rationality of production" would solve the problem.

Another kibbutznik confided that the aspect of kibbutz life most difficult for that individual to accept was the leisurely attitude many people took toward work. Most people were conscientious, but in that person's opinion there were too many exceptions—people obviously not working up to their ability. This view was substantiated recently by Judith Glickman, who was once a member of Or Haner, a small kibbutz composed of approximately 80 couples and 100 children.[75] At least 10 members of this settlement were completely insensitive to the normal social incentives of the kibbutz. Most had been rotated from job to job but were unable to adjust to any. In most cases the community "made a job" for them, at which they worked half heartedly when they worked at all. Usually they stayed home "sick." Three of these malingerers were men and 7 were women, but all 10 were married to individuals who either had highly responsible jobs in the kibbutz or who were exceptionally good workers. Or Haner, in effect, was willing to carry these persons in order to keep their spouses and children.

From the evidence available, no one would predict an early or even a distant demise for the Israeli communes. But they are certainly changing and in ways that directly parallel the route previously taken by the successful 19th-century eutopias. They are moving toward a corporation type of structure despite every effort to keep them from doing so. They are now being molded by Israeli society far more than they are molding the new state.

As Alan Arian has noted, most kibbutzim have taken a position similar to Martin Buber's with regard to socialism. They have believed in a socialist order built up community by community rather than by revolutionary capture of the state. But Israeli communists consider this "Jerusalem" road "utopian" in the most pejorative sense of the word. They maintain that the larger capitalistic society cannot be converted to socialism by small communalistic settlements. Instead, the settlements themselves will become involved in the capitalistic mode of production and their ideology will be gradually subverted.[76] So far, the evidence confirms this communist view.

Summary

Israeli communes have provided a further test of Communist Man (Millennial Man) incentives, this time in the context of an allegedly secular, but strongly nationalistic, social movement. Although viable commune movements still in the prime of life, kibbutzim and shitufim arranged along a common gradient of change seem to be following the same general path taken by the 19th-century communes. They seem to be changing from communes to juristic persons or corporations. The tendency of all such group games is to dissolve into individual players as the latter get caught up in the larger game of the civilization of capitalism. Although intentional part-societies can achieve a degree of planning far more comprehensive than anything ever attempted in traditional communities, they prove incapable of averting the very consequences they set out to avoid.

The communes discussed here and in Chapter 5 have shown that under unusual circumstances and within relatively small social units Communist Man incentives work for a limited period of time. It is most unlikely that they could be successfully applied to entire states or even to the stateless world envisioned by the anarcho-communists. Chapters 7 through 9 show why in more detail.

Chapter Seven

Utopia: Millennial Man in Fiction

IN CHAPTERS 5 AND 6 we saw how Homo ludens manages to play the group game of Millennial Man. In view of its limited occurrence throughout history, it is an improbable game that depends on fortuitous and unusual circumstances. It works best as a counterculture game played by small part-societies against larger "host" societies permissive enough to put up with them but antagonistic enough to enhance the contest. In the Israeli case the larger society has been actively supportive and promotive, a situation that might have seriously corrupted the community game by now, were it not for the precarious nature of the nationalistic game being played by the host state as well as for the closely overlapping Zionist goals of both.

In all our Millennial Man cases, the units were small enough that with the help of unusually strong commitment they achieved high visibility within their memberships. Under these conditions social predictability was able to effect the selective individual reinforcement necessary for successful team play. Could an entire state ever play the Millennial Man game?

In Chapter 8 we compare two state eutopias, Russia and China, that would have liked to play the Millennial Man game but have had to settle for the Socialist Man form. In the absence of real-world examples, we shall settle for fictional ones here; but the exercise of comparing utopian, Millennial Man states is far from frivolous. We live at a time when "futurology" has come of age; utopian schemes of all sorts are inundating us. Even prophets of doom who prescribe a corrective course of action are detailing conditions for "utopia" in the minimal sense, at least, of a world society capable of surviving. Opponents of these "ecodoomsters" consider them messianic chiliasts who are really "utopians at heart" despite their gloomy "scientific" prognostications.[1] World breakdown and chaos become the ecodoomsters' route to world salvation. Yet their peculiar brand of stationary-state utopia, as their opponents point out, may be nothing more than the justification of a planetary status quo that maintains the favored position of the First World's affluent "middle" classes.

Although an ecodoomster's model of a stationary state capable of avoiding his own prognostications of Armageddon is not what most people associate with the notion of utopia, the two are much the same when viewed as games. Utopia, of course, is quite a different kind of game from eutopia. The latter, we have just seen, can actually involve members of a real society as full, game-playing participants. People in the eutopian games reviewed in Chapters 5 and 6 were primarily subjects of play rather than objects of play. But fictional utopias are designs or models. Were such designs applied to the real world, would the people in them play them as subjects or be played by them as objects? If the intention of the designer is social engineering, then the people playing his game would have to conform to his design. They would, in a sense, become counters moved about on a chessboard according to the utopian's rules.

Michael Holquist draws just such a parallel when he says the relation of chess to battle is much like the relation of utopia to actual society.[2] Both chess and utopia are stylized abstractions that provide a limited but graphic perfection. Utopian laws like chess rules, however, are inflexible. A real state could no more be run according to the logic of utopia than a real battle could be won by following the logic of chess. The purpose of both games is to achieve a peculiar kind of freedom, like that of the laboratory or the theater, by withdrawing at least partially from reality. This kind of game frees the designer from the irreversibility of real-world consequences and allows him to make exploratory calculations to his heart's content. But in fitting real societies to the rules of a utopia, the designer or social engineer must wittingly or unwittingly reduce them to police states.

The authors of the five fictional societies we are about to compare were men of good intentions: all five wanted to eliminate despotism and corruption—not portray it. Yet as we compare these fictional utopias to the real-world eutopias of the preceding chapters, we shall see that Holquist is right. These idealistic "chessboard" societies would probably all be despotisms if put into practice. Since utopians of all persuasions, even ecodoomsters, are usually well intended, we must learn to view them all with the utmost caution.

Like our eight successful communes, the five utopias chosen for comparison in this chapter have stood the test of time. Plato's *Republic* has been part of our intellectual history for over two thousand years, and Thomas More's *Utopia* is still being discussed and analyzed after almost five centuries. Etienne Cabet's *A Voyage to Icaria* was a bestseller in early 19th-century France where it even inspired a brief social movement in the form of working-class study groups to discuss his ideas.[3] Edward Bellamy's *Looking Backward* became one of the top three bestsellers in the United States during the late 19th century, eventually sold millions of copies, was translated into over twenty languages, and, similar to Cabet's book, stimulated a brief political mass movement through the more than 150 Bellamy Clubs that sprang up in North America in 1890 and 1891.[4]

Since its original publication in 1948, B. F. Skinner's *Walden Two* has sold over a million copies. This utopian novel and the author's later philosophical defense of its views in *Beyond Freedom and Dignity* (1971) have raised him to controversial prominence.

The first and last of our five cases are not Millennial Man states in the strictest sense. In Plato's *Republic* there is no collective production at all, and the only collective consumption is that practiced by the Guardian, or governing, class. But this ancient fictive example of collective consumption is still relevant and too instructive to ignore. Skinner's Walden Two society, on the other hand, includes comprehensive collective production as well as consumption, but it is a small community, not a state. If our purpose is to test the implications of Millennial Man utopianism for state-size groups, by what logic do we include it here?

There are two reasons for including Walden Two. First, the community can be viewed as a pilot project for social engineering on a much larger scale, for its small size is an experimental convenience, not a strategy to achieve conditions of social predictability. Second, it is the strongest and most contemporary case of utopian behaviorism, a behaviorism quite different from that serving as an underlying theme of this book. The time has come to make the kind of behaviorism endorsed here explicit and to differentiate it from Skinnerian utopianism.

Behaviorism in Utopia

All of our five authors are "behaviorists" in a primitive and partial sense at least; all indicate ways of engineering society to reduce behavior they dislike. In this regard, Plato sets a course followed by the others to varying degrees. After examining the dislikes of our five authors, we compare their views of human nature and finally their "behavioristic" techniques.

The words and labels he used are different from those we use today, but Plato, like many agrarian-minded Greeks of his time, was disturbed by the incipient version of Capitalist Man that had grown up in the trading cities of Asia Minor and had spread to the Ionian and Corinthian Greeks. By the 6th century B.C., coinage was in use in the great Ionian commercial city of Miletus where a new bourgeois or businessman cult of the individual had developed. That the influence of this new doctrine of individualism was already strong in Athens by Plato's time is evidenced by the teachings of the Sophists, who emphasized the motive power of self-interest.

To the agrarian Greek, his merchant brothers were lazy, self-indulgent people who overate and overdressed. The agrarians saw them "pompously stalking about" at their markets in bright colored robes, elaborate hairdresses and strong perfumes and considered their behavior excessively ostentatious as well as ridiculously effete.[5]

The rich, according to Plato, devote all their reasoning powers to calculating how to make money breed more money, and Plato saw little virtue in this. Even though many work hard to become rich and in their youth economize to reduce unnecessary expenses, such commonly admired behavior is motivated by the pursuit of money and is therefore a sign of avarice. And with their fortunes made, the rich and their children serve society in no useful way, becoming merely consumers of goods. Even worse, if they loan their capital out, the rich become usurers who multiply their wealth and with it the number of drones who live off it in effeminate indolence with no higher motive than their own immediate pleasure.[6]

As Allan Bloom has noted, Plato's concern over the reasonable distribution of the good things in life stems from the fact that they are viewed as always in short supply.[7] Thus, as someone's gain becomes another's loss, the harmony of the good society is constantly threatened. This preindustrial zero-sum view of the world is very much like Thomas More's.

Although Thomas More designed his *Utopia* (1516) almost two thousand years after the *Republic* (300 B.C.), his dislikes sound much the same as those of Plato, a thinker he greatly admired.[8] The disturbing element in More's world, as it was in Plato's, is a preindustrial version of Capitalist Man, for it seemed to More that the wealthy few obtained their riches at the expense of a disadvantaged majority. Everything is "divided among a few . . . while the rest are utterly miserable." Through "conspiracy" the rich seek their own private advantage in the name of the "commonwealth" (the collective good). They pay as little as possible for the labor of the poor people they oppress, and they manipulate the government and its laws to safeguard for themselves all that they have unjustly acquired. Thus, through their "insatiable greed" they "divide among themselves the goods which would have been enough for all."

More is particularly hostile to the "idle" nobility who live like "drones" off the labor of their tenants. Why, he wonders, should nobles and moneylenders, who do "nothing at all for a living" or at least nothing of any "use to the public," live such a "sumptuous and elegant life"? Farmers, blacksmiths, and servants work "as hard as a beast at labor," and the "commonwealth could not last a year without them." Yet they are forced to live under conditions worse than those of "draft animals," and after they are "worn out by age and sickness" the "thankless state" leaves them to their "miserable death."[9]

The height of infamy is the enclosure movement by which cultivated lands are turned into pasture for sheep so that nobles and abbots can make even more profit than before. Thus, the rich are not only "no longer satisfied to live in idleness and luxury without benefiting society," they must now deliberately "injure the commonwealth" to satisfy their "insatiable gluttony." And the poor, miserable people forced out of their homes, what happens to them? They want to work but can find no one to hire them. If they beg, they are thrown in jail as vagabonds; if they steal, they are hanged. Yet to make the situation even worse, "wanton luxury is yoked" to their misfortune. In the houses of the rich, expensive clothing and extravagant eating add insult to injury. "Pride," says More, "measures her prosperity not by her own goods *but by others' wants*" (emphasis mine). More's vivid, zero-sum view clearly applies to personal property with as much force as to productive property.[10]

All this sounds exactly like Rousseau in his most antiprogressive moments. Yet it was written some 250 years before Rousseau's progress-minded time. The base of the English economy in More's day was still peasant agriculture, and manufacturing was still largely domestic, part of a putting-out system in which the employer was more merchant than manufacturer. No wonder the father of antiprogress has been labeled anachronistic.

Since More's *Utopia* was a primary inspiration of *A Voyage to Icaria* (1840), it is not surprising that Cabet uses the same techniques, as we see below, to correct the same vices. Although Bellamy's book (1888) is in this same zero-sum tradition, the description now sounds Marxist. The Capitalist Man villain is no longer just a merchant or landed aristocrat, but is now a stockholder living in idleness off investments made by his father or grandfather, investments that have increased in value over the years due to the work of others but not to any effort on his part. In Bellamy's famous metaphor of the coach driven by hunger and pulled by the masses, the fortunate few who ride at the expense of those who toil come to believe they do so by natural superiority, an "hallucination" that produces "indifference" to the suffering of those in harness.[11]

Even 60 years later in Skinner's *Walden Two* (1948), we find vestiges of the same zero-sum view of scarce goods.[12] How can people get what they need to be happy "without stealing it from somebody else"? The "competitive society" outside Walden Two, we are told, is one in which each person who gains a "reward" does so through some punishing "expense" to another. On periodic field trips to the "outside world," Walden Two children are shown the "connection" between the "fine residences" and beautiful public buildings on the one hand and the "depravity" of the "saloons," "jails" and "slums" on the other. In his most recent popular book, *About Behaviorism* (1974), Skinner wonders if a culture will eventually evolve in which no individual will be able to accumulate power harmful to others or be so engrossed in his private pursuits as to be oblivious to the future and present needs of his fellows.[13]

On what do our utopian behaviorists place the blame for such injustices? Do they blame human nature or the social environment? Actually, they blame both, but it is society rather than human nature which is directly altered by their chessboard designs. Human nature involves constants, some of which must be bypassed.

Even our contemporary utopian behaviorist, Skinner himself, finds troublesome aspects to the human character.[14] In the evolution of the human species there was a time when anger, fear, rage, jealousy, and other forms of aggressive behavior were advantageous to survival and were therefore "phylogenetically reinforced" through natural selection. But it is dangerous to explain all present behavior on such grounds, for now that these aspects of human nature have "served their evolutionary purpose," they may prove "lethal" unless replaced by good emotions such as "joy and love." By building a cooperative society, destructive emotions such as jealousy can be made to atrophy as the need for them disappears. On the other hand, a society that gives a great deal of attention to competitive games is not simply channeling aggressive tendencies, it is reinforcing them.

Some strong drives, however, can be channeled or released to make them less destructive. Adolescent sex need not be repressed; in Walden Two people marry in their teens, and most women have borne all their children by the age of 22. The potential of some basic drives or motivations can be expanded to fill the vacuum left by those no longer reinforced. Once students, for example, are no longer motivated by fear of family reactions to low grades or by public esteem for scholastic honors, the motive of natural curiosity will have a chance to break through and replace the previous "spurious needs." Skinner opposes explanations of human behavior that rely on nebulous psychic processes inside the head because they do not lead to control of behavior as does operant conditioning based on environmental explanation. Yet here in the case of natural curiosity we have an internal psychic force that guides behavior once "operant conditioning" has eliminated the effects of spurious, fortuitous conditioning.[15]

Our "primitive" utopian behaviorists did not have Skinner's sophisticated 20th-century vocabulary (disrespectfully referred to by some as "pigeon English"), but was their reasoning any different? The phylogenically selected aggression of Skinner's individual is the acquisitiveness and avarice that eventually overcomes reason in Plato's.[16] Thomas More uses the medieval word "pride" for the innate force underlying all forms of greed and conspicuous consumption.[17] "Pride," writes More, is "the first and foremost of all evils"; and were it not for pride, the whole world might live like his Utopians. Because of it, however, some may consider themselves superior just because their clothes are made of fine wool thread instead of coarse; because of it they will pursue their own advantage to the point of surpassing others in conspicuous consumption; and because of it they may be induced to commit "any sort of crime."

Bellamy's individual has several basic motives including fear, love of luxury, and desire for security, gratitude, and honor.[18] In addition this person has the motives of patriotism and "inspiration of duty" which in time of war may lead him to die for his country. The opportunity structure within which an individual acts, however, determines the expression of these basic motivations. For example, people love money and pursue it for several reasons including security, luxury, power, and high social position while "higher motives" such as patriotic service are left grossly underdeveloped. But if everyone's needs could be abundantly provided for, the quest for luxury would be obviated. Only the higher motives, patriotism and honor, would be left to be exploited and developed by Bellamy's utopian society. Though it sounds naive in retrospect, his "patriotism" works much the same as Skinner's benign aggression and natural curiosity.

When it comes to engineering the kind of society in which "good" behavior will be favored and "bad" behavior "extinguished," our five utopias belong to a single historical tradition. More admittedly borrowed from Plato and Cabet from More. To Lewis Mumford the structural implications of Cabet's industrializing utopia seem so close to the fully developed industrial army described by Bellamy that he considers the second only a variant of the first.[19] As for Skinner's *Walden Two*, it is clearly a descendant of its precursors.

In all five of our utopias the common denominator of dislike is competitive materialism, the selfish pursuit of property, be it productive or personal. Therefore all five utopians set up conditions to minimize material incentives.

The collective good of Plato's utopian city-state is the organic morality of a perfectly functioning social whole. Combatting the social-contract views of the Sophists, Plato argues that men are not self-sufficient creatures bound together "unnaturally" by society.[20] On the contrary, since men have different aptitudes which fit them for different jobs, mutual exchanges among them are beneficial to all. One specializes in the task for which one's natural endowments have best prepared one, and each person thereby becomes a functional part of the social whole.

The size and internal variety of Plato's social whole is determined by the civilization of his day, a reformed version of his own city-state, Athens. He begins by having Socrates sketch the outlines of a primitive but "healthy" version of the ideal society with only five main occupational categories.[21]

In this "healthy," primitive state needs are met adequately though minimally, but such a level of reasonable need seemed quite unreasonable to Socrates's students, who labeled it a community fit only for swine. So Plato has Socrates relent and raise reasonable need to what all can consider a "civilized" level, one approximating the living standards of Athens circa 300 B.C. The society's "health" is thereby reduced, however, for the addition of luxuries raises its "temperature." The state, moreover, must now be enlarged to accommodate all the new occupations, none of which are really necessary: artists, poets, furniture manufacturers, bankers, cooks, and ladies' maids. Raising the level of needs raises the level of acquisitiveness, the source of most evil among both individuals and states.[22] If needs at this level of luxury are to be deemed reasonable, how can individuals be restrained from seeking more than their just share?

Plato's solution is the creation of a special administrative class, the guardians. They see to it that the state does not become too large, and they prevent both poverty and excessive wealth. A potter, for example, too poor even to acquire the tools of the trade would surely turn out an inferior product. On the other hand, the craftsmanship of a rich potter would be no better, for a rich potter would grow "idle and careless." [23] Since the poverty of some members of society is a consequence of the excessive wealth of others, the guardians use their superior reasoning powers to counter the baser appetites of the masses and thus keep acquisitiveness within bounds.

But what keeps the guardians from pursuing the same base appetites? At this point Plato institutionalizes collective consumption and unwittingly creates a managerial elite of primitive Christians three hundred years before the birth of Christ. Provided only with the bare necessities of life by the citizens they govern, the guardians consume communally and own no private property beyond essentials. They are not allowed to acquire land or money and are forbidden even to touch silver and gold. Without such restrictions Plato reasoned they would soon become farmers and merchants and would seek their own advantage at the expense of their fellow citizens. Private property is the undermining evil of the city-state, and where its ownership is not controlled, it divides the city into two parts, the rich city and the poor city, each hostile to the other.[24]

Agreeing with Plato, that needs must be limited to reasonable levels under conditions of equality and that private ownership of property is inevitably corrupting, Thomas More extends Plato's institutionalized collectivism to production as well as consumption and to all the inhabitants of his chessboard society.[25] Organizing Utopia in the form of a state commune, he makes all its citizens into millennial men, all participating equally in collective production and sharing equally according to need. But consumption is even more austere than in the Republic. Personal property of all citizens is restricted to bare essentials; no ornaments, jewelry, fancy clothes, or luxuries are condoned.

Second only to the abolition of private productive property and the restriction of personal property is the abolition of money. With money gone, greed disappears; "frauds, thefts, quarrels, uprisings, murders" and even poverty "wither away" and eventually "vanish." The old laws "too numerous to be read and too obscure to be readily understood" disappear along with the crimes they were supposed to control. Utopian law becomes so simple and clear that every citizen can serve as his own counsel; lawyers become only an unpleasant memory.[26]

Thus, the state commune removes contingencies of reinforcement for greedy antisocial behavior. But Thomas More is full of additional behavioristic suggestions. In the case of theft in 16th-century England, for example, More does not advocate a new moral man; his solution is much more direct and positive in its reinforcement: provide everyone with a chance to work and no one will be forced to steal. And if theft is punished by execution (as it was in More's day), thieves have nothing to lose by murdering their victims; on the contrary, they are far better off to have eliminated all witnesses. To decrease the number of bloodthirsty thieves, let the punishment fit the crime.[27]

Sir Thomas More even designed contingencies for kings. By putting a low ceiling on the amount of money a king could accumulate in his treasury and by requiring him to distribute periodic surpluses among his subjects, he would find it impossible to invade foreign countries (as most kings like to do); yet at the same time he would become so loved by his subjects that he would learn to prefer their prosperity to his own selfish ends.[28]

To discourage conspicuous consumption in the form of jewelry, precious metals in Utopia are used for chamber pots. Thus degraded, gold and silver turn anyone wearing them into the laughing stock of the community.[29]

Even More's treatment of religion is behavioristic to judge from Skinner's recent statements on "laws of religion." Such laws, says Skinner, merely "codify contingencies of reinforcement" that are "maintained by social environments."[30] An individual may feel acutely uncomfortable when threatened with eternal damnation; but subsequent behavior will be shaped by the same contingencies that account for the discomfort, not by the feelings per se. More illustrates the same relationships between feelings, contingencies and behavior when he reduces supernatural sanction in Utopia to social sanction. Any Utopian who does not believe in rewards and punishments in the afterlife is not permitted to hold public office or argue this heresy in public. Even worse, his fellow citizens look down on him "as a man of worthless and sordid nature."[31]

It was More's *Utopia*, according to Etienne Cabet, that first called his attention to the importance of communal ownership and eventually led him to see that the "vices and unhappiness" of people are due to an improper organization of society.[32] The human is rational and perfectible, say Cabet, but true happiness can be achieved only through the perfect equality provided by "community of goods."[33] In Icaria all capital is the property of the entire community. Everyone participates in collective production and receives an equal share of the goods produced.

For Cabet as for More, collective production and consumption provide a social structure that eliminates the zero-sum game. Money and commercial transactions become completely unnecessary. Since there is no money and everyone possesses the same goods as everyone else, the incentive to steal is eliminated along with most reasons for murder, arson, and suicide. With the elimination of crime there is no longer any need for trials, lawyers, judges, and penal codes.[34]

Approximately half a century after the publication of *Icaria*, Edward Bellamy published (1888) his description of the utopian future he later called "Nationalism,"[35] a utopia located in the United States in the year 2000. By this time technological progress has created many new wonders, but Bellamy's American future is basically the same state commune as Utopia and Icaria. Everyone works for the state, which owns and controls all productive property, and everyone receives the same share of annual production. The zero-sum consequences of private ownership have been eliminated in all three as has *un*reasonable need in the form of greedy, ostentatious, competitive consumption.

In Bellamy's behaviorist view, the remarkable differences between the world of 1888 and that of 2000 are not based on changes in human nature but on changes in the "conditions of human life" which have affected humanity's motives for acting as it does. The old society was so organized that officials were constantly tempted to misuse their power for their own advantage. The social system of the year 2000, however, no longer rewards dishonesty; there is no longer any opportunity for an official to misuse power or seek personal advantage at other peoples' expense. In the old days almost all crime was provoked by inequalities of wealth and the desire for money; now that everyone is equal and money has been eliminated, crime has vanished and with it the need for lawyers, state legislatures, taxes, and even legislation. Almost all laws in the old days were concerned with private property and commercial transactions; and with both of these eliminated, there is no longer any need to make new ones. Buying and selling, moreover, was an "antisocial" activity, "an education in self-seeking at the expense of others." [36]

All the above can be found in the behaviorism of Thomas More. Bellamy's unique contribution to the structuring of human behavior and motives is his "industrial army." All citizens become employees of one single employer, the nation, as a kind of universal military service. Such service is not "compulsory" but "a matter of course"; for when an action is inevitable, it is regarded as natural. There is no other way to survive in the new society except as a member of the industrial army; to attempt otherwise would, in effect, be "suicidal." Since there is no alternative to joining the industrial army, no one has to be compelled to join it! [37] As we see in Chapter 7, this is precisely why Chinese and Russian collectives are more "successful" than the Third World experiments. Belonging to a collective becomes "natural" and a "matter of course" when the alternatives have all been eliminated. This is behavioral engineering on the grand scale.

Our most recent utopia, Skinner's *Walden Two* (1948), employs the same collective-consumption, collective-production design for extinguishing material incentives. It, too, thereby achieves the harmonious absence of ostentatious consumption, pursuit of power, crime, legal problems, and even legislation. Although this utopia is a relatively small social unit of only a thousand people, it seems more like Plato's city-state than one of our 19th-century eutopian communes. In fact, as a meritocracy run from the top, it could even be considered a miniature version of Bellamy's industrial army. And if Plato's Republic seemed at times nonbehavioristic because it was run by guardians making mentalistic decisions, we find that the behaviorist utopia par excellence also has its guardians—now called "planners." Since democracy might leave too much to chance, planning in Walden Two is accomplished by specialists skilled in behavioral engineering. [38]

Unfortunately, Walden Two provides no meaningful examples of how the behavioral engineering Skinner advocates would be put into daily practice. Take, for instance, the problem of the farmers who picked up "objectionable odors" working around livestock. When the community began to ostracize these dedicated individuals, something obviously had to be done. How did behavioral engineering solve the problem? Showers (for the farmers) were installed in the barns.

In Walden Two's only other example of behavioral engineering techniques, children are taught to build tolerance for disagreeable, frustrating situations by standing tired and hungry for five minutes before their soup bowls and by postponing consumption of lollipops placed in their possession.[39] Since reinforcement is always positive in Walden Two, we must by definition accept the classification of these situations as nonpunitive. Skinner never tells us what the psychologist in charge does when children ignore his orders and start eating their soup and lollipops.

Despite the poverty of these examples, they are sufficient to indicate the asymmetry that typifies Walden Two's behaviorism. And this asymmetry is altogether justified, Walden Two's visitors are told, because people are no more qualified to operate the behavioral technology being applied to them than are children in a "group nursery." Once you have a technology, it must be controlled by those skilled in its use. Moreover, amateurs never appreciate the need for experimentation; they want the assurance that their experts know the outcome in advance. And since the masses are incapable of evaluating experts, the latter cannot be elected; they must be self-appointed.[40]

According to Plato, the guardians of his Republic would be compelled to serve it out of fear, the fear of what would happen if those with lesser qualifications were to serve in their place.[41] Skinner's planners also serve because they alone have the unique qualifications to do so. If instead of attributing their devotion to Plato's fear reduction we attribute it to rational decision or to the positive reinforcements of running a social experiment, is the explanation any less mentalistic or the act itself any less authoritarian and egotistical?

Before trying to answer this question, we compare our five utopias to our previous eight eutopias within the same commitment and social-predictability frameworks used previously. I add one other case, however, to the comparative data: the intentional community of Twin Oaks at Louisa, Virginia. Although the community was only five years old at the time its founder Kathleen Kinkade published *A Walden Two Experiment* (1973), her book is probably the best report on a contemporary "commune" to date.[42] As an attempt to apply Skinner's chessboard society to the real world, it is useful to the discussion that follows.

Commitment

Persecution is not a factor in any of our utopias. In our real-world communes, however, it is usually associated with social-movement origins, a concept partially developed by two of our authors, Cabet and Bellamy.

Cabet tells us that the rich and poor of Icaria had been fighting for centuries and the country had been constantly disrupted by revolutions and massacres.[43] But about half a century before Cabet's visit, the last despot had been overthrown by the glorious leader, Icar, who founded the imaginary commune-republic. Even in the presence of foreign visitors an Icarian family might suddenly join together in a spirited hymn offered to the memory of their revered national hero. In this respect Cabet's fictional account reads like the report of a journalist visiting Maoist China during the Cultural Revolution.

Bellamy gives considerable attention to current labor problems in his first chapter.[44] Since the early 1870's, he explains, labor unrest in the United States had been growing increasingly acute, and labor's demands for a greater share of the good things of life had reached heights impossible to satisfy. In the words of one of Bellamy's characters, "The working-classes all over the world seem to be going crazy at once." These labor "disturbances" finally culminate in a "great movement" that ushers in the "modern industrial system." Bellamy's hero awakens from a Rip Van Winkle sleep lasting over one hundred years to view the results of these events in the year 2000.

Much of the appeal of Bellamy's utopia was its nonviolent resolution of the threatening labor situation. Only one year earlier, in his preface to the 1887 edition of *The Conditions of the Working Class in England*, Engels reported enthusiastically that during the previous ten months a revolution had taken place among the American working class that would have taken "at least ten years" anywhere else.[45] The movement, as he saw it, was spreading like a "prairie-fire" and striking "terror" in the hearts of the American "ruling classes." We now know that Engels misread the signs, but in 1888 we might not have been so sure.

Instead of a class revolution, Bellamy gave his readers a "logical evolution" culminating in what he was to label elsewhere "nationalism." Labor unrest, as he saw it, was provoked by the increasing concentration of capital in ever larger corporations that treated labor impersonally and tyrannically. To have retreated to the older system of small businesses and industries would have decreased the growing inequalities, but it would have done so only at the cost of increasing poverty and arresting progress. The people of the United States finally realized that the only rational solution was to consolidate all the productive capital of the nation into a "single syndicate representing the people" to be operated for "the common profit." By the time the decision was made, the public was "fully ripe for it" and fully supported it. Without bloodshed or violence the nation itself became the "sole corporation."[46]

Skinner gives no indication that Walden Two is the result of a social movement or involves the intense individual commitment that normally accompanies one. Surely a deep commitment to the experimental approach by all involved would be necessary to carry out such a project using only positive reinforcement. Yet only once does Skinner come close to a conceptualization of social-movement conditions. In the context of a discussion of Walden Two's appeal for new members, he says it must approach "conversion" and in some cases may even involve "rejection" of the external society. He fails to develop this insight further since he is more interested in the indoctrination of Walden Two's second generation than in the recruitment of their parents. Instead, Walden Two specifically rejects political action as a viable means of achieving the "good life," for such action implies power and force. Religion and belief in the supernatural are similarly dismissed. The community, moreover, does not propagandize its members because a scientific experiment is not compatible with proselytizing.[47]

Yet the real Walden Two experiment, just like our other real communes, was very much the product of a social movement. The founding of Twin Oaks in 1967 and its growth in membership in 1970 coincided with a counterculture movement among American youth. Within this movement Twin Oaks had a special appeal to college dropouts familiar with *Walden Two* and interested in its future-oriented, experimental approach to a better life.[48]

That Skinner is truly oblivious to the crucial importance of social-movement origins is perhaps best revealed by his discussion of "vertical cleavage," a Walden Two phenomenon resembling Hutterite branching. In contrast to the Hutterites, however, whose population expansion is due to internal growth, Walden Two and its projected daughter communities will grow through assimilation of new members from the outside. Subdividing every 2 years, the number of Walden communities is expected to reach 60 within 10 years.[49] Such a rapid assimilation rate would match or surpass the unique record of the kibbutz movement but without any of the extraordinary social circumstances that gave rise to it.

Though their reasons are different, Plato and More share Skinner's lack of concern for social creation. As authors of preindustrial, preprogress utopias they are less action oriented than the postprogress authors. Elizabeth Hansot has tried to make a case for a "classical" versus a "modern" mode of utopian thinking along mentalistic lines sometimes difficult to follow.[50] The classical utopians, she feels, thought on a more ideal plane that differed from reality in kind whereas the modern utopians have been more intent on criticizing a contemporary world from which their own model differs only in degree. Along these lines, Plato and More were not concerned with how to bring about a utopia; they never expected it to come about. Certainly both Plato and More were explicit in their final skepticism regarding the workability of their models.[51] But the differences here between early and recent utopians are a reflection of two quite different social environments with two quite different sets of expectations. Once the notion and expectation of progress were widely accepted, people could more readily link social criticism to social action.

As Mumford pointed out long ago, utopias after Charles Fourier are vastly different from those preceding Francis Bacon.[52] The more recent ones are dominated by mechanization, and in them means begin to dominate ends. Mumford finds the earliest mention of mechanical improvements in Campanella's *City of the Sun* and considers it an anticipation of the inventions and "whirring machinery" that were to have such a drastic impact on 19th-century utopias. A utopian author no longer had to locate a better world in some distant land, but could put it in a future that humanity conceivably might achieve through industrial and political ingenuity.

One can readily agree with Bloom that a major goal of Plato's ideal city-state is to eliminate the civic strife caused by competition for scarce goods.[53] Harmony within the organic, social whole—the perfect working together of its various occupational parts—is insured by a low level of reasonable need. The model is perfectly static. Needs maintained at a minimal level require neither technological nor social innovating. Simplicity of needs becomes the foundation of the utopian goal, organic harmony.[54]

In the sheer austerity of his Utopia More is close to Socrates's minimal version of reasonable need. Everyone works to provision the communal storehouse where all goods are in free supply for all citizens equally. There is no scarcity or want, but needs are limited to bare essentials. For example, Utopians are "indifferent to fineness of texture" in their clothing and are satisfied with "one cloak every two years." They care nothing for those differences in style and color that "fastidious men" in other countries employ for ostentatious purposes.[55]

In Utopia, as in the Republic, the goal is one of static harmony and egalitarian justice. But in its vital concern with the afterlife, Utopia seems closer to the 19th-century religious communes. Like them too, it achieves some degree of social isolation, in this case by its insular location and treacherous harbors. Utopians, moreover, are very receptive to labor-saving inventions. They quickly adopted the technology of printing and the making of paper and welcomed any visitors with unusual abilities.[56] This openness to change not only resembles our 19th-century communes, it is indicative of the times. It was in More's day that craftsmen were beginning to develop the modern idea of progress, as noted above. But full development of this idea would take another two hundred years. The predominantly static quality of Utopian technology and society is in keeping with the times.

According to H. G. Wells, Cabet was the first utopian to free humanity "from irksome labors through the use of machinery." [57] As the first to incorporate the industrial revolution into utopia, Cabet's Icaria (1840) became, for Wells, "the great primitive of modern utopias." Icaria's "immense storehouses" add vast quantities of manufactured goods to the agricultural and handicraft products of More's day, but everything is still distributed in equal amounts to all families.[58]

A dynamic element, however, has now penetrated utopia—an elastic new view of reasonable need. An example is a new item of furniture the Icarian republic decides to mass produce for every household; its production requires an additional 5 minutes labor daily for one year from a hundred thousand workers. Although the workday in Icaria was once 10 to 18 hours long, it has since been shortened to 6 hours through the development of machinery. But Icarians believe 6 hours will be their minimum; instead of decreasing work time further, they prefer to increase their consumption of manufactured goods. Utopia itself has now moved from leisure preference to work preference. Through mechanization this rational-secular utopia has opened the door to a continual increase of material "pleasures." [59]

Machines in Icaria not only perform all dangerous, boring, and disagreeable tasks, they increase the goods available for family enjoyment. Happiness, therefore, is increasing progressively in Icaria with no forseeable limit to its expansion. Only one limitation is enforced; material satisfactions increase at the same rate for everyone. Items, such as carriages, that cannot be produced in sufficient quantities for all citizens are manufactured only for collective use. But when the citizenry decides to enjoy some new material good, like the furniture item above, the item is produced in quantities sufficient to supply every household.[60] Goals coalesce with needs as the citizens of Icaria, like the members of the modern kibbutz, play the game of "going up together."

Bellamy's United States of the year 2000 also uses labor-saving machinery to provide an elastic but egalitarian material abundance. Each family, however, is allowed to use its own budgetary discretion in selecting those items of personal property it chooses to consume. Some families own more clothes than others; some acquire larger houses. But such differences never become ostentatious because they represent only differences of discretion, not differences of discretionary income.[61] The United States has become a giant shitufi, and our utopias to this point have followed the same labor-saving, expanding-need route to privatization that our eutopias did.

While Skinner's utopia moves in the same direction, it goes by a different route. Most people, according to Skinner, do not want to participate in planning; they are satisfied to live from day to day as long as their future is made secure by the intelligent few concerned with long-term goals. Happiness is therefore the first goal of Walden Two, and active future orientation is second.[62]

The priority of immediate over long-term goals in Walden Two is consistent with the virtual absence of social-movement characteristics, but such a situation is inconsistent again with the characteristics of successful eutopian communes. This ranking of priorities is precisely the reversal that led to their breakdown. Adherence to Walden Two objectives led to a continuing "debate" at Twin Oaks between those favoring expansion of the community and its social-experiment objectives and those favoring immediate improvements in material living standards. As Kinkade was writing her book, the "quality of life" contingent was winning out, and per-capita living costs were doubling.[63]

Skinner's utopia differs from all the rest in being totally progressive; it is a continuing social experiment under the direction of its planner-psychologists. This gives us three types of utopia along a continuum from totally static to totally progressive. Plato's Republic is both technologically and socially static; and since only the faintest stirrings of technological progress are evident as yet in More's utopia, it can be classified with Plato's. Icaria and Bellamy's future states, however, are socially static but materially progressive. They capably stimulate and manage technological progress without ever disturbing or altering the static perfection of their social orders. And finally we have Walden Two, which accepts technological change—even making labor-saving inventions of its own—while continually working to improve human social behavior.[64]

If there are any long-term goals in Walden Two, they belong to its planners, who are concerned primarily with social progress. The masses are more concerned with short-term need satisfactions. When such differences lead to problems in a totalitarian eutopia, the planners can resolve them by force. But under conditions of voluntary membership, Twin Oaks demonstrates as well as any of our previous eutopias the implausibility of Skinner's model.

With the exception of Walden Two, the sheer size of our utopian states would tend to make high frequency of membership interaction difficult and the growth of individual competitiveness relatively easy. Plato's ideal city-state was limited to some five thousand families, a small enough republic for all members of the state's smallest occupational class, the guardians, to be recognized on sight. But this is not a state commune, and only within the small, collectively consuming guardian class does Plato fight competitive individualism directly. By outlawing the nuclear family among the guardians, he tries to make his entire ruling elite into a single, cohesive "family." All "wives" are "held in common," children are raised apart, and parents are never permitted to know which children are theirs or vice versa.[65]

Only Skinner follows Plato in trying to weaken the family. The community is said to replace the family not only as an economic unit but also as a social and psychological unit.[66] Husbands and wives are assigned separate rooms, but this is done to preserve their sense of privacy, not to facilitate group marriage as at Oneida. Monogamy is the rule at Walden Two. The relationship between parent and child, however, is deliberately weakened by raising children in a fashion that combines features of the kibbutz nursery with those of Oneida's "pa- and ma-hood." In effect, the relationship is a very close approximation of Plato's scheme for child raising. At Twin Oaks, however, sexual freedom proved far more popular than monogamy, and the community's attempt to copy Walden Two's child-rearing techniques was so unsuccessful that it decided not to accept any more children until it became better established.[67]

More does not attempt to strengthen the unity of his Utopia at the family's expense. The family in Utopia is as patriarchal and age graded as that of Amana or the Hutterites. Wives take their orders from their husbands and children from their parents. In the communal dining halls the elders are served first and receive the best food. The principal communal unit in Utopia is a magistracy of 30 households sharing a common kitchen and dining hall. Each household within this unit is an extended family of not more than 16 or less than 10 adults.[68]

More's hierarchically organized state based on the patriarchal family resembles, as J. H. Hexter has noted, the public order of Confucian China, which was also built on the patriarchal extended family.[69] More, however, was simply following the traditions of his own society and rejecting along with Plato's imaginative elimination of the family the alternative suggested by that popular medieval commune, the monastery. More wanted neither a celibate society that could not reproduce itself nor a society practicing group marriage. He may not have been as imaginative as Plato, but he was much more practical; Amana lasted three times as long as Oneida.

Living in small neighborhood units the size of a kibbutz or an Amana village, Utopians worked and interacted frequently with the other members of their collective unit. The communal dining hall of each magistracy helped to maintain such interaction as well as high visibility. Women took turns working in the communal kitchen; and though taking food home to eat was "not forbidden," it was "not thought proper" either.[70]

There was little chance for internal competition in Utopia except in the social mobility of its scholars. Sex and age determined most of the ranking as it did among the Hutterites and in Amana; and as in the kibbutz, among the Shakers and in most of the other successful communes, there was minimal symbolization of status. Distinguished persons were honored, but they were honored "willingly" because they deserved it, not because they demanded it. Even the elected prince of Utopia had no official "robe or diadem." Anyone, moreover, who overtly sought a public office was certain not to win it. As for treatment of children, it was even more strict than among the patriarchal Hutterites.[71]

Some 5 times as large as Utopia, the Icarian state would be large even by modern standards: 50 million inhabitants evenly distributed among 100 provinces subdivided into 10 counties each. The population of each county, approximately 50,000 persons, was about that of a Utopian city. But instead of subdividing each county into smaller residential units like More's magistracies, Cabet describes a modern division into all kinds of democratic associations. Icarians annually elect all local officers including factory, hospital, store, theater, and school officials. Total participation in local government takes place at the county level through open assemblies. Government by elected representatives occurs only at the provincial and state levels. At the county assemblies all public officials may be held accountable for their acts at any time by the "sovereign people." And since all officials including even the president of Icaria pursue their regular occupations in addition to their government responsibilities, their double burden is lightened by giving each as many subordinates as possible. This practice spreads the work of government and greatly increases the extent of popular participation even at the highest levels.[72]

Cabet's huge state is very Rousseauean in its attempt to involve the public as much as possible in government and to make it truly sovereign. Icarian democracy has one foot in the agrarian, preindustrial utopia of Thomas More and one foot in the highly industrialized one of Edward Bellamy. It tries to preserve the face-to-face quality of the small agrarian community while opening its arms to a future characterized by mass production and uninhibited industrialization.

Cabet is at least partially aware, however, of the drift toward individualism entailed by the industrial process. No longer is everyone a farmer as in More's Utopia. There, all took their turn at two-year periods of farm service, and city-dwellers were recruited for corvée harvest labor like they are today in Castro's Cuba. And when a Utopian grew bored with one trade, others could be mastered and changed off as desired, in a very Marxian fashion.[73] But Cabet is impressed with the need for specialization, not rotation. The number of workers needed for each occupation is "statistically determined," and young men are invited to take the competitive examinations necessary to qualify for training in the profession of their choice.[74]

To counter the competitive consequences of specialization, Cabet makes everyone's lifestyle the same. Citizens are equal in clothing, housing, food, eligibility for office, and leisure pastimes. In addition, all occupations are given the same status; all dirty and "repulsive" jobs are done by machinery, and the rest are "esteemed equally." A shoemaker is as good as a doctor because both occupations are equally necessary, and both individuals work equally hard for their country.[75]

Bellamy carries Cabet's industrial, Millennial Man society another step beyond the patriarchal, family-based version of Thomas More. In Bellamy's "nationalized" industrial state even Cabet's counties with their town-meeting type assemblies have been superseded by a hierarchical social structure patterned on military organization. The industrial army is a giant meritocracy, and even the "general-in-chief," the President of the United States, must work up through the ranks on the basis of performance. Promotion in the lower grades is by appointment and in the higher grades by election, but voting is limited to citizens who have completed their years of industrial service and are in honorary retirement. In any case, the candidate is judged on merit including the results of tests; favoritism and politicking are not condoned. The procedures of the hierarchical organization are so standardized and all-encompassing that little is needed in the way of formal legal structure.[76]

Since specialization is encouraged by the very structure of the industrial army, changes of occupation are now deemed "capricious"; only the "poorer sort" of worker is inclined to seek a change. Bellamy is not concerned with problems of alienation, for all kinds of labor-saving inventions have reduced the drudgery of work. Most of the tasks once done by domestic servants are now performed by collective services such as the public laundries and public kitchens. In the public dining hall of each ward, however, tables are waited on by young people, who spend the first three years of their industrial service as "common laborers." No stigma is attached to this personal and unskilled service; it is a stage through which all citizens must pass.[77]

After three years of service as a common laborer each person chooses an occupation. Those who choose a profession must take further training at schools so difficult that no one would attend simply to escape work. Students who fail to make the grade and have to return to industry are not stigmatized in any way. Again we have a highly competitive, mobile occupational structure in which all failure and disappointment are eliminated purely by literary license. For example, patients are allowed to seek the physician of their choice; but to the question what do bad doctors do when everyone bypasses them for the better ones, Bellamy assures the reader there are no bad doctors in his utopia.[78]

In the new society creative individuals such as authors must behave in a manner very much like capitalists. There is no money; but everyone in the industrial army earns the same labor credits, and these are traded for consumer goods according to each item's labor value, the labor invested in each. Authors publish their own books and put whatever labor value on them they please. Like any private entrepreneur they must be careful not to overprice the item and thereby discourage sales. The first book must be written after working hours, and the cost of printing it must be saved from the author's annual labor credits. If the book sells well, enough labor credits are accrued to permit the author to spend all working hours writing. Inventors are said to work the same way, but clearly it would not be possible to amass the necessary research capital for modern inventions in this manner. Bellamy's utopia endorses change in principle, but in practice he leaves its initiation largely to an impractical form of the competitive, individualistic capitalism he wishes to eliminate.[79]

As we have seen, families in Bellamy's world of the future spend their incomes differently. They do not all have the same material possessions as do the citizens of Icaria and Utopia. All incomes are the same, however, so such differences in Bellamy's view cannot foster competitive consumption. But what about the family that has difficulty budgeting its annual income, that spends on frivolities and ends up without the necessities? In such cases the state puts the family on a monthly or even a weekly allowance as the situation requires. Apparently Bellamy does not anticipate any widespread need for such close supervision. He also allows material goods to be inherited, but this practice does not create inequities or spark jealousy since it applies only to personal property, which is usually redundant. Rather than spend for storage space to keep inherited articles, people give them away.[80]

Walden Two in many ways is a miniature version of Bellamy's giant meritocracy. For one thing it appoints, rather than elects, its planners and managers. The latter are specialists who run economic or service divisions much like branch managers in a kibbutz. But while kibbutz managers and officials are elected by popular vote, Walden Two managers are said to "work up" to their positions like members of a "civil service" on the basis of demonstrated ability.[81] A civil service, however, is a formal structure necessary in large states, not in small communities where individual differences in abilities and aptitudes are manifest to all. Skinner uses a civil-service system in his small community to make sure his directors are selected solely on the basis of technological competence.

As we have seen, technically competent kibbutz branch managers may be replaced if the members of the branch find them too overbearing. Social expertise may be just as crucial to the survival of a community as technical expertise. Twin Oaks has found that the most competent members are often the ones most likely to be demanding, pushy, and intolerant of others. While the community continues to appoint its officers on the basis of ability, it rotates them every 18 months and takes their social as well as technical skills into account. Twin Oaks also shifted very early from "private planners meetings" to "public planners meetings." It found it expedient to include the membership in decision making to the extent of publicly discussing all major issues and eliciting popular support for them.[82] In other words, Twin Oaks has found it necessary to substitute a great deal of "simple democracy" for the formal meritocracy of its fictional counterpart. Of course, the Walden Two argument is that its planners are, in fact, social technicians who can do no wrong. This is the same kind of fictional license which makes all doctors equally good in Bellamy's utopia and all guardians social-organism minded in Plato's.

Walden Two planners, moreover, maintain such a low profile that most of the members do not even know who they are.[83] At Twin Oaks, as in any of the real-world communes, everyone knows the community leaders.[84] The fact that Walden Two members do not is consistent with the community's low frequency of interaction and high degree of privatization. Again Walden Two is very unlike the successful real-world communes.

Despite Walden Two's cooperative housing, common recreation facilities, dining hall, and library, there is seldom any occasion when the entire community comes together. There are no general assemblies; and to save construction costs, the theater and dining hall were made so small that members eat or attend in shifts.[85] Walden Two sounds more like William Hinds's description of Zoar just before it disbanded than like any of the successful 19th-century eutopias in their prime.[86] At Twin Oaks on the other hand, the high degree of interaction, the frequent community meetings, and the deliberate attempts to achieve "ritualization" of behavior are all characteristics strongly reminiscent of the successful communes.[87]

Social or Legal Predictability?

All of our utopians, as we have seen, want to eliminate property incentives in order to bring out the best in humanity. What sort of selective incentives, if any, do the utopians put in their place? For the most part, our authors do not work out clear incentive structures for their good societies. And when they mention punitive measures, they do so in an offhand manner, for they clearly do not expect their societies to be coercive. In cases of last resort, punitive action might be taken in utopia, but such cases are clearly to be exceptional. Each chessboard society has been so well designed that the human counters must just naturally be good.

In Plato's Republic everything depends on the unselfish rule of the guardians, who are kept unselfish by being deprived of all property and all income except for the minimal subsistence provided by the community. But who would want their job? That is precisely the question put to Socrates by his student, Adeimantus. Everything about the life of the guardians seems unappealing to him. Their consumption is austere, and they are not permitted a normal family life. What good, he wonders, do they get out of the system they control? Rulers of other states have large houses with magnificent furnishings where they entertain lavishly and enjoy many sumptuary privileges. In this Republic, however, the rulers do not even have the same advantages as the common citizen. Socrates counters at first with an organismic argument. He is trying to devise a society in which the good of all is the first consideration. Farmers will not wear royal robes nor crowns, nor will potters sit around their fires drinking and carousing. Guardians, like all other functionaries of this society, must perfect themselves at the job for which they have a special and natural aptitude. The nature of this compulsion lies in the organic quality of Plato's social system. Each part of the social body must perform its function for the body's well-being.[88] A condition of chessboard society is that it be played in the fashion prescribed by its author. Again, the name for such compulsion is "literary license."

Later in the elaboration of his argument, however, Socrates returns to Adeimantus's objection, and at that point stresses moral or social incentives. Guardians are honored by their fellow citizens while they live, and when they die they receive a public funeral and an "appropriate memorial." Says Socrates, they will be more honored than an Olympic victor. Distinguished young men also have the right to sleep more frequently with young women; but aside from this one "material" incentive, honors and rewards appear to be mainly social.[89] The feasibility of applying such incentives to an entire class is enhanced by the fact that its numbers are few and the city-state is small. The guardians are highly visible and will find it difficult to acquire property or carry on unauthorized business clandestinely. Allan Bloom is so unimpressed by these answers to Adeimantus that he suggests Plato is not only indicating how impossible such dedication would be, he is deliberately pointing to a problem for which utopia has no solution.[90]

Thomas More, early in his book, asks his fictional informant how men could possibly live well while holding everything in common. It seemed likely to him that everyone would stop working, since without the "hope of gain" to "drive" one, each would rely on the rest and "become lazy." [91] More thereby raises the perennial question: What motivates Millennial Man?

He partially answers his question through the size of his communal units and his emphasis on high visibility. He stresses that no loafing can take place because everyone lives "in full view of all." Distinguished men, furthermore, are "publicly honored" through statues erected to help the public remember their virtuous deeds. It is said that unless an individual's misbehavior is sufficiently severe no public punishment occurs, but neither the nature of public punishment nor the crime that merits it is specified. For lesser infractions, again unspecified, husbands punish wives, and parents their children.[92]

The major duty of each magistrate is to make sure that everyone in the magistracy works hard, for no one is allowed to sit idle. But what happens to someone caught loafing we are not told. Moreover, the first time a person leaves his place of work to take an unauthorized trip without an internal passport from the city prince, he is said to be "severely punished." And if he ever does it again, he is made a bondsman; in other words, sentenced to forced labor. If he still does not work, he is killed.[93]

Forced labor and internal passports, to say nothing of capital punishment, add a Stalinist flavor to More's account, but one has the feeling that a despotism is not what he really had in mind. He would rather remove temptation wherever possible than punish people for falling into it. All taverns, "ale houses," "brothels," and "hiding places" for "secret meetings" are eliminated as in Maoist China; ideally there is no alternative to work or to "honorable leisure" in either.[94] Thus the incentive structure of Utopia adds up so far to: (1) positive moral or social incentives in the form of social acclaim for a few outstanding individuals; (2) possible negative social incentives due to high visibility and supervision; (3) strong negative material incentives such as death and forced labor at unpleasant work; and (4) the removal of distracting alternatives (opportunity costs) so that recourse to negative incentives will be minimal.

More is not oblivious to positive material incentives. In fact, as measured by its success in 19th-century and modern communes, his major material incentive is eminently credible; Utopia offers its inhabitants security.[95] More's informant sounds like a modern Hutterite or kibbutznik in asking what could be better than to live in a society where one never has to worry about having enough to get by, even in old age. More's Utopia is the kind of commune-state one might imagine a Hutterite or Amana state to be like were such a thing possible. Given the Reformational origins of all three, More's utopia comes as close to plausibility as any ever devised.

The social controls of Icaria resemble both the social predictability of a small community and the "socialist emulation" goals of such contemporary eutopias as Russia, China, and Cuba. Cabet even comes close to the label "socialist emulation" with his term "useful emulation." By this he means the social esteem and public distinction given those individuals whose service to the republic goes beyond the call of duty. Conversely, an individual who does not do his part is subjected to public disapproval and condemnation. The offender may be deprived of some rights as a citizen; exclusion from certain public places, for example, constitutes a kind of secular excommunication.[96]

While there are no police in Icaria, all citizens act as such by watching each other. But the high visibility of the small traditional community can become very sinister if deliberately organized on a statewide scale. Cabet certainly has nothing sinister in mind, for he is obviously thinking of small-group situations. Individual offenses against the community and the republic are always judged in local groups, the popular county assemblies, the schools, the factories, the communal dining halls, and even the family itself.[97] But regardless of Cabet's good intentions, the scale of his communal organization is closer to contemporary Socialist Man eutopias than to past or present Millennial Man communities; and "socialist emulation" on a national scale generally requires third-party force external to the local community or small group. Mumford deems all the provisions for popular government in Icaria an "epiphenomenon" since in a society of this size and structure they would be only a veneer for the dictatorial power underlying them.[98]

In any case, Cabet is certain that all would work according to their abilities in this paradise. When he asks what happens to the lazy in Icaria, he is told they do not exist. Not only are all Icarians happy at their work, but all despise laziness as other people despise thievery.[99] Here again we encounter the socialist zero-sum view: the free-riding malingerers cost their fellows extra effort.

For many of his critics, one of the most ominous aspects of Cabet's utopia is government domination of the press. In the Icarian view a private press is necessary only to oppose kings and aristocracies; but in a truly democratic country people are best served by a press entrusted to their own elected officials. The function of the Icarian press is to publish disinterested, objective news accounts without the lies and internal contradictions so common elsewhere. Each county has its own newspaper, which reports fully the deliberations of its county assembly. Since these town-meeting-type assemblies constitute the popular voice, reporting that voice is the perfect expression of public opinion.[100]

Again we can be sure that Cabet intended no suppression of a free press as we understand the meaning of that phrase today. No man exiled five years from his native land for opinions he printed in his own newspaper could have had such an intention. He undoubtedly was convinced that he had designed such a perfect democracy that a critical private press could be safely replaced by a government organ which faithfully recorded public opinion and criticism. Had he lived to see the socialist eutopias of the 20th century and the development of an antipress executive branch in the United States government, he would probably have shared the misgivings of his critics. Cabet illustrates the danger of taking chessboard societies seriously.

In Bellamy's utopia of the year 2000, each citizen tries to work up the promotion ladder of the industrial meritocracy. But Bellamy specifically rejects the Socialist Man system of rewarding according to work.[101] Material rewards— the distribution and sharing of the "wealth" produced by the state—is what he actually has in mind. To Bellamy it would be "immoral" to give one citizen more of the national product than another simply because he has more natural ability. Everyone in the new society is expected to work up to the ability level given him by "The Creator"; and if one citizen happens to have twice the ability of another, his productivity should be twice as great too. "All men who do their best do the same." Members of society who fail to make full use of their native abilities are in debt to all the rest. Society must see to it that no one becomes such a debtor. Those who produce twice as much as others because they are twice as able deserve no reward; but if they fail to produce twice as much, they deserve to be punished.[102]

How does society know what the ability level of each citizen is? Bellamy avoids this question while showing that his system can in fact pay greater rewards for greater ability; payment, however, is social, not material.[103] The question he tries to answer, then, is how people can be induced to do their best when no matter how much effort they expend their income always remains the same. Again, "income" in this context means wages and material goods.

The entire promotion system of the industrial army, including the performance records kept on each individual, appeals to the desire for social honor and esteem. For those unable to achieve high rank in the system, ranks are subdivided into grades so that all can achieve some upward mobility during their working years. An additional advantage of the higher grades is the privilege they give the worker to choose the branches of his specialty in which he prefers to work.[104]

Everyone wears a badge or insignia that shows his rank, grade, and branch of industry. No one is supposed to be invidious of anyone else's rank, yet all are encouraged to achieve the next grade above their own! Except for a few people employed in the arts and professions, rank thereby becomes the dominant source of social distinction in the new society. In addition, public acclaim and special "prizes" are given for outstanding individual accomplishments. Special honor is paid those accepting unusually disagreeable and dangerous work. The highest of all honors—even higher than the presidency—is the "red ribbon" awarded through popular vote to outstanding artists, authors, engineers, and inventors.[105]

Bellamy's social incentives sound very much like the socialist-emulation prizes Russia, China, and Cuba were to experiment with several generations later. But his most original selective incentive is the insignia of branch, grade, and rank. No socialist society to date has endeavored to use a ranking system so universally visible except, of course, in its military organizations. Nor has any utopian ever come so close to Joseph Schumpeter's "penny stamp." It was Schumpeter's belief, as noted in Chapter 2, that in a society in which the privilege of sticking a penny stamp on one's trousers was sufficiently exclusive it could provide as much motivation as a million-dollar-a-year income does now.[106] Bellamy's insignia of rank is not only a form of Schumpeter's penny stamp, it meets the same criteria of ostentation as competitive material consumption does in a society characterized by transience. One's status becomes universally visible to anonymous others everywhere. Just a simple insignia on one's lapel could obviate Cadillac, gold wrist watch, diamond ring, and extravagant apparel simultaneously. And as people turned from conspicuous consumption, they could find other ways more socially and personally fulfilling to spend their time and money.

But what about those who refuse to play this new game, who have no interest in working hard for promotions, insignia and red ribbons? Such people, "incapable of generous motives" are dealt with very strictly by the industrial army. People who refuse to work or to work well are "sentenced to solitary confinement on bread and water" until they mend their ways.[107]

On the positive side, however, an important incentive is leisure time. Hours of labor vary according to the attractiveness or disagreeableness of a task, and the degree to which it may be either the one or the other is decided by popular opinion through the job recruitment process. For a job everyone wants, hours are increased until its popularity declines. Conversely, the working hours for disagreeable employments are reduced until recruitment meets demand.[108]

Despite Bellamy's good intentions, his utopia has seemed ominously totalitarian to many. What in 1888 was an Americanized brand of socialism proved by mid-20th century to be an amazingly close approximation to Soviet socialism, alias "state capitalism" or "statism." There, too, the state is the "sole corporation" and its socialism "patriotic" or "nationalistic" rather than the product of an international proletarian movement. And Russia was the first of the socialist countries to experiment heavily with "socialist emulation," rewarding workers through public esteem in place of material incentives.

That Bellamy's book was immensely popular in Russia during the years prior to the Bolshevik revolution may be of more than anecdotal interest. According to Alexander Nikoljukin, Bellamy was instrumental not only in introducing socialist ideas to all levels of Russian society, he also helped destroy many popular prejudices against those ideas.[109] In its story form, Bellamy's message may have been more influential than Marx's; and like Marx, he may have been writing mainly for Russians without knowing it.

All of our four state utopias substitute social for material incentives, and all four have been widely criticized for totalitarianism. Only More's conditions of local control or social predictability have seemed sufficiently credible to be viewed favorably by some. But the very way in which More achieves permanent, face-to-face groups within his large state—through close supervision, an internal passport system, and forced labor for those who do not cooperate—would seem to require tight centralized control. In other words, all four disharmoniously combine incentives appropriate to the social predictability of the small traditional community with conditions of highly centralized legal predictability. Selective social incentives applied on such a mass scale would certainly require close supervision of each citizen by the state. As we saw in Chapter 3, any modern state that attempted to revive labor taxation would necessarily intrude into people's lives far more than one collecting money taxes.

Our fifth utopia, Walden Two, has only one thousand inhabitants.[110] Surely we would expect it to give us the conditions of social predictability that fit so well with the social incentives of our real-world communes. Quite the contrary, Walden Two comes no closer to our real-world cases with respect to social incentives and the conditions of social predictability than it did with respect to commitment factors.

Although Walden Two is not the product of a social movement, it does not benefit from charismatic leadership either. It is said not to require strong leadership because of its "culture." [111] While this is true of the kibbutz, it is true only because kibbutz "culture" is so much a product of the Zionist social movement. Yet the kibbutzim, which are open to the outside like Walden Two, have had to adjust to a relatively high recruitment and turnover rate. How does Walden Two select its recruits, and how does it screen them? Does it have a candidacy period? Skinner is oblivious to all these problems.

Even Twin Oaks has a candidacy period although it is only two weeks long. At the end of it, each candidate is judged by an "entrance poll," a questionnaire filled out on the applicant by all members. The procedure does help in screening out persons likely to be socially difficult or disputatious. Although very small in 1973—only 40 members—Twin Oaks has endured a turnover rate as high as 70 percent per annum.[112]

Walden Two avoids nearly all the selective incentives that were so effective in our successful communes. If an individual works poorly, for example, another job is simply assigned. In a kibbutz this procedure, as we saw, could lead to expulsion if the person did poorly at everything, eventually being regarded as a malingerer. At Walden Two, however, an individual who works badly at everything is sent to a psychologist. What the psychologist does we are not told because such cases are as scarce as "leprosy." [113] We are back again to literary license, for just as Plato's guardians were compelled by Plato's social requirements to be perfect rulers, so Skinner's psychologists must elicit total support of the collective good through a science of behavior that obviates all punishment.

The Walden Two Code, which each new member must agree to follow, is "enforced" without any selective incentives either positive or negative. When necessary, rules are brought to the attention of the membership through meetings and public posters. Gossip and criticism, those negative incentives so powerfully selective in the small community, are banned in Walden Two. And that powerful positive incentive, gratitude, is "generalized" toward the whole community rather than made selective for the individual. Simple thank-yous from one person to another are taboo. Gratitude is expressed toward the society at large, and members are always ready to "do for all" in return for the endless benefits "received from all." The group gives no special approbation to individual members, for it has nothing to gain from one person's glory. On the contrary, to single out one individual for public acclaim neglects all the rest and makes their achievements appear "unexceptional" by comparison. Thus individual fame and honor are perceived as being won only at the expense of others.[114]

Like his predecessors, Skinner the utopian is opposed to the zero-sum game, but he has extended the field of play far beyond that of Plato, More, Cabet, and Bellamy, who concentrated on property and "unearned" income. Obviously they did not regard the social incentives they substituted for these material incentives as constituting a zero-sum game, but Skinner does. Even public acclaim of the deserving scientist or scholar is "unfair" because it fails to reward all the other individuals whose achievements are worthy of the same attention. Skinner's reform goals go far beyond the socialist's concern with property. His Man is Millennial Man par excellence, rewarded according to needs that do not even include a desire for social approbation. In Walden Two people are not taught to take joy in "personal triumph," says Skinner, because such joy is at the expense of someone else's pain of defeat. "Triumph over nature and over oneself, yes. But over others, never." [115]

Curiously, Skinner's utopia employs one important material incentive borrowed from Bellamy, the labor-credit system. Since jobs have different labor-credit ratings according to their popularity or unpopularity, an individual is rewarded with increased leisure for performing disagreeable work.[116] But if additional leisure still has high marginal utility in a community where no one works more than four hours a day, that community would surely have a strong leisure ethic—not the work ethic characteristic of most successful communes in their prime. This particular selective incentive is consistent, however, with the goals of a utopia in which all social incentives are obsolete and most menial labor is performed by labor-saving machinery.

Twin Oaks has experimented with the labor-credit system, but members still average about 40 hours of work per week. Additional labor credits are rewarded for work that has to be assigned, but the increment for any one week is limited to 10 percent. Moreover, many tasks unanimously disliked when Twin Oaks was small became the preferred choice of some members once it reached the size of 40. Kinkade believes the community may even be drifting toward specialization of work and away from job rotation.[117] If so, this development will parallel the experience of the kibbutz.

Although selective incentives are called "reinforcements" at Twin Oaks, the community is much closer to the successful communes in its social controls than to its fictional model, Walden Two. A member who does not work is asked to leave; expulsion is the ultimate threat here as in all the successful cooperative groups discussed earlier. But as in those cases it is seldom necessary to implement the threat. The malingerers mend their ways or leave of their own accord, for the group becomes cold and restrained in its behavior toward them. Moreover, the community makes it clear to the malingerers that in failing to do their share of the allotted work they are, in effect, asking the other members to do it for them. Here, again, the zero-sum stigma is applied to labor contributions. To remain economically viable, the community cannot, as Kinkade sees it, support too many "parasites." [118]

One form of negative social incentive that Walden Two was especially proud of eliminating was gossip, and Twin Oaks has tried hard to emulate its fictional model in this regard. Members are not supposed to make critical or disparaging remarks about others, not even about their work habits. In practice, however, Twin Oaks has found it necessary to attempt the same kind of sanction in other ways. People write out criticisms of others and drop them in the "bitch box." The "bitch manager" then acts as intermediary by calling an individual's attention to personal traits annoying to other members. But while Kinkade feels this system has helped, she does not believe it has much effect on strong personality traits. Group-criticism sessions were instituted to get at these, but unlike the Oneida case in which the presiding presence of John Humphrey Noyes made everyone's participation inevitable, attendance at the Twin Oaks sessions was voluntary. Some members rejected the experiment as an attempt to get around the no-gossip rule, and the very members who most needed criticism elected not to participate. Some Twin Oaks members feel all these measures are devious and that straightforward, spontaneous honesty would be better than a no-gossip rule. Their judgment is supported by the histories of the successful communes.[119]

The fact that Twin Oaks has never been able to achieve economic independence is undoubtedly due in part to inadequate social controls and relatively weak commitment. All such judgments are relative, of course, and in this context I am comparing Twin Oaks with our successful commune examples. Compared with most modern intentional communities or with our fictional utopias, especially Walden Two, it has relatively strong controls and commitment. Since 1968, however, members have been taking turns working for wages in the city, mainly at construction and office jobs. They would all rather work full time at Twin Oaks, but the farming and industrial enterprises have been unable to maintain the community. At their city jobs, members must meet competitive work standards much more strict than at Twin Oaks. For example, at home in the community, members "control" the undesirable trait of "bossiness" in their managers by refusing to "reward" them with obedience. Since these kinds of sanctions and behaviors could not work in the external job market, it may be that Twin Oaks' economic solvency is ultimately dependent on external wage–labor sanctions it is unwilling or unable to apply within the community. To the extent this is true, Twin Oaks remains, like so many intentional communities, a bedroom "commune" with a collective-consumption lifestyle rather than a full-fledged commune based on successful collective production.[120]

The same parasitic dependence on external sanctions applies to traffic tickets at Twin Oaks. The community began by paying its members' fines until the expense became so excessive that it decided to make members individually responsible. Now each member must earn the money to pay fines by wage work in town.[121]

Theoretically Walden Two solves all such mundane problems by scientific social engineering; but as Kinkade points out, when Skinnerian behaviorists are dealing with the real world, not fictional situations, they usually employ "token economies." The situations in which they work involve school children or hospital patients, and the staff rewards them for performing desired behavior with tokens that can be saved and exchanged for special privileges. This kind of social engineering would never work at Twin Oaks, she says, because the members would never accept such high-handed, presumptuous manipulation by their planners and managers. Members would destroy the tokens and demand their rights.[122]

We must agree with Holquist that chessboard societies would be highly totalitarian if applied to the real world. Despite the good intentions of all our behaviorist utopians, their fictional societies would require strong central control. Social incentives under such conditions would require close supervision of individual behavior.

Walden Two, however, spurns even social incentives. Skinner says such "reinforcers" are largely unplanned and "aversive" (negative). Praise and blame, moreover, work best in small communities, not in large, mobile societies in which one is never likely to see the same blamer or praiser twice.[123]

We now see even more clearly why the relatively small size of Walden Two was irrelevant in the context of Skinner's larger view of utopia. There is no reason why it should have had the attributes of our successful communes, for it is only a smaller version of the larger, transient society of which it is a part. Its size is simply a matter of experimental convenience. If face-to-face social incentives (reinforcers) are ineffective in modern, heterogeneous society, why make them important in a pilot-project utopia for the modern world?

But there is another and even more important reason why Skinner turns his back on social incentives. They are not under the control of his experiment. As he says in his foreword to Kinkade's book, she and her friends did not use "scientific principles" at Twin Oaks; they "simply muddled through." [124] In the perfect scientific experiment the psychologist-planners would have to design all reinforcements. People could not use selective social incentives on one another as in real societies without "muddling," in other words without rewarding some individuals at the expense of others. All reinforcements must be an integral part of a planned experiment directed by experts of social engineering. While in most respects Skinner is far less innovative and imaginative than our other four authors, in the end he is the most original in a very special sense; in its implications for the real world, his chessboard society is the most totalitarian ever conceived.

Utopian Behaviorism

Like most utopians whose schemes seem totalitarian to their readers, Skinner does not really mean to be totalitarian. This is clear from his examples of bad behavioral engineering. Russia, for instance, bases its social engineering on "power" and "punishment"; and while the Nazis are offered as an illustration of the effectiveness of behavioral engineering, they also illustrate what happens when this remarkable social technology falls into the wrong hands. Walden Two is saved from despotism by the fact that the planners know it would wreck their scientific experiment. They will be sensitive to the wishes of the people just as the pilot of an airplane is sensitive to the sputtering of the engine. Neither laws nor police are necessary to call the pilot's attention to the dangers of the situation.[125] Stalin, however, relaxed his collectivization drive when peasant discontent threatened Russian grain harvests, but ruthlessly renewed it once this danger was past. A totalitarian state can tolerate large amounts of "insensitivity" before the "sputtering engine" affects the pilot's behavior.

As Skinner has recently acknowledged, his behaviorism is not "the science of human behavior" but merely a "philosophy of that science." [126] It is a philosophy, moreover, that has developed as much from his utopian convictions as from his scientific research. Articles he wrote to rebut the critics of *Walden Two* became an important chapter in his textbook *Contingencies of Reinforcement*. *Beyond Freedom and Dignity*, to which *About Behaviorism* is a recent "philosophical" sequitur, is simply an expanded version of the argument of that chapter.[127]

Skinner's utopian behaviorism, like much of philosophy, is strongly hortative, for he believes the rules of his chessboard society can and should be applied to the real world. In the closing statement of *About Behaviorism* he affirms that the human animal is now able to control its own destiny because it knows what has to be done and has the behavioral technology to do it.[128] But in Skinner's behaviorist philosophy, as in most utopianism, people become object players in the social game, not subject players. There are at least three reasons why this is so: (1) the peculiarities of Skinner's behavioral data; (2) his perception of the difference between present reinforcements and future rewards; and (3) his concept of cumulative knowledge. Let us examine each of these reasons in turn, for they show why we must reject utopian behaviorism.

John Platt has recently called attention to a basic weakness in Skinnerian reinforcement studies.[129] They have concentrated on such asymmetrical relationships as those of teacher-child, doctor-patient, and psychologist-pigeon. Much more needs to be done, Platt believes, in the study of reinforcement behavior within groups of different sizes and between friends and peers—situations in which participants alternate in controlling and being controlled. This is precisely the subject matter of the social sciences; but as we have seen, Skinner largely ignores social data.

This neglect is very surprising since Skinner wants to avoid the blind alleys of "mentalistic" explanation by sticking to environmental factors. Certainly for his and our purposes social behavior is the most important part of the human environment. What is left to a psychologist who rejects most of psychology for sociology and then ignores sociology? What is left is precisely what that psychologist started with, the sociology of asymmetrical dyads. Skinner's chessboard is literally for two players, one of whom is the subject of play and the other the object.

Now we can see more clearly why Skinner avoids the problem of utopian creation and concerns himself chiefly with the operant conditioning of utopia's children. This is also why Twin Oaks, in his opinion, is not yet a fair test of Walden Two.[130] It does not yet have a second generation; it is still a society of peers. The first generation is a hurdle easily circumvented in utopia through literary license, but in the real world it is a veritable mountain. Before he can get to his self-perpetuating culture, Skinner must start with a generation of peers in which a few are parental or psychologist surrogates and the rest children, mental-patient, or pigeon surrogates. Since the latter surrogates do not reward one another but are rewarded only by the psychologists, Skinner's utopia is comprised of a multitude of two-person, zero-sum games in which most of the participants are object players.

Object-player masses, moreover, are much more likely to take appropriate present actions to get future rewards than are subject-player masses. According to Skinner, the worst "immoralists" are those who insist on judging a culture as it appeals, or fails to appeal, to them in the here and now. Rather, we must design a world to "be liked not by people as they are now" but as they will be in the planner's design. To design for the present would only "perpetuate the status quo." [131]

In Chapter 8 we see how the Bolsheviks decided to shape Russia for future generations over the objections of the peasant masses. The kulaks, who best represented the contemporary "status quo" in the rural areas, became the "immoralists" sacrificed for that greater good perceived by the planners. Skinner would probably consider any such comparison between the Russian eutopia and his utopia as grossly unfair; for he has clearly labeled the Russian use of power and punishment bad engineering. But how do planners take long-range action over short-term objections without it being perceived as "aversive" by the masses?

It is worth noting at this point that Skinner has altered the priorities of Walden Two in his later books. Happiness in the present no longer takes first place over interest in the future; for if deferred punishments are often the price of immediate rewards, then, says Skinner, immediate punishments may also be the price of deferred rewards. [132] That being the case, how can the "goodness" of Skinner's controllers or planners be gauged by the happiness of the present? They may now have to use "aversive" methods for a higher morality— the survival of the culture and the happiness of future generations. Even if the masses accept this view of morality, how can they know for sure when aversive planning techniques are to benefit posterity and not just the planners? While peasants were starving to death by the millions during the great Russian famine that followed collectivization, the Bolshevik planners never missed a meal.

Although in *Walden Two* Skinner contemptuously disposes of democracy as a "pious fraud," he concedes more recently that self-government provides one way of "identifying the controller with the controlled." Democracy thus becomes a way of subjecting designers and controllers to the same contingencies they design and operate. But he still insists that designers and controllers, as specialists, must have "contingencies" necessarily different from the controlled. [133]

For one thing they must have enough authority to put into effect the "conditioned" and "supplementary" reinforcers that can link remote beneficial consequences with present acts. But this kind of reinforcement requires programming subjects through "a series of intermediate contingencies" before they reach the terminal state of happiness. [134] And the final rub here is that the terminal contingencies for this remote "happiness" will be of such a nature that the subject would have had to pass through the programming before finding them acceptable!

Finally, utopian behaviorism needs object players because the designers or planners are experts, specialists upon whom the nonspecialist players must rely.

It is certainly true that the more specialized society becomes the more each of us has to rely on the technical skills of everyone else. Even in Plato's Republic, it was up to the potters to pot, the weavers to weave, and the managers to manage. One of the most important timesavers in modern society is leaving important decisions wherever possible to those specialists qualified to make them. To exemplify the criterion of competence in the relegation of authority, political scientist Robert Dahl uses the relationship between an airplane pilot and passengers.[135] The latter, he says, do not want to vote on the operation of the aircraft; they trust the pilot to do the job or they go by train.

Similarly, Skinner says most people do not try to repair their own cars. They leave that job to a mechanic and use their time to do what they do best. But everyone, Skinner notes, "fancies himself an expert in government."[136] The technology of behavioral engineering deserves to have its experts too and along with it the popular trust that competence merits in other areas of specialization. The main reason such experts do not have the public's confidence, however, is that to date knowledge in the "technology" of human management has not been cumulative.

Were Aristotle brought back to life, says Skinner, he would understand nothing of modern physics but would have little difficulty following a contemporary discussion of human affairs. There is no excuse for such backwardness in the science of behavior; a technology of operant behavior is ready to meet our problems, and once we allow it to do so, cumulative knowledge will develop so fast in the field of human behavior that our dependence on the social engineer will become complete.[137] In other words, cumulative knowledge in human behavior is not an accomplished fact; but it could be, and in Skinner's utopia it already is. So the reason his illustrations are either poor or metaphorical is because the accomplishment is a fiction. To believe that he has a technology of operant behavior ready to solve our problems is his test of the reader's credulity.

Yet so convinced is Skinner of the merits of his technology that he feels justified in crossing the boundaries between the technical and the moral order. He opposes the view that problems of applying science involve value judgments which scientists have no more right to make than anyone else. No behavioral scientist, he says, should accede to such a view.[138]

Dahl's example is too simple to serve us here; airplane pilots cannot "cheat" (endanger) their passengers without endangering themselves. But if jet-aircraft noise becomes more than the people living around an airport can take, who decides whether the airport or the homeowners have to move? Would anyone want to leave such decisions entirely to experts? Certainly we always want expert studies made in such situations so the best possible moral (or situational) assessments are available to all responsible for the final moral judgments. But moral judgments should never be the exclusive prerogative of experts, for cumulative knowledge can be of direct help only for the situational assessments.

As I implied above in comparing Skinner's planners to Plato's guardians, his utopian behaviorism ends up espousing what his methodological behaviorism spurns—mentalistic explanation. As moral philosopher and spokesman for his utopian behaviorism, he advocates decision, action, and planning. While ambivalent and self-contradictory on the subject of democracy, he is clearly distrustful of laissez-faire economics. He considers this a philosophy that leaves everything up to the "inherent goodness and wisdom of the common man," whom he prefers to see as object player rather than as subject player.[139] Laissez-faire is a policy of fortuity that leaves the common people prey to accidental and idiosyncratic forces in the environment. But what Skinner fails to make clear, or perhaps fails to fully understand, is that most of his so-called environment is made up of common people for whom he would substitute uncommon planners, his "technicians" of moral judgment.

In discussing "countercontrol," Skinner comes very close to contradicting himself, for here he shows some understanding of the dangers of asymmetrical two-person games. Five fields which have become "classical examples of mistreatment" include care of prisoners, psychotics, the mentally retarded, the aged, and the very young. In all such cases in which the objects of control are relatively powerless, the compassion, devotion, and benevolence of the subjects of control tends to deteriorate. Skinner's point is that kindness and compassion depend on "reciprocal action." [140] We are less likely to hurt others if we are hurt in consequence. Or to put it in the terms of Chapter 2, to prevent cheating we must oppose it with counter-cheating.

No behaviorist could be anything but a reciprocal altruist unless he begins to advocate a chessboard society for which he designs the rules. Then he or his planner-surrogates become the rational technicians of nonreciprocal altruism. The fortuitous laissez-faire of common-man reciprocity is replaced with non-reciprocal planning in which experts purposively determine human "destiny." This is teleological mentalism of the most obvious kind.

Most of the mentalism Skinner objects to as a methodological behaviorist is the unconscious tension-reduction reasoning (aggression, sex, cognitive dissonance, guilt, fear, and so on) that has dominated clinical psychology and functional sociology for so long. But he also objects to conscious or teleological mentalism.[141] A behaviorist, however, does not have to forsake all forms of mentalism as partial explanation. The methodological danger lies in accepting them as total explanations, for the investigator who does so is likely to close an investigation prematurely and miss key environmental factors—consequences of behavior or contingencies of reinforcement—that are often easier to change than internal functions.

Let us illustrate with an example of teleological mentalism used by R. B. Braithwaite in his *Scientific Explanation*.[142] Braithwaite is trying to show how teleological explanations differ from other causal explanations. The explicandum (thing to be explained) in a causal explanation occurs either simultaneously with or after the explicans (the efficient cause) as in "The pedestrian was killed by a car." The death of the pedestrian (explicandum) is simultaneous with or follows the collision with a vehicle (explicans). In a teleological explanation, however, the explicandum is "causally related either to a particular goal in the future or to a biological end which is as much future as present or past." In either case the explicans is a final cause, and usually we regard Braithwaite's second type of final cause as illegitimate and the first type as legitimate.

Suppose, says Braithwaite, he replies to someone's question as to why he is going to stay in Cambridge all summer with the explanation "to finish writing my book." The explicandum (staying in Cambridge all summer) precedes, rather than follows, the explicans (completion of the book). But the explicans is a goal or intent verifiable through the verbal behavior of the subject. Were we to say, on the other hand, that humanity is the result of a grand evolutionary design, we would be assigning intent to forces in which intent has no verifiable locus.

While teleological mentalism can be quite legitimate when its locus is human, it can still halt productive research prematurely. Professor Braithwaite has given a legitimate and acceptable explanation; but if we stopped there, we might not ask why so many other college professors throughout the world also stay home during the summer months to finish books. We would fail to uncover the entire university promotion system based on publication. Only within a group of college professors would Braithwaite's mentalistic explanation be complete. Since they would all be aware of the contingencies of reinforcement in this case, it would be banal to mention them. Teleological mentalism is therefore a useful short-hand form of explanation when the environmental contingencies are so familiar to everyone that they need no investigation or restatement. As long as we can keep mentalism around just for purposes of short-hand and partial explanation, methodological behaviorism as a form of explanatory, investigatory, and corrective procedure makes good sense. This aspect of behaviorism can be accepted and adhered to while rejecting its utopian philosophy completely.

Philosopher Robert Nozick has recently made a distinction between "invisible-hand" and "hidden-hand" types of explanation which helps elucidate the difference between utopian behaviorism and the humanistic variety endorsed here.[143] The term "invisible hand" comes of course from Adam Smith and refers to a market process that produces an overall pattern or "design" which is not teleological. All the individuals acting in the marketplace are behaving purposively or "teleologically," but the sum of all their teleological actions forms a pattern that is not teleological. As Adam Smith put it, each individual intentionally pursues his own gain, but in so doing is "led by an invisible hand" to contribute to a result that was "no part of his intention." What Nozick calls a "hidden-hand explanation" refers to cases in which the alleged intent of an individual or group is used to explain a set of facts that otherwise seem (and usually are) completely unconnected. So-called "conspiracy theories" are a popular form of hidden-hand explanation.

The planners in the Walden Two chessboard society certainly fit the hidden-hand form of causal explanation. Contemporary American society, on the other hand, could be viewed as an ongoing behavioral experiment in which the overall design or pattern has invisible-hand origins. That is to say, its citizens reciprocally reinforce each other in many different ways and each for individual reasons; but the composite outcome is not the product of anyone's intent. It is a "muddling-through" experiment, a giant Twin Oaks if you will. Power could be more evenly balanced than it is at present, a prospect suitable for more utopian exploration. But as the "invisible hand" slowly raises levels of awareness through information and education media, hopefully citizens will act with a broader and longer-range view of the consequences of their acts. This kind of ongoing, muddling-through, invisible-hand game is the one most likely to engage its citizen-players as the subjects, rather than the objects, of play.

Summary

Designers of utopian commune-states mean well. Each wants to engineer a chessboard society in which the masses will happily subject-play his game without oppressive supervision. Despite good intentions, great ingenuity, and some surprising insights, these social engineers were either oblivious to conditions of commitment and social predictability essential to the success of our real-world examples, or their social orders were just too large for any plausible accommodation to them. Their chessboard, Communist Man societies would necessarily be despotisms. Under the guiding hand of guardians or planners, the masses would be the objects—not the subjects—of play. Levels of reasonable need would be imposed from above along with severe punishments for free riding. Because players could not conceivably win more than their fellows without cheating them, material equality would have to be pervasive. A centralized command economy under stern guardianship would make sure all players stayed equal.

Such total planning in a monoecological future would obviously involve grave dangers for those who prefer to live in subject-player societies. One of the gravest dangers is exemplified by utopian behaviorism with its specialists of moral judgment. While specialists in the open-ended game of humanistic behaviorism would be encouraged to render their best moral assessments, the moral judgments leading to public action would be those of subject-playing masses. Improvements could only take place gradually as members of the subject-playing masses accommodated to one another through reciprocal altruism. They would all have to "muddle" (struggle) toward "utopia" (a better world) together. Is humanistic behaviorism compatible with utopian socialism of either the statist or stateless variety? That is the underlying question of Chapters 8 and 9.

Chapter Eight

Russia and China: Socialist Man in Eutopia

IT HAS BEEN more than a hundred years since the "father of modern liberalism" eloquently defended the rights of the individual against the collectivity. Each of us, said John Stuart Mill, in his essay *On Liberty* (1859), should be free to pursue his own opinions, inquiries, and course of action.[1] Only when a citizen in pursuit of individual self-fulfillment becomes a danger to his fellows should freedom be curtailed. But Mill was talking about "civilized" citizens, for he was also a believer in progress. A backward society has few tools for self-improvement, and the impediments to "spontaneous progress" within it are too great to allow much choice in overcoming them. "Despotism is a legitimate mode of government" when dedicated to the improvement of such a society, said Mill, for in this case, and this case only, the end justifies the means. The backward society's best course of action is to give complete obedience to a powerful and capable leader, if it is lucky enough to get one.

We cannot know whether John Stuart Mill would have applied his notion of backwardness to what we today refer to as "underdeveloped," "developing," or "Third World" nations, much less to Russia in 1917 or China in 1949. But there are many who make just this kind of distinction to justify the application of utopia by whatever means. To acquire the intellectual tools essential for successfully performing as the subject players of eutopia, the citizens of backward nations must first, as object players, be "civilized" through applied utopianism.

By word and deed the leaders of the Bolshevik revolution followed Mill's recipe for progress in a backward society. Russia, they concluded, was not only backward but fortunate, indeed, to have their leadership. In his *The State and Revolution,* written at the beginning of the Russian revolution, Lenin declared the abolition of the state his ultimate aim and looked forward to a final classless stage of communism in which the state had withered away and with it "the subordination of one man to another." [2] All members of the final communist society will have "learned to administer the state themselves" so that "the need for government of any kind" will "disappear altogether." There is even an element of utopian behaviorism in Lenin's prediction that a "new generation" will grow up with new "habits" reinforced by the social contingencies of communism. People will then live together without violence or exploitation.

After three years of civil war and the problems of organizing defense and industrial production, the emphasis of Bolshevik theorizing switched from long-range millennial goals to the immediate rules of the game. Trotsky, the great Bolshevik organizer, illustrates that change well in his *Terrorism and Communism*, written in 1920.[3] Replying to foreign critics of Soviet repression, Trotsky described the state before its final disappearance as "shooting up in a brilliant flame" just like "a lamp before going out." At that moment in history, in the "form of the dictatorship of the proletariat," it becomes "the most ruthless form of State" and "authoritatively" guides "the life of its citizens" in "every direction." This "ruthless" final "flame," however, is necessary only long enough to achieve the material progress that precedes the communist millennium. For a short while applied utopia must be the opposite of its goal.

One of many Russian revolutionaries and former Bolsheviks repelled by this applied utopianism was Yevgeny Zamyatin, the Russian author who wrote what some of Orwell's critics have regarded as the original version of *1984*.[4] Zamyatin's novel, *We*, written between 1920 and 1921 was such a scathing satire of the new totalitarian state that to this day it has not been published in Russia. But George Orwell, that great enemy of all totalitarianisms and especially the Soviet variety, wrote a more readable and frightening book. He so convincingly converted the Russian eutopia into a threatening, malevolent dystopia that the communist menace has become almost synonymous with *1984*. I show why our reaction to that picture has been unjustifiably severe.

How does a great leviathan comprised mainly of illiterate peasants play catchup progress? What game strategy can the designers employ to build a real-world eutopia? These are questions that concern us in the first section of this chapter as we compare the overall development "plans" of Russia and China. Next we turn to factors of commitment. To what extent do the masses act as subject players? What factors make them pliable object players? Does material consumption threaten the socialist game? Third, we consider conditions of social predictability. How has China used them more effectively than Russia in the losing battle both countries are fighting against material incentives? Finally, we look for conditions of legal predictability in two eutopias that have achieved a certain "lawlessness." Here we come to grips with all the problems of legal predictability deferred until now. In the context of this chapter we begin to consider their importance for our future as well as for the eutopian state.

Strategy

Developing countries are predominantly agricultural. This is so almost by definition since development usually implies industrialization, a process that expands the nonagricultural labor force. To support this process, the farming sector must not only provide initial resources for capital investment in industry, it must provide food in ever increasing amounts for the growing urban markets. How can a state get its peasantry to participate in a deliberate industrialization program? Does it coerce them, tax them, or entice them? Does it treat them as object players to be sacrificed if necessary for the millennial dream or as subject players in a working partnership?

The Bolsheviks were among the first to be faced with these kinds of catch-up decisions. As the new revolutionary masters of Russia, they found themselves responsible for developing a nation over 80 percent peasant. Moreover, since the expected socialist revolution in Europe had not taken place, Russian socialism was all on its own, a condition Stalin was to label "socialism in one country."

The Bolsheviks came to power at a time when strong central authority was necessary to wage a civil war against the antirevolutionary White and foreign armies. During the years of "war communism," 1918–1921, they subjected the relatively small, encircled area under their control to an economy of total war. "Committees of the poor" were organized at the village level to requisition grain from "rich" peasants or kulaks, a practice of little help to the cities when the Committees ate most of it themselves. So factory-worker food detachments or "commandos" were also organized to reconnoiter rural areas and requisition grain by force. When famine and peasant insurrections threatened to overwhelm the new state in 1921, the first problem was met by the American Relief Association and the second by the Red Army.[5]

Under these economic and insurrectionary pressures, Lenin in 1921 acknowledged a partial and temporary retreat from socialism to "state capitalism," and initiated his New Economic Policy (NEP). Taxes were reduced, land tenure was guaranteed, hiring of labor and land leasing were allowed and enterprises generally decentralized and commercialized for greater market competition. Money economy was reestablished as were private trade and small industry.[6] By 1926 the total agricultural area was within 5 percent, and grain production within 10 percent, of prewar levels. Yet, by some accounts, less than half as much grain was coming to market.[7] In any case, the Bolshevik leaders wanted a bigger share of the peasants' product than they were getting.

Prior to World War I Russia had been the world's leading exporter of grains, and half of that exported had come from peasant holdings. The other half had been produced on the large estates, which were broken up and expropriated by the peasants at the outbreak of the revolution. No longer saddled with rent or mortgage payments, peasants were eating better and using more of their grain for animal feed than before the war.[8] But the state needed to regain this source of foreign exchange to finance industrialization. By 1924 it was clear that the postwar recovery in industrial production had gone as far as it could by re-activating and rebuilding factories and that new and costly industrial construction was essential for future growth.[9]

After Lenin's death in January 1924, two major opposing views developed on how to achieve this continued development. One of these was the strategy of Nikolai Bukharin of the party right wing, who supported continuation and elaboration of Lenin's NEP. The other was the strategy of Evgeny Preobrazhensky, economist and theoretician of the Trotskyite opposition on the left. Considered by many the greatest Bolshevik theorist—even greater than Lenin—Bukharin in his early, prerevolutionary writings seems strongly antistatist, even utopian. But revolutionary conditions, and later those of war communism, led Bukharin and other Bolsheviks to emphasize a transitional period between capitalism and communism when a strong proletarian state must fight the enemies, "internal and external," of the working class. Joining with the left, Bukharin went so far as to endorse the collectivization of agriculture and "compulsory labor service." Capitalism was a "spontaneous" process, but "building communism" had to take place through plan, organization and even "proletarian coercion." Toward the end of the war-communism phase, however, Bukharin began to move away from the left and the coercive aspects of a final and transitional "brilliant-flame" state.[10]

Lenin's NEP was a complete change in party policy from war communism, and its results had a profound effect on Bukharin. His earlier antistatism reasserted itself as he became the leading proponent of NEP on the party right. The state's and party's role should be one of persuasion, not coercion, in his view. Thousands of small, voluntary associations among workers and peasants would be the best decentralized offense against the creeping return to centralized rule by a degenerate, czarist-type bureaucracy (*chinovniki*). He advocated less state interventionism and more reliance on the spontaneous action of the market and on participation by the masses.[11]

In place of "Genghis Khan" planning by a new ruling proletariat class monopolizing all authority and privilege, greater reliance would be placed on a consumer-oriented economy. By meeting the needs of the masses and attending to an expanding market for consumer goods, industrial growth could be accomplished through spontaneous popular participation instead of chinovnik prodding. The masses would follow their private pursuits, but state socialism would ultimately benefit most as greater competitiveness and efficiency resulted.[12] In exchange for industrial goods peasants would willingly produce a food surplus, and cumulative growth would accelerate in both sectors. Nor would a prosperous, petty-bourgeois peasantry undermine the proletariat basis of the communist state, for a careful policy of public investment would develop the public sector of the economy faster than the private. Finally, the kind of marketing and service cooperatives that had been so successful in rural Russia prior to World War I—not farm collectives—would become the major form of peasant voluntary associations.[13]

Preobrazhensky's strategy was much closer to the spirit of war communism than was Bukharin's. He argued that unless industrialization took place rapidly, Russian socialism would be devoured by the private sector, which NEP was encouraging. In a country as backward as Russia, rapid industrialization would have to be effected through "primitive socialist accumulation," a process analogous to what Marx had called "primitive capitalist accumulation." The latter was based on expropriation of colonies and the surplus of precapitalist forms of production.[14] While Preobrazhensky eschewed "colonial plundering" by a socialist state, he believed that during the period of primitive socialist accumulation the state must exploit its petty-bourgeois peasants by expropriating part of their surplus product.[15] The analogy, as well as his vocabulary, brought charges from Bukharin and the right that such methods would debase the countryside in the same parasitic fashion as capitalism.[16]

While Bukharin's strategy favored enticing the peasants' surplus into the market in exchange for consumer goods produced by light industry, Preobrazhensky's favored capitalization of heavy industry by taxing or requisitioning peasant "surpluses." Unfortunately for Bukharin's strategy, a series of crises in 1927 led to a "goods famine" and a subsequent "grain crisis." The state was unable to provide the variety and quality of cheap consumer goods to expand peasant interest in the market and was unwilling to pay more for the peasants' grain. The so-called "scissors" phenomenon, the difference between the high prices charged for industrial goods and the low ones paid for agricultural products, constituted a "voluntary" tax peasants were unwilling to pay. Within two years Stalin had begun his "revolution from above" and, as Stephen Cohen so well puts it, had not only adopted Preobrazhensky's reasoning, "but his draconian rhetoric as well." [17] The Russian peasantry would pay a "tribute" or "supertax" as a kind of internal colony. Moreover, collectivization of the peasantry into large-scale farming units would make agricultural production more efficient and provide the easiest means of applying the supertax. Farm products thus "pumped" out of the countryside would support the industrial work force in Russian cities while in the export market they would buy the capital goods necessary for developing heavy industry.[18]

To Bukharin this represented a return to the official lawlessness and "military-feudal exploitation" of czarism, an accusation which could hardly have disturbed Stalin, who openly admired Peter the Great. Stalin's strategy worked, moreover, for by 1933, state grain procurements were twice what they had been in 1928, even though the harvest was five million tons less.[19] As anarchist Bakunin had feared over half a century earlier, "statist" revolutionaries on the throne of Russia could impose a "red bureaucracy" worse than suppression under the czars.[20]

In terms of the intellectual debate that preceded Stalin's total usurpation of power, Bukharin belonged with the "geneticists" and Stalin with the "teleologists." The former, who advocated using spontaneous forces of growth and were later liquidated by Stalin, included most of Russia's prominent economists. The latter, who preferred plan and direction to spontaneous growth, were mainly engineers. In terms of Nozick's distinction between invisible-hand and hidden-hand causality (introduced in Chapter 7), both groups of opponents in the debate were teleologists in a sense. The geneticists espoused invisible-hand or market causality in which the purposive behavior of many individuals determines an outcome that is unpredictable and therefore unplanned. The outcome itself is not teleological although generated by what might be called "pluralistic teleology." This is the "muddling-through" game in which a maximum number of participants are subject players.[21]

The "teleologists" of the Russian debate were too impatient to play muddling-through; they wanted to accomplish rapid development by directing the masses as the object players of a totally planned game. Since there was certainly nothing secretive or clandestine about this policy, Nozick's "hidden-hand" or conspiratorial teleology is not an appropriate label for it. I therefore call the openly totalitarian form "directing hand." I prefer not to call it "controlling" because true control is never really accomplished despite the implicit assumption or hope that it will be.

Right and left factions within China's Communist Party have also emphasized invisible-hand and directing-hand teleologies respectively. Liu Shao-chi has been equated with Bukharin and Mao Tse-tung with Stalin, although admittedly the differences between these two Chinese leaders were greatly exaggerated by the Cultural Revolution when Liu was made a Maoist target for mass criticism. For 30 years Liu and Mao worked successfully together, the former building up an effective governing organization while the latter provided charisma and ideology.[22]

Both men accepted the Marxist–Leninist Soviet view that a strong state based on a dictatorship of the proletariat must necessarily precede the stateless condition of full communism. It had been Sun Yat-sen's conviction even earlier that each individual Chinese would have to sacrifice personal freedom to help unify a China that throughout history had been a "sheet of loose sand."[23] But Liu, like Bukharin, preferred to make use of spontaneous forces based to some degree on the pursuit of self-interest. This led him to accept market forces and differential wage scales more readily than Mao. He did not think differences in income would corrupt the masses as long as these inequities had progressive consequences for all, including the less advantaged. Liu Shao-chi tended to take a positive-sum view of invisible-hand causality.[24]

Although Liu-Shao-chiism bears some striking resemblances to Bukharinism, Maoism diverges in many ways from Stalinism. Liu-Shao-chiists have been called "pragmatists" and Maoists "ideologists," but the Russian right and left were both highly pragmatic.[25] Stalin unequivocally endorsed income inequality in the form of differential wage scales as a necessary incentive structure during socialism while Maoists have tended to prefer moral incentives and material egalitarianism. Moreover, Mao never viewed the Chinese peasantry as objects for "colonial" exploitation by a socialist bureaucracy. Quite the contrary, the bureaucracy was to become the target for continuing revolution by the masses.

In fact Mao's distrust of bureaucracy is in some ways reminiscent of Bukharin's fear that the Soviet party bureaucracy would revert to the exploitive chinovniki form of czarist days. The memory of dynastic China's bureaucratic gentry of scholar-officials may have inspired Mao's hatred of bureaucracy as much as any threat of "revisionism." [26]

Other authorities, however, are impressed by the similarities between Mao and Stalin. Like Stalin, Mao could attack the very bureaucracy he helped to build while remaining strongly centralist in conviction and method. He believed in strong state power with strong authority; and to help legitimize his highly personal dictatorship of the proletariat, he allowed and encouraged a "cult of personality." [27]

Mao's views and actions with regard to collectivization were also close to Stalin's. While Liu Shao-chi (like Bukharin) allegedly favored enticing peasant grain to market through the production of light-industry consumer goods, Mao favored more direct requisitioning. He did not believe, moreover, that a socialized industrial sector could survive in a sea of petty-bourgeoisie capitalism; and if socialism did not quickly win its battle in the rural areas, capitalism would.[28] Following land reform, many party members and cadres began withdrawing from politics to become enterprising farmers. Some were even acting like rich peasants and "exploiters." [29] Thus, when a crisis made it possible to justify the act, Mao, like Stalin, initiated his collectivization drive. As a result of flood damage to harvests, peasants during the winter of 1954–1955 panicked and began to hoard grain and buy up state reserves. Cadre investigations to appraise "real" need and apprehend hoarders only aggravated the situation. Obviously peasant production had to come under tighter control, particularly since the capital accumulation necessary for rapid industrialization was not proceeding on schedule. Industrial goods were too few and expensive to tempt the peasants into the marketplace.[30] The Russian story was repeating itself; and although Mao had no wish to repeat the more inhumane aspects of the Russian program, he decided on rapid collectivization.

Differences between Maoism and Liu-Shao-chiism that have no counterparts in the Russian policy debates are indicative of some major strategy differences in the Chinese case. While Liu, for example, might be called a behaviorist in the invisible-hand sense, Mao always tended strongly toward mentalism; his brand of behaviorism was, at best, highly utopian. And while Liu's "altruism" seems to have been strongly reciprocal, Mao's by comparison was nonreciprocal or idealistic.

Liu Shao-chi's more calculating approach to human nature allowed him to make use of its self-enhancement aspects and thereby to emphasize the reciprocity of altruistic behavior; if you help others, they will help you. He did not concern himself primarily with internal feeling states or the power of ideas.[31]

Mao, on the other hand, believed that each citizen must become selfless. Thinking must be revolutionized to create a new "ethic of intention" that annihilates self and creates in everyone a dedication to the masses and their collective good. Through creative application of Mao's thought the objective world could be transformed by a subjective world of correct ideas. Citizens who became truly selfless in their dedication to the collective interest did not calculate the consequences of their acts for their own well-being, but concentrated on the well-being of others.[32]

Instead of punishing self-centered wrongdoers, Mao preferred to transform them through education. Moreover, party members, properly indoctrinated in Mao's thought, would have a special kind of political knowledge and social experience that justified centralist control as compared to decentralized management by mere experts of science and technology.[33]

Although the Russian and Chinese socialist eutopias are far from identical, their basic strategies of development were much the same, and in their own terms both have been highly successful. Collectivization of agriculture made it easier in each case to collect an agricultural "surplus" and to allocate it to the industrial sector.[34] Russia has had much longer than China to develop her industries, and though the production of consumer goods is not up to the level many Western economists feel it should be, the production of military hardware has been spectacular.[35] Between 1926 and 1974, the percentage of industrial workers and white-collar employees in the working population rose from less than 20 to over 60 while the percentage of peasants fell from more than 80 to less than 40. No longer dependent on the agricultural sector for capital accumulation, the Soviet Union has at last begun to invest heavily in agriculture and to raise rural incomes and living standards.[36]

The growth rate of China's GNP since 1949 has been, by some accounts, much greater than India's for the same period and apparently exceeds England's between 1750 and 1850 as well as Japan's between 1878 and 1936. In controlling pestilence and famine, China has outperformed all other underdeveloped countries. For a generation, the entire Chinese populace has been adequately housed, clothed, and fed. No longer do millions starve to death or suffer from chronic malnutrition and disease as is the case still in India and Pakistan.[37] Just in the last decade, over ten million acres of land have been added to those under irrigation. By developing its own high-yield wheats and dwarf varieties of rice, as well as by importing the new "miracle" strains developed in the United States and Mexico, China has quietly sponsored its own "green revolution." The catastrophic famines that hit different parts of China almost every year are merely a bad memory today.[38] Since 1950 the agricultural tax has dropped from a third to only seven percent of government revenues.[39]

To those critics who object to the human costs—the millions of Russian kulaks who died during collectivization, the millions of Russian peasants who starved to death afterwards, or the hundreds of thousands of landlords executed during the Chinese land reform—Charles Wilbur has pointed out that development in the West paid its human price as well.[40] Were the cruelties of the British enclosure movement or of the early factory system any less inhumane?

And what about the famines and pestilence that repeatedly swept across Western Europe, Russia, and China before development and that might still be taking millions of lives today except for those initial human costs? Perhaps the major difference between East and West is that the cruelties of a directing hand seem more intentional and deliberate than those of an invisible hand. But are they? As Wilbur says, the costs in the Russian case were not inherent in the development model; they were fortuitous or historical aspects of its application.

What seems like deliberate cruelty in retrospect may have been the unexpected results of planning errors. That China's collectivization program was able to proceed as smoothly as it did was due in part to the intentional avoidance of Russian mistakes. In an applied utopian game of catch-up progress, in which the masses are played as objects, heavy human costs will often be a consequence of blunders. If these costs are perceived as only short-run payments for long-term benefits, they are seen as a contribution to success. Such is the moral ecology of the game.

Commitment

Both of our state eutopias grew out of social movements so intense that Michael Barkun classifies them as "millennial" in his recent analysis of the causal relationship between chiliastic movements and the disasters such movements usually follow.[41] Social upheaval, crop failures, famines, and warfare preceded both the Bolshevik victory of 1917 and the Chinese Communist victory of 1949. According to Barkun, multiple disasters and an essentially rural-agrarian environment are the two situational factors most conducive to such total social movements.

Lenin and Mao were much impressed by the power, mass participation and spontaneity of peasant movements each had occasion to observe in 1905 and 1927 respectively, and their reactions to the experience were typical of subsequent differences in official Russian and Chinese attitudes toward peasants and mass movements.[42] Peasants made up over 80 percent of the population of each of these countries at the time of communist takeover; and while in the Russian case this situation was considered a severe handicap, to the Chinese it became the opportunity for a new communist approach to Third World development.

Historian G. F. Hudson traces the modern version of peasant activism back to the 19th-century Russian populists, or Narodniks, who saw in the discontent of the Russian peasantry a latent but potentially explosive force for social transformation.[43] Some Narodniks believed the peasants could accomplish the transformation on their own, but others considered them too unsophisticated, too bound by inertia, and too dispersed and unorganized to transform society without a guiding elite of socialist intellectuals. But populism failed, and as Marxism began to take its place, the proletariat became the new revolutionary hope of the elite. Lenin made his greatest contribution to practical socialism, however, when he combined Marxism with populism in his worker–peasant (hammer and sickle) alliance, the "dictatorship of the proletariat and the peasantry."

The Bolsheviks preserved none of the Narodnik sentimentality; peasants, they knew, were only after more land and their own self-interest. Bolshevik dislike and contempt for the peasantry was in keeping with Marx's disdain for "rural idiocy." In practice the dictatorship would work through the proletariat while firmly in the grasp of Lenin and the party. Maoism came much closer than Bolshevism to the Narodnik philosophy. To Maoists, Russia might be a useful revolutionary model in industrial countries with urban proletariats; but the Chinese case, while unique in its historical particulars, is closer to the preindustrial conditions of all the oppressed and exploited agrarian countries of the world.[44]

Lenin and the Bolsheviks tended to distrust mass spontaneity.[45] They came to power, as Alec Nove has put it, on the "flood-tide of peasant revolt," and for a while it was all they could do to keep from being swept away by it.[46] On their own the peasants spontaneously carried out a land reform the Bolsheviks could do no more than legitimize after the fact. The Russian Revolution was an authenic mass movement of libertarian proportions. Worker councils as well as peasant village assemblies were part of a spontaneous anarchism the Bolsheviks were later to defend as a materially destructive stage essential to the revolutionary cause; the chaos and organizational breakdown it created made possible their own ascent to total power.

Once in charge, the Bolsheviks had to fight a civil war against White armies supported by Czech, British, French, Japanese, and United States troops. This struggle helped the Bolsheviks justify the highly centralized control they established in the name of war communism. Moreover, the participation of foreign troops in behalf of the enemy enhanced the Bolshevik appeal to national pride and patriotism.[47] Despite its disastrous economic consequences, war communism's military success made it "the heroic period" of "revolutionary enthusiasm" for the party. A ruthless, authoritarian militarization of all social life that destroyed the libertarian movement and initiated security-police repression by the dreaded Cheka became for the Bolsheviks an idealized period in their history, on which Stalin could later model his own "revolution from above."[48]

In China neither peasants nor mass movements were distrusted. By deliberately instigating and directing social movements, the party worked to transform peasant inertia into peasant activism. Once caught up in mass campaigns designed to realize party objectives, peasants became "voluntary," subject players whose enthusiasm could accelerate the development process. As Benjamin Schwartz has aptly phrased it, Maoism worked to maintain "an unremitting Revival atmosphere."[49]

Popular activism stimulated through mass movements became in James Townsend's opinion the most typical form of political participation in communist China.[50] Of course, party leaders or cadres were essential to keep such movements within the bounds of party goals and objectives. The social movement thus became an instrument for activating the masses to perform like subject players while still guiding and using them as object players. As long as a social movement operates according to direction, such subject-player masses do not act with invisible-hand spontaneity. In response to directing-hand influences, they may evince a guided "spontaneity" and unanimity reminiscent in some ways of Rousseau's general will.

Just as foreign aggression helped give Bolshevism a patriotic and nationalistic flavor, the Japanese invasion of China in 1937 helped make Chinese communism into a nationalistic social movement. During the Yenan period, as the party carried guerrilla warfare to the Japanese, it came closest to the ideals of its mass-line approach. Popular support achieved a degree of spontaneity requiring minimal party control. The United States, by supporting the losing Kuomintang government against the communists in the ensuing civil war, and by remaining hostile to the Chinese People's Republic long after, helped maintain external pressures useful for the communist mass line.[51]

Robert Bernardo has called attention to the similarities between Russia's war communism and Cuba's period of partial mobilization during and after the Bay of Pigs incident.[52] The rise in ideological commitment precipitated by this act of United States aggression greatly increased individual initiative and for a while virtually eliminated industrial absenteeism. Che Guevara was so impressed that he urged continuation of the state of emergency as a permanent method of "moral" stimulation. In the same vein Bernard Kiernan devotes an entire book to exposing the way in which the United States unwittingly promoted communism around the world by aggressively opposing what Chalmers Johnson calls "peasant nationalism." [53] By providing communist revolutions with an external threat, the United States helped them develop into mass movements with a high degree of internal commitment. The very breadth of the attack, moreover, increased the international quality of revolutionary "comradeship" and helped to create and strengthen the "communist conspiracy" the United States so quixotically worked to contain. One result is that the Maoist brand of agrarian socialism became increasingly appealing to Third World countries as a "command" or directing-hand model for social and economic development.

Foreign aggression not only helped stimulate nationalism and patriotism in the Russian and Chinese revolutions, it also helped to lock the Bolsheviks and Chinese communists into two different adaptations. When the Chinese Communist Party (CCP) looked back on the Yenan period as its "heroic" phase, it looked back on procedures and attitudes much different from those of the "heroic" war communism of the Bolsheviks. Instead of idealizing coercive statism and the suppression of popular forms of political action, the Chinese could look back on an ideal time when peasant activism flowed easily into the channels set for it, a time when party and popular goals were so close that object and subject players were hard to tell apart. Just as the Bolsheviks tended to return to war communism in their brutal collectivization program and police-state tactics, the CCP preserved its Yenan techniques of mass mobilization and revolution even at the expense of administrative and economic stability. In Victor Funnell's words, the CCP became the "prisoner of its own experience," [54] a judgment equally applicable to the Bolsheviks.

The land-reform movements of the two countries were important in shaping the revolutionary experience to which each subsequently became a "prisoner." The Bolsheviks could take little credit for a redistribution which the peasants carried out on their own. In China, on the other hand, land reform became the first in a series of mass movements directed by the CCP. It had already been initiated in areas held by the communists prior to 1949, but in the summer of 1950 the Agrarian Reform Law officially made it a national movement under the direction of the party. As a consequence the Chinese peasantry had far more reason than its Russian counterpart to feel grateful to the new government.

On the heels of its land reform, the CCP launched a series of movements beginning with a campaign to enforce the new marriage law followed by the "Resist America—Aid Korea Movement," the "Suppression of Counterrevolutionaries Movement" and movements against corruption, bribery, tax evasion, and so on. In each case the party attempted to elicit active participation by the masses to stimulate greater political awareness, concern, and commitment. Movements on an even grander scale, of course, included the collectivization drive of 1950–1957 and the Great Leap Forward of 1957–1960.[55]

Russia during the 1930's employed similar social-movement techniques to raise worker productivity. Authorities instigated the so-called shock-brigade, socialist-emulation and Stakhanovite movements and manipulated them in such a way as to make them appear spontaneous outgrowths of worker initiative and enthusiasm. While the emphasis of these programs was primarily on material incentives, most workers, according to Swianiewicz, felt inconvenienced rather than benefited by the campaigns and remained cool or hostile toward them.[56] In China, too, cadres and masses alike tend to become inured over time to repeated mass movements. People learn to go through the motions without making the same emotional or psychological commitment as in earlier years. As they do, says Barnett, it becomes increasingly difficult to involve them.[57]

Yet even in Russia, as Alec Nove points out, there was genuine enthusiasm for some projects particularly among the younger workers during the 1930's.[58] He cites as one example the great metallurgical center built at Magnitogorsk under conditions of pioneering hardship by workers and technicians "fired by a real faith in the future." Nove does not believe Stalin's revolution from above could have been carried out without the help of the many devoted men both inside and outside the party who were enthusiastically dedicated to industrialization. Beyond the desire to maintain themselves in power, they were sincerely committed to rapid modernization even if it required ruthless leadership at the top.

While in both countries "enthusiasm" was probably always greater among party members than the masses, the amount of interaction between party and masses and the amount of popular participation in mass organizations has undoubtedly been higher in China. It was Mao's conviction that the party should go directly to the masses, concern itself with their problems, and arouse them to action. Beginning with the village mass meetings held to survey and redistribute local lands, the party urged direct contact between cadres and masses in the formation of mass organizations such as peasant associations, trade unions, women's groups, and youth groups. And although not genuine decision-making bodies, according to Townsend, people's congresses organized at all levels from province to township became a way of giving people a sense of political involvement.[59]

Both the people's congresses and the mass organizations, however, have been a means of mobilizing popular participation in the execution of party policies, not for influencing the decisions on which they are based. Nevertheless, the degree of popular interaction especially at the lowest levels is probably greater than in Russia where, for example, kolkhoz (collective farm) assemblies exist only on paper, even today. Where they convene, these supposedly popular institutions are simply vehicles for party activism and control. In China, too, as the revolution grows older, the people's congresses tend to become increasingly symbolic.[60]

In the eutopian game of catch-up progress it is the goals of the directing-hand elite which are generally long term; the masses tend to be more concerned with short-term needs. The more immediate nature of the latter usually makes them personal and familial, and therefore vulnerable to such opprobrious labels as egotistical, bourgeois, and materialistic. Elite or party goals, on the other hand, are presented as being in the best long-term interests of the public as a whole.

Soviet textbooks admit that the Russian people have had to make great sacrifices for the rapid development of heavy industry. Production of mass consumption goods has had to wait and with it any appreciable expansion of workers' needs or increase of real wages.[61] Some members of society, moreover, have had to sacrifice more than others, for rural income and living standards have lagged far behind those of urban workers. The per-capita income of collective farmworkers, for example, is still about half that of unskilled urban laborers. Not only does the rural population of Russia get much less than its proportionate share of consumer goods, even public goods such as utilities, transportation, health, and education fall far below urban standards.[62]

Chinese policy, especially when dominated by Maoism, has been more egalitarian in its emphasis than Russian. Need levels, it was believed, should be kept much the same for everyone; only that kind of development should take place which allows everyone to rise together.[63] Ideally at least, China has been like a giant shitufi.

Consumer-goods production in China has focused on items everyone could afford to buy. Few would ever save enough to buy a motorcycle, and those who did might well be inclined to consider themselves better than others. Bicycles, however, are within everyone's reach, so they are manufactured in great numbers. Maoists have been opposed to production of items that would increase inequality. They rejected "trickle-down" development in favor of the going-up-together variety. Reasonable need was therefore limited to adequate food, clothing, housing, and articles such as bicycles, wrist watches, sewing machines, and cameras that could be purchased with a few months' savings. The level of reasonable need should be kept low enough to prevent the competitive consumption that makes people strive for private, rather than collective ends.[64]

Since Khrushchev's time the main target of Chinese attacks on consumerism has been the Soviet Union rather than the United States. In the Maoist view, Russia's emphasis on material incentives and a self-interested consumer mentality could be a greater threat to the future of communism than the United States because it represented a revisionist drift toward capitalism within the world communist movement itself.[65] But Russia's drift toward material incentives and differential wage rates goes a long way back, as far at least as Stalin's famous critique of wage egalitarianism in 1931. To get workers to stay at their jobs and learn special skills, he believed they would need appropriate material incentives.[66] New wage scales came into being; and though differences at first were only as high as 4 to 1, by 1940 the highest-paid workers were earning more than 30 times the income of the lowest paid.[67] Today the incomes of top managers, engineers, scientists, writers, and so on, are more than a hundred times those of unskilled workers.[68] Even in the countryside, the chairman of a collective farm may earn 5 times as much as a common field worker.[69]

There is no longer any ambivalence in Soviet policy with regard to material incentives. To get efficiency and industry in production, incomes must be unequal. But wages by themselves are ineffective; the state now recognizes that workers will strive to raise their incomes only if this enables them to buy more consumer goods. And the quality and diversity of these goods cannot be too restricted without weakening wage incentives. The contemporary emphasis is not on a "new communist man" but on ways of perfecting the material-incentive structure.[70]

Cars, television sets, refrigerators, and washing machines are gradually coming within the reach of the Russian masses. Recent visitors to the Soviet Union report traffic jams and parking problems. Children of upper-echelon officials are seen with transistor radios, motorcycles, and mod clothes. American news stories reporting this consumer-goods explosion invariably emphasize the disparities that still exist between Russians and ourselves. There is only 1 car for every 100 Russians compared to 1 for every 2 Americans or only 1 refrigerator for every 8 Russians compared to 1 for every 3 Americans. What these reports overlook is the amazing growth in Soviet production over the past 15 years. While the number of cars and television sets per 1,000 of population increased in the United States 45 and 66 percent respectively between 1960 and 1975, in Russia during the same period they increased 300 and 1,000 percent respectively.[71] And this expansion was accomplished while building a war machine second to none.

Hedrick Smith claims that the number of Russians aspiring to a way of life approaching that of middle-class America is steadily growing even though the leadership still views the masses primarily as producers rather than consumers.[72] So far below demand are the quantity and quality of goods available that Russians have become expert at "competitive shopping." They queue in any department store line that forms on the assumption that something worth the trouble is being sold. If it turns out they do not need the item, they buy it for a friend who does. The gap between consumer demands and the supply of goods and services available has become so great that a vigorous "counter economy" has grown up to fill it. Not only does illegal private enterprise flourish in the service sector, complete private industries operate underground.

Perhaps Maoist fears were justified; the Russian masses do seem to be getting caught up in the game of competitive consumption. Even some Russians are highly critical of a growing trend they pejoratively label "careerism." Careerists work hard to climb the job ladder not out of a desire to serve society as they should but to obtain better apartments and more material goods. Susan Jacoby found the trend particularly strong among young people.[73] Although oblivious to Western notions of "liberty" and "democracy," they are very much attracted to Western forms of material consumption. Jacoby found this growing consumerism doing more to undermine the collectivist ideology than any direct ideological attack could have done. In her opinion it has become the "most powerful, long-range force" working against an educational system that continually tries to put the group ahead of the individual. Moreover, to Russian teenagers as well as their parents, higher education itself has become the one visible avenue to successful careerism and the consumer goods they desire.

The new consumer game, however, is only a substitute for older, more traditional forms of consumption that survive in many places to the displeasure of authorities. For example, peasants on some collective farms still hold large wedding celebrations at which the hosts, according to critical Soviet newspaper accounts, compete in providing guests with alcoholic beverages. Even among industrial workers, reciprocal drink-buying is common on paydays, and anyone who fails to participate is shunned by workmates.[74] Another indication that wage goods are still not plentiful and appealing enough to attract discretionary income is the impressive growth of savings accounts among both rural and urban families.[75]

In China, on the other hand, Maoist ideology strongly opposed consumerism and the growth of a competitively consuming "middle class." [76] It also opposed the traditional forms of conspicuous-giving consumption that peasants and even some rural cadres still cling to in the form of "wasteful" wedding banquets and traditional celebrations.[77] The Maoist ethic called for self-sacrifice and self-abnegation in almost primitive Christian fashion. It extolled simple, unpretentious living spent in devoted service to others rather than in the pursuit of "pots and pans." [78] As a result, wage scales have remained closer to the egalitarian ideal than in Russia. The difference between Mao Tse-tung's monthly salary and that of the lowest government employee was on the order of only

15 to 1 although in 1955, according to Christopher Howe, it reached 30 to 1.[79] At factories visited by John Kenneth Galbraith in 1972, he found plant managers' salaries only 3 to 4 times that of the lowest apprentices.[80] According to figures collected by Barry Richman at the beginning of the Cultural Revolution in 1967, the top-paid managers of most enterprises earned about 5 times as much as the lowest-paid employee.[81] Even Mao at this time earned only 10 times as much as the lowest. By 1972, however, the wage span of the bureaucracy had jumped back up to 20 to 1 according to Howe.

While the range of these wage scales has been more compressed than in Russia, it has certainly provided unequal rewards for unequal skill and effort. And as in Russia, consumer goods have been made available so these wage differences would have incentive value. During the 1960's, conspicuous consumption was actually promoted to some extent according to Richman.[82] Workers were induced to be more productive and improve their skills so they could increase earnings and buy the "four good things," bicycles, watches, sewing machines, and radios. In addition, greater varieties of clothing were made available as well as cosmetics, cameras, and other items. Richman found all these wage goods in widespread evidence in 1967. People proudly told how they had worked and saved to buy them. They showed every sign of a strong motivation to acquire personal property.

Cuba during the 1960's provided an instructive contest between Soviet pragmatism and the "Sino–Guevarist" version of Maoist idealism. We saw in Chapter 3 how hard Cuba tried to substitute social for material incentives as consumer goods became relatively unattainable. Since 1970, however, Cuba has returned to the production and importation of consumer goods in order to reduce the amount of money in circulation. As long as there was nothing to buy with wages except food—and even much of that rationed—the incentive to earn wages decreased, absenteeism increased, and labor productivity plummeted. According to Mesa-Lago, the total income of Cuban workers in 1970 was about twice what it should have been given the available supply of goods.[83] As a result many items in the black market were selling at five to ten times their official price. By making more goods available, the amount of money in circulation began to drop and by the end of 1973 had begun, according to Castro himself, "to have some value." Now workers were becoming more interested in earning wages, and labor productivity was swinging upward.

By 1974, Castro was even advocating greater inequality of material rewards to increase the productivity of skilled technicians. The new "socialist emulation" would link material rewards more closely to individual productivity. Though not yet available in the stores, such wage goods as radios, bicycles, refrigerators, pressure cookers, watches, and sewing machines were being distributed directly to enterprises. The latter periodically posted lists of these goods on bulletin boards and encouraged workers to fill out purchase-application forms. Those applicants judged most productive by their worker committees were then allowed to buy the items of their choice.[84]

An especially interesting aspect of the Cuban experiment was the expansion of the free supply system during the Sino–Guevarist phase. Probably no other socialist state has ever moved as close to collective consumption in this regard. A deliberate policy of the Sino–Guevarists, as Mesa-Lago shows, was to increase the distribution of free services in the form of education, housing, medical treatment, water, gas, electricity, public transportation, and recreation.[85] A major assumption of the Sino–Guevarist line was that workers would learn to associate effort directly with the collective good instead of their private interest. Instead, however, the free supply system opened the door to a massive free-rider effect. Not only did productivity go down, but wasteful consumption increased. The same phenomenon illustrated by Amana food consumption, the kibbutz soap story, and the waste of electricity in the shitufim, took place on an even grander scale in Cuba. An appropriate label for all such phenomena might be "free-supply free riderism."

Cuban officials now regret their earlier decision, for once public services are free or too cheap, it is hard to impose charges or to increase them. Yet that is precisely what Cuba has had to do in the 1970's to combat consumer waste and unnecessary overloading of the telephone and transportation systems. Moreover, the old Sino–Guevarist plan to abolish house and apartment rents has been shelved indefinitely.[86]

Even in China the 1970's brought a renewed emphasis on consumer goods and the construction of the light industries necessary to produce them. More household appliances, better clothing, and leather shoes were promised. Attacks on materialism in the Chinese press seemed to be directed more at the special privileges of government officials and party functionaries than at consumption per se. Functionaries get all sorts of special perquisites such as cars, sometimes with chauffeurs, free housing, medical attention, servants, and special entertainment and recreational facilities. On trains they get to ride in the comfortable compartments while the masses are crowded into hard seats.[87]

But while these attacks on privilege have often had official sanction in China, in Russia they take the form of antigovernment leaflets printed and distributed by a "citizens' committee" of underground dissidents. Russian officials get rent-free country houses, medical attention at the best hospitals, and special purchasing privileges. They are far more likely than most citizens to have automobiles and houses of their own.[88] In a leaflet distributed in the summer of 1972, Kremlin officials were accused of living better than bureaucrats under the czar.[89]

At the time of communist takeover, both Russia and China had high rates of illiteracy. By some estimates Russia's was nearly 60 percent and China's over 90 percent.[90] In both cases this gave the existing intelligentsia and their children a tremendous advantage over the masses. Skills and knowledge are always in short supply under pressures of catch-up progress, a situation which must inevitably bestow some power on those who have them. The intelligentsia, moreover, were far more likely to motivate their children to want an education than were workers or peasants. While the new educational opportunities increased social mobility, they nevertheless left the children of workers and peasants in a less competitive position. For one thing, rural schools did not provide the same quality of preparation as their urban equivalents.[91]

Although for a while in the late 1920's and early 1930's, Russia promoted proletariat education, the demands of catch-up progress resulted in examinations gradually taking precedence over social origins in the selection of candidates for advanced training. Children of peasants and workers could still move up the social ladder through formal education, but their background put most at a disadvantage when they were no longer specially recruited. After 1957, two years of job experience was favored for entrance to universities, but families of the upper social strata found ways to circumvent such requirements.[92] They also have the means to hire tutors for their children, a practice increasing in the cities to the disadvantage of young people whose blue-collar parents cannot afford the expense.[93]

Today, despite official acknowledgment of background disparities, the prevailing policy is not to lower entrance standards for social reasons but to gradually eliminate the social reasons. The quality of rural education, for example, will eventually be raised to the urban level; and until it is, the quality of university education will not be lowered to accommodate it.[94] Jacoby found this attitude reminiscent of the reaction to the quota system by some educators in the United States.[95]

Given the much narrower knowledge base with which communist China began and the strong fear that the old gentry class would simply maintain itself at the top of the social order, Chinese educational policy endeavored to maintain priorities different from the Russian. To have judged students simply on universalistic criteria of competence, such as examinations and job performance, would have given the bourgeois and landlord classes too great a head start. Such criteria were avoided, therefore, in qualifying people for cadre ranks and promotions. Two career patterns consequently developed. The first stressed competence in specialized technical skills and general intellectual ability while the second stressed political activism and party loyalty. People of bourgeois or landlord background were more likely to be prominent in the first while the second provided rapid mobility for persons of proletariat and peasant background.[96] The "red versus expert" antithesis in China was part of the Maoist attempt to open up avenues of mobility at the lowest social levels while keeping the power of the old ruling class contained. For this reason criticism of bureaucratic privileges as well as "experts"—a subversive activity in Russia—often had official support in China.

Social Predictability

Despite the strong Millennial Man overtones of Maoist ideology, in practice the Chinese eutopian experiment has applied Socialist Man incentives almost as strongly, though not as consistently, as the Russian experiment. During the

Great Leap Forward of 1958 and 1959 an attempt was made to reduce and deemphasize material incentives in favor of socialist-emulation campaigns. Production suffered, however, and by 1961 material incentives were as much in force as ever. Nonmaterial incentives were again stressed during the Great Proletarian Cultural Revolution of the late 1960's, but this time Maoist ideology affected practice even less than during the earlier campaign.

Some observers found the Maoist antagonism to material incentives perplexing inasmuch as Mao denounced Millennial Man egalitarianism even before Stalin. In 1931 Stalin wrote it off as "primitive peasant communism" and later as "petty-bourgeois absurdity." He stressed the necessity of rewarding skilled labor more than unskilled and of paying wages according to work rather than need. This, he claimed, was the true Marxist–Leninist approach to wages in a socialist state. Only when the communist millennium was achieved and the state had disappeared could people be expected to work according to ability while receiving according to need.[97] Mao, however, had already opposed "extreme egalitarianism," in a 1929 essay, advocating instead the distribution of goods according to work. In his 1942 book on "Economic and Financial Problems" he went even further; he gave his support to progressive piece-rate systems. As Christopher Howe has pointed out, piecework systems of the progressive kind can lead to some of the most extreme cases of income differentiation.[98]

In some of their earliest collective experiments the Bolsheviks distributed proceeds according to need and blamed the poor quality of the results on inadequate rewards for effort and skill.[99] Since then they have consistently rewarded according to work. In industry a variety of incentive wage systems have been used including the straight piece rate, the progressive piece rate, and the premium, or bonus. These incentive payments are added to a basic wage that varies with the job. The share of average earnings represented by basic wages has increased over the years, and today the incentive-wage share is only about 10 percent of average earnings. Some 90 to 95 percent of all Soviet workers, however, still receive part of their earnings in incentive wages, determined in most cases by piece rates. This is over 3 times the percentage of U.S. factory workers still covered by incentive-wage systems. The United States, however, is ahead of Russia in industrial automation, a trend that renders piece-rate systems less effective.[100]

China has never used piece-rate systems in industry to the degree Russia has. A peak coverage of 42 percent of the industrial work force was achieved in 1956; but during the Great Leap Forward of 1958, when all material and wage incentives were under attack, the system was abolished in many places. With the resurgence of wage incentives in the 1960's, premium-wage systems were favored over piece rates although the purpose was the same—to improve work performance. The result is not very different from the current Russian wage system in that both base their rewards primarily on the job and the worker's qualifications. For the most part only a minor share of the industrial worker's income is determined by piece rates or premiums.[101]

For many years Russian collective-farm (kolkhoz) workers were paid on the *trudoden* or labor-day system. The trudoden was an arbitrary unit of work, rarely a true labor day, which was assigned to each job in such a way that workers would earn not only in relation to output but to skill. Basically it was a piecework system that used both straight and progressive rates. It paid off, however, in trudodni credits instead of rubles. Records were kept of the trudodni accumulated by each kolkhoznik, and at the end of the year each received a share of the farm's annual surplus equal to his share of the total number of work credits (trudodni) earned by all the members of the kolkhoz. State-farm (sovkhoz) workers, in contrast, received a guaranteed minimum income with an additional amount determined by piece-rate performance, in other words a wage comparable in structure, if not in amount, to that used in industry. The state-farm sector has increased its share of Russia's arable land from roughly 10 percent in 1953 to well over half today. Most of this expansion has been through the conversion of collective farms, whose members welcome the change. They are said to prefer a predictable wage to a harvest share that reflects vagaries of the weather more than effort.[102]

In the late 1960's all the collective farms were put under the same wage system as the state farms. The basic or guaranteed minimum wage is an advance payment equivalent to only 60 to 70 percent of the wage norm for each job; the remaining 30 to 40 percent of the norm is determined by piece-rate performance. This differs from the industrial wage system only in the lower basic-wage percentage of the former. The difference between kolkhozes and sovkhozes is now largely nominal; given the meaning of the word "collective" in this book, they are all state farms.[103]

Except for some state farms established in frontier regions of Inner Mongolia, Sinkiang, and Manchuria, Chinese farming is performed within small land-holding groups known as "teams" comprised of some 20 households. Various work-point systems are used to divide harvest surpluses according to time, effort and skill. For jobs like weeding, a field can be divided into mou (1/6 acre), and each worker credited with so many work points per mou. When jobs cannot be conveniently divided into piecework units, work points are assigned on the basis of individual ratings. Team assemblies may periodically classify all their members into labor grades on the basis of strength and ability, the various grades receiving different numbers of points for a day's work. In the so-called "Tachai" model of evaluation all piece rates and time rates are discarded in favor of monthly team evaluations of each member. Each must first evaluate himself, an initial appraisal that is later discussed and revised by his teammates, who then assign him his work points for the period in question. Criteria used for evaluation in this model include political attitudes. As in all true collective-farming systems, the harvest surplus or profits are distributed in portions equal to each worker's share of all the work points earned within the collective unit—in this case the team or a work group within the team. If Martin Whyte's data on the Tachai model are representative, peasant antagonism to the system led cadres in most cases either to drop it or to alter work-point assignments in such a way as to make effort the deciding criterion rather than political attitudes.[104]

Not only are work incentives primarily material and individualistic in China and Russia, but both countries try to avoid tax systems that would directly conflict with incentives based on wage differentials. Either little or no use is made of the income tax, as in China, or it is kept small and only very slightly progressive, as in Russia. Since over half the average household income goes for taxes in Russia, all or most of this in the form of a progressive income tax could badly undermine the incentive structure. The principal source of revenue, therefore, is a turnover tax levied mainly on consumer goods. A profit tax levied on all state enterprises constitutes more than half of China's revenues, and a turnover tax levied mainly at the retail level provides most of the rest.[105]

It would be interesting to know just how effective Russian and Chinese incentive systems are, but data on labor productivity, especially in the case of China, leave much to be desired. Russian factories designed and constructed by Western firms end up employing far more workers than those same factories would require in the West. In three cases cited by Wilczynski, the Russian plants used from three to eight times the number of workers for which they were designed.[106]

One frequently cited gauge of productivity is the private agricultural plot. In both countries each farm household privately cultivates a small plot of land to supplement its income from the collective or state sector. In Russia this private sector includes some 3 percent of all cultivated land and in China about 7 percent.[107] China, however, has a much larger and denser farm population so the private household plots of team members are usually mere fragments of an acre, just one-hundredth or two-hundredth in many cases. In Russia the household plots on state farms range somewhat under a third of an acre in size and those on collective farms around an acre. Although relatively small in total area, the private sector produces much more per unit of land than the collective sector.[108]

Household plots in China produce 80 percent of the nation's hogs and 95 percent of its poultry; according to some estimates they may supply as much as 20 percent of China's food. In Russia they produce about half the country's meat and vegetables, over half its milk and eggs, and about two-thirds of its potatoes. Farm households in both countries prefer labor intensive crops on their private plots because labor is the input over which they have the most control.[109]

Chinese peasants not only devote much labor and time to their plots, they also favor them—much to official displeasure—with most of the available natural fertilizers. Some cadres rotate household plots to discourage this practice. In other cases peasants are known to work as little as 30 days a year on the collective sector while devoting most of their time to their garden plots and to market transactions.[110] According to one report, peasants fulfilled as much as half their collective-work obligations at night so they could spend the daylight hours on their own plots.[111]

For Russia it has been estimated that more than a third of all agricultural labor goes into the private sector. While this results in yields on the household plots that are anywhere from one- to two-thirds higher per acre than in the collective sector, plot yields per worker-day of labor run 30 to 50 percent lower due to the labor-intensive quality of the product. Despite the lower productivity of labor on the private plot and despite the fact that the Soviet government doubled worker incomes on state farms and tripled them on collectives between 1953 and 1967, work on the plot is much more profitable than collective work. Peasants can earn almost twice as much from a day's work on their plots as from a day's work in the collective sector. The reason for this seeming inconsistency is the high price which they get for their products in the free market and the high prices they avoid by consuming home-produced food. The high market values are created in turn by the high prices the government pays to purchase state and collective farm products. But these purchase prices are necessarily high to cover the high production costs. In the end, the high production costs are due to many inefficiencies not the least of which is apathetic work in the collective sector.[112]

The guaranteed wage for Russian collective farmers, as well as the rise in farm incomes, was supposed to increase work efficiency; but during the period when state-farm wages doubled and collective wages tripled, productivity rose only 80 and 100 percent respectively. One explanation for this lag in productivity is that the lag in the rural availability of goods and services blunts wage incentives. Another explanation is that the relation between reward and effort is still far too indirect in the collective sector. Seldom do peasants even understand how their wages are computed.[113] In other words, incentives in the socialist eutopia tend to be strongly materialistic and individualistic, but not materialistic and individualistic enough. The private plot, therefore, continues to appeal to the farm household because the labor input is fully under its control and the relation between what the family does and what it gets is eminently clear. Russia would like to eliminate the private sector entirely, and eventually probably will. The impediment is not some overriding productive-property incentive in the rural psyche that ties peasants to their plots. If the productivity of labor in the collective or socialist sector can be increased to the point where labor-intensive household gardening becomes a waste of time, the garden plot will disappear.

There is little doubt that the productivity of Russian farm labor is capable of dramatic increases. While it is true that Russia, for the most part, has poor soil, unreliable rainfall, and a very short farming season,[114] some observers do not believe these handicaps account for more than 25 percent of the difference between Soviet and U.S. productivity; and by most estimates—even Russian—U.S. farm labor is 4 to 6 times more productive.[115] However, Russian experiments with the so-called *zveno* (link) method of production have demonstrated that spectacular increases both in farm-labor productivity and per-acre yields are possible.

Where it occurs within collective or state farms, a zveno is a minimum work unit of four to eight people. In its most common and officially acceptable form, the group works together regularly on specific job assignments. This form of zveno apparently has little affect on productivity. In the second form, the small group is responsible for an assigned share of the farm's land on which it regularly carries out the entire production cycle and sells the product to the farm at a contract price agreed upon at the beginning of the season. Between harvests, zveno members receive advance payments for living expenses. In effect this zveno becomes a miniature, small-group collective within the larger farm. It is this form of zveno to which I refer henceforth whenever I use the word. Where studies have been made of it, productivity per acre increases at least threefold and productivity per worker at least fivefold.[116]

There seems little doubt that this spectacular rise in productivity is due to the small-group nature of the zveno. In the first place, it meets the conditions of social predictability. The groups are formed of individuals who elect to work together and are usually relatives and close friends. This is precisely the kind of free-forming small group that can effectively control its membership as we have seen in previous chapters. Second, by being completely responsible for the production of its own small subfarm, the relation between reward and effort is unambiguous. All the "numerous controllers, supervisors, and auditors" normally essential to check on peasant field work are obviated. This would reduce production costs enormously since for some crops on Russia's giant farms the costs of indirect labor alone may exceed all labor costs for those same crops on U.S. farms.[117]

Despite the efficiency of the zveno and its popularity with peasants and agricultural economists, it has been vigorously resisted by the Soviet leadership. Most stable and effective when comprised of close relatives, it seems to Soviet leaders like a retrogression toward "nonsocialist" bourgeois farming. In fact, as Pospielovsky has pointed out, a collective farm subdivided into zveno farming units comprised mainly of close relatives would constitute a group-land-tenure body not unlike the 19th-century mir.[118]

Some of the earliest Russian collective farms were actually very much like the contemporary zveno. During the early and middle 1920's, kolkhozes averaged under 12 households each and were comprised of relatives and close friends. It was undoubtedly owing to these conditions of social predictability that some of them actually worked. The vast majority, however, even well into the late 1920's were apparently land consolidation associations and only nominally collective. In reality each household was individually farming its consolidated parcel. With forced collectivization under Stalin, the objective became mechanized farm "factories," large "industrial" farms on which the peasants could eventually be proletarianized. This fixation on large size both in agriculture and industry has been labeled "gigantomania" by Russia's critics. By 1938, average kolkhoz size had increased to 78 households and by 1966 to 417. Sovkhozes grew even faster over the same period, and by 1966 averaged 651 workers. Within these huge farm enterprises the work force is normally divided into "brigades" which often number over a hundred members.[119]

One of the most interesting casualties of the gigantomania movement was the commune form of kolkhoz, for during most of the 1920's it was officially regarded as the "highest" form. Because of its collectivized consumption and egalitarian distribution of income, it was furthest along the road to true communism. But of those few early kolkhozes that were truly communal, that rewarded according to need in Millennial Man fashion, most were tiny associations of less than a dozen deeply religious families often closely related. These sectarian communes belonged to such faiths as the Adventists, Baptists, Dukhobors, and Molokanes and were probably very much like contemporary Hutterites or the 19th-century religious communes described in Chapter 5.[120] By the late 1920's the official attitudes began to turn against them, and distribution according to need was accused of contributing to low labor productivity; in 1928 piecework was recommended for all kolkhozes. Collective forms of consumption were prohibited in 1930, the year Stalin declared the time was not yet ripe for communes. After 1931 there were no more procommune statements or further references to communes as the highest form, and by 1934 they were no longer listed separately in Soviet statistics; all had been converted to collectives.[121]

One reason for official disenchantment was the strongly religious nature of the most stable and enduring memberships. These groups sheltered their young from the political influence of the state, sometimes by keeping them out of the public schools. The most important reason for the demise of the Russian communes, however, was the conflict between their consumption goals and the state's grain procurement program. Soviet authorities wanted the kolkhozes to produce for the cities and for export but the communards were more interested in their own collective consumption. According to one 1926 survey, they consumed 14 times as much meat and twice as much milk as the national peasant average, statistics resembling those for Amana before and after incorporation. In a judgment made more than 30 years later, Khrushchev claimed communards had expected to live well while working as little as possible for the collective good. Their motto, he claimed, was "work when you feel like it, receive as you need." But a communard's collective good was the small-group game of subject players; Khrushchev's was a state game for object players.[122]

The collectivization drive with its accompanying gigantomania increased the size of kolkhozes so drastically that conditions of social predictability were greatly weakened if not destroyed. The population per commune kolkhoz jumped about 700 percent between 1918 and 1930, and memberships lost their homogeneous, self-selective quality. The sectarian communes, for example, were forced to admit members not of their faith, which soon undermined their religious leadership and group commitment.[123]

Although the Chinese communes failed in the end for much the same reasons as the Russian, the two experiments had little else in common. Many of the Russian communes lasted several years, but few of the Chinese communes lasted even one. And while the former occurred early during collectivization and were very small, the latter were formed at the height of collectivization and culminated in enormous units averaging some five thousand households each.[124]

Apparently the first Chinese communes were not the deliberate result of central planning. They were developed by cadres at the local level as a solution to labor shortages brought about by the Great Leap Forward movement. The communistic nature of the new organization was not recognized by the rural activists who originated it until pointed out to them by the party intellectuals. The motives of the original organizers were practical rather than ideological.[125]

As a result of the giant corvée labor projects organized to construct water-conservation and irrigation works during 1957 to 1958, rural China actually began to experience labor shortages. Local cadres had to find new ways of obtaining extra labor, and two presented themselves as a result of experiments used in water-conservation construction. Corvée armies of farm workers had been created by pooling the labor of several collectives. These made possible a more "rational" deployment of the labor supply for agriculture as well as construction. A second solution was the public dining hall which standardized eating hours and allowed work teams to be deployed more efficiently. Women released from household cooking could spend more time in the fields, a communal-service notion of efficiency that led to public nurseries, laundries, and even tailor shops. Communal services resulted in a free-supply system that obviated much of the work-point accounting so disagreeable to inadequately trained cadres. But Chinese communards proved just as hearty diners as their Russian equivalents had been, and again at the expense of state grain procurements. Everyone, moreover, wanted a full share of free supplies, but no one wanted to work any harder than anyone else to get it.[126]

Work organization was militarized on corvée patterns. Although all workers were still living in their home village, they were assigned to specialized work squads comprised of people with whom they were not accustomed to working. The previous informal work groups were broken up to form brigades for water drawing, rice-shoot plucking, ground preparing, and so on, on a "factory" basis. Intimate, informal, "particularistic" relationships and procedures were replaced by those of a more "universalistic," "mechanistic," and rational nature. This brief phase of Chinese gigantomania had disastrous effects on production. But the dangers were immediately recognized and led quickly to drastic revisions. Free supply was abolished and the communes decentralized.[127]

In China today "communes" are administrative units combining economic and political functions between the "district" and "administrative village" levels.[128] As collectively consuming and producing social units—the meaning used in this book—"communes" do not exist anywhere in China. China depends mainly on farm collectives and very small ones at that. In fact, the size of collective farming units makes for one of the most striking differences between the Chinese and Russian experiments.

The Chinese communists initiated their collectivization drive in 1950 with mutual aid teams of 4 to 8 households based on traditional exchange-labor practices. Beginning in 1952 these were combined into "elementary" APCs (agricultural production cooperatives) of some 20 or fewer households. By 1958 most of these had been converted into "advanced" APCs ranging in number of households from 50 to 200. During this consolidation process, however, the smaller units persisted. Production teams were comparable in size to the lower APCs and work groups to the old mutual-aid teams.[129]

After the abortive commune movement the production team became the basic accounting and production unit with "minor" or de-facto ownership rights over its land, tools, and animals.[130] Actually "three levels of ownership," commune, brigade, and team, were instituted. Within this group-land-tenure hierarchy the commune is still nominally the largest ownership unit, but in practice the brigades and teams decide questions of use and allocation. The latter were given the right to self-management and to the direction of their own labor. They became responsible for organizing and carrying out their production activities and for distributing income among their members.[131]

Today over 80 percent of the Chinese population is divided into teams comprised of 20 to 30 households. Groups of teams, in turn, make up brigades of 100 households or more. Brigades are sometimes coterminous with villages, but in any case the members of a team make up natural neighborhood groupings within the village and seldom extend beyond it. Households within a single team may all have the same surnames and are often closely related.[132]

Apparently when a team is small in size it is more likely to be the collectively producing unit. But most teams seem to be subdivided into work groups roughly equal in size to the old mutual-aid teams and traditional exchange-labor groups. These units of 4 to 10 households farm land allotted to them for an indefinite period by their team. Under some arrangements they contract to meet specified production quotas with the agreement that everything they produce above those quotas is theirs. As Barnett notes, this decentralization of authority was in line with the renewed emphasis of economic incentives; production responsibility was returned to a level at which peasants could clearly see the relationship between increases in effort and increases in rewards.[133]

Not only are these collective farming units small enough to relate reward and effort, they are even more likely than the team to be comprised of close friends and relatives as in the precommunist exchange-labor groups. They are social groups which meet the conditions of social predictability, and in effect are Chinese versions of the Russian zveno. But while Russian leaders have suppressed the zveno, in China it has become the standard collective-farming unit.

What is even more remarkable about the Chinese situation is that individual households and at times "consortiums" of two friendly households (one with a deficiency and the other with a surplus of labor) may be given responsibility for fields assigned to them within the "collective" sector of a team or work group. Both the individual households and the consortiums carry out all the work on their fields from planting to harvesting except during periods of peak labor load when the entire work group rotates its labor among the plots in the same fashion as traditional exchange-labor groups.[134] In the family responsibility system, known also as "household contract production," the individual household subcontracts with the team or work group to meet its share of the production quota with the right, again, to keep whatever it produces above the quota.[135]

Household, or family, farming is, of course, the ultimate in piecework production. It is the form of piecework most characteristic of American agriculture, which is still dominated by family farming. And American farm labor is the most productive in the world. To what extent Chinese farming has reverted to this ultimate form of piecework is anyone's guess, but during the Cultural Revolution many prominent agricultural officials came under attack for encouraging the expansion of private plots as well as the household contract system. Since agricultural agencies and even local cadres are judged on the basis of production statistics, they tend to favor methods that provoke the most enthusiastic response from the peasants. Moreover, small-group and household farming, as in the case of the zveno, obviates much or all of the work-point accounting that is such drudgery even for the most literate of local cadres.[136]

During the years of the Chinese New Economic Policy (1961–1965), the private sector expanded far beyond the legal limit of 7 percent in many parts of China. The private grain harvest in Yunan is believed to have surpassed the collective harvest as early as 1962 when privately cultivated land rose to 50 percent of the total.[137] In southwestern China more than 20 percent of the collective land was diverted to the private sector; and in 1964 private cultivation is said to have exceeded collective cultivation in the provinces of Kweichow and Szechuan.[138] Maoist reaction to these revisionist tendencies began as early as 1963 in the form of warnings about the capitalist dangers inherent in the private sector. By 1964 indoctrination programs were underway to remind the peasant once again that a good communist pursues collective good, not individual advantage.[139]

Instead of restricting peasant individualism, however, the initial effect of the Cultural Revolution was to increase it. As central authority broke down, local cadres began to give in more than ever to peasant pressures. Communal property was often divided up, and in some cases private plots were extended at the expense of the collective sector. Underground private industrial and handicraft enterprises came into being as well as underground construction teams which filched their raw materials from state supplies. Considerable private initiative generated spontaneously in many places. By 1969 the government was demanding a reduction in the size of private plots, but there is no certainty that these policies were ever put into practice on any extensive scale.[140] In fact, there is little evidence that the Cultural Revolution had much intentional effect on the countryside except for Maoist propaganda campaigns conducted through study groups. The social upheaval and the activist demonstrations so prominent in the cities seem to have bypassed most of the rural areas.[141]

The tendency in rural China for small-group production to drift toward family farming would seem to justify Russia's distrust of the zveno. But the impressive accomplishments of communist Chinese agriculture would also tend to justify the claims made for the efficiency of zveno-type production units. China's willingness to make use of such units is in keeping with another very characteristic difference between the People's Republic and the Soviet Union. Russia, as Martin Whyte points out, has emphasized hierarchical relationships along with strong material incentives.[142] Worker is pitted against worker through individual competition and secret police terror in such a way as to fragment primary and informal work groups of a horizontal nature. In spite of that fact, informal groups have arisen in the Soviet Union which oppose rate busting and otherwise obstruct government production and political objectives. China, on the other hand, has attempted to create new primary groups that employ social incentives horizontally. Members of these small groups, or *hsiao-tsu*, are thus encouraged to support official objectives rather than the norms of traditional or natural primary groups, that is, the family, extended kinship groups, neighborhood groups, friendship groups, and informal co-worker groups.

Whyte, Townsend, Barnett, and other authorities agree that in China the small group has become one of the most pervasive instruments ever used for exerting political and social pressures on the masses.[143] On a regular day-to-day basis it is supposed to do for the mass line what the social movement is supposed to do for it through periodic campaigns. Hsiao-tsu units of not more than 15 people are organized everywhere, government offices, schools, factories, urban neighborhoods, to carry out political study and to engage in mutual and self-criticism. Among peasants, however, the production teams or work groups within them are normally the small-group vehicles for such activities.

In his 1924 characterization of Chinese society as "a sheet of loose sand," Sun Yat-sen reasoned that China had never achieved true nationalism because the unity of the Chinese people had never gone beyond "family-ism and clan-ism." The communists have deliberately attempted to rectify this situation by using their new groupings to undermine traditional institutions such as the village clans and religious societies. By joining the peer-group pressures of their own small groups with hierarchical control, the communist leaders have extended their centrally organized bureaucracy directly into the natural village to a degree far beyond that achieved by any other state government in Chinese history. And according to Whyte, the Chinese communists have worked to combine "regimentation and mass enthusiasm" through the hsiao-tsu organizational system.[144] Ideally, mass participation and enthusiasm take the place of coercion and material incentives without preventing the authority structure from watching and controlling each person's behavior.

Through what Whyte calls the political rituals of the hsiao-tsu, political study, mutual criticism, and mutual surveillance, all deviant behavior becomes public knowledge and a target for social pressures to bring about conformity. Negative opinions are criticized as well as disputatious behavior, malingering at work, and failure to participate enthusiastically in political discussions and mutual criticism. Cadres are not supposed to use compulsory techniques; without slipping into the errors of "commandism," they must get hsiao-tsu members to attend meetings "voluntarily" and to apply social pressures "spontaneously" and enthusiastically. But the spontaneity of such procedures seems to derive mainly from each individual's desire to avoid being criticized.[145]

In China mutual criticism has achieved a degree of importance and social control never dreamed of by John Humphrey Noyes. In a part-society such as Oneida, membership and participation are truly voluntary in the sense that everyone is free to leave; but as Townsend notes, in China "there is no freedom to abstain."[146] Only a relatively few manage to defect to Hongkong (where they become informants for scholarly studies by men like Whyte and Barnett). Despite the charisma of a leader like John Humphrey Noyes, as long as his converts are free to abandon his little part-society game at any time, they are all subject players. In China, however, the same small-group techniques are applied on a scale and under circumstances in which subject playing is a contrived mass charade acted out by participants who are still objects of play.

The attempt by China's leaders to apply small-group social controls on the most massive scale in history undoubtedly helped, in Whyte's view, to unify and organize the populace in the pursuit of national goals. But as his data show, it failed both to displace material incentives and to create a new communist man. It helped to achieve behavioral conformity and to get people to work harder, but it did not appreciably alter basic attitudes. There were several reasons for this failure.[147]

First, basic attitude changes were not nearly as easy to effect as were temporary alterations in behavior patterns. As Whyte found, individuals adapted their behavior to small-group social pressures in the same way they adapted to mass movement pressures. They learned to go through the motions, to play the game, and to pretend activism in routine fashion without the spontaneous commitment they may have experienced in earlier years when all such programs were still a novelty. Second, for the two largest sectors of the population, the peasants and the workers, production was too important to be disrupted by political activities that conflicted with work, that added strain to an already heavy work schedule, or that provoked interpersonal conflicts which diverted attention from the serious business of producing the necessities of life. Cadres were less inclined to demand conformity when the means of doing so were more likely to disrupt production than to stimulate it.[148]

Third, not all so-called primary or small groups embodied what have been labeled in this book the conditions of social predictability. The act of creating new primary groups to cut across and compete with natural or traditional ones often obviated those very conditions. In fighting family, kinship, and friendship ties, the memberships of the manufactured groups were not likely to be comprised of individuals who would normally reciprocate favors and confidences. Hsiao-tsu memberships were deliberately "heterogeneous," to stimulate better criticism. People who knew each other well were considered less likely to criticize each other enthusiastically or sincerely and more likely to outmaneuver their leaders than individuals less predictable to one another.[149]

Finally, small and primary groups of a natural or traditional nature persisted alongside the new, especially in rural areas. To the extent teams and work groups were allowed to form freely for reasons of greater production efficiency, conditions of social predictability within these groups tended to reinforce the same traditional and natural loyalties the regime was trying to weaken or neutralize. Whyte found some evidence that clan and kinship ties, for example, actually strengthened after each mass-movement campaign passed its peak and individual involvement in them began to fall off. Moreover, by aggravating existing cleavages between village clans and kinship groups, the political rituals of small groups, as well as competition for leadership positions within them, often reinforce the traditional loyalties they were meant to weaken.[150]

In the case of the extended family, William Parish believes that the conditions of improved health and greater economic security achieved by the communist regime has actually brought the Chinese family closer than ever to the traditional ideal.[151] A large extended family composed of grandparents, parents, and married children was an ideal seldom achieved in the past because of poverty and high mortality. Today the grandparents live longer, and married sons continue to reside in the same compound with their parents or next door to them. Households with a large hand-to-mouth ratio (many adult workers and few dependents) are the most affluent, and within a single production team may enjoy a per-capita income more than five times that of households with low hand-to-mouth ratios.

Hsiao-tsu groups seem to be most effective among cadres. In some contexts the word "cadre" refers to all persons occupying leadership positions anywhere in the hierarchy from head of state down to the head of a farm production team. It may also refer, however, to bureaucrats without leadership positions. Since political dedication is at the core of cadre occupational life and the major criterion for cadre advancement, the social pressures of mutual surveillance and criticism have considerable influence on attitudes as well as behavior.[152] Study sessions for cadres tend to be more frequent and better attended than those for other groups. Frequent movement of cadres to combat bureaucratization increases their feelings of insecurity, makes them more dependent on the party, and prevents them from entering easily into free-forming primary groups that would compete with the hsiao-tsu. Daily political study sessions, weekly evaluation meetings, annual self-evaluations with group assessment, constant surveillance, and periodic rectification campaigns with their intense mutual criticism, "struggle sessions," and public censure have all worked to maintain cadre conformity and loyalty.[153] The guardians of Plato's Republic served the public good simply because the social organism depended on their dedication; the guardians of the People's Republic serve the public good because their social position and personal well-being depend upon it.

In addition to the selective incentives of small-group pressure, Chinese cadres are exposed to a nationwide ranking system divided into some 24 salary grades. The egalitarianism of the early years was soon replaced by a system of ratings that bestow great differences in personal power and income. For the most part cadres are extremely rank conscious, and the degree of deference and respect they receive from others depends on their position in the hierarchy.[154]

If it is fair to say that the Chinese system of ranking bears some resemblance to the grades and ranks within Edward Bellamy's industrial army, then the Soviet system of service ranks could be called a close approximation indeed. The Russians, like the Chinese, also replaced their earlier egalitarianism with a system of ranks that has steadily grown in complexity and in the number of occupations included. Patterned largely on the Soviet military, the system includes ranks, insignia, and in some cases even uniforms for such occupational groups as the diplomatic corps, railroad service, public prosecutor service, police, navigational service, mining technicians, merchant shipping personnel, banking and finance officials, communication personnel, state inspection officials, geological services, oil and gas technicians, and civil aviation personnel. According to Boris Meissner, no other country in the world comes close to Russia in the number and complexity of its orders, titles, and ranks.[155]

While in Bellamy's utopia everyone received the same material income, and selective incentives were entirely in the form of grades, ranks, and social honors, the Russians and Chinese have found it necessary to back up these social incentives with significant differences in material income. Even honorary titles such as "Distinguished Scientist" and "Hero of Socialist Labor" entitle their recipients to material prizes and privileges. In China and Cuba as well as in Russia, honorary awards and titles conferred in "socialist emulation" campaigns have quickly lost their incentive value when unaccompanied by material bonuses or prizes. Pennants and hero medals are extremely vulnerable to the phenomenon of "prize inflation." An incentive system that relies heavily on such social incentives must award them generously enough to make them obtainable at wide levels. The more generously they are awarded, however, the more trivial they become.

The socialist eutopian experiments raise some doubts concerning Schumpeter's penny-stamp theory. While they support previous evidence that ranking systems provide effective social incentives, they also indicate that it may be utopian to expect such systems to stand entirely on their own within a progressive economy. It would certainly be safe to say, however, that they make it easier to restrict the range and amount of material incentives without eliminating the need for them altogether. While it bothers some Chinese cadres, for example, that their salaries are not very high, they find their privileged status sufficient compensation for this inadequacy.[156] Utopians like Cabet and Bellamy believed members of a progressive society could be motivated to invest effort in the acquisition of skills by social incentives alone, but eutopians like Stalin and Liu Shao-chi did not. Since Stalin and Liu Shao-chi were men in a hurry, they may not have provided the final test. Perhaps Castro came closer to such a test than either of them.

Another aspect of utopianism tested by the Chinese is the Skinnerian goal of subjecting controllers to the same contingencies of reinforcement as the controlled. Cadres were required to practice the "four togethers," "eating, living, working and consulting with the masses," as well as the "six to's," going "to fields, nurseries, happiness homes, hospitals, mess halls, and members' homes." [157] Leaders, according to Maoist doctrine, were supposed to make themselves inseparable from the masses and thus available to them for constant scrutiny and appraisal. Such procedures, it was hoped, would keep cadres from treating the masses indifferently and impersonally. In the eutopian experiment, however, the masses supposedly reinforced the cadres, and the latter supposedly kept their actions highly visible to the masses, neither of which was practiced in Skinner's utopia. But even the Chinese masses, as Schwartz points out, were supposed to judge their cadres from a correct Maoist position determined by the top leadership. And when the masses were wrong, their cadres were to lead them to the Maoist truth.[158] In the end, the Chinese came to just what Skinner's utopian behaviorism would be in practice. When such a circle of reinforcements finally closes, power returns to its locus—not in spite of all the leadership's good intentions but precisely because of them.

Some check or control of leadership through the high visibility of guardians or magistrates was considered or implied in the preindustrial utopias of Plato and Thomas More. The city or the neighborhood groupings were small enough that utopian cadres, like their communist Chinese counterparts, would be highly visible along with everyone else. The populations were also sedentary, and in Utopia were kept that way by an internal passport system. Both China and Russia have similarly employed internal passport systems to keep their rural populations in place. Russia has used the system intermittently to check migration to urban areas while China has used it more consistently. Neither communist government has been successful, however, in halting urban migration completely. Forced collectivization in Russia caused considerable shifting of population, sometimes from one rural area to another. The greatest shift was from rural to urban localities; about 25 million people migrated to towns and cities between 1927 and 1939, almost 10 million of these between 1930 and 1932 when the collectivization drive was at its peak.[159] Flight of labor from rural areas to the cities has remained a severe problem for Russian agriculture to the present time.[160] But even when the passport system has been used to slow down internal migration, its effectiveness has been undermined by passport forging.[161]

Chinese peasants cannot travel without permission from their brigade office. When they reach their destination, they must register at the nearest public security substation; and for authorization to make food purchases at the new location, they must take their grain-ration tickets to the nearest Grain Management Office.[162] While even these regulations have not proved foolproof, most Chinese are still living in the same villages where their families have resided for generations. The conditions of social predictability traditional to the natural village have not yet been disrupted by the transience of modernization to anything like the degree they have in Russia. According to Russian dissident Andrei Amalrik, even those people remaining in the Russian countryside have been "proletarianized" into an "alien class" that is today neither peasant nor genuinely working class in character.[163]

The Chinese attempt to use small-group conditions of social predictability to effect control and consensus within their huge population is reminiscent of utopian Icaria. There everyone watched everyone else through the high visibility of small-group relations at all levels and in all situations. As we saw in Chapter 7, Lewis Mumford was highly critical of Cabet's utopia.[164] Writing in 1922, long before the Chinese were to put his criticisms to the test, he saw that the Icarian associations could not possibly be as democratic as Cabet intended. Universal consensus on a mass scale in such a large population would certainly have to be manipulated by a strong, highly centralized power structure. The Chinese experience has borne him out. It also gives support to those critics of Rousseau who see something ominous in a "general will," particularly one effected within a confederation of republics even though small enough to rely on face-to-face, general-assembly, total-participation forms of government. The very scale of such a superimposed polity would suggest a centrally manipulated consensus of the kind Whyte feels the Chinese guardians accomplished through their small-group mass-movement political rituals.

Legal Predictability

Another recurring theme in our utopias was the distrust, even hatred, of formal law. The perfectly engineered utopia can dispense with laws, courts, and especially lawyers. Popular hostility toward law and lawyers, however, has by no means been confined to fiction. It was strong, for example, in the American colonies during the 17th and early 18th centuries.[165] Legal historian Seagle cited three attempts by national governments to abolish lawyers prior to World War II: Prussia in 1780, France in 1790, and the Soviet Union under Stalin.[166] Since then, China has followed a similar course, particularly during the Cultural Revolution when law and professional lawyers were vigorously condemned as bourgeois.[167] But even when Maoists went so far as to advocate "lawlessness," they were simply reflecting a characteristic Chinese hostility toward law that goes back to earliest imperial times over two thousand years ago.[168]

Although Peter the Great, after seeing lawyers for the first time on a visit to Westminister Hall in 1698, vowed to hang at least one of Russia's two legal scholars as soon as he returned home, Russia has not advocated lawlessness as much as she has been accused of it.[169] "Endemic lawlessness" permeates Russian history, according to Richard Pipes, especially in "relations between those in authority and those subject to it." [170] For "endemic lawlessness" Julius Jacobsen substitutes "law of lawlessness," particularly with reference to the Stalinist period.[171] And Russian dissenter Andrei Amalrik is convinced that the one common aim of all the various opposition movements in Russia today is to achieve "the rule of law." [172]

By "rule of law," Amalrik refers to a conception of law that grew up in the West, particularly in the tradition of English law as a result of constitutional struggle between courts and crown. According to this conception, law sets constitutional limits to executive power and denies special privilege.[173] Thus, the "lawlessness" to which Pipes and Jacobsen, as well as some critics of Chinese history, refer is a condition of relatively unrestrained executive power and capriciousness. This capricious quality of unrestrained executive or royal power is quite the opposite of what we have referred to as "legal predictability." The latter is a characteristic of the rule of law. Is it possible that entire states can exist in some kind of no-man's land between legal and social predictability?

In a sense there are two sources of legal predictability, and Adam Smith characterized the difference between them very well by using a game metaphor, that of chess.[174] He said "the man of system" would like to manipulate all the members of the great human society as if they were pieces on a chessboard. To such a man, "the principle of motion" of the pieces is simply the guiding hand that moves them. He fails to recognize that each piece has "a principle of motion of its own," often quite distinct from that which the lawgiver might wish "to impress upon it." On the great chessboard of human society, therefore, the first principle of motion must adjust to the second if harmony is to prevail.

Here, in essence, Smith vividly illustrates the distinction legal scholars make between "objective law" and "subjective law." [175] In the former instance law is viewed as conferring rights on individuals; or, as Max Weber put it, individuals and their interests tend to be viewed by government as "objects rather than bearers of rights." [176] In the case of subjective law, however, the legal rights asserted by individuals are considered the legitimate source of law. Thus we find our existentialist distinction between object players and subject players even in legal philosophy.

To carry this distinction further still, we might say that public law, at least in its most primitive forms, approximates objective law while private or civil law approximates subjective. In its broadest and most modern sense, of course, public law acts to limit state power, but this has not always been so.[177] In that authoritarian model of government Max Weber labeled "patrimonial," public and private become "indistinguishable;" for the former devours the latter as all law becomes the personal privilege of the head of state.[178] In a patrimonial state, in which adjudication takes place by administrative decree, law and administration are the same. Individuals are the objects of commands, says Weber, that abide by no "fixed forms" and occur at "arbitrary times."

Whatever the predictability of "patrimonialism" it is clearly on the side of a governing elite rather than the members of society at large and is not a form congenial to the growth of the civilization of capitalism. For society at large patrimonialism replaces "predictability" with sheer capriciousness. Capitalism demands "legal predictability" in the sense we have used it throughout this book, a conforming to "rule of law" in which contract law has come to dominate the substance of private law.

Up to this point I preferred to leave "legal predictability" simply a general category for contemporary written law within the civilization of capitalism. Therefore, I leave the Russian and Chinese case material momentarily to review some general statements on law that will help to clarify my category of legal predictability. A major concern of previous chapters was the testing of Millennial Man incentives, which led to a concentration on what were called conditions of social predictability, conditions mainly of high, interpersonal visibility. These conditions conform roughly, as I noted earlier, to Max Weber's "customary law." [179] The "coercive apparatus" of customary law, according to Weber, derives from "consensus" rather than the "enforcement machinery" of "specialized personnel" as in the case of formal law.

Some scholars have found a rough correspondence between Sir Henry Maine's status-contract distinction and that between customary and formal law. But as even Maine was aware, some notion of contract exists in all societies, including those dominated by personal and familial relationships.[180] For this reason Max Weber preferred to emphasize the continuity of contract by altering Maine's distinction to one of "status contract" versus "purposive contract," the first being characteristic of familial and feudal relationships and the latter of relationships within a market economy.[181]

Recently Lon Fuller has reemphasized this same continuity but in a slightly different way.[182] For him, the line between customary law and contract law is very fluid; both kinds of law find their roots in what he calls "stable interactional expectancies." Highly repetitive modern contracts, especially in commercial law, become "standard" or customary practice. Frequently they serve as little more than a framework for an "ongoing relationship" resembling "a kind of two-party customary law." In a primitive situation, on the other hand, in which the community boundaries of customary rules are never clearly defined, Fuller feels that something like two-party customary law "can and does exist." The data on exchange labor presented in Chapter 3 certainly bear him out.

Max Weber seemed to have something very similar to Fuller's "interactional expectancies" in mind when he spoke of a "force" additional to both law and convention.[183] This force is rooted in each party's "self-interest in the continuation of a certain agreed action," in other words, in reciprocal altruism. Thus, each "partner to an exchange" counts "upon the other party's conduct to conform with his own expectations." Such a transaction can acquire a "certainty" that needs no reinforcement of either a customary or formally legal nature. It would seem that Weber's additional "force" is essentially what Fuller makes the common denominator of customary and contract law. It also seems very close to the dyadic form of social predictability.

By expanding these reciprocal expectations beyond the dyad, however, Fuller allows his common denominator to pull the two legal extremes closer together.[184] His "stable interactional expectancies" are those which have diffused from dyadic exchanges or specific contracts to general practice or "standard clauses" and conversely are borrowed from general practice and standard clauses for negotiating a particular exchange or drawing up a particular contract. And if I understand Fuller correctly, the "stable interactional expectancies" that grow up horizontally in the context of a civil law dominated by freedom of contract inspire a very general form of public law that also depends on "stable interactional expectancies," this time vertically between lawgivers and citizens. In short, Adam Smith's harmonious chess game is achieved because the directing hand, such as it is, accommodates to a "principle of motion" residing in the pieces themselves. This is all very close conceptually to Hayek's harmonious state in which law also develops through "mutual correspondence of expectations." [185]

Fuller, it would seem, is linking customary law with contract and enacted law at least partly through a common denominator of social predictability. Even in a large, complex, modern society people may form voluntary associations to which conditions of social predictability apply. To the extent this is true, a kind of customary law symbiotically persists within the framework of contract and enacted law, all three forms reciprocally exchanging with and reinforcing one another. This expands the social predictability of small-group, face-to-face conditions to the "stable interactional expectancies" or "predictabilities" of larger and more anonymous groupings under "rule of law." What is imperative to "rule of law," however, is that enacted law remain loose enough to foster the persistence of "undercover" customary law and that this undercover form of customary law becomes more voluntary and free forming than its traditional counterpart.

In both imperial Russia and China, despite national legal codes, customary law persisted at the village level in a very traditional form. Well over 80 percent of both populations were comprised of peasants living in small villages averaging less than 400 inhabitants. The strong anarchistic tendencies or potentialities that some modern writers find endemic to these populations are undoubtedly related to the fragmented character of their peasant masses. The social solidarity of the village rarely extended beyond it; there was little or no unity among villages, and peasants had no national organizations. Villages enjoyed a certain degree of autonomy almost by default; as long as they met state tax requirements, they were left to manage their own affairs.[186]

There seems to be more disagreement on this point in the case of China than in that of Russia. Chu, for example, claims there was no autonomy in towns and villages of dynastic China and no self-government in them of any kind.[187]

The official administration that governed rural China under the Ch'ing was highly centralized. Together the gentry and local officials, according to Chu, "determined local policy and administration and shared the control of society." There was no popular participation in the governing process. The crucial question is to what extent traditional informal and unofficial governing processes persisted. Balazs tended to agree with Max Weber that, whereas towns in dynastic China were occupied by government officials and had no autonomy, villages preserved at least some of theirs if only by default.[188] Van der Sprenkel believes village autonomy was a product of official policy, not official negligence.[189] Hsiao feels that whatever autonomy the village enjoyed it was not the product of either of these factors, but resulted, instead, from the sheer inability of the central government to control it completely.[190]

According to van der Sprenkel, Chinese villagers relied on mediation for settling civil disputes, and litigants went to court only as a last resort.[191] In south China the boundaries of the village and the clan often coincided although villages with two or more clans were not unusual in the north. Composed of people closely related or who had known one another all their lives, the traditional village fulfilled important conditions of social predictability.

Clans actually forbad members from going to the official court before giving clan leaders a chance to settle differences. And for maintaining internal order, clans used selective social incentives very reminiscent of our communities in Chapter 5. To be summoned before the whole clan and its leaders was a form of public humiliation that everyone preferred to avoid. To be omitted from the clan genealogy or denied access to clan rituals was similar to excommunication. Finally there was expulsion with loss of all clan privileges.[192]

Craft and merchant guilds also pressured members to let guild leaders mediate differences before resorting to a magistrate's court. Disputes of an inter-clan nature were adjudicated when possible by village leaders; and the village had its social controls, too, public derision and ostracism being two of the most powerful. On the positive side was concern for "face." An individual's quest for prestige and reputation in the community was a quest for social approval. And as van de Sprenkel says, each individual was forever "acting" on a community "stage" before an audience of fellow villagers continuously judging his performance.[193]

Much of the village leaders' time was spent mediating and settling disputes, in other words, administering customary law. It was important not to disturb the harmony of the village; the permanence of group relationships was stressed over any short-term personal advantage. Consequently the laws of the land seldom intruded into village life. And villagers by and large preferred it that way since the consequences of legal action in the magistrate's court could be unpleasant for everyone. Given the corruption that prevailed at the official level as well as the vagueness of imperial law, the prevailing attitude was to avoid civil courts and formal law whenever possible.[194] According to Bodde and Morris, the ordinary man regarded "involvement in the formal system" as "a road to disaster." [195] They quote two popular Chinese proverbs as illustration: "Win your lawsuit and lose your money," and "Of ten reasons by which a magistrate may decide a case, nine are unknown to the public."

Distrust of lawyers, courts, formal law, and corrupt officials was as true of the precommunist Russian village as its Chinese counterpart. While Chinese villagers were bound together by their clan relationships and the need to cooperate in the maintenance of local irrigation works, Russian villagers were bound together by the group-land-tenure arrangements of the mir and its collective responsibility for taxes. And although a mir would occasionally include more than one small community, it was usually coterminous with the inhabitants of a single village. Customary law and conditions of social predictability were strong in rural Russia, too; and again an overriding concern of the peasantry was the maintenance of harmonious, neighborly relations within the local community.[196]

So strong was the Russian rural community that it survived both the Stolypin reforms aimed at breaking up the mir and the early Bolshevik attempts at reorganization through the rural soviets. As both Shanin and Taniuchi have shown, the mir and its traditional assembly, or "gathering," enjoyed a remarkable revival following the Bolshevik revolution.[197] These communities continued to collect their own taxes and to meet many of their own local needs even after such practices were declared illegal by the state. Studies conducted by the central government during the 1920's revealed that the rural soviets were not only having little influence on the countryside, they had, in fact, lost their authority to the traditional gatherings. Peasants ignored all meetings of the soviets, and the officials of these bodies had become dependent on the village gatherings for the collection of taxes and their own financial support.

As in China, the Russian rural community imposed strong selective incentives on its members, typical of traditional communities. Life could be made unbearable for the nonconformist; and though some gatherings illegally imposed fines on recalcitrant members, these would not think of complaining to government officials. Peasants were not interested in what went on outside their communities; they resented the interference of officials they considered outsiders, and they complained that the central government collected their taxes but contributed nothing to local services.[198]

Not only was customary law strong in the Russian village, its population was far more homogeneous socially and economically than Bolshevik political leadership would admit. It created a kulak enemy to account for peasant resistance, but peasant revolts and resistance were actually, says Shanin, a product of peasant cohesion.[199] He demonstrates the strong interdependence between the size and wealth of peasant households and shows that socioeconomic differences were a product of "cyclical mobility." Households tended to rise economically for a time; and the poorer they were to start, the more probable that their position would improve. But after reaching a peak, a household would tend to decline; again, the wealthier a particular household became, the more probable that its position would begin to deteriorate. Wealthy households tended to break up through internal friction while poor households that increased their worker–consumer ratio through biological growth tended to convert this into economic expansion. Differences among households were never very great, and positions could change relatively fast. Purely chance factors in the life histories of particular families had exaggerated effects on economic differences. All of this resulted in what Shanin calls "multidirectional mobility"; it did not result in a peasantry divided into socioeconomic strata as visualized by Soviet leaders.

Apparently cyclical and multidirectional mobility were also characteristic of rural China in the 19th and early 20th centuries. At this time, according to Mark Elvin, Chinese rural society was "one of the most fluid in the world"; with luck a poor household could achieve "landlord" or "rich peasant" status in as little as three years.[200] Nor has the collectivization of agriculture entirely altered this situation; for as Parish has recently shown, the per-capita income of households in the same production team can vary as much as seven to one as a result of differences in their hand-mouth ratios.[201]

During imperial times, both Russia and China achieved an accommodation between the directing hand and the movement of the "pieces" themselves by leaving the latter to operate within the traditional context of customary village law. Meanwhile, the central government operated in a manner characteristic of Weber's patrimonial state. In fact, Weber frequently used Russian and Chinese data to illustrate this political type in which the differences between law and administration tend to disappear above the village level.[202]

Using Weber's concepts in his historical analysis of Russian polity, Richard Pipes shows that the Russian "patrimonial regime" followed the Weberian model by concerning itself only with crimes committed by subjects against the interests of the state, not with those committed against a subject by the state or by another subject.[203] Even when this patrimonial regime was partially dismantled during imperial times, Russian citizens were never invited to participate in the making of laws. The state continued to deny society any legal or political foothold that might challenge its omnipotence. And as early as the beginning of the 18th century, it created for the first time in history a separate police bureau to deal "exclusively with political crimes."

A class of state officials developed which became notorious for its venality. Underpaid by the state, the provincial chinovniki were especially corrupt. True public service was completely alien to this bureaucracy, which served only itself and the czar—in that order. While the state remained largely oblivious to injuries against ordinary citizens by these officials, it was merciless against officials who injured the state. Because of the close parallels between the Criminal Code of 1845 and those of 1927 and 1960, Pipes declares the first to have had the same importance for the history of totalitarianism as the Magna Carta had for the history of human freedom.[204]

Most of the patrimonial characteristics Pipes finds in imperial Russia, other scholars have noted for imperial China. Written law, claim Bodde and Morris, was "overwhelmingly penal in emphasis" although civil law was largely ignored.[205] Official law was only "secondarily interested" in the rights of citizens versus other citizens and not at all in the rights of citizens versus the state. It "operated in a vertical direction" from state upon citizen rather than horizontally. The rural masses were completely submissive to their superiors; they were passive, not active, participants in the making of government. Balazs and Hsiao both write of an atmosphere of mutual surveillance and suspicion permeating society and the entire administrative structure.[206] Chinese officials, also underpaid, made up the difference through "customary fees" permitted by law and through graft called "squeezing" or "satiation at the middle," the latter at the expense of the rural taxpayer and the imperial government. As in Russia the rural bureaucracy was the most unscrupulous of all and tended to serve itself first, the state second, and the public last. The Chinese state was also less concerned with the extortion of its citizenry than with embezzlement of state funds or neglect of duties by its officials.[207]

According to Weber, capitalism could develop in only minor, restricted ways under patrimonial regimes because of its acute sensitivity to any and all "irrationalities" of law, which "upset the basis of calculability."[208] Modern capitalism required a legal system free from capricious, unpredictable interference by government. Rule of law provides this essential legal predictability by reducing the capriciousness of official acts. Central to this growth of legal predictability, however, was the growth of freedom of contract, which in turn was directly related to market expansion.[209]

At this point it is helpful to return to Lon Fuller and a social-interaction distinction he makes between customary and contract law.[210] Using a "scale of relationships" extending from "intimacy" at one end to "hostility" at the other with a condition of "friendly strangers" in between, Fuller finds customary law "at home" across the entire "spectrum of social contexts" including kinship societies, modern commercial dealings, and international relations. Contract law, on the other hand, has found its special adaptive niche in the middle ground of friendly strangers. Persons hostile to one another do not have enough mutual trust to negotiate, and those very close to one another have so much that they do not need explicit contracts.

We can use the example of exchange labor again to help illustrate this spectrum. When close relatives, such as brothers or father and son, exchange labor, they are less likely to worry about an exact equivalence. They are reciprocating so many favors over such an extended period that there is usually little reason to quibble over particular units of exchange. On the other hand, people hostile to one another would not think of exchanging because they would expect cheating. Exchange labor is likely to achieve its most contractual—as compared to customary—form when it is deliberately instituted by a group of "friendly strangers" in a new land settlement, for example. As in the case of the Venezuelan cooperatives discussed in Chapter 9, a small group of farmers in a new land-reform settlement may agree to exchange their labor on principles of customary labor exchange known to all of them. But since these individuals are not yet well known to one another, they must watch each other closely during the shakedown period that determines the success of the experiment. Free riders must be spotted quickly and expelled early. In this situation, participants are extremely sensitive to inequities of exchange due to malingering, neglect of duty, and poor work. The atmosphere becomes much less "customary" than that of labor exchange among kin in a traditional village and much more like the "contractual" atmosphere of hired labor.

In parts of Europe such as England and France, where agricultural-extension agents help farmers form "machinery rings" to exchange labor and machinery, agents first study examples of traditional labor and machinery exchange. They see what customary practices seem to work best and then draw up written rules for forming successful rings. These rules seem almost like formal contracts, but a study made of marketing-cooperative contracts by the University of Reading concluded that in the absence of those conditions which make a cooperative successful, a written contract will not change the outcome.[211] It serves only as a useful guide or plan. A ring formed on such guidelines is still a face-to-face small group, and its success is determined by conditions of social predictability. The "contract" aspects of customary law necessarily graduate to fully formal, contract law when the exchanging parties cannot maintain the high degree of personal interaction, visibility, and mutual sanction required by these conditions.

Exchange labor also helps in illustrating the useful reconciliation Fuller makes between Malinowski's view of customary law and that of Max Gluckman.[212] While reciprocity of favors and services is central to the former's position, the notion of "the reasonable man" is central to the latter's. The first Fuller characterizes as "the trader" and the second as "the conscientious tribesman with a sense of trusteeship for the welfare of the group." He then shows how the two positions stem from the differences between Malinowski's Trobriand Islanders, who were keen traders, and Gluckman's Barotse, who organized their economy primarily on a kinship basis. But Fuller then suggests that Malinowski would probably have been just as successful finding reciprocity among the Barotse as Gluckman would have been applying his "reasonable man" concept to the Trobrianders.

I would carry this comparison even further. Malinowski and Gluckman have hit upon the two most important categories of customary law. Malinowski's reciprocity is that aspect of customary law which develops into contract law while "the reasonable man" notion includes that aspect which develops into enacted and administrative law. The latter category not only produces customary rules of the game whose "rationality" is specific to a particular environment, as during the multiecological stage, it also produces rules which are broadly applicable to many environments. When rules of exchange labor are written down and deliberately formalized, they prove to be remarkably similar around the world. They demonstrate a basic pragmatic "rationality" common to all people—an ability to formulate the broader rules within which the "pieces" on the chessboard can follow their own "principles of motion" everywhere. But the lifespan or applicability of the rules depends on the duration of those conditions under which they can still provide the exchange incentives of reciprocal altruism.

Rationality, of course, does not always imply freedom or justice. Similarities of extreme patrimonialism in widely separated states may reflect nothing less than the common rationality of that bureaucratic despotism Weber called "sultanism." [213] In such cases the "principle of motion" of the common "pieces" is confined to the limits of the peasant village. There the "pieces" play their traditional games of cyclical mobility and reciprocal feasting while above them those who have made it into the bureaucracy play the "career" game of upward mobility in the hierarchy. A major limit to the power of the directing hand is the clear impossibility of completely controlling all the "pieces." And the major limit to the "principle of motion" within the "pieces" is the fragmented, horizontal structure of peasant society. Splintered into tiny village units, peasants lack the knowledge, overview, and organization to curtail patrimonial power through rule of law.

Under freedom of contract, however, voluntary associations and corporations of friendly strangers not confined to village or even national boundaries form overlapping networks that pervade the entire social structure. The "principle of motion" within the "pieces" expands into a wider field of social interaction that diffuses knowledge, overview, organization, and power. For Max Weber, money was the crucial agent in the process by which contract law grew out of the soil of custom.[214] Once money has been accepted by all parties to a degree that its desirability to them becomes continuous, says Weber, it creates a new kind of community unlike either a traditional community or a deliberately formed organization. This new kind of community depends not on participants focused on each other's persons, but persons focused only on a commodity. This is not a fraternal community nor a group with clear boundaries. On the contrary, it is an impersonal community of strangers who are "actual and potential participants in the market" and who have a common "material interest" in certain market payoffs. This is a "community" in which conditions of social predictability can be present but in which they seldom prevail.

Thus the growth of contract private law becomes a "legal reflex" to the expansion of a market economy. Purposive contracts among strangers (Weber actually used the word "enemies") must replace the status contracts of fraternal society. As the market economy expands under freedom of contract conditions, increasing numbers of legal specialists with adequate knowledge and experience become necessary to handle legal transactions continually growing in number and complexity as they keep pace with business expansion. Utopian hostility toward lawyers necessarily gives way to acceptability, particularly on the part of the business interests who require the legal predictability they represent.[215]

Our own American colonies illustrate this transition. The small, homogeneous communities of Massachusetts were able to get along with a minimum of written law and a hostility toward legal specialists much longer than the more heterogeneous New York colonies. New York consequently became a leader in juristic development for the new country, a development made increasingly unavoidable by the rapid expansion of commerce during the 18th and 19th centuries.[216]

But this transition must take place under the rule of law if "the rules of the game" are to have the legal predictability required by the civilization of capitalism. This kind of legal predictability did not occur in the patrimonial states of imperial Russia and China. Why, unlike the West, did these two countries fail to break out of the patrimonial mold?

In the case of China, Mark Elvin has recently provided a provocative explanation through his concept of "high-level equilibrium trap." [217] Finding a rough correspondence of technical and economic developments in Europe and China up to the 14th century, Elvin asks why the Chinese economy subsequently fell into a decline while that of the West took off in an industrial revolution. He first counters some previous explanations. Inadequate capital could not have been the cause since there were large concentrations in merchants' hands. Markets were by no means inadequate; in fact very large markets were available for the mass consumption of goods. The political obstacles imposed by the bureaucratic structure of the empire were severe, but perhaps they were more a symptom than a cause of the failure to develop. Similarly the absence of contract law was as much a symptom as a cause.

Basically, Elvin's explanation is one of excessive population growth. A relatively advanced technology and agriculture permitted population expansion to become excessive in the sense that it limited the available resources upon which an easy, pristine transition to industrialization depends. Most of the available land had to be devoted to food crops. This meant fewer forests to provide the lumber essential for housing, ships, and simple machinery. And it meant less land for growing the clothing fibers on which the West based its initial industrial takeoff. It also reduced the amount of grazing land on which the supply of draft animals depends; farmers were left to be the beasts of burden, and cheap transportation was restricted entirely to waterways.[218]

Intensive rice agriculture made possible a population growth that trapped China in a high-level equilibrium between human fertility and soil fertility. It had to wait for some other area of the world to show the way out and then catch up through deliberate, collective action on an enormous scale.

Russia was not trapped in a patrimonial box in the same way as China. To explain the Russian case, I depend on the provocative "world-system" model of Immanuel Wallerstein.[219] Let us begin with his distinction between "empire" and "world economy." The empire is primarily a political unit using primitive techniques of economic domination to guarantee an economic flow from periphery to center. Its techniques are primarily those of tribute and taxation supplemented by tradition monopolies. A world economy, however, is an economic unit within which the "core" states avoid the waste caused by the repressive, exploitive form of bureaucracy that typically runs an empire. Instead of running its economy as a single centralized enterprise, the capitalistic state fosters "terms of trade" that increase market incentives.

The world economy is an expanding multiple-state economy in which some states occupy a position "peripheral" to those in the "core" area. Towns, industries, and merchants all flourish in the core states where labor becomes free and specialized, agriculture intensive, the population relatively high in density, and the social system relatively noncoercive. Those states enrich their economies by draining entrepreneurial profits from the peripheries. In the peripheral states, on the other hand, a very labor-intensive mining and agricultural (usually monocultural) technology is organized under a coercive and labor-exploitive social system which provides the core area with necessary raw materials and food staples. This combination of a free, specialized core and an exploited, coercive periphery is essential to the capitalistic world economy. The entrepreneurial profits resulting from this asymmetrical system are shared between "groups in the core areas, international trading groups, and local supervisory personnel" in the peripheral areas including aristocrats, bureaucrats, and hacendados. It is Wallerstein's position that the modern world system originated during the 16th century as Western Europe became the core and Eastern Europe the periphery of a "European world economy." [220]

A state with patrimonial, empirelike characteristics that, through geographic position and historic accident, ends up in the peripheral area of a world economy is likely to be subjected to economic forces that will perpetuate its patrimonialism. In Wallerstein's involved historical explanation, Russia starts out attempting to create its own world economy but ends up peripheral to Western Europe. In his recent book (which appeared simultaneously with Wallerstein's), Richard Pipes's Russia seems to fit Wallerstein's "empire" just as well as China does. [221] This is a classificatory problem I do not wish to pursue here, however. The point I wish to make is simple: Wallerstein provides a useful and testable explanation of the political and economic forces that trapped Russia in a prolonged patrimonial type of social order. And, like China, Russia finally found it expedient to catch up to the First World through a massive mobilization of human capital. Both are catch-up eutopias. But the character of their eutopian endeavors was predetermined by the patrimonial quality of their precommunist social orders. They might also be called "catch-up patrimonial empires."

Mass mobilization of human capital is a logical eutopian game for a catch-up, patrimonial state. And it is only natural that the great mass of village peasants should seem to those in authority like a sheet of loose sand or a breeding ground for anarchy. The peasant village could no longer be left to its own customary devices; central authority had to take charge. The directing hand had to become the dominant principle of motion for all the pieces on the chessboard.

In Russia the Bolsheviks finally realized that neither the party nor the soviets were making headway in the rural areas; the village community had grown stronger, not weaker. Not only was collectivization in keeping with the taxation and tribute strategies of empire, it provided a comprehensive attack on customary law and the traditional village through total organization. The peasantry was forcibly recruited into a pervasive agricultural-and-industrial army run by the state. New production and administrative units were created that could compete more effectively with the traditional village and finally overwhelm it. A structure was created in which administrative law could directly confront customary law with virtually no contract law between. As various observers have noted, in communist Russia, as in communist China, contract is a part of central planning, and its sanctions are a way of disciplining the management of enterprises—all of which belong to government.[222]

In China, recruitment of the peasantry into total organization was more persuasive and less coercive than in Russia. And although by 1957 China had drawn up its own civil and criminal codes, these were pushed into the background during the Great Leap Forward. Law has been left mainly to local administration, and mediation is still the favorite way of settling disputes. Since civil, and especially contract, law was never highly developed in precommunist China, the legal profession was extremely small. It was not possible on short order to mass produce the number of legal specialists needed to administer law uniformly throughout such a vast population. Besides, the newer cadres objected to the Western ideas of the older legal specialists, who came under increasing attack after the Hundred Flowers campaign showed lawyers to be among the severest critics of the communist regime. Since the central government, moreover, could not control the way in which cadres at the lower levels administered the law, it has had to allow them considerable freedom to make their own interpretations and decisions, often in the light of local custom.[223] One wonders to what extent customary law has actually changed in rural China under the communists. Certainly administrative law has made considerable inroads simply as an adjunct of collectivization.

Some scholars believe the ancient distinction between *fa* and *li* still has a bearing on Chinese law even under communism. Fa is the legalist term for law as opposed to the Confucian term, li. The former is an administrative concept of law appropriate to empire conditions. A strong government, according to the legalist position, should publicize its laws and apply them equally to all members of society. This was not a law that bestowed "rights"; it was an objective or public law that would effectively control the population of an expanding empire.[224]

In the Confucian view, fa represented control by force and punishment, whereas li encouraged the natural good in people to dominate reciprocal relationships within the family, between friends, and between superiors and inferiors. Confucian law was a kind of codified, ideal form of customary law that served as a cushion between real customary behavior in the villages and the abstract public law of the empire. It prescribed ideal face-to-face relations spanning and linking the kin-dominated village and the patrimonial bureaucracy.[225] According to Balazs, Confucianism defended best the interests of the gentry, those in the middle between bureaucracy and family.[226]

It is said that Maoism preserved the traditional Chinese hostility to legalism by resisting codification and legal specialization. And in emphasizing morality and the internalization of rules of conduct, Maoism came close to Confucianism.[227] If the character of China's catch-up eutopianism was sometimes softer than Russia's, it is possible to find the roots of such a difference in China's own traditional brand of patrimonialism.

Maoism diverged farthest from Confucianism in its pervasive egalitarianism. In emphasizing proper reciprocal relations between superior and inferior, elder and younger, and noble and humble, Confucianism emphasized "status contract" relations characteristic of a hierarchical patrimonial order.[228] Ironically, in opposing this nonegalitarian aspect of China's past, Maoism retarded the transition from patrimonial to modern bureaucracy.

For Weber, the most efficient modern bureaucracy was a meritocratic type that added to technical knowledge through a high degree of specialization, and by recruiting and promoting its personnel on the basis of technical competence instead of the personal considerations that tended to dominate the patrimonial form.[229] Maoism, on the contrary, opposed technical competence as a criterion for advancement or differential reward and gave equal or greater weight to political criteria.[230] The ideal Maoist bureaucracy could become only a modernized, egalitarian version of the traditional patrimonial form. Commitment and dedication to the goals of the catch-up eutopia replaced personal loyalty to the emperor. But if Mao was the personification of the eutopian goals, the differences between old and new were small indeed.

At this point it is helpful to return once again to the example of the 17th-century American colonies with their Chinese-like antipathy for formal law and lawyers. They too emphasized layman participation in adjudication and lawmaking. And just as Chinese at the local and neighborhood level came to rely on Mao's little red book as a source of moral–legal guidance, American colonists relied on divine law revealed by Scripture as their "binding subsidiary law."[231] The significant difference is that the American participation was spontaneous. The American "pieces" were following a "principle of motion" residing within themselves. They were not put in motion by a vast cadre organization.

I do not make this comparison to belittle the Chinese accomplishment. Eighteenth-century conditions of pristine industrial development must be compared *to*, not *with*, 20th-century China. The catch-up, patrimonial empire must follow its own game plan. It should be obvious by now, however, that it cannot completely dictate the movement of the "pieces" any more than the primitive patrimonial empire could. It has had to depend, as we have seen, on differential wage scales and the materialism of increasing consumer-goods production. To enlist the principle of motion within the pieces themselves, this becomes inevitable.

According to Andrei Amalrik, a zero-sum view of living standards and material success is still endemic in the "Russian psyche."[232] Average Russians are more concerned with the probability that others are likely to gain at their expense than the possibility of improving their own position. Consequently Russians have a "destructive" sense of justice: "Nobody should live better than I do." They do not imitate the individual among them who excels or stands out; they make every effort to bring that person down to their level. This zero-sum view he blames most on the peasants and those of peasant background who often "find someone else's success more painful than their own failure." It is a behavior pattern he finds least typical of the "middle class," the class of educated specialists with higher than average income.

No doubt this behavior has its roots in the cyclical mobility patterns so characteristic of the Chinese as well as the Russian peasants. There, too, it produced an atmosphere of perpetual hostility and jealousy.[233] And there today it undoubtedly contributes to the extreme egalitarianism that has opposed every meritocratic advancement within the bureaucracy. It is a symptom of the early stages of catch-up patrimonialism and is a testimony to the fact that development has not yet produced a positive-sum view. That must await expansion of consumer-good production and the material incentive structure that goes with it. Whatever the West does to stimulate commercial interaction with the eutopian states should enhance the growth of internal positive-sum behavior and the principle of movement within the "pieces."

Hedrick Smith disagrees with this Western "notion" that trade "will soften the Soviet police state" and lead to greater liberty.[234] He thought so once, but after living in Russia for three years, he realized that the notion "naively ignores" history. The "accumulated weight of Russian history," Smith believes, makes "fundamental change" unlikely. He concludes in his final paragraph that Russians today are "the same people" as those who lived "under the czars." Yet the preponderance of data in his insightful and fact-filled book fairly shouts against such a Lamarckian conclusion.

Of course Russia is a product of her history. This is precisely why she fulfilled anarchist Bakunin's prophecy that a "red bureaucracy" would result in a statist despotism worse than that of the czars.[235] But the Bolshevik revolution is little more than half a century old and China's even less. Amana, Zoar and Economy lasted twice as long, and they were only tiny populations with relatively short histories. According to Robert Kaiser, Russians are only just now leaving the "era of poverty," for most still live close to the "subsistence level." [236]

As Smith himself shows, the Russian privileged class, which comes closest to enjoying a life style similar to that of our middle class, practices "discreet" rather than conspicuous consumption. They buy their goods at unmarked stores to which only they have access or buy in the "counter-economy" what only they can afford. And most of this consumption takes place behind a "curtain of privacy." Even Western films, forbidden to the general public, are shown privately to members of the privileged class by the Ministry of Culture. According to Smith, those Russians privileged to view them feel a special excitement in being able to enjoy what most of their countrymen are denied.[237]

Despite the distance traveled, the Russian masses are still living somewhere between Thomas More and Bernard Mandeville. More, as we saw in Chapter 7, found the privileged class of his day measuring its enjoyments "by others' wants." Mandeville, two hundred years later, described a conspicuous consumption that had become competitive all the way from the butcher's wife to the ladies at court. The zero-sum behavior of More's day was being transformed into the keeping-up-with-the-Joneses of ours. That the Russian masses are still closer to More's day is supported by Amalrik's contention that the zero-sum view of the world he attributes to peasant mentality still predominates. Although Russians are still behind the Yugoslavs, who are already "keeping up with the Jovanovičes," [238] this is no time to despair about the intransigence of their psyches. The Russian people are on the threshold of profound social changes. The seeming slowness of this development for those who impatiently await it, or those who have given up far too soon, is a subject to which I return in Chapter 10.

In any case, the fear that catch-up eutopias doom us all to *1984* has surely become quixotic. This was not George Orwell's view. In an analysis of Orwell's writings, William Steinhoff shows that the author of *1984* was basically an optimist.[239] Orwell had great faith in the future of mankind as long as the masses had a "chance to bring their innate decency into the control of affairs." Something of a humanistic socialist, he emphatically rejected the "myth" that the Soviet Union was a socialist country. He despised all forms of totalitarianism and was especially hostile to the tendency prevalent among intellectuals to endorse it. *1984* is not what we are coming to, it is a picture of what life is like when the predelictions of these intellectuals are carried to their logical conclusion. As he saw it, intellectuals want to make an untidy world more orderly by reducing it to "something resembling a chessboard." For many who call themselves socialists, revolution is not a mass movement to which they lend their services. It is, rather, "a set of reforms which 'we,' the clever ones, are going to impose upon 'them,' the Lower Orders." Thus, *1984* is not a prediction; it is an indictment of egotistical, power-hungry intellectuals and a warning to ordinary, decent men not to buy their utopian schemes.

But Orwell did his job too well. He provided a frightening picture of the existentialist's nightmare, and he hit the wrong target. He intensified the Western world's fear of totalitarian socialism or "communism," a fear that these social structures will diffuse to us. Actually Orwell once speculated in print that the Russian regime might eventually "become more liberal and less dangerous." [240] He was right. But unfortunately the pathological fear he helped stimulate only retards the liberalization process by keeping the catch-up state on the defensive. These eutopian modernizations of the patrimonial empire are not in our future; they are nowhere in the long-term future of mankind. *1984* is a hell which the people of many countries are still trying to outgrow. We can help them, or we can continue to fight and harass them whenever and wherever they try to play catch-up eutopianism.

Summary

Although the Communist Man (Millennial Man) ideal was a strong component of early Russian Bolshevism as well as Chinese Maoism, it has resisted practical application in both eutopias. Socialist Man has been an unavoidable compromise with reality, and rewards have become increasingly material and unequal. That this state of affairs can lead to the pursuit of individual advantage and to competitive consumption is recognized in both China and Russia. China, however, has pushed a fight-self ideology longer and harder than Russia by deliberately organizing and manipulating mass movements. China has worked harder and more successfully to promote total commitment and has even tried to create conditions of small-group predictability to support the eutopian objectives. But this simulation of the group game does not result in the authentic subject playing encountered in the communitarian examples of previous chapters.

Within the moral ecology of catch-up eutopianism this is not necessarily bad. It may have been the most expedient way to propel these huge societies out of their economic and social "traps" into the modern world. And as they make this transition, they seem to change in ways similar to the communitarian eutopias. Fight-self ideologies give way more and more to the individualistic and competitive pursuit of material rewards. The masses begin to turn from a group game manipulated by a guiding hand to one in which the principle of motion becomes increasingly their own. Materialism, then, tends to have the same liberating consequences in socialist eutopias that it has had in the West. Russians and Chinese belong to the same reciprocally altruistic species we do. Change is slow, but it can accelerate through the kinds of commercial and cultural interaction that open these eutopias to the external world. Opposing them can prolong patrimonialism by strengthening the guiding hand that moves the pieces on the board.

Large, state societies need much more than conditions of social predictability to effect eutopian changes. They also need conditions of legal predictability, which range between two distinct poles. At the so-called "lawless" extreme a centralized state expands public law, extending downward from the top. Private and contract law may exist only in "customary" village form under conditions of social predictability beyond direct manipulation by the state. At the "rule-of-law" extreme, private and contract law—growing out of conditions of social predictability—expand up and outward at the expense of public law. Catch-up eutopias, by recapitulating the centralist, asymmetrical organizations of the patrimonial states they replace, start off close to the "lawless" pole. In no way compatible with humanistic behaviorism, they provide living illustrations of what utopian behaviorism really implies. Such patrimonial states frighten us by claiming to portend our future when actually they are but desperate attempts to break out of a past to which their habits and institutions are still captive.

The catch-up eutopias portend neither our future nor their own; the West, in fact, is much closer than they to whatever future we may have in common. Such an "exploratory" judgment does not please the kind of intellectual so detested by the George Orwells and the Eric Hoffers. That kind of utopian always knows what is best for mankind. In his choice of games we all become mere pieces on the board and he the principle of motion.

Chapter Nine

Worker Management and Utopian Anarchy

IN OUR EXAMPLES of community and state eutopias, Homo ludens has been a team player. "Team" in this context implies working together for the collective good by the membership or population. When the eutopian community or state is under the pervasive influence of a social movement, the team is composed of subject players to the degree its members or citizens are sincerely committed to the movement. To the degree the social movement is not pervasive or to the degree the membership grows cynical, team play becomes less spontaneous and in the eutopian state more directed. In the latter case participants become object players.

Since the eutopian community is a part-society, its members can defect more easily than can the citizens of a eutopian state. Homo ludens therefore remains a subject player in the eutopian community even as commitment cools so long as he freely chooses to stay. Some observers believe the Hutterites are at least a partial exception to this open quality of the eutopian community since they deliberately reduce the chances for their young people to make a successful transition to the larger society. With only minimal formal education, young Hutterites cannot hope for more than unskilled jobs on the outside. The practice of "breaking" their children's will, moreover, tends to make them nonaggressive and puts them at a competitive disadvantage if they try to "make it" on their own. In this hidden-hand or conspiratorial explanation of Hutterite success, the adult generation effectively trims the "wings" of its children and makes it harder for them to leave the nest. Against this argument, however, is the fact that no young Hutterite attains full, official membership in the community until voluntarily willing to do so during a baptism ceremony considered the most important event in one's life. On this ritual occasion one publicly wills to exchange one's private will for the "common will of the group," and "great stress," says Deets, "is placed upon the autonomous character of [this] act of willing." [1]

To what extent Hutterites are subject players and to what extent they are object players guided by a hidden hand is an interesting empirical question. It is also an important legal question for the larger society. Should the state enforce the same educational requirements for Hutterite children as it does for other children? To Hutterite parents, such enforcement may seem like a totalitarian infringement upon Hutterite self-determination. But to some members of the external society, all children of the state need safeguards against any totalitarian indoctrination by parents that could limit a child's range of free choice in later life.

To the extent a eutopian state is a total society and defection difficult or impossible, Homo ludens must be a team player regardless of cynicism. When one's major alternatives are the forced labor camps of a Gulag Archipelago, reindoctrination in a Seventh of May school, incarceration in an insane asylum or even "death by shooting," one learns to play the game assigned. Homo ludens becomes an object player in the eutopian, progressive, catch-up society. With the expansion of a cadre bureaucracy one may even be manipulated in ways to make one's object playing simulate subject playing. "Spontaneous" participation can be contrived through directed mass movements and through small groups engineered to effect face-to-face social incentives. With its singleness of purpose the eutopian catch-up state opposes any other games that distract participants from its progressive goals. It may oppose traditional, festive forms of competitive status-seeking even more assiduously than the competitive consumption of modern industrial society. One form of game playing held over from pre-eutopian, agrarian-state days may be the competitive upward mobility of a meritocratic or pseudomeritocratic bureaucracy. But despite bureaucratic expansion, this game is restricted to an elite minority on which a strong fight-self ethic is superimposed—at least for a while—in keeping with the curtailment of other forms of individual competitiveness. In this sense, the team play of the eutopian state simulates the more voluntaristic, fight-self form of the eutopian community.

Most people would probably not choose to live in either of these two kinds of fight-self eutopias, and some of them have seen in Rousseau's notion of general will an Enlightenment version of modern fight-self totalitarianism. According to this view of Rousseau, the Lawgiver, or Legislator, of the *Social Contract* is a Mao-like figure who sets out to change human nature by making each individual a part of a larger whole. This figure performs for the *Social Contract*, says Maurice Cranston, what the tutor performs for *Emile*. In the end the individual either conforms to the general will or is, in Rousseau's words, "constrained to do so by the whole body" such that he is "forced to be free." [2]

There are others, however, who read quite a different meaning into Rousseau. For them, the lawgiver is more like a specialist, a person qualified by special experience, special training, and special ability to make the best moral assessment of a given situation. But final judgment, the act of legislation itself, must still be left up to the members of the "whole" social body. In the same chapter of the *Social Contract* in which he discusses the lawgiver, Rousseau makes this distinction clear. The best moral assessment should take the general will (the collective good) fully into account. But even those individuals best qualified to make our moral assessments are only mortal men, not gods. If allowed to make the judgments, in effect to legislate, they might be corrupted by special interest. They might pursue an individual or particular will rather than the general will. Judgments in the form of legislation must be made by the sovereign, ideally a general assembly of all the citizens. While their majority vote is by no means the same as the general will, it is the best insurance we have that laws will conform to the general will rather than to any particular will.[3] Rousseau is careful to point out that the general will of a subgroup or interest group is only a particular will within the larger society.[4]

According to Charles Sherover, some scholars view Rousseau as the "father of the theory of the positive state" because he wanted the state to actively promote the collective good (general will) through public education and the elimination of excessive inequalities of wealth and power.[5] This position is clearly taken in *Political Economy*, in which Rousseau states that responsible government will "accomplish" the general will by bringing "all the particular wills into conformity with it." It will make men "what there is need that they should be." [6] Such a view of good government would seem to fit the eutopian catch-up state very well. Through its one-party system contemporary communist China, for example, organizes, educates, and manipulates the masses to become what they should be—to conform to the general will as conceived by its guardians and to actively support it.

Rousseau, however, was something of a cultural relativist, for as Sherover points out, he posited no single utopian system of government.[7] Quite the contrary, he indicated that different circumstances might require different systems. This flexibility makes it possible to join Rousseau and Mill in relativistic context. The catch-up eutopian state needs more activist lawgivers than we do. Its guardians have to be strong lawgivers because of the huge gap between them and their illiterate peasant constituencies. Their assessments of long-term collective good cannot be quickly understood or appreciated by the masses. Yet these assessments must be acted upon rapidly if the nation is not to fall further and further behind the rest by falling deeper into its systemic trap. Perhaps we can agree with Mill that these states are fortunate indeed to have such guardians.

We can afford to be more generous toward the catch-up eutopia than we have been in the past. We can afford to recognize its need for stronger fight-self leadership. We do not have to bomb it, fight it, and harass it. The eutopian experiments of catch-up states unnecessarily threaten us when we view them as dystopian projections of *our* future instead of rationalized versions of *their* past.

The fight-self side of Rousseau lends itself to a more compassionate and tolerant view of catch-up eutopianism. But the other side of Rousseau, the fight-for-self side, is more appropriate to our own needs. The fight-for-self side emphasizes the need for each citizen to help keep moral assessments honest—although for the collective good rather than for vested interests. This requires active participation by an educated and informed citizenry in passing moral judgment through legislation. And if these judgments are to take proper cognizance of long-term consequences, education and communication are vitally important.

Long before Rousseau's day, states had grown much too large to be governed by town-meeting type assemblies. He therefore saw no hope for "true democracy" since it would be impossible for all citizens to meet in "perpetual assembly." For citizens to elect deputies to represent them was no solution, for the general will and sovereignty of the whole social body would soon be alienated. By responding to particular wills, representatives open the door to cheating and excessive inequality. States would have to be small enough for all citizens to participate in the enactment of legislation, which would make them vulnerable to larger predatory states. For their protection such "true" democratic communities would have to be joined together in some kind of confederacy (minimum state). In a footnote and the concluding paragraph Rousseau admitted that he had planned to end the *Social Contract* with a study of this subject but had given up when it proved "too vast" for his "weak vision." To go beyond the "range" of his competence would have been too utopian for Rousseau.[8]

In his *Anarchy, State, and Utopia* (1974) Robert Nozick has, in effect, provided just the kind of utopian, minimum-state "framework" that Rousseau was too modest to attempt.[9] Nozick's minimal-state utopia would be a smorgasbord of utopias. It would allow individuals to choose the way of life they find most satisfying by freely joining any one of an unlimited range of free-forming utopian communities. People would have the right to try different communities or to participate in forming new ones. And each community would have the right to impose any rules—including egalitarian redistribution of wealth—on its members as long as it had only a voluntary membership on which to impose them and as long as it did not try to force them on other communities.

As a philosopher, Nozick presents us with an elegant argument. The weakness of his utopian design lies in his anthropology, or more correctly, in his total lack of any. No one can fault his intent to provide individuals with a maximal range of self-determined choices within the minimal restrictions of a protective state. But the data of the preceding chapters have shown us that individuals in a modern, industrial state do not gravitate toward eutopian communities except as participants of temporary and relatively limited social movements. According to the computations of one student of intentional community movements, Harold Barclay, the number of such communities per million population is still less in today's community movement than it was during the early 19th-century movement. The current widespread interest in intentional communities does not in itself hold out much hope for an all-inclusive smorgasbord of same. To bring about such a situation, Nozick's minimal-state would have to be prescriptive; and once prescriptive it would no longer be minimal. Nor does Nozick concern himself with such potential problems as that of hidden-hand, indoctrinational totalitarianism, illustrated by our Hutterite example or by Skinner's utopian behaviorism.

With industrialization and modernization, Homo ludens expands the field of play, and the small community gives way to associations and corporate groups that are distinctly nonresidential in character. There is no convincing evidence yet that this trend is about to reverse itself. James S. Coleman has recently emphasized the historical importance of the "juristic person" or "corporate actor" as an instrument for greater individual freedom.[10] It offered an alternative to the hierarchical organization of medieval "corporate bodies."

As an organization of coequals the corporate actor made it possible for many men to act as one and be treated as one. When the medieval "social organism" began to break down, the modern corporation filled a "power void," says Coleman, between the increasing power of the state and the increasing freedom of the individual. Through the juristic person individuals found a power base as coequals to help insure the preservation of their freedoms against the increasingly powerful state. Moreover, as a bureaucratic structure, whose component parts were now positions rather than persons, the corporate actor freed natural persons from the organiclike bonds of previous corporate bodies. Natural persons became free to change membership or employment in corporate associations because their positions could be filled by other natural persons also free to associate by choice.[11]

Modern corporations, however, have grown enormously in size and number since their "invention." Today corporate actors wield enormous power, which has grown at the expense of the power, and in some cases the freedom, of natural persons. The utopian anarchist must now reckon with the modern corporation as well as the state. Perhaps some kind of utopian corporations that return power to natural persons would be more worthy of consideration than a Nozick-like smorgasbord of utopian communities. The former have already proved a more effective instrument than the small community or the organic corporate body as a power buffer between individuals and states.

The next section briefly reviews three major directions of utopian anarchism: anarcho-capitalism, anarcho-communism and anarcho-socialism or syndicalism. We then turn our attention to a recurring form of social experiment, collective farming, that illustrates why the corporate form is indispensable to a world in which legal predictability must supplement and often replace social predictability.

Utopian Anarchism

The classic example of anarcho-communism in utopian fiction is William Morris's *News From Nowhere* (1890).[12] Written as a counter-reaction to

Edward Bellamy's *Looking Backward*, it provides a futuristic picture of England early in the 21st century. Government has reverted to town-meeting type assemblies at the parish level; since central government and civil law had existed only to protect "the rich from the poor, the strong from the weak," both have become unnecessary in this new egalitarian world. Criminal law has disappeared along with crime since both had depended on the defense of private property usurped by the wealthy, privileged few.

All material and industrial progress ended late in the 20th century after strikes, lockouts, and a massacre of workers provoked revolution. Some advanced machines were retained to perform unpleasant tasks; but for all work more pleasurably done by hand, machinery was abandoned. The "age of inventions" ended, and people relearned handicrafts through an "instinctive," "spontaneous" revival of "work-pleasure." England decentralized as the population gradually moved back into country villages. Houses, clothes, towns, and craftware took on a 14th-century appearance and people adopted the "clean," "orderly," "trim" habits of medieval times. Ugly iron bridges were rebuilt in "handsome" stone and oak, and parts of London once choked with slums and factories were now covered with wild and beautiful forests.[13] In Morris we find one of the earliest examples of what Victor Ferkiss had recently called the "ecoanarchist." [14]

Money is a quaint relic found only in museums. When the visitor to this utopia goes into a store to buy a pipe and tobacco, they are handed over free. Some people grow tobacco, some carve pipes, and some operate stores. All productive, distributive, and service activities are carried on as a public good without any individual rewards but the pleasure of work. Just the right amount of everything needed is provided even without money or barter to regulate supply and demand. Since Morris's utopia is not a market economy, it is not the product of an invisible hand; it operates like a command economy but without either a directing or hidden hand to run it.[15]

Corvée labor on roads, bridges, or in the fields is done in a festive atmosphere. People who do not show up to do their share are not free riders; they are simply persons who decided to perform some other useful chore instead. Enough people are always present to complete the necessary work.[16] In this egalitarian society where labor is no longer coercive and exploitive, the natural goodness of humanity at last breaks through to dominate all social and economic relations. All problems are solved, work becomes a joy, and everyone lives in a harmonious social paradise in which individuality is expressed through arts and crafts. This society is obviously the product of a noble ideal—the author's. But since all the players conform to his purpose through fictional license, the society is utopian in the most pejorative sense. According to H. G. Wells, such an "Olympian" utopia could only have been imagined by an "irresponsible rich man ... playing at life" while living off stock dividends.[17] Art for fun is one thing, but "digging potatoes" to keep from starving is quite another.

The most famous advocate of "anarchist communism" was Prince Peter Kropotkin, a Russian nobleman and revolutionary who spent most of his last

40 years of life (roughly 1880 to 1920) writing from exile in England. Although a friend and admirer of William Morris, he differed from him in being a firm believer in progress and labor-saving machinery.[18] Like Rousseau, he was not opposed to material progress as long as it was secondary to moral progress. Kropotkin, however, saw no similarities between himself and Rousseau, for true to his time, he labeled Rousseau's view of primitive life an exaggerated, "unscientific . . . idealization."[19] But as we saw in Chapter 3, Rousseau clearly disclaimed any historical accuracy for his "model" of the primitive condition. Kropotkin, on the other hand, was an evolutionist who considered his own version of primitive communism an historical link between animal social organization and humanity's anarchistic future. He also differed from Rousseau in espousing complete equality. For anarchistic society to be successful, its citizens would have to live in close contact and take a "lively interest" in one another. Such a society could be large enough to defend itself only if the "free federation" of independent communities of which it was comprised achieved complete equality through communism—through rewarding labor according to need rather than work.[20] Thus, community anarchism would succeed only if joined with communism. Martin Buber, as we saw in Chapter 6, came to this same mistaken conclusion half a century later.

Darwin, according to Kropotkin, emphasized the competitive aspects of natural selection especially among individuals of the same group without nearly the "wealth" of documentation he had employed to support other assumptions. On the contrary, argues Kropotkin, natural selection avoids competition, for the "fittest" species are the most sociable ones.[21] He then marshals his evidence for mutual aid among primitives and "barbarians" and for survivals of such proclivities "among ourselves." The most reliable data in his *Mutual Aid* consist of various examples of what we discussed above as group land tenure, exchange and festive labor, and corvée labor. At best, however, his data are highly superficial, and as George Woodcock has pointed out, he avoids discussing the "tyranny of custom," endemic to small communities.[22] In other words his data lack the depth to illustrate the highly negative side of most selective incentives used by primitives and peasants to control free riders. Ironically, his treatment of primitive sociability is more strongly skewed toward romanticism than Rousseau's. Those who still use "Rousseauean" as a pejorative adjective to indicate the romanticization of primitive or peasant life would be more correct to substitute the word "Kropotkian."

There is even a Maoist flavor to much of Kropotkin's writing. In addition to his preference for rewarding according to need rather than work,[23] he wanted to alternate mental and manual labor and combine industry and agriculture at the village level to achieve regional self-sufficiency and decentralization.[24] And because written law was created only to protect private property and to keep workers subordinate to employers, he advocated a return to village customary law and mediation. He repeatedly associated the rise of written law with the usurpation of power by "landlords," "warriors," "priests," "bullies," and "rulers." Yet he also said that written law and capitalism developed together. For Kropotkin, the law that established the authority of the imperialist state over its subjects was no different from the law that protected the bourgeois capitalist and the juristic person from the monarch. "Millions of transactions," he argued, are carried on everyday "without interference by government." For Kropotkin, a "feeling of honor" and the importance of keeping one's word were enough to bind a contract and make "trade possible." [25]

Because he did not emphasize the behavioral reinforcements of selective social incentives and because he never made clear distinctions between learned and "instinctive" behavior in his treatment of the evolution of sociability among animals and people, Kropotkin's view of human nature seems much like Morris's. Examples of ant, bird, and human behavior are treated so similarly that the propensity for mutual aid and sociability seems closer to what we previously called nonreciprocal altruism than to any learned reciprocal form. He also drifts toward mentalism in reference to the "feelings of solidarity" in the "morality" that links our evolution to that of the social animals. In any case, this propensity that developed through natural selection provides a causal engine absent from Morris's utopian anarchism. Although Kropotkin's anarcho-communism also lacks any invisible, hidden or directing hand, it promises to be the evolutionary culmination of the better side to human nature. The causal teleology is therefore finalistic and illegitimate; its locus is in a self-directed evolutionary process whose goal is Kropotkin's utopia. We are all urged to give the process a helping hand, which in the absence of any power to direct it would have to be a receptive frame of mind so general as to constitute a universal consensus.

Alexander Berkman struggled hard with the anarchist problem of achieving universal consensus in his *ABC of Communist Anarchism* (1929).[26] Kropotkin and Berkman were both greatly disillusioned by the Bolshevik dictatorship; but Kropotkin died in 1921, and it was left to Berkman to write a definitive manual on anarcho-communism that would take into account the Bolshevik usurpation of the Russian revolution.

The first half of Berkman's book is one of the most unambiguous, "hidden-hand" explanations of capitalism ever written. The entire capitalist system is a giant conspiracy to rob the workers of the profits of their labor. Unemployment is a deliberate policy to keep a ready supply of strikebreakers on hand, a "whip" to threaten the workers; and wars are deliberately instigated by the quest for profits. Meanwhile, church, school, and even unions work on the side of the capitalist masters to keep labor contented with the system. The government and all law-making agencies continually serve the interests of capitalism and come to its aid against any social or ideological threat.

Three conditions favor the anarchists, who want to change all this. First, all the real power is in the hands of the people; they simply do not realize it. Neither capitalism nor the government and laws supporting it could last a day if people stopped believing in them. Second, evolution is on the side of the anarchist, as Kropotkin showed in his *Mutual Aid*. The whole trend of society's development is inevitably toward "brotherhood" and "good will." Third, revolution is the "boiling point" of evolution when underlying economic and political problems create pressure for radical changes in ideology. Through the use of the general strike, the masses achieve ideological consensus and assert their real power; even the most modern army must bend to their will. Once free, the workers run all their "shops and factories" through special committees, and all goods produced are distributed according to need rather than work, thus preserving complete equality.[27]

There are two problems with this paradigm as Berkman sees it. First, revolutions are likely to appear where they are not expected. Russia, for example, had the revolution that the United States was supposed to have. Berkman has no overt solution to this problem, but the activist role of the anarchist seems to be to educate masses everywhere as he is doing with his "ABC" manual. Second, the Russian revolution showed that a political party of dedicated conspirators can enlist the support of the masses initially through an anarchistic ideology that endorses expropriation and advocates "all power to the soviets" (local groups). But once it gains control, this same party can establish a personal dictatorship that suppresses individual freedoms even more than the previous czar or capitalist conspirators did. In short, revolution may replace a hidden-hand despotism with a directing-hand despotism (state capitalism) that is worse. What can anarchists do to prevent this subversion of the true evolution-revolution process?

According to Berkman the principle of the soviet—"equal rights and representation of all members alike"—was an anarchist idea with a long history in Russia, and one of its most notable expressions was the village public assembly, or mir.[28] So strong was this ideology that the Bolsheviks could not fight the soviets head on. They had to infiltrate them to gain control. Berkman wrote the *ABC of Communist Anarchism* before the full thrust of Russian collectivization. He did not know then that when the Bolsheviks failed to gain control of the village gatherings, they would smash them head on through a complete reorganization of the countryside. As we saw in Chapter 8, there was indeed a kind of peasant anarchism prior to collectivization, in part because it involved no effective peasant organization above the village level. This lack of organization makes peasant "anarchism" highly vulnerable to manipulation and even to ruthless coercion.

In fairness to Berkman, he is not primarily interested in peasant or village anarchism. He dutifully follows Kropotkin in a few brief remarks on eventual decentralization with increasing regional independence. But the major thrust of Berkman's response to the Bolshevik type of challenge is a call for organization beyond the local level. Moreover, the local units that occupy his attention are not communities but worker associations: "shop and factory committees," "labor councils," "workers' committees," "workers' councils," and "house committees." These various voluntary associations for production and distribution are organized by district, region, and state and are federated nationally. Yet this hierarchical organization does not constitute a government or state for Berkman because it develops "from the bottom up" in free, "libertarian" unions of "equal parts." [29]

This brings us back to the whole problem of consensus. The anarcho-communists need some kind of organization to protect against takeover by a directing-hand state. They want at least the degree of individual participation characteristic of the invisible hand but without the market mechanism. Moreover, they want a predictable, directed outcome. In short, the legitimate teleological components of the invisible hand, individuals, must achieve a unity of purpose that achieves the productive, distributive and self-protective consequences of a directing-hand without the state. Berkman mentions the "idealism," "heroic self-sacrifice," and "deep-felt brotherhood" that "must be roused by the social revolution." [30] Thus, a social movement must awaken underlying "instinctive" qualities of nonreciprocal altruism so that they become universally active within the population. Berkman's consensus ends up as utopian as Kropotkin's.

As we have seen in the case of communist China, mass revolutionary movements are best sustained by the directing hand of a strong state. In Berkman we not only find the same Maoist characteristics noted for Kropotkin but several others resulting from his negative reaction to Bolshevism: federating all units through a hierarchy of face-to-face groups, preparing the masses where possible prior to revolution, making the masses feel they are full participants in the revolutionary process, treating counter-revolutionaries humanely, arming workers and peasants to resist invasion, keeping "great moral principles" before the masses at all times, and combatting shirkers through the negative incentives of small-group social control.[31] In short, nearly all the characteristics of Berkman's anarcho-communism are found in Maoism; but to the extent they are part of the mass behavior of communist China, they are also the product of the strongest centralized state China has ever known.

Berkman's emphasis on worker associations rather than communities has a syndicalist flavor. Through him anarcho-communism overlaps to some extent on anarcho-socialism. Anarcho-capitalism may overlap on either of these to the extent it emphasizes decentralization into small communities or increasing control by workers of productive property. The criterion for distinguishing among the three is the system of rewards—whether they are distributed according to need, work, or capital.

Although to some readers H. G. Wells' *A Modern Utopia* (1905) has seemed socialistic, it is actually a classic anarcho-capitalist utopia in many important respects.[32] Wells does not claim to be an anarchist because he believes some planning would be necessary to initiate a utopian society; it could not come about by accident. Nevertheless he creates conditions for a minimal-state in several ways. First, since his utopia is a world-state that includes the entire planet, it is spared the problems of defense and aggression so prevalent under nationalism. Second, although the state owns all land and most natural resources, it leaves control over these as well as public services to local government. Third, much of the governing is left to a voluntary nonhereditary "nobility," deliberately patterned on Plato's guardians. They are people of exceptional ability who do not engage in the pursuit of profit or wealth. Like Plato's guardians they put the public good ahead of their own private interest, but unlike them they allow individuals in the private sector complete freedom to experiment and initiate progressive changes particularly in science, technology, and labor-saving machinery.

This emphasis on private initiative and enterprise as the engine of progress is strongly capitalistic and individualistic. Wells considers money essential to progress; no other "device," in his opinion, combines such strong incentives to achieve with such great freedom of action. In short, he considers money the best positive selective incentive ever devised. No society worthy of being called a "civilization" could exist without it, and within his utopia "to be moneyless will be clear evidence" of an individual's "unworthiness." [33]

Wells is trying to devise a game in which "individual freedom" achieves a "universal maximum" under conditions which generate technological progress through individual enterprise. Individuals can accumulate as much wealth during their lifetimes as their ambition and ability permit, but upon their death their productive properties, including stock shares, are sold by the state. This prevents wealth accumulations that would give some players too great an hereditary advantage over others. Similarly, all finite forms of wealth such as land and natural resources are owned by the state (though controlled and leased by local government); for in these areas one individual's accumulation of wealth vis-à-vis other players is zero sum rather than positive sum (creative and progressive). Finally, to discourage "safe investment" and to maximize the creative, progressive dynamic of the positive-sum game, the state assures each citizen that in the event of an untimely death one's dependents will be properly educated and cared for, and that in the event of severe financial loss a citizen will still receive a generous income in old age. Without such worries to inhibit them, people are more likely to become innovative, risk-taking players.[34]

Wells allows his world-state to interfere in people's lives only enough to intensify the participation of subject players while keeping object players to a minimum. He cannot decentralize government completely because an important dimension of freedom in this utopia is its unlimited spatial mobility. Its mobile, heterogeneous population would not lend itself to Nozick's smorgasbord of communitarian utopias.[35]

To avowed anarcho-capitalists like David Friedman, Wells's utopia must seem just another harebrained product of Fabian socialism.[36] It allows government to do too many things. And minimal as its government might seem to some, it is nevertheless guided by a special class of nonreciprocal altruists—the most romantically utopian aspect of Wells's design. Friedman would not rely on any social-security system to help increase risk-taking; he would leave social security to private charity. There would be no restrictions on ownership of property nor on the inheritance of wealth. Schools would operate on free market principles; and through the voluntary individual purchase of private protection services, police and courts and law would all be thrown "on the market." If some people, however, wanted to establish "virtuous societies" with their own laws and social-security programs, they would be free to set up separate communities as long as they had no right to force their way of life on their neighbors. Unlike Nozick, he obviously does not expect significant numbers of people to take the communitarian route.

Except for such communities everything is accomplished by private enterprise in Friedman's anarcho-capitalist utopia because government, by his definition, is nothing but "an agency of legitimized coercion." Moreover, according to Friedman's law, "it costs any government twice as much as it should to do anything." Government, therefore, has "no proper functions" whatsoever. The only reason people give it functions is because they mistakenly believe it necessary to do so. Here Friedman parallels Berkman, and true to similar anarchist principles he would "educate" people toward his utopia through writing books and giving public lectures rather than force anyone to accept it.[37] It is impossible to do justice to Friedman's arguments in so brief a sketch.

Anarcho-capitalists like Friedman do not view large private corporations as a threat. There is an optimum size for any type of business organization; and once that optimum is surpassed, the organization is made increasingly vulnerable to competition through its own internal inefficiencies.[38] Government organizations such as the United States Post Office are exceptions because they are protected from competition. But while the inefficiencies of the post office are dramatized by its inability to earn as much as it spends, many government agencies are not in a position to charge consumers for their services even on a monopoly basis. This leads to the useful dichotomy between businesses and public-service institutions made by Peter Drucker in his book, *Management*.

The purpose of business, says Drucker, is to "supply the wants and needs of a consumer." To speak of the "profit motive" of business is to mistake its "test of performance" for its purpose. The profit of a business is simply a measure of its effectiveness in performing its purpose of meeting customer needs. If it does not satisfy customers, it does not get paid. The operation of a business is thus tied to customer response through the feedback or self-regulatory effects of its profits.[39]

The public-service institution, unlike a business, has no such self-regulatory test of performance. Typically paid by means of budget allocations, it learns to measure success by the size of its budget and staff. Since public-service institutions have become the fastest-growing sector of modern society, there is urgent need to subject them to performance standards. Free of the test of market competition, such institutions, according to Drucker, tend to become bureaucracies in a pejorative sense—that of institutions run chiefly for the convenience of their managers and employees. Drucker believes the objectives of public-service institutions must be rigorously defined so that effective performance measures can be applied. Such institutions should have managerial autonomy and be exposed, where possible, to sufficient consumer choice and competition to maintain performance standards.[40] Unfortunately, however, when an institution does not have to create customers, its perception of customer needs is more likely to conform to its own convenience than to market reality. The institution becomes a directing hand, Friedman's "legitimized coercion," instead of an instrument of the invisible hand. For this reason the anarcho-capitalist would prefer to transform all "public-service institutions" into "businesses."

James S. Coleman's "corporate actor" includes both business and Drucker's public-service institution.[41] Coleman, however, sees growth for growth's sake as a dominant characteristic of all corporate actors or "juristic persons," although he agrees that those subject to highly competitive market conditions are less likely to be alienated from the needs and goals of natural persons than those which are not. The latter type of organizations should be broken down into coalitions of countervailing corporate actors within the larger corporate whole.

E. F. Schumacher is strongly opposed to growth for growth's sake, though he does not want to forsake all entrepreneurial freedom and creativity.[42] He also sees an advantage to breaking large organizations down into semiautonomous units to allow for greater entrepreneurial freedom and greater response to profit tests of consumer satisfaction. However, the profit index of success too narrowly restricts the focus of private enterprise. Consequently, private enterprise gives far less consideration to conservation than it does to limitless economic growth. At this point Schumacher comes much closer to ecoanarchism than to anarcho-capitalism. To maximize the decentralization of decision making in corporate enterprise, he would place half the ownership shares of each company in the hands of the local government where the industry resides. This would force enterprise management to be more responsive to the broader public interest.

Schumacher also favors employee ownership of enterprises, an idea that is currently gaining increasing attention due, in part, to Louis Kelso's "Employee Stock Ownership Plans" (ESOP).[43] The United States Tax Reduction Act of 1975 provided a tax incentive (economist Paul Samuelson calls it "another tax loophole") to encourage the spread of worker ownership in the United States. While this scheme would increase worker participation in ownership, it would not necessarily lead to greater worker participation in management as it has in those few cases in which small industries have actually been purchased by their employees.

David Friedman, our model anarcho-capitalist, has no objections to worker-owned enterprises.[44] In a capitalist society, workers have as much right as anyone to buy the stocks of the company that employs them. And Friedman sees no financial reasons why they could not obtain the capital to do so. The fact, therefore, that very few corporations are owned by their employees may indicate that, for some reason, this type of organization is not as successful or feasible as the more conventional kind.

Enthusiasm for worker-owned and -managed enterprises is nothing new. In the 1852 edition of his *Principles of Political Economy,* John Stuart Mill described various instances of worker-owned industries in Europe and concluded that "if mankind continues to improve," this "form of association," in which the workers collectively own the capital and work under the management they elect, will eventually "predominate." [45]

There were innumerable experiments in worker-owned industries during the second half of the 19th century, but they certainly did not live up to Mill's expectations. Most failed, and the few that survived usually changed into conventional joint-stock companies. Fred Boggis has recorded the major reasons for their high rate of failure.[46] Worker insubordination was one big problem, and corrupt management another. Workers tended to quarrel with their elected managers and begrudged them their higher pay. Workers wanted to become "their own masters," but at the same time wanted to increase their income while decreasing their effort. All quickly tired of going to the endless meetings where group decision making turned into group arguments. In most cases, too, workers were simply not sophisticated enough to understand accounting systems and marketing arrangements. In cases in which the manager was more sophisticated than the other workers and they grew dependent, the manager might pawn the enterprise's assets without their knowledge and disappear with the cash.

In those rare instances in which worker or production cooperatives are successful, as Paul Blumberg points out, they tend to "degenerate" into profit-seeking enterprises that close off their memberships.[47] Members turn into partners or shareholders who begin hiring whatever additional labor they need. Max Weber found this process operating as far back as the Middle Ages among production cooperatives of German mineworkers.[48] Members set themselves up as co-owners who began employing new workers instead of admitting them as members with equal shares. Paul Bernstein has recently noted the same process for the famous worker-owned plywood factories of Oregon.[49]

Despite such lessons of the past, there are many utopians who still believe it possible to make worker-owned and worker-managed enterprises successful on a world wide scale. It is at this point that the highly decentralist versions of anarcho-communism and anarcho-capitalism converge with anarcho-socialism. This last, at least for purposes here, is indistinguishable from anarcho-syndicalism. Workers are limited to some kind of use rights to the productive capital of their enterprise which prevents them from being labeled "capitalists"; but since they pay themselves according to work rather than need, they are not "communists" either.

The classic fictional utopia which comes closest to anarcho-socialism is Theodor Hertzka's *Freeland* (1890).[50] Hertzka wanted to eliminate what Marxists call "unearned" income of interest and rent, while preserving the entrepreneurial function of capital. Each enterprise in Freeland is controlled by its workers' association, all members of which have equal right to the productive capital of the enterprise, regardless of seniority. New members have the same rights in this regard as founding members.

A group of workers with a good idea for a profitable enterprise act like a single entrepreneur. They form a workers' association and go to Freeland's bank for loan capital. Once the business is established, the workers' association pays back the loan out of profits. The bank builds up its supply of loan capital through taxes on the net income of all Freeland workers' associations—in other words all Freeland enterprises.[51]

Each enterprise is managed by a directorate elected by the workers' association from its own membership. The highest authority, however, is the general meeting of the association. Freeland itself is governed by 30 "specialist parliaments" that allow inhabitants to focus their political activities in the areas of their greatest competence.[52]

Most of the "dirty" jobs in Freeland are done by "ingenious" machines, since this is a highly progressive, industrial society. But all unpleasant jobs which must be done by human labor are performed by a workers' association that has built a profitable and satisfying enterprise on this social need. However, all pollution of air and water have been, or are soon to be, eliminated.[53]

Workers share in the profits of their enterprises on the basis of work, not need. One measure of work is labor time, but the labor day of one worker may be more valuable than the labor day of another worker since income varies with ability, experience, and responsibility. A plant director may be credited with 24 hours of work for every 8-hour day logged by a manual laborer. During Freeland's early years, income differentials went as high as 6 to 1; but with rising affluence, incomes at the bottom rose to the point where top incomes were only 2 or 3 times the average earning of manual laborers. The citizens of Freeland do not believe that all are born equal and therefore do not reward equally. But they do believe in equal "rights" and opportunities. Everyone gets a good basic education, and those who go on for further specialization do so on merit alone. However, the combination of equal rights, industrial progress, and increasing wealth eventually produce a general "leveling off" of income with relatively small differentials.[54]

No productive property can be owned privately, but all own personal property including their homes. The owner of a house has only usufruct rights to the land on which it is built though the heir to the personal property is heir to this right as well. As in so many of the utopias we have examined, Freeland needs no judges, police, courts, or formal law. Given full employment without any private ownership of productive property, the country is free of all theft, robbery, and murder. Anyone incapable of work, moreover, is provided with a decent standard of living by the Freeland bank. Yet there are no free riders here, for the natural good in humanity achieves its full development. Freelanders live well but do not indulge in frivolous competitive consumption. Like modern kibbutzniks, they prefer to spend on travel. Anyone who bought diamonds, for example, would be treated with the same compassion as the mentally retarded.[55]

Factories

When we turn to real-world tests of anarcho-syndicalism, we are hampered by the inadequacy and inconclusiveness of most of the relevant data. The period of anarchist "control" in parts of Spain during 1936 has been considered evidence by some of the feasibility of spontaneous worker-managed factories and peasant-run collective farms. In Barcelona from July through October, factories and public services operated under worker management with what some observers considered "surprising" success. In some rural areas, meanwhile, extensive collectivization of agriculture is thought to have taken place. This was a period of revolution and the kind of social-movement conditions when extraordinary things can happen. But because Franco's troops won the war, these experiments did not last long enough to prove their feasibility under normal circumstances. Since contemporary descriptions of the events were journalistic reports, not intensive field studies, no one really knows how "efficiently" the factories operated. And as George Woodcock has pointed out, no one knows to what extent peasant participation in the farm collectives was a product of local coercion or just how successfully the collectives operated.[56]

Another famous experiment, now more than a quarter of a century old, is the Yugoslavian "self-management" program. To avoid Stalinist statism, on the one hand, without succumbing to capitalist exploitation, on the other, industry was nominally put under the control of local government and the workers themselves. The instrument of worker control in each plant is the workers' council, which supposedly has all formal power and makes all vital decisions including appointment of managers, hiring and firing, establishing salary scales, and long-term planning. Studies by outsiders, now acknowledged and confirmed by Yugoslav scholars as well, have shown that, in practice, power is still at the top of the Yugoslav factory organization. Sturmthal found that some very small factories were close to the democratic ideal because all the workers were members of the council, but such cases were exceptional.[57] However, Bucar claims that Yugoslav firms are generally smaller in scale than in the West, which helps to make self-management seem more practical there than it could ever be under fully developed, modern industrial conditions.[58]

But those who have had an opportunity to look closely at Yugoslav firms agree that management makes the important decisions. The crucial dividing line in plant membership is between that 65 percent falling in the unskilled and semiskilled categories and the remaining 35 percent comprised of management, white-collar employees, and skilled workers. A disproportionate number of worker-council members come from the second group, and these are the members who are most likely to participate at worker-council meetings. They are also the ones most apt to understand the more complex problems and decisions facing management, particularly those of a long-term nature. In any case, the worker council ends up accepting those measures in which management is interested. The bulk of the workers, who make up the first group, are poorly educated and unable to follow technical discussions. Most of them think of themselves as wage laborers, do not feel the factory is theirs, and are ready to take a better job somewhere else at the first opportunity.[59]

Most of the workers, then, remain primarily short-term oriented toward increases in wages and are least likely to be interested in long-term investment and modernization goals. Even if the enterprise does well, workers may oppose expansion of the labor force because it will mean sharing the growing income with others. The rank and file in large Yugoslav plants tend to be much the same as their counterparts in large industrial organizations everywhere. They are more interested in their pay packets than in managerial problems.[60] Descriptions of worker-council meetings by Kolaja and Jenkins resemble C. Northecote Parkinson's illustration of the "Law of Triviality," that "the time spent on any item of the agenda will be in inverse proportion to the sum involved." [61] With less than five minutes of discussion a board approves a $1 million development plan which no one but the director understands. But the next item on the agenda, the office water cooler, is a $50 expense that engages the entire board in acrimonious debate for over an hour.

Kolaja and others feel that the worker councils have opened up channels of communication between management and workers and thereby perform important educational and informative functions.[62] But as Adizes says, there are limits to the educational benefits of self-management.[63] Kolaja thinks the participation and interest of workers would be far more intense if they had a genuine organization of their own, but the labor unions have become financially dependent on the councils, which also overlap on the personnel and social-agency functions of the unions.[64] Emery and Thorsrud agree with Sturmthal that strong unions would protect worker interests better than weak representation within management.[65] And on the basis of his own studies, Zupanov is convinced that Yugoslav employees are unwilling to assume responsibilities beyond the limits of their own jobs, and that effective worker participation will have to take the form of "strong," "autonomous" labor unions.[66]

Recent students of Yugoslav self-management have emphasized the effects of market forces on the decentralized socialist economy. Zupanov feels the distribution of executive power is no different in Yugoslav than in American firms, and that in the long run the emphasis on a market economy has had the effect of reducing worker participation and of increasing executive power.[67] Organization executives were not assigned their present entrepreneurial role by the formal structure; they appropriated it themselves because under competitive market pressures someone had to and they were best prepared. Hunnius complains of the "enterprise particularism" produced by market competition.[68] Characterized by a "profiteer mentality," it leads all to concern themselves primarily with monetary benefits. Similarly, Wachtel refers to an increasing "efficiency fetishism" that has accelerated the power and status of experts and technicians "at the expense of blue-collar workers." [69] In his opinion, the growing contradiction between the collectivist spirit and the individual pursuit of material rewards has become the greatest threat to "participatory socialism" in Yugoslavia.

Adizes found Yugoslav executives under double pressure as the result of decentralization.[70] First, they now have to demonstrate their managerial competence independently of their political connections. Requests for investment funds, for example, have to be submitted to banks instead of government planning agencies, which means they have to be supported by impressive performance records. Banks can demand the replacement of incompetent executives before making a loan.

In addition to these competitive market pressures to demonstrate efficiency and profitability, executives in many cases have to put up with worker-council interference as well, since they can no longer act as autocratically as when they counted on political support. Some company directors quit, and others develop "dysfunctional" syndromes such as apathy. In other cases effective directors who know their own worth threaten to resign unless their worker councils give them the authority and free hand they need. Even more dramatic was Adizes's discovery of a new movement toward what he calls "contractual management." A management expert, for example, may approach a plant in financial difficulties, perhaps even on the verge of bankruptcy, and offer to correct the situation if the workers' council will meet the expert's conditions for unencumbered authority. As a consequence of all these forces, individuals with degrees, specialized knowledge, and expertise are gaining status as that of the participative system declines. By comparing their wages with those of comparable personnel in other factories, moreover, workers are able to appraise the effectiveness of their executives and to see the importance of competent authority. The drudgery of attending meetings, which constantly conflict with family life, is also making worker-council membership increasingly unattractive.[71]

The trouble with a Freeland-type utopia is that it combines competitive market socialism with worker self-management. That the members of each enterprise or "workers' association" will work together harmoniously and democratically is assumed because the success of the enterprise will depend on it, and because all members will be able to measure that success through their pocketbooks. But the Yugoslav-type eutopia shows us that under competitive market pressure an effective "workers' " enterprise must develop a strong vertical structure to achieve entrepreneurial flexibility. And pocketbook sensitivity under these conditions is more likely to produce worker acquiescence to authority than to enhance participative decision making.

According to Peter Westerlind, even kibbutzim make no "pretense that their industrial enterprises are 'democratically' led." [72] Some even hire experienced managers who are not members and give them authority similar to that described by Adizes for Yugoslav contractual management. The worker-owned plywood factories of Oregon also hire their general managers "from outside the firm" because the relative success of these firms, says Bernstein, depends in large measure on the business ability of their managers.[73] Within the membership of a worker-owned enterprise that ability can, indeed, be in short supply. Moreover, one of the severest tests of this ability in the Oregon examples is the degree to which the manager can persuade his worker-owners to pursue their long-term interests as owners against their short-term interests as wage earners. The nature of the (softwood) plywood industry, however, obviates any need for authoritarian management. Enterprise units are small (50 to 450 workers) and labor intensive with relatively low levels of capital and a rather narrow range of skills, a worker-owner environment that tends to be egalitarian as well as highly visible to all. In this environment strong group pressures make free riders feel like they are "stealing from the others."

In their comparative study of industrial organizations in five countries, Tannenbaum and his collaborators found that all systems, regardless of country, showed some "hierarchical effect." [74] In other words all the plants had vertical structures, and the higher the position of any member in that structure the greater his authority and influence were likely to be. This proved true of the highly participative kibbutzim and Yugoslav plants as well as the less participative plants in the United States, Austria, and Italy. Mass production and plant expansion result in a universal "logic of the machine"; authority increases at the top of the structure, and repetitive, specialized jobs increase at the bottom. While formal participative systems can give lower-echelon members more influence, those systems never result in equal distribution of power.

Tannenbaum rejects, however, the extreme view of hierarchical universalism represented by Michels's "iron law of oligarchy." According to this view, an exploitive elite inevitably develops in any organization because leaders tend to appropriate a disproportionate share of rewards which they then protect by restricting advancement into their privileged group. The kibbutzim plants are his major reason for rejecting this "law," because they function efficiently without any stratification of material rewards and social prestige. Social approval may go to specific persons for displaying effective leadership, but no one gets prestige just by occupying a position.[75]

There may be good reasons to question the iron law of oligarchy, but the kibbutz is not one of them; for a social-science "law" can certainly be no more than a probability statement. Because a communitarian experiment like the kibbutz, as we have seen, tests the very limits of collective behavior, it is an improbable phenomenon at best, and, therefore, a poor source of data for challenging a probable "law." Moreover, the comparative data collected by Tannenbaum and his associates were questionnaire responses; for social data he relied on other sources. His claim, for example, that the highly participative kibbutz factories are as efficient as their nonparticipative American counterparts is based on an earlier study in Israel by Seymour Melman. But Melman excluded from his sample any kibbutz enterprises relying substantially on hired labor.[76] This limited him to relatively small, face-to-face factory groups comprised of fellow commune members with the high degree of commitment characteristic of their unusual movement.

Although the United States, Italian, Austrian, and Yugoslav plants were selected to match the limited industrial types available in the kibbutzim, Tannenbaum is not totally oblivious to the distortions made possible by such procedures.[77] He admits that the kibbutz factory may not be "*the* model of socialism" although many of its features fit socialist "conditions." Its small size, he feels, probably helps account for the success of its highly participative organization. Large organizations, on the other hand, are affected by complex technological and administrative conditions that level out ideological and cultural differences and thereby tend to produce a more "universal rationality."

The small size of the kibbutz organizations, as well as their unique social-movement characteristics, cannot be overemphasized. Twice, Tannenbaum makes the point that workers in the highly egalitarian kibbutz factory do not compete for office and often have to be pressured by their peers to assume leadership responsibilities. Almost 40 years ago, Chinese sociologist Li An-che took Ruth Benedict to task for her caricature of Pueblo Indian passivity.[78] Like kibbutzniks, Pueblo Indians did not seek office; leadership was thrust upon them. But as Li pointed out after living among the Zuñi, a Pueblo farming community was like its counterpart in China. Everyone in such a small, face-to-face community knows who its competent leaders are, and no one has to belabor the obvious. The rare individual who actively seeks office under such circumstances is usually incompetent.

A test case in Israel, with much broader applicability than the kibbutz to problems of industrial organization, would have been the Histadruth factories. The Histadruth is the Israel Federation of Labor, and it owns and operates enterprises more typical of large-scale industrial conditions. Although the Histadruth ideologically favors worker participation in the management of its factories, it has faced, in practice, the same obstacles and problems other production cooperatives have faced since the early 19th century. According to Tabb and Goldfarb, Histadruth factory workers feel that because these enterprises "belong" to them they should not only be better paid than other workers, they should not have to work as hard.[79] This attitude had led to a steady deterioration in the relationship between workers and management. Although the latter is increasingly preoccupied with productivity and profitability, poor work discipline continues to result in low productivity and inflated production costs. Workers resist management attempts to improve discipline and even strike against the factories they supposedly own, much to the embarrassment of the Histadruth. Once highly ideological, management has gradually been changed by the economic pressures of the competitive market into a professional elite that concentrates on technological efficiency while growing increasingly distrustful of worker participation.

Large organizations tend to be alike no matter what countries they are in or what ideologies they espouse; and as Tannenbaum notes, these tendencies are not conducive to self-management.[80] In the view of some of his collaborators, however, a socialist country that adopts industry on this scale is compromising its socialism. To be truly socialist, an enterprise must be small. This is the "small is beautiful" theme again; the best capitalism, socialism, and communism are all small. We are right back to Kropotkian and Buberian utopianism.

Farm Collectives[81]

A problem with eutopian tests of anarchy is that, in being imposed or regulated from above, they cease to meet conditions of spontaneity. Joze Gorciar, for example, accepts as true self-management only that which develops from the creative, spontaneous effort of the masses.[82] If it takes place by "decree" as in Yugoslavia, it is not the real thing. The form of self-management to which we now turn is also a product of government manipulation, but it is a form that will help us to appreciate the importance of group size for self-management. We have already seen the importance of group size under social-movement conditions in the chapters on communes. But farm collectives provide examples of similar social experiments under more mundane conditions. Moreover, the farm collective illustrates behavioral difficulties generic to self-management experiments regardless of the type of enterprise involved.

Farm communes and farm collectives, as noted earlier, both produce collectively, but only the first consume collectively. In fact, the collective consumption of the commune, as we have seen, is the quality most closely associated with social-movement origins and strong commitment. Successful communes are spontaneous; if government initiates them or interferes with them, they are almost sure to fail. They are truly spontaneous forms of self-management and are the closest real-world approximations of the anarcho-communist utopia. Farm collectives, on the other hand, are almost always initiated by government. In fact, they are practically certain to fail if government does not support them.

In an anarchist utopia, of course, everyone must be a subject player in the fullest sense. If a government deliberately tries to institute such subject play through some form of worker self-management, the attempt is bound to strike many observers as a charade. Government, in the act of creating socialist self-management, replaces the conspiratorial, hidden hand of the capitalist exploiter with its own directing hand, and the workers remain just as much object players as before.

In socialist eutopias such as Russia and China, where collectivization is complete, peasants have no choice; they must play the prescribed game. But members of most Third and First World collectives have the option of leaving whenever they want. In the sense of having other alternatives, they are much closer to subject players than their socialist counterparts.

Farm collectives in the First and Third Worlds are usually instruments of social welfare rather than compulsion. They may be part of land-distribution programs or simply a way of providing work for the unemployed and landless. Positive incentives such as free land, farm machinery, and low interest loans are used to get people to join.

Governments, of course, can redistribute land in separate family parcels; they need not require or induce people to work land collectively. Then why do they? One of the most common reasons is to effect economies of scale. Machinery too expensive to be amortized on a small farm where it would lie idle most of the year can be put to full use by a large collective, and the high level of mechanization already achieved on some expropriated farms can be retained through collective production. Managing accounts and production for a large collective is also simpler and less expensive for supervising and lending agencies than if the same area were divided into a great number of small family farms. Both Mexico and Venezuela have sponsored land-reform collectives. Sometimes they have formed them to preserve economies of scale on the large, mechanized farms they have expropriated, and sometimes they have formed them on new lands developed by costly clearing and irrigation projects that the countries felt could best be amortized by industrial, commercial farming.

In addition to effecting economies of scale, governments may sponsor farm collectives to provide as many jobs as possible for landless, unemployed, or underemployed laborers. A case in Africa was the Ol Kalou Salient Project in the former "White Highlands" of Kenya. Here about 140,000 acres of cattle and dairy land, abandoned by 104 European and South African owners following independence, was formed into 19 group-land-tenure bodies, each consisting of 100 Kikuyu families. The 19 groups operated their holdings as collectives under government administration. The intention of government was to provide full employment for as many tribesmen as possible, while maintaining the commercial and "rational" quality of this highland farming.

During the Great Depression in the 1930's, the United States and the United Kingdom independently founded farm collectives for unemployed laborers organized in group land-tenure associations. In the United States, 24 "cooperative corporation farms" under the jurisdiction of the Farm Security Administration were put into operation in 12 states between January 1937 and December 1942.[83] Between March 1936 and March 1939, the British Ministry of Agriculture established 5 agricultural production cooperatives or "settlement societies" for unemployed Welsh coal miners, with the objective of employing as many of them as possible. Specializing in intensive vegetable production, these farms were worked as collectives because the Ministry felt that unemployed coal miners with no experience at farming would have a better chance for success under unified management.[84]

The 33 "workers' agricultural cooperatives" located around Ravenna in the Po Valley of Italy provide the most unusual example of the employment-type collective. These farms have a history that goes back to the late 19th century, and to the best of my knowledge are the only successful farm collectives not initiated by government. They have never offered full employment to the bulk of their members; they provide only part-time work as a hedge against unemployment or underemployment, and have among the lowest per capita acreage of any collectives on record—about three acres of cultivable land per member. This low ratio of land to worker is possible because the farms provide only part-time employment and specialize in the most labor-intensive crops. In these collectives, economies of scale that reduce labor inputs are avoided until labor costs become too high for the farms to remain competitive.

Well over half the active members are women, most of whose husbands are employed full time in nearby factories. Collective membership, according to Alison Sánchez, parallels local membership in the communist labor union, which works closely with the federation of cooperatives.[85] Extensive technical assistance is provided by the federation including appointment of the college-trained farm managers who administer the collective farms. Corporate tendencies are held in check by Italian law, which prevents the collectives from using salaried workers for more than four percent of their total labor needs and from paying members on the basis of capital shares. In spite of this, collectives since 1951 have been helping to finance their operations with a deferred wage-payment fund which, in effect, becomes capital from which members withdraw their shares upon retirement.

Just the opposite situation is represented by the Swedish experience. Between 1949 and 1959 Sweden established five experimental collective farms in its search for means of improving the economic situation of its landless farm laborers. These were all large farms of over 1,000 acres, but no more than six families were settled on any one of them. The ratio of land to workers on these collectives was among the highest on record: 100 to 250 acres of cultivated land per member, plus pasture and timber forest. The purpose of this Swedish experiment, however, was to see if the member families could achieve middle-class living standards through mechanized, rational farming methods. I return to this case below.

Finally, governments may sponsor collective farms for purely ideological reasons. Julius Nyerere's collectivization program in Tanzania is one of the best and purest examples. Nyerere wants Tanzanian agriculture to modernize and commercialize, but not by the capitalist route.[86] Under capitalist development some Tanzanian farmers expand their farms and begin employing other Tanzanians. This is exploitation, and Nyerere prefers that Tanzanians develop by helping, not exploiting, one another. He advocates, therefore, an African form of socialism he calls "*ujamaa* socialism" and which he models on the solidarity and communality of the traditional African family or lineage.

As anthropologist Raymond Apthorpe and others have pointed out, however, the *jamaa*, or extended family, in the traditional rural community may have cooperated well for funerals and marriages, but it never cooperated for any other purpose, and especially not for collective food production.[87] Tanzanian tribesmen were no different from natives anywhere; they practiced group land tenure, but neither collective production nor the communal ownership of tools, utensils, or livestock. Tanzanian peasants, moreover, have not taken to Nyerere's game of ujamaa, so he must employ increasing amounts of force to get his way. As he does, he turns his subject-playing peasants into the object players of his ujamaa utopianism.

Since most First and Third World countries shy away from outright coercion in their collective-farming experiments, how do they involve players in this game? What are the inducements? In the case of land-reform programs or land-distribution programs for landless farm workers the inducement, of course, is the land itself. For peasants who already have land, inducements have included irrigation projects, farm credit at low interest rates, tax advantages, the opportunity to acquire farm machinery under favorable credit arrangements, and the consolidation of badly fragmented land holdings by means of government technical assistance.

But if peasants and farmers find they do not like to play the game of collective farming, how do they get out of it? Even in the Second or Socialist World, individuals withdraw to play their own game if the choice is theirs. When Poland and Yugoslavia dropped their collectivization programs, the collectives broke up immediately. At the peak of Poland's drive approximately 10 percent of all cultivated land was collectivized. Yet by 1957, only one year after liberalization, 83 percent of Poland's collective farms had dissolved leaving in collectives less than 1 percent of the nation's cultivated land. The collectives that disbanded first and universally were those which had been formed by joining together the holdings of independent farmers. Collectives formed on estate lands with memberships comprised of landless proletariat, unaccustomed to working for themselves, tended to last the longest.[88]

Yugoslavia pressured so many farmers into collectives between 1946 and 1951 that 20 percent of all agricultural land had been collectivized by the latter date. But after the liberalization decree of 1953, collectives all but disappeared in most regions. Only 39 were left by 1963, and as in Poland, those that survived were mainly landless proletariat in origin.[89]

In Russia during the late 1920's, before the major collectivization drive began, there were great fluctuations in kolkhoz memberships. At times up to 30 percent of kolkhozes being formed would unofficially disappear as soon as they were officially established.[90] At the very height of the collectivization drive in March, 1930, Stalin relaxed the campaign because of peasant unrest and his fear that the spring planting might be seriously disrupted. Lower-echelon officials were blamed for pushing collectivization too fast, and voluntary membership was emphasized. In only a few weeks 9 million households withdrew their lands from collectives to return to individual farming. The percentage of rural households in collectives dropped from 60 to 23 percent. By fall, collectivization was once more underway and was never to be "voluntary" again.[91]

Since First and Third World countries do not have collectivization "drives" of this magnitude, individual and group withdrawal is usually a gradual, rather than abrupt, process. Venezuelan collectives I visited in 1964 had averaged a

37 percent loss of membership in the less than 5 years since the program began. On the family-farm-type settlement, however, membership loss averaged only 6 percent. On the United States FSA farms, individual withdrawal took the form of very high turnover rates, as high as 30 to 40 percent per annum in some cases. This was not the direct cause of their demise, however; the FSA experiment was terminated during the second World War by the United States congress for being impractical, communistic, and un-American. The average age of the 24 farms was only about 4 years at the time of termination.[92]

In Mexico, where land is scarce, individuals who withdraw from a collective, land-reform association (collective *ejido*) give up a very precious property right. Members of a collective prefer to petition and agitate for an equal division of the land into family parcels. Since the overwhelming majority of Mexican ejidos are of the family-parcel variety anyway, there is a clear precedent for such division. Collective farmers sometimes argue that they are being discriminated against and that they deserve to have their land in separate family plots "like everyone else." Eventually the government gives in to the pressure, and land surveyors divide the collective into equal parcels, one for each member.

In the lowland areas of Venezuela members of collectives could always go back to slash-and-burn farming by squatting on undeveloped private or government land nearby. This had accounted for most of the drop in membership on Venezuela's 11 collective farming experiments by 1964. In the highland areas, where population pressures were more like those in Mexico, I visited 3 collectives that had also converted to individual farming by group withdrawal. Only one of these had done so with government approval and assistance. The members of the other two had divided the land on their own initiative in open defiance of the land-reform bureaucracy. One of these, Cascarí in Táchira, declared the settlement off bounds to all employees of the Agrarian Institute and posted armed sentries at the gate.

The Bolivian agrarian reform consisted mainly of giving the serfs of expropriated haciendas permanent use rights to what had been their perquisite plots. The former hacendado's commercial demesne (usually about a third of the estate's cultivated land) was assigned to the emancipated work force as collective land. At none of the many properties I visited throughout southeastern Bolivia in the summer of 1963 (ten years after the reform), did I find the collective sector under collective production. In all cases it had been illegally divided by the group-land-tenure body into tiny parcels. Usually these had been given to the ex-serfs' children.

Many of the expropriated estates had orchards which were also supposed to be exploited collectively. But jealousies invariably arose at fruit-picking time, when members accused each other of picking more than their fair share. In successive years the competition "to get mine first" became so great that fruit was harvested green. Independently at many widely separated farms, the problem was resolved in the same way—an equal division of the trees.

First and Third World reactions to collective-farming experiments are simply exaggerated versions of those that take place in the socialist states, exaggerated because they are allowed to run their full course. This is just as true of what we might call "partial withdrawal" as it is of individual and group withdrawal. The most common form is withdrawal into garden-plot cultivation. As in Russia and China some Third World collective-farming experiments allow part of the group-held land to be used for individual production by members. Usually these household plots are devoted to subsistence farming, and if they are large enough to meet much of a family's needs, the heads of household may eventually contribute little or no labor to the collective sector.

The process is well illustrated by two collectives in Venezuela, both of them expropriated haciendas turned over to their former workers. Only a fourth to a third of these extensive estates was under cultivation. This was the collective sector, and it was devoted to such plantation crops as coffee, cacao, and sugarcane. The rest of the land was covered with forest, and here members cleared *conucos* (slash-and-burn subsistence plots) of 2 to 6 acres, a privilege continued from the days when the haciendas were privately owned. Eighty percent of the families worked less than half the time on the collective sector, 30 percent less than a sixth, and some not at all. Most members sent their wives and older children to work in their place while they labored on their conucos. Wage laborers were being depended on more and more by those in charge to get work done on the collective sector.

Complete garden-plot withdrawal was by far the most common denouement to most of the collective-farming experiments I visited in Ghana and East Africa in 1968. Members ended up spending all their time on their subsistence plots while ignoring the collective sector completely. Two collective-farming settlements in the Tanga region of Tanzania, similar in many respects to the two Venezuelan cases mentioned above, were typical of what so often happens in Africa. The collective sector in each case was devoted to sisal production and occupied only a small part of the total land area, most of which was in brush and forest. Between 60 and 80 percent of the original members had defected, and those who remained were no longer working on the sisal at all. They had cleared private shambas (slash-and-burn plots) and were spending full time growing maize, cassava, and other food crops for subsistence and supplementary cash.

The most unusual case of partial withdrawal was achieved by the Welsh collectives, simply through their ability to keep work-output levels under group control. As former miners the new settlers retained their antagonistic attitudes toward management, which they now directed against Ministry of Agriculture officials. Unlike the FSA collectives, the Welsh farms had a low turnover rate because the ex-miners did not mind working under supervision as long as they could effectively resist all efforts to raise labor productivity and farm profitability. When the government tried to raise them by admitting younger, more ambitious members, the old miners used the same group tactics on them that they had formerly used against rate busters in the mines. Although the Welsh farms lasted nearly 20 years, they became so noncompetitive and unprofitable that the Ministry of Agriculture liquidated them in 1960 rather than subsidize them further.[93]

As these examples indicate, collective-farming experiments have a high rate of failure when not backed by force. The reasons are not elusive. First, the social-movement commitments that accompany successful farm communes are seldom present in the case of collectives. Even when they are present under revolutionary or semirevolutionary conditions they do not last long. Of all the collective farms established in the Yaqui and Mayo River valleys of north-western Mexico during the late 1930's, only one remained by 1958, and that one, Quechehueca, was becoming something else as we see below. The ex-collectives I surveyed in 1958 had lasted 1 to 9 years, 5 years on the average. I visited all 11 of Venezuela's collective farming experiments during the winter of 1963–1964 when the land-reform program was still less than 5 years old. Three, as we have seen, had already converted to individual farming, and the rest were suffering from high membership losses and garden-plot withdrawal. The rate of failure of Tanzanian collectives by 1968—before force was employed—was said to be over 98 percent.[94]

Second, a major reason strong commitment is usually absent in the case of collectives is that conditions of social predictability seldom apply either. Because farm collectives are usually initiated by government to achieve economies of scale, they are almost never small, face-to-face groups. More often than not they begin with over a hundred members. These memberships, moreover, constitute associations which are not necessarily communities.

The Mexican collective, for example, is simply a type of ejido, a group of individuals (20 or more) who have been made the beneficiaries of a grant of land, usually obtained by expropriation. This association constitutes a group-land-tenure body in that no member can alienate his share from the rest. Ejido members, moreover, must personally work the land, for according to ejido law they cannot sharecrop, rent, or sell it.[95] Of the two types of ejido, individual and collective, the first has always predominated. The group-held land, in this form, is divided into equal-size parcels among the members, who manage and work them individually.

In northwestern Mexico, members of collective ejidos as well as individual ejidos usually belonged to several neighboring villages. These associations were not coterminous with communities nor were members likely to all belong to the same community. Even in the case of new settlements in lowland Venezuela, where collectives were sometimes organized as single communities, members were from many different parts of the country, and began their association virtually as strangers. Moreover, in Bolivia or those parts of Mexico and Venezuela where collectives are formed from existing communities, such as the resident laborers of an expropriated estate, there were seldom tight bonds of mutual cooperation and exchange. Not even the residents of closed, traditional, peasant villages exchange labor with one another indiscriminately.

As deliberately created associations, farm collectives seldom have the conditions of social predictability that would allow members to apply selective incentives to difficult members either by tradition or by the rules prescribed for the association. The result is inequality of effort on the part of members. Free riders, in other words, undermine and gradually destroy the collective.

Without exception, members of ex-collectives I talked with in both Latin America and Africa described the free-rider phenomenon as the main cause of failure. As the informants usually explained it to me, they had worked hard; they had wanted the experiment to succeed. But too many other members showed up for work assignments just to get a day's labor credit. On the job they worked at their own slow pace and spent a lot of time "leaning on their hoes. So I began to ask myself: 'Why should I work hard to support those lazy bastards?' " The following are other typical informant statements: "Most workers went out to the fields to report for payment, but did no work" (Mexico); "Some worked more than others, but all were paid the same" (Venezuela); "Collectives will always fail because some people do not work hard and others then become angry" (Ghana).

At the two Tanzanian sisal collectives, where everyone had withdrawn into private food-crop production on individual clearings, members explained the labor-inequality phenomenon by comparing collective farming with exchange labor. They were all practicing traditional labor exchange for the clearing and cultivation of their individual shambas. Usually two to four men, but sometimes as many as eight, worked a day or two on each other's food plots in rotation. Each man chose friends to exchange with, men he knew well, whom he trusted, and who worked at the same pace he did. This, I was told, was why work done on the shambas was better than that done on the collective sector. One informant, struggling for the words to carry the explanation further, said: "Working in a collective is like trying to exchange labor with everyone. There are too many people. You cannot be such good friends with everyone."

Even illiterate peasants do not actually have to experience collective farming, however, to appreciate the basic problem. Ocurí, a Quechua community in the Chuquisaca highlands of Bolivia, is a case in point. At the time of my visit in 1964, this Indian comunidad of 74 households was a very "closed" peasant community that, since colonial times, had managed to defend its lands against the encroachments of the haciendas. Much of the comunidad's 700 hectares were comprised of communal pasture, but individual households had permanent use rights to their cultivated parcels. No one, however, could sell or rent those parcels to outsiders. Group land tenure, in short, was strong in this community, as were the traditional practices of exchange and festive labor. Households also collaborated each year in corvée labor projects to maintain such public goods as church, roads, and cemetery.

I was curious to test the reaction of such a closed community to the idea of collective farming, and I had a chance at a meeting of all heads of household. I described the ideal Mexican collective ejido, being careful not to color my description with any judgments pro or con. After a brief discussion, the group reached a consensus: people have different customs in different places so this collective way of laboring together might work in Mexico. But it would not work in Ocurí. The head elder pointed to the three men nearest him and said: "These men work hard and well. I, on the other hand, am slow and lazy. Why should we share alike?" In this closed and intimate peasant community the speaker referred to himself as the lazy one. Everywhere else informants identified with those who worked the hardest. The social climate of this small, traditional community came through in the style of the answer but not in the meaning. The meaning was the same as everywhere else: equal reward for unequal effort is not social justice.

Because members of collectives need some income between harvests to purchase family food supplies, advances are usually paid against future profits. However, the government financing agencies that provide operating credit for collectives cannot usually afford to pay an advance equal to the lawful minimum wage; for due to the free-rider effect, labor productivity tends to be so low that labor costs are high in spite of the small advance. Often they are so high that no profits are realized at all. Under these circumstances the advance becomes, in effect, a substandard wage which aggravates feelings of injustice and adds to an already vicious circle of disincentives.

One of the great ironies in the operation of collectives is that they can obtain high productivity per acre along with low productivity per worker. Records kept for the FSA collectives, for example, showed precisely this relationship when compared with the average for private farms in the same states.[96] Part of the reason for the low labor productivity of collectives is their social purpose of providing as many people as possible with land or employment. To the extent a collective is oversupplied with labor, the earning potential and incentives of its members will be limited.

In the absence of profits, collective members soon become suspicious. The Welsh miners, for example, were always convinced that Ministry of Agriculture officials were "fiddling" them.[97] Similarly, Mexican ejidatarios believed Ejido Bank officials were practicing the *mordida,* literally the "bite." Such suspicions are compounded by ignorance, for collective members seldom know the exact size of harvests, costs of production, or even the prices at which crops are sold. When a collective ejido would fail even to pay its debts, members would compare it to a tienda de raya (the old hacienda store), where costs were deliberately piled on workers to keep them in debt slavery.

Members' perception of management as a malevolent hidden hand eventually encompasses their own leaders as well. Bitterness can result from the practice of counting administrative time as equal to that spent at field labor. When the farm manager and the office staff work all year and the other members only seasonally, a great disparity can result between the number of advances received by the administrative staff and that received by the field workers. When profits are distributed, the differences become even more apparent; for profits are divided on the basis of each member's labor-time percentage (total number of an individual's labor days divided by the total for the entire collective).

Within farm collectives, management and leadership by members are usually weak and ineffectual. Field managers, for example, are regarded as peers by their fellows, a fact which often makes it impossible for them to reprimand workers. When they do, they are accused of feeling self-important and of treating their companions as inferiors. A manager who tries to get a normal day's work out of a crew may only provoke their derision. As members of Mexican collectives would remind their work bosses, "We are no longer living in the days of Porfirio Díaz."

To protect their investments, government lending agencies try to find ways of their own to reestablish discipline. In Venezuela this was done by appointing salaried managers who were not members. Invariably these were former hacienda bosses who began asserting, under land-reform conditions, the same capricious authority they had enjoyed before the reforms. At one collective, the government-appointed manager instituted a system of work norms and deliberately set the norms for some jobs so high that they could be used for punitive work assignments to anyone who challenged his authority. In the face of this kind of external management, members perceive their own status as reverting to that of farm laborers, and the collective looks more and more like a state-owned farm. This was true of many of the Mexican and Venezuelan land-reform collectives, African settlement schemes, and the FSA and Welsh depression farms.

Members of the FSA farms complained of being treated "like kids" and thought of themselves as government-employed farm laborers. In Venezuela, collective members were fond of saying that the Agrarian Institute had simply replaced the private owner while everything else had remained the same. And as far as members of Mexican collectives were concerned, the Ejido Bank was far more impersonal, unpredictable and inefficient than their former patrón. At least the patrón always saw to it that they had enough to eat: "The Bank does not care if we starve. They [the Bank personnel] are just employees. They get paid no matter what happens, so why should they care about us?" In Africa, where the management of collective schemes was often expatriate as late as 1968, centralized control sometimes seemed like neocolonialism. The outgoing expatriate manager of one Kenya collective included the following admonition in the instructions to a successor: "You will need to ensure that at all times you have a 'feeling' for the likely reaction of the populace in any given set of circumstances, and you will need to react with complete ruthlessness against any self-seeking individual or minority group which starts to set up any agitation."

The few instances in which collective farming is at least a temporary success are just as instructive as the many failures. A case in point is the collective credit society La Parchita, at the Pimpinella land-reform settlement in the Venezuelan state of Portuguesa. When I visited it in 1964, it was about 3 years old, and its 12 members were among the few original Pimpinella settlers still remaining. This settlement had been founded mainly with unemployed urban workers from Caracas, most of whom had long since returned. Parchita members, however, had adapted to the rural life and preferred to stay. The society had originally consisted of 20 members, but 8 had been expelled in the process of narrowing the group down to those who worked well together and trusted one another. Members felt that small-group size and prompt expulsion of malingerers were major factors in their successful cohesion to date.

Parchita members were proud of the fact that they had "invented" a system of successful "cooperation" through trial and error. Although initiation of the credit society had been promoted by a young agronomist of the Agricultural and Livestock Bank, the group had been left to develop its own procedures. Pimpinella was an individual-type settlement, and Parchita members' plots were not contiguous. All their separate holdings were now worked as a single common holding, however, with everyone contributing equal amounts of work and dividing income equally. The main problem was to prevent the free-rider syndrome. How could Parchita members make sure they all contributed equal amounts of work? In solving this problem, these uneducated, unsophisticated workers independently discovered both the Russian trudoden and the Chinese family-responsibility systems.

Jealousy was rampant in the early stages; each thought everyone else had an easier job or was working less. They decided to rotate all tasks, including that of field boss, every week; but this proved much too often. A useful consequence of these rotations, however, was the familiarity members developed with all jobs. This enabled them to plan work schedules as a group and eliminated the need for a manager. The elected head of the society began contributing administrative time for free, and only manual labor was remunerated. Due to the rotation experience the group was readily able to agree on what constituted a fair day's work for each job, and all members were assigned weekly chores on a piecework basis.

Some men completed their weekly assignment in one or two days of concentrated effort with the help of their wives and children. Others worked a few hours each day. (Parchita members all worked as day laborers on construction projects and nearby private farms for their major source of income.) At the end of the week, however, members critically appraised each other's work; and if judged negligent, one had to make up one's deficiencies. While this had led to the expulsion of some members, it had eliminated jealousies over work assignments and complaints about unequal work among those who remained.

Because of bad technical advice from a government agronomist, Parchita was developing economic problems that promised to overwhelm it eventually.

But the example shows that collective farming can succeed at least for a while if it meets small-group conditions of social predictability. A similar instance of small-group collectives were the eight credit societies I visited in northwest Mexico during 1967. They are of special interest because they illustrate an additional adaptive tendency.

These collective credit societies were located in Ejido Cuauhtémoc in the Yaqui River Irrigation District of Sonora, where they are extremely rare except for some in the Yaqui Indian reservation. They did not actually include entire credit societies but only small "work-group" subdivisions. The eight work groups averaged only six members, in each case relatives or close friends who were well known to one another and long accustomed to working together. Again, conditions of small-group social predictability prevailed.

Cuauhtémoc was a former collective ejido that had long ago converted to the individual type. At the time of division, however, relatives and friends were given contiguous plots. Because of this, the work groups in question were able to join their contiguous parcels into single blocks farmed with jointly owned machinery across plot boundaries. While these "work groups" had started out as true collectives in the sense that all member households worked on the joint farms, by the time of my visit, nearly all had changed into corporate operations. Administration was being left to one or two members who were hiring landless farm laborers to do most of the manual labor, a practice that began when some ejidatarios died and their widows were unable to do the heavy farmwork. Other members meanwhile found more rewarding employment off the ejido and preferred not to continue farming.

Those members who administered the block farms also maintained and operated the jointly owned machinery and were paid wages from profits for their time. After deduction of all expenses including wages of administrative and hired labor, profits were divided equally among all the members on the basis of equal participation in the *capital* of the group. Ironically, ejido land was the lion's share of each group's capital. Again, the Cuauhtémoc examples illustrate at least the temporary workability of collective farming under small-group conditions of social predictability. But they also show that when such groups are economically successful they readily and spontaneously transform into small corporate farms.

The same process is illustrated by the Swedish experiment in collective farming. Of the five Swedish collectives formed between 1949 and 1959 only two survived in 1968 at the time of my visit. As noted above, in all five experiments the government had made the membership small, originally five or six families each. Nevertheless, poor management and internal dissension had led to the abandonment of two of the cooperatives. The third had been located too close to a city and had been sold for residential subdivision. The two successful societies had only four members each by 1968, and were made up of relatives and close friends. The friendships had been of long standing even before the societies were created. Both farms had operated since they began under the same member-managers, exceptional individuals who had previously worked as farm managers and had been important leaders in the farm labor union.

Each collective paid salary advances to its members. At Hornsjofors it was assumed that all members worked equally and all were equal owners of the accumulated capital, so wages and profits were distributed equally among them. At Kungsgarden, records were kept of labor time, and wages and profits were distributed accordingly. An attempt was made, however, to assign chores so as to equalize as much as possible the time worked by all members. Both groups considered themselves small corporations, and Kungsgarden had started to pay each member seven percent interest per share of the accumulated capital regardless of annual work time. This farm also had three permanent employees.

In recent years several Western European countries have tried to encourage the formation of agricultural-production cooperatives with inducements of inexpensive credit especially for the purchase of farm machinery. Small credit societies are thereby created that jointly own machinery, and in many cases pool their labor as well. In some countries the members of these cooperative groups go a step further by also pooling their lands and distributing profits to capital and labor according to various arrangements. In 1968 I visited many such cooperatives and talked with government officials involved in their formation in England, Norway, France, and Spain. The Spanish experiments are discussed separately in the next section. In all these cases, we are dealing with production cooperatives that have achieved some degree of success, not by a reduction in size from some larger grouping, but because they were based on small-group social predictability from the start.

Western European countries were encouraging such cooperatives in 1968 because of the great migration of labor from rural to urban areas since World War II. The average age of the farm population had increased significantly while farm labor had become relatively scarce. To alleviate the situation, governments were trying to speed up the trend toward larger, more mechanized farms. Machinery rings, based on traditional exchange-labor practices, were being pushed by government in England, Norway, and France. Those that were successful were small and selected their membership on the basis of propinquity and friendship.

Great Britain had hundreds of these rings, called "syndicates," most of which exchanged labor in addition to sharing the ownership costs of their machinery. And as one Hampshire farmer put it, "You have to pick your partners carefully. Some people cooperate well and some don't; they have to have the face for it. It has to be a congenial group, so you pick people you've known most of your life." According to a group of Norfolk farmers, those who thought mainly in terms of profitability were most likely to join a syndicate. "Today if you're not big, you have to join a group and get big."

In the process of "getting big," a few farmers had moved beyond the machinery syndicate to form "production syndicates," small land-pooling partnerships or corporations. Such groups existed in Surrey, Hampshire, Norfolk, and Scotland. Sometimes whole farms were pooled. In other cases members contributed only portions of their farms. Some syndicates exchanged their labor, paid themselves wages, and distributed profits and costs according to capital. Others hired all their labor, and capital (land and equipment) became the sole basis for distributing costs and profits.

In addition to achieving economies of scale, another purpose of this corporate farming was to "spread risks." Given the short planting season at these latitudes and the need to rotate machinery among a group of joint owners, those who got the machinery too early or too late might be considerably disadvantaged. But when land and harvests were pooled, the order in which individual farms were planted or harvested was no longer important. If the crop did badly on one farm, the loss was absorbed by profits on the rest.

A similar government program in Norway had resulted in the formation of four hundred machinery rings (maskinring) by 1968. These groups averaged three to four members in size and were comprised again of friends and neighbors who had worked together frequently in the past. Only nine Norwegian machinery rings had pooled their land as well as their machinery. In these experiments the members rented their lands to their "cooperative," which then paid them an hourly work rate agreed upon by all in advance. Profits were divided on the basis of one-third to capital (distributed in proportion to the size of member farms) and two-thirds to labor (distributed in proportion to the total hours of each member). Since the Norwegian small-group production cooperatives distributed profits mainly to labor, they were closer to collectives than to corporate farms, according to our criteria.

France had gone much further than either Norway or Great Britain in sponsoring production cooperatives. Here, too, experiments began with machinery rings, of which there were over ten thousand by 1968. From these the government progressed to "work banks" based on traditional exchange labor and ranging in size from five to ten members. Both forms had the advantages of small size and social predictability.

The most interesting aspect of the French program has been the collective production unit known as the "gaec" (groupement agricole d'exploitation en commun). During my visit officials were celebrating the founding of the thousandth gaec, but by December, 1975, according to Josette Murphy, the number had grown to 5629.[98] A major inducement for joining a gaec was the availability of low-interest loans for the purchase of machinery. However, since 1970, gaec members have not been favored over other farmers in this regard. Farmers continue to join gaecs, says Murphy, because the more economical use of machinery thereby made possible reduces dependence on hired labor, which continually grows scarcer and more expensive. Members can also specialize in activities they prefer and can rotate unpleasant chores such as caring for dairy cattle on weekends. They are still required to work their joint farm personally and may not, as occurs in many of the English cases, expand their operations by becoming administrators who hire all their labor. As a result, gaecs continue to be very small in size, averaging only 2.7 members, consisting predominantly of close relatives, such as brothers or fathers and sons. The number of non-kin members, never very large, has been steadily decreasing since 1968, according to Murphy. Arrangements for the distribution of income continue to be highly variable and show the same tendency for small-group production cooperatives to drift from a collective to a corporate structure. The following facts, collected in 1968, still apply.

All members of a gaec are paid the same monthly allowance (an amount decided upon by the group) on the premise that all contribute equal amounts of time to the cooperative. If the members all rent their lands, the gaec simply pays all the rental fees as a cost of the operation. When members own their own farms, however, they are not always willing to rent to the gaec. If they are, profits are divided equally after paying 5 percent interest on capital (the land, machinery, and buildings contributed by each member). This can occur if farms are of about the same size. But the larger the differences in capital contributed, the greater is the tendency in practice to distribute part of the profits on the basis of capital. Usually half goes to capital and half is equally divided among the members on the basis of their equal contributions of labor. But if differences in capital contributions are large, as much as two-thirds of the profits may be distributed to capital. In these cases the gaecs are "collective" in their use of labor, but "corporate" in their distribution of profits.

All of these examples show that a form of agricultural production cooperative that fits our definition of a collective can occur with just the right inducements if it is small and meets the conditions of social predictability. But the examples also show that such associations readily transform into the more probable corporate form because of its greater flexibility. If all these .cases are illustrative of general principles, why are there so many large collective ejidos in Mexico?

Mexican collective farms are largely an illusion despite the impression created by some writers that they are widespread and still very much alive. One reason for this general misunderstanding is the very imprecise, often colloquial, usage of the word "collective." In Mexico an ejido may be "collective" long after it has changed to the individual form. Understandably, what has become a customary part of a proper name continues in use. Ten years after the Bolivian agrarian reform, expropriated haciendas turned over to their peasant labor forces were still being called Hacienda Camargo, Hacienda Bella Vista, and so on. The word "hacienda" continued in use as part of the customary title. In Mexico many ejidos no longer collective, still are called by such names as Ejido Colectivo Juárez or Ejido Colectivo Todos Santos.

Today when collectives occur, they are not entire ejidos but subdivisions called "credit societies" that work with credit, machinery, and technical direction provided by the Ejido Bank. The memberships of these societies are often quite small. Simply counting the number of such credit societies can give the illusion that collective farming in Mexico is prevalent and vigorous. Actually, these so-called "collectives" are less extensive and involve fewer farm families than the production cooperatives of England, France, and Spain. And when one looks closely at Mexican credit-society collectives, one finds that like the production cooperatives of Europe most are not true collectives anyway.

Confusion also stems from the phrase *responsabilidad colectiva* used as a synonym for *responsabilidad solidaria*. These terms refer to the joint responsibility of all members of a credit society for the losses of any one member. Consequently some ejidatorios will designate a credit society as "collective" on the basis of joint-credit responsibility even when the members are separately working their individual plots.

Another common confusion is illustrated by the sugarcane areas around Los Mochis, Sinaloa, where ejidatorios claimed they were working collectively. Pressed further, they explained that they were working collectively (en colectivo) with the Los Mochis Sugar Company, a collaboration involving corporate, "semicollective" farming with no collective production whatsoever. Ejidatarios in semicollective credit societies funded by the Ejido Bank also use the expression "en colectivo" on occasion, a confusion that permeates Salomón Eckstein's book on the collective ejido.[99] Using questionable statistics gathered from old government questionnaires filled out by unsophisticated ejidatarios, he uses semicollective credit societies to show that the number of "collectives" is increasing. But if we take a close look at the so-called semicollective, we see that it is not a collective at all.

Actually, the semicolectivo has been the most common decollectivization route to corporate farming in Mexico. It is, in a way, a kind of corporate reciprocal farming that often follows the individualization of a collective through group withdrawal. The commonly held land is divided so that all the members of the ejido receive parcels of equal size. But then, rather than carry out the entire cycle of agricultural activities separately on each parcel, the Ejido Bank persuades the ejidatarios to permit major farming operations to be carried out across the boundaries of the individual plots. Land is prepared, planted to a single cash crop, and cultivated and fumigated by the latest mechanized procedures. Irrigation and a few other manual operations are left to the individual ejidatarios and harvesting takes place within their parcel boundaries.

This "semicollective" farming follows the procedures of reciprocal farming with one very important difference. The ejidatarios do not form an exchange-labor team to carry out the farming that takes place across the parcel boundaries. The Bank hires a specialized labor force to do it—tractor drivers, crop dusters, and so on. Qualified ejidatarios have preference at time of hiring, but most prefer to let the Bank employ others. Of the total production costs for an average "semicollective" crop in the Yaqui River Irrigation District of Sonora, the Bank spends about 80 percent on mechanized operations performed by private contractors, 13 percent on administrative, interest, and social-security overhead, and only 7 percent on manual operations that could be performed by the ejidatarios. Frequently ejidatarios hire landless day laborers to do even this small part of the work.

There is little difference between a semicollective operation and one labeled "collective" that involves complete garden-plot withdrawal. For example, in Coahuila and Durango many ejidos have allocated individual garden plots to members, while retaining most of the land in the collective sector. In some cases ejidatarios devote all their time to their individual plots and leave the Ejido Bank to work the "collective" sector. The latter hires its own work force and carries out all stages of the farming operation including harvests.[100] This in turn is very similar to the illegal renting of large blocks of contiguous ejido plots by private entrepreneurs. In neither case do most ejidatarios participate in the farming, yet in both they derive an income from the land. The major difference is that the private operator pays a fixed rent whereas the government endeavors to return all profits to the ejidatarios. But why does the government turn over the income from expropriated land to people who have only use rights to it and are not farming it themselves?

The Bank, ironically, is assuming that each member of the group-land-tenure body, the "collective" ejido, has equal rights to the undivided lands, that each has an equal share in it as capital. The net profit is then divided among the members of an association that has not actually used the land, only loaned it back to the government to use. Profits are no longer divided on the basis of labor time but on the basis of property rights. Land decapitalized by expropriation and group tenure has been recapitalized, and labor decommoditized by collectivism has been recommoditized. Such collective ejidos, or credit socities, have become corporate farming organizations and their members equivalent to shareholders in a joint-stock company in which all have equal shares. The government has reintroduced capital into a socialized sector, and provisioning of the collective good has been returned to the labor market.

The most famous collective in Mexico is probably the ejido Quechehueca in the Yaqui River Irrigation District of Sonora, Mexico. Its fame is due to its prosperity; by 1967, 30 years after it began, its capital assets in machinery and buildings alone totaled 30 million pesos. It is often used as an example of what can be accomplished by collective farming. In one sense it is very atypical of Mexican collectives, and in another sense very typical.

It is atypical in the amount and quality of its farmland. Quechehueca lies in an exceptionally fertile sector of a very fertile irrigation district. The group land holdings total almost three thousand acres, approximately 65 per member. Given the high quality of the land, this per-capita ratio compares favorably with that for the FSA collectives and must be considered one of the highest among all the many collective experiments that have been attempted anywhere in the world. Even in 1959, when I first visited Quechehueca, all the families had electric lighting and gas stoves, and each received a daily food ration at Quechehueca's "cooperative" store. In addition to these benefits and the wage advances paid to those who worked, member families also received 20 to 30 thousand pesos annually as their share of crops. Many had bought their own trucks and cars.

Two adaptive processes in Quechehueca's history make it very typical, however, of collectives in general. First, it underwent a drastic reduction in size before it became prosperous. Thoroughly disenchanted with the collective system for the usual reasons, 75 members split off in 1948 with their share of the collective land and formed a separate individual-type ejido. Six years later another 65 members did the same. The collective was now reduced to a credit society of 42 members, half of whom were Indian and all of whom were highly dependent on a charismatic leader by the name of Bernabé Arana. This was a much more manageable group than the original membership; and to help matters, Arana proved an exceptionally gifted farm manager and businessman.

Second, the collective gradually became corporate. In 1959, Quechehueca was still dividing profits on the basis of work, but it had made a modification that was to become important. It allowed members who did not want to work to name "replacements" to serve in their place for half the members' wages and share of profits. By 1961 the "collective" was dividing profits equally among all its members regardless of labor contributions, and 60 percent of the work was being done by wage laborers. By my last visit in 1967, wage laborers were performing 80 percent of the work. Only ten members still did agricultural work; these operated the farm machinery and received skilled workers' wages.

When I asked Bernabé if his collective was not in fact becoming a capitalist enterprise, he agreed by disagreeing: "We are not *becoming* a capitalist enterprise; we already are one!" The members of the Quechehueca "collective" were, in his opinion, a group of stockholders in a small farming corporation. To prove his point, he told of a recent meeting of the "collective" at which a topic of discussion had been the possibility of admitting two new members. The reaction had been strongly and unanimously negative. Any new members, it was decided, would have to buy in, pay an amount equivalent to the current percapita share of the total capital. That figure in 1967 would have been about $60,000 (U.S.), a totally impossible sum for any potential candidate.

One final confusion about Mexican collectives is illustrated by Raymond Wilkie's book, *San Miguel: A Mexican Collective Ejido* (1971).[101] In the first place, the title gives the impression that the ejido is still collective. Yet, as Wilkie's data show, San Miguel had become an individual-type ejido nine years before his first visit in 1953. Were Wilkie more familiar with the individual-type ejido in other parts of Mexico, he would realize that since 1944 the significance of the collective label for San Miguel has been more historical than taxonomic. Production has become both individual and corporate.

The confusion in this case, as with many persons who write about the Mexican ejido, is between group land tenure and collective production. Wilkie says at one point that subdivision of San Miguel land introduced a major change in its "collective land tenure." Elsewhere he says "ownership" of the land remained largely "collective" because the ejidatarios still could not buy or sell it after the labor was individualized.[102] Wilkie is obviously using the word "collective" synonymously with group land tenure, but even members of individual-type ejidos cannot buy, sell, or legally rent their parcels. Both types of ejido are group-land-tenure associations.

The Spanish Case [103]

Our excursion into the self-managed farm enterprise or "collective" brings some of the underlying problems of worker management into sharper focus. The basic problem is the same as for any group endeavoring to provision a collective good, the problem of the free rider. In this case the success of an enterprise becomes the collective good of all those employed in it. One could say this is true of any business enterprise, but under ordinary circumstances such an interpretation is irrelevant since the employees are working for a wage; and if they fail to do their share, they are fired. Authority in the form of management defines the collective good and each employee's proper contribution. Under self-management, workers must ideally set their own material incentives (wages) and provide effective social incentives including expulsion (firing). As we have seen repeatedly in this book, the latter is feasible under conditions of social predictability, and we are most likely to find these conditions either in very small, permanent, self-selective groups or somewhat larger ones that for social-movement reasons have strong enough commitment to raise the social visibility.

Without these conditions the collective good will not be provisioned unless some hierarchical organization is present. In the simplest case, that of corvée labor in a primitive community, the "chief" or "headman" becomes a surrogate for general other. This provides enough asymmetry in his relationship with each individual in the community to help keep potential free riders within bounds.

Experiments in collective farming, we saw, display the same characteristics of failure and adaptation as 19th-century and contemporary experiments in industrial self-management. Members lack the knowledge and expertise to make sound management decisions; they find it impossible to discipline one another, effort decreases, and bankruptcy ensues. A very few are successful because for some fortuitous and improbable reason they are small enough to effect conditions of social predictability. But whether small or large, the inevitable adaptive process of any successful "collective" is toward corporate farming. Members become administrators or they retire from the active farmwork, which is performed by wage laborers. The hierarchical structure of the corporate form increases its flexibility and permits a range of size that goes beyond conditions of social predictability.

All of these processes are clearly demonstrated by an unusual and largely fortuitous experiment sponsored by the Spanish government. It crystallizes all that has been said and shows precisely why the juristic person has become so predominant a form of enterprise under conditions of legal predictability.

In Spain, the post-World War II migration of agricultural workers into the industrial sector has been even greater than in the rest of Western Europe. Between 1950 and 1967 the percentage of the Spanish working population engaged in agriculture decreased from 47.8 percent to 27.8 percent. As men and women between the ages of 25 and 45 have left the rural areas to find employment in the cities, 50 has become the average age of those actively engaged in agriculture. Farmers find it more difficult to keep their grown children on the farm and harder to do the work themselves. Adding to the problem is the extreme degree of fragmentation of holdings in the poorest areas. In Castilla la Vieja, for example, the average farm holding is divided into 34 separate parcels, which are often widely scattered. Ninety percent of all Spanish farms have less than 50 acres of land and two-thirds of them less than 12 acres.

To consolidate fragmented land holdings and to help small farmers achieve greater economies of scale through mechanization and the pooling of lands, the Spanish government has created an agency of the Ministry of Agriculture known as the Servicio Nacional de Concentración Parcelaria y Ordenación Rural (National Service of Land Consolidation and Rural Development). The major activity of this agency is to consolidate farm parcels in areas where fragmentation is most severe. The servicio persuades entire communities to consolidate their holdings simultaneously.[104] All the farmlands of a community are carefully mapped and their value appraised. Each farmer is then given a single piece of farmland equal in value to that of all the parcels he formerly owned. The advantages of consolidation are so clear to the peasants that the servicio has had more requests for help than it has been able to meet. In the process of consolidating farm parcels, the servicio also encourages the formation of cooperatives for working farms "in common." As an added inducement low-interest credit is provided these cooperatives for farm improvements and for the purchase of machinery. So popular have these cooperatives become, that most of them are formed even before land consolidation takes place. By 1965, only 5 years after the program had begun in earnest, there were some 3,250 of these agricultural production cooperatives in Spain. About 3,000 were grupos sindicales de colonización and 250 were cooperativas del campo.

The difference between grupos and cooperativas is mainly one of size. The minimum number of members allowed for a grupo is 3 and for a cooperativa 15. The production on their land holdings (either owned or rented or both) must be appropriate for the machinery they propose to buy. The larger the grupo or cooperativa, the more money it can borrow and the more equipment it can purchase.

Neither type of cooperative conforms to the laws under which they are established. The law for grupos sindicales says nothing about working land collectively. The law for cooperativas specifies that members must all work in the coop and that all must have equal rights. Few if any cooperativas del campo meet these specifications.

The government has remained flexible in the interpretation and enforcement of its laws on cooperatives to avoid classifying these farming organizations as corporations. So classified, they would be subject to taxes that in some cases would cut profits by as much as half, and would reduce the incentive for farmers to join them. The main concern of the Spanish authorities is to encourage economies of scale through mechanization, without interfering in any way that might deter the process. No investigations are made to determine the percentage of members actually participating in the work of their cooperatives or how profits are divided. The servicio feels that to do so would antagonize the farmers. The dominant official attitude favors an experimental approach—provide opportunities and encouragement for farmers to pool their lands and let appropriate organizational procedures evolve.

The most immediate incentive for farmers to join or form a cooperative is to obtain machinery. The servicio obtains 80 percent of the cost as a loan from the Credit Bank of the Ministry of Agriculture at low interest (2.75 percent), and donates the remaining 20 percent as a subsidy. The labor-saving advantages of machinery are readily perceived by the farmers. Farm labor has grown increasingly scarce in recent years, and wages have gone up proportionately. As many farmers explained to me, and as servicio studies have verified, the cooperative organizations do not appreciably raise productivity, but they can dramatically lower labor costs. Individuals with jobs or businesses that are more remunerative than farming find it advantageous to place their land in a cooperative where they work less, or not at all, and thereby free themselves for more profitable pursuits.

Servicio-sponsored grupos outnumber the servicio-sponsored cooperativas about 10 to 1; farmers prefer to join the smaller organizations. Since cooperativas must begin with at least 15 members, they are harder to organize initially. A major reason is that most farmers want to form an association to acquire machinery long before land consolidation takes place; and the greater the number of members, the more scattered will be the fragmented holdings of the society. Cooperativas are easier to form during or after consolidation, and large grupos are usually the result of expansion following a consolidation project.

Since the land owned by the three, four, or five members of a small grupo is not usually enough to qualify for loans, the members must rent additional parcels. Most often they rent from relatives, but they attempt to select plots of convenient size and location. Moreover, the farmers of a small grupo usually work together and share profits on the basis of equal contributions of labor. The larger the grupo, the more difficult it becomes to find congenial partners who can be trusted to contribute equal amounts of time and effort. Since the members of the small grupo are renting most of their land, inequalities of land holdings are not important. The grupo simply rents all its lands including that of its members and distributes profits equally after paying all farming costs including rents.

The emphasis of the small grupo is on labor contributions capitalized with machinery to exploit an optimum supply of rented land. The members are those who want to farm the land personally and realize a maximum return for their labor. The objectives of landowners who do not work their land are just the reverse. They want to minimize the return to labor and maximize the profit from their land (capital). They are better off with their land in a cooperativa, most of whose members do not participate in the farmwork and whose profits, after paying wages and other costs, are divided according to the value of the lands contributed. But fewer cooperativas exist, and they are not available to most landowners.

The differences between grupos and cooperativas in the amount of land worked per member reflect this difference in the importance placed on labor versus capital. The 65 cooperativas operating in the province of Burgos in 1968 averaged 20 acres per member, which is close to the average for the nation as a whole. Most of the land in cooperativas is owned by the members; little is rented. A landowner would rather join the cooperativa and participate directly in the division of profits than rent his land for a much lower amount. Because of the large number of members, the total acreage of most cooperativas is great enough to qualify them for large loans. The average size of the Burgos cooperativas was 1,100 acres and 46 members.

A sample of 88 grupos in Burgos average 4.2 members each, 90 acres per member, and 400 acres per grupo. Those 75 grupos with only 4 members or less averaged 110 acres each. Large grupos, however, work per-capita holdings close in size to the average for cooperativas, because large grupos in their operations are usually indistinguishable from cooperativas. Like the cooperativa, the large grupo distributes profits on the basis of capital, and few members participate in the labor. Grupos that begin as small societies distributing profits on the basis of equal contributions of labor and later expand into large grupos change to a distribution based on capital. Because grupos and cooperativas become indistinguishable as they overlap in size, the degree to which labor or capital is emphasized in a society is clearly a function of membership size and is not determined simply by the "grupo" and "cooperativa" labels.

During 1968, I visited a sample of 20 grupos and 8 cooperativas of varying sizes in the provinces of Cuenca, Segovia, and Burgos. These 28 societies arranged in order of size from smallest to largest show clearly the relationship of structure and operations to group size. The 8 cooperativas varied in size from 17 to 240 members and averaged only 15 acres per member. The 4 grupos ranging from 15 to 57 members (equivalent to cooperativas in size) averaged 26. The 11 grupos with 5 or fewer members averaged 85 acres per capita. The 5 grupos ranging from 7 to 12 members averaged 75.

All grupos with more than 6 members, as well as all the cooperativas, divided profits on the basis of capital, paid wages to all workers, kept formal accounts, and had a work boss of some kind. From one-fourth to two-thirds of the members of the 4 largest grupos and all but the smallest cooperativa (that of 17 members) were absentee landowners. The percentage of active members in the same societies averaged less than one-fourth, and almost none of the societies' lands were rented.

All of the 12 grupos with 6 members or less divided profits on the basis of equal contributions of labor and did not pay themselves wages. Only 2 kept formal accounts. The others simply shared costs and profits as they came along. All operated by consensus with a division of responsibilities; none appointed any of their number to serve as work boss. Only 1 group had an absentee member. Two others had an inactive member (due to advanced age), and in each case a son worked in his place. In all but 1 of these 12 societies half or more of the land was rented.

The flexibility of the Spanish government in its sponsorship of agricultural production cooperatives has led to the evolution of two major types determined primarily by the size of membership. The first, accounting for about 60 percent of all the societies, is a small-group collective, usually with six or fewer members. The second is a predominantly corporate farming type that varies in size from seven to over two hundred members and includes about 40 percent of all the societies.

The significance of this typology is reflected further in the way in which the two types control their workers. Members of the small-group collectives seldom complain about inequalities of effort. A typical statement by one farmer was: "This is a small community, and everyone knows everyone else. We all know which people are lazy and which are industrious. Why would hard workers join with lazy ones?" The small-group collectives meet the conditions of predictability and high visibility.

At the other end of the continuum are the very large corporate farming societies with a hundred or more members. Those I visited made a clear, explicit distinction between the roles of a member as a worker and a shareholder. "A member who works for us is like any other hired hand. If he works well, fine; if not, we fire him. He still gets his share of profits like any other member, but either he does his job or he works elsewhere. If this treatment offends him, he can withdraw his land at the end of the contract period."

The corporate farming societies between these two extremes were the ones that complained the most about the inequality of member effort. Some societies in this range fail because of it. Most of the society heads felt it was easier to control hired laborers than members, and many would have preferred to use only outside labor. Some societies use ridicule as a negative selective incentive to bring malingerers in line. Some hire predominantly members' grown sons, whom they can fire more easily than the members themselves if they do not work well. The work of one society of 57 members is done mainly by 6 industrious young men who are sons of members. In this case incentives are positive. The society pays them wages far above scale to keep them from migrating to the city. Another society of 8 members practices a form of mutual criticism. Members regularly review each others' work and point out inadequacies.

One society was endeavoring to employ all of its 63 members, for all but the widows wanted to work. In this case, jobs were rotated to give each member an opportunity to work in proportion to his capital, and wages were scaled according to age and strength. Don Aureliano Francisco, president of this unusually successful *cooperativa*, was an exceptional leader and farm manager. Moreover, the society comprised an entire small village in which selective social incentives for status and ridicule were strong.

The tendencies predominant in the corporate societies are best illustrated by a *grupo* at Garcinarro in the province of Cuenca. All 10 members of this society had originally been members of a larger *grupo* that failed "because some didn't work as hard as others." The new *grupo* established a special condition for membership I encountered nowhere else. No one could be a member who also wanted to work on the farm. The best farmer among the 10 was elected administrator and paid a special salary. The other members did not work at all, but received their share of profits based on land contributed. All members had at least 125 acres each, and the 9 who did not participate in the farming operation had other full-time employment or businesses.

The villagers had nicknamed this society "El Grupo Telefónico" (the telephone group) because the members "se pueden hablar pero no se pueden ver" (can talk to each other but cannot see one another). This is a pun on the phrase "cannot see one another," which in Spanish carries the double meaning "cannot stand one another." In other words, the members were known locally as persons who were not the best of friends. As the members explained it to me, "We do not have to be friends. Now that members are no longer workers, this is purely a business operation. Do people who buy stock in the same corporation have to be friends?"

Although only a small association in a small Spanish village, the Grupo Telefónico illustrates the same change from status contract to purposive contract that Max Weber writes about in connection with the "joint hands" associations of the Middle Ages.[105] These early forms of the juristic person constituted a "single community of risk" among individuals joined in a common specific business venture. A "business relationship," says Weber, replaced "fraternal" relationships. But the juristic-person type of corporation allows individual participants greater freedom of choice. They can participate in several or many associations on a "purposive" or business basis, whereas only one association of a status and fraternal nature could easily consume all their time.

The greater freedom of choice and action that individuals may acquire through the juristic person is inherent in the increasing specialization of interest and function. An association of investors is primarily interested in returns on capital, not labor. Once invaded by the civilization of capitalism, even a village will reflect the change from fraternal to business relationships. And those people who join an association to maximize returns on capital will have different objectives from those who join it to maximize returns on their own labor or to maximize the leisure they can combine with labor. By restricting its interests and functions to returns on capital, the Grupo Telefónico avoided the kinds of fraternal relations necessary to meet the social-control conditions of social predictability. Not only were fraternal relationships among the investors (land owners) unnecessary, but labor could now be cold-bloodedly hired and fired at will. Specialization of interest and function narrows the scope of a corporate group's collective good and thereby reduces the social interaction necessary to control free riders.

The interests and functions of the owners or managers of capital and those of labor are too distinct to allow any easy accommodation to a simple or lopsided view of the collective good. Organizational hierarchy is necessary to contain free riding. The collective good of management is best served when malingerers and incompetents can be fired. The collective good of labor is served when workers are treated well and fairly rewarded. In a society where most people are the employees of juristic persons, they can change employers and employments much more readily than they did under the paternalistic employment of status contracts. While employees do tend to become objects of play manipulated by juristic persons, they can change employers, and they can join juristic-person unions to fight their juristic-person employers. If this seems less than ideal, how much freedom does an individual have in a traditional village, in an intentional, social-movement community practicing a fight-self philosophy, or in a patrimonial eutopian state in which workers nominally own all productive capital but are accused of "exploitation" through malingering?

Giving workers part ownership of the businesses that employ them will not necessarily make them work any harder. Quite the contrary, if management's right to fire workers were impaired by the co-ownership status of wokers, malingering could very well increase. In Japan, lifetime employment is practiced in many companies even without co-ownership, and worker commitment remains high. Japanese companies, however, are unusual in the degree to which they effect conditions of social predictability even in large factories by organizing workers in networks of small groups.[106]

The need for management to control malingering stems, of course, from each company's competitive position vis-à-vis other companies in eliciting "consumer votes." In buying that product which seems to offer the best quality for the most reasonable price, the consumer ultimately fires the malingerers (or incompetent managers) in those concerns which are least competitive. But those juristic persons which provide a public good not governed by consumer votes are in an entirely different position. These juristic persons expand the employment of personnel as a measure of organizational success. Since their survival does not depend directly on consumer choice, management lacks the external pressure to fight malingering. Thus, entire government bureaucracies become free-riding juristic persons.

Summary

Communist Man (Millennial Man) is most probable in small communities and least probable under statism. The utopian solution of anarcho-communism, therefore, is to create large stateless societies composed of small production cooperatives and communes. But without a state to initiate and maintain such a stateless condition, men must either be nonreciprocal altruists or they must achieve a degree of unanimity possible only within some kind of permanent and highly intense mass movement. Anarcho-communism requires a degree of universal commitment and consensus that only a genetic ecology—not a moral ecology—could provide.

Capitalist Man works well in large societies, tends to expand beyond and to blur national boundaries, and allegedly is the enemy of statism and big government. But without some sort of state to regulate growth, anarcho-capitalism, many fear, would lead to government by giant corporations. Although anarcho-capitalism assumes reciprocal altruism and favors diversity of behavior and differences of opinion, it does not convincingly obviate the state.

Anarcho-socialism would have us solve the problem by allowing workers to own and "self-manage" industries, a solution whose appeal is enhanced by the current fashionableness of the small-is-beautiful theme. Moreover, by overlapping on worker-management aspects of anarcho-communism and anarcho-capitalism, it provides an area of convergence for all three forms of anarchism. Worker management, therefore, has become the most popular form of utopian anarchism at present, the reason it was the major concern of this chapter.

As a form of collective production, worker management is open to the same assessments as previous case material in this book, as well as the additional evidence presented here on collective farming. Except under unusual circumstances, enterprise units are too large or too heterogeneous to make possible conditions of social predictability. While the high commitment of a mass movement might provide precisely the unusual circumstances necessary, the deliberate instigation and manipulation of such movements would presuppose a highly centralized state. Worker- or self-management is, therefore, susceptible to the same external influences of competitive consumption as other forms of collective production. Without collective consumption and the social-movement conditions that usually accompany it, worker- or self-management is even more vulnerable. When it does not fail altogether, it is most likely to survive as corporate production.

Chapter Ten

Participatory Evolution

THIS BOOK BEGINS with several ambitious questions. How and why do people provision collective good? Is progress coming to an end, or will it continue? In either case will the necessary adjustments reduce human freedom and individuality? Or to put it in other words, can humanity control its technology and economy for either a progressive or steady state without Hobbesian overlords? To what extent can humanity depend on other than purely material incentives? Are material incentives of growth and progress essential to the maintenance of collective good? Implicitly at least, the preceding chapters have endeavored to answer these questions. There my chief concern was to stick to moral *assessments*, leaving moral and "exploratory" *judgments* of a personal nature until the end. This chapter, then, goes beyond moral assessment to moral judgment. Having stated this at the outset, I see no need to load my sentences with qualifiers. Opinions expressed firmly and directly are not commands. I write as citizen, never as Planner. Objective certainty has never been an attribute of opinions, so the purpose of expressing them firmly is simply to provoke a healthy exchange of views.

Recapitulation

In a recent article in *Science*, biologist W. H. Murdy has taken the position that man must participate in his own evolution to overcome the current knowledge crisis.[1] Humanity's cumulative knowledge appears to have outgrown its collective wisdom, a situation that threatens its very survival. Since man has more power than any other species to affect his evolution, he must learn to identify with human destiny and what Murdy calls the "greater wholes" of "society and nature." Man must learn to restrain the "unbridled self-indulgence" which has been typical of past generations and learn to identify with future generations. To effect this collective bond with the future, man must embrace an anthropocentric faith in his own destiny.

Here we come back to the problem of collective good in a monoecological world. In a way Murdy, like Boulding, is asking us to let future generations "vote." Again we encounter an example of the broadest possible extension of the liberal interpretation of Rousseau's general will. The new moral man will act for his own good only after first asking if it is in the best interest of everyone else, *including* future generations. But moral assessments of the future are a problem of prediction or "exploratory calculation." Who presumes the omniscience of knowing how future generations will vote?

Ron Dare, a physical anthropologist who has replied to Murdy, is disturbed not by the problems of prediction inherent in this view of participatory evolution but by Murdy's call for anthropocentric faith.[2] This he regards as a "biomystical teleology" worthy of a Teilhard de Chardin. On the contrary, Dare is confident that people do act for the good of future generations and will continue to do so because of *phylogenic* altruism of both reciprocal and kin-selective forms. We have nothing to worry about; our genes are programmed to take care of us.

This kind of faith in man's genetic predisposition to support the greatest of collective goods has recently drawn fire from economist Paul Samuelson, who accuses the new field of sociobiology of reviving social Darwinism in a new form.[3] The old social Darwinism, says Samuelson, "regarded altruism as dysgenic"; but the new form not only revives Kropotkinism, it gives it biological survival value. So completely do I sympathize with Samuelson's position that I have been careful, first, to distinguish between reciprocal altruism and what I have labeled "nonreciprocal" altruism and, second, to employ the reciprocal form predominantly in a cultural or ontogenic sense. To trust to phylogenic altruism resulting from reciprocal and kin-selective adaptations is biomystical phylogeny in my view.

Some might wonder why, if I employ the concept "reciprocal altruism" in an adaptive context that is primarily cultural, I do not simply speak of exchange. The reason I do not is that this sociocultural phenomenon had phylogenic roots which help explain how social life itself may have been instrumental in the development of the unique, knowledge-building, human brain. But the great marvel of human reciprocal altruism is that by helping to develop the cognitive abilities of the mind it became uniquely cultural or ontogenic. It is important to remember this. The only altruism we can seriously depend upon for future cultural adaptation is this ontogenic or exchange form. To some, "exchange" may seem a more neutral, and therefore a better, term than "reciprocal altruism." But in that "neutral" sense, exchange is often opposed to altruism with the implication we should rise above the self-interest inherent in exchange to achieve a higher level of morality. This is why I stay with "reciprocal altruism"; it is not only the highest form of altruism, there would be no moral ecology without it. Moreover, the essential cognitive nature of this altruism continually expands the boundaries of moral ecology via its moral assessments. Any hope for "participatory evolution" must take this uniquely cognitive form of reciprocal altruism into account. To do otherwise would be phylogenic utopianism.

In all the societies we looked at in this book, no matter how eutopian, we found strong selective incentives. Even the small fraternal communities with their powerful commitments to group goals were not immune. Despite a fight-self general will that could make members ponder the consequences for the collective good of their every individual act, there was both a positive exchange of rewards between Ego and Group and an effective sanctioning capability on the part of the community.

The collective good in a capitalist utopia is presumably the product of an invisible hand that results in turn from millions of individual transactions motivated by the selective incentive called "profit." And when the invisible hand is replaced by the directing hand of a socialist eutopia, severe social "costs" may be engineered to motivate selectively support for the collective good. Nowhere do we find a collective good maintained without self-interest. Nowhere, in other words, do we find "altruism" without some form of individual reinforcement.

At the biosocial level a second crucial factor of concern to us in this book has been the "play" aspect of human behavior. Again, I refer primarily to a cultural or ontogenic phenomenon that is biosocial only in the sense of its ultimate origins. If certain aspects of man's behavior seem playful, they are certainly in keeping with his biological past both as primate and mammal. If we assume that play behavior has afforded those forms in which it arose some adaptive advantage and that this advantage is associated with learning, then it is not too surprising that man should remain playful most of his life; he continues to learn throughout it.

For culture the adaptive advantage of human playfulness, in my view, is general rather than specific. At the level of specific societies and their specific cultures there is a broad range of tolerance for playful behavior that may not be specifically adaptive. During the multiecological era as humanity spread over the biosphere, many forms of cultural play developed. In their entertaining book about human pecking orders, *The Dominant Man,* Maclay and Knipe provide a possible link between the play of humans and other primates.[4] For scholars like Donald Symons who have studied primate play believe its most important adaptive consequence is the reproductive success of the individual animal due to enhancement of defensive motor skills.[5] Dominance rank within the social orders of these animals is therefore a function of individual—not social—"survival."

When I speak of human "play," I am not limiting the word to the behavior of children; I am using it in the broad sense Huizinga did when writing of Homo ludens. Thus, such "dominance competitions" of primitive peoples as horse-stealing raids, counting coup, ceremonial exchange, potlatching, and so on can be viewed as adult games or forms of play. And while the games of industrial society may seem much less romantic than those of the "affluent" savage, there is no reason, as we have seen, to stress arbitrarily the "leisure preference" of affluent savagery over the "work preference" of "protestant," bourgeois industrialism. By seeing them all to some extent as "play," we can be more detached and universally critical.

We must not make the mistake, however, of assuming socially specific human forms of play to be specific in an adaptive sense. Among all animals forms of play are species specific. In other words, the exact forms of play behavior vary with each species, and one must legitimately ask to what extent these differences have adaptive significance. The rich variety of human play forms we must attribute to their cultural character. The variety of play rather than any particular form is what is species specific about Homo luden's play. It is the variety, therefore, rather than particular cultural manifestations, that has adaptive significance. The current tendency to find a "materialistic" explanation for all cultural "irrationalities" by brainstorming some "ecological system" in which they can be given an adaptive "function" is just another human game, one momentarily fashionable in some academic circles.

The adaptive significance of highly variable play behavior is its potential for innovation and change. It is a major part of humanity's general adaptive character which has made it successful in so many environments and under such different ecological stresses and pressures. A particular environment may tolerate a certain range of human-play forms that preserve this general adaptive character without any of them being specifically required by that "ecological" adaptation. An advantage of viewing human behavior this way is that we open all culture and therefore all societies to more intense moral inspection and assessment. Fortunately our long period of "cultural relativism" in the social sciences has given us more than sufficient sophistication to judge cultures without ethnocentric naiveté. In other words, while a specific form of human play may not be maladaptive (socially destructive) in its given time and place, it may not be the best adaptive response to the situation either. In that event citizens may judge it a game they can very well do without; they may judge it "maladaptive" to the moral ecology they wish to build as participants in their own evolution.

Human game playing in the long run has enhanced cultural development by providing motivational energy as well as a context in which cognitive innovation is more likely. Thus, while reciprocal altruism and play behavior have biological roots in the species, their expansion has been an integral part of ontogenic development. They have both been crucial factors in the new evolution.

In the old evolution what some biologists would call "the tendency for life to reproduce itself" combines with mutation to provide the energy and change components of adaptive radiation. The physical environment provides the selective reinforcement. In actual practice, however, explaining evolution is a very idiographic form of historical reconstruction in which the selective reinforcements peculiar to each speciation must be identified. It is on these that attention centers; for while the "energy" and change components may be necessary to a completely satisfying explanation of speciation, as constants they are much less interesting.

Similarly in the new evolution the motivational and cognitive components of culture change become uninteresting constants as one focuses on the "ecological" reinforcements that tend to vary with each situation. In the new evolution as in the old, explanation must rest ultimately on painstaking idiographic analysis. Both evolutions are the product of nonpredictive determinism. They are the long-term directions that result from short-term histories.

Both the old and new evolutions are therefore invisible-hand consequences of idiographic events. The invisible "hand" of both evolutions is, of course, purely metaphorical. To imply intent in either case would be teleological in the pejorative sense. What makes the new evolution seem less metaphorical and therefore more mysterious is that human beings act with purpose. But the sum or consequence of all the individually purposive acts is far removed from any single purposive act and therefore far removed from any "predictable" control.

Man became aware of the invisible hand of the new evolution long before he was willing to acknowledge a similar hand in the old evolution. He looked back over his history and saw a progress that had unintentionally resulted from millions of purposive acts over millions of years. This judgment coincided with the supraecological era and the spread of the civilization of capitalism. The new game of market exchange and money economy began to eclipse all the older games. The growth of science correlative to that of the new game and the belief in progress provided the evidence and inspired the confidence that enabled man to renounce the "hidden hand" of divine providence as an acceptable explanation of the old evolution.

As man enters the monoecological era, he dreams more and more of participatory evolution. He dreams of shifting progress from invisible hand to directing hand. He hopes to bring the future within the scope of plan and thereby make it totally benign and totally predictable. Such dreams often presume a controlling hand rather than a directing hand. The directing hands of catch-up, socialist eutopias sometimes create the illusion of control because the goal has already been reached by others via a well-trodden path. But the dream of a controlling hand is but a modern version of the old utopian dream, for the future is still as unpredictable as ever. Although the purposive acts of groups under the label of "planning" become ever more comprehensive, the directing hand can never achieve "control" without omniscience and omnipotence; and it will never achieve either. The idea of letting future generations "vote" or of trying to form a "bond" with future generations presumes the predictability of omniscience. We must be skeptical of anyone who claims to know the votes of future generations, for he is simply justifying his own demands and predilections in their name. The collective good that such a utopian wishes the rest of us to support is usually little more than a personal judgment.

Moreover, it is likely to be a collective game in which we are invited to act as object players, for the rules of play depend on the utopian's authority.

Participation in Evolution

As long as we preserve a strong, healthy skepticism of utopian demands, they cease to be a danger and become instead a contribution to the collective good. I say that because the collective good should always be a matter of public debate and discussion. Human crises, of which the current so-called knowledge crisis is only one, are an important condition for cultural growth. Even arguments over the inevitability and desirability of growth are symptomatic of syntropic development toward more direction and experimental planning. Notions of collective good, progress, and evolution overlap more and more.

The idea of progress began as a positive appraisal of the past and an optimistic projection of that appraisal into the future. But there was never total agreement on the substance of progress. Rousseau, whom we have dubbed the father of antiprogress, is a case in point. For him the progress of his day was not a collective good because it did not benefit everyone equally. He wanted a progress that would be a true collective good in this egalitarian sense; and to insure that it would be, he wanted all people to participate in lawmaking. The moral judgment of each citizen should have equal weight in deciding the rules of the game.

Before we could even attempt to decide whether progress is coming to an end, we would first have to agree that it has ever existed. Total agreement on this point is impossible, for just as individuals hope for different kinds of futures, so do they differ in their appraisals of the past. We can more easily agree that there has been evolution or change, for that requires only the acceptance of history—not a moral judgment of it. But it is important that we go beyond the mere acceptance of history and of its moral assessment by experts. We must all prepare to make our own moral judgment of the past and to argue our own moral preferences for the future.

As forms of social criticism even dystopian portrayals of the future are pedagogically useful to arguments about progress. They help spread awareness of alternatives and help involve us as subject players in active moral judgment. It is this concern for progress, rather than any particular notion of it, that is likely to influence evolution. Concern for progress inspires ever more exacting moral assessments of development processes and environmental opportunities. To the extent such assessments contribute to directed change, ideas about progress and collective good become a part of evolution.

It is in much this sense that George Land, in his *Grow or Die,* sees continuing positive growth in human culture.[6] Growth is so much a part of life that any attempt to return to a past state or to conserve a balanced or stationary state would be a setting for extinction rather than survival. To date, says Land, the history of life knows no exceptions to this rule. However, the improper application of an electric-feedback model to life systems has contributed to a homeostatic view of organisms and culture, which in fact are heterostatic. Thus, the positive feedback that magnifies distortion to the point of instability and disintegration in an electrical system is an essential nutritive aspect of growth in life systems.

Land distinguishes three forms of this growth through positive feedback: accretive, replicative, and mutual. The first is simply growth in size; the second is growth in numbers as in cell division; but the third involves information exchange that is not only heterostatic but syntropic in its consequences. Nutritive, positive feedback through information exchange opens a system to dynamic adaptive growth. In society and culture such information exchange depends on "dynamic human relationships" that are "mutually enriching" in the sense that they generate both "evaluation" and "new information." Growth through mutualistic information exchange is always greater than the sum of its parts and is therefore syntropic rather than entropic.[7] Thus, we might say that at the level of information exchange reciprocal altruism becomes the genesis of cultural syntropy.

Land takes an additional step, however, that seems to me unnecessary. To give his book a more argumentative and challenging tone, he exhorts us to action. We must continue to grow and develop or face extinction; he places the entire outcome in our hands.[8] In short, the syntropy of mutualism has reached a crucial point where its further evolution depends entirely on our decision to resist some entropic tendency within us to withdraw from the game of life. I do not believe he can have it both ways. Either the information exchange of mutualistic feedback and growth is syntropic or it is not. If it is, the process is too established, too gradual, and too universal to be under our control. It is another case of invisible-hand determinism.

If syntropic, mutualistic evolution is another case of nonpredictive determinism, humanity will continue to be the beneficiary of progressive collective good no matter what anyone claims or does. Then why do anything about this collective good at all? Why not be free riders? That, of course, is the beauty of all long-run collective goods produced by an invisible hand. We must all be free riders in their provisioning, for that is the only way they come to us. But they do not really come to *us*, they come to our descendents. Or at least we hope so, since we will not be there to see for ourselves. So we play our short-run games and let the long run take care of itself. Why not? We live, as Keynes said, in the short run. The only long-run collective goods we actually enjoy are those we review—not predict—which means their goodness is, more often than not, a matter of opinion.

If we choose to provision a collective good at all, we would do well to pick one of the short-run variety we can enjoy. There are always plenty of this kind to provision. But what about the short-run collective good that may be a long-run collective disaster? Who says it will be a long-run disaster, and what are that person's credentials? Why is it that such dangers, if real, do not offer enough short-run threats to provide short-run negative incentives? Is it rational to worry about catastrophes so far in the uncertain future that we could not possibly live to experience them? On the other hand, who says we have to be rational?

We have already said that people play many games which are not "rational" in the sense of being essential for survival. Working and arguing for the collective good of future generations is becoming an interesting game with many participants. It provides another way to get public visibility and attention and to interact pleasurably with interesting people. And the participants may be sincere performers who feel strongly about the issues. Is this not the way that life should be played? Should not each one find the game or games he can play with enough sincerity to get caught up in their enjoyment?

Games of which to beware are those that demand participation as object players. One can be open to persuasion from those who work for future generations; one can listen to their arguments, and on some issues join their game as subject player. On other issues one may find the arguments unconvincing. In that event should we let experts or authorities dictate to us in the name of posterity? If they did, would we not be justified in doing Patrick Henry one better by voting for the death of future generations as well as our own? Is it not better to "muddle through" (see Chapter 7) together either into oblivion or into syntropy than to be planned into utopia?

It was the conviction of the great existentialist Kierkegaard that exploration and development of self was most likely to occur during those demanding periods in an individual's life when he was most involved in the "pathos of choice."[9] The freedom to make one's own decisions and to add thereby to personal growth is the freedom of the subject player as contrasted with the object player. But the complex modern world offers us far more choices than we have the time and emotional capacity to experience. Even the subject player must take short cuts.

Perhaps the most marvelous of all humanity's shortcuts to choice is habit rationality. Many people think of habit as a retarding, conservative force with which we fight a constant running battle that is never won. Actually, habit is one of our most rational attributes as a simple example of consumer choice well illustrates. A young couple's small children wear out several pairs of jeans per year. The couple goes back again and again to one particular store because its location is convenient and both the product and the price are competitive. Why bother to do extensive research on the price and quality of jeans? Why make this decision into a big, time-consuming issue? The same couple, however, decides to buy a freezer so it can buy meat and other products in bulk quantities to save money. But the price of a freezer represents a large percentage of the couple's annual income. So it carefully compares quality and price and even investigates the costs of freezer maintenance to compare with estimated savings on bulk purchases.

If we tried to research every choice we have to make in an average day, we would not only accomplish little, we would become hopelessly neurotic.[10] To conserve our time, energy, and concentration for choices of importance, we let habit rationality be our "automatic pilot" in making those that matter less. Where past reinforcements have been sufficiently positive, we expediently return for more. Not only individuals but whole societies use this automatic pilot, which Max Weber called "usage" and "convention."[11] These terms include the uniform behaviors people follow unreflectively and collectively because they are accustomed to do so. Different societies, however, can have very different automatic pilots depending on past social experience and the patterns of reinforcement these engender. The mutualism of information exchange has an enormous effect on the level and quality of this automatic pilot, a point to which I return below.

A second important time saver for choice in a modern complex society is the specialization that makes possible both cumulative knowledge and syntropic mutualism. But specialists in a society of specialists must depend on each other. The big question is how they can monitor each other for cheating behavior without leaving their own areas of competence. In all the many fields outside our own we must rely on moral assessments made by competent strangers. And when differences of opinion between experts in the same field are crucial to the moral judgments we as subject players want to make about the present or future, how do we even know which experts to believe? If we decide to trust experts in those areas of cumulative knowledge most crucial to our welfare, are we not likely to end up being played by planners and guardians?

The best way to watchdog experts is to insist they make the best possible moral assessment of a situation and then leave the final moral judgment to society at large. But this means a great deal of intelligent voting requiring tremendous amounts of time. The kibbutz is a good illustration. In the early days, as we saw, it was small, relatively unspecialized and strongly committed. General meetings were enthusiastically attended and everyone kept up on everything that was going on. But a kibbutz in the early days was an intense group game at which members tirelessly played for 12 to 16 hours a day. As kibbutzim grew older, larger, more specialized and less intense, the group game became less interesting. Now general meetings are often poorly attended, for members have come to resent the great amount of time consumed by group decisions in a community that tries to apply them to everything. So by sheer default, community government becomes less participatory and more representational.

The kibbutz was a great test of Rousseauean democracy. It showed how hard it is to avoid representative government. How could we all attend town meetings every night to decide local, regional and national issues? So the third important time saver for choice is to delegate part of our decision making to congressional representatives and bureaucratic administrators. As Rousseau saw, however, this makes us all vulnerable to insidious forms of cheating by powerful persons and groups.

An alternative to the representative form of time saving is to shift voting as much as possible from the arena of group decision to that of "consumer choice." All societies do this with the automatic pilot of habit rationality, usage, or convention. But not all encourage this automatic pilot to work through the market. A utopian ideal of laissez-faire capitalism is that it permits all members of society to vote directly, constantly and effortlessly simply by the way in which they spend their discretionary time and money. It is for this reason that libertarians or anarcho-capitalists advocate replacing government services with private ones as much as possible. Unfortunately we cannot plug all our social problems into the marketplace in such a fashion that subject-playing "consumers" can "vote" on competing solutions through their pocket-books. All things considered, how can we possibly play such a cosmic game as participatory evolution without converting most of the public into object players?

Inequality and Participation

The biggest obstacle to distributing power equally, as Rousseau himself was aware, is the fact that some people are born with more intelligence than others. If they want to cheat and "exploit," they are better equipped to do so. Since material progress increases the cheating opportunities of the gifted, Rousseau wanted to counterbalance material progress with social progress. It is in this sense that we labeled Rousseau the father of antiprogress. He was not really antiprogressive per se; he was opposed to a lopsided version that benefited the few. Rousseau was not so blinded by the long-run panorama of history that he failed to see all the misery persisting in the short run. We can speak categorically of "Rousseau's Man" as the one who opposes material progress without social progress—progress in the long run without enough in the short run. Rousseau's Man insists on a more equitable distribution of the material benefits of evolutionary change *now*, in *this* lifetime.

One of the oldest justifications for Rousseau's Man has been Pascal's Man. French mathematician Blaise Pascal left us one of the most widely quoted renditions of the 17th-century idea of progress.[12] So far as science or cumulative knowledge was concerned, he saw the entire succession of human beings over the ages as like "a single man who persists forever" and never stops learning. Pascal's Man is at once cumulative culture, syntropy, and the so-called "social fund."

Edward Bellamy was probably the most famous utopian to apply the social-fund idea in support of egalitarianism.[13] As the argument goes, all the good things of our age have been bequeathed to us by the peoples of the past. These goods constitute an inheritance, one might say, from our common father, Pascal's Man. It was he who created all these goods and left them to us, so why should some of his children live in palaces and others die in the gutter? Should not the inheritance, this social fund, be divided equally among the heirs? The rational citizens of Bellamy's utopia designed it as a commune on just this logic. But did they have their facts straight? Did all the people of the past contribute equally to the fund, or did a tiny, gifted few down through the ages bequeath most of it? Did just a brainy elite make up the intelligence of Pascal's Man?

Jonathan and Stephen Cole recently put the social-fund notion to the test strictly within the profession of physics.[14] Does the great physicist build on the contributions of all the lesser physicists? Their results do not so indicate. The Coles found that creative work in physics takes place within a small elite at the top of the profession. The nutritive feedback of creative-information exchange in physics is restricted overwhelmingly to this group. To judge from the Coles's study, only the brain of Pascal's Man contributes to the new evolution.

Is this so surprising? The variability of human aptitudes is a significant part of human adaptability, for the very inequality of our genetic endowment enhances our survival. If the contribution Pascal's Man makes to our well being is a product of inequality, to what extent can Rousseau's Man eliminate social inequality without destroying that contribution?

Even Bellamy, who thought the gifted individual should voluntarily make a contribution to society in proportion to his abilities, not rewards, designed a meritocratic utopia that gave highest status for greatest ability. The equal-opportunity meritocracy has become the egalitarian's favorite compromise with inherent inequality.

In the view of some, however, a meritocracy that really worked would have dystopian, not utopian, consequences. Peregrine Worsthorne, for example, cannot imagine any stratification system more dreadful than that resulting from an effective meritocracy.[15] Eventually all the members of the upper class would be truly superior and would know it, and all those in the lower class would be truly inferior and know it. The individuals at the bottom as well as those at the top could rest assured that their positions in society were precisely what they deserved.

British sociologist Michael Young had a lot of fun with this idea in his dystopian novel, *The Rise of the Meritocracy, 1870–2033*.[16] Not only did all the brains rise to the top in his story, the best brains of both sexes intermarried and stayed there. And as the technology became increasingly complex, the permanently stupid lower-class families ended up as the domestic servants of the intelligentsia because they were not competent to do anything else. Thus, the social stratification that the meritocracy of equal opportunity had been established to destroy was recreated in the form of a caste system so hopelessly rigid that not even opportunity could ever be equal again. What Young is saying, of course, is that opportunities are never really equal as long as some people start out with a hereditary advantage.

Geneticist Dobzhansky believes that contemporary Western society is already sufficiently meritocratic to allow a "tendency" for high-ability people to concentrate at the top of the social ladder.[17] But he does not believe this will ever result in genetically fixed classes. Human abilities are too qualitatively diversified for one thing, and for another, performance levels continue to remain "fluid" between generations. He suggests that we may get "aptitude aggregations" rather than fixed socioeconomic classes. These aggregations would simply be concentrations of individuals genetically appropriate for their jobs. But unlike traditional social classes, they would not become permanent strata.

According to the results of the much publicized study of inequality by Christopher Jencks, heredity has much less to do with success than we have been accustomed to believe.[18] Income differences among brothers, for example, are surprisingly close to those for the population as a whole. In the same vein, the Coles found that while it does take considerable intelligence to get a Ph.D. in physics (the average IQ of Ph.D.s in physics is 140), performance in the profession beyond that point does not correlate with IQ scores.[19]

Admittedly IQ scores are an imperfect measure of intelligence, but something besides native ability is important to success and would continue to be even in a perfect meritocracy. Individual life histories will always vary and will always result in different personalities. Birth order alone can make for enormous differences in the social environment and social reinforcements of children in the same family. Only in behaviorist utopias (or dystopias) like that depicted by Aldous Huxley in his *Brave New World* are people turned out all alike in assembly-line fashion.[20] As long as personality factors are "scrambled" or randomized by accidents of life history, social mobility should remain highly fluid even in a meritocracy. An effective meritocracy might have just the results Dobzhansky speculates it would have—a great many highly fluid aptitude aggregations.

It seems unlikely that individual performances in a meritocratic society could ever be so clearly related to native ability that unsuccessful people would have to admit to being "truly" inferior. The common face-saving procedure today is to blame one's situation on bad luck, and according to Jencks's study this common explanation is correct. Luck and "personality" are probably more important determinants of success or lack of it than native ability, family background, or education. It is extremely doubtful that any meritocracy could be so perfect as to eliminate the influence of luck and personality.

Even if performance and native ability could be closely matched in a meritocracy that reduced the factor of luck, would this situation necessarily be harder to take than one like ours with all its uncertainties? The Coles found that physicists can size up their career chances fairly well at an early age because the criteria for measuring a successful performance in "hard" sciences like physics tend to be "universalistic" and unambiguous.[21] In other words, by its very nature physics tends to be more meritocratic than most other professions. Yet those physicists who can see by the age of 30 that they are going to be "minor league" performers the rest of their lives do not turn into frustrated failures suffering from acute anomie. The Coles suggest that "failure" may be easier to accept within a reward system everyone considers fair.

In a sense, the ability one is born with is the first "luck" or chance factor in any individual's life. And if one's career ends at a point clearly and justly commensurate with one's native ability, could this not also be viewed as the final result of that initial luck? Such an ultimate form of luck, however, allows little room for anger at the unfairness of the social order. Perhaps the major reason the people of 19th-century England seemed so content with their class system was because so many at the bottom still thought it fair for one man to be "born" a gentleman and another to be "born" a butler. If a meritocratic system could provide the same sense of fairness on "rational" grounds, we might all be more content with our lot than ever before.

It is most unlikely, however, that we shall ever have a meritocracy in which performance criteria throughout the society could be as universal and unambiguous as in physics. Not even all so-called "sciences" have performance criteria of this quality. Stanislav Andreski has written a delightful book lampooning social science on just these grounds.[22] Because social science is closer to an art form—and some like Andreski would say a very bad art form—the criteria for judging excellence are often personal and ambiguous. Consequently social scientists are able to play a game which tolerates the influence of luck and personality far more than physics. This circumstance leads to the ludicrous play fads of jargon, methodology, and so-called "theory" that occupy the ambitious, industrious mediocrities of these professions. Presumably a study of sociologists similar to the Coles' study of physicists would show a much lower average IQ and a much slower, later, and more anomic reaction to failure. Social scientists often speak of "late bloomers," and those who speak of them are usually in middle life still hoping to "bloom."

Performances by the different members of society are always going to be unequal, and we will never be certain that we have given the best or most deserving people a fair chance to show what they could do. We must stand by Rousseau's Man, however, in continually advocating improvement of the system so that each person can more fully realize his potential if he so desires. In doing so, we help to improve the brain of Pascal's Man for short-run as well as long-run payoffs; we help to improve it for the esoteric moral assessments on which we base our short-run, exoteric moral judgments. But we can always be certain, too, that no matter how good the brain of Pascal's Man becomes, it will always be imperfect as will its moral assessments. And that is why we, like Rousseau's Man, must continue to insist that each of us actively contributes to the final moral judgments.

Visibility and Participation

To get the best possible moral assessments, we must allow and encourage the most talented people to achieve their full potential. But "encouragement" must not include rewards that give them the power to convert their moral assessments into action judgments. We must never tolerate specialists of moral judgment; for that is the road to all totalitarianisms including, as we have seen, behavioral utopianism. Pascal's Man must not be rewarded with the power to so dominate Rousseau's Man that he becomes a guardian or planner who plays the rest of us on his utopian chessboard.

When the Coles discovered that more than 80 percent of the creative work in physics was accomplished by less than 20 percent of the profession, they speculated that economy might be served by producing at least 50 percent fewer physicists.[23] Such a reduction, they felt, by increasing demand and selectivity, would also improve the product. But the Coles's research also showed that the less distinguished physicists tend to be more widely read than their more creative fellows and tended to have a greater awareness of all the new developments taking place. These are primarily teachers, and they produce primarily teachers. But those who keep abreast of what is going on in any field are in the best position to monitor its creative elite. Would we really be better off to eliminate two-thirds of these watchdogs? Or should we have twice as many?

Pascal's Man has to be monitored by someone. He has to be visible to people who can understand and interpret what he is doing. In the syntropic world of mutualistic information exchange, education and understanding are as vital to visibility as they are to exchange. The argument that the masses are over-educated, that few really need a college education, that more people should be directed into vocational schools at an earlier age has become increasingly popular of late. For the nurture of Pascal's Man, not Rousseau's Man, this argument may be valid. Nazi Germany, for example, economized in the education of its masses. The very best students got the very best scientific training, and by the age of 14, the poorer performers were shunted into occupational schools to learn mechanical skills. Pascal's Man was fed while Rousseau's Man was starved. And we all know the result. A country with remarkable scientific and technological expertise became morally bankrupt. Modern Russia is similar except that there a growing body of dissidents is now crying for Rousseau's Man to be fed. Higher education must never be viewed as purely occupational and its results weighed only on wage scales. In a world of increasing specialization, we must all become increasingly sophisticated in judging the moral assessments of other specialists. It is the job of Rousseau's Man to keep Pascal's Man from cheating. Our peace and prosperity in the short run depend on it.

Pascal's Man never cheats in the long run, for in the long run he is cumulative, syntropic culture. Only in the short run is he flesh and blood, and only in the short run—the time space in which we live—does he draw blood. So difficult has the job become of monitoring Pascal's Man, that increasing numbers of utopians are turning to Kropotkin's Man for their solution. The Bubers, Schumachers, Nozicks, Nisbets, and countless others advocate a return to a world in which visibility is more direct. The small-is-beautiful theme is mainly a mirage, however, for small can be ugly indeed.

All those of anarchistic persuasion, whether they be anarcho-communists, anarcho-socialists or anarcho-capitalists, would like to make our social units in some way smaller. Certainly they should continue to argue their convictions, for this is one important way in which human play brings about information exchange. And if Nozick's smorgasbord of utopian communities were to become a reality, we would all do well to take our pick and make the best of it. But if there is one thing I feel safe in "predicting," it is that no such smorgasbord will ever occur. It is the high visibility of the small community from which people have been escaping for hundreds of years.[24] As one who has spent considerable time in village communities, I can readily understand why. It is a stifling world in which everyone monitors everyone else; it is the only real world in which Big Brother (the group) is forever watching each and every member. And communist China is the only large state to simulate this degree of monitoring by organizing the entire population in small groups and keeping it as far as possible in small communities.

We have had community movements, and we will have more; and those people who find communes and other intentional communities congenial should be allowed to enjoy them. The percentage of people who choose to live in such societies even for the duration of a social movement will always be small. In Zionist Israel, where all the conditions for Buber's total cooperative were so ideal, only a very small percentage of the population has chosen this way of life.

As a part society, moreover, the intentional community is vulnerable to the same external influences as the traditional community. The opportunities for personal growth and freedom of expression outside the little community eventually become overpowering. I have talked to people in some of the most uninviting squatter settlements around Latin American cities and found them not only optimistic about their future but determined never to return to their rural villages. One of the most common reasons given for this preference is greater freedom. People find a new freedom from kinship obligations and the continual interference of the small community in their daily lives.

Robert Nisbet, in his *Twilight of Authority,* laments the "decay" of the family in modern times.[25] For him, the importance of strong kinship systems was primarily economic and political, not affectional or moral. In those societies where the extended family was strong, says Nisbet, the power of the state was correspondingly limited. The state, in fact, became an "association of families, not of discrete individuals." Does he have in mind the patrimonial empire of dynastic China?

A lifetime is a very limited good, and each day is precious. Do we want to spend that time with companions picked for us by the accident of birth? Do we really want to commit our time to people with whom we have genes in common rather than to persons whose interests and backgrounds make them desirable companions by choice?

Nisbet rues the day humanity moved toward legal predictability, and his major target in that transition is Roman law, which he believes is reasserting itself today.[26] Modern "Romanist" tendencies within United States law, according to Nisbet, have become an active force for redesigning the social order not as judicial power per se but by usurping legislative and executive powers. Fear of central utopian planning under the guise of law, particularly its administrative form, is shared by many thoughtful persons. But whatever the dangers and difficulties that face us in the realm of legal predictability, we cannot live in a complex modern world without it. We cannot return to a world that relies entirely on the small-group conditions of social predictability.

As Elizabeth Colson shows in her recent study, the growth of codified law in Africa has definitely strengthened central power by reducing the flexibility of customary law.[27] The codified law leaves less to the discretion of the local court because of its impersonal nature. Yet this same impersonal quality makes it far more equitable and easier to administer. As courts and their judgments become more standardized, people travel more easily without fear of being at the mercy of a strange and biased court. Even in their home community they gain a new sense of freedom, for they no longer have to devote time to the social demands of a highly personal (status) form of law. They do not have to worry as much about local opinion and can go straight to court without having to win their kinsmen to their cause. In the old days they had to invest great amounts of time maintaining close cordial relationships with all their kin just so they could count on kin support in time of legal trouble. The new impersonal system, says Colson, allows each person to "live more freely."

Despite resentment of a perceived increase in central power, the village Africans have no desire to go back to the world of customary law. They value their greater spatial freedom as well as the new social freedom to pick friends and companions on other than kinship grounds. To those already removed from it by at least half a dozen generations, the small kinship society can have the strong appeal of Kropotkian romanticism. But those born to it, or only one generation removed, see it through entirely different eyes.

The social freedom that comes with legal predictability comes at the sacrifice of the high visibility characteristic of the small community. What we have to achieve is a form of high visibility that is impersonal, equitable, and, yet, not an invasion of personal privacy or a threat to individual liberties. Science provides an excellent example of this kind of high visibility. Individuals who meet for the first time at a professional meeting may already be well known to one another professionally through their published papers. Science, by its very nature, makes its active participants highly visible to one another in this impersonal fashion. Yet the sanctions of this impersonal form of high visibility are every bit as effective as those of an intentional or traditional community. Each scientist's published contributions are open to criticism and verification by colleagues. And in no social group is excommunication more final or devastating than that of a scientist caught "cheating"; the culprit is never fully reaccepted by the profession. So open is science for the purpose of information exchange that *flagrant* cheating rarely occurs; the probability of escaping detection is much too low to make it tempting.

The peculiar nature of the game of science makes it easy for the players to monitor one another in an impersonal way that neither invades privacy nor restricts freedom of movement or creativity. In Efremov's utopia *Andromeda,* where everyone has become a creative scientist, the rules of the game operate purely on public opinion and impersonal visibility with little need for formal law.[28] Since it is not likely that all people will ever have the opportunity or ability to be scientists, impersonal visibility must be obtained by other means. Besides, most scientists never publish, and even those who do may cheat in "acceptable" ways like fudging on their income tax returns.

H. G. Wells gave serious consideration to visibility in his *A Modern Utopia* (1905), although he called it "identification." [29] The "homely methods of identification" that served so well "in the little communities of the past where everyone knew everyone" could no longer suffice in a modern world where so much spatial mobility prevailed. A "responsible" modern world, Wells believed, would have to be able to locate and identify people at all times. Files, indexed by "some unchanging physical characteristic such as the thumb-mark" would be kept on everyone, and there each person's last location would be recorded. Wells supposed that many readers might find this notion of complete surveillance highly objectionable. But he urged them not to assume that such a government would be evil. The one he had in mind would be discreet, and he referred to its benevolent surveillance as the "quiet eye of the state."

Wells was certainly correct in anticipating a negative reaction to this quiet-eye concept for benevolent government. It became the underlying theme of two famous dystopias, Zamyatin's *We* and Orwell's *1984.*[30] Both did such a marvelous job of frightening everyone that for most people today benevolence and surveillance are mutually exclusive concepts. "Big Brother is watching you" has become a favorite symbol of sinister, totalitarian malevolence.

In 1890, 15 years before Wells's notion of the quiet eye, utopian Theodor Hertzka proposed a very different kind of visibility for a complex industrial society, one much closer to that of science.[31] In his utopia, Freeland, citizens could monitor officials and organizations whether public or private. As in science, this visibility was accomplished through publication and unrestricted information exchange. The "fundamental condition" for the successful operation of this utopia, declared Hertzka, was the complete elimination of secrecy and complete public exposure of all transactions in both government and business. The weakness of Wells's system of visibility lay in his failure to balance it with Hertzka's. The benevolence of a quiet eye can only be guaranteed by reciprocal public monitoring, in other words, a completely open system with visibility in both directions.

The Hertzkian direction is enjoying some popularity at the moment through current investigations of secrecy and collusion in business, government, and even such agencies as the FBI and CIA. But as Weisband and Franck have recently pointed out, the thefts of secret papers that initiated this investigative climate are only "the tip of the Ellsberg." [32] In the United States, they argue, the structure of the executive branch of government is such that the publication of stolen documents by a "politicized" free press has come to replace normal political dissent and public discussion. British ministers, for example, are much more likely to resign in protest than are top officials in the United States; and when they do, they not only publicly disagree with their prime minister, they often make public the official information necessary to justify their decision. While British law is far less permissive than United States law to "going public" with official information, the British characteristically reveal much more when resigning than do their American counterparts. An American official who resigns, no longer able to support presidential policy in good conscience, continues to remain "loyal" to the Chief and keeps his reasons to himself.

This difference in behavior reflects important structural differences of the two systems. Top United States officials in the executive branch come predominantly from big business or the law and are characteristically team players. To act in a way that appears disloyal, no matter how convincing the reasons, brands the protester a poor risk for anybody's team. The protester's career, business, law, or government, is permanently damaged. A British minister, on the other hand, is also a member of parliament and has a public constituency to impress. And if he sees himself as a prospective prime minister, he will be anxious to extend this political base. The minister is likely to be positively reinforced for showing "ethical autonomy." Instead of ruining his career, he tends to enhance it.[33]

Weisband and Franck, like others before them, advocate a United States cabinet composed only of members of congress. But if such a structural change proves long in coming, we must not in the meantime make the existing situation worse. The lower-echelon officials who clandestinely xerox government documents and mail them to their favorite newspaper columnist have become a vital lifeline to freedom within our system. While the motives of bureaucratic malcontents who make disclosures to the press may more often be personal and vindictive than public spirited, we must not pass laws to make such actions criminal or to impair either freedom of the press or the confidentiality of its sources.

It may seem inconsistent to defend one form of secrecy while arguing against secrecy in general. Certainly, if the day ever came when we had Hertzkian openness, there would be no need for confidentiality of newspaper sources because disclosure of all transactions would be mandatory and automatic. Disclosure would become so routine as to be completely unnewsworthy except when cheating was exposed. But with cheating so much easier to detect, as in science, it would become less tempting. In the meantime, however, we must preserve the one form of secrecy that provides a weapon to attack the rest.

The usurpation and abuse of power through secrecy finds its strongest justification in arguments of national defense. The Watergate affair made this truth more evident than ever before. Fear of "communism" drives us into international strategies beyond the control of popular government and straight into the hands of those who would reduce us all to object players. Gradually, however, we are learning that "communism" is only a dystopian (for us) name for a utopian (for others) form of catch-up capitalism. None of its eutopian expressions ever match its utopian goals or ever will. With time, they are all doomed to the same kinds of "corrupting" influences that eventually undermine or change eutopian communities.

Secrecy must not only be challenged in government, it must be fought as well within those huge juristic persons we call "corporations." The main thrust of James Coleman's book on this topic is that the behavior of corporate actors should be made as visible to real persons as the latter are to the corporate actors.[34] He would accomplish this by equalizing the flow of information in both directions. At present the flow is too one-way: the corporate actor can get more information on persons than persons can get on the corporate actor. Barnet and Muller have made an even more compelling argument for corporate disclosure in their recent critique of multinational corporations.[35]

But while many persons can clearly see the advantages of a Hertzkian attack on secrecy at the top, they are antagonistic to any quiet-eye approach to secrecy at the bottom. They use the mystique of "privacy" to defend secrecy for the individual in the same way that those at the top cover up malfeasance in the name of national defense. Nisbet's arguments are again a useful case in point.[36] After decrying how government has become increasingly invisible to the public, he condemns the "gross violation" of former Vice President Rockefeller's "privacy" following his nomination. That this public figure should have been required to make such an extensive disclosure of his "economic, family and personal life" is viewed by Nisbet as a "litmus test" of our loss of freedom. If this persists, says Nisbet, we will have no more heroes; for if those of the past, like George Washington and Franklin D. Roosevelt, had had to make such disclosures, they would have been made too human to be worthy of our veneration!

Hertzka was right in assuming that the major purpose of all secrecy is cheating. Why should anyone guard the "privacy" of a tax return or business transaction if there is nothing to hide? If all tax returns and negotiations were equally available for everyone else's inspection, most of the cheating would end. The objection so often heard that "I don't want other people to know my business" is a precious subterfuge devised by Homo ludens to circumvent the rules of the game. If all citizens were equally exposed, their common nakedness would soon become a matter of mutual indifference. Again, exposure would be too general and common to be newsworthy except where it revealed cheating or social injustice. Prominent persons are always newsworthy; and if, as a result of complete exposure, those who seek public office learned to lead a private life in keeping with their public image, we might yet see real "heroes" in public office.

For most people this exposure would not be an invasion of "privacy" because no one would be interested in their records. This kind of public-record visibility would remain far more anonymous for the most part than the invasions of privacy that take place daily in small communities of either the traditional or intentional variety. Yet when Director of the Passport Office Frances Knight advocated a national registration of all citizens that would insure their personal identity through a national identity card, many people accused her of nothing less than the advocation of *1984*. All Knight wanted, in fact, was one form of benevolent quiet eye to end the use of false identification papers for criminal purposes. Not only are government losses in social security and welfare programs enormous, but false documents are a cover for drug traffickers, swindlers, fugitives from justice, tax evaders, and confidence men.

The impersonal quiet eye is needed not only to defend society against cheaters, it is more than ever essential to defend it against the so-called "crazies," members of revolutionary social movements who are willing to kill any number of innocent victims in pursuit of their utopian goals. Society must achieve the visibility necessary to defend itself against dangerous utopians at the bottom as well as the top of the social scale. One would hope that society wherever possible will monitor things—explosives, guns, and so on—rather than people. But if atomic-explosive devices ever make the danger from crazies severe enough, we shall have to invent quiet-eye defenses. Like H. G. Wells, I do not believe such steps would produce *1984* conditions.

As we saw in Chapter 8, *1984* was modeled indirectly on the catch-up, patrimonial empire. It is a place some people are coming from; it is not where *we* are headed. Only Spenglerian pessimists like Nisbet can seriously believe otherwise. Spenglerians renounce progress and sometimes even cultural evolution. They think in cyclical terms although they are seldom interested in the progressive side of even a cultural cycle. They choose, instead, to dwell on its downward slope, for they are characteristically doomsters.

Thus Nisbet sees nothing in the uncovering of Watergate to warrant praise for our "system." [37] The argument that our system saved us he labels "nonsense." Quite the contrary, the "revelations of Watergate" were simply the "products of accident." For Nisbet they merely confirm a downward trend toward further corruption and absolute power. This is an amazing statement of social causation. Initiating causes are usually accidental; but as any event unfolds, hundreds of factors contribute to its complete explanation. To make an initiating cause both necessary and sufficient for an event of this magnitude is far closer to "nonsense" than the view of which Nisbet is so contemptuous. In fact, when enough situational factors have contributed to the probability of a certain general outcome, any number of initiating causes, including the "luck" of one or more investigative reporters, may provoke the same general result.

This argument can be further illustrated by one long used to minimize the indispensability of any particular inventor. In the case of Edison's inventions, for example, the time was ripe for them, and had he not performed as he did, someone else would have. Two hundred years earlier, on the other hand, Edison might have invented something, but not the incandescent lamp. In the case of the executive branch of the United States government, some observers have wondered why a Watergate did not take place eight years earlier. Perhaps the initiating causes were late, rather than early. The exact time and many or all of the actors could have been different, but the self-corrective consequences for society would have been much the same. In how many countries of the world could an event like Watergate have unfolded at all, much less in the manner in which it did?

The growth of administrative law and the increasing use of extralegal facts in the process of judicial review are threatening developments to many people. They see in such trends a real danger that we shall all become objects of play on the chessboard of Pascal's Man; specialists will end up deciding everything according to a comprehensive plan. But a modern complex society cannot leave everything to the slow unfolding of common-law precedent. A modern society is necessarily segmented into many organizations which must establish rules of operation in order to plan. Purposive action is important to these kinds of rules and goals. These trends are not as dangerous as they sometimes appear for at least three reasons.

First, administrative law can and must be kept under legislative and judicial review. In this way specialized knowledge benefits society without the specialists turning us into object players. Second, the use of extralegal facts in judicial review does not mean that sociologists or economists are going to make our laws. There are bound to be cases so complex that courts will have to rely entirely on the testimony of experts they are not even able to understand. Scientific experts with equally impressive credentials will be called to testify on each side of a particular issue, and the courts will have to decide which to believe. This is precisely the problem of moral judgment that faces all of us in those decisions where we must weigh conflicting moral assessments made by different experts. Judges are only human, and the overwhelming indication at present is that they tend to follow, rather than lead, public opinion.

As any field of science makes the results of its research known to society, it slowly but inexorably alters public opinion. Paul Rosen shows in his book, *The Supreme Court and Social Science,* that even before the court admitted to using extralegal facts it was making moral judgments based on the social Darwinism of 19th-century social science.[38] But the "new social science" that began in the 1920's at the University of Chicago eventually altered public opinion, and court decisions responded to that change.

This is precisely what judicial review must do. It must bring the purposive, planning type of law deriving from legislative and administrative action in line with public knowledge and acceptability. It must interpret the vague moral principles of constitutional law in the light of popular moral judgment (public opinion) as this adapts to the syntropic consequences of mutualistic information exchange.

Third, the realm of public opinion as a kind of collective moral judgment and habit rationality must remain the basis of a spontaneous order over which no organization, plan, or administrative law can ever claim dominion. In his useful distinction between spontaneous order and organization, F. A. Hayek identifies private and contract law with the spontaneous order of a free society and codified public law with organization.[39] As he says, the whole purpose behind codification has been to make legal decisions more predictable, but when they invade the spontaneous order they become capricious. To invade the spontaneous order of the total society with administrative law would be to turn it into an organization, a planned eutopia. As we have seen, an intentional community can accomplish this through strong membership commitment under conditions of social predictability while a eutopian, catch-up state is more likely to achieve it through a neopatrimonial form of public law "predictable" to the planners but often capricious and manipulatory from the standpoint of the masses.

In the spontaneous order, according to Hayek, a "mutual correspondence of expectations" develops through the social interaction of private persons. The judge most likely to render "predictable" legal decisions is the one who tries to ascertain what private persons have "legitimately" come to expect of one another through interaction in a complex, dynamic society. Much if not most of these legitimate expectations will have become a part of a "diffused" public opinion as to what is right. In Hayek's view, ultimate power in a free society is public opinion, a power which "determines nothing directly" but which controls all determining power by tolerating only those forms it finds acceptable.[40]

In other words the predictability of both public and private law must be their flexibility in adjusting to public opinion as this in turn adjusts to the growth of cumulative (syntropic) knowledge. I do not think, moreover, that "public opinion" has to be taken mystically or mentalistically. It is in large part a "habit rationality" that is continually changing and adapting. It is, therefore, in part a learning process accomplished through social interaction and information exchange. It is a form of large-group social predictability based upon the "mutual correspondence of expectations" which people in a large society arrive at through interaction with others in the many small and large groups in which they participate from day to day. It boils down to the "muddling-through" (see Chapter 7) kinds of mutual reinforcements people give one another in the grand behavioral experiment of a free society in which, ideally at least, every individual is planner and guardian.

Hayek laments the fact that the words "utopia" and "ideology" have fallen into disrepute, for even a free society needs some guiding model of "overall order" which may not be wholly "practicable" or "achievable." [41] If Hayek implies by "utopia" and "ideology" a dynamic concept of collective good in the broadest sense, I could not agree more wholeheartedly. In that sense, utopia implies neither a technology nor a static social order but a continuing experiment in their mutual accommodation, an experimental game in which everyone is at least a willing if not always an enthusiastic subject player. And it is a game in which the players become increasingly aware of expanding contingencies, a realization that moves anywhere on the global chessboard affect all the rest. Thus, the universal otherhood gradually moves back toward the universal brotherhood, but this time the latter will not be an impractical, unrealizable religious ethic but a practical, behavioral bond between self-interest and the collective good of all humanity. Utopia thus becomes a mutual accommodation between Pascal's Man and Rousseau's Man, an ideal of progress of the broadest and most humanitarian kind.

The peoples of the world are not advancing toward this universal brotherhood evenly; for their habit rationalities, public opinions, automatic pilots, or whatever we choose to call them, are not at the same level. The habit rationality of Russia, for example, is still far different from that of the United States. When Andrei Amalrik says all the distinct dissident groups in Russia have one common aim, "the rule of law," he puts his finger precisely on the difference.[42] With its historical roots in the patrimonial order of an empire state, Russia failed to develop the civil or private side of its law as did the West. The kind of habit rationality and mutual expectations that grew up around contract law never had a chance to develop in Russia. When it went through its period of anarchist "crazies" that culminated in the murder of Alexander II in 1881, its patrimonial tendencies were reinforced with a codification of repressive legislation that has characterized the public law of Russia ever since.[43] Thus, as we have seen, 1984 was born in a country with the habit rationality and public opinion of a patrimonial state. When its quiet eye went to work under Lenin and Stalin, it took over like rabbits took over Australia. It found an environment, a moral ecology if you will, with no natural predators.

Throughout his *Gulag Archipelago*, Solzhenitsyn seems to marvel at the passivity of his fellow Russians in the face of oppression.[44] But they had never developed the quality of mutual expectations that would provide a spontaneous resistance. People in the United States have, however, and that is why the United States would be able to tolerate quiet-eye defenses against crazies without fear of 1984 consequences. The people of the United States have developed a habit rationality and a public opinion incompatible with patrimonial public law. We all had the opportunity recently to observe this incompatibility when, for the first time in history, the cannon fodder of a great nation took to the streets against a patrimonial war and brought it to a close. Even the justices of the Supreme Court know that ultimately the very existence of the Court depends on the extent to which they follow, not lead, public opinion.

The differences between Russia and the United States are reducible largely to differences in the habit rationalities of their masses. That habit rationalities are in turn a product of the reinforcements of social history does not mean that any population is inexorably governed by "the weight of tradition," "centuries of oppression," or a "cultural force." When such phrases are used to argue that Russians, for example, will never change, the argument often sounds either Lamarckian or teleological in its implications. Habit rationalities are affected mainly by the expansion of individual choice and the greater subject playing it involves. This is the process that creates a public opinion incompatible with patrimonial public law. It is a process that builds momentum very slowly, but as we have seen repeatedly in this book, it is virtually impossible to stop once it has begun. Nor is it a process compatible with extended-family life in small Kropotkian communities.

Incentives and Participation

I see no evidence in the history of Homo ludens to indicate that he would ever play the game of eutopian communities on a mass scale. It is conceivable that some catastrophe such as an acute fuel shortage could precipitate a "state of emergency" in which the public might mobilize in the "fight-self" spirit of a national social movement to lick the crisis. But fighting self will never become a permanent way of life, not in a single country nor in the world at large.

Homo ludens will always need selective incentives to become involved in a game, whatever it may be. So the next question is whether these incentives can be made less materialistic than they are today. We discuss the question of why they should be below. In contemporary society the scholar is a favorite example of a fully involved player who is relatively insensitive to material incentives, putting in long hours at research and writing for a modest material return. According to the common mentalistic explanation, he is motivated by curiosity. Curiosity is characteristic of the human animal, but some members of the species work much harder than the rest to reduce this cognitive tension. Differences in ability and environmental reinforcements—not the constant—explain the behavioral variety. Professional and public acclaim for creative work are powerful reinforcers. In Andromeda, Efremov's utopia of the distant future, everyone is a scientist motivated by this kind of social incentive.[45]

As we have already seen, academics is an unusual kind of community with a high visibility that applies to its members' work rather than their persons. It would be hard to imagine an entire social order which could achieve this unusual form of visibility so that rewards could be mainly social. But are academicians as oblivious to material rewards as this ideal model suggests? In the first place, only a small percentage regularly publish, and among those that do, a large proportion may be motivated as much or more by pecuniary gain than by scholarly acclaim. Book royalties are obviously a primary consideration of the textbook "scholar." But even the producer of scholarly professional papers is often motivated by the desire for tenure or for salary increments.

The Coles suggest that one reason why those physicists who "sink to their level of competence" are not more unhappy than they are is that in "sinking" they may actually increase their material gains.[46] In the larger society, say the Coles, individuals often demonstrate the Peter Principle by rising to their level of incompetence. But physicists, who cannot fool their fellows so readily, are more likely to fall to that level most commensurate with their ability. This follows because they tend to crowd at the top when on trial as young assistant professors. But as it becomes clear which of the contenders are best, the losers go off to third-rate departments for full professorships at two or three times their previous salary. They "fall up" as it were. They shift from the bottom of a game emphasizing social rewards to the top of one emphasizing material rewards. So far as this example is concerned, physics is a microcosm of society at large. If one has to be a garbage collector, it is better to be one with a high standard of living. We are back again to the problems of innate inequalities within a meritocracy.

And this in turn brings us back to Bellamy, who proposed the most original solution to the problem of incentives in a society that allowed no differences in income.[47] He had a complex system of status and rank with appropriate insignia so that everyone's relative success in life was readily ascertainable. Insignia in Bellamy's utopia replaced the big cars and expensive clothes of our world. It is a solution that has never fully been put to the test. Socialist eutopias which try to replace material incentives with these kinds of "social" alternatives—especially Russia with its elaborate development of ranks and insignia—never succeed in making a complete conversion. Those people with the best and most responsible jobs also have the highest incomes and the most and best material possessions.

Even in a society like the shitufi where all families have the same income, some become more affluent than others purely on differences in ability to manage household budgets. No matter what design is used to make people the same, some manage to stand out. Societies that try to apply only social incentives while keeping material consumption the same for all are "command economies" whether they command through the social predictability and intense commitment of a eutopian community or the administrative law of a eutopian state. Neither is ever completely able to command equality. Material incentives which are nonselective, the going-up-together kind, can work for a while in some intentional communities under unusual conditions. But these conditions eventually change; and as they do, material incentives again become selective. The probability that material incentives will ever be completely eliminated would seem to be extremely small.

Unquestionably the most devastating "cost" of such an ingenious, social-incentive system as Bellamy's is the requirement of total organization. An "industrial army" that encompassed all society would mean the end of any larger spontaneous order. Such a society is typical of all those utopias, from Cabet's to Efremov's, that would presumably allow technology and science to progress while freezing the social order in a state of static perfection. It is a society in which all contracts become a part of Plan, all law becomes Public and Admintrative, and Utopia becomes the Patrimonial State.

If Mandeville could return to see such a state, one wonders if it would please him. The spontaneous order that intrigued and confused him as it began the industrial era would be gone. The lady in the Easter crowds could no longer fool him by wearing clothes out of keeping with her station. An insignia would now be on her sleeve, and her dress would be no better than anyone else's. But would the smile still be on her face? Would her new self-confidence be replaced by resignation? Or would she look condescendingly down on Mandeville from some higher status? If we were all engaged in one big game of chess, would the board and the rules be playing us? Do we all need some roulette in our lives?

In his *Economics and the Public Purpose*, Galbraith converts the invisible hand of the market into a conspiratorial hidden hand by inventing a teleological force or culture pattern he calls the "convenient social virtue." [48] It is a kind of latter-day puritan work ethic kept alive by the planning sector to provide invaluable services in areas that are least amenable to economies of scale. Because of it, millions of small entrepreneurs in farming and service enterprises exploit themselves unmercifully by working long hours for a relatively small hourly return. At first glance it would seem that he is describing a kind of public opinion or habit rationality, but there are no selective reinforcements to maintain the pattern. While it is certainly true that family farms and small service businesses tend to consume a great deal of family labor, their proprietors are not puppets of an ideological force.

An often noted appeal of small business is the freedom of being one's own boss. To Galbraith this is no freedom at all because the proprietor is the slave of his customers. His freedom is that of one "who is pecked to death by ducks." [49] Are we to believe from this that most proprietors find no rewards in serving customers? Curiously, Galbraith notes that some communist countries have returned to small, privately owned enterprises to increase the quality of services. In these countries our "convenient social virtue" has somehow proven more powerful than their prevailing political ideology. Obviously there are reinforcements here quite independent of either one.

Not only do small proprietors have more freedom, but up to a point they can even control income through inputs of their own labor, their so-called "self-exploitation." The crucial point is that the decision is theirs. And while the odds may not be great, there is always the expectation among young proprietors that they will eventually expand their enterprise and win big—the "roulette" factor. The older proprietors, like older physicists who accept lack of renown, become reconciled to their level of achievement and stand pat. They may even wish they could work shorter hours, but feel more secure staying with what they know—what has become predictable to them. Again, the choice of game is theirs.

Let us return, now, to the question of why we should want to reduce or eliminate material incentives. This is essentially the problem of "reasonable need," a notion we have found cropping up repeatedly in utopian schemes and eutopian experiments. A common utopian belief of the preprogress and anti-progress variety is that people have more material wants than are good for them or the environment and that life would be simpler and purer without them. Great quantities of material goods are likely to result in great inequities of possession with all the "pride" and "envy" that accompany this condition. As an alternative to the progressive utopia where everyone goes up together, in these everyone stays down together. But both types are alike in two overriding ways. They are compulsively egalitarian, and they require a command economy. Some reasonable-need level must be decided upon and then enforced. But who decides and who enforces?

In the catch-up eutopian state the cornucopia of material plenty is merely postponed while heavy industry is developed first. But heavy industry in the eutopia soon becomes dominated by military objectives, and the needs of military experts are insatiable. Their needs define the games that dominate society and set the levels deemed reasonable for others.

But in no society have needs remained for long within the limits that any utopian deemed reasonable. Even in Plato's fictional Republic, the level of reasonable need had to be raised at the very outset when Socrates's students objected to a level of austerity that seemed thoroughly unreasonable to them. Eutopian communities, as part-societies, are inevitably "corrupted" by rising levels of need in the larger society which undermine their standards of what is reasonable. The command economy of a group game eventually splinters into the corporate economy of individual players.

Eutopian states prove to be part-societies, too. Members, never so completely involved in the group game as in a eutopian community, are vulnerable to outside influences. The guardians must be eternally vigilant in insulating them from external sources of contamination. But even eutopian states must commerce and negotiate with the outside world. No matter how hard such writers as Barnet and Muller try to ridicule what they call the "global shopping center," [50] economy has continued to lead polity since it first jumped ahead of it in Western Europe with the rise of the civilization of capitalism. Arbitrary need levels will grow more and more unreasonable to the masses of state eutopias as these become increasingly integrated into a global economy. Wage goods will inevitably outweigh contrived social incentives as the major impetus to work.

Our own society, however, has seen the development of a new phenomenon, an antiprogressive, proegalitarian, antimaterialistic utopianism among college-educated young people. It is the conviction of these utopians, as it has been with many in the past, that materialism goes hand in hand with destructive competition, selfish egotism, and unrestrained cheating. What economists and some political scientists refer to as "consumer choice" they regard as producers' control. Like Galbraith's, their objective is to make the world a better place for "the people." But, like Orwell's intellectuals, they clearly disclose their contempt for all who need their help and refuse to admit it. Citizens, to the utopians, are not free consumers making free choices. They are mere automatons who do everything Madison Avenue tells them to do. Some of these young intellectuals who have traveled outside the United States even decry the growing materialism of Third World countries. The innocent everywhere are being corrupted by the hidden-hand, conspiratorial machinations of Wall Street and Madison Avenue. There is no genuine demand anywhere, only coercive supply.

Actually, this is the kind of controversial utopianism that stimulates increasing information exchange. It is healthy utopianism as long as we do not get administrators and elected officials who decide to impose it upon us. As a point of view to be argued and sold to as many as can be converted, it is stimulating and welcome. After all, some society, somewhere, someday, must surely reach a saturation point in the consumption of trivia. But it must be a saturation point arrived at by the spontaneous order and the give and take of debate and consumer choice, not by administrative decree.

Many young intellectuals want the world to become a better place today, right now. They see the average worker as too unperceptive to realize what is best for him and his environment and too bound by inertia to act in time. The workers must be made to do what is best for themselves *now* before time runs out. These young intellectuals with their higher education and greater wisdom must take control. They cannot wait to sell their ideas; that takes too long. The same antimaterialism that so often justifies its views in the name of equality can be very inegalitarian where it matters most, the power to make decisions. To increase material equality, power must be unequal; so we are back to the command economy.

The degree of material inequality that our society can tolerate will depend on how successfully we continue to maintain a positive-sum economy. If our economy slows down and our living standards tend to level off at home and to decline relative to improving conditions in other parts of the world, the zero-sum form of social comparison will gain in strength. Those toward the center as well as the bottom will be more likely to join the cause of the egalitarians. They will be more likely to view the material advantage of those at the top as advantages gained at the expense of the rest. Only then will society at large act to limit extreme differences in material consumption.

Long-run developments are not always visible in short-run political behavior. To increase inheritance tax exemptions, even when the alleged intent is to help low- and middle-income groups, is certainly not the most direct route to complete death duties on productive property. Meritocratic capitalism must move toward zero exemption and eventually the elimination of all inherited wealth. Children of successful parents will be better off raised under the constant admonition that they will have to achieve success in their own right, that they cannot expect to inherit a free ride.

Children of exceptional parents will, of course, always have some advantages. Even in Russia, as we have seen, successful technocrats can afford tutors for offspring who might not otherwise meet university entrance requirements. Despite the absence of private productive capital, children of high-ranking bureaucrats have a better chance of excelling at "careerism" than the children of kolkhozniks and blue-collar workers.[51] Meritocratic societies of the future must find ways of neutralizing the effects on children of unequal incomes. While income differentials could be radically reduced in the United States without eliminating material incentives, such a reduction would not cancel out all stratification effects without mechanisms to equalize opportunities for children of low achievers.

A major excuse for doubling the inheritance-tax exemption is to help preserve the family farm, but we should seriously ask whether children of farmers are always the best persons to carry on these enterprises. The very small percentage of communal farmers in Israel should not obscure the fact that farming there is competitive, efficient, and productive even though most of the land is owned by the state. I am inclined to agree with John Stuart Mill and H. G. Wells that such "nonmoveable" wealth as land and natural resources should be owned by all the members of society and should be exploited for the benefit of all by those best qualified to do so. There is no reason why our agricultural schools and a meritocratic examination and review system could not select better farm managers to lease "family farms" than one that assigns farmland through inheritance-tax exemptions. Children of farmers would still have a tremendous advantage under a meritocratic farm-leasing system if they were competent and appropriately motivated.

As Galbraith has noted, "geographically dispersed" activities favor small enterprises in the form of family farms or personal-service enterprises including franchise proprietorships.[52] Such activities tend to be unstandardized, performed in isolation without supervision and/or located in relation to the persons who use their services. They benefit only slightly from increased organization. The incentive structure of market capitalism tends to survive more strongly in these primary and tertiary sectors than in the secondary sector of manufacturing and those related extractive industries where organization leads to corporate concentration and centralization. The so-called postindustrial society is characterized by an expansion of employment in the tertiary sector, but as Heilbroner has recently pointed out, the expansion of the service sector has been due mainly to an employment shift from agriculture, since the industrial sector has long been stabilized at approximately one-third of the total work force.[53] Contraction of the agricultural work force has been accomplished through the ability of individuals and families to work larger farms by increasing their mechanization rather than the size of their organizations.

Curiously this tertiary-sector expansion results in some of the same benefits for household economy often ascribed to communes. Women are free to work as specialists in the larger economy as they are freed from household "drudgery." Children can be left at nurseries, dirty clothes at laundries, and meals can be eaten in "collective" dining halls. But in modern industrial society, as compared to the commune, services are privately owned and run. The advantage of the first lies in consumer choice and the reduction of free-rider behavior in both production and consumption. Consumers use those enterprises which render the most satisfactory service. Moreover, instead of the same institutional food day after day, families can pick among competing restaurants and fast-food franchises with specialized menus. Like kibbutzniks who take the communal fare "home" to their apartments to eat in privacy, members of the giant, Capitalist Man "commune" can carry home prepared pizzas, fish and chips, or fried chicken. In the second case, however, consumers have an infinitely greater selection; and they are less likely to take home more than they can eat, for waste reduces each family's discretionary income. These improved "communal" advantages thus operate as wage-good incentives in a society too large to effect controls of social predictability.

Differences in discretionary income are a function of differences in income, and they remain an important material incentive even in a society in which most of the work force is employed in the service sector. For this reason the degree to which income differentials can be reduced without damaging incentives is an empirical question that has no quick or easy answer. According to Christopher Jencks, income disparities within occupations contribute far more to income inequities in American society than do those between the average incomes of different occupations.[54] He therefore favors procedures to reduce income differences within, rather than among, groups. Since people are more likely to compare themselves with peers and those closest to them in the occupational structure, dissatisfaction about unequal rewards is greatest within occupations. It would seem to me, however, that precisely because comparisons are most acute within occupations these income disparities are the most "natural" of all. Here is where material incentives have greatest strength and where any collapsing of disparities calls for greatest caution. This is the arena in which Homo ludens plays the income game most intensely.

Many services in our industrial society are not exposed to the sanctions of consumer choice operating through market competition. Economists of Keynesian persuasion, who favor full employment through the creation of government services in the form of parks, libraries, museums, health facilities, highways, recreation areas, and so on, assume consumer choice. What they want for the people, the people will surely want for themselves. While the anarcho-capitalist dream of plugging all social problems into the market where people can vote on issues with their pocketbooks is clearly utopian today, we would be foolish to abandon consumer choice especially for services best provided by small firms. The problem is how to achieve the sanctions of consumer choice for services requiring large organizations.

Many jobs within large organizations will probably always be "instruments" for leisure-time pursuits rather than subject-player games for those who fill them. How much better in such cases to keep productivity high and working time low, so that leisure can be enjoyed off the job instead of through coffee breaks and malingering. Sanctions somehow have to be applied. If the market is not always an appropriate vehicle, consumer choice must be implemented in some other fashion. But monitoring large organizations brings us right back to the problems of visibility and incentives for public vigilance.

In his *Defense of Anarchism,* Robert Wolff suggests that the technology is already available to raise the visibility of government as well as citizen participation in modern society.[55] An "in-the-home voting machine" attached to each family's television could be set to the thumb or voice prints of all registered voters in the household. Local and national issues could be debated at certain hours followed by mass voting or polling. Computers would tabulate results fast enough to make everyone feel like active participants in the political game.

I share Wolff's optimism that popular interest and participation in the political process would be greatly enhanced by such a technology. Politics and the debating of public issues could, through the added inducements of partial audience participation, become a form of public entertainment more popular even than spectator sports. Visibility of the political process could be raised far beyond most utopian expectations. I do not share, however, the fear of some Planners that a new polling and voting technology would lead to the capricious, unstable rule of a "democratic" mob. Like Plato's Guardians, Planners want to save the common man from himself. The more effective the technology, the more prepared and informed would become the moral judgments of the public. Participatory democracy in the great society would not be instantaneous, for debate and discussion would precede action.

Despite Wolff's optimism regarding such a form of "direct democracy," he remains pessimistic about majoritarian rule.[56] He ends up espousing anarchistic decentralization of economy and polity to achieve a small-community world in which "unanimous democracy" would be feasible. For Wolff, the inherent difficulties of a majoritarian democracy are illustrated by a basic confusion in Rousseau's concept of general will. In one sense the general will is a "will issuing laws which aim at the general good," but in another sense it implies majority opinion or group consensus. Because he confused these two meanings of his concept, says Wolff, Rousseau falsely assumed that the moral judgments of the majority will best express the general or collective good for both the dissenting minority and the preponderant majority. As Wolff points out, a majority of citizens may vote out of a concern for their own self-interests rather than from any overriding concern for the collective good. Even if the majority strives for the greatest general good, its ignorance or its inability to predict outcomes may lead to bad legislation. Through better knowledge or a better calculation of contingencies, the moral judgment of the minority may actually come closer to the general good than that of the majority.

The extent of Rousseau's confusion we will never know, but there is a way of reconciling the two implications of his general will. First, we must view legislation dynamically, not statically. In a small, face-to-face community "unanimous democracy" is subject to changing opinion and legislation. A small minority may begin agitating for some change of community rules through private discussion and persuasion. As long as the innovators remain a distinct minority, they may never even bother to raise the issue at a general meeting. They may prefer, instead, to preserve the atmosphere of community unanimity. But as the innovators convince others of the worthiness of their cause, their numbers may swell to a size large enough to justify public discussion. If they still fail to persuade a majority, they may drop the issue again, out of deference to community "unanimity," while still using argument and persuasion in private. Eventually they may become a new majority whose preponderance of numbers is so visible to all that proponents and former dissenters alike unanimously agree to the new legislation, again in a show of public harmony.

A losing minority may be right in the long run, but if its knowledge and its arguments are sound, it should be able to find a way through the give and take of information exchange to grow into a winning majority. When we view majority rule as a dynamic, everchanging response to information exchange and the growth of knowledge, we eliminate the seeming inconsistency in Rousseau's paradigm. Only "instant democracy" and "unanimous democracy" are usually incompatible, and in this sense Rousseau is right in saying that as a member of a minority he realizes his true "freedom" by accepting the majority view. To do otherwise in the short run would be to replace discussion, argument, persuasion, and conciliation with either chaos or force.

Second, the general will is an ideal that assumes not only the progressive growth of knowledge but a humble realization that its dissemination requires, more often than not, a dedicated patience. Such patience is born in respect for the autonomy of others and the certainty that in the long run the best guarantee of one's own autonomy lies in the preservation of that respect. Thus, the general will in practice becomes indistinguishable from what Rousseau called the "aggregate will," the will of a citizenry voting on the basis of self, or private, interest. Through growth of knowledge and information exchange, reciprocal altruism brings collective good and self-interest into closer harmony. A dedicated minority must show how the self-interest of all will be better served by its position than by the position of the majority. By leaving the burden of proof to the dedicated minority, aggregate will is most likely to move toward general will without sacrificing individual autonomy.

New technology or new uses of existing technology may provide positive incentives for raising visibility and participation, but negative incentives will also have to be provided through laws that attack secrecy within government and large organizations. To make leaking of government secrets a criminal act, as recently proposed, would be another step in the wrong direction. What we need is more of the kind of executive leadership provided by recent governors of Florida and Georgia in making government more visible through financial disclosures of officeholders, abolition of secret government meetings, and televising important legislative sessions. Here lies one of the most important routes toward effecting Rousseau's Man. As consumers of government services, we must have all the information on which to base our choices as well as the means to sanction those who would cheat us.

Perhaps the most difficult incentive problem of all, and one increasing rapidly today, concerns what Robert Lekachman regards as a new form of property— property in work.[57] He is referring to the "guaranteed income" provided by "guaranteed jobs" such as those enjoyed by members of strong unions, civil-service workers and the tenured faculty of universities. How can consumer choice bear directly on services and products provided by the owners of this kind of property? Yet the security it provides is demanded more and more by workers, the same kind of security that members of our communes prized so highly. In fact, the communes examined in this book are perfect examples of property in work as long as highly unusual circumstances maintained their social incentives. When those circumstances were altered, free riding not only reduced member productivity, it increased the waste within free supply.

It may be that we shall have to drastically rethink economics in some such fashion as that recently proposed by Eugen Loebl in his *Humanomics*.[58] Loebl discounts the importance of productive-property ownership in a developed economy while emphasizing humanity's creativity as the true source of wealth. He would encourage creativity while strengthening the power of consumer choice. Socialist planning does not achieve these goals; under comprehensive planning, enterprise targets provide the wrong incentives. Managers conceal enterprise capabilities to keep production assignments easy and meet assignments quantitatively by sacrificing quality. Planning must be restricted to a "macroorgan" that does not interfere with enterprise or consumer decisions, yet is able to effect full employment, stable prices, and high efficiency through manipulation of the money supply and the taxation system. Loebl believes this kind of planning would lead enterprises to increase profits through greater efficiency rather than higher prices, a reinforcement structure in which profit sharing would have far more incentive value for workers than it does now. Finally, to keep the "macroorgan" honest, it would be controlled by the consumer-citizens themselves through "economic democracy." A public trained in economics would participate in budget decisions by direct vote.

Any such scheme as Loebl's assumes maximal visibility within the economic as well as the political and social orders. It therefore assumes changes in technology, legislation, and habit rationality that will make possible this high degree of reciprocal visibility. It also assumes a great shift in public services from government to enterprise management to make them more responsive to consumer-citizen choices.

Such assumptions may be utopian, but they are utopian in a constructive, information-exchange sense. They are also optimistic because they rest on an Orwellian faith in the good sense of common people. They challenge the Spenglerian views of those who see only centralist, statist planning ahead or some kind of Kropotkian anarchy. What is constructive about the kind of long-range dystopian prophecies at least one well-known economist is currently making? [59] Why believe humanity is doomed to object playing in a planned, chessboard society in which the principle of motion becomes a new mass-movement "religion"? Since none of us will be in that distant future to test such prophecies, why not choose an optimistic denouement based on faith in humanity's real wealth—creativity? Instead of one final S curve, why not look ahead to a ladder of S curves? I, for one, believe Pascal's Man and Rousseau's Man have barely begun to collaborate and that this collaboration marks only the beginning of progress. Participatory evolution has only started, and the end is nowhere in sight.

Notes

Notes to Chapter One: *Introduction* (pp. 1–10)

1. V. Gordon Childe, *Man Makes Himself* (New York: New American Library, 1936), pp. 9–15.
2. Donella H. Meadows, Dennis L. Meadows, Jorgen Randers, and William W. Behrens, *The Limits to Growth* (New York: Universe, 1972), p. 29.
3. Robert L. Heilbroner, *An Inquiry into the Human Prospect* (New York: Norton, 1974), pp. 32–35, 42–54, 75–76.
4. Roberto Vacca, *The Coming Dark Age* (Garden City, N.Y.: Doubleday, 1973), pp. 127–32.
5. H. S. D. Cole, Christopher Freeman, Marie Jahoda, K. L. R. Pavitt, eds., *Models of Doom: A Critique of the Limits to Growth-* (New York: Universe, 1973), pp. 9–10, 193, 210–11.
6. George T. Land, *Grow or Die: The Unifying Principle of Transformation* (New York: Dell, 1973), pp. 73, 184, 194.
7. E. F. Schumacher, *Small Is Beautiful: Economics as if People Mattered* (New York: Harper and Row, 1973), p. 214.
8. Richard S. Peters, Introduction to *Leviathan* by Thomas Hobbes (New York: Macmillan, 1962), p. 12.
9. William Ophuls, "Leviathan or Oblivion?" in *Toward a Steady-State Economy*, ed. Herman E. Daly (San Francisco: Freeman, 1973), p. 216. G. Hardin, "The Tragedy of the Commons," *Science* 162 (1968):1243–48.
10. Joseph A. Schumpeter, *Capitalism, Socialism and Democracy* (New York: Harper and Row, 1950), pp. 121–30.
11. Johan Huizinga, *Homo Ludens: A Study of the Play Element in Culture* (Boston: Beacon, 1950), p. ix.

Notes to Chapter Two: *Altruism, Progress, and Utopia* (pp. 11–42)

1. George Gaylord Simpson, *The Meaning of Evolution* (New Haven: Yale University Press, 1949), p. 287.

2. Erich Fromm, *The Anatomy of Human Destructiveness* (New York: Holt, Rinehart, and Winston, 1973), pp. 2–4, 16. See for example Robert Ardrey, *The Territorial Imperative: A Personal Inquiry into the Animal Origins of Property and Nations* (New York: Dell, 1966), and Konrad Lorenz, *On Aggression* (New York: Harcourt, Brace, and World, 1963).

3. B. F. Skinner, *Contingencies of Reinforcement: A Theoretical Analysis* (New York: Appleton-Century-Crofts, 1969), p. 51.

4. Howard Gardner, *The Shattered Mind: The Person After Brain Damage* (New York: Knopf, 1974), pp. 206–19, 451–55.

5. Immanuel Kant, "Idea of a Universal History from a Cosmopolitan Point of View," in *The Idea of Progress Since the Renaissance,* ed. W. Warren Wagar (New York: Wiley, 1969), p. 63.

6. Thomas Hobbes, *Leviathan* (New York: Macmillan, 1962), p. 131.

7. Sources on social insects: Wilhelm Goetsch, *The Ants* (Ann Arbor: University of Michigan Press, 1957); O. W. Richards, *The Social Insects* (New York: Harper, 1953); Edward O. Wilson, *The Insect Societies* (Cambridge: Belknap, 1971); and Edward O. Wilson, *Sociobiology: The New Synthesis* (Cambridge: Harvard University Press, 1975).

8. A. R. Louch, *Explanation and Human Action* (Berkeley: University of California Press, 1966), p. 161.

9. Wilson, *Insect Societies,* pp. 320–22.

10. Wilson, *Sociobiology,* pp. 117–18.

11. Robert L. Trivers, "The Evolution of Reciprocal Altruism," *Quarterly Review of Biology* 46 (1971):35–43.

12. For "cooperative breeding" see Wilson, *Sociobiology,* p. 125.

13. Trivers, "Reciprocal Altruism," p. 36.

14. Ibid., pp. 46–47.

15. Ibid., p. 49.

16. Ibid., p. 54.

17. Theodosius Dobzhansky, "Ethics and Values in Biological and Cultural Evolution," *Zygon: Journal of Religion and Science* 8 (1973):277.

18. Eric Hoffer, *The True Believer: Thoughts on the Nature of Mass Movements* (New York: Harper and Row, 1951), pp. 21, 60–65.

19. Michael A. Jochim, *Hunter-Gatherer Subsistence and Settlement: A Predictive Model* (New York: Academic Press, 1976), p. 19.

20. John F. Martin, "The Estimation of the Sizes of Local Groups in a Hunting-Gathering Environment," *American Anthropologist* 75 (1973): 1448, 1463.

21. A. Paul Hare, *Handbook of Small Group Research* (New York: Free Press, 1962), pp. 227–30.

22. George A. Miller, "The Magical Number Seven, Plus or Minus Two: Some Limits on Our Capacity for Processing Information," *The Psychological Review* 63 (1956):86, 88, 91, 95.

23. Hare, *Handbook,* pp. 227–30.

24. Abraham H. Maslow, *Toward a Psychology of Being* (New York: Van Nostrand, 1968), p. 12.

25. K. E. Read, "Morality and Concept of the Person Among the Gahuku-Gama," *Oceania* 25 (1955):260, 276–77, 281–82.

26. Herbert Kaufman, *The Limits of Organizational Change* (University: University of Alabama Press, 1971), p. 73. Michel Crozier, *The Stalled Society* (New York: Viking, 1973), pp. 31, 64–65, 156–57.

27. Jean Bodin, *Method for the Easy Comprehension of History,* trans. Beatrice Reynolds (New York: Columbia University Press, 1945), pp. 296–302.

28. Bernard le Bovier de Fontenelle, "Digression on the Ancients and the Moderns," trans. W. Warren Wagar in *The Idea of Progress Since the Renaissance,* ed. W. Warren Wagar (New York: Wiley, 1969), pp. 48, 55. For Bodin and Fontenelle see also J. B. Bury, *The Idea of Progress* (New York: Dover, 1932), pp. 37–43, 98–112.

29. Crane Brinton, *The Shaping of Modern Thought* (Englewood Cliffs, N.J.: Prentice-Hall, 1963), pp. 116–17, 141.

30. Peter Gay, *The Enlightenment, Volume II: The Science of Freedom* (New York: Knopf, 1969), pp. 22–23.

31. Sidney Pollard, *The Idea of Progress: History and Society* (Baltimore: Penguin, 1968), p. 31.

32. ·E. R. Dodds, *The Ancient Concept of Progress and Other Essays on Greek Literature and Belief* (London: Clarendon, 1973), pp. 1, 8, 10, 24–25.

33. Carl L. Becker, "Progress," *Encyclopedia of the Social Sciences Volume XII* (New York: Macmillan, 1934), pp. 497–99.

34. Carl L. Becker, *The Heavenly City of the Eighteenth-Century Philosophers* (New Haven: Yale University Press, 1932), pp. 138–50.

35. Edgar Zilsel, "The Genesis of the Concept of Scientific Progress," *Journal of the History of Ideas* 6 (1945):326, 329–33, 336–37, 346.

36. Bertrand Russell quoted by W. Warren Wagar in *Good Tidings: The Belief in Progress from Darwin to Marcuse* (Bloomington: Indiana University Press, 1972), p. 270.

37. Henryk Skolimowski, "The Scientific World View and the Illusions of Progress," *Social Research* 41 (1974):52–82.

38. Henry M. Pachter, "The Idea of Progress in Marxism," *Social Research* 41 (1974):140.

39. Joseph A. Schumpeter, *Capitalism, Socialism and Democracy* (New York: Harper and Row, 1950), pp. 122–26.

40. Ivan Efremov, *Andromeda: A Space-Age Tale,* trans. George Hanna (Moscow: Foreign Language Publishing House, 1960).

41. Bernard P. Kiernan, *The United States, Communism, and the Emergent World* (Bloomington: University of Indiana Press, 1972).

42. Benjamin Nelson, *The Idea of Usury: From Tribal Brotherhood to Universal Otherhood* (Chicago: University of Chicago Press, 1969), pp. 78–79.

43. Christopher Hill, "Protestantism and the Rise of Capitalism," in *The Rise of Capitalism,* ed. David S. Landes (New York: Macmillan, 1966), pp. 45–49.

44. Abraham H. Maslow, "A Theory of Human Motivation: The Goals of Work," in

The Future of Work, ed. Fred Best (Englewood Cliffs, N.J.: Prentice-Hall, 1973), pp. 24, 28–31.

45. Bernard Mandeville, *The Fable of the Bees: Or, Private Vices, Public Benefits* (Baltimore: Penguin, 1970), pp. 98, 151, 200–201, 219, 255, 258–59, 368–70. See also Phillip Harth, Introduction to *The Fable of the Bees,* pp. 18–23.

46. Adam Smith, *The Wealth of Nations* (New York: Modern Library, 1937), p. 14.

47. From Adam Smith's *Moral Sentiments* (1759) quoted in the Editor's Introduction to *The Wealth of Nations,* p. lii.

48. Smith, *Wealth of Nations,* p. 508.

49. Ibid., p. 13.

50. Ibid., p. 423.

51. Kant, "Universal History," pp. 63–65.

52. Baron Charles Louis de Secondat Montesquieu, *The Spirit of the Laws,* trans. Thomas Nugent (New York: Hafner, 1949), pp. 3–5.

53. Jean-Jacques Rousseau, *The First and Second Discourses,* ed. Roger Masters, trans. Roger Masters and Judith Masters (New York: St. Martin's Press, 1964), pp. 132, 156–57, 174–75, 180, 193.

54. Ibid., pp. 109, 111, 147, 179.

55. Ibid., pp. 159–60, 172.

56. Ibid., pp. 156, 175, 194, 199.

57. Smith, *Wealth of Nations,* pp. lviii.

58. Kant, "Universal History," p. 65.

59. Lucio Colletti, *From Rousseau to Lenin: Studies in Ideology and Society,* trans. John Merrington and Judith White (New York: Monthly Review Press, 1972), pp. 157–62.

60. Hobbes, *Leviathan,* pp. 11, 108, 113, 160.

61. John Locke, *Of Civil Government: Second Treatise* (Chicago: Regnery, 1955), pp. 25, 33.

62. Ibid., pp. 38–39, 102.

63. Smith, *Wealth of Nations,* pp. 669–70.

64. Mandeville, *Fable of the Bees,* pp. 188, 208–9.

65. Smith, *Wealth of Nations,* pp. 70–72, 82–83.

66. Kenneth E. Boulding, "The Economics of the Coming Spaceship Earth," in *Toward a Steady-State Economy,* ed. Herman E. Daly (San Francisco: Freeman, 1973), pp. 127–29.

67. E. F. Schumacher, *Small Is Beautiful: Economics as if People Mattered* (New York: Harper and Row, 1973), pp. 14, 24–31, 61, 70.

68. A. L. Morton, *The English Utopia* (London: Lawrence and Wishart Ltd., 1952), p. 11.

69. Ibid., pp. 12–20. See also F. Graus, "Social Utopias in the Middle Ages," *Past and Present* 38 (1967):3–19.

70. Friedrich Engels, *Socialism: Utopian and Scientific,* trans. Edward Aveling (New

York: International, 1935), pp. 72–73. Montesquieu, *Spirit of the Laws,* pp. 1–5.

71. See for example Becker, "Progress," pp. 497–98.

72. Pachter, "Progress in Marxism," pp. 136–61.

73. George Gaylord Simpson, "Evolutionary Determinism and the Fossil Record," *The Scientific Monthly* 71 (1950):263.

74. John Stuart Mill, *Principles of Political Economy* (New York: Augustus M. Kelley, 1965 reprint of 1871 edition), pp. 746–51.

75. John Maynard Keynes, *Essays in Persuasion* (London: Macmillan, 1931), pp. 371–72.

76. Schumpeter, *Capitalism,* pp. 131, 143, 146.

77. Ibid., pp. 207–8.

78. Gunther S. Stent, *The Coming of the Golden Age: A View of the End of Progress* (Garden City, N.Y.: Natural History Press, 1969), pp. 87, 132–33.

79. Ibid., pp. 111, 127.

80. Peter B. Medawar, *The Hope of Progress* (Garden City, N.Y.: Doubleday Anchor, 1972), p. 137.

81. Hoffer, *True Believer,* p. 68.

82. Kant, "Universal History," p. 66.

83. Jean-Jacques Rousseau, *The Social Contract,* trans. Maurice Cranston (Baltimore: Penguin, 1968), pp. 84, 141.

84. Ibid., p. 64.

85. Crane Brinton, *The Shaping of Modern Thought* (Englewood Cliffs, N.J.: Prentice-Hall, 1963), p. 129.

86. Ellen M. Wood, *Mind and Politics: An Approach to the Meaning of Liberal and Socialist Individualism* (Berkeley: University of California Press, 1972), pp. 153–71.

87. Gay, *Enlightenment,* p. 551.

88. Hobbes, *Leviathan,* pp. 113, 132–33.

89. Rousseau, *Social Contract,* pp. 96, 113.

90. Ibid., pp. 91, 143.

91. Ibid., p. 149.

92. "A Blueprint for Survival," *The Ecologist* 2 (1972):1–44.

93. Jean-Jacques Rousseau, "Essay on the Origin of Languages," in *On the Origin of Languages,* eds. John Moran and Alexander Gode (New York: Ungar, 1966), pp. 32–33.

94. Ibid.

95. Kant, "Universal History," p. 72.

96. Schumacher, *Small Is Beautiful,* pp. 61–70. Alvin Toffler, *Future Shock* (New York: Random House, 1970), pp. 18–19.

97. Martin Buber, *Paths in Utopia,* trans. R. F. C. Hull (Boston: Beacon, 1949), p. 136.

Notes to Chapter Three: *Mutual Aid: Preindustrial Forms* (pp. 43–72)

1. Rousseau, *First and Second Discourses,* pp. 117, 128, 130–32, 137. See also Colletti, *Rousseau to Lenin,* pp. 151, 171–74; Gay, *Enlightenment,* pp. 535, 537–39; and Wood, *Mind and Politics,* pp. 80–82.

2. Thomas Hobbes, *Leviathan* (New York: Macmillan, 1962), p. 100.

3. Rousseau, "Origin of Languages," p. 33.

4. Rousseau, *First and Second Discourses,* pp. 103, 150.

5. Emile Durkheim, *Montesquieu and Rousseau: Forerunners of Sociology* (Ann Arbor: University of Michigan Press, 1960), pp. 66–67, 102.

6. For the importance of selective incentives in provisioning collective good see Mancur Olson, *The Logic of Collective Action: Public Goods and the Theory of Groups* (New York: Schocken, 1965), pp. 21, 34, 43–44, 51, 60–64. See also James Buchanan, *The Bases for Collective Action,* General Learning Corporation Module (New York: General Learning Press, 1971).

7. Locke, *Civil Government,* p. 16.

8. Montesquieu, *Laws,* pp. 3–5.

9. Napoleon A. Chagnon, *Yanomamo: The Fierce People* (New York: Holt, Rinehart, and Winston, 1968), pp. 15, 34, 40, 91, 96, 98.

10. Robert L. Trivers, "The Evolution of Reciprocal Altruism," *Quarterly Review of Biology* 46 (1971):49.

11. Hsiao-tun Fei and Chih-i Chang, *Earthbound China* (Chicago: University of Chicago Press, 1945), p. 36. Robert B. Hall, "The Société Congo of the Ile à Gonave, Haiti," *American Anthropologist* 31 (1929):691.

12. Morton Deutsch, "Cooperation and Trust: Some Theoretical Notes," in *Interpersonal Dynamics: Essays and Readings on Human Interaction,* eds. Warren Bennes, Edgar Schein and David Berlew (Homewood, Ill.: Dorsey, 1964), pp. 580–81.

13. Ibid.

14. Ibid.

15. H. Ian Hogbin, *Experiments in Civilization* (London: Routledge, 1939), p. 58.

16. John H. Provinse, "Cooperative Ricefield Cultivation Among the Siang Dyaks of Central Borneo," *American Anthropologist* 39 (1937):85.

17. Morton H. Fried, *Fabric of Chinese Society: A Study of the Social Life of a Chinese County Seat* (New York: Praeger, 1953), p. 118.

18. Conrad M. Arensberg and Solon T. Kimball, *Family and Community in Ireland* (Cambridge: Harvard University Press, 1940), p. 77.

19. John W. Monette, *History of the Discovery and Settlement of the Valley of the Mississippi* (New York: Harper, 1846), p. 16.

20. Wendell C. Bennett and Robert M. Zingg, *The Tarahumara: An Indian Tribe of Northern Mexico* (Chicago: University of Chicago Press, 1935), p. 11.

21. Hobbes, *Leviathan,* pp. 132, 160.

22. Melville J. Herskovits, *Life in a Haitian Valley* (New York: Knopf, 1937), pp. 70–73.

23. S. F. Nadel, *A Black Byzantium, The Kingdom of Nupe in Nigeria* (London: Oxford University Press, 1942), p. 243. Jomo Kenyatta, *Facing Mount Kenya, the Tribal Life of the Gikiuyu* (London: Seeker and Warburg, 1938), p. 59. Araucanian Indians of Chile: author's field notes.

24. Herman Clarence Nixon, *Possum Trot* (Norman: University of Oklahoma Press, 1941), p. 27.

25. Author's field notes.

26. Melville J. Herskovits, *Dahomey* (New York: Augustin, 1938), p. 72. Daryll Forde, "Land and Labour in a Cross River Village, Southern Nigeria," *Geographical Journal* 90 (1937):40. William R. Bascom, "Acculturation among Gullah Negroes," *American Anthropologist* 43 (1941):44. K. L. Little, "The Mende Farming Household," *Sociological Review* 40 (1948):48.

27. A. I. Richards, *Land, Labour and Diet in Northern Rhodesia* (London: Oxford University Press, 1939), p. 147. Hugh A. Stayt, *The Bavenda* (London: Oxford University Press, 1931), p. 34.

28. I. Schapera, "Economic Changes in South African Native Life," *Africa* 1 (1928):175. Monica Hunter, *Reaction to Conquest: Effects of Contact with Europeans on the Pondo of South Africa* (London: Oxford University Press, 1936), p. 88.

29. S. F. Nadel, *The Nuba: An Anthropological Study of the Hill Tribes in Kordofan* (London: Oxford University Press, 1947), p. 54.

30. Hogbin, *Experiments,* p. 73. Bronislaw Malinowski, *Argonauts of the Western Pacific* (London: Routledge, 1922), p. 161. Bronislaw Malinowski, *Coral Gardens and Their Magic* (New York: American Book, 1935), p. 157.

31. Provinse, "Cooperative Cultivation," pp. 86–87.

32. Nadel, *The Nuba,* pp. 54–56.

33. Donald Pierson, *Cruz das Almas: A Brazilian Village,* Institute of Social Anthropology Publication No. 12 (Washington, D.C.: Smithsonian Institution, 1951), p. 70. Julio de la Fuente, *Yalalag: Una Villa Zapoteca Serrana,* Museo Nacional de Antropología Serie Científica No. 1 (México: Imprenta Nuevo Mundo, 1949), p. 123. Alfred Metraux, *Making a Living in the Marbial Valley, Haiti,* UNESCO Occasional Papers in Education (Paris: Education Clearing House, 1951), pp. 70–71, 74, 86.

34. Ibid.

35. Nadel, *Nupe in Nigeria,* p. 250. Elizabeth Colson, "The Plateau Tonga of Northern Rhodesia," in *Seven Tribes of British Central Africa,* eds. Elizabeth Colson and Max Gluckman (London: Oxford University Press, 1951), p. 105. Jenson E. Krige and J. D. Krige, *The Realm of the Rain-Queen: A Study of the Pattern of Lovedu Society* (London: Oxford University Press, 1943), p. 60. Cornelius Osgood, *The Koreans and their Culture* (New York: Ronald Press, 1951), p. 66.

36. George C. Homans, *English Villagers of the Thirteenth Century* (Cambridge: Harvard University Press, 1941), p. 261.

37. Rowland E. Robinson, *Danvis Folks* (Boston: Houghton Mifflin, 1894), p. 117.

38. Joseph A. Schumpeter, *Capitalism, Socialism and Democracy* (New York: Harper and Row, 1950), pp. 123–26.

39. Rousseau, *Social Contract*, pp. 140–41.

40. Olson, *Collective Action*, p. 13.

41. Fedor Belov, *The History of a Soviet Collective Farm* (New York: Praeger, 1955), p. 103.

42. Aleksandr I. Solzhenitsyn, *The Gulag Archipelago 1918–1956: An Experiment in Literary Investigation,* trans. Thomas P. Whitney (New York: Harper and Row, 1973).

43. S. Swianiewicz, *Forced Labour and Economic Development: An Enquiry into the Experience of Soviet Industrialization* (New York: Oxford University Press, 1965), p. 39.

44. Kang Chao, *Agricultural Production in Communist China 1949–1965* (Madison: University of Wisconsin Press, 1970), pp. 60–61. E. L. Wheelwright and Bruce McFarlane, *The Chinese Road to Socialism: Economics of the Cultural Revolution* (New York: Monthly Review Press, 1970), pp. 26–27.

45. Robert M. Bernardo, *The Theory of Moral Incentives in Cuba* (University, Alabama: The University of Alabama Press, 1971), pp. 72–74. Roberto E. Hernández and Carmelo Mesa-Lago, "Labor Organization and Wages," in *Revolutionary Change in Cuba,* ed. Carmelo Mesa-Lago (Pittsburgh: University of Pittsburgh Press, 1971), p. 230. Carmelo Mesa-Lago, "The Revolutionary Offensive," *Transaction* 6 (1969):27.

46. Carmelo Mesa-Lago, "Material and Moral Incentives," *Journal of Interamerican Studies and World Affairs* 14 (1972):83.

47. Hernández and Mesa-Lago, "Labor Organization," pp. 235–37. Bernardo, *Moral Incentives,* p. 58.

48. José A. Moreno, "From Traditional to Modern Values," in *Revolutionary Change in Cuba,* ed. Carmelo Mesa-Lago (Pittsburgh: University of Pittsburgh Press, 1971), pp. 473, 485, 488, 490–91.

49. Ibid., p. 490.

50. Bernardo, *Moral Incentives,* pp. 43, 49, 56, 123–26. Joseph A. Kahl, "The Moral Economy of a Revolutionary Society," *Transaction* 6 (1969):32.

51. Bernardo, *Moral Incentives,* pp. 54–55. Hernández and Mesa-Lago, "Labor Organization," pp. 235, 237.

52. Ibid., p. 221. Moreno, "Modern Values," p. 490. Bernardo, *Moral Incentives,* pp. 67–68.

53. Ibid., pp. 94, 116–17.

54. Ibid., p. 88. Carmelo Mesa-Lago, "Economic Policies and Growth," in *Revolutionary Change in Cuba,* ed. Carmelo Mesa-Lago (Pittsburgh: University of Pittsburgh Press, 1971), pp. 286, 327. René Dumont, "The Militarization of Fidelismo," in *Dissent* 17 (September–October 1970):411–28.

55. Hernández and Mesa-Lago, "Labor Organization," pp. 239, 243.

56. Bernardo, *Moral Incentives,* p. 88.

57. Fidel Castro, "This Shame Will Be Welcome," *The New York Review of Books* 24 (September 1970):18–33.

58. Lowry Nelson, *Cuba: The Measure of a Revolution* (Minneapolis: University of Minnesota Press, 1972), pp. 102–16. Carmelo Mesa-Lago, "Typología y Valor Económico del Trabajo No Remunerado en Cuba," *El Trimestre Económico* 159 (1973):682–86.

59. Ibid., p. 689.

60. Bernardo, *Moral Incentives*, p. 45. Hernández and Mesa-Lago, "Labor Organization," p. 224.

61. Nelson, *Cuba*, p. 119.

62. Ibid., pp. 121–24.

63. Dumont, "Militarization of Fidelismo," pp. 411–28. K. S. Karol, *Guerrillas in Power: The Course of the Cuban Revolution* (New York: Hill and Wang, 1970).

64. Mesa-Lago, "Economic Policies," pp. 63–64. Carmelo Mesa-Lago, *Cuba in the 1970's: Pragmatism and Institutionalization* (Albuquerque: University of New Mexico Press, 1974), p. 6.

65. Ibid., p. 9.

66. *Santa Barbara News Press,* 23 June 1974, p. 1.

67. Charles Hillinger, "Whitewing Without Portfolio," *Los Angeles Times,* 9 December 1971, p. 1.

68. Albert Brisbane, *Social Destiny of Man; or, Association and Reorganization of Industry* (New York: Burt Franklin, 1968 reprint of 1840 edition), pp. 121–24, 136–38.

69. David F. Belnap, "Chile Firemen All Volunteers and They Pay for the Honor," *Los Angeles Times,* 29 December 1971, pp. 1, 23.

Notes to Chapter Four: *Property Incentives: Origins of Capitalist Man* (pp. 73–112)

1. H. Ian Hogbin, "Tillage and Collection, A New Guinea Economy," *Oceania* 9 (1938–39):291–97. H. Ian Hogbin, *Transformation Scene: The Changing Culture of a New Guinea Village* (London: Routledge and Kegan Paul, 1951), p. 63.

2. Karl Marx, "Critique of the Gotha Program," in *Basic Writings on Politics and Philosophy: Karl Marx and Friedrich Engels,* ed. Lewis S. Feuer (Garden City, N.Y.: Doubleday, 1959), pp. 118–19.

3. Karl Marx and Friedrich Engels, "Manifesto of the Communist Party," in *Capital, The Communist Manifesto and Other Writings by Karl Marx,* ed. Max Eastman (New York: Modern Library, 1932), pp. 335–36.

4. John N. Hazard, *Communists and Their Law: A Search for the Common Core of the Legal Systems of the Marxian Socialist States* (Chicago: University of Chicago Press, 1969), pp. 202, 204, 222, 226. William Hinton, "Reflections on China," *Monthly Review* 25 (June 1973):30–31.

5. Tse-tung Mao, *Quotations from Chairman Mao Tse-tung* (Peking: Foreign Languages Press, 1966), p. 195.

6. Hazard, *Communists and Their Law,* p. 200.

7. Ibid., pp. 225–30.

8. Leo Huberman, "The ABC of Socialism," in *Introduction to Socialism,* eds. Leo Huberman and Paul M. Sweezy (New York: Monthly Reader Paperbacks, 1968), pp. 24, 71.

9. Leo Huberman and Paul M. Sweezy, "Lessons of Soviet Experience," in *Introduction to Socialism,* eds. Leo Huberman and Paul M. Sweezy (New York: Monthly Reader Paperbacks, 1968), pp. 118–20.

10. Michael Harrington, *Socialism* (New York: Saturday Review Press, 1972), pp. 295, 302, 306.

11. Norman Thomas, "Humanistic Socialism and the Future," in *Socialist Humanism,* ed. Erich Fromm (Garden City, N.Y.: Doubleday, Inc., 1965), pp. 353–55.

12. Johan Huizinga, *Homo Ludens: A Study of the Play Element in Culture* (Boston: Beacon, 1950), pp. 46–47.

13. Ibid., pp. 48–49, 58, 63–64, 89, 104, 156.

14. Ibid., pp. 46–47, 191–210.

15. Ibid., p. 191.

16. Jacques Ehrmann, "Homo Ludens Revisited," in *Games, Play, Literature,* ed. Jacques Ehrmann (Boston: Beacon, 1968), pp. 20–21, 51.

17. Ibid.

18. Erving Goffman, *The Presentation of Self in Everyday Life* (Garden City, N.Y.: Doubleday, 1959), pp. 17–18.

19. Alfred L. Kroeber, *Anthropology* (New York: Harcourt, Brace, 1948), pp. 27–30, 355–57, 552.

20. Thomas Hobbes, *Leviathan* (New York: Macmillan, 1962), p. 113.

21. John Locke, *Of Civil Government: Second Treatise* (Chicago: Regnery, 1955), p. 102.

22. Adam Smith, *The Wealth of Nations* (New York: Modern Library, 1937), p. 670.

23. Jean-Jacques Rousseau, *The First and Second Discourses,* ed. Roger D. Masters (New York: St. Martin's Press, 1964), pp. 158–59.

24. Marx and Engels, "Manifesto," p. 355.

25. Locke, *Civil Government,* p. 22.

26. For a good summary of primitive property rights see Max Gluckman, *Politics, Law and Ritual in Tribal Society* (New York: New American Library, 1965), pp. 65–110.

27. Alfred G. Meyer, *Marxism: The Unity of Theory and Practice* (Ann Arbor: University of Michigan Press, 1954), p. 56.

28. Karl Marx, *Pre-Capitalist Economic Formations,* trans. Jack Cohen, ed. E. J. Hobsbawn (New York: International, 1964), pp. 67, 69, 75, 88, 90, 94, 143. Friedrich Engels, *The Origin of the Family, Private Property and the State in the Light of the Researches of Lewis H. Morgan* (New York: International, 1942), pp. 52, 57, 151–52. Karl Marx and Friedrich Engels, "The German Ideology," in *Marx and Engels: Basic Writings on Politics and Philosophy,* ed. Lewis S. Feuer (Garden City, N.Y.: Doubleday, 1959), p.

250. Lewis H. Morgan, *Ancient Society* (New York: Henry Holt, 1907), pp. 526–44.

29. Jozo Tomasevich, *Peasants, Politics and Economic Change in Yugoslavia* (Stanford: Stanford University Press, 1955), pp. 178–88.

30. Marx, *Pre-Capitalist Formations,* p. 88.

31. Engels, *Origin of the Family,* p. 53.

32. James Dow, "On the Muddled Concept of Corporation in Anthropology," *American Anthropologist* 75 (1973):904–8.

33. Locke, *Civil Government,* pp. 21–40.

34. Sir Gerard Clauson, *Communal Land Tenure,* FAO Agricultural Studies No. 17 (Rome: Food and Agricultural Organization of the United Nations, 1953), p. 44.

35. Locke, *Civil Government,* pp. 29, 36, 38.

36. Rousseau, *First and Second Discourses,* pp. 154–57.

37. John Stuart Mill, *Principles of Political Economy* (New York: Augustus M. Kelley, 1965 reprint of 1871 edition), p. 230.

38. William Bradford, *Of Plymouth Plantation 1620–1647,* ed. Harvey Wish (New York: Capricorn, 1962), pp. 101–2.

39. Donald Mackensie Wallace, *Russia on the Eve of War and Revolution* (New York: Random House, 1961), pp. 285, 355–56.

40. Rousseau, *First and Second Discourses,* pp. 154–55.

41. Mill, *Political Economy,* pp. 231–35.

42. Ibid.

43. Jean-Jacques Rousseau, *The Social Contract,* trans. Maurice Cranston (Baltimore: Penguin, 1968), pp. 66–68.

44. Douglass C. North and Robert Paul Thomas, *The Rise of the Western World: A New Economic History* (London: Cambridge University Press, 1973), pp. 1–2.

45. Ibid.

46. Ibid., pp. 56–57, 65–66, 92.

47. Ibid., pp. 62–64.

48. Ibid., pp. 152–56.

49. Joseph A. Schumpeter, *Capitalism, Socialism and Democracy* (New York: Harper and Row, 1950), pp. 131–34.

50. David S. Landes, "The Structure of Enterprise in the Nineteenth Century," in *The Rise of Capitalism,* ed. David S. Landes (New York: Macmillan, 1966), pp. 99–102.

51. Neil McKendrick, "Josiah Wedgwood and Factory Discipline," in *The Rise of Capitalism,* ed. David S. Landes (New York: Macmillan, 1966), pp. 65–81.

52. Ben R. Finney, *Big-Men and Business: Entrepreneurship and Economic Growth in the New Guinea Highlands* (Honolulu: University Press of Hawaii, 1973), pp. 80–82, 101–9.

53. Hazard, *Communists and Their Law,* p. 214. Klaus Mehnert, *China Returns* (New York: Dutton, 1972), p. 93.

54. Gerhard E. Lenski, *Power and Privilege: A Theory of Social Stratification* (New York: McGraw-Hill, 1966), pp. 311–13, 355–56.

55. Adolf A. Berle and Gardiner C. Means, *The Modern Corporation and Private Property* (New York: Harcourt, Brace and World, 1968), pp. ix–xi.

56. Peter F. Drucker, *The Unseen Revolution* (New York: Harper and Row, 1976), pp. 1–4.

57. Field notes of the author.

58. Ibid.

59. Harrington, *Socialism,* pp. 302–3.

60. Hedrick Smith, *The Russians* (New York: New York Times Book Co., 1976), pp. 86, 101. Murray Seeger, "Poland Looks to West for Economic Solution: Shift from Orthodox Communism," *Los Angeles Times,* 9 May 1976, pp. 1, 2, 3. Murray Seeger, "Knowing When to Back Down: Hungarian Leader a Master of Timing," *Los Angeles Times,* 9 July 1976, pp. 1, 9, 10. Sharon Zukin, *Beyond Marx and Tito: Theory and Practice in Yugoslav Socialism* (New York: Cambridge University Press, 1975), pp. 22–23.

61. Rousseau, *First and Second Discourses,* p. 147.

62. Richard G. Wilkinson, *Poverty and Progress: An Ecological Model of Economic Development* (London: Methuen, 1973), pp. 84–85, 173–74.

63. J. H. Boeke, *Economics and Economic Policy of Dual Societies as Exemplified by Indonesia* (New York: Institute of Pacific Relations, 1953), pp. 37–40.

64. Kenneth E. Carpenter, ed., *Labour Problems Before the Industrial Revolution: Four Pamphlets 1727–1745* (New York: Arno, 1972), pp. 41–42.

65. Wilkinson, *Poverty and Progress,* p. 173.

66. Smith, *Wealth of Nations,* pp. 82–83.

67. Bernard Mandeville, *The Fable of the Bees: Or, Private Vices, Public Benefits* (Baltimore: Penguin, 1970), pp. 200–201, 208–9.

68. Marshall Sahlins, *Stone Age Economics* (Chicago: Aldine, 1972), pp. 1–39. Richard B. Lee, "What Hunters Do for a Living, or, How to Make Out in Scarce Resources," in *Man the Hunter,* eds. Richard B. Lee and Irven DeVore (Chicago: Aldine, 1968), pp. 33–40.

69. Ester Boserup, *The Conditions of Agricultural Growth: The Economics of Agrarian Change under Population Pressure* (Chicago: Aldine, 1965).

70. North and Thomas, *Rise of Western World,* pp. 41–43.

71. Charles J. Erasmus, "Monument Building: Some Field Experiments," *Southwestern Journal of Anthropology* 21 (1965):277–301.

72. Schumpeter, *Capitalism,* p. 123.

73. Harrington, *Socialism,* pp. 345, 371–72.

74. North and Thomas, *Rise of Western World,* pp. 25–26. See also Robert-Henri Bautier, *The Economic Development of Medieval Europe* (New York: Harcourt Brace Jovanovich, 1971).

75. L. A. Clarkson, *The Pre-Industrial Economy in England 1500–1750* (London: Batsford, 1971), pp. 45–47, 75–77, 105–6.

76. Ibid., pp. 113–16, 119–21.

77. Alan David Dyer, *The City of Worcester in the Sixteenth Century* (Leicester, England: Leicester University Press, 1973), pp. 157–61.

78. Eric Kerridge, *The Farmers of Old England* (Totowa, N.J.: Rowman and Littlefield, 1973), pp. 163–67.

79. Mandeville, *Fable of the Bees,* pp. 152–54.

80. Ibid.

81. Ibid., p. 154.

82. David Lockwood, "Sources of Variation in Working-Class Images of Society," in *Comparative Perspectives on Stratification: Mexico, Great Britain, Japan,* ed. Joseph A. Kahl (Boston: Little, Brown, 1968), pp. 100–101, 106–113.

83. Ibid.

84. Alvin Toffler, *Future Shock* (New York: Random House, 1970), pp. 47–161.

85. Clarkson, *Pre-Industrial Economy,* pp. 31–32, 40–41.

86. David S. Landes, "Introduction," in *The Rise of Capitalism,* ed. David S. Landes (New York: Macmillan, 1966), pp. 12–15.

87. Boeke, *Dual Societies,* pp. 37–40.

88. Clifford Geertz, *Agricultural Involution: The Processes of Ecological Change in Indonesia* (Berkeley: University of California Press, 1968), pp. 48–49, 52–53, 63, 70.

89. Manning Nash, *Machine Age Maya: The Industrialization of a Guatemalan Community* (Washington, D.C.: American Anthropological Association Memoir No. 87, 1958), pp. 13–15, 18, 20, 23.

90. Ibid., pp. 34–42, 65–74.

91. Ibid., pp. 16–17.

92. Waldemar Richard Smith, "The Mesoamerican Fiesta System: A Behavioral Analysis" (Ph.D. diss., University of California at Santa Barbara, 1973), pp. 135–36, 140–41.

93. Ibid., pp. 145–46, 164–66.

94. Ibid., pp. 170–71, 232–34.

95. Charles J. Erasmus, *Man Takes Control: Cultural Development and American Aid* (Indianapolis: Bobbs-Merrill, 1961), pp. 238–62.

96. David S. Landes, *The Unbound Prometheus: Technological Change and Industrial Development in Western Europe from 1750 to the Present* (London: Cambridge University Press, 1969), p. 49.

97. Frank Parkin, *Class Inequality and Political Order: Social Stratification in Capitalist and Communist Societies* (New York: Praeger, 1971), pp. 33–36.

98. David R. Mettee and John Riskind, "Size of Defeat and Liking for Superior and Similar Ability Competitors," *Journal of Experimental Psychology* 10 (1974):333–51.

99. Charles Nordhoff, *The Communistic Societies of the United States* (New York: Schocken, 1965 reprint of 1875 edition), pp. 11–13.

100. Erasmus, *Man Takes Control.*

101. John Maynard Keynes, *Essays in Persuasion* (London: Macmillan, 1931), p. 372.

102. Leonard Plotnicov, "The Modern African Elite of Jos, Nigeria," in *Social Stratification in Africa,* eds. Arthur Tuden and Leonard Plotnicov (New York: Free Press, 1970), pp. 269–302.

103. Stanislav Andreski, *Parasitism and Subversion: The Case of Latin America* (London: Weidenfeld and Nicolson, 1966). Stanislav Andreski, *The African Predicament* (London: Michael Joseph, 1968).

104. André Gunder Frank, *Lumpenbourgeoisie: Lumpendevelopment* (New York: Monthly Review Press, 1972).

105. Bernard P. Kiernan, *The United States, Communism, and the Emergent World* (Bloomington: University of Indiana Press, 1972).

106. E. L. Wheelwright and Bruce McFarlane, *The Chinese Road to Socialism: Economics of the Cultural Revolution* (New York: Monthly Review Press, 1970), pp. 212–15.

Notes to Chapter Five: *Nineteenth-Century Communes* (pp. 113–166)

1. Lewis S. Feuer, "The Influence of the American Communist Colonies on Engels and Marx," *The Western Political Quarterly* 19 (1966):459–60.

2. Jean-Jacques Rousseau, *The First and Second Discourses,* ed. Roger D. Masters, trans. Roger Masters and Judith Masters (New York: St. Martin's Press, 1964), p. 113.

3. James G. March and Herbert A. Simon, *Organizations* (New York: Wiley, 1958), pp. 67–73. I have substituted "commitment" in the empirical or behavioral sense for March and Simon's "group identification." Their term emphasizes individual perceptions and has, therefore, a mentalistic quality I prefer to avoid.

4. Karl Kautsky, *Foundations of Christianity: A Study in Christian Origins* (New York: Monthly Review Press, 1925), p. 310.

5. Ibid., pp. 409–11.

6. Ibid., pp. 327–31, 339–41.

7. Ibid.

8. Ibid., 415–47.

9. Ibid., 449–51. Herbert B. Workman, *The Evolution of the Monastic Ideal: From the Earliest Times Down to the Coming of the Friars* (London: Epworth, 1927), pp. 25–37.

10. Jean Decarreaux, *Monks and Civilization: From the Barbarian Invasions to the Reign of Charlemagne,* trans. Charlotte Haldane (London: Allen and Unwin, 1964), pp. 70–116. Workman, *Monastic Ideal,* pp. 113–24.

11. Workman, *Monastic Ideal,* pp. 155–57.

12. Dom. Paul Delatte, *The Rule of Saint Benedict* (Latrobe, Pa.: Archabbey, 1921), p. 374.

13. Ibid., 71, 205–11, 244, 253–55, 288. Anthony C. Meisel and M. L. del

Mastro, *The Rule of St. Benedict* (Garden City, N.Y.: Doubleday, 1975), pp. 70, 75, 77, 85–86.

14. Delatte, *Rule of Saint Benedict,* pp. 212–27. Meisel and Mastro, *Rule of St. Benedict,* pp. 71–74, 84.

15. Delatte, *Rule of Saint Benedict,* p. 477.

16. Meisel and Mastro, *Rule of St. Benedict,* pp. 93, 105. Workman, *Monastic Ideal,* pp. 68–69, 150.

17. Kautsky, *Christianity,* pp. 454–57. Workman, *Monastic Ideal,* pp. 219–24.

18. Delatte, *Rule of Saint Benedict,* pp. 201, 245, 251, 344, 351. Meisel and Mastro, *Rule of St. Benedict,* p. 76.

19. Workman, *Monastic Ideal,* pp. 233–34.

20. Ibid., pp. 238–46. Bennett D. Hill, *English Cistercian Monasteries and Their Patrons in the Twelfth Century* (Urbana: University of Illinois Press, 1968), pp. 5, 8, 11, 53, 78–79, 147–48, 153.

21. Workman, *Monastic Ideal,* pp. 271–72.

22. Hill, *Cistercian Monasteries,* pp. 12–13.

23. Kautsky, *Christianity,* pp. 452–54.

24. Major works used in the comparative analysis of the six communal movements (Shakers, Rappites, Zoar, Amana, Oneida and Hutterites) are arranged below alphabetically. Page numbers refer only to materials covered in "Commune Profiles."

ANDREWS, EDWARD DEMING. *The People Called Shakers: A Search for the Perfect Society* (New York: Dover, 1963), pp. 3–93, 224–40.

ARNDT, KARL J. R. *George Rapp's Successors and Material Heirs 1847–1916* (Cranbury, N.J.: Associated University Presses, 1971), pp. 61–84, 318–70.

————. *George Rapp's Harmony Society 1785–1847* (Cranbury, N.J.: Associated University Presses, 1972), pp. 30–34, 44–52, 69–77, 379–81.

BENNETT, JOHN W. *Hutterian Brethren* (Stanford: Stanford University Press, 1967), pp. 25–34.

BOLE, JOHN ARCHIBALD. *The Harmony Society: A Chapter in German American Culture History* (Philadelphia: Americana Germanica, 1905), pp. 34, 72.

CARDEN, MAREN LOCKWOOD. *Oneida: Utopian Community to Modern Corporation* (Baltimore: Johns Hopkins University Press, 1969), pp. 1–45, 165–212.

CONKIN, PAUL K. *Two Paths to Utopia: The Hutterites and the Llano Colony* (Lincoln: University of Nebraska Press, 1964), pp. 3–48.

DOBBS, CATHERINE R. *Freedom's Will: The Society of the Separatists of Zoar—An Historical Adventure of Religious Communism in Early Ohio* (New York: William-Frederick, 1947), pp. 26–44, 83–89.

DUSS, JOHN S. *The Harmonists: A Personal History* (Harrisburg: Pennsylvania Book Service, 1943), pp. 1–118.

GROSS, PAUL S. *The Hutterite Way* (Saskatoon, Canada: Freeman, 1965), pp. 1–14.

HINDS, WILLIAM ALFRED. *American Communities* (New York: Corinth, 1961 reprint of 1878 edition), pp. 7–22, 23–38, 49–58, 81–116, 118–20.

HOSTETLER, JOHN A. *Hutterite Society* (Baltimore: Johns Hopkins University Press, 1974), pp. 1–118, 295.

——— AND HUNTINGTON, GERTRUDE ENDERS. *The Hutterites in North America* (New York: Holt, Rinehart, and Winston, 1967), pp. 1–4.

JOHNSON, CHARLES A. *The Frontier Camp Meeting* (Dallas: Southern Methodist University Press, 1955), pp. 25–68.

MELCHER, MARGUERITE FELLOWS. *The Shaker Adventure* (Cleveland: The Press of Case Western Reserve University, 1941), pp. 3–83, 227–65.

NORDHOFF, CHARLES. *The Communistic Societies of the United States* (New York: Schocken, 1965 reprint of 1875 edition), pp. 26–31, 63–81, 99–103, 117–19, 125–35, 259–62.

PETERS, VICTOR. *All Things Common: The Hutterian Way of Life* (Minneapolis: University of Minnesota Press, 1965), pp. 9–50.

RANDALL, E. O. *History of the Zoar Society: A Sociological Study in Communism* (New York: AMS Press, 1971 reprint of 1904 edition), pp. 2–12, 52–71.

ROBERTSON, CONSTANCE NOYES, ed. *Oneida Community: An Autobiography, 1851–1876* (Syracuse: Syracuse University Press, 1970), pp. 1–26.

SHAMBAUGH, BERTHA M. H. *Amana That Was and Amana That Is* (New York: Benjamin Blom, 1970 reprint of 1932 edition), pp. 31–55, 372–405.

WEISBERGER, BERNARD A. *They Gathered at the River: The Story of the Great Revivalists and Their Impact upon Religion in America* (Chicago: Quadrangle, 1958), pp. 20–50.

WILLIAMS, AARON. *The Harmony Society at Economy, Penn'a* (Pittsburgh: W. S. Haven, 1866), pp. 14, 28, 33, 48–95.

WILLIAMS, RICHARD L. "The Shakers, Now Only 12, Observe Their 200th Year," *Smithsonian*, September 1974, pp. 40–41.

YAMBURA, BARBARA SCHNEIDER. *A Change and a Parting: My Story of Amana* (Ames, Iowa: Iowa State University Press, 1960), pp. 20–36.

25. Andrews, *Shakers*, p. 224. Melcher, *Shaker Adventure*, p. 227. Nordhoff, *Communistic Societies*, pp. 179–214.

26. Shambaugh, *Amana That Was*, p. 81.

27. Robertson, *Oneida Autobiography*, p. 89. Carden, *Oneida*, p. 41.

28. Arndt, *Rapp's Society*, p. 121. Hinds, *Communities*, p. 26.

29. Bennett, *Hutterian Brethren*, p. 151. Conkin, *Two Paths*, p. 90. Joseph W. Eaton and Albert J. Mayer, *Man's Capacity to Reproduce: The Demography of a Unique Population* (Glencoe, Ill.: Free Press, 1954) pp. 15, 20. Hostetler and Huntington, *Hutterites*, p. 44. Peters, *Hutterian Way*, p. 152.

30. *Alberta Report on Communal Property* (Edmonton, Alberta: Queen's Printer, 1972), p. 13. Eaton and Mayer, *Capacity to Reproduce*, p. 9. Hostetler and Huntington, *Hutterites*, pp. 44, 47.

31. Bennett, *Hutterian Brethren*, pp. 155, 256. Hostetler and Huntington, *Hutterites*, p. 103.

32. Carden, *Oneida,* pp. 19, 85, 99.

33. Arndt, *Rapp's Society,* pp. 340–41. Duss, *Harmonists,* p. 84.

34. Andrews, *Shakers,* pp. 35–53. Duss, *Harmonists,* pp. 7–13. Dobbs, *Separatists of Zoar,* pp. 26–35. Yambura, *Story of Amana,* pp. 21–26. Carden, *Oneida,* p. 26.

35. Shambaugh, *Amana That Was,* p. 110. Dobbs, *Separatists of Zoar,* p. 64.

36. Nordhoff, *Communistic Societies,* pp. 144–45. Carden, *Oneida,* p. 79.

37. Andrews, *Shakers,* pp. 243–48.

38. Nordhoff, *Communistic Societies,* p. 395.

39. Williams, *Society at Economy,* p. 55. Lee Emerson Deets, *The Hutterites: A Study in Social Cohesion* (Gettysburg, Pa.: Times and News Publ., 1939), pp. 46–47. Hostetler, *Hutterite Society,* p. 245. Hostetler and Huntington, *Hutterites,* p. 86. Andrews, *Shakers,* p. 179. Shambaugh, *Amana That Was,* p. 241.

40. Conkin, *Two Paths,* p. 16. Deets, *Social Cohesion,* pp. 46–47. Hostetler, *Hutterite Society,* p. 245. Peters, *Hutterian Way,* p. 159. Dobbs, *Separatists of Zoar,* p. 66. Randall, *Zoar Society,* p. 12. Andrews, *Shakers,* p. 262. Shambaugh, *Amana That Was,* pp. 241, 270. Yambura, *Story of Amana,* p. 137.

41. Carden, *Oneida,* pp. 74–75. Robertson, *Oneida Autobiography,* pp. 147, 313.

42. Williams, *Society at Economy,* p. 41. Shambaugh, *Amana That Was,* p. 247.

43. Shambaugh, *Amana That Was,* pp. 60–61, 113. Yambura, *Story of Amana,* pp. 29, 168.

44. Yambura, *Story of Amana,* pp. 135–36.

45. Hinds, *Communities,* p. 122.

46. Duss, *Harmonists,* pp. 66–70. Arndt, *Rapp's Harmony,* p. 77.

47. Shambaugh, *Amana That Was,* pp. 27–30, 91. Yambura, *Story of Amana,* p. 25.

48. Hostetler, *Hutterite Society,* p. 256. Hostetler and Huntington, *Hutterites,* p. 95.

49. Andrews, *Shakers,* pp. 43, 91, 120–35, 232–34. Melcher, *Shaker Adventure,* pp. 24–30, 178, 188.

50. Nordhoff, *Communistic Societies,* pp. 387, 408.

51. Ibid., pp. 399, 407, 409.

52. Duss, *Harmonists,* p. 51.

53. Nordhoff, *Communistic Societies,* p. 410.

54. Bennett, *Hutterian Brethren,* p. 129.

55. Nordhoff, *Communistic Societies,* p. 410.

56. Conkin, *Two Paths,* p. 16. Peters, *Hutterian Way,* p. 104.

57. Robertson, *Oneida Autobiography,* pp. 48, 62.

58. Conkin, *Two Paths,* p. 81. Peters, *Hutterian Way,* p. 167.

59. Andrews, *Shakers,* pp. 136, 181–85.

60. Shambaugh, *Amana That Was,* p. 269.

61. Carden, *Oneida,* p. 45.

62. Kautsky, *Christianity,* pp. 311–12, 347.

63. Carden, *Oneida*, pp. 47, 52–53. Robertson, *Oneida Autobiography*, pp. 321, 323.

64. Andrews, *Shakers*, pp. 106–7. Melcher, *Shaker Adventure*, pp. 47–48.

65. Duss, *Harmonists*, pp. 28–29, 121. Dobbs, *Separatists of Zoar*, pp. 53–56. Randall, *Zoar Society*, p. 46.

66. Bennett, *Hutterian Brethren*, pp. 118, 257. Hostetler and Huntington, *Hutterites*, p. 47. Hostetler, *Hutterite Society*, pp. 203–6. John A. Hostetler, "Education and Marginality in the Communal Society of the Hutterites," mimeographed (University Park: Pennsylvania State University, 1965), p. 120.

67. Williams, *Society at Economy*, p. 62.

68. Andrews, *Shakers*, p. 150. Bole, *Harmony Society*, p. 146. Shambaugh, *Amana That Was*, pp. 127, 142. Randall, *Zoar Society*, p. 32. Dobbs, *Separatists of Zoar*, pp. 53–55. Nordhoff, *Communistic Societies*, p. 312. Bennett, *Hutterian Brethren*, p. 108.

69. Carden, *Oneida*, p. 43.

70. Nordhoff, *Communistic Societies*, p. 40.

71. Melcher, *Shaker Adventure*, pp. 140–41.

72. Meisel and Mastro, *Rule of St. Benedict*, p. 93.

73. Bennett, *Hutterian Brethren*, pp. 146, 149, 156, 159.

74. Williams, *Society at Economy*, p. 42. Randall, *Zoar Society*, p. 34. Carden, *Oneida*, p. 87.

75. Andrews, *Shakers*, p. 193.

76. Ibid., pp. 57–59, 253–60.

77. Ibid., pp. 105–6.

78. Ibid., pp. 106, 193.

79. Shambaugh, *Amana That Was*, pp. 94–101.

80. Ibid., pp. 102–4.

81. Hostetler and Huntington, *Hutterites*, pp. 27–30.

82. Ibid., pp. 10, 62, 66. Conkin, *Two Paths*, p. 28.

83. Bennett, *Hutterian Brethren*, p. 128. Conkin, *Two Paths*, pp. 87, 93.

84. Shambaugh, *Amana That Was*, pp. 169–72.

85. Margaret Mead, "Communes: A Challenge to All of Us," *Redbook Magazine*, August, 1970, pp. 51–52.

86. Julia Elizabeth Williams, "An Analytical Tabulation of the North American Utopian Communities by Type, Longevity and Location," M.A. diss., University of Iowa, 1938.

87. George B. Lockwood, *The New Harmony Movement* (New York: Dover, 1971 reprint of 1905 edition), pp. 58, 83.

88. Ibid., pp. 98, 100–101, 140, 148–49, 157. Arthur Bestor, *Backwoods Utopias: The Sectarian Origins and the Owenite Phase of Communitarian Socialism in America, 1663–1829* (Philadelphia: University of Pennsylvania Press, 1970), pp. 162–64.

89. J. F. C. Harrison, *Quest for the New Moral World: Robert Owen and the*

Owenites in Britain and America (New York: Scribner's, 1969), pp. 178–79. Lockwood, *New Harmony,* pp. 90–91.

90. Bestor, *Backwoods Utopias,* pp. 163–64. Harrison, *New Moral World,* pp. 184–85. Lockwood, *New Harmony,* pp. 120, 140, 178–79.

91. John Humphrey Noyes, *History of American Socialisms* (New York: Dover, 1966 reprint of 1870 edition), pp. 64–65.

92. Ibid., pp. 326, 348, 369, 402, 445.

93. Ibid., pp. 243, 349, 445, 648.

94. Ibid., pp. 306–7, 493.

95. Ibid., pp. 235–36.

96. Mark Holloway, *Heavens on Earth: Utopian Communities in America, 1680–1880* (New York: Dover, 1966), pp. 136–37.

97. Noyes, *American Socialisms,* pp. 402–3, 445, 496.

98. Bestor, *Backwoods Utopias,* p. 84. Harrison, *New Moral World,* pp. 180–82.

99. Harrison, *New Moral World,* p. 93.

100. Robert Houriet, *Getting Back Together* (New York: Coward, McCann and Geoghegan, 1971), p. 47.

101. Judson Jerome, *Families of Eden: Communes and the New Anarchism* (New York: Seabury, 1974), pp. 21–22. Benjamin David Zablocki, *The Joyful Community: An Account of the Bruderhof, A Communal Movement Now in Its Third Generation* (Baltimore: Penguin, 1971), p. 304.

102. Houriet, *Back Together,* p. 134.

103. Jerome, *Familes of Eden,* p. 22.

104. Rosabeth Moss Kanter, "Communes," *Psychology Today,* July 1970, p. 57.

105. Jerome, *Families of Eden,* p. 22.

106. Houriet, *Back Together,* pp. 144–45.

107. Zablocki, *Joyful Community,* pp. 308–9, 311.

108. Ibid., p. 319.

109. Herbert A. Otto, "Communes: The Alternative Life-Style," *Saturday Review,* 24 April 1971, pp. 20–21. Jerome, *Families of Eden,* p. 23.

110. Zablocki, *Joyful Community,* p. 304. Houriet, *Back Together,* pp. 152, 209.

111. Kanter, "Communes," p. 57.

112. Zablocki, *Joyful Community,* p. 300.

113. Jerome, *Families of Eden,* pp. 16–20.

114. Ibid., pp. 78, 82–83.

115. Ibid., p. 184.

116. Nordhoff, *Communistic Societies,* p. 408.

117. Jerome, *Families of Eden,* pp. 96–98, 191.

118. Ibid., p. 83.

119. Ibid., pp. 52, 173, 199.

120. Nordhoff, *Communistic Societies,* p. 397.

121. Robertson, *Oneida Autobiography,* pp. 262–63. Duss, *Harmonists,* p. 51.

122. Nordhoff, *Communistic Societies,* p. 161.

123. Noyes, *American Socialisms,* p. 19.

124. Adam Smith, *The Wealth of Nations* (New York: Modern Library, 1937), p. 424.

125. Andrews, *Shakers,* pp. 113–15. Melcher, *Shaker Adventure,* p. 134.

126. Carden, *Oneida,* p. 85. Robertson, *Oneida Autobiography,* p. 213.

127. Duss, *Harmonists,* pp. 46–47. Williams, *Society at Economy,* p. 65.

128. Dobbs, *Separatists of Zoar,* pp. 46–48.

129. Shambaugh, *Amana That Was,* pp. 157–58, 167.

130. Robertson, *Oneida Autobiography,* p. 217. Duss, *Harmonists,* pp. 46–47. Dobbs, *Separatists of Zoar,* pp. 46–48. Shambaugh, *Amana That Was,* p. 157.

131. Shambaugh, *Amana That Was,* pp. 125, 142, 153, 156. Yambura, *Story of Amana,* p. 34.

132. Shambaugh, *Amana That Was,* pp. 154, 160.

133. Ibid., pp. 151, 156, 158.

134. Melcher, *Shaker Adventure,* pp. 254–55, 302.

135. Duss, *Harmonists,* p. 227.

136. Williams, "Now Only 12," pp. 40–41.

137. Dobbs, *Separatists of Zoar,* pp. 63, 75–76. Hinds, *Communities,* p. 28.

138. Randall, *Zoar Society,* pp. 35–37, 51.

139. Robertson, *Oneida Autobiography,* pp. 73, 226, 244, 251, 254–59.

140. Ibid., pp. 89–90, 215.

141. Nordhoff, *Communist Societies,* p. 393.

142. Shambaugh, *Amana That Was,* pp. 137, 156, 158, 407. Yambura, *Story of Amana,* p. 94.

143. Andrews, *Shakers,* p. 115.

144. Ibid., pp. 152–56.

145. Nordhoff, *Communistic Societies,* p. 161.

146. Duss, *Harmonists,* pp. 48, 84.

147. Robertson, *Oneida Autobiography,* p. 125. Carden, *Oneida,* pp. 91, 98.

148. Hinds, *Communities,* pp. 36–37.

149. Randall, *Zoar Society,* p. 45.

150. Shambaugh, *Amana That Was,* pp. 269–70.

151. Ibid., pp. 106–7.

152. Yambura, *Story of Amana,* p. 277.

153. Shambaugh, *Amana That Was,* pp. 343–45. Yambura, *Story of Amana,* p. 229.

154. Ibid., pp. 224, 227.

155. Ibid., pp. 238–40.

156. Randall, *Zoar Society,* pp. 49–50.

157. Duss, *Harmonists,* p. 236.

158. Randall, *Zoar Society,* pp. 49–50.

159. Ibid., pp. 53–54, 63, 68.

160. Shambaugh, *Amana That Was,* p. 346.

161. Yambura, *Story of Amana,* pp. 107, 143–47. Shambaugh, *Amana That Was,* p. 396.

162. Ibid., pp. 406–8.

163. Ibid., p. 413.

164. Nordhoff, *Communistic Societies,* p. 385. Nordhoff actually listed eight movements or "societies" instead of seven because he separated Bethel and Aurora. I consider these both part of the same movement.

165. Hostetler, *Hutterite Society,* pp. 285, 296.

166. Lee Emerson Deets, *The Hutterites: A Study in Social Cohesion* (Gettysburg, Pa.: Times and News Publ., 1939), pp. 52–54.

167. Ibid., pp. 55–56.

168. Bennett, *Hutterian Brethren,* pp. 169, 189. Joseph W. Eaton, "Controlled Acculturation: A Survival Technique of the Hutterites," *American Sociological Review* 17 (1952):335. Joseph W. Eaton and Robert Weil, *Culture and Mental Disorders: A Comparative Study of the Hutterites and Other Populations* (Glencoe, Ill.: Free Press, 1955), pp. 193–94. Hostetler, *Hutterite Society,* pp. 269–76, 359–72. John A. Hostetler, "Education and Marginality in the Communal Society of the Hutterites," mimeographed (University Park: Pennsylvania State University, 1965), pp. 85–116. Hostetler and Huntington, *Hutterites,* p. 102.

169. *Alberta Report on Communal Property* (Edmonton, Alberta: Queen's Printer, 1972), p. 13. Hostetler, *Hutterite Society,* pp. 42–45.

170. *Alberta Report,* pp. 22–23, 27–28. Hostetler, *Hutterite Society,* p. 196.

171. *Alberta Report,* p. 22. Bennett, *Hutterian Brethren,* pp. 161–65, 212–14. Eaton, "Controlled Acculturation," pp. 336–38. Hostetler, *Hutterite Society,* pp. 181–82.

172. Ibid., pp. 185–90, 255–59, 268–69.

173. Diane Bray Heiken, a teacher in Newbury Park, California, is a candidate for the Ph.D. in anthropology at the University of California, Santa Barbara.

Notes to Chapter Six: *Israeli Communes* (pp. 167–196)

1. Charles Nordhoff, *The Communistic Societies of the United States* (New York: Schocken, 1965 reprint of 1875 edition), p. 408.

2. Jean-Jacques Rousseau, *The Social Contract or Principles of Political Right plus the Dedication from the "Second Discourse" and "On Political Economy,"* edited with commentary by Charles M. Sherover (New York: New American Library, 1974), pp. 113, 151, 165, 239.

3. Ibid., pp. 31, 264–67.

4. Martin Buber, *Paths in Utopia,* trans. R. F. C. Hull (Boston: Beacon, 1949), pp. 13–14, 128, 132, 149.

5. D. Weintraub, M. Lissak, and Y. Azmon, *Moshava, Kibbutz, and Moshav: Patterns of Jewish Rural Settlement and Development in Palestine* (Ithaca: Cornell University Press, 1969), pp. 6–13. Dan Leon, *The Kibbutz: A New Way of Life* (London: Pergamon, 1969), p. 44. Yonina Talmon and E. Cohen, "Collective Settlements in the Negev," in *Agricultural Planning and Village Community in Israel,* ed. Joseph Ben-David (Paris: UNESCO, 1964), pp. 168–69. Michael Frank, *Cooperative Land Settlements in Israel and their Relevance to African Countries* (Tubingen, Germany: Kylos-Verlag Basel, 1968), pp. 28–29.

6. Alan Arian, *Ideological Change in Israel* (Cleveland: Press of Case Western. Reserve University, 1968), p. 75. Haim Darin-Drabkin, *The Other Society* (New York: Harcourt, Brace and World, 1962), pp. 280–81. Boris Stern, *The Kibbutz That Was* (Washington, D.C.: Public Affairs Press, 1965), p. 92.

7. Population estimates have been interpolated from the author's field notes and the following sources. Darin-Drabkin, *Other Society,* pp. 79, 81–82, 275–76. Haim Darin-Drabkin, *Patterns of Cooperative Agriculture in Israel* (Tel Aviv: Department for International Cooperation, Ministry of Foreign Affairs, 1962), pp. 36, 39. Eliyahu Kanovsky, *The Economy of the Israeli Kibbutz,* Harvard Middle Eastern Monographs, No. 13 (Cambridge: Harvard University Press, 1966), pp. 19–21, 147. Leon, *Kibbutz Way of Life,* p. 201. Stern, *Kibbutz That Was,* p. 85.

8. Kanovsky, *Economy of Kibbutz,* pp. 18, 20. Weintraub, Lissak, and Azmon, *Moshava, Kibbutz, Moshav,* pp. 30–31.

9. Darin-Drabkin, *Other Society,* pp. 79–80. Darin-Drabkin, *Cooperative Agriculture,* pp. 16–17.

10. Kanovsky, *Economy of Kibbutz,* p. 126.

11. Stern, *Kibbutz That Was,* pp. 114–15.

12. Kanovsky, *Economy of Kibbutz,* p. 49. Uri Leviatan, "The Industrial Process in Israeli Kibbutzim: Problems and their Solutions," in *Israel: Social Structure and Change,* eds. Michael Curtis and Mordecai S. Chertoff (New Brunswick, N.J.: Transaction Books, 1973), pp. 159–64.

13. The following historical material on the shitufim was gathered from several informants, but it benefits particularly from the help of Shlomo Kenan and his unpublished manuscript, "Life in the Shitufim," mimeographed (Gilboa, Israel: Moshav Shitufi Moledeth, 1965).

14. Melford E. Spiro, *Kibbutz: Venture in Utopia* (New York: Schocken, 1970), p. 5.

15. Kanovsky, *Economy of Kibbutz,* p. 11.

16. Jill Cordover Byron-Cooper is a candidate for the Ph.D. in anthropology, University of California at Santa Barbara.

17. Internal composition of kibbutz interpolated from author's field notes and the following sources. Leon, *Kibbutz Way of Life,* p. 203. Stern, *Kibbutz That Was,* p. 96.

18. Darin-Drabkin, *Other Society,* pp. 60–62, 70, 77. Kanovsky, *Economy of Kibbutz,* p. 127.

19. Joseph Ben-David, "The Kibbutz and the Moshav," in *Agricultural Planning*

and Village Community in Israel, ed. Joseph Ben-David (Paris: UNESCO, 1964), pp. 50–52. Joseph W. Eaton and Michael Chen, *Influencing the Youth Culture: A Study of Youth Organizations in Israel* (Beverly Hills, California: Sage Publications, 1970), pp. 56–67. Michael Gorkin, *Border Kibbutz* (New York: Grosset and Dunlap, 1971), p. 56. Stern, *Kibbutz That Was*, pp. 4–13, 88–89. Talmon and Cohen, "Collective Settlements," p. 60. Weintraub, Lissak, and Azmon, *Moshava, Kibbutz, Moshav*, p. 110.

20. Spiro, *Kibbutz*, p. 85.

21. Murray Weingarten, *Life in a Kibbutz* (Jerusalem: Publishing Department of the Jewish Agency, 1959), p. 159.

22. Gorkin, *Border Kibbutz*, p. 14. Stern, *Kibbutz That Was*, pp. 4–8, 16–18, 22. Weintraub, Lissak, and Azmon, *Moshava, Kibbutz, Moshav*, pp. 1–8.

23. Spiro, *Kibbutz*, pp. 39–40, 98.

24. Nordhoff, *Communistic Societies*, p. 40.

25. Yonina Talmon, "Differentiation in Collective Settlements," in *Scripta Hierosolymitana*, ed. Roberto Bachi, Publications of the Hebrew University, Vol. 3 (Jerusalem: Magnes Press, 1956), pp. 171–75.

26. Nordhoff, *Communistic Societies*, pp. 281, 393.

27. Arian, *Change in Israel*, p. 178. Ben-David, "Kibbutz and Moshav," p. 53. Talmon and Cohen, "Collective Settlements," p. 61. Weintraub, Lissak, and Azmon, *Moshava, Kibbutz, Moshav*, p. 120.

28. Stern, *Kibbutz That Was*, pp. 23–25. Talmon and Cohen, "Collective Settlements," p. 68.

29. Seymour Melman, "Industrial Efficiency under Managerial vs. Cooperative Decision-Making: A Comparative Study of Manufacturing Enterprises in Israel," *Review of Radical Political Economics* 2 (1970):27.

30. Frank, *Settlements in Israel*, pp. 23–24. Leon, *Kibbutz Way of Life*, pp. 48–50.

31. Kanovsky, *Economy of Kibbutz*, p. 84.

32. Eaton and Chen, *Youth Culture*, p. 115. Kanovsky, *Economy of Kibbutz*, pp. 60–64.

33. Leviatan, "Industrial Process in Kibbutzim," p. 164. Menahem Rosner, "Worker Participation in Decision-Making in Kibbutz Industry," in *Israel: Social Structure and Change*, eds. Michael Curtis and Mordecai S. Chertoff (New Brunswick, N.J.: Transaction Books, 1973), pp. 145–46.

34. Stern, *Kibbutz That Was*, p. 42.

35. Talmon and Cohen, "Collective Settlements," p. 68.

36. Arian, *Change in Israel*, p. 109.

37. Leviatan, "Industrial Process in Kibbutzim," p. 164. Stern, *Kibbutz That Was*, p. 51.

38. Ibid., pp. 88–91. Talmon and Cohen, "Collective Settlements," pp. 61–62.

39. Ibid. Eaton and Chen, *Youth Culture*, pp. 63–67, 119–24.

40. Ibid., pp. 77, 225.

41. Gorkin, *Border Kibbutz*, p. 97.

42. Stern, *Kibbutz That Was*, p. 73.

43. Information on volunteer laborers provided by Katherine Wyckoff, who worked as a kibbutz volunteer during 1973.

44. William Alfred Hinds, *American Communities* (New York: Corinth, 1961 reprint of 1878 edition), p. 28.

45. Stern, *Kibbutz That Was*, pp. 45–47.

46. Talmon and Cohen, "Collective Settlements," p. 92.

47. Constance Noyes Robertson, ed., *Oneida Community: An Autobiography, 1851–1876* (Syracuse: Syracuse University Press, 1970), p. 125.

48. Ben-David, "Kibbutz and Moshav," p. 56.

49. Arian, *Change in Israel*, pp. 117–18.

50. Stern, *Kibbutz That Was*, pp. 52–57.

51. Ibid., pp. 137–38. Arian, *Change in Israel*, pp. 88–89.

52. Leon, *Kibbutz Way of Life*, p. 86.

53. Stern, *Kibbutz That Was*, p. 62.

54. Yonina Talmon, "The Family in a Revolutionary Movement—The Case of the Kibbutz in Israel," in *Comparative Family Systems*, ed. M. F. Nimkoff (Boston: Houghton Mifflin, 1965), p. 271.

55. Weintraub, Lissak, and Azmon, *Moshava, Kibbutz, Moshav*, pp. 108, 114, 120.

56. Robertson, *Oneida Autobiography*, p. 49.

57. Talmon and Cohen, "Collective Settlements," p. 84.

58. Darin-Drabkin, *Other Society*, p. 133. Weingarten, *Life in Kibbutz*, p. 160.

59. Darin-Drabkin, *Cooperative Agriculture*, pp. 234–35.

60. Talmon, "Family in Revolutionary Movement," p. 276.

61. Stern, *Kibbutz That Was*, p. 141.

62. Ibid., p. 133. Ben-David, "Kibbutz and Moshav," p. 54.

63. Talmon, "Family in Revolutionary Movement," p. 261.

64. Ibid., pp. 271–72. Stern, *Kibbutz That Was*, pp. 120–22.

65. Talmon, "Family in Revolutionary Movement," p. 280.

66. Kanovsky, *Economy of Kibbutz*, pp. 87–124.

67. Leon, *Kibbutz Way of Life*, pp. 56–57.

68. Ibid., p. 39.

69. Talmon and Cohen, "Collective Settlements," p. 67.

70. Arian, *Change in Israel*, p. 87.

71. Stern, *Kibbutz That Was*, p. 105.

72. Harry Viteles, *The Evolution of the Kibbutz Movement, Vol. 2, A History of the Cooperative Movement in Israel* (London: Vallentine, Mitchell, 1967), p. 555.

73. Arian, *Change in Israel*, p. 74.

74. Viteles, *Kibbutz Movement*, p. 552.

75. At the time of writing, Judith Glickman was an anthropology student at the University of California, Santa Barbara.

76. Arian, *Change in Israel*, pp. 79–80.

Notes to Chapter Seven: *Utopia* (pp. 197–231)

1. Wilfred Beckerman, *In Defense of Economic Growth* (London: Cape, 1974), pp. 49–53. Harvey Simmons, "System Dynamics and Technocracy," in *Models of Doom: A Critique of the Limits to Growth,* ed. H. S. D. Cole (New York: Universe Books, 1973), p. 207.

2. Michael Holquist, "How to Play Utopia: Some Brief Notes on the Distinctiveness of Utopian Fiction," in *Game, Play, Literature,* ed. Jacques Ehrmann (Boston: Beacon, 1968), pp. 106–8, 110, 121–22.

3. Marie Louise Berneri, *Journey Through Utopia* (New York: Schocken, 1971), p. 222.

4. Erich Fromm, Foreword to *Looking Backward* by Edward Bellamy (New York: New American Library, 1960).

5. Miriam Beard, *A History of Business, Volume I: From Babylon to the Monopolists* (Ann Arbor: University of Michigan Press, 1938), pp. 18–20.

6. Plato, *The Republic,* trans. Francis MacDonald Cornford (New York: Oxford University Press, 1941), bk. 8, sec. 550–56.

7. Allan Bloom, "Interpretive Essay," in *The Republic of Plato,* trans. Allan Bloom (New York: Basic Books, 1968), pp. 18, 341, 364.

8. Thomas More, *Utopia,* ed. and trans. H. V. S. Ogden (New York: Appleton-Century-Crofts, 1949), p. 81.

9. Ibid., pp. 8, 80.

10. Ibid., pp. 10–11, 82.

11. Edward Bellamy, *Looking Backward: 2000–1887* (New York: American Library, 1960), pp. 26–28.

12. B. F. Skinner, *Walden Two* (New York: Macmillan, 1948), pp. 8, 206, 261.

13. B. F. Skinner, *About Behaviorism* (New York: Knopf, 1974), p. 206.

14. Skinner, *Walden Two,* p. 102. B. F. Skinner, *Contingencies of Reinforcement: A Theoretical Analysis* (New York: Appleton-Century-Crofts, 1969), pp. 50–51, 56, 195–96.

15. Skinner, *Walden Two,* pp. 123–24, 129–33. Skinner, *Contingencies,* p. 4.

16. Plato, *Republic,* bk. 4, sec. 434–41.

17. More, *Utopia,* pp. 50, 65, 81.

18. Bellamy, *Looking Backward,* p. 77.

19. Lewis Mumford, *The Story of Utopias* (New York: Viking, 1962), pp. 151–69.

20. Plato, *Republic,* bk. 2, sec. 368–76.

21. Ibid.

22. Ibid.

23. Ibid., bk. 3, sec. 421–22.

24. Ibid., sec. 416–17.

25. More, *Utopia,* p. 25.

26. Ibid., pp. 61, 81.

27. Ibid., pp. 7, 13.

28. Ibid., p. 22.

29. Ibid., pp. 43–45.

30. Skinner, *About Behaviorism,* pp. 124, 193.

31. More, *Utopia,* pp. 72–73.

32. Berneri, *Through Utopia,* p. 220.

33. Etienne Cabet, *Voyage en Icarie* (Paris: Editions Anthropos, 1970 reprint of fifth edition, 1848), pp. 35–36.

34. Ibid., pp. 36, 96.

35. Edward Bellamy, "Some Account of the Propaganda Work in America Which Has Followed *Looking Backward,*" and "The Programme of the Nationalists," in *Edward Bellamy Abroad: An American Prophet's Influence,* ed. Sylvia E. Bowman (New York: Twayne, 1962), pp. 439–48.

36. Bellamy, *Looking Backward,* pp. 56, 72, 139, 144.

37. Ibid., pp. 57–58.

38. Skinner, *Walden Two,* pp. 23, 91, 264, 266.

39. Ibid., pp. 79, 107–12.

40. Ibid., pp. 266–67.

41. Plato, *Republic,* bk. 1, sec. 347.

42. Kathleen Kinkade, *A Walden Two Experiment: The First Five Years of Twin Oaks Community* (New York: Morrow, 1973).

43. Cabet, *Icarie,* pp. 39–40.

44. Bellamy, *Looking Backward,* p. 30.

45. Friedrich Engels, *The Condition of the Working Class in England,* trans. W. O. Henderson and W. H. Chaloner (Stanford: Stanford University Press, 1958), pp. 352–53.

46. Bellamy, *Looking Backward,* pp. 53–55.

47. Skinner, *Walden Two,* pp. 162, 193, 210, 260.

48. Kinkade, *Twin Oaks,* pp. 13, 117, 267–68.

49. Skinner, *Walden Two,* pp. 223–24, 228.

50. Elisabeth Hansot, *Perfection and Progress: Two Modes of Utopian Thought* (Cambridge: MIT Press, 1974), pp. 11, 16.

51. Plato, *Republic,* bk. 9, sec. 592. More, *Utopia,* pp. 82–83.

52. Mumford, *Story of Utopias,* pp. 104, 115, 147.

53. Bloom "Interpretive Essay," p. 364.

54. Plato, *Republic,* bk. 2, sec. 367–74.

55. More, *Utopia,* pp. 36–38.

56. Ibid., pp. 28, 56.

57. H. G. Wells, *A Modern Utopia* (Lincoln: University of Nebraska Press, 1905), p. 100.

58. Cabet, *Icarie,* p. 100.

59. Ibid., pp. 100–103.

60. Ibid.

61. Bellamy, *Looking Backward*, p. 84.

62. Skinner, *Walden Two*, pp. 166–67, 209, 270.

63. Kinkade, *Twin Oaks*, pp. 90, 226, 228.

64. Skinner, *Walden Two*, pp. 29–30, 49, 61, 290.

65. Plato, *Republic* (Cornford), p. 159, note 2; bk. 4, sec. 429; bk. 5, sec. 457, 465–66. Bloom, "Interpretive Essay," p. 385.

66. Skinner, *Walden Two*, pp. 138–46.

67. Kinkade, *Twin Oaks*, pp. 130–46, 164–71.

68. More, *Utopia*, pp. 28–29, 32, 37–40, 58–59.

69. J. H. Hexter, *The Vision of Politics on the Eve of the Reformation: More, Machiavelli, and Seyssel* (New York: Basic Books, 1973), p. 42.

70. More, *Utopia*, p. 39.

71. Ibid., pp. 40, 60.

72. Cabet, *Icarie*, pp. 161, 200–201.

73. More, *Utopia*, pp. 29–30, 34.

74. Cabet, *Icarie*, p. 106.

75. Ibid., pp. 38–39, 101–2.

76. Bellamy, *Looking Backward*, pp. 63, 131–33, 142.

77. Ibid., pp. 61–62, 90, 112–13.

78. Ibid., pp. 63, 92.

79. Ibid., pp. 116–18.

80. Ibid., pp. 72–73, 89.

81. Skinner, *Walden Two*, pp. 54–55.

82. Kinkade, *Twin Oaks*, pp. 104–5, 242–44.

83. Skinner, *Walden Two*, p. 235.

84. Kinkade, *Twin Oaks*, p. 244.

85. Skinner, *Walden Two*, pp. 41–45, 163–64.

86. William Alfred Hinds, *American Communities* (New York: Corinth, 1961 reprint of 1878 edition), p. 37.

87. Kinkade, *Twin Oaks*, pp. 248–55.

88. Plato, *Republic*, bk. 4, sec. 417–21.

89. Ibid., bk. 5, sec. 460, 465–66.

90. Bloom, "Interpretive Essay," p. 370.

91. More, *Utopia*, p. 26.

92. Ibid., pp. 42, 59–60.

93. Ibid., pp. 34, 41–42, 59.

94. Ibid., p. 42.

95. Ibid., p. 80.

96. Cabet, *Icarie*, pp. 102, 131.

97. Ibid., pp. 132–33.

98. Mumford, *Story of Utopias,* p. 158.

99. Cabet, *Icarie,* p. 102.

100. Ibid., pp. 197–98.

101. Bellamy, "Programme of Nationalists," p. 447. Bellamy, *Looking Backward,* pp. 60, 75–77, 93–96, 118.

102. Ibid., pp. 75–76.

103. Ibid., p. 77.

104. Ibid., pp. 93–94.

105. Ibid., pp. 60, 95–96, 118.

106. Joseph A. Schumpeter, *Capitalism, Socialism and Democracy* (New York: Harper and Row, 1973), p. 208.

107. Bellamy, *Looking Backward,* p. 95.

108. Ibid., p. 60.

109. Alexander Nikoljukin, "A Little-Known Story: Bellamy in Russia," in *Edward Bellamy Abroad: An American Prophet's Influence,* ed. Sylvia E. Bowman (New York: Twayne, 1962), p. 85.

110. Skinner, *Walden Two,* p. 23.

111. Ibid., p. 235.

112. Kinkade, *Twin Oaks,* pp. 106–8.

113. Skinner, *Walden Two,* p. 173.

114. Ibid., pp. 82, 161, 164–65, 168–72.

115. Ibid., pp. 112, 169.

116. Ibid., p. 52.

117. Kinkade, *Twin Oaks,* pp. 41–45.

118. Ibid., pp. 45, 79–81.

119. Ibid., pp. 151–58.

120. Ibid., pp. 55, 72–80.

121. Ibid., pp. 197–98.

122. Ibid., pp. 148–49. Skinner, *Walden Two,* p. 270.

123. B. F. Skinner, *Beyond Freedom and Dignity* (New York: Knopf, 1971), pp. 108–11, 150.

124. B. F. Skinner, Foreword to *A Walden Two Experiment: The First Five Years of Twin Oaks Community,* by Kathleen Kinkade (New York: Morrow, 1973), p. x.

125. Skinner, *Walden Two,* pp. 255–56, 269, 271, 274–76.

126. Skinner, *About Behaviorism,* p. 3.

127. B. F. Skinner, "Utopia and Human Behavior," in *Moral Problems in Contemporary Society,* ed. Paul Kurtz (Englewood Cliffs, N.J.: Prentice-Hall, 1969); *Contingencies of Reinforcement* (New York: Appleton-Century-Crofts, 1969), pp. 29–49; *Beyond Freedom and Dignity* (New York: Knopf, 1971); *About Behaviorism* (New York: Knopf, 1974).

128. Skinner, *About Behaviorism,* p. 251.

129. John R. Platt, "The Skinnerian Revolution," in *Beyond the Punitive Society*, ed. Harvey Wheeler (San Francisco: Freeman, 1973), p. 54.

130. Skinner, Foreword to *Twin Oaks*, p. x.

131. Skinner, *Contingencies*, p. 41; *Beyond Freedom*, p. 164.

132. Skinner, *Contingencies*, p. 39.

133. Skinner, *Walden Two*, p. 265; *Beyond Freedom*, p. 172; *Contingencies*, p. 43.

134. Ibid., p. 40.

135. Robert A. Dahl, *After the Revolution?* (New Haven: Yale University Press, 1970), pp. 30–38.

136. Skinner, *Walden Two*, p. 269.

137. Skinner, *Beyond Freedom*, pp. 6–25; *Walden Two*, p. 266.

138. Skinner, *Beyond Freedom*, p. 102.

139. Skinner, *Walden Two*, p. 273; *Beyond Freedom*, p. 98.

140. Skinner, *About Behaviorism*, pp. 190–92.

141. Ibid., pp. 148–66; *Beyond Freedom*, pp. 10–15.

142. Richard B. Braithwaite, *Scientific Explanation* (New York: Harper, 1953), pp. 324–25.

143. Robert Nozick, *Anarchy, State, and Utopia* (New York: Basic Books, 1974), pp. 18–21.

Notes to Chapter Eight: *Russia and China* (pp. 232–281)

1. John Stuart Mill, "On Liberty," in *The Utilitarians* (Garden City, N.Y.: Anchor, 1973), pp. 483–87.

2. V. I. Lenin, *Selected Works: One-Volume Edition* (New York: International Publ., 1971), pp. 322–23, 337.

3. Leon Trotsky, *Terrorism and Communism: A Reply to Karl Kautsky*, trans. Max Schacktman (Ann Arbor: University of Michigan Press, 1961), p. 170.

4. Yevgeny Zamyatin, *We*, trans. Mirra Ginsburg (New York: Viking, 1972). George Orwell, *1984: A Novel* (New York: Harcourt, Brace, 1949).

5. Lazar Volin, *A Century of Russian Agriculture: From Alexander II to Khrushchev* (Cambridge: Harvard University Press, 1970), pp. 147, 164, 174.

6. Stephen F. Cohen, *Bukharin and the Bolshevik Revolution: A Political Biography, 1888–1938* (New York: Vintage, 1973), p. 124.

7. Volin, *Russian Agriculture*, pp. 166–88.

8. Ibid., pp. 110, 143–60.

9. Cohen, *Bukharin*, pp. 244–45.

10. Ibid., pp. 17, 72, 90–103.

11. Ibid., pp. 140–47.

12. Ibid., pp. 173–208.

13. S. Swianiewicz, *Forced Labour and Economic Development: An Enquiry*

into the Experience of Soviet Industrialization (New York: Oxford University Press, 1965), pp. 79–81.

14. M. Lewin, *Russian Peasants and Soviet Power: A Study of Collectivization,* trans. Irene Nove (Evanston, Ill.: Northwestern University Press, 1968), pp. 150–51. Cohen, *Bukharin,* pp. 161–65. Swianiewicz, *Forced Labour,* pp. 81–83.

15. Edward Hallett Carr, *Socialism in One Country 1924–1926,* Vol. 1 (New York: Macmillan, 1958), pp. 202–5. E. Preobrazhensky, *The New Economics,* trans. Brian Pearce (Oxford: Clarendon Press, 1965), p. 88.

16. Cohen, *Bukharin,* pp. 170–71.

17. Ibid., pp. 263–64, 290.

18. Lewin, *Russian Peasants,* pp. 257–58.

19. Cohen, *Bukharin,* pp. 320, 340.

20. Daniel Guerin, *Anarchism: From Theory to Practice,* trans. Mary Klopper (New York: Monthly Review Press, 1970), p. 25.

21. Alec Nove, "Soviet Political Organization and Development," in *Politics and Change in Developing Countries: Studies in the Theory and Practice of Development,* ed. Colin Leys (Cambridge, England: Cambridge University Press, 1969), pp. 69–70. Swianiewicz, *Forced Labour,* pp. 139–40.

22. Lowell Dittmer, *Liu Shao-chi and the Chinese Cultural Revolution: The Politics of Mass Criticism* (Berkeley: University of California Press, 1974), p. 211.

23. James R. Townsend, *Political Participation in Communist China* (Berkeley: University of California Press, 1969), pp. 29, 37–42, 60.

24. Dittmer, *Liu Shao-chi,* p. 193.

25. Klaus Mehnert, *China Returns* (New York: Dutton, 1972), pp. 241–43.

26. Dittmer, *Liu Shao-chi,* p. 289.

27. Ibid., p. 233. Victor C. Funnell, "The Metamorphosis of the Chinese Communist Party," in *Communist Systems in Comparative Perspective,* eds. Lenard Cohen and Jane Shapiro (Garden City, N.Y.: Doubleday, 1974), pp. 125–28.

28. E. L. Wheelwright and Bruce McFarlane, *The Chinese Road to Socialism: Economics of the Cultural Revolution* (New York: Monthly Review Press, 1970), p. 37.

29. Thomas P. Bernstein, "Keeping the Revolution Going: Problems of Village Leadership after Land Reform," in *Party Leadership and Revolutionary Power in China,* ed. John W. Lewis (New York: Cambridge University Press, 1970), pp. 243–44.

30. Richard Lowenthal, "Development vs. Utopia in Communist Policy," in *Change in Communist Systems,* ed. Chalmers Johnson (Stanford: Stanford University Press, 1970), p. 46.

31. Dittmer, *Liu Shao-chi,* pp. 193–94, 216–19.

32. John G. Gurley, "Capitalist and Maoist Economic Development," in *America's Asia: Dissenting Essays on Asian-American Relations,* eds. Edward Friedman and Mark Selden (New York: Pantheon, 1969), pp. 332–38.

33. Dittmer, *Liu Shao-chi,* p. 338. Townsend, *Political Participation,* p. 71.

34. Charles K. Wilber, *The Soviet Model and Underdeveloped Countries* (Chapel Hill: University of North Carolina Press, 1969), p. 52.

35. Paul Gregory, *Socialist and Nonsocialist Industrialization Patterns: A Comparative Appraisal* (New York: Praeger, 1970), p. 146.

36. Boris Meissner, "Social Change in Bolshevik Russia," in *Social Change in the Soviet Union: Russia's Path Toward an Industrial Society,* ed. Boris Meissner (Notre Dame, Ind.: University of Notre Dame Press, 1972), p. 74. Alexander Vucinich, "The Peasants as a Social Class," in *The Soviet Rural Community,* ed. James R. Millar (Urbana: University of Illinois Press, 1971), p. 318.

37. Gurley, "Maoist Economic Development," pp. 345–47. Thomas E. Weisskopf, "China and India: A Comparative Survey of Performance in Economic Development," *Economic and Political Weekly* 10 (1975):175–85.

38. Sterling Wortman, "Agriculture in China," *Scientific American,* June 1975, pp. 13, 15–16, 19.

39. Barry M. Richman, *Industrial Society in Communist China* (New York: Random House, 1969), p. 503. Byung-Joon Ahn, "The Political Economy of the People's Commune in China: Changes and Continuities," *Journal of Asian Studies* 34 (1975):648.

40. Wilber, *Soviet Model,* pp. 117–27.

41. Michael Barkun, *Disaster and the Millennium* (New Haven: Yale University Press, 1974), pp. 6, 186–99.

42. G. F. Hudson, *Fifty Years of Communism: Theory and Practice 1917–1967* (Baltimore: Penguin, 1968), p. 46. Townsend, *Political Participation,* p. 45.

43. Hudson, *Fifty Years of Communism,* pp. 31–35.

44. Ibid., pp. 46, 97, 194.

45. Townsend, *Political Participation,* p. 87.

46. Alec Nove, *An Economic History of the U.S.S.R.* (Baltimore: Penguin, 1969), pp. 48–50, 58.

47. Hudson, *Fifty Years of Communism,* p. 71.

48. Cohen, *Bukharin,* p. 79.

49. Benjamin Schwartz, "Thoughts of Mao Tse-tung," *The New York Review,* 8 February 1973, p. 31.

50. Townsend, *Political Participation,* p. 185.

51. Ibid., p. 84.

52. Robert M. Bernardo, *The Theory of Moral Incentives in Cuba* (University: University of Alabama Press, 1971), pp. 124–25.

53. Bernard P. Kiernan, *The United States, Communism, and the Emergent World* (Bloomington: University of Indiana Press, 1972), pp. 183–84. Chalmers Johnson, *Peasant Nationalism and Communist Power* (Stanford: Stanford University Press, 1962).

54. Funnell, "Chinese Communist Party," p. 108.

55. Townsend, *Political Participation,* pp. 87–88.

56. Swianiewicz, *Forced Labour,* pp. 156–58.

57. A. Doak Barnett, *Cadres, Bureaucracy, and Political Power in Communist China* (New York: Columbia University Press, 1967), pp. 70, 438.

58. Nove, *Economic History of U.S.S.R.,* pp. 190–91; "Soviet Political Organization," pp. 70, 72.

59. Townsend, *Political Participation,* pp. 49–51, 114–15.

60. Ibid., pp. 3, 114. Vucinich, "Peasants as Social Class," p. 321.

61. Gregory, *Industrialization Patterns,* p. 149.

62. Vucinich, "Peasants as Social Class," p. 313.

63. Gurley, "Maoist Economic Development," p. 332.

64. John Kenneth Galbraith, *A China Passage* (Boston: Houghton Mifflin, 1973), p. 136. Gurley, "Maoist Economic Development," p. 332. Mehnert, *China Returns,* pp. 205–6.

65. Ibid., p. 202. Richman, *Industrial Society in China,* p. 318.

66. Nove, *Economic History of U.S.S.R.,* p. 208.

67. Meissner, "Change in Bolshevik Russia," p. 49.

68. J. Wilczynski, *Socialist Economic Development and Reforms* (New York: Praeger, 1972), p. 121; *Profit, Risk and Incentives under Socialist Economic Planning* (London: Macmillan, 1973), p. 129.

69. Karl-Eugen Wadekin, *The Private Sector in Soviet Agriculture* (Berkeley: University of California Press, 1973), p. 24.

70. Wilczynski, *Socialist Economic Development,* pp. 112–13; *Profit, Risk,* pp. 127, 148.

71. Ibid., p. 150.

72. Hedrick Smith, *The Russians* (New York: Quadrangle, 1976), pp. 55, 67, 86, 93–95.

73. Susan Jacoby, *Inside Soviet Schools* (New York: Hill and Wang, 1974), pp. 115, 134, 229–33.

74. Walter D. Connor, *Deviance in Soviet Society: Crime, Delinquency, and Alcoholism* (New York: Columbia University Press, 1972), pp. 40, 52.

75. Robert C. Stuart, *The Collective Farm in Soviet Agriculture* (Lexington, Mass.: Heath, 1972), p. 128.

76. Gurley, "Maoist Economic Development," p. 349.

77. William L. Parish, "Socialism and the Chinese Peasant Family," *Journal of Asian Studies* 34 (1975):615.

78. Schwartz, "Thoughts of Mao," p. 30.

79. Christopher Howe, *Wage Patterns and Wage Policy in Modern China: 1919– 1972* (London: Cambridge University Press, 1973), p. 40.

80. Galbraith, *China Passage,* pp. 135–36.

81. Richman, *Industrial Society in China,* p. 799.

82. Ibid., pp. 317–20.

83. Carmelo Mesa-Lago, *Cuba in the 1970's: Pragmatism and Institutionalization* (Albuquerque: University of New Mexico Press, 1974), pp. 39, 41.

84. Ibid., pp. 43–45.

85. Carmelo Mesa-Lago, "Material and Moral Incentives," *Journal of Inter-american Studies and World Affairs* 14 (1972):63.

86. Sergio Roca and Robert E. Hernández, "Structural Economic Problems," in *Cuba, Castro and Revolution*, ed. Jaime Suchlicki (Coral Gables, Fla.: University of Miami Press, 1972), p. 91.

87. Robert S. Elegant, *Los Angeles Times*, August 4, 1974: 15 and January 1, 1975: 1.

88. Smith, *Russians*, pp. 26–47.

89. *Newsweek*, June 26, 1972: 38.

90. Oskar Anweiler, "Educational Policy and Social Structure in the Soviet Union," in *Social Change in the Soviet Union*, ed. Boris Meissner (Notre Dame, Ind.: University of Notre Dame Press, 1972), p. 178. Ezra F. Vogel, "Politicized Bureaucracy: Communist China," in *Communist Systems in Comparative Perspective*, eds. Lenard Cohen and Jane Shapiro (Garden City, N.Y.: Doubleday, 1974), p. 162.

91. Vucinich, "Peasants as Social Class," p. 314.

92. Anweiler, "Educational Policy," pp. 181–200.

93. Jacoby, *Soviet Schools*, pp. 139–40.

94. See note 91.

95. Jacoby, *Soviet Schools*, p. 165.

96. Vogel, "Politicized Bureaucracy," pp. 162–64.

97. Carmelo Mesa-Lago, *The Labor Sector and Socialist Distribution in Cuba* (New York: Praeger, 1968), pp. 14–15.

98. Mehnert, *China Returns*, p. 208. Howe, *Wage Patterns*, p. 59.

99. Naum M. Jasny, "Production Costs and Prices in Soviet Agriculture," in *Soviet and East European Agriculture*, ed. Jerzy F. Karcz (Berkeley: University of California Press, 1967), p. 402.

100. Leonard J. Kirsch, *Soviet Wages: Changes in Structure and Administration since 1956* (Cambridge: MIT Press, 1972), pp. 15–18, 23, 41–42.

101. Howe, *Wage Patterns*, pp. 119–25.

102. John N. Hazard, *Communists and Their Law: A Search for the Common Core of the Legal Systems of the Marxian Socialist States* (Chicago: University of Chicago Press, 1969), p. 151. Naum M. Jasny, *The Socialized Agriculture of the USSR: Plans and Performance* (Stanford: Stanford University Press, 1949), pp. 402–5. Lazar Volin, *A Century of Russian Agriculture: From Alexander II to Khrushchev* (Cambridge: Harvard University Press, 1970), pp. 425–27, 519.

103. David W. Bronson and Constance B. Krueger, "The Revolution in Soviet Farm Household Income, 1953–1967," in *The Soviet Rural Community*, ed. James R. Millar (Urbana: University of Illinois Press, 1971), p. 220. Peter B. Maggs, "The Law of Farm-Farmer Relations," *The Soviet Rural Community*, ed. James R. Millar (Urbana: University of Illinois Press, 1971), pp. 151–54.

104. Byung-Joon Ahn, "The Political Economy of the People's Commune in

China: Changes and Continuities," *Journal of Asian Studies* 34 (1975): p. 647. Kang Chao, *Agricultural Production in Communist China 1949–1965* (Madison: University of Wisconsin Press, 1970), p. 56. Charles Hoffman, *Work Incentive Practices and Policies in the People's Republic of China 1953–1965* (Albany: State University of New York Press, 1967), pp. 48–53. Martin King Whyte, *Small Groups and Political Rituals in China* (Berkeley: University of California Press, 1974), pp. 143–53.

105. Michael Kaser, *Soviet Economics* (New York: McGraw-Hill, 1970), pp. 132, 148. Barry M. Richman, *Industrial Society in Communist China* (New York: Random House, 1969), pp. 381, 495, 503–4.

106. J. Wilczynski, *Profit, Risk and Incentives under Socialist Economic Planning* (London: Macmillan, 1973), p. 142.

107. C. S. Chen, *Rural People's Communes in Lien-Chiang* (Stanford, Cal.: Hoover Institution Press, 1969), p. 18. Boris Meissner, "Social Change in Bolshevik Russia," in *Social Change in the Soviet Union: Russia's Path Toward an Industrial Society,* ed. Boris Meissner (Notre Dame, Ind.: University of Notre Dame Press, 1972), p. 102. Jan S. Prybyla, *The Political Economy of Communist China* (Scranton, Pa.: International Textbook, 1970), p. 35.

108. Barnett, *Cadres, Bureaucracy,* p. 423. Bronson and Krueger, "Soviet Farm Income," p. 23.

109. Arthur E. Adams and Jan S. Adams, *Men Versus Systems: Agriculture in the USSR, Poland, and Czechoslovakia* (New York: Free Press, 1971), p. 25. Meissner, "Change in Bolshevik Russia," p. 102. Nancy Nimitz, "Farm Employment in the Soviet Union, 1928–1963," in *Soviet and East European Agriculture,* ed. Jerzy F. Karcz (Berkeley: University of California Press, 1967), p. 193. Wadekin, *Private Sector,* pp. 48, 88.

110. Barnett, *Cadres, Bureaucracy,* p. 423. Chao, *Agricultural Production in China,* p. 67.

111. Chen, *People's Communes,* p. 13.

112. Barnett, *Cadres, Bureaucracy,* p. 423. Bronson and Krueger, "Soviet Farm Income," pp. 233–34, 238–39. Nimitz, "Farm Employment," pp. 191, 202. Wadekin, *Private Sector,* pp. 66, 197, 377.

113. Bronson and Krueger, "Soviet Farm Income," pp. 48, 238–39.

114. Richard Pipes, *Russia Under the Old Regime* (New York: Scribner's, 1974), pp. 1–9.

115. Jasny, "Costs and Prices," pp. 236, 250. Volin, *Russian Agriculture,* p. 428.

116. Hazard, *Communists and Their Law,* p. 154. Roy D. Laird and Betty A. Laird, *Soviet Communism and Agrarian Revolution* (Baltimore: Penguin, 1970), p. 97. Alec Nove, *An Economic History of the U.S.S.R.* (Baltimore: Penguin, 1969), pp. 303–4. Dimitry Pospielovsky, "The 'Link System' in Soviet Agriculture," *Soviet Studies* 21 (1970):411–35.

117. Jasny, "Costs and Prices," p. 236.

118. Pospielovsky, "The Link System," pp. 411–35.

119. Adams and Adams, *Men Versus Systems,* pp. 7, 22. George L. Yaney, "Agricultural Administration in Russia from the Stolypin Land Reform to Forced

Collectivization: An Interpretive Study," in *The Soviet Rural Community,* ed. James R. Millar (Urbana: University of Illinois Press, 1971), pp. 19–21.

120. M. Lewin, *Russian Peasants and Soviet Power: A Study of Collectivization,* trans. Irene Nove (Evanston, Ill.: Northwestern University Press, 1968), p. 110. Robert G. Wesson, *Soviet Communes* (New Brunswick, N.J.: Rutgers University Press, 1963), pp. 73–77, 161–67.

121. Jasny, *Socialized Agriculture,* p. 402.

122. Wesson, *Soviet Communes,* pp. 73–77, 224, 232–34.

123. Ibid., p. 121.

124. Chao, *Agricultural Production in China,* p. 59.

125. Ibid., pp. 61–62. Franz Schurmann, *Ideology and Organization in Communist China* (Berkeley: University of California Press, 1968), pp. 467–78. E. Zurcher, "The Chinese Communes," *Bedragen Tot de Taal-, Land-, en Volkenkunde,* Deel 118 (1962):75–83.

126. Ibid.

127. Schurmann, *Ideology and Organization,* p. 471.

128. A. Doak Barnett, *Cadres, Bureaucracy, and Political Power in Communist China* (New York: Columbia University Press, 1967), pp. 313–24.

129. Ibid., pp. 323–24.

130. Schurmann, *Ideology and Organization,* p. 492.

131. Gargi Dutt, *Rural Communes of China: Organizational Problems* (New York: Asia Publ., 1967), pp. 112–14. John C. Pelzel, "Economic Management of a Production Brigade in Post-Leap China," in *Economic Organization in Chinese Society,* ed. W. E. Willmott (Stanford: Stanford University Press, 1972), pp. 394–95, 407. Prybyla, *Political Economy of China,* pp. 297, 352.

132. Ahn, "People's Commune," p. 637. Barnett, *Cadres, Bureaucracy,* pp. 415–17. Pelzel, "Production Brigade," p. 395. Schurmann, *Ideology and Organization,* p. 493. James R. Townsend, *Political Participation in Communist China* (Berkeley: University of California Press, 1969), pp. 169–71.

133. Barnett, *Cadres, Bureaucracy,* pp. 364, 421. Dutt, *Rural Communes,* pp. 112, 114. Pelzel, "Production Brigade," p. 407.

134. Ibid., p. 408.

135. Chen, *People's Communes,* pp. 34, 44. Michel Oksenberg, "Occupational Groups in Chinese Society and the Cultural Revolution," in *Communist Systems in Comparative Perspective,* eds. Lenard Cohen and Jane Shapiro (Garden City, N.Y.: Doubleday, 1974), p. 339.

136. Ibid.

137. E. L. Wheelwright and Bruce McFarlane, *The Chinese Road to Socialism: Economics of the Cultural Revolution* (New York: Monthly Review Press, 1970), p. 68.

138. Prybyla, *Political Economy of China,* p. 351.

139. Chao, *Agricultural Production in China,* p. 68.

140. Prybyla, *Political Economy of China,* pp. 521–22, 566.

141. Oksenberg, "Occupational Groups," p. 342.

142. Whyte, *Small Groups in China,* pp. 22–28.

143. Ibid., pp. 2–3.

144. Ibid., pp. 17, 33, 35. Barnett, *Cadres, Bureaucracy,* p. 412.

145. Whyte, *Small Groups in China,* pp. 3, 42, 66, 211, 233.

146. Townsend, *Political Participation,* p. 183.

147. Whyte, *Small Groups in China,* pp. 214, 233–34.

148. Ibid., pp. 187, 214, 232.

149. Ibid., p. 39.

150. Ibid., pp. 95, 136, 165, 227.

151. William L. Parish, "Socialism and the Chinese Peasant Family," *Journal of Asian Studies* 34 (1975):613–16.

152. Whyte, *Small Groups in China,* pp. 58, 229.

153. Barnett, *Cadres, Bureaucracy,* pp. 102–3, 162–71, 177.

154. Ibid., pp. 40–47.

155. Meissner, "Change in Bolshevik Russia," pp. 52–59.

156. Barnett, *Cadres, Bureaucracy,* p. 57.

157. Townsend, *Political Participation,* p. 177.

158. Benjamin Schwartz, "Thoughts of Mao Tse-tung," *The New York Review,* 8 February 1973, pp. 30–31.

159. S. Swianiewicz, *Forced Labour and Economic Development: An Enquiry into the Experience of Soviet Industrialization* (New York: Oxford University Press, 1965), pp. 121–22.

160. Adams and Adams, *Men Versus Systems,* p. 191.

161. Fedor Belov, *The History of a Soviet Collective Farm* (New York: Praeger, 1955), p. 108.

162. Barnett, *Cadres, Bureaucracy,* p. 396.

163. Andrei Amalrik, *Will the Soviet Union Survive Until 1984?* (New York: Harper and Row, 1971), p. 36.

164. Lewis Mumford, *The Story of Utopias* (New York: Viking, 1962), p. 158.

165. Paul S. Reinsch, *English Common Law in the Early American Colonies* (Madison, Wis.: Da Capo, 1970 reprint of 1899 edition), p. 30.

166. William Seagle, *The History of Law* (New York: Tudor, 1946), p. 146.

167. Victor H. Li, "The Evolution and Development of the Chinese Legal System," in *China: Management of a Revolutionary Society,* ed. John M. Lindbeck (Seattle: University of Washington Press, 1971), p. 251.

168. Derk Bodde and Clarence Morris, *Law in Imperial China* (Cambridge: Harvard University Press, 1967), pp. 13–16.

169. Seagle, *History of Law,* p. 146.

170. Pipes, *Russia Under Old Regime,* p. 51.

171. Julius Jacobson, "Russian Law Enters the 'Final Stages of Communism,' " in *Soviet Communism and the Socialist Vision,* ed. Julius Jacobson (New Brunswick, N.J.: New Politics Publ., 1972), p. 165.

172. Amalrik, *Will the Soviet Union Survive?* p. 13.

173. Seagle, *History of Law*, pp. 209, 226.

174. Adam Smith, *The Theory of Moral Sentiments* (Indianapolis: Liberty Press/ Liberty Classics, 1976), pp. 380–81.

175. Seagle, *History of Law*, p. 267.

176. Max Weber, *Law in Economy and Society*, ed. Max Rheinstein (New York: Simon and Schuster, 1954), p. 45.

177. Seagle, *History of Law*, p. 267.

178. Weber, *Law in Economy and Society*, pp. 44, 46.

179. Ibid., pp. 20–27.

180. Henry Sumner Maine, *Ancient Law* (Boston: Beacon, 1963 reprint of 1861 ed.), pp. 163–65, 316–21.

181. Weber, *Law in Economy and Society*, p. 105.

182. Lon L. Fuller, "Human Interaction and the Law," in *The Rule of Law*, ed. Robert Paul Wolff (New York: Simon and Schuster, 1971), pp. 188, 191.

183. Weber, *Law in Economy and Society*, p. 33.

184. Fuller, "Human Interaction and Law," pp. 92, 199–201.

185. F. A. Hayek, *Law, Legislation and Liberty, Volume I: Rules and Order* (Chicago: University of Chicago Press, 1969), p. 110.

186. Amalrik, *Will the Soviet Union Survive?* pp. 31, 41. Etienne Balazs, *Chinese Civilization and Bureaucracy: Variations on a Theme*, trans. Arthur F. Wright (New Haven: Yale University Press, 1964), pp. 70, 156. Sybille van der Sprenkel, *Legal Institutions in Manchu China: A Sociological Analysis* (London: Athlone, 1962), pp. 18, 121. Teodor Shanin, *The Awkward Class: Political Sociology of Peasantry in a Developing Society: Russia 1910– 1925* (London: Oxford University Press, 1972), pp. 34, 198.

187. Tung-tsu Chu, *Local Government in China under the Ching* (Cambridge: Harvard University Press, 1962), pp. 1, 4.

188. Balazs, *Chinese Civilization*, p. 70.

189. Sprenkel, *Legal Institutions*, pp. 18, 100–103.

190. Kung-Chuan Hsiao, *Rural China: Imperial Control in the Nineteenth Century* (Seattle: University of Washington Press, 1960), p. 263.

191. Sprenkel, *Legal Institutions*, p. 88.

192. Hsiao, *Rural China*, pp. 342–43.

193. Sprenkel, *Legal Institutions*, p. 99.

194. Phillip M. Chen, *Law and Justice: The Legal System in China 2400 B.C. to 1960 A.D.* (New York: Dunellen, 1973), p. 13. Balazs, *Chinese Civilization*, p. 154. Hsiao, *Rural China*, p. 416. Sprenkel, *Legal Institutions*, pp. 65, 70, 72, 78.

195. Bodde and Morris, *Law in Imperial China*, p. 6.

196. Pipes, *Russia Under Old Regime*, p. 158. Shanin, *Awkward Class*, pp. 34, 41. Donald Mackensie Wallace, *Russia on the Eve of War and Revolution* (New York: Random House, 1961), p. 270.

197. Shanin, *Awkward Class*, pp. 165–68. Yuzuru Taniuchi, *The Village Gathering in Russia in the Mid-1920's*, Soviet and East European Monographs No.

1 (Birmingham, England: University of Birmingham Press, 1968), pp. 4, 7, 10, 12–14, 19–20, 23–26.

198. Shanin, *Awkward Class,* pp. 195–97. Taniuchi, *Village Gathering,* pp. 35–39, 48, 51–52.

199. Shanin, *Awkward Class,* pp. 63–121.

200. Mark Elvin, *The Pattern of the Chinese Past* (Stanford: Stanford University Press, 1973), pp. 258–59.

201. Parish, "Chinese Peasant Family," pp. 616–17.

202. Weber, *Law in Economy and Society,* pp. 141, 184–86, 237, 264, 282. Max Weber, *Economy and Society,* eds. Guenther Roth and Claus Wittich (New York: Bedminster, 1968), pp. 228, 243, 248.

203. Pipes, *Russia Under the Old Regime,* pp. 109, 114, 129–30.

204. Ibid., pp. 282–84, 287, 294–95.

205. Bodde and Morris, *Law in Imperial China,* pp. 3–4.

206. Balazs, *Chinese Civilization,* pp. 5–6, 9, 57. Hsiao, *Rural China,* pp. 8, 119, 124, 414–15, 504.

207. Chu, *Local Government,* pp. 7, 32, 194.

208. Weber, *Economy and Society,* p. 240.

209. Weber, *Law in Economy and Society,* pp. 40, 96, 100. See also: Max Rheinstein, Introduction to *Max Weber on Law in Economy and Society,* ed. Max Rheinstein (New York: Simon and Schuster, 1954), p. 1; William J. Chambliss and Robert B. Seidman, *Law, Order and Power* (Menlo Park, Cal.: Addison-Wesley, 1971), pp. 187, 218.

210. Fuller, "Human Interaction and Law," pp. 204–9.

211. L. G. Bennett and K. J. McCready, *The Use of Contracts in Co-operative Horticultural Marketing,* Department of Agricultural Economics Miscellaneous Studies Number 45 (London: University of Reading, 1968), pp. 16, 44, 51, 53–54, 58–59.

212. Fuller, "Human Interaction and Law," pp. 210–11.

213. Weber, *Economy and Society,* p. 232.

214. Weber, *Law in Economy and Society,* pp. 105, 116, 192.

215. Ibid., pp. 96, 100, 229.

216. Reinsch, *Common Law in American Colonies,* pp. 12, 30.

217. Elvin, *Pattern of Chinese Past,* pp. 203, 286–306.

218. Ibid.

219. Immanuel Wallerstein, *The Modern World-System: Capitalist Agriculture and the Origins of the European World-Economy in the Sixteenth Century* (New York: Academic, 1974), pp. 15–16.

220. Ibid., pp. 100–102, 127–28.

221. Pipes, *Russia Under the Old Regime.*

222. W. Friedmann, *Law in a Changing Society* (Berkeley: University of California Press, 1959), pp. 111–12. Barry M. Richman, *Industrial Society in Communist China* (New York: Random House, 1969), pp. 366–68.

223. Luke T. Lee, "Chinese Communist Law: Its Background and Development,"

in *Government of Communist China,* ed. George P. Jan (San Francisco: Chandler, 1966), pp. 312, 316–22. Li, "Evolution of Chinese Legal System," pp. 225–41.

224. Bodde and Morris, *Law in Imperial China,* pp. 18–29.

225. Ibid.

226. Balazs, *Chinese Civilization,* p. 7.

227. Li, "Evolution of Chinese Legal System," p. 223.

228. Tung-tsu Chu, *Law and Society in Traditional China* (The Hague: Mouton, 1961), p. 236.

229. Weber, *Economy and Society,* pp. 223–25.

230. Martin King Whyte, "Bureaucracy and Modernization in China: The Maoist Critique," *American Sociological Review* 38 (1973):150.

231. Reinsch, *Common Law in American Colonies,* p. 14.

232. Amalrik, *Will the Soviet Union Survive?,* pp. 34–35.

233. Elvin, *Pattern of Chinese Past,* p. 259.

234. Hedrick Smith, *The Russians* (New York: Quadrangle, 1976), pp. 502–4, 507.

235. See note 20.

236. Robert G. Kaiser, *Russia: The People and the Power* (New York: Pocket Books, 1976), p. 55.

237. Smith, *Russians,* pp. 33, 46, 51.

238. Sharon Zukin, *Beyond Marx and Tito: Theory and Practice in Yugoslav Socialism* (London: Cambridge University Press, 1975), p. 119.

239. William Steinhoff, *George Orwell and the Origins of 1984* (Ann Arbor: University of Michigan Press, 1975), pp. 51, 80–81.

240. Ibid., p. 199.

Notes to Chapter Nine: *Utopian Anarchy* (pp. 282–327)

1. John W. Bennett, *Hutterian Brethren* (Stanford: Stanford University Press, 1967), pp. 442–43. Lee Emerson Deets, *The Hutterites: A Study in Social Cohesion* (Gettysburg, Pa.: Times and News Publ., 1939), pp. 25–26. John A. Hostetler and Gertrude Enders Huntington, *The Hutterites in North America* (New York: Holt, Rinehart, and Winston, 1967), pp. 66–67, 107.

2. Jean-Jacques Rousseau, *The Social Contract,* trans. Maurice Cranston (Baltimore: Penguin, 1968), pp. 64, 84. Maurice Cranston, Introduction to ibid., pp. 42–43.

3. Charles M. Sherover, Introduction and commentary to *The Social Contract,* by Jean-Jacques Rousseau (New York: New American Library, 1974), pp. 62, 84, 86.

4. Jean-Jacques Rousseau, *The Social Contract or Principles of Political Right Plus the Dedication from the "Second Discourse" and "On Political Economy,"* ed. with commentary Charles M. Sherover (New York, N.Y.: New American Library, 1974), pp. 257–58.

5. Sherover, Introduction, pp. xx–xxii.

6. Rousseau, *Social Contract or Principles,* pp. 263–64.

7. Sherover, Introduction, p. xv.

8. Rousseau, *Social Contract or Principles,* pp. 112, 141, 143, 165, 239.

9. Robert Nozick, *Anarchy, State and Utopia* (New York: Basic Books, 1974).

10. James S. Coleman, "Social Inventions," *Social Forces* 49 (1970):163–64.

11. James S. Coleman, *Power and the Structure of Society* (New York: Norton, 1974), pp. 14–15, 25–28, 35–38.

12. William Morris, *News from Nowhere* (Boston: Routledge and Kegan Paul, 1970 reprint of 1891 edition), pp. 65, 68, 74–75.

13. Ibid., pp. 19, 57–60, 62, 82, 87–111, 114, 137, 146, 153.

14. Victor Ferkiss, *The Future of Technological Civilization* (New York: Braziller, 1974), p. 75.

15. Morris, *News from Nowhere,* pp. 7–8, 30–31.

16. Ibid., pp. 39–40, 149.

17. H. G. Wells, *A Modern Utopia* (Lincoln: University of Nebraska Press, 1967 reprint of 1905 edition), p. 101.

18. James Joll, *The Anarchists* (New York: Grosset and Dunlap, 1964), p. 151. George Woodcock, *Anarchism: A History of Libertarian Ideas and Movements* (New York, World, 1962), p. 211.

19. Peter Kropotkin, *Mutual Aid: A Factor of Evolution* (Boston: Extending Horizons Books, reprint of 1914 edition), p. 111.

20. Roger N. Baldwin, ed., *Kropotkin's Revolutionary Pamphlets* (New York: Dover, 1970), pp. 72–73, 163, 172, 185.

21. Kropotkin, *Mutual Aid,* pp. 57–61, 74–75.

22. Woodcock, *Anarchism,* p. 216.

23. Peter Kropotkin, *The Conquest of Bread* (New York: Blom, 1968 reprint of 1913 edition), pp. 214–31. Baldwin, *Kropotkin's Pamphlets,* p. 58.

24. Peter Kropotkin, *Fields, Factories and Workshops or Industry Combined with Agriculture and Brain Work with Manual Work* (New York: Blom, 1968 reprint of 1913 edition), pp. 78, 352, 369.

25. Baldwin, *Kropotkin's Pamphlets,* pp. 64, 80, 147, 175, 203, 205, 210–13. 267.

26. Alexander Berkman, *What Is Communist Anarchism? Now and After: The ABC of Communist Anarchism* (New York: Dover, 1972 reprint of 1929 edition).

27. Ibid., pp. 102–3, 193, 197, 210, 223, 226, 246–59.

28. Ibid., p. 152.

29. Ibid., pp. 249, 259, 267, 276, 283–88.

30. Ibid., pp. 278–79.

31. Ibid., pp. 246, 266–68, 275, 283, 290–91, 294–95.

32. Wells, *Modern Utopia,* pp. 12, 33, 76–77, 88–89, 98–102, 128, 152, 259.

33. Ibid., pp. 73, 149.

34. Ibid., pp. 91–96.

35. Ibid., pp. 23, 47.

36. David Friedman, *The Machinery of Freedom: Guide to a Radical Capitalism* (New York: Harper and Row, 1973), pp. xiii–xiv, 64, 73–89, 155.

37. Ibid., pp. 24, 116, 152, 218.

38. Ibid., pp. 140–41.

39. Peter F. Drucker, *Management: Tasks, Responsibilities, Practices* (New York: Harper and Row, 1974), pp. 60–61, 71, 141.

40. Ibid., pp. 39, 131, 133, 158, 163.

41. Coleman, *Power and Structure*, pp. 49, 64.

42. E. F. Schumacher, *Small Is Beautiful: Economics as if People Mattered* (New York: Harper and Row, 1973), pp. 230–34, 247.

43. Ibid., pp. 258–68. Clayton Jones, "Turning Workers into Capitalists," *Christian Science Monitor,* 13 May 1975, pp. 14–15.

44. Friedman, *Machinery of Freedom*, pp. 133–35.

45. John Stuart Mill, *Principles of Political Economy* (New York: Kelley, 1965 reprint of 1871 edition), pp. 772–73.

46. Fred Boggis, "Workers' Co-operatives: A Vital Experiment," in *Participation in Industry,* ed. Campbell Balfour (Totowa, N.J.: Rowman and Littlefield, 1973), pp. 33–40.

47. Paul Blumberg, "On the Relevance and Future of Workers' Management," in *Workers' Control: A Reader on Labor and Social Change,* eds. Gerry Hunnius, G. David Garson, and John Case (New York: Vintage, 1973), p. 153.

48. Max Weber, *General Economic History*, trans. Frank H. Knight (New York: Collier, 1961), p. 145.

49. Paul Bernstein, "Run Your Own Business: Worker-Owned Plywood Firms," *Working Papers for a New Society,* 2 (Summer 1974):29.

50. Theodor Hertzka, *Freeland: A Social Anticipation* (New York: Appleton, 1891), pp. 1–2, 97.

51. Ibid., pp. 1–2, 93, 109.

52. Ibid., pp. 97, 145.

53. Ibid., pp. 120–21, 193–94.

54. Ibid., pp. 96, 100, 247, 281, 295, 299.

55. Ibid., pp. 97, 111, 137, 212, 279, 284.

56. Woodcock, *Anarchism,* pp. 393–98.

57. Adolf Sturmthal, *Workers' Councils* (Cambridge: Harvard University Press, 1964), pp. 176, 178.

58. France Bucar, "The Participation of the State and Political Organizations in the Decisions of the Working Organizations," in *First International Conference on Participation and Self-Management, Reports, Volume I,* Institute for Social Research, University of Zagreb (Zagreb, Yugoslavia: Zrinski, 1972), p. 47.

59. F. E. Emery, and Einar Thorsrud, *Form and Content in Industrial Democracy* (London: Tavistock, 1969), pp. 40–42. Jiri Kolaja, *Workers' Councils: The Yugoslav Experience* (New York: Praeger, 1966), pp. 16, 21, 41–42,

76. Joze Goricar, "Workers' Self-Management: Ideal Type—Social Reality," in *First International Conference on Participation and Self-Management, Reports, Volume I,* Institute for Social Research, University of Zagreb (Zagreb, Yugoslavia: Zrinski, 1972), pp. 20–24. David Jenkins, *Job Power: Blue and White Collar Democracy* (Baltimore: Penguin, 1973), pp. 100–101, 105, 111. Sturmthal, *Workers' Councils,* pp. 113, 189. Howard M. Wachtel, *Workers' Management and Workers' Wages in Yugoslavia* (Ithaca, N.Y.: Cornell University Press, 1973), pp. 73, 181.

60. Ichak Adizes, *Industrial Democracy: Yugoslav Style* (New York: Free Press, 1971), pp. 222–23. Gerry Hunnius, "Workers' Self-Management in Yugoslavia," in *Workers' Control: A Reader on Labor and Social Change,* eds. Gerry Hunnius, G. David Garson, and John Case (New York: Vintage, 1973), p. 309. Jenkins, *Job Power,* p. 105. Kolaja, *Yugoslav Experience,* pp. 60, 64, 76.

61. Jenkins, *Job Power,* p. 101. Kolaja, *Yugoslav Experience,* pp. 46–49. C. Northcote Parkinson, *Parkinson's Law: And Other Studies in Administration* (Boston: Houghton Mifflin, 1957), pp. 24–32.

62. Kolaja, *Yugoslav Experience,* pp. 64, 76.

63. Adizes, *Industrial Democracy,* pp. 222–23.

64. Kolaja, *Yugoslav Experience,* pp. 22, 31–34, 67.

65. Emery and Thorsrud, *Form and Content,* p. 42. Sturmthal, *Workers' Councils,* p. 194.

66. Josip Zupanov, "Employees' Participation and Social Power in Industry," in *First International Conference on Participation and Self-Management, Reports, Vol. I,* Institute for Social Research, University of Zagreb (Zagreb, Yugoslavia: Zrinski, 1972), pp. 37, 40.

67. Ibid., pp. 38–40.

68. Hunnius, "Self-Management in Yugoslavia," p. 309.

69. Wachtel, *Workers' Management,* pp. 186–87.

70. Adizes, *Industrial Democracy,* pp. 198–203.

71. Ibid., pp. 209, 215, 223–25, 231.

72. Personal communication from Peter Westerlind, Ph.D. candidate in anthropology, University of California at Santa Barbara.

73. Bernstein, "Run Your Own Business," pp. 25–27. See also Katrina V. Berman, *Worker-Owned Plywood Companies: An Economic Analysis* (Pullman: Washington State University Press, 1967).

74. Arnold S. Tannenbaum, Bogdan Kavcic, Menachen Rosner, Mino Vianello, and Georg Wieser, *Hierarchy in Organizations* (San Francisco: Jossey-Bass, 1974), pp. 120, 126, 183–84, 209.

75. Ibid., pp. 121–22.

76. Seymour Melman, "Industrial Efficiency under Managerial vs. Cooperative Decision-Making: A Comparative Study of Manufacturing Enterprises in Israel," *Review of Radical Political Economics* 2 (1970):12.

77. Tannenbaum, Kavcic, Rosner, Vianello, and Wieser, *Hierarchy in Organization,* pp. 15, 125–26, 212.

78. An-che Li, "Zuñi: Some Observations and Queries," *American Anthropologist*

39 (1937):63, 68. Ruth Benedict, *Patterns of Culture* (New York: Penguin, 1934), pp. 52–119.

79. J. Yanai Tabb and Amira Goldfarb, *Workers' Participation in Management: Expectations and Experience* (London: Pergamon, 1970), pp. 92–93, 95–96, 280.

80. Tannenbaum, Kavcic, Rosner, Vianello, and Wieser, *Hierarchy in Organization*, p. 224.

81. Unless otherwise indicated, data in this section are from the author's field notes.

82. Goricar, "Self-Management: Ideal—Reality," p. 20.

83. I am indebted to Mr. Stephen Hughes, Missouri state director of the Farm Security Administration during 1942 and 1943, for a personal account of this experiment. See also: Edward C. Banfield, *Government Project* (Glencoe, Ill.: Free Press, 1951), pp. 29, 36, 60, 62, 77, 100, 105, 108–9, 111, 128, 223; Joseph W. Eaton, *Exploring Tomorrow's Agriculture* (New York: Harper, 1943), pp. 65–172; Henrik F. Infield, *Cooperative Communities at Work* (New York: Dryden, 1945), pp. 51–71.

84. I am indebted to Mr. A. J. S. Cox, a former technical officer with the Welsh Land Settlement scheme for a personal account of this experiment. See also M. J. Wise, H. W. Durrant, D. J. Palmer, and D. A. Hole, *Final Report of the Departmental Committee of Inquiry into Statutory Smallholdings,* Ministry of Agriculture, Fisheries and Food (London: Her Majesty's Stationery Office, 1967).

85. Since my visit to the Po Valley in 1968, Alison Bland Sánchez, candidate for the Ph.D. degree in anthropology at the University of California at Santa Barbara, has made a detailed ethnohistorical study of these collectives. Her Ph.D. thesis will explain how special political support and unusual historical, economic, and membership conditions have contributed to their longevity.

86. Mwalimu J. K. Nyerere, *Socialism and Rural Development* (Dar Es Salaam: Government Printer, 1967), pp. 6–10, 15, 17, 21, 24, 30.

87. Raymond Apthorpe, "A Survey of Land Settlement Schemes and Rural Development in East Africa," mimeographed (Kampala, Uganda: Makerere College, 1966), p. 4.

88. Arthur E. Adams and Jan S. Adams, *Men Versus Systems: Agriculture in the USSR, Poland, and Czechoslovakia* (New York: Free Press, 1971), pp. 104, 109. Theodor Bergmann, "Cooperation and Changes in Land Tenure," in *Year Book of Agricultural Cooperation,* The Plunkett Foundation for Cooperative Studies (Oxford: Blackwell, 1963), p. 11. Margaret Digby, *Cooperative Land Use: The Challenge to Traditional Co-operation* (Oxford: Blackwell, 1963), p. 39.

89. Ibid., pp. 34–36. Otto M. Schiller, *Cooperation and Integration in Agricultural Production* (London: Asia Publ., 1969), p. 206.

90. M. Lewin, *Russian Peasants and Soviet Power: A Study of Collectivization,* trans. Irene Nove (Evanston: Northwestern University Press, 1968), p. 112.

91. Ibid., p. 515. Naum M. Jasny, *The Socialized Agriculture of the USSR: Plans and Performance* (Stanford: Stanford University Press, 1967), p. 308.

92. See note 83.

93. See note 84.

94. Griffiths Cunningham, "Socialism and Rural Development in Tanzania," mimeographed (Dar es Salaam, Tanzania: Kivukoni College, 1968), p. 4.

95. Rafael Piña, *Código Agrario* (México, D. F.: Ediciones Cicerón, 1954), pp. 70–74. Sergio Reyes Osorio, Rodolfo Stavenhagen, Salomón Eckstein, and Juan Ballesteros, *Estructura Agraria y Desarrollo Agrícola en México,* Centro de Investigaciones Agrarias (México, D. F.: Fondo de Cultura Económica, 1974), pp. 484–535.

96. See note 83.

97. See note 84.

98. Josette Murphy is a candidate for the Ph.D. in anthropology, University of California at Santa Barbara. Her Ph.D. thesis on French gaecs will be available by fall, 1977.

99. Salomón Eckstein, *El Ejido Colectivo en México* (México: Fondo de Cultura Económica, 1966), pp. 92, 127, 169.

100. Ramón Fernández y Fernández, "La colectiva ha muerto; viva la colectiva," *Chapingo: Revista de la Escuela Nacional de Agricultura,* Epoca II, 1, no. 3 (1961):10–13.

101. Raymond Wilkie, *San Miguel: A Mexican Collective Ejido* (Stanford: Stanford University Press, 1971), pp. 39, 45.

102. Ibid., pp. 58, 65, 72.

103. Unless otherwise indicated, data in this section are from the author's field notes.

104. Miguel Bueno, Jaime Lamo, and Fernando Baz, *Explotación en Común de la Tierra y Concentración Parcelaria,* Servicio Nacional de Concentración Parcelaria y Ordenación Rural Serie Monográfica No. 13 (Madrid: Ministerio de Agricultura, 1966).

105. Max Weber, *Law in Economy and Society,* ed. Max Rheinstein, trans. Edward Shils and Max Rheinstein (New York: Simon and Schuster, 1954), pp. 156–63.

106. Ronald Dore, *British Factory—Japanese Factory* (Berkeley: University of California Press, 1973).

Notes to Chapter Ten: *Participatory Evolution* (pp. 328–361)

1. W. H. Murdy, "Anthropocentrism: A Modern Version," *Science,* 28 March 1975, pp. 1168–72.

2. Ron J. Dare, "Anthropocentrism and Evolution," *Science,* 22 August 1975, p. 593.

3. Paul A. Samuelson, "Social Darwinism," *Newsweek,* 7 July 1975, p. 55.

4. George Maclay and Humphrey Knipe, *The Dominant Man* (New York: Delacorte, 1972).

5. Donald A. Symons, *Play and Aggression: The Function of Aggressive Play in Rhesus Monkeys* (New York: Columbia University Press, 1977).

6. George T. Land, *Grow or Die: The Unifying Principle of Transformation* (New York: Dell, 1973), pp. 73, 91.

7. Ibid., pp. 87, 101.

8. Ibid., p. 187.

9. William Barrett, *Irrational Man: A Study in Existential Philosophy* (Garden City, N.Y.: Doubleday, 1958), pp. 162–63.

10. On the subject of choice and time see Robert A. Dahl, *After the Revolution?* (New Haven: Yale University Press, 1970), pp. 8–56.

11. Max Weber, *Law in Economy and Society,* ed. Max Rheinstein, trans. Edward Shils and Max Rheinstein (New York: Simon and Schuster, 1954), p. 20.

12. Blaise Pascal, "Fragment of a Treatise on Vacuum," trans. Leona Fassett, in *The Idea of Progress: A Collection of Readings,* ed. Frederick J. Teggart (Berkeley: University of California Press, 1949), p. 167.

13. Edward Bellamy, *Looking Backward: 2000–1887* (New York: New American Library, 1960 reprint of 1888 edition), pp. 26–29.

14. Jonathan R. Cole and Stephen Cole, *Social Stratification in Science* (Chicago: University of Chicago Press, 1973), p. 228.

15. Peregrine Worsthorne, *The Socialist Myth* (London: Cassell, 1971), pp. 231–33.

16. Michael Young, *The Rise of the Meritocracy 1870–2033: An Essay on Education and Equality* (London: Thames and Hudson, 1958).

17. Theodosius Dobzhansky, *Genetic Diversity and Human Equality* (New York: Basic Books, 1973), pp. 40–49.

18. Christopher Jencks, *Inequality: A Reassessment of the Effect of Family and Schooling in America* (New York: Basic Books, 1972), p. 220.

19. Cole and Cole, *Stratification in Science,* pp. 255–60.

20. Aldous Huxley, *Brave New World* and *Brave New World Revisited* (New York: Harper and Row, 1965).

21. Cole and Cole, *Stratification in Science,* p. 69.

22. Stanislav Andreski, *Social Sciences as Sorcery* (London: Deutsch, 1972).

23. Cole and Cole, *Stratification in Science,* pp. 175, 228–34.

24. In my experience rural peoples in Latin America move to the cities for higher income and more things on which to spend it. Once there they defend their greater freedom and strongly denounce the constraints of the rural village.

25. Robert Nisbet, *Twilight of Authority* (New York: Oxford University Press, 1975), p. 81.

26. Ibid., pp. 170–75.

27. Elizabeth Colson, *Tradition and Contract: The Problem of Order* (Chicago: Aldine, 1974), pp. 69–81, 113.

28. Ivan Efremov, *Andromeda: A Space-Age Tale,* trans. George Hanna (Moscow: Foreign Language Publ., 1960).

29. H. G. Wells, *A Modern Utopia* (Lincoln: University of Nebraska Press, 1967 reprint of 1905 edition), pp. 162–66.

30. Yevgeny Zamyatin, *We*, trans. Mirra Ginsburg (New York: Viking, 1972). George Orwell, *1984: A Novel* (New York: Harcourt, Brace, 1949).

31. Theodor Hertzka, *Freeland: A Social Anticipation* (New York: Appleton, 1891), p. 104.

32. Edward Weisband and Thomas M. Franck, *Resignation in Protest: Political and Ethical Choices Between Loyalty to Team and Loyalty to Conscience in American Public Life* (New York: Grossman, 1975), pp. 169–70.

33. Ibid., pp. 60, 96, 119, 145–47, 157.

34. James S. Coleman, *Power and the Structure of Society* (New York: Norton, 1974).

35. Richard Barnet and Ronald E. Müller, *Global Reach: The Power of the Multinational Corporations* (New York: Simon and Schuster, 1974).

36. Nisbet, *Twilight of Authority*, pp. 195, 227.

37. Ibid., pp. 45–46.

38. Paul L. Rosen, *The Supreme Court and Social Science* (Urbana: University of Illinois Press, 1972).

39. F. A. Hayek, *Law, Legislation and Liberty, Volume I: Rules and Order* (Chicago: University of Chicago Press, 1973), pp. 116–19.

40. Ibid., pp. 93, 95, 98.

41. Ibid., pp. 64–65.

42. Andrei Amalrik, *Will the Soviet Union Survive Until 1984?* (New York: Harper and Row, 1971), p. 13.

43. Richard Pipes, *Russia Under the Old Regime* (New York: Scribner's, 1974), pp. 295–317.

44. Aleksandr I. Solzhenitsyn, *The Gulag Archipelago 1918–1956: An Experiment in Literary Investigation*, trans. Thomas P. Whitney (New York: Harper and Row, 1973).

45. Efremov, *Andromeda.*

46. Cole and Cole, *Stratification in Science*, pp. 73, 260.

47. Bellamy, *Looking Backward*, pp. 93–95.

48. John Kenneth Galbraith, *Economics and the Public Purpose* (Boston: Houghton Mifflin, 1973), pp. 30, 40–51, 55–56, 68–77.

49. Ibid., p. 75.

50. Barnet and Müller, *Global Reach*, pp. 26–44.

51. Susan Jacoby, *Inside Soviet Schools* (New York: Hill and Wang, 1974), pp. 139–40.

52. Galbraith, *Economics and Public Purpose*, pp. 55–57.

53. Robert L. Heilbroner, *An Inquiry into the Human Prospect* (New York: Norton, 1974), pp. 64–65.

54. Jencks, *Inequality*, pp. 226, 249.

55. Robert Paul Wolff, *In Defense of Anarchism* (New York: Harper and Row, 1970), pp. 34–35.

56. Ibid., pp. 38–58, 81–82.

57. Robert Lekachman, *Economists at Bay* (Hightstown, N.J.: McGraw-Hill, 1976), pp. 78–79.

58. Eugen Loebl, *Humanomics* (New York: Random House, 1976).

59. Heilbroner, *Human Prospect*.

Index